HISTORY
OF AFRICA
From 1800
to present

HISTORY OF AFRICA
From 1800 to present

HARRY A. GAILEY, JR.
San Jose State College

HOLT, RINEHART and WINSTON, INC.
New York, Chicago, San Francisco, Atlanta, Dallas,
Montreal, Toronto, London, Sydney

Cover Photo: Brooklyn Museum

Copyright © 1972 by Holt, Rinehart and Winston, Inc.

All rights reserved

Library of Congress Catalog Card Number: 72–169611

ISBN: 0–03–086249–3

Printed in the United States of America

2345   090   9 8 7 6 5 4 3 2 1

for

LAUREL, KAREN, NANCY, RICHARD, and JENNIFER

Preface

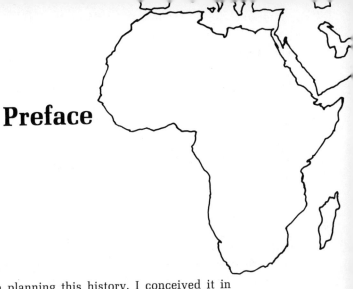

Three years ago when planning this history, I conceived it in terms of a single volume. It soon became obvious that such a book would be overly long unless I wanted to ignore large portions of the continent and treat other segments in a very cursory fashion. The decision was then made to issue the work in two separate but complementary volumes. The first was published early in 1970 as a *History of Africa from Earliest Times to 1800*. Although this decision solved one set of problems, it introduced new ones concerning redundancy and continuity. This introduction is an example of the former since I have already stated the reasons for writing the text, what audience it is aimed toward, and what goals I hope to achieve. Those statements are equally applicable to this volume. There are still few general studies of the continent available for teachers of basic courses in African history. Interest in the subject continues to grow on all levels including secondary education. It was partially to relieve my frustrations as a teacher because of the lack of good supporting material that I undertook the long task of writing this history.

In a single volume, continuity of theme and time is relatively automatic. In any multivolume history the author must compromise coverage and continuity in return for other advantages offered. Therefore, in this volume I have not attempted to reintroduce the reader to materials already covered in greater detail in the first book. Thus it may appear that I give little attention to such matters as the origins and development of the Bantu, the Sudanic state, or African religious systems. To have attempted a paraphrase of subjects already delineated in the earlier book would only have increased the size of an already large text and made its organization more difficult and complex.

Any historian imposes an order and unity upon the events he surveys which may not in fact have been true. Nevertheless, some organizational scheme must be used when one is attempting to survey the history of a continent over a period of almost two centuries. The pattern of geographic division utilized in the first book has again been followed with some modifications. Because of the increasing complexity of African societies and polities, it was necessary to introduce chronological subdivisions to each of the major segments. In most cases this has caused few problems since much of sub-Saharan Africa fits into a logical chronological framework without an author forcing one upon the subject matter. Thus the pre-1870 period, the scramble, organization of European control, and the period of devolution of power to African leaders are, in point of time, common to the bulk of African territories. The most glaring exceptions to this type of periodization are the two polities, Ethiopia and Liberia, which maintained their independence throughout much of the nineteenth and twentieth centuries. In surveying these areas, therefore, a different chronological pattern was utilized.

Two decisions were made early in planning this volume. One concerned the need to include events occurring south of the Limpopo River. Some histories of sub-Saharan Africa arbitrarily exclude the complex interactions of Bantu, Hottentot, Indians, and whites. This seems indefensible since southern Africa has been so important, not only because of the mélange of peoples resident there, but because of the effect which they have had upon the rest of Africa. By including southern Africa, the length of the book has been increased. Further, because of the dominance of whites in South Africa, it has been necessary to devote more space to the evolvement of their power structure than to the Bantu or Colored residents. Apartheid is one of the key potentially explosive facts of modern Africa. It seems incumbent upon a general history to elucidate the complex background of this attitude.

The second decision was to exclude any detailed history of the North African areas. Although physically a part of Africa, they are culturally, religiously, and politically more associated with the Middle East and the Mediterranean world. I wanted to avoid an expansion of the text to include the complex problems of the Ottoman Empire and its connections with European diplomacy of the nineteenth century. Obviously one could not ignore the influence of Egypt upon the Sudan, northeastern and eastern Africa, and upon the diplomacy of the scramble for Africa. Thus some attention has been given to events in Egypt in the forty-year period after 1870.

The amount of information available on almost any African area is now so great that it is impossible for one person, or for that matter a team, to be equally knowledgeable in all areas. African studies is in the fortunate state where hundreds of specialists are active in research in many fields. New books and monographs are added weekly to the already impressive list of materials available to the student, teacher, and generalist. However laudatory, this presents the author of a textbook with many problems. One cannot read all the new books and articles, much less be aware of the large body of unpublished information, known only to specialists, which might seriously modify his interpretations. Every attempt has been made in this work to minimize outright error and to guard against overspeculation. Wherever there is adequate information, I have tried to qualify my statements in such a way as to indicate the tentative nature of the conclusion.

It is an impossible task to construct a list of acknowledgments for those persons who, either directly or indirectly, aided in the production of a general text. However, I should be remiss if I did not express my thanks to Dr. G. Wesley Johnson of Stanford University who read the complete manuscript and commented extensively and fairly upon it. My wife, Rosalie, as usual was indispensable, acting as critic, proofreader, and chief typist for the many drafts of the manuscript.

Harry A. Gailey

Los Gatos, California
September 1971

Contents

List of Maps

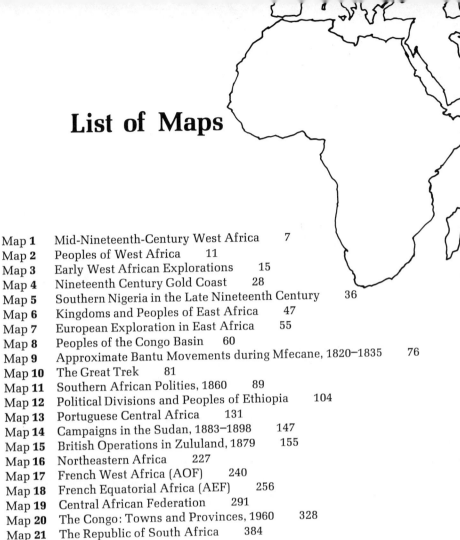

HISTORY
OF AFRICA
From 1800
to present

ONE

West Africa
before the scramble

Islamic resurgence in the Western Sudan

The Western Sudan was in a state of flux after the Moroccan conquest in the sixteenth century. No power arose to take the place of Songhai. Rather the territory was contested by a large number of smaller polities. Trade declined partially because of the unstable political conditions and partially because European traders along the African coast diverted large amounts of goods away from the interior. The Sudan was as divided religiously as it was politically. The power of Islam was actively challenged by the states of Segu, Kaarta, Macina, and Tekrur. Nevertheless, the dream of a Dar al-Islam, a haven for Islam in the Western Sudan, persisted in the minds of Islamic teachers and holy men. They looked back at the golden age of Mali and Songhai and worked actively to foster in the minds of the people a return to the imagined purity of those days. A realization of a purified religious state was, in practice, modified by the nature of Islam in the Western Sudan. It had been strongly infiltrated by traditional religious beliefs. The carriers of the Islamic revolution in the eighteenth century were Marabouts who were teachers and holy men. However orthodox individual Marabouts might have been, they were viewed by the populace as men endowed with magical and supernatural powers. The visions of the Marabouts had particular meaning for the Fulani and the related Tucolor people. Their acceptance of the ideal of reformation created in the nineteenth century a series of Islamic states stretching from the Upper Senegal to Hausaland.

Early in the reign of Askia Muhammad, some Fulani pastoralists rebelled against their Songhai overlords. Driven out of the empire, they moved southwestward and settled in Central Guinea. Gaining adherents from non-Fulani groups, particularly the Mandinka, some of them moved northward in the mid-sixteenth century, skirted the Wolof states, and overthrew the rulers of Tekrur. Here in the Upper Senegal regions they estab-

1

lished their own non-Islamic dynasty, the Denianke, which remained in control of the new state of Futa Toro until the 1770s.

The Fulani who remained behind in the Futa Jallon settled down and took on many attributes of townsmen. Among those elements absorbed by these Fulani in the next century was Islam. In the first quarter of the eighteenth century Fulani holy men, "revivers of Islam," created a new type of state in the Futa Jallon. An imam who claimed to rule the state in the name of God was the religious, political, and military leader of the state. The imam was selected from religious teachers who were members of a few important families, and he ruled for only a specific period of time. The state was divided into nine provinces and these into further subdistricts. Each unit was administered by officials directly responsible to the imam. Located in the hilly country of Guinea, this theocratic state continued to prosper and its system remained relatively intact until the French invasions of the latter nineteenth century. During this long period, Futa Jallon acted as a training ground for religious teachers and as a practical example for Islamic reformers everywhere in the Western Sudan.

Further to the north in Futa Toro, the Denianke dynasty was challenged in the 1770s by their Tucolor subjects. The Tucolor people, basically Fulani with slight admixtures of Wolof and Serer, had long been converts to Islam. Thus the reforming movements in North Africa and the Western Sudan in the eighteenth century found early adherents among the Tucolors. Suleiman Ba was the leader of the reformers in Futa Toro and in 1776 his followers succeeded in overthrowing the Denianke rulers. The imamate of Futa Toro was subsequently created to further the goals of a revived theocracy. After the death of Suleiman, the rulers of Futa Toro were elected. Under Muslim leadership, trade which had languished was revived with other areas of the Sudan and with the French on the coasts.

Other Muslim states were created farther to the east in the same period. One such state was Bondu, located between the two Futas. Another area was Macina where the Muslim Fulani in the eighteenth century created an alliance with their still pagan rulers. In the latter eighteenth century the Islamic Fulani in Macina were almost completely free from control by the pagan rulers. The Islamic revolution was brought to the borders of the Hausa states by the creation of the town of Say. This was the work of a Marabout, Alfa Muhammad Diobo, who wished to create a center for a purified Islam. All this intellectual, religious, and political ferment was the necessary preliminary to the largest and most successful of Islamic revolutions—the Fulani jihad in northern Nigeria.

The Fulani jihad in Hausaland

The Fulani had long been resident in the Hausa city-states. Many who had forsaken the wandering pastoral life had risen to positions of prominence as teachers, traders, and public officials. The majority of these town Fulani had been converted to Islam long ago. They were not insulated from the current wave of reformism in the Western Sudan. The preaching of Muslim reformers and the practical example of the implementation of the Shari'a or Muslim law in Futa Jallon and Futa Toro gave hope of change in the same direction in the various Hausa states. Although religious motives were primary in the overthrow of the Hausa rulers, there were also many other grievances which the Fulani and many Hausa had against their government. Excessive taxation, raids on cattle herds, and unfair courts were some of the reasons why Usuman dan Fodio, the moving force behind Fulani protest, could appeal to the masses who could not become excited over the religious issue.

Usuman dan Fodio, a Fulani of the Torodbe clan, was born in Gobir in 1754. As a young man he had received an excellent Islamic education in western and northern Africa. He became a convert to the reform movement then stirring in Western Sudan. Usuman was a teacher in Gobir, and later preached his message of social and religious reform throughout Hausaland. He became famous for his learning and piety, and was selected by the ruler or sarkin of Gobir as a tutor for the royal children. He thus was in a position to convince a number of nobles of the need to reorder the state on the basis of justice and a purified religion. In 1802 the king died and Usuman's pupil, Yunfa, became sarkin Gobir. However, the new ruler, instead of putting into effect reforms suggested by Usuman, launched a campaign against him and his followers.

The sarkin Gobir's increased efforts against Muslims brought on the civil war. By 1802 Usuman had drawn a large number of followers to his base at Degel. In 1804 he was attacked by Gobir armies and forced to flee from Degel. He then proclaimed a jihad against the proven infidels. Almost immediately his army defeated a large force sent by the sarkin. With this success his fame grew among both Hausa and Fulani.

Usuman did not take part in the battles; rather he acted as the spiritual and political head of the faithful. He distributed flags to certain leaders to indicate his faith in them and charged them with supplanting the old order in various parts of Hausaland. Usuman's armies were convinced of the divine justice of their cause and quickly overran most of the north. Kebbi fell in 1805, Zaria in 1806, Katsina and Kano in 1807, and Daura and Gobir in 1808. The wars continued—particularly against Nupe, Ilorin, and Oyo in the south. However, after 1810, the largest and richest portion of Hausaland was controlled by Usuman's forces. Eastward the chief of Bauchi, although not a Fulani, received a flag and subdued the people of the plateau area. In Adamoua, the Fulani pastoralists gave their support to one of Usuman's lieutenants, Modibba Adama, and they carried the jihad into the northern Cameroun.

Eventually only Bornu, after a seven-year war, was able to resist the Fulani armies. Once one of the greatest powers in the Sudan, Bornu, by the early nineteenth century, possessed only a shadow of its former influence. In 1805 adherents of Usuman led a revolt and carved out a number of small emirates in western Bornu. Then revolt struck the southern areas and the emirate of Gombe was created. Finally in 1808 the Fulani drove the mai from his capital of Birni N'Gazargamo. Bornu was eventually saved by the appearance of irregular forces led by Al Kanemi. This army, which was composed of cattle herders from the old province of Kanem and reinforcements from the royal forces, was powerful enough to retake the capital in 1810. The final campaign was waged by the Fulani in the following year. After initial victories, the Fulani were defeated by Al Kanemi's forces and the royal army and were driven back toward the west. For all practical purposes the boundaries thus established remained throughout the nineteenth century.

The young Dunama, mai of Bornu, who had come to the throne in 1810, was retained although Al Kanemi held most of the power in the state. Dunama was deposed in 1814 and later killed; however, Al Kanemi did not seize the throne since he preferred to control affairs secretly. He consolidated what remained of Bornu, restored authority over Kanem, reformed the administrative structure, and vainly sought to recapture the territories lost to the Fulani. At his death in 1835 his son, Umar, replaced him as the power behind the throne.

In 1846 the subject state of Zinder revolted in association with the sharif of Wadai. Mai Ibrahim attempted to use this rebellion to throw off Umar's control of the state, but his army was defeated. Umar crowned his victory with the execution of Mai Ibrahim, thus extinguishing one of the longest-ruling dynasties in African history.

Umar ruled Bornu until 1880. The later years of his reign were relatively peaceful, and he retired to a life of contemplation, allowing the state to be governed by palace favorites. During this period, Kanem and a number of western tributary states broke away from centralized control and the reduced kingdom suffered from raids by Wadai. After Umar's death the corrupt bureaucracy proved incapable of efficient rule. In 1891 the slaver Rabeh, fleeing with his followers from the Bahr el Ghazal region of the Sudan, invaded the kingdom and within five years brought the whole state under his domination. Rabeh's power was finally broken by the French army in a major campaign in 1900.

Usuman dan Fodio had been the revolutionary, idealistic religious leader who had inspired first the Fulani and then a portion of the dominant Hausa to revolt against their traditional rulers. It was his son, Muhammad Bello, who consolidated the conquests and created the political structure of the Fulani empire. Even before his death Usuman, as Commander of the Faithful, had left the administration to Bello and his brother Abdullahi. The provincial rulers paid allegiance to either Abdullahi at Gwandu or Bello at Sokoto. At Usuman's death in 1817 there was a brief period of unrest until Bello assumed the title of sultan. Abdullahi remained an emir with, however, political control over one half of the empire. In both sections the empire was divided into areas which were each ruled by an emir. In normal administrative matters the emirs were supreme in their territory; however, they were required to defer to the political judgment of Sokoto and Gwandu. In religious matters the Commander of the Faithful at Sokoto was supreme. Each emir was required to obey the orders of his superior and to pay tribute to him. The viziers of Gwandu and Sokoto visited the emirates regularly to settle disputes and to review the administrative practices. The Fulani retained to a very large extent the administrative machinery found in the Hausa states revising it only to make it more amenable to centralized control and a purified Islamic state. Usuman and Bello did not discriminate against the numerically more powerful Hausa. In most cases the emirs were Fulani but the other offices within the emirates were open to men of piety and talent whether Hausa or Fulani.

The sultan was forced to garrison some of the emirates—such as Katsina, Kebbi, and Zamfara—more heavily than others, because in the period before 1830 a significant portion of the population of these cities had not accepted the new system. Forty times, Sultan Bello in his twenty-year reign led the Fulani forces against dissidents within the empire and against unbelievers in the south. By the time of his death resistance against Fulani rule had been broken in all areas except the south. The Fulani emir of Nupe had forced back into two small towns the adherents of the traditional rulers. Eventually the entire area became subject to the emir who ruled the area from Bida. In the extreme south the Fulani, during the height of the jihad, were halted at Ilorin, a predominantly Yoruba town. It wasn't until 1829 that a Fulani commander was given a flag in recognition of his conquest. Despite the weakness of the Yoruba after the breakdown of the kingdom of Oyo, the Fulani were not able to occupy much Yoruba territory permanently. The forest line and the tsetse fly acted as allies of the Yoruba and limited the effectiveness of the Fulani cavalry.

The unification of the competing city-states resulted in an economic resurgence in the north. Kano became the most important trading city of the Western Sudan. The major export product was cloth which was produced in the villages and major cities. It was then dyed and some of it made into clothing. Such cloth from the north found its way into markets throughout the Western Sudan and also into the forest states. Other important manufactures were finished leather goods, metal products, and dyes. Horses and cattle also provided the north with considerable income as did the slave trade. Many slaves were taken to Kano for transport to the oases of the Sahara, North Africa, and to the Eastern Sudan. A far larger number collected as spoils of war against pagans from the southern border areas were sent southward and eventually found their way to the European slavers at Badagry, Lagos, Bonny, and Calabar.

Many European observers in the nineteenth century reported that the centralized control of the sultan began to wane after the death of Bello in 1837. Recent research has indicated that this assessment is only partially true. As late as 1860 the sultan had the power to depose the emir of Zaria and select a new man for the position. All emirs, even those most distant such as Adamoua, needed the sanction of the sultan to rule. Where there were rival claimants to the throne each would, if necessary, travel to Sokoto to secure the sultan's underwriting of his legitimacy. The united empire without doubt underwent a number of changes in the years after Bello's death. The fervor of the jihad died away and the emirs became increasingly materialistic. There were attempts by individual emirs to rid themselves of the practical links that bound them to the sultan and there was open jealousy between emirs. However, when the British forces under Lugard in the last years of the century occupied the north, they found a well-ordered, stable Islamic empire. Far from being decayed, it functioned so well that the British modified only a portion of its administration and were content to allow the sultan and emirs to continue their rule relatively unchanged into the twentieth century.

The Tucolor empire and other reform movements

The successful Fulani jihad in Hausaland spurred on religious reformers elsewhere in the Western Sudan. In the early nineteenth century Sheikh Ahmadu bin Hammadi Boubou who had studied with Usuman at Sokoto returned to Macina and opened a Koranic school there. This became the centrum of a reform movement designed to create an Islamic state in Macina. His activities worried the rulers of Macina and their overlords, the Bambara of Segu. In defense of the faith, Ahmadu proclaimed a jihad in 1818 which overthrew the old government of Macina. Ahmadu's forces took the city of Djenne and even held the city of Timbuktu for a short period. The reconstructed Islamic state followed an organizational pattern similar to that established by Usuman and Bello in Hausaland. There were five emirates with each ruler responsible to Ahmadu at his new capital city of Hamdullahi. The government based upon the Shari'a was puritanical and efficient, but the revised laws and their implementation were more fair to the people than the laws of the previous regime. Although Timbuktu was soon lost, the greater portion of the new state remained faithful to Ahmadu's successors until it was incorporated briefly into the empire of Al Hajj Umar after 1862.

Al Hajj Umar was a Tucolor born and educated in Futa Toro. Like so many of his learned contemporaries, he traveled a great deal in order to study with renowned teachers. In 1820, when about thirty years of age, he undertook a five-year pilgrimage to Mecca and Medina. On his return to North Africa he came under the influence of the Tijaniyya brotherhood. This movement created by Ahmad al Tijani stressed the special place reserved by Allah for the faithful ones. Despite their sins they were destined for salvation. Thus a member of the Tijaniyya believed himself to be superior to all Muslims who did not subscribe to the teachings of al Tijani.

Al Hajj Umar was appointed caliph of this movement in the Western Sudan. However, his wanderings were not yet completed. He resided in Sokoto in the golden years of Sultan Bello's rule and there absorbed the details of political and military organization. While in Hausaland he gained considerable wealth and presumably a number of faithful followers. The respect shown to him is indicated by his marriage to one of Bello's daughters.

In 1838 Umar left Sokoto and established a religious center in the Futa Jallon. His teachings and the attitudes of his followers frightened the orthodox imams and he was expelled. Umar then established a religious

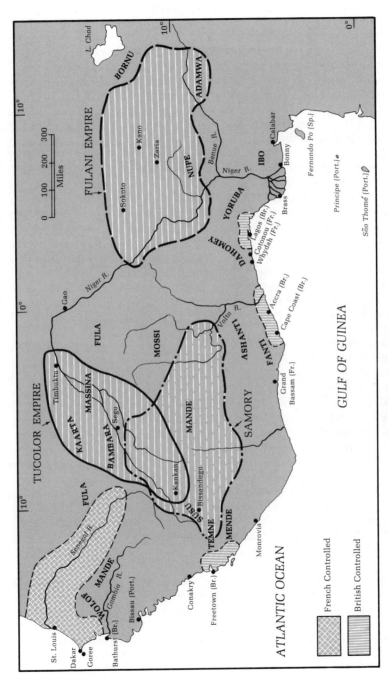

Mid-Nineteenth-Century West Africa

7

and military base at Dinguiray near the source of the Niger River. There he continued to attract followers and prepare for war. Many of his Tucolor and Fulani recruits were armed with modern weapons acquired from European traders along the coast. In 1852 some of his soldiers clashed with the forces of a local Bambara chief. Proclaiming a jihad, Umar's armies in 1854 swept northward conquering Bambauk and humbling the Bambara state of Kaarta. Turning his attention eastward Umar sought to gain a hold in the middle Senegal area. However, the French under Governor Louis Faidherbe blunted this drive in the two-year period after 1857. Thwarted there, Umar then attacked Segu, the most powerful Bambara state. Segu capitulated in 1861.

Umar's Tijaniyya forces then confronted the Islamic state of Macina that was ruled by Ahmadu III, a grandson of the founder. Despite much provocation, Ahmadu III appealed to Umar in a manner similar to that of Al Kanemi of Bornu when under attack by the forces of Usuman dan Fodio. He wished to know how it was possible for one Muslim leader to make war against another under the excuse of a jihad when this was expressly reserved for conversion of pagans. Umar's reply was that Ahmadu III had given help to the pagan rulers of Segu and thus could be considered an ally of those who struggled against the faithful. Umar's armies subsequently defeated those of Ahmadu in 1862 and Macina was incorporated into the empire. With the taking of Timbuktu in 1863 his personal empire reached its zenith.

The Tucolor had conquered a vast territory, but they had not gained the allegiance of the people. The Bambara remained obstinately pagan. In Macina the new rulers were hated because of Umar's breach of Islamic law in attacking them. Further a policy of forced conversion to the concepts of Tijaniyya was attempted. The unrest in Macina resulted in a revolt against Umar's authority in 1863 and he was killed trying to repress the uprising. With the loss of its charismatic leader, the Tucolor empire began to fall apart. In the extreme west the French were actively undermining Tucolor authority. In the north the empire had to thwart periodic Tuareg attacks. Throughout the empire the conquered rebelled against the rule of Umar's son, Ahmadu; but by the early 1870s he had regained nominal control over most of his father's empire. However, the constant fighting had disrupted trade and left some areas such as Macina little more than desert. Ahmadu and Tucolor rule were so hated by subject peoples that large segments of the population welcomed the French in the 1880s and 1890s, not as conquerors, but as deliverers.

Although not specifically a part of Islamic state building, the Mandingo empire of Samory Touré must be mentioned briefly. It was created at the same time that Ahmadu's Tucolor empire was crumbling. Samory controlled only a small chiefdom in the Kankan region of Guinea in the early 1860s. In fifteen years, through his administrative and military skills, he had transformed this tiny, weak state into the most powerful interior state west of Hausaland. He first incorporated the small neighboring Mande states within his kingdom and in 1873 conquered Kankan. From this date he was continually at war until his power was broken by the French twenty-five years later. At its greatest extent in the early 1880s, Samory's well-administered domain extended from the Futa Jallon in the east to the area of the Upper Volta in the west. Samory, not Ahmadu, provided the French with their most implacable opponent in their drive to occupy the interior of West Africa.

In the Senegambia area there was also a spilling over of reforming Islam. The juxtaposition of Wolof, Mandingo, Jola, Serer, and Fulani in the area as well as the presence of the French and British along the coast prevented the creation of a single Islamic polity. However, the fifty-year period of struggle between the protagonists of Islam, the Marabouts, and the traditional leaders, the Soninke, had important ramifications for the future of the area.

The first religious reformers appeared in the Gambia area in the early 1850s. These teachers had been involved in similar movements in Algeria or other parts of the Sudan. They found the majority of the population of the Wolof kingdoms of Jolof, Cayor, Sine, Saloum, and chieftaincies along the Gambia relatively untouched by Islam. Those chiefs who had accepted Islam were at best occasional conformists, and religious observances among them were highly colored by animistic practices. Those who listened to the teachers and followed the war chiefs in the 1850s and 1860s were a minority of the population, but an organized and at first inspired minority. However, along the Gambia River the only way to convert the Soninke was by conquest. As the internecine wars continued the religious motivation of some of the leaders dimmed and many of the small wars were caused by political and economic desires of individual leaders.

The only leader to emerge with attributes similar to the most successful religious revolutionaries, Usuman dan Fodio and Al Hajj Umar, was Maba. During a brief career in the early 1860s he sought to create a large Islamic state in southern Senegal. His objective was thwarted not only by the Soninke but by the French and British. After Maba's death in 1867, the leaders of the Marabout movement such as Fodi Kabba, Fodi Silla, and Musa Mollah were content with expanding their own small kingdoms and engaging in the slave trade. The religious motive by the 1880s had become secondary. Continuing warfare along the Gambia River destroyed many of the traditional ruling houses and left a vacuum of power that was easily filled by the British and French in the 1890s. Despite the inability of the early Muslim reformers to create a single purified state, they were successful in this period of warfare in converting the mass of the riverine population to Islam. In the Wolof states the successors of Maba in Sine and Saloum continued his work of conversion. Lat Dior, another of Maba's disciples, came to power in Cayor as did Alboury N'Diaye in Jolof. Thus by the time of the French occupation much of the population of these areas had been converted to Islam.

European attitudes toward West Africa

European interest in Africa from the first hesitant coastal voyages of the Portuguese in the fifteenth century had been primarily economic. The original impetus for the Portuguese crown to underwrite these explorations was the hope of by-passing the Mediterranean and thus undercutting the Italian states that controlled trade in Eastern luxury goods. Profits from gold, ivory, pepper, feathers, and gum from Africa justified the investment and danger to the pioneer explorers. The Portuguese, from their trading stations and forts in West and East Africa, were the first beneficiaries of the demand for slaves without which the plantations of the New World could not have functioned. The slave trade, a trickle in the sixteenth century, reached flood tide in the eighteenth and displaced thousands of Africans every year. French, Danes, Brandenbergers, Courlanders, Dutch, and British all were eager to tap these riches. At the opening of the eighteenth century the French, Dutch, and Portuguese, although active in the slave trade, had confined the bulk of their activities to restricted areas in West Africa. British merchants dominated the trans-Atlantic carrying trade.

Coastal African societies came to depend largely upon the export of slaves. This interaction between native polities and European legitimate slave merchants belongs to the period before 1800. It is sufficient to note that states such as those of the Ibibio and Ijo east of the Niger had completely reoriented their political and social systems because of the slave trade. In areas such as the Senegambia, Gold Coast, and Angola, where Europeans were firmly established in towns or forts, the lives of neighboring African people came to be centered on the slave trade. Inland states, which could not be conquered by Europeans, tended to develop into large autocratic militaristic polities. The creation of the Ashanti Union, Dahomey, Oyo, and Kasanje depended upon issues other than the slave trade, yet the profit motive of increased trade with Europeans was an important factor in their development.

The reversal of British attitudes toward slavery in the early nineteenth century had ramifications which, in time, affected most of Africa. On the most obvious level it restricted British merchants from engaging in the trade after 1807. All British governments in the nineteenth century were committed to halting the traffic in slaves. Due in large measure to British pressure, other European states eventually outlawed it thus placing most European slavers beyond the law. The logic of commitment led British governments to support a series of activities designed to enforce the paper decrees of abolition. These included the maintenance of a permanent West African squadron to seize suspected slave ships, establishment of permanent stations along the coast, and treaties with native rulers that elicited promises to cease selling slaves. Inevitably Britain was drawn more deeply into the internal affairs of African states to secure compliance with these agreements.

The abolition of the slave trade was but one offshoot of a more generalized development within British society. The Evangelical movement, a reinterpretation of Protestant Christianity, was the dominant theme of British life in the nineteenth century. Biblical Christianity became the driving force for political, economic, and social change. One area almost totally neglected by the Established Church in the eighteenth century was mis-

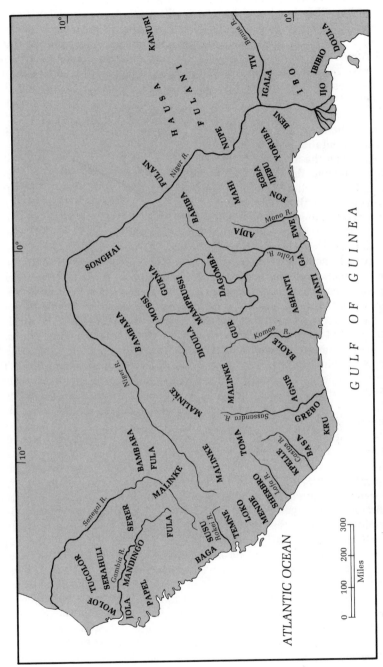

Peoples of West Africa

sionary activity. Evangelicals, however, took seriously the call to preach the word to "heathen" peoples. To facilitate this, proselytizing Baptists, Wesleyans, Independents, and Anglicans established missionary societies. Within a few years these agencies had missionaries placed in territories from Africa to the Pacific Islands. This phenomenon coincided with and reinforced official activities to end the slave trade. By the end of the first five decades of the century British-sponsored missionaries were at work throughout West Africa. They expected and received active support for their efforts from their government. Thus, despite official statements to the contrary, the missionaries drew the government into deeper intervention in the internal affairs of African polities.

Although the abolition of the slave trade did not immediately end the traffic in human beings, it did result in cutting back British trade with Africa. Large trading firms in Liverpool and London lost very little from the reversal of policy. The British empire was large enough and its manufacturers and bankers so dominant that it was a simple matter to reorient the direction of their trading activities. However, smaller trading houses were damaged and began to seek out new African products to substitute for slaves. In some areas this search was short. East of the Niger Delta, oil palm products became the major trade items even before the African middlemen had been forced to abandon completely the sale of slaves. Elsewhere it took longer to develop alternate exports. Exports of peanuts, cocoa, and rubber from West Africa did not assume major proportions until the latter years of the nineteenth century. With the increasing effectiveness of measures to limit the slave trade, Africa became an economic backwater for Europe. As first Britain and later other European states embraced free trade they began to reduce government expenditure by closing down unprofitable stations. Government officials at those permanent bases that were retained for noneconomic reasons were under orders not to expand the territory under their jurisdiction.

Another set of factors closely joined to evangelical and economic motives also worked to undermine the official position against expansion. Curiosity about the unknown parts of the world had been growing in the eighteenth century and had resulted in government sponsorship of many exploratory ventures. Perhaps the most fruitful of these had been the three Pacific Ocean voyages of Captain Cook. Africa, whose periphery was so well known, became the focal point for private and government-sponsored explorations in the early nineteenth century. The African Association, formed in 1788, led the way by underwriting efforts to unlock the secrets of the interior of West Africa. Their most successful venture, Mungo Park's journey from the Gambia to the Niger, was but a prelude to a series of explorations which by 1850 had solved most of the geographic mysteries of West Africa. The British government sponsored many of the expeditions for the dual purpose of checking the slave trade and discovering, if possible, new sources of wealth that could be exploited by British merchants.

The generalized picture of European activities in West Africa is a strange picture of increasing involvement limited by the official attitudes that stressed noninvolvement. Explorers, missionaries, and officials working for the destruction of the slave trade committed European states, particularly Britain, to greater intervention in the affairs of African rulers. At the same time the economic facts dictated an official policy that would minimize expenditures. The resultant tension between these divergent factors produced inconsistent government activities that confused Europeans concerned with Africa as much as they did the Africans. Although it is not totally possible to separate the many European activities, it will be convenient to survey each area in some detail.

European exploration in West Africa

In 1788 the African Association was founded, due largely to the efforts of Sir Joseph Banks who had accompanied Captain Cook on his first voyage to the Pacific. Although the association had economic motives and later developed humanitarian overtones, its primary purpose was the scientific collection of data concerning the unexplored world. The first major question that its members sought to answer was the riddle of the great river mentioned in Arabic texts of the Western Sudan. Although Europeans had been active along the coasts for 350 years, no European had observed such a river. There were many theories about this mysterious stream. Some geographers believed as did Herodotus that it was the same as the Nile. Somewhere beyond the limits of European knowledge, the river, flowing eastward, changed its course to become the Nile. Another theory stated that the two rivers were separate. The one in the Western Sudan flowed eastward and lost itself in a great lake where the bulk of its waters simply evaporated. Yet others thought that its direction of flow was not eastward but westward. It branched into three rivers—the Senegal, Gambia, and Rio Grande (Jeba)—whose mouths were already familiar to Europeans. All of these elaborately developed theories rested on no firm foundation. No one knew whether there was such a stream, let alone its source, direction, and outlet. It was to solve these problems that the African Association dispatched its first explorations.

By 1793 the association had sponsored three expeditions into the Western Sudan. All had failed although Major Houghton who used the Gambia River as a point of departure had, before his death, communicated enough to the association to convince them that there was a river and it flowed eastward. A young Scots doctor, Mungo Park, undertook to complete Houghton's work. Arriving at Pisania on the Gambia River in the summer of 1795, he studied the language and talked to as many Africans as possible before departing for the interior. After enduring hardships and sickness that would have killed most men, he reached the Niger near Segu almost a year later. The broad river did exist and it flowed eastward. Exhausted and without supplies, he was forced to turn back to the coast. The results of Park's first expedition were modest, but they fired the imaginations of many powerful Englishmen. The association boldly announced that the way was open for commercial penetration of the hinterland.

By 1805 the Colonial Office had been convinced of the worth of further detailed explorations of the Niger. It financed a large utterly inexperienced expedition led by Park whose purpose was to uncover the remaining secrets of the Niger. Thirty-eight Europeans, including Park's brother-in-law, accompanied the explorer on the second expedition. They carried with them the equipment necessary to construct boats that would presumably carry them down the Niger to its outlet. Arriving during the rainy season, the expedition soon discovered the perils of travel in West Africa. By the time they reached the Niger near Bamako, in August 1805, only ten Europeans were alive and most of these were in no condition to continue. Ultimately Park, four Europeans, and four Africans set off from Sansanding to float down the river on a raft. Later Park and his surviving companions were lost in the rapids near Bussa after a fight with the inhabitants of that town. Park's Mandingo servant, Isaaco, fortunately managed to carry Park's manuscript back to the coast where it was subsequently delivered to the British government.

The Napoleonic Wars brought a halt to further explorations and it was not until 1820 that Dr. Walter Oudney was invited by the British government to undertake a new expedition. Associated with him in the venture were Major Dixon Denham and Lieutenant Hugh Clapperton of the Royal Navy. The group left Tripoli in early 1822, crossed the Sahara via the Fezzan and Tibesti, and arrived at Kuka in Bornu. Denham moved southeast from there exploring Bornu and the regions of the Shari River. Oudney and Clapperton proceeded westward. Oudney died at Murmur in January 1824, but Clapperton reached the great trading city of Kano and eventually Sokoto. He was kindly received there by Sultan Bello, spiritual and temporal head of the all-powerful Fulani empire. However, Bello would not allow him to explore southward toward the Niger only 150 miles away. He then retraced his steps to meet Denham at Kuka and together they recrossed the desert to Tripoli. Arriving in England in June 1825, he was almost immediately commissioned by the colonial secretary, Lord Bathurst, to lead a further expedition to the Fulani-Hausa states following a new route northward from the coast of Guinea. One reason for the Colonial Office's haste was the naïve belief, fostered by Sultan Bello's request for a treaty, that he would be willing to abolish the slave trade in his empire.

Clapperton's second expedition included four other Europeans. One of these was Clapperton's twenty-one year old Cornish servant, Richard Lander. The small group landed at Badagry near the end of 1825. Very soon after leaving the coast two of the Europeans died and another decided to explore Dahomey, thus leaving Clapperton and Lander to proceed northward alone. Their journey took them through Bussa to Zaria and Kano and thence to Sokoto. Clapperton was dismayed to discover that Bello had no intention of abolishing a lucrative and traditional source of income on the basis of the arguments of a wandering European. Clapperton became ill in December 1826, and died the following March. Despite evidence that the rulers of Hausaland in the midst of their troubles with Bornu were becoming suspicious of him, Lander decided to travel southeast toward

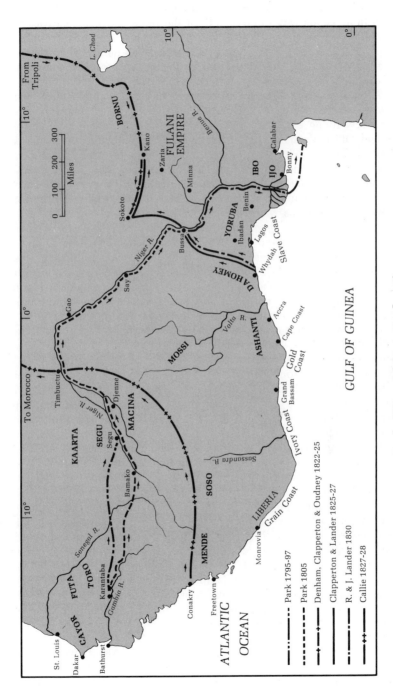

Early West African Explorations

15

what he believed to be a town on the Niger called Funda. From there he hoped to make his way to the mouth of the river. However, he was halted by soldiers of the emir of Zaria before he reached his objective and was compelled to return to the coast by the same way he and Clapperton had come. In April 1828 Lander arrived in Britain with all the notes of the expedition.

After delivering Clapperton's papers to the Colonial Office, Lander wrote two accounts of his adventures. No longer just a servant, but one of the few living experts on West Africa, he was able to convince the Colonial Office to underwrite a further attempt to trace the Niger from Bussa to the sea. The government subsidy was far from munificent. It consisted of £100 each for Richard and his brother John, and a guarantee of an additional £100 for the maintenance of Richard's wife in his absence. The two brothers landed at Badagry in March 1830, and from there they followed the previous route taken by Clapperton to Bussa. Richard was remembered by the ruler of the town and they were warmly welcomed. Procuring two canoes and the men to row them downstream, they left Bussa and had few problems with the riverine Africans until they reached the vicinity of Asaba. Despite difficulties with the Ibo, they eventually reached Brass in November and persuaded a British captain to transport them to Fernando Po. From there they sailed via Brazil to Britain and did not arrive home with the news of their discovery until July 1831.

Other explorers had also been active in the period immediately after the Napoleonic Wars. The Frenchman Gaspard Mollien in 1818 had investigated the Futa Jallon and discovered the sources of the Sengal, Gambia, and Rio Grande rivers. Four years later Major Alexander Laing had identified the source of the Niger. In the two years after 1827, René Caillie traveled from the Senegambia via the mysterious Timbuktu to Morocco. Caillie exposed the low level to which the once great trading city of the Western Sudan had fallen.

In the decade and a half after Waterloo, the hinterland of western Africa had been exposed to Europe by the exploits of a few intrepid, lucky explorers. Each of them had upon their return to Europe put down their adventures in writing and had found an eager market for their books about the unknown continent. The British government, which had sponsored many of the expeditions, was particularly receptive to the information about peoples, their activities, and particularly the economic possibilities of the new territories. It is possible, however, to overstate what the early explorers had done. Much of West Africa remained a mystery to Europeans. The later activities of the Landers, Macgregor Laird, Dr. Baikie, and Heinrich Barth would provide more information to solve the puzzle of the hinterland. Nevertheless, large segments of the interior remained a mystery until after the scramble for Africa had been completed seventy years after the Niger River ceased to be a mystery.

Enough of the territory had been explored by the 1830s to indicate several things. The various expeditions had exploded the myth of the great wealth of the interior cities such as Timbuktu and Kano. This tended to confirm the dominant attitude of European governments that trade in most of the areas was not worth the trouble and expense of any territorial expansion. Some businessmen, however, saw in a few of the areas opportunities to expand preexisting trading activities. The most important of these areas were believed to be those adjacent to the Niger River northward to the Fulani states.

Trade and exploration along the Niger

European activities along the Niger coast in the nineteenth century were a complex amalgam of old and new forces. The slave trade continued to play an important role until the British occupied the area in the latter decades of the century. Coastal African rulers and middlemen, particularly in the Ijo and Ibibio states, at the same time were dealing with legitimate trade products. In some areas, such as Bonny, the oil palm trade had become more important by mid-century than slaving. However, the economic and political structures created for the exploitation of the slave trade remained intact; only the trading materials changed. Most European traders respected the coastal merchants' claim to the sources of supply and did not seriously attempt to bypass them and trade directly with the interior. New merchant entrepreneurs such as Macgregor Laird did not. Intrigued with the potential of the hinterland as reported by the explorers, they became active in further exploratory ventures designed to establish trading centers in the interior. Although not necessarily connected to the latter movement, the growing missionary interest tended to reinforce attempts to open up the hinterland. Missionaries and business interests concerned with activities that were hostile to the traditional closed system of the African middlemen expected and grudgingly received the support of the British government.

The first attempt to take advantage of the newly discovered Niger route for trade proved a disaster. In 1832 a Liverpool merchant, Macgregor Laird, dispatched two iron oceangoing steamships to the Niger with forty-eight Europeans including Richard Lander on board. The purpose was to reconnoiter the river and establish a trading station. Although the party traveled past the Benue confluence, it was forced to return to the coast because of the heavy death rate. Thirty-nine Europeans including Lander died of malaria. This expedition dampened enthusiasm until 1841 when the Church Missionary Society sent another large group to the Niger to establish a permanent station upriver. Representatives of European merchants trading with African coastal cities vainly protested this attempt to bypass them. The society, supported by the government, believed that such a station would enable missionaries to reach many thousands of interior Africans. The station was to be converted into a model farm. Thus European technology would reinforce Christianity. Hopefully in the future the station would be but one of many and would stimulate direct trade with Europe. This costly experiment also failed since over one-third of the Europeans involved lost their lives. The disaster convinced the directors of the Church Missionary Society that, because of the appalling European death rate, the major hope of Christianizing the interior lay in sending more African missionaries such as Samuel Ajayi Crowther who had been one of the missionaries on the 1841 venture. The Church Missionary Society also changed the focus of their attention from the Niger to the Yoruba states to the west.

Meanwhile the Church of Scotland in 1846 had sent Hope Wadell and a contingent of Jamaican Christians to work at Calabar. They established a mission near Duke Town and later one in Creek Town. These missionaries, in the following decade, worked to subvert some inhumane practices of the Ibibio society such as the killing of twins and human sacrifice. In this struggle they enlisted the reluctant support of European traders of Calabar. Their success can be measured by the fact that in 1858 upon the death of the ruler of Creek Town there were no official sacrifices of slaves.

Beginning in the 1830s large numbers of freed Yoruba slaves began to return from Freetown to their homeland. Many of these people had become Christians and formed colonies of Westernized Africans at Badagry and Abeokuta. There they established trade and cultural links with Freetown and the Gold Coast. Soon Methodist, Baptist, and Church Missionary Society missionaries followed them. In 1842 Thomas Freeman, a part African Methodist minister, established a mission station at Badagry. In the same year Henry Townsend of the Church Missionary Society visited Abeokuta prior to opening missionary work there. In the following year Townsend and Crowther set out to bring Christianity to Abeokuta. The disturbed affairs of the Egba states and a war with Dahomey prevented this and they had to be content with working at Badagry until 1846. Even after that date it was extremely trying and dangerous for the missionaries at Abeokuta. By the 1850s there were many missionaries from England representing most of the mission societies at work throughout southern Yorubaland.

In 1850 the British government commissioned an Englishman, James Richardson, and two Germans, Adolf Overweg and Heinrich Barth, to explore Hausaland and the Western Sudan. This expedition was a belated continuation of the efforts of Oudney, Denham, and Clapperton of over two decades before. Richardson and Overweg died, but the indomitable Heinrich Barth spent five years crossing and recrossing the Sudan from Timbuktu to Bornu. His book recounting these adventures in extraordinary detail became the standard work on the Western Sudan almost immediately. In response to a letter from Barth in 1852 concerning the Benue River, the British government in conjunction with Macgregor Laird sponsored a new expedition designed to collaborate with Barth. This venture commanded by Dr. Baikie, a naval surgeon, discovered little of geographic note and never contacted Barth. Nevertheless, it was one of the most important of all the explorations of West Africa because Baikie insisted upon the daily use of quinine. As a result none of the Europeans died. With such protection, the way was clear to open the Niger for further European economic and missionary activity.

One of the members of Dr. Baikie's expedition was the Reverend Samuel Crowther who with other African missionaries established the Niger River mission of the Church Missionary Society at Onitsha. Later smaller stations were begun at Lokoja and Gbebe. Despite early problems, the Niger River mission prospered and in 1864 Crowther was nominated as the Bishop of Western Equatorial Africa. By this time the missionary ventures of all the societies were flourishing throughout southern Nigeria. At the close of the first half of the nineteenth century, missionaries were at work in almost all of the major towns and cities from the Cross River to Badagry. Wherever they were they exercised an influence far beyond their numbers. Because of their success at conversions, the missionaries undermined the traditional closely knit African political, socioeconomic systems. They brought sorely needed medical knowledge to the people under their charge. Most important for the future, they opened schools and thus developed an ever-growing number of Western-educated Africans. Missionary influence on education continued to be dominant in all Nigerian areas even after British annexation later in the century.

West African naval patrols and the slave trade

British Evangelicals who succeeded in pressuring Parliament to end the slave trade naïvely believed that the trade would soon end and with this slavery itself would wither away. It became quickly apparent that neither of these goals would be accomplished easily. In order to enforce the ban on British subjects engaging in the slave trade, the crown assumed jurisdiction over the colony of Freetown and sent two old ships to patrol the West African coast. An admiralty court was established at Freetown to deal with captured ships whose captains were charged with engaging in the trade. Eventually courts of mixed commission were also created as Britain entered into treaties with other European powers who had also outlawed the trade. In 1810 four ships were assigned to the slave patrol. Although old and slow, their activities caused a series of protests from other European states that Britain was interfering with their trade.

Immediately after Waterloo, British statesmen brought diplomatic pressure to bear on all European powers then active in the trade. The result was that Portugal in 1815 and Spain in 1817 agreed to limit the activity of their slave ships to south of the equator. France outlawed the trade in 1818 and Brazil, which was one of the great markets, agreed in 1826 not to import any more slaves. The United States had declared the slave trade illegal in 1808. Thus in the ten years following the close of the Napoleonic Wars, almost all of the nations concerned with slave trading had either outlawed the practice or agreed to limit its scope.

There were a number of interrelated factors that made these treaties and agreements almost worthless. The first was the increasing demand for slaves in the New World. The sugar industry in Cuba was expanding and needed more men to work the plantations. In Brazil, where vast new territories were being opened, the economy depended upon tobacco, cotton, and coffee culture—all of which demanded a cheap labor force. In the

United States, the invention of the cotton gin completely changed all but the most liberal attitudes toward slavery. New lands in Alabama, Mississippi, Louisiana, and later in Texas were given over to the production of cotton. Thus the demand for slaves increased greatly after the trade abolition. Government officials charged with upholding the laws openly condoned the importation of slaves. African rulers had no intention of abandoning the profitable enterprise of gathering and selling slaves. Most African middlemen were eager to sell as long as there was someone to purchase the commodity. Much later in the 1880s, the emir of Kontagora expressed the feelings of so many African rulers when he said: "Can you stop a cat from mousing? I shall die with a slave in my mouth." The price of slaves on the west coast remained generally stable, actually declining in many areas, in the 1830s and 1840s when the West African patrol became more effective. At the same time, the price of slaves increased in the markets in Cuba and the United States. By 1850 the price of a good field slave in the New World had more than quadrupled since the opening of the century. With such profits to be gained, slave traders of all nationalities were willing to take chances to secure their share.

The British West African Squadron, even had there not been such a demand for slaves, would have had a near impossible task. There were over 4,000 miles of deeply indented coastline to patrol. The rivers of West Africa tend to lose themselves in a number of mouths or swampy mangrove delta land. These provided many excellent hiding places for the slavers. By the 1820s Britain was maintaining an average of twenty ships on the patrol, and all available statistics indicate that many more slaves were being shipped than before the abolition. It was not until the mid-1820s that the ships of the Royal Navy were fast enough to apprehend some of the better-equipped slave ships. In some cases the slavers were as well armed as warships; one of the larger slave ships mounted twenty guns. There were many instances of slave captains fighting after being overtaken. During the chase the slaves might be thrown overboard because until 1839 they were the only evidence that could convict a captain of slaving.

The problem had hardly begun when a slave ship was captured. A prize crew was put on board and the ship and its cargo sailed to a port where there was a mixed commission. In West Africa this port was normally Freetown. The voyage could be thousands of miles long. The sufferings of the slaves on board did not stop with its capture since these ships were normally packed with slaves. Upon landing, the senior naval officer filed his papers and in due time the case would be heard by the commission. Unless everything had been done exactly right and there was no question of the nationality and the purpose to which the ship was put, the commission would find for the ship owner. Until 1839, when the British law was amended, slaves had to be found on the captured ship. Equipment or other circumstantial evidence as to the ship's purpose was not considered. Captains of British warships could be held personally responsible for losses to the owners of ships brought into port when the navy could not prove their charges. Ships of the United States that were apprehended by the American squadron were sent to United States ports. Most American captains and owners who were found guilty were given relatively small fines.

One obvious answer to the problems of patrolling waters where slavers of different nationalities operated was reciprocal search agreements. Britain obtained treaties allowing this from Portugal and Spain in 1817, from the Netherlands in 1818, and from Sweden in 1824. In 1831 France agreed to allow British naval vessels to search French ships in the restricted area from 10° south to 32° north latitude extending from 0° to 30° west longitude. However, an attempt in 1841 to extend the area was refused by France. The official position of the United States, stated prior to the War of 1812, that no naval vessel of a foreign power had the right to stop an American trading vessel on the high seas, remained until the Civil War. This position gave American slavers a relatively free hand in West Africa. Furthermore, it led to the use of the American flag by slave captains of all nationalities. The United States sent four warships to West Africa in 1820 to maintain its own patrol. These were withdrawn within three years. The Webster-Ashburton Treaty of 1842 provided for joint cruising by British and United States warships. In 1843 two ships under the command of Lieutenant Matthew Perry were assigned to this duty. In the 1840s the United States never had more than seven ships on station compared with Britain's twenty or more. The United States ships were based on Cape Verde, 1,000 miles from the slaving areas. It is, therefore, little wonder that the joint cruising concept did not work. The United States squadron in the ten years following its reestablishment took only nine slave ships.

Despite the difficulties, the antislave patrols began to make real progress in the 1850s. This was partly because of the more active role of the British government and the missionaries on the mainland. Another reason was that the equipment treaties with most nations allowed slave ships to be taken even if there were no slaves on board. France began to maintain its own naval patrol off the Senegambia after 1845. Britain increased the numbers of its ships. Many of these were new, well-armed, fast steam vessels. In the early 1850s, the United States squadron of five ships was under the command of Lieutenant Andrew Foote who cooperated more fully with his British counterparts than any other previous American commander. However, the turn of the tide against the slave trade did not come until the American Civil War. All the major countries except the United States had by then abolished slavery in their territories. This became an accomplished fact in the United States in 1865. Brazil alone of western hemisphere areas recognized the legal status of slavery until 1888. Denied markets where great profits could be made, the slaving entrepreneurs were forced to turn to other areas for profitable investment. The practical abolition of the trans-Atlantic slave trade, far from being the simple process envisioned by Evangelicals, took almost sixty years. It had cost the British government millions of pounds and thousands of lives. Despite the difficulties encountered, the British squadron, in the forty years after 1825, had captured over 1,250 slave ships and released over 130,000 slaves alive. However, the slave patrol and the diplomatic maneuvering of the British government were only two facets of the total problem. Another phase of the antislave trade movement concerned the maintenance of bases on the African coast, the resettlement of captured slaves, and the attempt on the part of abolitionists to return freed slaves to African colonies. In this context the two areas of Freetown and Liberia became extremely important.

Freetown

The small settlements of what later became Freetown were located in the hills abutting upon the mouth of the Rokel River and had been promoted by Evangelicals in 1787. They visualized a haven for freed slaves in Africa. These settlers, already committed to Christianity and Western ideas, not only found a good future in Africa, but acted as carriers of civilization. As detailed elsewhere, the original plans of the Evangelicals foundered because of the hostility of local Africans, the inexperience of the original colonists, and the unhealthy climate. In 1791 the Sierra Leone Company was formed to continue the work of colonization. New settlers were brought from Nova Scotia, England, and Jamaica, and by the beginning of the nineteenth century, despite all difficulties, there were over 1,500 settlers in the Freetown area. The cost of administering the private colony, however, was prohibitive, and the directors of the company were delighted to turn their responsibilities over to the crown in 1808.

After 1808 the history of the settlement was tied closely to the drive to end the slave trade. Freetown became the major British naval base in West Africa. The British squadron was stationed there and the majority of the captured slave ships were taken to Freetown. The great increase in the population of the colony was due almost entirely to freed slaves. By 1822 the population of the area was estimated at 22,000, and by mid-century over 70,000 captives had been liberated at Freetown. Throughout most of the century the government was autocratic with the governor and his staff appointed by the Colonial Office. Until mid-century the governors were almost always military men.

The most active governor in the early history of the colony was Sir Charles MacCarthy who was appointed in 1814. He was deeply committed to eradicating the slave trade and to accomplish this he enlarged the territory responsible to the crown. MacCarthy wanted to annex islands that were known slaving territory and to extend the government's influence over the native peoples immediately adjacent to the colony. The Colonial Office refused to sanction most of MacCarthy's schemes for the expansion of British influence. Even so, the expenses of administering Freetown increased fourfold during MacCarthy's administration.

In 1821 MacCarthy became the governor in charge of all British West African territories. Thus the governor's time was increasingly devoted to the affairs on the Gold Coast and in the Gambia. The major area of concern at this time was the Gold Coast and the danger of an Ashanti invasion. MacCarthy was killed there in 1824 while attempting to carry out an activist policy against the Ashanti. His death had wide ramifications for British policy, not only in the Gold Coast but throughout West Africa. Thereafter the governors at Sierra Leone were under direct instructions not to expand British territory or to enter into alliances with chiefs who might call upon the British for help in time of trouble. This policy was enforced through the 1880s. A parliamentary commission in 1865 investigated the feasibility of abandoning all British possessions on the west coast. It reluctantly recommended holding those areas that Britain already controlled because the government had assumed certain moral responsibilities to the people of these colonies, particularly those at Freetown. The British presence had to remain, but with the distinct understanding that no new territories were to be added. This policy was scrupulously followed and resulted in the French occupation in the 1880s of the coastal area northwest of Sierra Leone and the Isles de Los.

During the half century following the assumption of control by the crown, a homogeneous population owing more to the culture of Western Europe than to Africa developed in the colony. The original settlers from Britain, Nova Scotia, and Jamaica and their immediate descendants at first held aloof from the freed slaves who were brought in increasing numbers to the colony. Government and missionary groups attempted to provide these liberated slaves with land and a small amount of relief funds. Since the liberated slaves had come from all parts of West Africa, they tended to drift toward their countrymen who congregated together in small villages around Freetown or in specific areas of the city. Within a generation the gap between the early Christian settlers and the new arrivals had narrowed, because the latter had begun to adopt the dominant language, religion, and mores of the colony.

The early settlers of Freetown did not regard themselves as Africans. Most held the native people of the interior in contempt for their backward "pagan" ways. The ethos of Freetown was a blend of evangelical Christianity and the materialism of nineteenth-century Britain. Christian missions continued to play an important role in the colony. A "Christian Institution" of learning was established in 1827 and this became Fourah Bay College in 1845. From this institution came a long list of men who would distinguish themselves as ministers, doctors, lawyers, and tradesmen, not only in Freetown, but throughout West Africa. The merchants based in Freetown traded with the interior of Africa and Europe and many made large fortunes. Others became artisans or entered the lower echelon of government service. They built substantial homes and copied the dress and manners of the British middle class. The newly arrived freed slave, if he chose, could adopt Christianity, work hard, and perhaps be accepted by the dominant families of Freetown as almost an equal. By 1865 this process of assimilation had gone on so long that there was little practical distinction between descendants of the 1790 settlers and those of freed slaves of the 1820s and 1830s. This mixed, Westernized creole population, protected from the Mende and Temne tribesmen of the interior, thrived in a manner that could be envied by the freed slaves in Liberia who were sponsored by American Evangelicals.

Liberia

Many concerned public officials and Evangelicals in the United States had viewed the Freetown experiment with great interest. Resettlement in Africa appeared to offer a solution to the poor conditions under which many freed slaves were forced to live, particularly in the southern United States. The first attempt at colonization was by a Negro Quaker, Paul Cuffee, who led thirty-eight settlers to Freetown in 1816. Governor Mac-Carthy did not welcome adding the care and possible maintenance of large numbers of Americanized Negroes to his many other problems; therefore, he suggested to Cuffee, who relayed the information back to the United States, that the Cape Mesurado area southeast of Freetown would be an excellent locale for any further similar experiments.

In late 1816 the American Colonization Society was formed. Its major function was to sponsor colonies of free Negroes in West Africa. In addition to the many ministers and abolitionists attracted to the new society, it also had the support of influential men in government such as Henry Clay, Bushrod Washington, and Daniel Webster. There was considerable support for the resettlement scheme by many slave owners who wanted to get rid of the free Negroes in the South. The United States government reluctantly agreed to provide transportation for the colonists but disclaimed any direct responsibility for the undertaking. The first settlement attempt sponsored by the society was by a group of eighty who landed on Sherbro Island in 1820. Within a few months, disease had all but destroyed the experiment and the survivors were taken to Freetown. Another group of thirty-three tried to establish themselves on Sherbo Island in 1821 but also failed. In December 1821, Dr. Eli Ayres and a small number of settlers arrived at Cape Mesurado. Upon landing they negotiated the purchase of the area from a local Bassa chief for approximately $300 in trade goods. It is reported that the most effective argument Ayres had for the cession was a pistol aimed at the head of the unfortunate chief. The land thus obtained later became the site of the city of Monrovia.

The society had meanwhile formed state branches, some of which later would plant their own small colonies in West Africa. For the settlement at Mesurado the society issued a constitution that conferred upon its resident agent administrative, legislative, and judicial powers. The laws of the new colony were to be those of the United States. In 1822 Yehudi Ashmun arrived in Mesurado to assume the post of agent, and until his death in 1828 he was the most important influence within the colony. The new town was named Monrovia and Ashmun supervised its fortification against the raids of neighboring African peoples. From the beginning the Kru, Bassa, and Grebo had not wanted the settlement and their antipathy soon took the form of raids against the colonists. In 1823 there was a minor war when the Africans attempted to drive the settlers from Monrovia.

Another problem closely related to the hostility evinced toward the settlers that Ashmun tried to solve was the continuation of slave trading almost within sight of the settlement. In July 1824, he reported that over 800 slaves had been sold from the vicinity of Monrovia in a three-month period. The slavers, most of whom were Spanish, refused to recognize the jurisdiction of the society over the territory. Ashmun and the settlers, in conjunction with the United States Navy, eventually raided a number of slave centers, burned the barracoons, and released the slaves. However, the society did not possess the power to stop the activities of the slavers along the entire coast. They continued to operate even after Liberia had become an independent state.

Tension, similar to that which had disrupted the Freetown colony in its earlier years, quickly developed between the settlers and the agents of the society. Most of the settlers were unprepared for the hard life in Africa. Disease, threats from native Africans, and the hard work necessary to clear the ground and plant crops were the actual reasons for the colonists' dissatisfaction. The agent represented rules that governed the colony and many of the colonists' complaints were focused upon this symbol of authority. The situation became so bad that a special agent of the society was sent in 1824 to investigate settler charges against Ashmun. Despite this the society did little to mollify the settlers until the late 1830s when the agent's title was changed to that of governor and the settlers received a portion of legislative and executive authority by having a resident council to represent their views.

In 1834 the Maryland branch of the society established a small colony near Cape Palmas. Later the New York and Pennsylvania branches began one on the St. Johns River. In 1838 the Greenville colony was begun by the Louisiana and Mississippi societies. Each of these small establishments was governed separately from Monrovia until 1838 when the society merged all except the Maryland venture into one colony. This new unified entity called the Commonwealth of Liberia was administered by a governor and a council, but the society still retained veto power over their decisions. The Maryland settlement was not absorbed by Liberia until 1857.

The first governor, Thomas Buchanan, was white, but in 1841 J. J. Roberts, a Negro settler, was appointed governor. Roberts thus began a long career of service to Liberia. After independence he was elected president five times, the last time in 1872. The first governors attempted to raise revenue for the state by levying customs duties on imports and exports. This led immediately to protests to the society from missionaries and, most important, the British government. In 1843 Britain asked the United States to clarify its relationship with Liberia. Was it a colony or protectorate of the United States? The answer, although not definitive, indicated that Liberia had never been considered a possession of the United States. This imbroglio led directly to the severing of connections between the American Colonization Society and Liberia in 1846. In the following year, a constitutional convention met in Monrovia in June to consider adopting a declaration of independence and constitution. On July 26, 1847, Liberia proclaimed its independence.

The Liberian Constitution established a system of government patterned directly upon that of the United States. There was to be a president, vice-president, congress, and supreme court. The laws of Liberia were basically the laws of the United States. It also adopted United States currency, weights and measures, and, in theory, its educational system. Despite the close historical links with the United States and the establishment of parallel institutions, the governments of Presidents Taylor, Fillmore, Pierce, and Buchanan tried to ignore the new state. Britain and France recognized Liberia immediately, but the United States did not recognize it until 1862. Herein lies the major difference between Liberia and the similarly created British colony of Freetown. The Liberians were all but cut adrift in the nineteenth century whereas the creole population at Freetown received the support of British protection and British investment.

The survival of Liberia as an independent state, particularly in the period of the later scramble for Africa, is one of the minor miracles of the nineteenth century. In 1860 there were fewer than 10,000 settlers in Liberia. They did not think of themselves as Africans; they were Christian, had some education, spoke English, and attempted to live according to current standards in the United States. Posts in government service were restricted to these Americo-Liberians. No concrete attempts to associate Africans in the government were made until well into the twentieth century. Although there was at the beginning a two-party system, the Whig party came to dominate public life. There were wars with the adjacent African peoples. The Grebo War of 1857, which resulted in the incorporation of the Maryland colony, was particularly savage. By the close of the nineteenth century the Americo-Liberians controlled the narrow coastal strip, but they had no practical authority over the large hinterland area which they claimed.

Liberia had to depend upon agriculture for its existence. It had few exports of value; therefore, it had little enough money to operate the government let alone to undertake major developments. Foreign investments and loans were almost impossible to get. After the default on a British loan of 1871, Britain proposed a joint Anglo-American protectorate but was thwarted by United States and French opposition. During the last two decades of the nineteenth century when Africa was being divided up, Liberia was saved by the jealousy of the competitive powers. The United States, although not wishing to assume the responsibility for the area, did not want to see its independence liquidated. In 1906 a British development company, in return for a loan, gained brief control of the customs office and frontier forces. This led to the establishment of a consortium composed of Britain, France, and the United States which, until World War I, collected the customs duties.

Despite its long history as an independent state, Liberia is practically a twentieth-century phenomenon. Large-scale investment in rubber plantations during the 1920s rescued the finances of the state, and the discovery of iron in the 1950s made Liberia financially independent. The effective policy of integration of members of the twenty tribes of the hinterland into the state is only a generation old. The bulk of the important positions in government are still held by Americo-Liberians. The one great advantage Liberia possessed over the new African states created in the late 1950s was a long history of governing itself within the context of a constitution which allowed it to extend freedom and government participation to Africans without revolution or even major government reorganization.

The Gold Coast

Much of the history of the Gold Coast for the century following the accession of Osei Kojo as Asantahene in 1764 seems to be a series of repetitious actions. The rule of the Ashanti was supreme over kindred Akan clans in an area of approximately 100 miles north and south and 150 miles east and west with its center in Kumasi. Far beyond this nucleus the Ashanti controlled vassal states through a system of treaties and the fear of Ashanti armies. These dependent states were so different that they could not be assimilated into the Ashanti Union. Thus the Ashanti were continuously involved in punitive expeditions and small wars against chiefs who wished to sever their connections with the Asantahene. One objective of Ashanti was to dominate the coastal Fante, Wassaw, Akim, and Ewe people. Although none of these polities was powerful enough to stand alone against the Ashanti, they did ally themselves with the Europeans who dominated the export trade from their many coastal forts. The combinations of Europeans and native allies denied the Ashanti practical control of the coast. However, these combinations were short-lived and were not powerful enough to keep the Ashanti from trying repeatedly to dominate the coast.

European activities along the coast were divided between Danish, Dutch, and British merchants. Each group attempted throughout the early nineteenth century to secure the major part of the trade for themselves. This competition made it impossible to present to the Ashanti a common economic or political policy except in times of extreme crisis. There were no clearly demarcated spheres of trading influence. The Danes attempted to play the Fante and Ashanti off against the British, and British merchants intrigued against the Dutch. The only long range common trade policy concerned the restriction of trading firearms to the Ashanti. In order to obtain guns, the Ashanti turned their trade more toward merchants operating from the Ivory and Slave coasts. This became increasingly true after the British abolition of the slave trade.

It is a mistake to assume that the three European governments were greatly concerned with the Gold Coast. Merchants of each country kept alive the old claims to the coast and were responsible for the upkeep of the trading forts. The British areas after 1783 were administered by the Company of Merchants Trading in Africa. They received a small annual

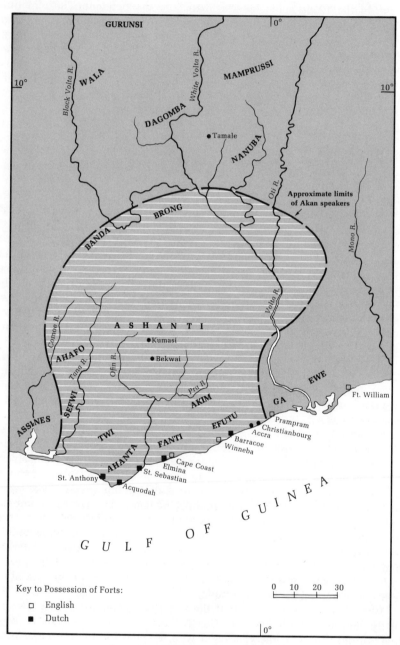

Nineteenth Century Gold Coast

subsidy from parliament for the upkeep of the forts. The company could not afford to maintain the military force necessary to counter Ashanti power or to act effectively against the slave trade. A complex combination of events in the first two decades of the nineteenth century eventually convinced the British government to assume direct control of the company's forts.

The period from 1800 to 1820 was probably the apex of the power of the Ashanti Union. The Ashanti claimed to be the overlords of the Fante middlemen living within the trading sphere of the European forts. In 1806 they defeated the Fante and European forces, captured the Dutch fort of Kormantin, and elicited from the chief representative of the British company the promise to pay the Ashanti rent for the continued occupation of the forts. By extension the Europeans had agreed that the Fante were vassals of the Ashanti. In the next ten years, the Ashanti armies continued to humble the divided Fante, Wassaw, and Akim peoples. In 1817 the British sent a mission to Kumasi and entered into an agreement whereby the Asantahene promised to protect the British forts. In return the British promised Ashanti traders along the coast equal treatment with the Fante.

The disturbed conditions in the hinterland, combined with evangelical pressure to end the slave trade, resulted in the reversion of the eight trading forts to the British crown. In 1821 Sir Charles MacCarthy assumed the responsibility of governing all British West African possessions. He began a more aggressive policy to rid the coast of the constant threat of an Ashanti invasion. MacCarthy obtained assurances of help from the Fante and Ga and rejected any idea of compromise with the Ashanti.

The result of this ill-conceived policy was war between Britain and the Ashanti. MacCarthy had underestimated his enemy and paid for this mistake with his life in 1824. After MacCarthy's death, Britain sent reinforcements to the coast to prevent the Ashanti from profiting from their previous victories. The British government then announced that it would stop all payments to the Ashanti for use of the forts. Despite victories over the Ashanti armies in 1826, the war dragged on. The following year the Colonial Office, in another reversal of policy, withdrew all British troops and officials from the Gold Coast, leaving their traders to extricate themselves from the results of the disastrous expansionist policy.

The British government, while still claiming the territory on which the forts were located, turned over actual administration of Cape Coast and Accra to three of the largest companies trading in the Gold Coast. Their representatives formed the London Committee, which made the general policy for the British Gold Coast. In the Gold Coast, resident executive authority was exercised by a Council of Seven. The president of the council, appointed by London, was the chief executive officer. Parliament paid the committee a small annual subsidy to help meet the expenses of maintaining the forts. In 1830 George Maclean, a young army officer, was appointed president of the council. He, more than any other person, was responsible for retaining the Gold Coast for Britain.

In 1830 the war still continued, trade with the interior was disrupted, and the Dutch and Danes were spreading their influence into areas that had been British spheres. Worst of all, the Fante and other allies had lost faith when British troops had been withdrawn. Maclean, who had served there during the disturbances of the mid-1820s, was no stranger to the territory. He was dynamic, shrewd, and relatively unhampered by unwanted, potentially harmful orders from London. He had only a small militia force and his intelligence with which to counter his enemies. In a short time he had restored the trust of the Fante in Britain by mediating quarrels between competing chiefs. He convinced the Dutch and Danes to abandon their differential policies that were ultimately harmful to all European traders. Finally he negotiated an end to the long war with the Ashanti. In return for recognition of their right to trade directly with the coast, the Ashanti relinquished their claims to be paid rent for the British forts. This was a trader's peace. Both the Ashanti and British merchants wanted to reopen the normal channels of trade. Therefore, there was no attempt to define the relationship of the coastal people with the British and the Ashanti.

Following this agreement with the Ashanti, Maclean interfered more in the affairs of adjacent people. He worked to stop such practices as human sacrifice, handed down rules that he considered binding on the Fante, and, if necessary, sent out punitive expeditions. He thus created an unofficial protectorate over the coast behind the British forts extending approximately forty miles into the interior. Exports during Maclean's rule increased fivefold. By 1840 they had risen to £325,000 per year and imports had increased threefold in the same period to £425,000 per year. Maclean's masterly tour de force was not applauded by all. Missionaries who arrived in the Gold Coast in this decade were very critical of Maclean. They believed he had not interfered enough to stop "heathen" practices, to end domestic slavery, and to spread Christianity. Other more legal-minded critics pointed, on the contrary, to the degree to which he had assumed control over the hinterland. To them the establishment of a de facto protectorate was illegal. Maclean had been given authority only over the affairs at Cape Coast and near Accra and should not have meddled in native affairs.

In 1841, in response to his critics, the Colonial Office sent a committed antislavery advocate, Dr. R. R. Madden, to investigate the charges. His report, despite the fact that he had spent little time in the Gold Coast, was so negative that in the following year a select committee of parliament was appointed to investigate the full range of British problems on the west coast. The report of the committee exonerated Maclean of wrongdoing and praised him for what he had accomplished with so little funds. The report stated the need for more money and for a more consistent policy for all British areas in West Africa. It suggested that this could be facilitated by a return to the system of one governor-general for all of British West Africa. In 1843 this system was approved and the Gold Coast reverted to direct administration by the crown through a lieutenant-governor. Maclean was retained as chief justice with special reference to native peoples. However, from this date until his death in 1847, he had little influence over major policy making in the Gold Coast.

The Foreign Jurisdictions Act of 1843 enabled the administration to legalize the de facto arrangements he had made with the hinterland chiefs. This was done by means of treaties, called "Bonds," with individual rulers. The chiefs promised to protect European property and lives, abolish certain practices repugnant to Europeans, and allow British judges to assist them in major cases such as murder and robbery. These "Bonds" did not convey to the British specific rights of government. However, in the Gold Coast, as elsewhere in West Africa, the administration of justice was difficult to separate from executive and legislative authority.

The resumption of authority by the crown did not succeed in establishing a consistent policy. Administration by the Colonial Office, through appointed officials who knew nothing of the peculiar problems of the area and who at best stayed for only a few years, could hardly have achieved what Maclean, acting without interference, could not do. Nor were the administrators given the money necessary to do much more than maintain the government establishment. The forts fell into even greater disrepair. In 1852 an attempt was made to improve finances by having chiefs collect a poll tax from their subjects. This plan never functioned well and was eventually abandoned. Dutch and Danish competition limited the funds that could be raised by increasing customs duties. In 1850 the Danes, after having struggled unsuccessfully to find enough profit from legitimate trade in troubled times, ceded their forts to the British. However, the Dutch continued to refuse to cooperate in establishing standardized policies.

Failure to clarify the relationship between the Europeans, the coastal people, and the Ashanti resulted in a series of minor incidents in the 1850s. The situation reached crisis proportions when Governor Pine refused to release to the Ashanti certain persons accused of various crimes. In 1863 Ashanti armies crossed into the area ostensibly under British protection. Pine was convinced that peace and prosperity would come to the coast only when the menace of the Ashanti was removed; therefore, he recommended launching a major counterattack against the invaders. The British government refused to authorize the expenditure. The coastal people again lost faith in the British ability to protect them, and trade, which had steadily declined in the 1850s, came almost to a complete halt.

These were the conditions which inspired the Colonial Office to send Colonel H. St. George Ord in 1864 and a select committee of parliament in 1865 to study the feasibility of a complete British withdrawal from West Africa. Both reports applauded this as a long-range objective but agreed that it was impossible to achieve immediately. The main proposals implemented were the restriction of the areas of British jurisdiction in West Africa, and once again the unification of all British West African territories under a governor-general at Freetown. In the Gold Coast, British authority was to be confined to the forts at Accra, Dixcove, Anomabu, and Christianborg, and to a five-mile radius around Cape Coast.

Educated Fante were encouraged to work for a meaningful association between the many competitive polities that would give them the ability to defend themselves against the Ashanti. In 1867 the British, in order to have their possessions on the Gold Coast grouped in one area, made a treaty with the Dutch. By this arrangement all British forts west of Cape Coast were to be exchanged for all Dutch forts east of Elmina. Although logical to colonial officials in London, this treaty set into motion events that destroyed the retrenchment policy of 1865. African chiefs and their subjects had not been consulted about the transfer. Many Africans did not want Dutch protection. The Denkara actually prevented the Dutch from occupying Kommenda. The inhabitants of Elmina were definitely anti-British and their attitude led to conflict with other nearby coastal polities. To complicate matters, the Ashanti reinvaded the coastal areas in 1868.

With such prevalent conditions and faced with a steadily declining trade, the Dutch in 1869 began negotiations for reversion of all their forts to the British. These complicated discussions were not completed until 1872 when the British, much to the dismay of some high officials, controlled all the Europeans forts on the coast. Complications arose immediately after the transfer. The people of Elmina were pro-Ashanti and encouraged the intervention of the Asantahene to prevent the British from occupying the fort. The Dutch had claimed that the rent that they paid to the Ashanti for their forts was simply another form of "dash" which enabled them to trade in peace. The Asantahene, however, claimed that all the forts were his. The Dutch had not consulted him about any transfer and he wanted them. The British attempted negotiations with the Ashanti and one of their envoys erroneously reported that Asantahene Kofi Kari-kari had renounced his claim to the disputed area. At this juncture the educated Fante proudly announced the completion of their attempts to create a meaningful federation. At Mankessim they had formed a confed-eration of thirty-three member states with a federal assembly and a king-president. Having been encouraged to do this, they were surprised and chagrined when the British government viewed this as a pro-Ashanti conspiracy and briefly arrested the leaders of the confederation movement.

In January 1873 the main Ashanti army invaded the coast once again with the express purpose of occupying the territory formerly ruled by the Dutch. Rains, an outbreak of dysentery, and smallpox halted the Ashanti and gave the British time to reassess their position and reluctantly accept the advice Governor Pine had given a decade before. Ashanti power in the coastal areas had to be eliminated. In October Major General Garnet Wolseley assumed the position of administrator and commander in chief of the Gold Coast. Over 2,500 British regular soldiers and large numbers of native auxiliaries gave General Wolseley enough strength to invade Ashantiland in early January 1874. Two major battles were fought in late January and early February. The Ashanti military organization and indi-vidual bravery proved no match for British firepower, and on February 5 Wolseley's forces entered Kumasi. Since the purpose of the expedition was not to occupy Ashantiland, Wolseley retired after burning the city. Repre-sentatives of the Asantahene soon after sued for peace. The terms dictated by the British demanded that the Ashanti pay an indemnity of 50,000 ounces of gold, renounce their claims over the coastal areas, promise to keep trade routes to the north open, and cease human sacrifice.

In July 1874 the conservative government of Disraeli proclaimed the direct takeover of the previously protected areas on the Gold Coast. Administration of the enlarged colony was separated from the authority of the governor-general at Freetown and placed under its own governor. These actions effectively killed any hope that the Fante might have had for a resurrection of their confederation schemes. Britain, despite its hesitant vacillating policies, had decided to increase its territory in the Gold Coast. Nevertheless, the Colonial Office was unwilling to sanction any further expansion at the expense of the Ashanti. The 1874 war thus did not settle in a final way the question of hegemony over the interior. The proud, warlike Ashanti still retained their land, organization, and military forces. Supremacy of the hinterland was not finally settled until 1900.

Oyo and the Yoruba states

The structures of government in Oyo were under stress in the eighteenth century. The system had been developed to rule directly over a much smaller area than that of the Oyo empire. Expansion of the empire and trading sphere brought a schism between the great councillors of state, the Oyo mesi, and the palace administration that the alafin used to carry out the government of the state. The alafin was theoretically a divine king, but in practice his power was considerably less than that of the kings of Dahomey, the Asantahene, or the Hausa rulers. If he abused his powers, he could be removed from office by the Oyo mesi and forced to commit suicide. By the mid-eighteenth century all the conditions were present for radical alteration of the way that Oyo was governed. This occurred when Prime Minister (Basorun) Gaha seized authority and became the real power in Oyo for over twenty years.

Before the mid-eighteenth century, the alafin directly controlled most of the western Yoruba towns and was represented there by officials charged with supervising tribute payments and securing the safety of trade caravans. The kingdoms of Borgu, Nupe, and the Egba states to the south were also tributaries of Oyo. Dahomey had finally agreed in 1747 to pay an annual tribute to Oyo and the alafin gave his protection to the trading cities of Porto Novo and Badagry. The power struggle in Oyo between Basorun Gaha and the alafins weakened the power of the central government. Finally in 1774 Alafin Abiodum killed Gaha and ended the power of the basorun's subordinates in the central government, but he was not able to purge the entire empire of Gaha's supporters.

The empire had been held together not only because of efficient administration, but also partly because the tributary monarchs feared retribution by the armies of Oyo. The armies' efficiency was also damaged by the long contest for central power on Oyo. The tempo of the slave trade had increased in the latter eighteenth century, and Oyo found that the few secure places for obtaining increased numbers of slaves were the Yoruba areas themselves and the adjoining non-Yoruba tributaries to the south and east of Oyo proper. The greater volume of trade in these areas increased the tensions between the central government and these territories. Beginning in the 1780s, the authority of the alafin was successfully challenged by a number of client rulers. In 1783 Borgu and in 1791 Nupe defeated the armies of Oyo and declared their independence. Dahomey ceased paying its tribute on a regular basis, and in 1818 King Gezo declared Dahomey's complete independence from Oyo. Armies dispatched by the alafin against territory dependent on the oni of Ife in 1796 refused to act and subsequently the alafin committed suicide. Afonja, the commander of the armies of Oyo, defected from Oyo and joined the Fulani armies in establishing a separatist rule over Ilorin.

These events coincided with an increase in the demand for slaves by Europeans along the coast due to increasing activity of the British Navy eastward from the Niger delta. Oyo's supply of slaves from the north had been cut off by the revolts of Nupe and Borgu and the actions of Afonja at Ilorin. The disturbances in Oyo, which had begun largely for reasons unconnected with the slave trade, degenerated into a long series of wars between competitive Yoruba rulers for the main purpose of gathering slaves. These Yoruba civil wars lasted until 1893 and resulted first in the fragmentation of the Oyo empire and later made it virtually impossible for the Yoruba to resist European incursion.

There are a few important developments in the early stages of these complex wars that must be mentioned. In 1827 a combination of Ife, Ijebu, and Oyo forces took and destroyed the powerful eastern city of Owu. Refugees from Owu returned to Egbaland and precipitated a decade of warfare that destroyed many villages and provided the victors with large numbers of slaves from the homeless. In 1829 some Ijebu, Ife, Egba, and Oyo refugees settled in the vicinity of the small town of Ibadan. Subsequent quarrels between factions at Ibadan resulted in migration southward of a sizeable portion of the Ibadan settlers. These established themselves at Abeokuta where they created a federal system of government that the Egba tended to dominate. In Ibadan itself there were a series of disputes throughout the 1830s that ended with the Oyo faction supreme. Ibadan soon became the most important of all the Yoruba towns, generally allied, but not subservient to Oyo.

During this period the Fulani at Ilorin were attempting to subjugate as much of Yorubaland as possible. If the Yoruba had not been so deeply divided, the Fulani would have posed no real threat. However, the internecine wars enabled Ilorin to conquer the previously powerful city-states of Ikoyi and Gbogun. The Fulani cavalry was halted in the hilly, wooded area of Ijesa, but there was no such protection for Oyo and the alafin fell under the domination of the Fulani rulers of Ilorin. In an attempt to throw off his control, Oyo allied itself with Borgu and Nikki. Oyo received no assistance from the rulers of other Yoruba states and in 1837 Muslim armies took and sacked Old Oyo so thoroughly that little remains today of the center of the once powerful Oyo empire. Ile Ife, the spiritual center for the Yoruba, was also abandoned temporarily during this phase of the wars.

Refugees from Old Oyo and nearby villages moved southward under their new alafin and settled in the small town of Ago Oja which henceforth became the capital of the Oyo kingdom. Soon after the founding of New Oyo, the Yoruba of Ibadan delivered a resounding defeat to the Fulani at Oshogbo in 1840. Although the Fulani threat remained active throughout the nineteenth century, they never afterward were able to mount a major offensive. However, the troubles of Yorubaland were not over. Wars between various city-states continued widening the gulf between Yoruba so that in some cases Muslims from the north were used in the fighting. In the mid-1840s the king of Dahomey, still deeply involved in the slave trade, began to encroach upon Yoruba territory. The greatest Dahomean threat came in 1851. King Gezo, taking advantage of Ibadan's preoccupation in a war with Ilesha, sent a strong army against Abeokuta. The Egba needed missionary assistance and ammunition supplied by the British Consul John Beecroft in order to repel the Dahomean invaders.

Southern Nigeria and Dahomey to 1865

In southern Nigeria the twenty-five year period after 1845 witnessed a curious liaison between three, at times, antagonistic elements—the traders, the missionaries, and the British government. As previously noted, the missionaries were very active among the Ijo and Ibibio east of the delta. The Atlantic slave trade was still present, but by mid-century had been greatly restricted by the British Navy. Even more important, the rulers of the leading coastal towns had found that oil palm products brought profits without the dangers attendant on the seaborne slave trade. Bonny soon became the most important city for this trade, while New Calabar and Brass also turned more in the direction of legitimate trade. African middlemen still controlled the bulk of the new trade. Although there were over 200 individual European traders along the coast, Liverpool traders predominated. They were content to allow the Africans to gather the oil so long as they could have the largest share in the trade. In the early 1850s, Europeans in most of the trading cities established courts of equity in order to discipline their members and to keep African rulers from retaliating against Europeans en masse for the activities of a few.

There were, however, Europeans who were not content with dealing with middlemen. Macgregor Laird and his associates were quick to take advantage of the interior discoveries of explorers. In 1857 he contracted with the British government to maintain a steamship on the Niger. The use of quinine made possible permanent trade stations such as Aboh, Onitsha, and Lokoja in the interior. Dr. Baikie established himself at Lokoja after his expedition in 1854 and pioneered new trading routes to Nupe and the north. These growing activities in the interior were resented by the Liverpool merchants along the coast as well as the African rulers. Between 1860 and 1870 Laird's ships were escorted on the river by naval vessels. The tension between the new European merchants and the traditional form of trading activity continued throughout the nineteenth century

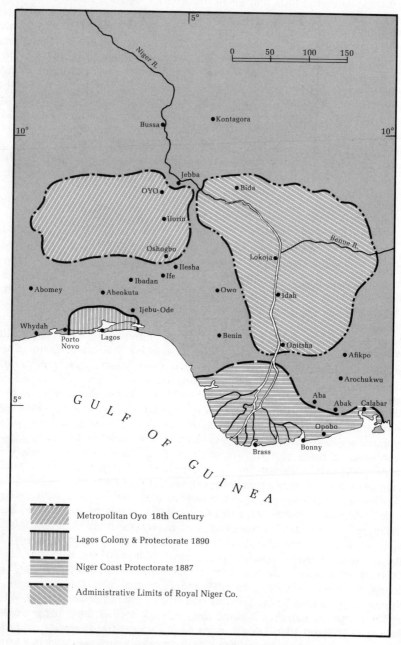

Southern Nigeria in the Late Nineteenth Century

Map labels:

5°
Niger R.

0   50   100   150

Kontagora
Bussa
10°   10°

Jebba
OYO   Bida
Ilorin
Benue R.
Oshogbo   Lokoja
Ilesha
Ife
Abomey   Abeokuta   Ibadan   Owo   Idah
Ijebu-Ode
Whydah
Porto   Lagos   Benin   Onitsha
Novo   Afikpo

5°   Arochukwu
Aba
G U L F   Abak   Calabar
O F   Opobo
G U I N E A   Brass   Bonny

Metropolitan Oyo 18th Century

Lagos Colony & Protectorate 1890

Niger Coast Protectorate 1887

Administrative Limits of Royal Niger Co.

until the great African trading houses were broken by the British invasions during the scramble. In the 1850s and 1860s these conflicts were open invitations for British officials to begin their intervention in African affairs.

In 1849 John Beecroft was named British consul for the Bights of Benin and Biafra. He had been active in west coast affairs since he left his ship at Fernando Po as a young sailor in 1827. In the intervening years he had explored the hinterland regions of the delta, become a successful trader, served the British government in a number of missions, and in 1843 had been named governor of Fernando Po by the Spanish. Beecroft favored more direct involvement of Britain in the affairs of African states to secure trade, advance missionary activity, and end the slave trade. In his six-year tenure as consul, he made the British presence felt in a variety of ways. Because of complaints of European traders and factionalism, he used British power in 1851 to depose and exile William Pepple, the ruler of Bonny, the most powerful delta trading state. Although Pepple was returned a decade later, the internal affairs of Bonny were never the same afterward. Beecroft also was very active in attempting to influence policy at Calabar.

It was at Lagos that his intervention had the most immediate effect. Continuing wars in the Yoruba states and the expansion of slave raiding activities by the king of Dahomey had made Lagos and Badagry major slave trading ports. British missionaries at these places and at Abeokuta continually bombarded the British government with pleas to end the internecine conflict, halt the slave traffic, and open the interior for legitimate trade. To them Kosoko, the ruler of Lagos, represented all that was wrong with the system because he was a confirmed slaver. However, his position was not secure because there were powerful factions within Lagos who resented the methods by which Kosoko had come to power. Beecroft interjected himself in this complex internal situation. He obtained a promise from Akitoye, Kosoko's uncle, that he would suppress the slave trade if he were selected oba. In 1851 Beecroft attempted to force Kosoko out by invasion, but failed. However, elements of the British West African squadron drove Kosoko from Lagos and Akitoye was later confirmed as the ruler. In 1853 after Akitoye's death, Docemo, his choice as a successor, was confirmed as oba. A full British consul was appointed for Lagos in the same year.

Kosoko, from his base at Epe, continued to harass interior traders. The Yoruba wars were an ever present deterrent to the establishment of legitimate trade, and Dahomey was a constant threat to the missionaries at Abeokuta. Thus in 1861, the British, in order to obtain a more permanent base in Yorubaland, gained the cession of Lagos from Docemo in return for an annual pension of £1,030. Soon afterward the governor at Lagos annexed the slaving town of Badagry and destroyed the town of Epe. The interior wars usually involving Ibadan continued in the 1860s unchecked by the growth of British influence on the coast. During one of these wars in 1867, the ruler of Abeokuta, angered at continuing interference from Lagos, expelled all European missionaries. For over a decade thereafter missionary activity among the Yoruba was almost nonexistent. In the same period, British trading firms became well established at Lagos and legitimate trade with the Yoruba in oil palm products and cotton increased. The reality of this trade with the Yoruba was at variance with the report of the 1865 select committee, which recommended a nonexpansive political policy. The combination of trading and missionary activities dictated a forward policy. When the British government decided to support such a policy in the 1880s, they found little opposition from the Yoruba states weakened by seventy years of civil war.

Westward from Badagry lay the coastal areas dominated by the powerful Fon kingdom of Dahomey. This well-organized, militaristic state had been checked in its expansion in the eighteenth century only by the Ashanti in the west and Oyo in the east. The ports of Whydah, Jaquin, Little Popo, and Porto Novo were most important for Dahomey's major export, slaves. European traders at these ports were never allowed to gain the power and influence that they exercised on the Gold Coast. Nevertheless, they played an important role in the complex competition for power between the kings of Dahomey, local rulers, and the alafin of Oyo. The kings of Dahomey managed to defeat the trading nobility at Whydah and Jaquin and to humble the European traders by the latter eighteenth century. By becoming a tributary of Oyo, they protected their eastern borders from invasions from this great Yoruba power. The focus of European slave trading activity in the latter eighteenth century moved from the Dahomean coast to Badagry and Lagos, and to the states east of the Niger delta.

The Dahomean state in the nineteenth century depended upon the slave trade, and its kings were, at first, helpless to reverse the trend of the trade away from Dahomey. The French, who were the dominant European traders in the area, also struck at the prosperity of Dahomey when in 1794 the republic banned the slave trade. However, in the early nineteenth century, a series of events gave the Dahomeans a chance to regain their supremacy in the trade of the Slave Coast. The French returned, to be sure, in lesser numbers after 1802. More important was the breakup of the mighty Oyo empire and the subsequent civil wars in Yorubaland. King Gezo of Dahomey felt secure enough to stop paying the annual tribute to the alafin of Oyo. The activities of the British West African patrol along the eastern Nigerian coast made Dahomey once again an inviting area for trade. Lagos, Badagry, and Porto Novo, because of the Yoruba wars, became almost independent entities. It, therefore, was only natural for King Gezo to try to absorb western Yorubaland into his sphere of influence.

When King Gezo actually began to attempt incorporation of Yoruba territory into his kingdom in the 1840s, he was opposed not only by individual Egba and Yoruba rulers, but also by Britain. Abeokuta was one of the major collection points for slaves in troubled Yorubaland, and Gezo attempted in 1845, 1848, and 1851 to absorb the Egba states into his kingdom. Reference has already been made to the contributions of Consul Beecroft and the missionaries to the defense of Abeokuta which foiled Gezo's plans. The establishment of British hegemony over Lagos and later

Badagry made it impossible for the Dahomean kings to incorporate these rich ports into their sphere of influence. Thus, due largely to the British, Dahomean efforts were only an additional cause for disorder in Yorubaland.

The Dahomean slave ports prospered during the first half of the nineteenth century because of restrictions on the trade elsewhere along the coast. British efforts to get Gezo and his successor, Gelele, to abandon the trade proved fruitless. A British mission in 1850 was flatly told that the king had no intention of giving up trading in slaves. In 1852 Gezo did sign a treaty but made no attempt to enforce it. All that could be done was to impose a rigid blockade on the Dahomean ports. The British government at one time considered military operations against Gezo but rejected it. Dahomey was one of the stronger powers in West Africa and could not be as easily defeated as the divided polities of coastal Nigeria. The active antislavery policy of Britain warned the Dahomean rulers that they had to maintain their military forces. Since they had not developed legitimate trade to any degree, the export of slaves was necessary to buy the guns that would assure their supremacy.

The history of the Slave Coast in the latter nineteenth century is bound up with the conflicting colonial ambitions of Britain and France. Britain had already staked out a sizeable sphere of influence from Badagry to Calabar. The French, after the abandonment of their fort at Whydah, were quiescent until the 1870s. However, when the scramble began, Dahomey became one of the major areas of French interest. Opposing this new imperialism, the autocratic rulers of Dahomey would be crushed in two bloody wars in the 1890s.

French activities to 1870

France, the second European power with considerable territorial and trading interest in West Africa, suffered from more handicaps than did Britain. The British government, despite changes of government, was stable throughout the nineteenth century. The French had been deeply divided ideologically and politically by the revolutions of the latter eighteenth century. These wide differences between conservative and liberal forces were reflected in the nineteenth century by the revolutions of 1830 and 1848. No less profound was the coup of Napoleon III in 1852 and the War of the Commune in 1871 following the Franco-Prussian War. Thus a succession of different governments based upon divergent theories of rule could hardly be expected to follow consistent imperial policies. French activity in Africa until the period of the Third Republic was very limited by comparison to its rival Britain. Two other factors should be remembered in discussing French imperialism. The first is the inferior nature of the French manufacturing and banking sectors in comparison to Britain. Thus mercantile and manufacturing pressure on French governments for overseas expansion was not great until the last quarter of the century. Another factor was that France had lost the bulk of her overseas territories in the wars with Britain in the eighteenth century. In Africa this meant that they had no substantial spheres until after the Napoleonic Wars. Even afterwards they were relatively restricted to the posts in the Senegambia which Britain had returned to them in 1817.

The major French enclave was St. Louis du Senegal which had been established in 1659. In addition the French controlled the island of Goree off Cape Verde and had a station at Albreda on the Gambia River. The major trade product in the early part of the century was gum gathered at Portendic and shipped from St. Louis. In the 1820s the French experimented with establishing a plantation economy based on cotton in Senegal. This venture was largely unsuccessful. Later peanuts were introduced, but this crop proved to be more suited to the land of the African kingdoms of Sine, Saloum, and Cayor. Peanut exports did not become significant until the 1850s. It is not surprising that the governments of Charles X and Louis Philippe were not eager to obtain any more territory of such dubious value.

Nevertheless, St. Louis had grown by 1851 into a small city of over 15,000 of whom almost 300 were Europeans. The myth of further riches to be gained by trade with the Niger territories had not been dispelled by the investigations of Mollien, Caillie, and British explorers. This expectation of wealth remained and became one of the reasons for Governor Louis Faidherbe's more active policy of the 1850s. In 1852 all the areas south of St. Louis were taken from the governor and placed under the authority of the naval commander on the west coast. At that period naval officers were extremely skeptical of the value of West Africa and resented the manipulations of French merchants to involve them more directly in African affairs. They acted as another brake on activist policies.

Some French merchants proved that they could compete with the British on the Ivory and Slave coasts. They brought pressure on the government to assure them protection from hostile Africans. Chief among these merchants was Victor Regis from Marseilles. He had been involved in the gum trade in Senegal until he quit in 1840 because of what he felt was government favoritism shown to his competitors. Subsequently he became involved in the palm oil trade further south. Due largely to his endeavors, the French became established on the Gabon coast and at Assinie and Grand Bassam on the Ivory Coast in 1843. Regis' company was also active at Lagos and Whydah. In 1850, when he withdrew from the Slave Coast, the navy stayed on to protect some of the smaller merchants involved in the scanty trade.

In 1841 Regis' agents secured a near monopoly of oil palm exports from Whydah in return for small payments to local officials and the king of Dahomey. His trading influence extended westward to Grand Popo. In 1851 he devised a scheme to export laborers from Africa for work in the West Indies. This was foiled by British opposition to what appeared to them as slavery in another form. Regis' position at Lagos was undercut by its transfer to the British crown in 1861 when almost immediately traiff rates on alcohol and tobacco drove him to seek an alternative port that would still allow his agents entrance to the trade of Yorubaland. His agents obtained a treaty of protection from the local ruler of Porto Novo and this was eventually approved by Napolean III's government in 1863. Regis' agent became the French consular agent for the area. However, the sandbar across the harbor there meant that another better port was needed. This led to the temporary occupation of Cotonou, which was directly ruled by King Gelele of Dahomey. The French government was in no position to undertake any real military action if Gelele moved against the European traders there. Because of the threat of possible war, the navy ordered the evacuation of Cotonou and Porto Novo in 1864. Although Regis had not been successful in his attempt to bypass Lagos, he had given the French a claim to Porto Novo. In 1868 Gelele ceded a small amount of territory at Cotonou to the French, and this together with Porto Novo gave the French bases from which much later they expanded northward into Dahomey proper.

Another place of growing French involvement during the 1860s was the Mellacourie and Scarcies River area northwest of Freetown. Creole merchants from Freetown and some French traders had been involved there for years since it was one of the outlets for trade from the Futa Jallon. In 1865 a civil war broke out between competing chiefs and protection for all European merchants became imperative. Almost all merchants trading in the Mellacourie signed a petition requesting British protection. The British government, operating on the philosophy of no expansion, was extremely reluctant to get involved. The French vice-consul at Freetown in conjunction with Governor Pinet-Laparde of Senegal decided to guarantee the security of the merchants. By using troops and naval vessels, a de facto French protectorate was established by 1868. Although British traders were in a majority in the Mellacourie, they lodged no great protests over the actions of the French authorities.

The French position in Senegal at mid-century was very weak. To the north, Moorish subgroups controlled the gum-producing areas and they charged French merchants what amounted to tribute to trade for gum. The Wolof states located between the Senegal and Gambia rivers were not controlled in any way by the governor at St. Louis whose military strength was such that he could not protect merchants even along the lower Senegal River. The rise of the Tucolor empire under Al Hajj Umar presented a definite threat to the French enclaves as well as to the Wolof. This was the situation when in 1854 a thirty-six year old engineering officer arrived in St. Louis to assume the position of governor. During his two periods as governor, Captain (later General) Louis Faidherbe's activist policies firmly established the French as the dominant force in the Senegambia.

His first area of difficulty was with the Moors. Faidherbe absorbed the Walo in 1855 and soon afterward defeated the powerful Trarza group. Thereafter the Moors could expect to be paid a standard three percent duty for gum exported through their areas. In 1857 an agreement with Britain exchanged the French post of Albreda on the Gambia for the relinquishment of British claims to the gum trade at Portendic. The French had established a fort at Podor in 1854 and one further east at Medina near the border of Tucolor territory. Faidherbe attempted to protect French merchants in the Wolof states and to further their dominance of the growing peanut trade. In the late 1850s he aroused the enmity of Portugal by establishing French claims to the Casamance north of Bissau. Faidherbe was provided with more troops and supplies from France than had any of his predecessors. He increased his potential military strength further by recruiting and training a Senegalese battalion in 1857. In 1857 Goree was returned to Faidherbe's jurisdiction, and a new town, Dakar, was established on the adjacent Cape Verde peninsula.

In 1855 Al Hajj Umar had proclaimed a holy war against the infidels in Senegambia. This did not pose any immediate threat to the French since it was directed primarily against Africans, and Umar was busy with his wars along the Niger. However, some of Umar's followers attacked French posts, and in 1857 a large segment of his army attempted to take Medina. After a siege of three months, the Tucolor were driven off. Faidherbe was concerned with the demarcation of French and Tucolor spheres of influence on the upper Senegal River and opening of trade routes to the Niger River. The first of these objectives was achieved by an agreement in 1859. During Faidherbe's second administration (1863–1865), he commissioned Lieutenant Abdon Eugene Mage to retrace Mungo Park's route to the Niger and to secure, if possible, a treaty with Umar that would encourage trade between St. Louis and the deep hinterland. Mage signed a very general agreement with Umar's son, Ahmadu, in 1866. Faidherbe's successor, Pinet-Laprade, did nothing to follow this up and there were no further French activities in that direction for over a decade.

The major sphere of French activity in the decade after 1857 was in the Wolof and Serer states. In 1859 Faidherbe, acting on many complaints from merchants, moved with approximately 350 well-trained troops against the alleged troublemakers in the kingdoms of Cayor, Sine, and Saloum. On March 18, the French defeated the army of Sine and soon afterward marched to Saloum. He dictated treaties to the two monarchs that gave the French a near monopoly of trade subject only to a three percent export duty. Each monarch granted extraterritorial rights to French citizens. Continuing threats from Sine and Saloum dictated another punitive expedition in 1861. The French established forts at Joal in Sine and Kaolack in Saloum in addition to the one previously constructed at Rufisque. In 1861 a quarrel erupted with the ruler of Cayor over French rights to build a telegraph line across his territory. The ruler, Macadou, was deposed and a puppet was installed. A strong Wolof leader, Lat Dior, disputed the throne of Cayor and it was not until January 1864 that the French were able to restore even their tentative position in Cayor.

In the mid-1860s the southern Senegambia was wracked by the religious upheavals called the Soninke-Marabout Wars. The rise of the religious reformer Maba threatened for a time not only "pagan" chiefs, but also the French presence. The kingdom of Rip, which he created, was constructed to recreate a powerful single government over the Wolof that had not existed since the breakdown of the power of the kingdom of Jolof in the eighteenth century. The growing crisis in Europe following the Austro-Prussian War meant that Governor Pinet-Laparde could not hope for replacement troops and certainly no reinforcements. Maba defeated the French a number of times and, if he had waited, he might have been successful in driving the French from the Wolof areas and thus assuring himself of the eventual domination and conversion of those states. However, he attacked Sine in 1867 and was killed in a battle against that king's forces. His death removed the greatest threat to French supremacy over the Wolof states.

The conquests of Faidherbe and Pinet-Laparde in Senegal gave France the largest European colony in West Africa. They had transformed what had been little more than a colony of two islands into extensive productive mainland possessions. In those territories where French merchants had once paid to trade, the governor at St. Louis in the 1860s claimed the right to control trade and, to varying degrees, the political life of those client states. France was thus in a very favorable position to expand control over the interior in the decades of the scramble.

Competition between Britain and France was not severe in the period 1860 through 1870. Contrary to usually stated reasons for economic conflict between the two states, it was free-trade Britain which was responsible for closed markets at this time. British territories were supposed to be self-sufficient; therefore, duties had to be imposed in order to provide the necessary funds. No such stricture was placed on French areas. The British placed high duties on alcohol and tobacco, the trade goods most used by the French. Thus, in effect, French traders were always at a disadvantage in British areas. In the mid-1860s the growing number of disagreements between British and French merchants all along the coast began to alarm both governments. Schemes for exchanges of territory and, by extension, spheres of influence were welcomed by both governments. Each wanted a grouping of areas. Most of Britain's interests were concentrated from Freetown to Lagos while the French were in the Senegambia. Thus plans for exchange involved trading Bathurst for French areas on the Ivory Coast. In 1866 and 1868 plans for such an exchange were foiled by a British parliamentary opposition that believed the compensation for British territory was not enough. Bathurst merchants and citizens also protested against being transferred to France. Despite this setback, plans for the exchange of the Gambia were revived after 1871 and this remained a possibility until World War I.

TWO
East and Central Africa before the scramble

The peoples of East Africa and the Arab traders

East Africa in the nineteenth century was inhabited by a bewildering number of differing Bantu, Nilotic, Nilo-Hamitic, and
Semitic people. Populated by a series of invaders from the north
and west over more than a thousand years, there was little
political unity. Only in the interlacustrine areas had there developed complex large-scale polities which could compare with
states in West Africa. Between the great lakes and the coast
the typical polity was small and generally clan oriented. Most of
the Bantu groups were agriculturists although wherever they
could they did keep and prize their cattle. Pastoralists such as
the Masai and Nandi with their more aggressive societies controlled a substantial portion of territory between the agricultural Bantu clans. However, they were never able to create a
state which functioned on the same high level as the interlacustrine kingdoms. Along the coast were the Zenj states dominated at the beginning of the century by local trading Arab
oligarchies. The population of these coastal towns was mixed,
the dominant language was Swahili, and the tempo of life considerably different from that of the interior villages and towns.

The most stable, affluent, and powerful of the East African
kingdoms was Buganda. Energetic rulers early in the century
had successfully declared their independence from Bunyoro.
Under Suna and later Mutesa—the greatest of the kabakas of
the century—its army and navy had brought Koki, Karagwe, and
western Busoga under Buganda control. The neighboring rulers
of Toro and Ankole were also directly affected by Buganda's
power. Buganda, blessed with excellent soil, its cattle herds
prospering, and with an already efficient government structure
improved by Mutesa, was invulnerable from outside attacks
until the arrival of the Europeans.

The kingdom of Bunyoro had by mid-century recovered
from the internal dissensions which had brought about the

separation of Buganda and Toro. Its rulers, Karmurasi and later Kabarega, strengthened the bureaucracy loyal to them and developed a powerful military force. They dominated trade and politics in the area between Lakes Kyoga and Albert. Arab traders, usually from the Sudan, traded freely with Bunyoro but only at the discretion of the ruler. It appears that a conflict between Buganda and the resurgent Bunyoro to determine dominance in the interlacustrine territory would have been inevitable had it not been for the arrival of Europeans. The entire energies of Bunyoro were taken up, throughout the two decades following 1870, with attempting to repulse the Europeans and Egyptians. And Kabarega did successfully fight off the attempts of Baker and Gordon to make Bunyoro an appendage of Egypt. However, in the late 1880s he attempted to supplant the kabaka's influence in Ankole and Toro and thus brought a coalition of Buganda and the British against him. Bunyoro was finally conquered in 1898.

East of the great lakes in what is modern Kenya there existed a multiplicity of Bantu and Nilo-Hamitic groups, many of them still unsettled. The Luo and Kikuyu were the most important of the agricultural Bantu of this area but neither group was well organized in a central state form. The Kikuyu of central Kenya were probably the largest Bantu group in eastern Africa. However, their clan system of government obscured their size and greatly reduced their potential power. The Kikuyu, hungry for land, were still in the process of moving into the Kiambu district in the latter nineteenth century. Harassed by the Masai, they had not fully brought this southern segment within the context of the Kikuyu land system by the time that the Europeans arrived. First Kikuyu contacts with Europeans were in this yet unstable region. Smallpox and rinderpest epidemics in the 1890s combined to depopulate large areas of the fertile highland, leading Europeans to believe that the territory was uninhabited. Herein lay the seeds of much future discord.

The proud Masai pastoralists were also still in the process of migration during the nineteenth century. By 1800 they were firmly established on the grasslands from an area west of Lake Rudolf south to Kilimanjaro. Few in number, the Masai's peculiar military-political system enabled them to fight effectively against strangers. However, they could not combine into larger, more powerful political units. Nevertheless, advance elements of the Masai reached deep into modern Tanzania until halted by the Bantu Gogo in the 1830s. At mid-century the Masai were driven out of the territory immediately to the west of Lake Rudolf by the southward migrating Turkana. Even with this loss the Masai clans controlled the bulk of the high hill country of central Kenya. Toward the end of the nineteenth century, partially weakened by smallpox and internecine struggles, one large segment of the Masai moved permanently into northern Tanzania.

Adjacent to the Kikuyu were located another pastoral people, the Nandi. Although not as aggressive as the Masai, they did raid their neighbors' lands and successfully defended their own grazing lands against everyone, even the Masai. It was the Nandi later in the century who caused the British government and the railroad builders the most trouble. But after

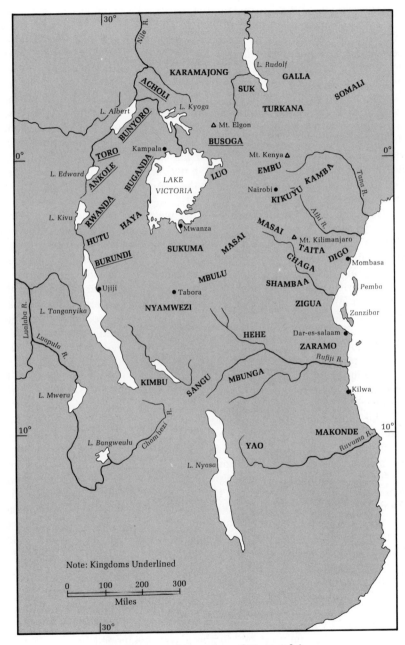

Kingdoms and Peoples of East Africa

47

many futile attempts by government forces, they were finally, in the early 1900s, induced to accept British rule.

The peoples of the Tanzanian area were no less complex in their numbers and differences than those of Kenya. There were no major states there until late in the nineteenth century when the Hehe and the Sambaa, responding to the outside threats of the Arabs and Europeans, created larger, more powerful entities. The Hehe located in the hill country near present-day Iringa were united by the work of two leaders, Myugumba and his son, Mkwawa. The Hehe not only helped block the further southward expansion of the Masai, but were later the chief opposition to German expansion. The powerful Sambaa kingdom was centered in the Usumbara Mountains and was the work of an early nineteenth-century ruler, Kimweri. The Sambaa ruler's control over his subjects was as firm as that of the kabaka of Buganda. The Sambaa, however, partially due to their location, did not play an important role in the history of East Africa during the latter nineteenth century.

Centered on Kaze (modern Tabora) were the many differing Bantu groups to which Europeans gave the common name, Nyamwezi. In actuality the Nyamwezi consisted of over one hundred separate clans each varying in size from a few hundred people to many thousands. They were basically an agricultural people, but the mark they left on the history of eastern Africa was due to their skills as porters. Arabs first, and then the Europeans, depended upon and trusted Nyamwezi carriers. Many of them were also long distance traders and were not adverse to selling their fellows into slavery. Partially because their country straddled the main slave route from the coast to the interior, many of the slaves sold on the coast were Nyamwezi. In southern Tanzania, the Yao and remnants of the Nguni in conjunction with Arabs carried on a profitable trade in slaves. The activities of these two Bantu groups spilled over into the territory of the Shire Highlands and Lake Malawi.

The movement and development of these hinterland peoples were hidden from European observers until the coming of explorers such as Livingstone, Baker, Speke, Burton, and Stanley later in the century. Europeans, however, had long known of the Zenj states. Ships in the lucrative India and China trade regularly called at these ports, although no European power after the Portuguese had attempted to dominate these cities. The British because of their position in India were particularly knowledgeable of the coastline and its Swahili-speaking inhabitants. The sultans of Oman and Muscat had long had a special interest in the eastern coast. However, the instability of their state prevented them from dominating the trading cities of the coast. Only after 1810 was Sultan Seyyid Said able to turn much of the energies of the Omani toward controlling East Africa. By 1820 his naval forces were successful in overawing all the coastal towns with the exception of Mombasa where his plans for domination were opposed by the ruling Mazrui family.

Sultan Said's conquest of Mombasa was postponed by the interference of Captain William Owen of the British Navy who in 1824 posted a small detachment at Mombasa and offered British protection to the Mazrui rulers. Owen did this without prior consultation with his government because he believed it the only way to significantly check the eastern seaborne slave trade. Said, not wishing to go counter to the most powerful naval power in the Indian Ocean, did not want to risk a confrontation at Mombasa. Finally in 1826 London repudiated Owen's policy and ordered all British personnel withdrawn from Mombasa. The British government did not want additional responsibilities in East Africa, and the Indian government preferred to see Said dominant on the coast. After the British withdrawal, Said's forces occupied Mombasa briefly in 1827 and 1828 and then permamently in 1837. Almost immediately the sultan entered into economic and political negotiations with the United States and Britain. The United States sent a consul to Zanzibar in 1837 and the British did so in 1841. This reflected Zanzibar's growing importance as a way stop in the Far Eastern trade. In 1840 Said transferred his residence to Zanzibar and began a policy which encouraged the planting of clove trees on the island and oil palms elsewhere along the coast. By these decisions he created a plantation economy which demanded an ever-increasing supply of slaves.

There was already extant trade routes which had brought interior products to the markets of the Zenj states for a thousand years. However, the urgings of Said and the increased demand for slaves caused adventuresome merchants to open new trade routes as they pushed farther into the hinterland. In 1842 the first Arab coastal caravan reached Lake Tanganyika and a few years later Arab merchants were trading regularly with Buganda. In 1852 an Arab caravan crossed the continent from Bagamoyo to Benguela. Tabora became a major interior entrepôt for caravans in the 1840s and a substantial number of Arabs established permanent residence there. One trader of mixed Arab and African descent from Tabora was Hamed bin Muhammad, better known as Tippu Tib. He became, for Europeans, the epitome of the wealthy, successful Arab trader. In the 1870s he had established himself southwest of Lake Tanganyika near the Lualaba River. There he built a vast commercial empire extending far westward into the Congo basin.

Despite the increasing importance of slaves during Said's reign, the main product which drew the Arabs into the interior was ivory. Slaves were either purchased or taken by force to provide the porters necessary to carry the equipment of the caravan and the heavy elephant tusks. After the completion of a trading venture, the slaves would then be sold.

An Arab caravan of the nineteenth century was a major undertaking which cost its backers a considerable investment. Depending upon the time and the route planned, caravans would stay in the field from one to two years before returning to Tabora or to the coast. On these long excursions Arab entrepreneurs preferred peaceful trading relations with the Africans. In most places they had little difficulty in obtaining ivory or slaves by offering a variety of goods for the desired products. In some places however, particularly when operating against Bantu people with a weak military organization, they utilized force in raiding for slaves. Trade with

Buganda and other similarly powerful states was on a more regularized basis. Tippu Tib and other major traders could not have operated successfully far into the interior with as few men as they had if powerful African states had not been well disposed toward them.

Arab merchants, by the time European explorers and missionaries began to arrive in great numbers, had established a complex system which tapped the interior trade from Gondokoro in the north to the Shire Valley in the south, and from the Congo River eastward to the coast. An integral part of the system was the involvement of Africans directly in the process of collecting slaves. In the south the Yao and Nguni were soon renowned for their slave raiding and in the north the Nyamwezi, Baganda, and Karagwe were deeply committed to the trade. One should note that these Arab princes of commerce owed no definite allegiance to any state or man. Some, like Tippu Tib, established their own interior states. The sultan of Zanzibar ostensibly was their overlord, but his power to punish stopped a few miles inland from the coast. His control over the activities of his subjects who could be absent for anywhere from one to five years was mostly economic. Until the Europeans by their interference diverted much of the trade, the best place to sell ivory and slaves was in the coastal towns. This gave the sultan a certain control over the traders—enhanced by the degree of his own investment in these interior ventures. But if the sultan could not effectively control all the activities of his Arab subjects, he was even less powerful in directing the political destinies of the African people. Until the 1880s he was relatively unconcerned with political power, being content to tap the riches of the interior. Despite this obvious fact, the British government throughout the early nineteenth century persisted in acting as if the sultan's edict would be enforced in the hinterland.

British antislavery activity

Britain early concerned itself with East Africa merely as an adjunct to its dominant position on the Indian Ocean. The British East India Company's government was deeply involved in the affairs of the Persian Gulf which in turn made events in Oman and Muscat important to them. After 1807 the new factor of the abolition of the slave trade was added to British policy toward territories abutting upon the Indian Ocean. It is important to note that while the British government recognized that it had certain interests in East Africa, it did not assign a very high priority to them. If the British could achieve their goals without undue expenditure of funds or risk of a major conflict, they would pursue them. If heavy expenses or the possibility of unnecessary open hostility with another European power intruded, Britain could retreat from her preestablished position. This latter development was particularly noticeable during the period of the scramble for Africa when Britain was confronted with German imperial ambitions in East Africa.

Early in the nineteenth century some British officials believed that the slave trade could be curbed by entering into formal agreements with rulers of territories which supplied slaves. In pursuance of such a goal Captain Fairfax Moresby, in 1822, acting for the governor of Mauritius negotiated a treaty with Sultan Said. By the terms of the Moresby Treaty the sultan promised to end the trade in slaves between his subjects and that of any Christian power. It did not interfere with the trade within the sultan's own possessions or with any Muslim state. Said also granted the British Navy the right to stop and search vessels suspected of being in violation of the treaty.

The next step in attempting to curb the slave trade was taken by a British naval officer who decided to act on his own initiative against the trade. Captain William Owen, while employed in charting the coastline of eastern Africa in 1822 and 1823, came to the conclusion that the sultan's agents were not complying with the terms of the Moresby Treaty. While in India in 1823 he tried to convince the governor of Bombay to intervene more directly in the sultan's affairs. Receiving no help from this quarter, Owen concluded that in the process of completing his survey he would strike at the malefactors whenever he could. On his return to eastern Africa he stopped at Oman and informed Said that on his return to Mombasa he would give protection to its Mazrui rulers if they requested it. Said, not wishing to offend a British naval officer, gave orders that all assistance should be given to Owen when he arrived on the African coast. Privately he later complained to the government of Bombay and other British representatives about Owen's contemplated action.

In February 1824, Owen was asked by the Mazrui rulers of Mombasa to offer them protection from possible conquest by Oman. Owen concurred and signed a treaty of protection on February 9 whereby the Arab leaders of Mombasa promised to give up the slave trade. Owen agreed to help Mombasa reinstitute its control over Pemba. He was not successful in this venture having to be content with the reopening of trade between the two areas. Owen soon sailed away to attempt to gain support for his undertaking from the governor of Mauritius. He left Lieutenant John Reitz, Midshipman George Phillips, a marine corporal, and three sailors behind to collect the customs and keep order in Mombasa. Reitz died in less than three months and Midshipman Phillips was left to deal with the Arab leaders, Indian merchants, and the slave trade. In August 1824, Phillips was replaced by Lieutenant James Emery.

Meanwhile Owen was having little success in convincing higher authority to support his protectorate. However, neither the government of Bombay nor Sir Lowry Cole, governor of Mauritius, ordered the abandonment of Mombasa. Rather, before taking a definite stand, they waited for instructions from London. Without active support from Britain and with the growing hostility of the Mazrui who were disappointed at the meager assistance they had received, Emery was forced to withdraw from Mombasa in July 1826 before orders to do so reached him from London. Thus ended the first, near comic, British protectorate in East Africa.

Once the British presence was safely removed, Said attacked Mombasa and his agents ruled there until the end of 1829 when the Mazrui once again asserted their independence. Said sent one more expedition against the town without success before turning to diplomacy to gain his ends. In 1836 on the death of Sultan Salim of Mombasa, Said allied himself with a strong faction within the town and forced the new sultan, Rashid, to accept the overlordship of Oman. A few months later with Omani troops garrisoning the town, Said had Rashid and many of his leading supporters murdered. Thus Said was able to end the local oligarchy and administer the town directly from Zanzibar. Said's control over Mombasa and the other coastal towns increased immeasurably when he moved the seat of government from Oman to Zanzibar in 1840.

The increase in the number of slaves taken in the interior in the 1830s and early 1840s showed clearly that the Moresby Treaty was not working. The primary task of Consul Hamerton, the first British permanent representative to Zanzibar, was to rectify this situation. Said depended upon continual British support to ward off encroachments by other powers, particularly the French, on his territories. Thus Hamerton exercised great influence over the sultan from the beginning. Hamerton on direct orders from Lord Palmerston suggested as early as 1841 a new, more comprehensive agreement which would replace the Moresby Treaty. Said resisted, knowing how unpopular any restrictions upon the coastal trade would be with many of his most powerful subjects. He agreed to the new treaty only after it became obvious that Britain would make such an agreement the price of continuing to support the sultan's position in the Indian Ocean. In 1845 the Hamerton Treaty was signed which proscribed the seaborne trade by the sultan's subjects except between Lamu and Kilwa. It gave the British the right to search Zanzibari ships suspected of carrying slaves.

Negotiations for the Hamerton Treaty were carried out against a background of renewed French activity in the Indian Ocean. French planters on Bourbon Island needed to obtain more "free workers" from eastern Africa for their sugar plantations and thus French agents were active along the Zenj coast. A French naval patrol was posted to the Indian Ocean area in 1845 and the British squadron gave up its right to search French ships suspected of carrying slaves. The French attempt to gain dominance on Madagascar and their occupation of the island of Nossi Be frightened Said and certainly contributed to his willingness to accept the Hamerton proposals.

The French openly supported the claims of Said's elder son, Hilal, to succeed his father. Said had made it clear that he wished his empire divided between two other sons, Thwain and Majid. The opportunity for the French to intervene to their advantage in this question was briefly ended by the death of Hilal in 1851. However, when Said died in 1856 leaving Thwain to rule in Oman and Majid in Zanzibar, the French once again attempted to gain influence by supporting one faction against another. They first supported Thwain, but soon shifted to uphold the claims to Zanzibar of a young brother, Barghash. In 1859 a French naval force visited Zanzibar and its commander and the French consul, presumably hoping for a coup, openly declared for Barghash. In response the British sent three warships to Zanzibar and General Rigby, the British consul, was able to convince the French representatives that they were creating a situation which would have serious diplomatic ramifications. After this brief sortie at rebellion, Barghash caused no more trouble and succeeded his brother as ruler of Zanzibar in 1870. French interest in the coast waned, and in 1862 they signed a declaration with Britain recognizing the independence of the sultan of Zanzibar.

In 1866 Dr. John Kirk, who had accompanied Livingstone on his explorations of the Shire Highlands, became consul. Partially because of Majid's need for British support and partially because of Kirk's skill as a physician, the new consul gained an influence over the sultan which none of his predecessors had enjoyed. This influence was continued after Barghash became sultan and it seemed at times that Kirk was more concerned about the political well-being of the sultan's empire than was Barghash. Despite this feeling of responsibility, Kirk was as convinced as his superiors that Barghash should be forced, if necessary, to sign a more definitive treaty concerning the slave trade as had been suggested by an 1871 parliamentary Commission of Inquiry.

In 1873 Sir Bartle Frere came to Zanzibar as a special commissioner to negotiate a comprehensive agreement. He wanted the sultan to forbid the export of slaves from any part of his kingdom and to close down all the slave markets. Barghash believed such an agreement would be economically disastrous and resisted until the presence of elements of the British Navy in the harbor and Kirk's threats to blockade the sultan's territory convinced him to capitulate. On Kirk's advice, Barghash later forbade marching slaves from one town to another along the coast. In order to make the new agreement more effective a new Zanzibari military force was created under the command of Lieutenant Lloyd Matthews of the British Navy and British ships quelled any signs of revolt from disaffected merchants in the coastal towns.

The agreement of 1873, although ending the bulk of the coastal and seaborne trade, did not stop the traffic in East Africa. Arab traders in the interior were merely forced to seek new and more difficult routes. Slaves from the Sudan became more important since one of the best markets for slaves in the early 1870s was Khartoum. The 1873 agreement showed how dependent the sultan was upon British support. His empire was a commercial one with little political control being exercised over interior African people. Barghash's tenuous control could be maintained as long as Britain was uninterested in expansion and would champion the sultan's cause against other European powers. In the 1880s the diplomatic scene changed radically and Britain slowly but definitely moved away from protecting the sultan, thus making possible the division of his empire.

European explorations

European curiosity concerning the mysteries of the East African hinterland did not become active until the mid-1850s. Until then West Africa had absorbed the attention of most geographers, adventurers, and missionaries.

True, there were continual speculations concerning the Nile source, but no one seemed willing to investigate the interior. The first European explorers of the hinterland of East Africa were German missionaries in the employ of the Church Missionary Society. Dr. Ludwig Krapf in 1844 had been given permission by the sultan to establish a mission on the mainland. Two years later he was joined by Reverend Johann Rebmann who opened a station fifteen miles west of Mombasa. Rebmann became interested in the people of the Taita hills and particularly the Chaga. In the course of one of his visits to them he sighted the snow-topped Mt. Kilimanjaro. Dr. Krapf, on a journey to the interior, was the first European to glimpse Mt. Kenya. When these reports reached Britain they were disbelieved. One noted geographer pointed out how impossible it was for snow to exist on the equator. A map drawn by another German missionary, J. J. Erhardt, who had obviously talked to Arab traders, introduced to Europe the possibility of a great inland sea which he called the Unyamesi.

These reports, particularly that of Erhardt, led Sir Roderick Murchison of the Royal Geographic Society to sponsor an expedition in 1856 to investigate these rumors. The two explorers chosen for this task had been officers in the Indian Army, and although possessing completely different personalities, they had already cooperated on one exploration in Africa. Richard Burton was a scholar, linguist, and adventurer, deeply attached to Eastern forms of life and to the exotic. Only thirty-six years old in 1856, he was already famous for his audacious visit to Mecca and later to Harar when in both cases he had disguised himself as a Muslim. John Hanning Speke had served ten years in the Indian Army and was regarded as a steady man and an excellent hunter. He previously, in 1854, had planned to investigate the source of the Nile. However, he had met Burton in Aden where he was persuaded to participate in the Harar and Somali venture on which he had been seriously wounded.

The two men, still good friends, left the East African coast on June 16, 1857, after forming their caravan. Following the southern slave route they reached Tabora in November. Both the explorers suffered constantly from a variety of illnesses. Despite such handicaps they reached Lake Tanganyika in February 1858, and returned to Tabora in June. Until this point the journey, although hard and reasonably productive, had not divided the two men. At Tabora they decided to trace the source of a rumor that there was a greater lake to the north. Since Burton was ill Speke proceeded alone and on August 3, 1858, at Mwanza he first glimpsed the huge lake which was later named Victoria. He was ill and low on supplies and, therefore, did not explore the shoreline of the lake. Nevertheless, he concluded that this vast expanse of water was the source of the Nile.

After hearing Speke's report, Burton dismissed the idea that the lake, named by them Victoria, could be the point of origin of the Nile. Speke had not investigated the lake and therefore there was nothing to substantiate his theory. This disagreement became the basis of hostility between the two men which developed into a hatred that lasted until Speke's unfortunate accidental death in September 1864. Speke who preceded Burton to

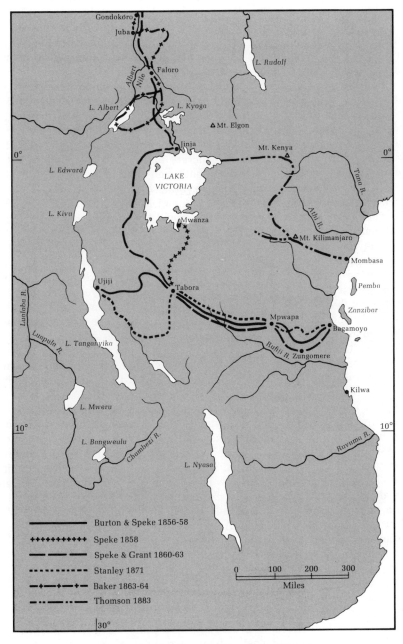

European Exploration in East Africa

Britain after their journey certainly did nothing to moderate Burton's dislike of him. He had promised not to discuss their findings until Burton had joined him. Despite this he gave interviews, delivered addresses, and was active in arranging government support for a new expedition. Thus when Burton arrived in London he found himself all but ignored. He never forgave Speke for breaking his promise and for years continued to agitate against Speke's conclusions concerning Lake Victoria.

Speke chose Captain James Grant as his companion on the new expedition. Grant was self-effacing and not likely to challenge Speke's authority or conclusions. They put together their party in Zanzibar and Bagamoyo in mid-1860, then followed the established southern route to Tabora and thence to Karagwe in November 1861. The journey was replete with the problems which were typical of explorers in East Africa. Supplies were lost and stolen, porters deserted, and both men were ill during much of the year which it took to reach Karagwe. Since Grant was ill in late 1861, Speke set out by himself to visit the court of Kabaka Mutesa of Buganda. His small party was welcomed by Mutesa and Speke had a number of long conferences with the ruler in the five months he spent in Buganda. Speke was the first European to visit this interlacustrine kingdom. His later description of Buganda, although in part unflattering, was important in introducing Europeans to this advanced but strange African state. After Grant joined Speke they proceeded northward to Bunyoro. On July 21, 1862, after having left Grant behind again, Speke encountered the Victoria Nile and one week later sighted Ripon Falls. The expedition then explored more of Bunyoro and, running low on supplies, moved northward according to plan to Faloro and thence to Gondokoro in the Sudan.

At Gondokoro Grant and Speke discovered that Samuel Baker and his wife were waiting for them. The Bakers had decided to spend their honeymoon exploring the Upper Nile. Speke and Grant because of lack of supplies had not been able to investigate rumors of another lake lying southwest of Victoria. They suggested to the Bakers that they should follow up this rumor. To facilitate their journey Speke gave Baker his own map of Bunyoro. In March 1863, the Bakers moved south toward Bunyoro. One year later, despite the usual difficulties with terrain, transportation, and illness, they arrived at the new lake which they named Albert. Traveling along the eastern shore they discovered a river flowing in from Victoria and followed this to the falls which they named Murchison Falls. They later confirmed that Lake Albert also contributed to the Nile. These discoveries which went far in vindicating Speke's theories could not be announced until after the Baker's finally reached Suez in October 1865. By that time Speke was dead and another expedition had been sponsored by the Royal Geographic Society to settle finally the questions of the lakes, mountains, and rivers of East Africa. This expedition was begun in 1866 by the most famous of the explorers of his time, David Livingstone.

Although Livingstone was only fifty-two years old when he began his third expedition, he had spent almost a quarter of a century traveling throughout Africa and popularizing the problems of Africa. He had come first to Kuruman station in Bechuanaland as a missionary for the London Missionary Society. Convinced of the need to search out routes for further missionary stations, Livingstone first explored the route to Lake Ngami and thence to the Makololo country of the upper Zambesi River. On these early journeys he was introduced to the interior slave trade and became obsessed with the need to develop legitimate trade with the interior people while at the same time opening routes for further missionary activity. It was in search of alternate routes into the interior that he undertook his solitary journey across the continent from Luanda to Quelimane. On this long (1853–1856), hazardous journey he discovered Victoria Falls and was the first European for centuries to venture into most of the lands bordering the Zambesi. Livingstone's book, *Missionary Travels and Researches,* describing these adventures was extremely popular and Livingstone became a celebrity. His activities inspired the organization of the Universities Mission to Central Africa.

In 1858 Livingstone was back in Africa as consul to Mozambique, a position which gave him free scope for explorations. The British government sponsored him on a detailed examination of the lower Zambesi and Shire rivers and Lake Malawi. From 1858 to 1864 in a series of explorations, aided by a substantial party of Europeans, he plotted out the significant features of the Malawi area. By their work in the field and then in subsequent books they laid the groundwork for the later missionary endeavors in Malawi.

Livingstone held aloof from the passions of the debate generated by Burton and Speke on the probable source of the Nile. Nevertheless, he did not believe that Lake Victoria was the source of the river. He appears to have thought that the river rose in an area west of that lake. On his third journey to Africa, Livingstone decided to operate from two bases, Zanzibar and Ujiji on Lake Tanganyika. His old friend, Dr. Kirk, the British consul in Zanzibar, was to be responsible for keeping Livingstone's interior base supplied. This link later broke down and left Livingstone grievously short of supplies. He found it difficult to recruit porters. The Arab slavers were suspicious of him and his letters from the interior in many cases were never delivered to Kirk. Nevertheless, Livingstone continued his investigations, discovering Lake Bangweulu in 1868, and the Lualaba River on a further journey.

If Livingstone's memory is that of a devoted Christian, Stanley's is that of *bula matari,* the breaker of rocks. Measured by the impact he had on both Africans and Europeans, he was the greatest of the explorers. An English orphan (born John Rowlands) who had made his way to the United States, Stanley had by 1871 clawed his way at age thirty to preeminence as a reporter for *The New York Herald.* He was commissioned in that year, as a part of a series assignment, to investigate whether the world famous Dr. Livingstone was lost and, if so, to find him. Despite the lack of cooperation of British officials at Zanzibar and his lack of experience in Africa, he put together a caravan on the coast and drove it by way of the southern slave route to Ujiji, making the journey in the record time of 104 days.

Here he found Livingstone who had just returned from his investigations of the Lualaba River to discover that supplies promised by Kirk had completely disappeared. The two men further explored Lake Tanganyika, but Livingstone refused to return to the coast with Stanley. Stanley left his newly discovered friend at Tabora with all the supplies he could spare in March 1872. However, Livingstone died near Lake Bangweulu in April 1873 before more aid could reach him.

Livingstone's contributions to European understanding of Africa were very great. In a long career of exploration he had been the first European in modern times to visit the Kalolo, see Victoria Falls, Lake Malawi, Lake Bangweulu, and the Lualaba River. He had popularized Africa by his books and speeches. More than all this, he had symbolized for his countrymen the selfless humanitarian who cared for Africans and sincerely wanted to improve their conditions.

On Stanley's return to Britain he wrote a best seller, *How I Found Livingstone*, which in connection with his brusque manner did nothing to endear him to the British upper classes. Nevertheless, he managed to convince *The New York Herald* and the *London Daily Telegraph* to finance him on further explorations of East Africa. Stanley left Britain for Zanzibar in August 1874, with three objectives in mind. He intended to circumnavigate Lake Victoria to determine, finally, its connection with the Nile. He then planned to do the same for Lake Tanganyika, and finally he hoped to check on Livingstone's theories that the Lualaba River was the true source of the Nile. Stanley's expedition which left the coast in November 1875, was the best equipped of any which had previously penetrated the hinterland. He had over 350 men to carry eight tons of supplies and the dismantled forty foot steel boat which was so important for his plans.

From the south shore of Lake Victoria in March 1875, Stanley and eleven others sailed along the east shore and in three weeks sighted Ripon Falls, then proceeded to Buganda in early April. Stanley was very impressed by the kingdom and by Mutesa. While he was at the kabaka's court, General Gordon's deputy, Linant de Bellefonds, arrived and agreed to take back a dispatch for the *Daily Telegraph* urging that missionaries be sent to Buganda. In early May, Stanley had proved Speke's theory that Victoria was a single, large lake and that it had only one major outlet at Ripon Falls. Later in 1875 after joining Mutesa in a battle with some natives on two islands in Lake Victoria, Stanley was provided by Mutesa with a guard for further explorations toward Lake Albert. The guard fled at the first opportunity and Stanley proceeded without them to Karagwe.

After returning to Ujiji and resting for some months, Stanley launched his boat on Lake Tanganyika in June 1876, to carry out the second of his objectives. In less than two months he had circumnavigated the lake and determined that there was no outlet which could be taken for the Nile. This discovery, combined with his investigations on Lake Victoria, finally confirmed Speke's and Baker's conclusions on the source of the Nile.

The third phase of Stanley's journey was begun in August 1876, when he set out with only about half of his original force to investigate the

Lualaba River. With the help of agents of the Arab slaver, Tippu Tib, he reached the river and launched his boat for the long voyage down river. After a series of adventures which included attacks from Africans, shipwreck, and loss of supplies, he reached the mouth of the Congo, 999 days after he had left Zanzibar. The African survivors of the journey were sent by boat back to Zanzibar and Stanley proceeded to Europe to write his book, *Through the Dark Continent*. He eventually accepted the offer to become Leopold II's chief agent on the Congo.

Other explorers at the time of Stanley's epic second journey were busy filling in the blank spaces of eastern Africa. Colonel Chaille-Long, one of General Gordon's assistants, traced the Nile from its source to Karuma Falls. He also discovered Lake Kyoga. Another of Gordon's lieutenants, Romola Gessi, circumnavigated Lake Albert and followed its course northward. With these discoveries European geographers could plot with great accuracy the major features of eastern Africa. Every explorer after Burton and Speke added new information, not only on the geography, but also on the people. Interior journeys which had been considered by Europeans to be the height of adventure and novelty in 1870 had become commonplace by 1890. The isolation of the hinterland peoples of eastern Africa from the European world had ended and in a short period of time they would become pawns of the Europeans in the scramble for Africa.

The Congo basin

Much of the history of Central Africa is concerned with the establishment of different Luba polities and various kingdoms and empires derivative of the Luba. Although the events relative to the creation of these states is crucial to the Congo basin, little is known of the complex migrations of Luba people or the genesis of individual chiefdoms. Some general background to nineteenth century Central Africa can, nevertheless, be abstracted. By the sixteenth century there had evolved in the Katanga area a major Luba kingdom. In time other smaller Luba states such as Kaniak and Kikonja also developed in the Katanga. All these states had a similar political structure. Power in each was exercised by a chief who was a descendant of one lineage. There was a relatively tight bureaucracy responsive to the will of the chief. However, the Luba kingdoms never evolved into large permanent empires since the chiefs were content only to gather tribute from subject people. The pattern of migration which had brought the Luba to the Congo originally continued, presumably because of population growth and political differences within the established states. The Bemba, Bisa, Lozi, Katanga Lunda, and Kazembe Lunda all developed from basic Luba stock.

The Katanga Lunda empire was established by the early seventeenth century. In contrast to the smaller Luba polities the early Lunda kings established a policy of politically incorporating neighboring people within the Lunda sphere. The ruler of this Sudanic-type state, the mwato yamvo, exercised tight control over his subjects. Chiefs of conquered people were

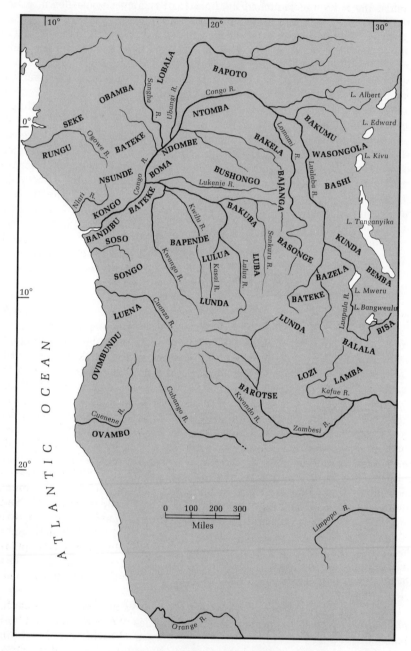

Peoples of the Congo Basin

allowed to retain their authority subject to good behavior and direct affiliation with the Lunda system of rule. Many of the smaller Luba polities of the Katanga were incorporated into the Lunda empire. In the 1740s one of the Lunda generals with a raiding force crossed into the Luapula Valley and conquered the Bantu people there. The new kingdom which developed from this conquest took the name Kazembe from its first ruler, Kazembe II, who established a strong centralized state. The Lualaba River became the frontier between these two Lunda empires although the Kazembe rulers continued to consider the mwato yamvo as their titular overlord well into the nineteenth century.

The Bemba were a Luba people who in the latter seventeenth century moved eastward across the Lualaba River. For over a century divisions within the original group and various complex migrations resulted in the settlement of the area between the Luapula and Luangwa rivers. The main group of Bemba after 1760 settled down in the territory between Lake Bangweulu and Lake Tanganyika. Another segment which became known as the Bisa established themselves east of Lake Bangweulu and south of the Chambesi River.

Another Luba migration was that of the Luyi, or as they were later called, the Lozi. They migrated southward to the upper Zambesi Valley in the late seventeenth century. In the following century they absorbed many of the other smaller Bantu groups into a federal type state. This peaceful, well-organized polity was by 1800 composed of over twenty distinct groups. The Luyi king, called the litunga, received ritual as well as political loyalty from his subchiefs who were drawn from leading Luyi families. The kingdom was divided into northern and southern segments. The north was directly under the control of the litunga while the south was ruled by a queen of the royal family and was sometimes almost completely free from northern rule.

There had been continuous trading contact for many centuries between all the hinterland kingdoms and the coastal towns of Angola and East Africa. These had increased after the arrival of the Portuguese in the late fifteenth and early sixteenth century. This trade had been one of the reasons for the creation of large, more aggressive Bantu polities in the Congo. Some of the early Luba-Lunda people had received guns in trade and this had given them the necessary power advantage over their neighbors allowing them to expand their influence. In the early nineteenth century due to a variety of factors, the trade between the interior and both coasts increased tremendously with ensuing revolutionary effects upon the Bantu states. The more centralized governments of the interior kingdoms allowed for more expeditious trade within a polity. In the immediate interior both in the east and west, certain African people reoriented their societies primarily toward trade. In the west the Imbangala of the Kasanje became the middlemen between the mwato yamvo's kingdom and the up-country trading agents of the Portuguese at Luanda. In the east the Bisa and the Yao were the first to act as intermediaries in trade with the east coast. Later the Nyamwezi became the dominant African long-distance traders. Africans were the primary agents in the upsurge of trading activities although the Portuguese and Swahili merchants still remained important for interior trade.

Portuguese demand on the Atlantic coast for African products remained relatively constant throughout much of the century. The great expansion in the volume of the slave trade occurred in the stable mercantile empire of the sultans of Zanzibar which demanded more slaves to work the clove and oil palm plantations. French planters on a number of sugar growing islands in the Indian Ocean were in great need of workers and they were willing to flaunt the regulations against the slave trade to obtain labor. The demand in Europe for ivory increased greatly in the nineteenth century. It is not surprising that African merchants and chiefs took advantage of such favorable conditions. The Nyamwezi are the best example of an African people who radically altered their society to meet the new economic demands. The Nyamwezi in the early nineteenth century were a collection of decentralized polities located in a most favorable position to dominate the east-west routes from Katanga to the east coast as well as the north-south interior trade toward Lake Victoria. In time Nyamwezi traders and porters became a fixture in most of the East and Central African territories. Under strong pressure from Swahili merchants in the early 1870s a Nyamwezi chief, Mirambo, using guns and Nguni mercenaries, created a powerful centralized state. This enabled the Nyamwezi to remain in control of the rich eastern trade in ivory, slaves, and copper from the Katanga. After Mirambo's death in 1884 the united kingdom fell apart and the Nyamwezi became easy prey to the Germans in the 1890s.

The increase in the demand for slaves in the mercantile empire of the sultan of Zanzibar spurred on the Swahili traders of the east coast to pioneer new trading routes into the interior. There traders, erroneously referred to as "Arabs," had by the 1870s already penetrated into the eastern Congo. Their outpost, Nyangwe, became a major trading entrepôt. The man who best exemplifies this new adventuresome attitude was Hamid bin Muhammad, better known as Tippu Tib. During the 1860s in a series of far-ranging ventures he pioneered trade routes into the Bemba sphere and became a Tetela chief in the Lomani area. In 1875 Tippu Tib established the center for his ivory and slave trade at Kasongo in the eastern Congo. From there by the strength of his administrative ability and a large force of well-armed retainers, he ruled a huge area of the Lomani and Lualaba valleys. In this empire he assessed taxes, built roads, regulated the hunting of elephants, and controlled all trade. In less than ten years he had extended his trading sphere as far down the Congo River as Stanley Falls. It was Tippu Tib who provided Stanley with the general knowledge and the physical support which enabled him to succeed in his exploration of the Congo River. Tippu Tib continued to be the most important political and economic force on the upper Congo River throughout the 1880s despite the inroads made by Stanley and other agents of the Congo Independent State. After he left the Congo permanently in 1890, no other "Arab" trader could gain supreme authority and very soon Tippu's territory was absorbed by the Congo Independent State.

Elsewhere in Central Africa the upsurge in trade also affected the state structures. The Bemba in the late eighteenth century had already developed an active trade with the people to the north for salt and with the Bisa for meat and fish. They also traded ivory to the Nyamwezi and Swahili. Traditionally the Bemba were ruled by a series of chiefs from one royal clan. Before the nineteenth century the paramount chief called the chitimukulu had performed mainly ceremonial and religious functions. In the first half of the nineteenth century the chitimukulus became paramount in political, military, and trading matters as well. Trade became a royal monopoly and the chief utilized the militaristic Bemba to secure more ivory and slaves. Much of the centralization was the work of Chitimukulu Chileshe who expropriated the throne at mid-century. From 1866 to 1887 the ruler was Chitapankwa who further extended the Bemba sphere of influence and the state became richer than ever. Bemba power continued even after the declaration of a British protectorate over their area in 1893. Quarrels over succession to the throne eventually weakened the Bemba and the British South Africa Company was finally successful after 1898 in making practical the paper claims to Bemba territory enunciated five years earlier.

An even more powerful polity than Lubemba was the Kazembe kingdom of the Luapula Valley. The Portuguese explorers, Monteiro and Gamitto, reported in the 1830s that the mwato kazembe had over 5,000 warriors, many well armed with guns. He also was a merchant prince controlling a major link in the trade which in the nineteenth century extended from the Atlantic to the Indian Ocean. Livingstone reporting his visit to this Lunda kingdom in 1868 indicated that the Kazembe's potential power had not waned. However, quarrels over succession weakened the Kazembes. This enabled a Nyamwezi merchant, Msiri, to build up a competitive state which stripped the Kazembe of much of their control over the Katanga trade. Msiri with a number of well armed Nyamwezi, later called Yeke, settled in Kazembe territory in 1856. Utilizing the Yeke and an extremely harsh rule, Msiri gathered slaves and ivory throughout the southern Congo basin. Many of the smaller Luba chieftancies to the north paid tribute to him.

The Lunda empire of the mwato yamvo was also deeply affected by the increase in trading profits. The king alienated large numbers of his people by his arbitrary use of power. He would designate whole villages to be sold into slavery. The dissatisfaction of his people combined with the ever-present centrifugal forces within a Sudanic type state caused a series of struggles for power at the center. This enabled the Chokwe, a seminomadic people from the south, to encroach upon the kingdom. Taking advantage of the disturbances and using guns obtained in trade, the Chokwe by the mid-1880s had taken over most of the territory formerly ruled by the mwato yamvo. Wars between the Chokwe and the Lunda continued for years and sufficiently weakened both sides so that they resisted very little the takeover of their territories by agents of the Congo Independent State.

Elsewhere in the Congo basin the agricultural Bantu who had not evolved larger, more elaborate state structures became the prey of African and Swahili slave raiders. European explorers and missionaries in the latter nineteenth century were witnesses to the side effects of the trading revolution which had done so much to transform the politics of Central Africa. Their reports of slave raiding and the huge ivory and slave caravans were important factors in creating the necessary climate of opinion in Europe which supported the new imperialism. Ultimately this European imperialism destroyed the great kingdoms whose existence was based largely upon the long-range trade.

THREE
Southern Africa
to 1872

British-Boer relations in Cape Colony to 1836

In June 1795, almost 150 years of rule by the Dutch East Indies Company was brought to an end by a British invasion fleet. The reasons for this occupation are closely tied to the upheavals in Europe begun by the French revolution. In 1794 the armies of revolutionary France invaded Holland, captured the Dutch fleet, and forced the aristocratic government to flee to Britain. The Prince of Orange entered into an agreement which allowed the British to occupy strategic Cape Colony before the French and the new Dutch revolutionary regime could do so. After minor resistance the Dutch commander at the Cape surrendered to General Craig and the British became responsible for the government of a territory with undefined boundaries, economic difficulties, independent frontiersmen, displaced Hottentots, and threats from the Bantu.

The European settlers, descendants of Dutch and Huguenot settlers of the seventeenth century, numbered approximately 20,000. The majority were concentrated in Cape Town and in the western Cape region. The settled burghers at Cape Town followed a variety of trades and professions, were in contact with the latest trends in Europe, and maintained schools and churches. The farmers of the western Cape were further removed from direct European influence but they, too, were generally prosperous and had developed various specialized agricultural pursuits. Both the Cape Town residents and those farmers located near such towns as Stellenbosch or Tulbagh were amenable to control by the central government. The Dutch East Indies Company had granted these interior areas a modicum of local government by the establishment of drotsdys. These were administered by an official, usually a local farmer, aided by a council of local government called the heemraaden. There was only one court for the entire colony located at Cape Town. Despite some tensions between these local authorities and the central government, the British took over a relatively well organized political system and found it necessary to make few changes.

A small group of Boers living far to the east of Cape Town near the settlements of Swellendam, Uitenhage, and Graaf Reinet, however, soon showed the British that their aims were far from those of the British governors. The basis of livelihood of these frontier areas was cattle farming. More than their settled kinsmen, these veld Boers exhibited characteristics which made it impossible for them to accept British rule in the nineteenth century. They disliked any authority, believed in their God-given superiority over all black men, were normally uneducated and fiercely Calvinistic, and wandered freely over the countryside to stake their claims to huge cattle ranges.

The frontier Boers in the eighteenth century had reduced their competitors, the cattle-keeping Hottentots, to a servile state of landless men. In the 1770s they encountered their first real African opposition from the southward moving Xosa clans of the Nguni Bantu. This began a series of conflicts over cattle and land which periodically exploded into general warfare. These so-called Kaffir wars will be treated in more detail later. It is only necessary to note here that the frontier Boers who resented authority and disobeyed government edicts expected first the company and later the British to help them exterminate the Xosa. When such aid was not forthcoming they were not immune to rebellion against central authority. In 1795 when the British first landed, the Boers at Swellendam and Graaf Reinet were in the midst of such a rebellion. The rebels reluctantly accepted the new government in hopes that the British would adopt an aggressive policy against the Xosa. Cattle raiding continued across the ill-defined borders and the Boer unrest in 1799 exploded in another rebellion by some of the disgruntled farmers at Graaf Reinet. British dragoons, infantry, and some Hottentot soldiers soon ended the experiment of a separate Boer government. No sooner had this been settled than a quarrel between two Xosa chiefs spilled over the frontier and began the third Kaffir war. The new liberal landdrost Maynier attempted to deal justly with all factions, forbade private military forays into Xosa land, was concerned with the condition of the Hottentots, and believed in the rule of law. The frontier war ended in 1802, but the Boers were again on the verge of rebellion against Maynier and he was recalled.

Maynier's problems on the eastern frontier can be viewed as prophetic of later British-Boer relations. Whenever a government official attempted to view problems objectively, particularly those connected with Hottentots or Bantu, he could expect no help from the frontier farmers. Government to the frontiersman should exist only to further his interests. A rule which was almost invariably true was that in a quarrel the native people were always in the wrong. Any government which did not subscribe to this could expect continuing problems from the Boers.

The first British occupation was ended by the terms of the Treaty of Amiens in 1802. The British governors had viewed their mission in almost completely military terms and had not attempted any major changes in the system of local and central government. Except where conflict was inevitable such as at Graaf Reinet, the British had left undamaged Boer presumptions of their superiority over blacks. The representatives of the reconstituted Dutch government (the Batavian Republic), Commissioner de Mist and General Janssens, who assumed responsibility for administration in February 1803, found themselves caught in an impossible dilemma. Imbued with ideas of liberty, equality, and fraternity, they wished to institute sweeping changes in government to regulate better the association between Boer, Bantu, and Hottentot. Little could be done to effect permanent change since war between Britain and France broke out once again in May 1803. Janssens, who was in charge at the Cape after 1804, could not afford to alienate the Boer population in the face of a potential second British invasion. In 1805 the British, acting once again to protect their trade routes, dispatched a large invasion fleet to the Cape. Early the next year after only a token resistance Janssens surrendered to the overwhelming British strength.

Although this second occupation was to prove permanent, British governors at the Cape did not know this until 1814. Therefore, the British governors in this interim period, Lord Caledon and Sir John Craddock, wanted to make as few changes as possible. However, it was necessary to intervene more directly into the lives of the Boer population. The abolition of the slave trade in 1807 applied to Cape Colony at a time when the economy was expanding because of the Napoleonic Wars. Thus a premium was placed upon the once despised Hottentot population. Many of the landless Hottentots had already been used by the farmers of the eastern Cape. After 1807 the Boers urged the government to pass legislation which would force the Hottentots to settle down in one place and work for them. Two Hottentot ordinances of 1809 and 1812 created the necessary rules to force the Hottentots to become workers and servants of the Boers. However, they also provided rules concerning contracts, terms, and conditions of employment of Hottentot workers. Although these regulations were largely ignored in practice, they did give theoretical protection to the Hottentots.

The London Missionary Society which had been active in Cape Colony after 1799 emerged as the champion of the Hottentots. The society had established a number of stations throughout the colony to minister to their needs. As the government policy and the farmers' attitudes began to press in upon the mission-station Hottentots, the missionaries appealed first to the governors and eventually to evangelical opinions in Britain. They represented the life of the Hottentot to be that of a slave who could expect no protection from the laws or officials of the colony. Particular charges made by the Bethelsdorp missionaries, combined with the obvious necessity of providing a court for the interior, led to the establishment of the circuit court in 1812. The second circuit court investigated the missionary allegations against fifty Boer farmers charged with everything from extreme cruelty to murder. The Roman-Dutch law of evidence and the wandering nature of Hottentots made the task of proving the charges almost impossible. Nevertheless, seven Boers were convicted of the lesser charge of mistreatment. More important, the precedent was established by the "Black Circuit" of accepting the testimony of natives against their white masters. Although the Cape government had been reluctant to alienate Boer opinion, the Boers had thus been introduced to the more liberal attitudes of the British.

At this time the eastern frontier was in turmoil with constant cattle raiding by both Boers and Xosa. In 1811 the fourth Kaffir war began and resulted in the Xosa being driven from the Zuurveld. After the war the British, instead of supporting the farmers' demands for continued commando and military action against the Bantu, ordered the Boers to retire behind a series of forts constructed west of the Fish River. The most important of these was Grahamstown which soon became an important white town. Although such a system, designed to keep contact between the races to a minimum, could not work, it could and did irritate the Boers. The Land Ordinance of 1812 revoked much of the old Dutch land law and tried to restrict individual landholding to 1,200 acres on which a high annual quit rent was required. This attempt also eventually proved unsuccessful, but it was another link in the chain of Boer grievances against a meddlesome British government.

By 1814 when the British government negotiated the permanent transfer of Cape Colony from Holland, there was already a deep estrangement between the British government and the Boer farmers. An example of this conflict which would assume an importance to many Boers far beyond its actual significance was the Slachter's Nek incident. A Boer, Frederick Bezuidenhout, was accused by a Hottentot servant of mistreatment. Pleading illness, Bezuidenhout did not appear in the circuit court to answer the charges. Subsequently a contingent of Hottentot police were sent to arrest him. Refusing to be arrested by blacks, he fired on them and was killed. Frederick's brother Johannes, a neighbor Hendrick Prinsloo, and other Boer farmers vowed vengeance for the killing. Prinsloo wrote to Gaika, one of the Xosa chiefs, proposing an alliance against the British. The message was intercepted by British authorities who then arrested Prinsloo. A few of the dissident farmers tried to rescue him. They could gain little support from most of the settlers and were easily beaten by the British. Those captured at Slachter's Nek were tried under the traditional Roman-Dutch law before Boer judges, found guilty, and sentenced to death. Their execution in 1815 was marred by the collapse of the gallows and the hanging had to be repeated. Very soon those who had been executed came to be viewed as martyrs, killed only because they stood for the traditional freedoms of the veld Boer against the autocratic British system.

Lord Charles Somerset became governor of Cape Colony in 1814. This descendant of Plantagenet kings represented the ambivalence of the British government. A Tory, he was extremely suspicious of radicals, humanitarians, and missionaries, yet his sense of order, propriety, and his autocratic nature guaranteed his estrangement from the frontier Boers. In 1818 a quarrel between clan leaders of the Xosa soon involved the British. Ndlambe and Makana, both unyielding enemies of the white settlers, challenged the more malleable Gaika for control of the western Xosa. Gaika was severely defeated and appealed to the British government for aid. In December white troops crossed the Fish River, burned huts, and captured over 20,000 cattle. Makana retaliated in April by invading the colony and with 10,000 warriors laid siege to Grahamstown. The war ended three months later after European reinforcements had arrived and Makana had surrendered. Gaika, for whose protection Lord Charles had used imperial forces, was forced to cede almost 3,000 square miles of Xosa territory to the British. The area between the Fish and Keiskama rivers was declared neutral territory. This action, far from ending the border crisis, was calculated to increase tensions since one of the major problems of the Xosa had been the necessity for them to find more land.

In 1813 the officer primarily responsible for the Xosa defeat in the Kaffir war, Colonel Graham, proposed that the government should underwrite the emigration of British settlers to the eastern Cape frontier. Significant numbers of sturdy British peasants would presumably dilute the Boer control of this region and they would provide a buffer against Xosa invasions. Lord Charles approved of the plan even before he left Britain. After the fifth Kaffir war of 1818 had begun, parliament voted £50,000 to subsidize sending out British settlers. As was usual for colonization schemes of the nineteenth century, this one was badly planned and poorly managed. Few of the settlers who arrived in 1819–1820 had any farming experience, and the area was suited to raising cattle, not to sedentary agriculture. Droughts, locusts, floods, and Xosa raiders in the first five years drove most of the settlers off their farms and into the towns. The major objectives of the plan outlined by Colonel Graham, therefore, were never achieved. However, the bulk of the 5,000 settlers did not return to Britain but remained in Cape Colony. Their demands that they be treated as British citizens struck at the very root of the autocratic unreformed government of Cape Colony. These British settlers demanded the primacy of the English language in legal transactions, English common law, a free press, and a curb upon the actions of the governor.

A series of personal confrontations with Lord Charles and sensation-provoking law cases brought by the government highlighted the Albany settlers' demands. Lord Charles quarreled with and secured the dismissal of his lieutenant-governor, Sir Rufane Donkin, and his colonial secretary, Colonel Bird. Each of these men upon their return to Britain joined the chorus of those already demanding Somerset's recall. Charges by two citizens against the collector of customs led to two long trials of the principals for libel. A printer, George Greig, whose paper was banned and his press seized, also became involved in litigation with the Cape government. Charges of maladministration of the relief funds for the Albany settlers also added to Lord Charles' discomfiture. The sum of all these allegations added to the depressed economic state of Cape Colony in the early 1820s and led the colonial secretary to send a commission of inquiry to investigate the whole range of government activity.

The man who came to personify to Lord Charles all the unprincipled radical activity was the newly appointed superintendent of the London Missionary Society in Cape Colony, John Philip. Although Somerset's assessment of Philip was untrue, the superintendent did become his most implacable opponent. In 1819 Philip believed that most of the trouble between the government and the mission stations was caused by the missionaries. Within two years he had completely reversed himself and was convinced that the missions could only begin to function as centers for Christianity when the Hottentots were treated as human beings. He criticized the government for being in league with the farmers to provide them with a steady, cheap Hottentot labor supply. To Philip, the Hottentot ordinances, far from protecting natives, guaranteed them a status as near slaves. Somerset used all his influence to have Philip removed. However, after 1826 Philip managed to convince the powerful parliamentary evangelical faction that Hottentot emancipation was only another facet of their struggle against slavery. Lord Charles was recalled to London to answer the many charges against him and eventually resigned in 1828.

The period after the arrival in Cape Colony of acting Governor Bourke in 1825 witnessed a series of near revolutionary changes which went far toward anglicizing the society. The Dutch language could no longer be used in the civil service, courts, or schools. The churches which were state established were also forced to adopt English for their services. The courts were reconstructed in the British mold with appointive judges, the jury system, and the common law. Roman-Dutch law was retained for civil cases, but business and criminal law followed the British model. Local government was completely changed. The office of landdrost gave way to magistrates appointed by the central government and responsible to it. The traditional commando leaders, the veld cornets, were stripped of their military and civil powers. Most of these changes recommended by the commission of inquiry were necessary for the modernization of the colony. However, they went far to convince the predominantly Dutch-speaking population that the British government aimed at the eventual destruction of all that was good and familiar in the old system.

The action of General Bourke which had the greatest impact and most lasting effect was Hottentot emancipation. Philip in the early 1820s had concluded that the only way that men of color in Cape Colony could be protected was to have the British government specifically grant them equality with whites. Toward this end Philip after 1821 devoted most of his energies. In 1826 he returned to Britain, met with Thomas Buxton and other parliamentary Evangelicals, and enlisted their support for his cause. He also wrote a two volume work on his experiences with the Cape government while championing the cause of the Hottentots. This served to enlist more influential support for his cause. In 1828 parliament passed a resolution which declared men of color equal to their European counterparts. Before the Colonial Office could put this resolution into effect word was received that General Bourke had already acted to achieve the same goal by issuing the Fiftieth Ordinance.

The ordinance allowed Hottentots, Griquas, and even Bushmen theoretical equal rights with white settlers. They no longer had to carry passes, could not be arrested for vagrancy at the whim of the police, and had easier access to the courts to complain of civil or criminal maltreatment. British and Boer alike protested that the ordinance had let loose on the colony a horde of indolent potential criminals and had robbed the farmers of the needed labor services of the Hottentots. Although most Hottentots continued to work for their employers, large numbers took advantage of their newfound freedom to wander from place to place living off relatives and stealing. Despite attempts by later governors, Lowry Cole and Benjamin D'Urban acting on the complaints of farmers to restrict the Hottentots, the Fiftieth Ordinance remained in force until the early 1840s. Its spirit was carried forth by a series of legislative acts which retained for the Hottentots, now generally called the Colored, equality in Cape Colony well into the twentieth century.

The Boer farmers had hardly recovered from the shock of Hottentot emancipation when the British parliament in 1833 abolished slavery. Although almost 40,000 of the ex-slaves were required to serve four years as apprentices, emancipation was a heavy blow to the affluent Boer farmers, particularly those of the western Cape. The money provided by parliament for compensation was not quite half the market value of the slaves. This sum was not paid directly to individual slave owners in Cape Colony but rather in drafts redeemable only in London. The Boer farmers thus lost even more in payments to London agents.

It has been commonplace to attribute the decision by thousands of Boers to trek away from the colony to the abolition of slavery. However, this action was seen by the Boers as only the latest of a long series of unwarranted tamperings with their attempt to live the good life. One other factor contributed heavily to the Boers leaving Cape Colony. The population of the colony had grown considerably in the decade and one-half after 1820, yet no significant land additions had been made. For cattle grazers on marginal lands who had large families, this lack of land was crucial. In response to the many-remembered grievances and the Boers' land hunger, three exploring parties or kommissie trekkes were sent north and east of Cape Colony. Their task was to investigate the new lands across the Orange River and report by the beginning of 1835 on such crucial matters as the presence of African tribes, the fertility of the land, and the availability of water.

It was at this crucial period that the sixth Kaffir war began. John Philip and other missionaries had urged upon Governor Benjamin D'Urban a policy of moderation toward the Bantu which would recognize the sovereignty of Xosa and Griqua states to the north and east of Cape Colony. Such a policy had little chance of success given the instability of the eastern frontier, continued cattle raiding, and the land hunger of the

Boers and Xosa. Along the coast northeast of the Kei River and in the deep interior the wars of Shaka and the mfecane had displaced tens of thousands of persons. The Xosa had also been affected by these events. Just before Christmas over 10,000 Xosa swept across the neutral territory and into the eastern Cape and with this invasion changed D'Urban's policy of moderation to one of force. In the first week of the war over one hundred Europeans were killed and the Xosa burned farmsteads and drove off thousands of cattle, horses, and sheep. Colonel Harry Smith who took command of the frontier found the bulk of the 7,000 European settlers concentrated in Grahamstown. However, imperial troops, Hottentot levies, and Boer commandos drove the Xosa across the Fish River and took the war to their kraals.

The sixth Kaffir war cost the farmers of the eastern Cape £300,000 and the imperial government over £150,000. To D'Urban this was a clear mandate to change previous policies which had not solved the problem of the unquiet frontier. He, therefore, declared all the land between the Keiskamma and Kei rivers to be British territory. All Xosa who stayed in this area which was named Queen Adelaide Province became British subjects. Africans friendly to Europeans such as the Fingoes (referred to by the Xosa as their dogs) were to be settled in the area. The Boers who had expected the bulk of the lands in the new area were disappointed, but they still confidently expected to be rewarded with land in the area between the Fish and Keiskamma rivers and in the Stormberg territory. However, they were totally disillusioned by the actions of the colonial secretary, Lord Glenelg. On the advice of Philip and other critics of D'Urban, Glenelg repudiated the annexation of Queen Adelaide Province. Instead D'Urban was ordered to withdraw behind the Fish River boundary. The eastern Cape was put under the control of a commissioner, Andries Stockenstrom, who was instructed to enter into treaties with various Xosa chiefs which would secure peace on the frontier.

Although some Boers led by Louis Trigardt and Janse van Rensburg had left the colony in 1835, no great numbers had departed until Glenelg's decision became known. Almost immediately Andries Potgieter and Sarel Cillers led the first large group northward away from ambivalent authority and really began the Great Trek. This wholesale movement of Europeans from Cape Colony will be discussed in more detail later. However, before a full understanding of how easy it was for the trekkers to occupy the area from the Orange to the Limpopo rivers one must survey the great changes which had taken place among the Sotho and Nguni groups in the forty years prior to the beginning of the Trek.

The rise of the Zulu and the mfecane

Before investigating the causes of the mfecane or "time of crushing," it is necessary to recapitulate briefly the general organization of the southern Bantu. Large groups of Bantu had moved across the Limpopo in the years after the sixteenth century. These people can be classified into two groups according to language and also by their place of settlement. The Nguni filled up the coastal strip east of the Drakensberg Mountains while the Sotho settled on the high plateaus of the interior west of these mountains. All the southern Bantu had similar social, political, economic, and military organizations. There were no extensive Bantu kingdoms in the south. Clans were the highest level of political organization. Originally members of a clan were denoted by kinship relations with the semi-mythical creator of the clan. However, by 1800 the larger clans had absorbed neighboring groups and there were hundreds of different clans in southern Africa. It has been estimated that in 1800 there were over 800 clans in the area of Natal alone. Clan size varied from a few hundred people to many thousands. Each clan was governed by a chief whose autocratic power was balanced by tradition, religion, and the unique limits placed upon him by other political institutions of the clan. The land itself dictated the type of economic development. In the rich valleys of Natal, sedentary agriculture was the basis of life and cattle keeping served primarily to indicate the richness of an individual and the clan. Further west and southward in marginal agricultural land, cattle and other livestock assumed a more important role. The stress placed upon different economic pursuits served along with language and customs to differentiate between the many Bantu groups. In the same locale because of constant regrouping of the clans and the practice of exogamy, there was cultural homogeneity.

The confrontation of some Xosa clans and Boer farmers along the Fish River in the 1770s was an event whose meaning transcended the series of Kaffir wars which followed. It indicated that the long period of Bantu wandering into open territory was almost at an end. No longer could the Bantu relieve population and political pressures by simply moving. Expansion into other areas after the 1770s would have to be done at the expense of other Bantu clans or white settlers. Thus all that was needed to set in motion a disastrous series of wars was the proper opportunity and the right African leaders. The opportunity presented itself in the first decade of the nineteenth century to the first of the great Bantu nation builders, Dingiswayo.

Dingiswayo (the troubled one) was a younger son of Jobe, chief of the Mtetwa clan. This clan of approximately 4,000 people was one of the largest in the Natal area. Fearing his sons, Jobe attempted to kill them all and believed he had succeeded. However, Dingiswayo was only wounded and took refuge with another clan, the amaHlubi. Tradition relates that during this short period he met and cared for a white man, probably a survivor of an expedition sent out in 1807 by Lord Caledon. After the death of his patient Dingiswayo took his horse and gun and with these established himself as the new chief of the Mtetwa. With the Mtetwa army he began to expand his authority. In his eight-year reign he established control over more than fifty adjacent clans. Dingiswayo's wars were designed to secure total submission of his enemies. Once his dominance had been accomplished he left the defeated clans in peace to be governed by their own leaders. His aim was not extermination but the creation of a larger, more viable state.

One of the smaller clans which fell under his overlordship was that of the amaZulu, the people of the heavens. They had been settled near the White Umfolozi River since the late seventeenth century. In the late 1770s the amaZulu, comprising not over 1,500 people living in a ten square mile area of rolling, grass-covered hills, were ruled by Chief Senzangakona. The chief was guilty of an indiscretion with Nandi, a woman of the neighboring eLangeni clan. Upon the announcement of her pregnancy the Zulu elders who had been shamed by their chief sent word to Nandi that she was mistaken. Her problem, they said, was caused by an intestinal beetle, *iShaka*. The child born to Nandi was given this name and lived most of his youth in the shadow of shame. About 1787 he was at his father's kraal, but he and his mother were driven out six years later and returned to the eLangeni. In 1802 because of famine, the eLangeni forced Nandi and her young son to leave and they finally found refuge in a clan directly controlled by Dingiswayo. About 1810 Shaka joined the other young men of the clan who had been called to serve in Dingiswayo's army. The embittered young man assigned to the izi Cwe regiment found his vocation since his bravery and innovations soon brought him to the attention of Dingiswayo and eventually he was given the izi Cwe to command. Shaka, during this period, evolved the military concepts which would later make his armies invincible.

The changes Shaka made are deceptively simple. The basic weapon of the southern Bantu had been the throwing spear. Shaka shortened the shaft and enlarged the blade, creating a stabbing spear. He increased the size of the shields for men in his regiment. He organized boys who were not yet warriors into a supply corps which was charged with keeping his men in food and drink. Shaka also threw away their oxen hide sandals and forced his men to toughen their feet. More important than any of these was the iron discipline and training techniques which enabled his men to cover over fifty miles in a day's march. These improvements created of the izi Cwe regiment first, and later all the Zulu armies, the most merciless and effective fighting machine in Africa.

In 1816 Shaka supported by Dingiswayo returned after Senzanga-kona's death to claim the chieftainship of the Zulu. He soon broke all opposition, destroying many of those who had ridiculed him when he was young. Shaka applied his military theories to the Zulu and in the early wars with his neighbors he evolved the ox-head formation. This formation which remained unchanged until the final destruction of Zulu power in 1879 was composed of four parts. The head met the enemy directly and held them fast while the horns, the left and right wings, fanned out and enveloped them. The fourth division, the body, was held in reserve and the commander could direct their attack wherever it could do the most good. After a victory, the Zulus killed all the enemy who could be found. By 1817 Shaka had incorporated some smaller clans and quadrupled the size of his kingdom. His army had grown to approximately 2,000 warriors.

Shaka was still the loyal servant of Dingiswayo when he was called

in 1818 to participate in an expedition against Chief Matiwane of the
emaNgwaneni clan to the north. Matiwane entrusted the bulk of his cattle
to an ally, the amaHlubi clan, who were located in the foothills of the
Drakensberg. Dingiswayo's campaign against Matiwane was inconclusive.
After peace had been restored Matiwane demanded his cattle from the
amaHlubi and was refused. At this juncture Chief Zwide of the
Ndwandwes who believed himself the equal of Dingiswayo attacked
Matiwane and drove the emaNgwaneni from their lands. This action
precipitated the mfecane. Zwide then began hostilities against the Mtetwa
by murdering Dingiswayo's son-in-law. In the ensuing campaign Dingiswayo was taken captive by Zwide and subsequently murdered. Without
their leader, the Mtetwa army retreated. Shaka, whose forces arrived after
Dingiswayo's death, could do nothing to reverse the Mtetwa defeat.
However, the death of Dingiswayo meant that the Mtetwa nation was
open for conquest by both Zwide and Shaka.

Meanwhile Matiwane, robbed of his cattle and lands, was blocked
by the Tembu, Xosa, and Boers in the south, the Zulu and Mtetwa in the
east, the Ndwandwes and Tonga in the north, and the Sotho in the
Drakensberg and beyond in the west. Matiwane could sit quietly and
watch his people starve or he could try to get cattle and food from his
neighbors. Matiwane's desperate people fell on the amaHlubi, massacred
the subclans, and took back their cattle. The remnants of the amaHlubi
retreated across the Drakensberg, striking against the small unorganized
Sotho clans. The mfecane had begun. Matiwane's people settled for about
four years in the lands vacated by the amaHlubi. By 1822 the Zulu were
dominant east of the Drakensberg and their impis had begun to raid into
the emaNgwaneni territory. Matiwane then led his people through the
Drakensberg passes in the wake of the amaHlubi who had been killing
and pillaging the Sotho for years. In 1823 Matiwane's forces caught up
with the amaHlubi remnants and in a five-day battle destroyed most of
them. The seven-year period following this event was one of chaos,
plundering, and killing which is nearly impossible to unscramble. It was
a time of confused coalescing and breaking apart of numerable clans.
Pillage and warfare became the way of life for the heretofore settled
Sotho clans.

One example of this desperate reshuffling is the career of Mantatisi,
the female ruler of the Sotho baTlokwa clan. They were among the first
to be driven from their homes by the amaHlubi. As the baTlokwa moved
in a generally southern direction, other scattered Sotho groups joined the
migration. It is estimated that by the time they neared the northern
borders of Cape Colony the "Mantatee horde" numbered over 50,000
people who literally ate up the country. Mantatisi's people were turned
back from the Cape by a combination of settled Bantu led by missionaries
and armed, mounted Griquas. Turning northward the horde began to
disintegrate. However, elements of the baTlokwa under Mantatisi's son,
Sikonyela, remained a threat to settled areas until destroyed by the Basuto
in 1852.

Mantatisi's group on their northward retreat displaced a small Sotho

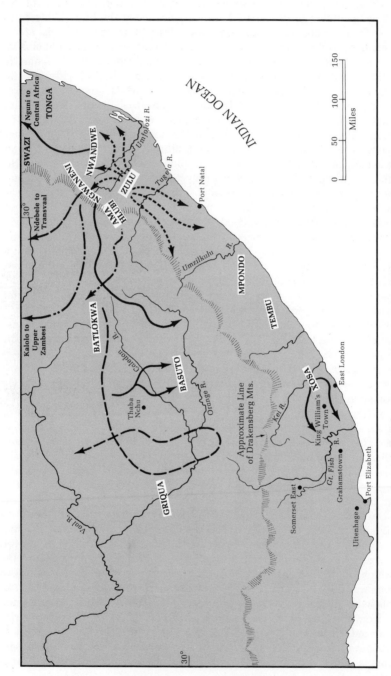

Approximate Bantu Movements during Mfecane, 1820–1835

clan led by a young chief, Mshweshwe. Instead of joining the landless pillagers, he led his people south to the western foothills of the Drakensberg. Here he found a flat-topped mountain, Thaba Bosiu, where he could locate his people and be able to defend them from the marauders. The area around Thaba Bosiu became an island of peace in the midst of disorder. In time other Sotho, sick of the wars and death, drifted to Mshweshwe. Out of such debris this remarkable man created the Basuto nation.

Matiwane, one of the chief architects of the mfecane, had by 1828 settled his people temporarily in Tembuland. Here misfortune continued to plague him. A Zulu impi that year had ranged far south into Xosa territory. Colonel Henry Somerset and a strong imperial force was dispatched to deal with this raiding column. Somerset's scouts confused the emaNgwaneni with the Zulu. Together with their Tembu allies they attacked and crushed Matiwane's force. The chief fled north where he was eventually captured, tortured, and killed by the Zulu.

After Dingiswayo's death an unquiet truce prevailed between Zwide and Shaka for a few months while the Mtetwa hegemony dissolved. Then in early 1819 Zwide moved his much larger army against Shaka. At Gqokoli Hill, Shaka abandoned his usual offensive tactics and fought a magnificent defensive battle. Zwide withdrew with most of the Zulu cattle. In the following months Shaka absorbed new elements into his armies, reorganized his regiments, and perfected his plans for the Ndwandwe invasion he knew was coming. When Zwide invaded Shaka's territory in May he found that Shaka had retreated, burning everything which could be used by the invaders. Shaka's supply corps kept the Zulu army well supplied with water and food while Zwide, without such a unit, could find little in the denuded country to assuage the hunger of his men. Shaka finally attacked and in two days of fierce battle destroyed the numerically superior Ndwandwe army. Shaka quickly followed up his advantage, invaded Zwide's territory, burned the chief's kraal, and ruthlessly smashed all possible future opposition. With this victory he had removed the only competitor to Zulu hegemony over the entire area of Natal. By 1820 Shaka could dispose of a finely tuned army of over 20,000 men and controlled directly over 10,000 square miles of territory. The later policy by which Shaka sent his impis to raid surrounding peoples made the Zulu power felt as far south as Xosaland. His regiments had humbled the Tembu and Cunu clans and cleared a hundred-mile-wide belt of all population south of the Tugela River.

The effects of Zulu nation building and the mfecane extended also far to the north. One of Zwide's generals, Soshangane, fleeing Shaka, drove the Portuguese out of the territory north of St. Lucia Bay and formed the basis there of the Shangan nation. The Ndwandwe refugees after the burning of Zwide's kraal retreated northward into the Transvaal area. Reorganized under Zwide's son, Zwangendaba, they scattered assorted northern Sotho tribes which added to the disorder of the mfecane. In the mid-1830s they crossed the Limpopo and cut their way across Rozwi territory destroying the Changamire empire. Eventually Zwangendaba's impis came to rest along the western shores of Lake Malawi. One of Shaka's generals, Mzilikazi, who had defied the great Zulu chief's orders, led approximately 300 Zulu warriors into the denuded central Transvaal area. There out of the scattered Sotho and his Zulu he created the militaristic Matabele nation. The Matabele remained dominant in this area until driven north across the Limpopo in 1837 by the Boers. The final northern offshoot of the mfecane was the Kalolo migration. They had been a part of Mantatisi's horde who found temporary safety in the area immediately south of the Limpopo River. By 1831 the Kalolo were a finely organized fighting force and had reached the confluence of the Zambesi and Chobe rivers. Their chief, Sebitwane, led them further into Luyi country and by 1838 they were masters of all Barotseland.

Shaka, the master of the Zulu, refused to relax the stringency of his rule after all his major enemies had been defeated. The armies were continually engaged in campaigns. Shaka, who had hundreds of wives with whom he had no contact, could not appreciate the attitudes of his warriors. The iron discipline of the Zulu military required them to remain celibate until given permission by Shaka to marry. Shaka in the past had rewarded victorious regiments with this permission. By 1828 it had been years since Shaka had waived his rules except for men too old to be of service in the field. In the security of his strength Shaka became unspeakably cruel. The death of his mother, Nandi, in October 1827, showed this trait more clearly than any other event. The people at the king's kraal taking their cue from Shaka began an orgy of grief which led to the indiscriminate killing of all those whose mourning did not seem genuine. Nandi was buried with ten live handmaidens whose arms and legs had been broken before burial. Shaka set an entire regiment to stand guard at her grave. He issued orders that in honor of his mother no crops were to be planted for the following year and no milk was to be used. Since sour milk was the main food of the Zulu this was tantamount to condemning the nation to a semistarvation diet. All women found to be pregnant in the period of mourning were to be killed. This blind, unreasoning reaction to Nandi's death continued for three months.

A plot to kill Shaka was devised in early 1828 by his two half brothers, Dingane and Mhlangana, and the chief of Shaka's household. In September the entire army was away on a campaign leaving only a small bodyguard at the king's kraal. The conspirators feigned illness and left the army. On September 22 while Shaka was receiving gifts from a delegation of Pondo, his brothers stabbed him to death. The assassins and people were so frightened by their deed that the scourge of the Zulu remained where he was killed for an entire night. The next morning he was dumped without ceremony into an empty grain pit.

After Shaka's murder there was a short period of joint rule of the brothers until Dingane, then thirty years old, determined that the army would be loyal to him. Most of the regiments which had been campaigning against Soshangane returned dispirited and low in morale. Dingane had already stopped the senseless slaughter at his court and he won the affection of the army by allowing a number of regiments to marry. As soon as he believed it safe he had his brother Mhlangana murdered along with a number of powerful nobles. The Zulu nation by 1829 was firmly in his hands. Dingane was for the Zulu an improvement over Shaka but his rule was still based on the strength of his army. He fought few major wars, but the regiments were kept busy since Dingane's normal response to problems was a violent one. Shaka had been an ascetic. Dingane was a hedonist who loved to eat, dance, and spend the majority of his time with his 300 wives. Dingane was not as consistent in the use of his power as was Shaka and was considered by Europeans to be more treacherous.

When the dissatisfied Boers began to leave Cape Colony for the north they found a largely depopulated land north of the Orange River. Only three major Bantu nations confronted them in their search for new land—the Basuto, the Matabele, and, most important, Dingane's Zulus.

The Great Trek

In 1823 following immediately after Captain Owen's survey of the coast-line of southeastern Africa, a group of traders and adventurers first established themselves at Port Natal. They found the land surrounding the harbor to be good and relatively free of Bantu. The first settlers were, however, not primarily concerned with farming or cattle raising, but with trade into the interior. Men such as John Thompson, Francis Farewell, James King, and Henry Fynn believed it possible to establish profitable relations with Shaka who controlled all of the land surrounding Port Natal. In July 1824, Farewell and Fynn visited the king's kraal. Shaka welcomed them, paraded his wealth and power before them, and gave them permission to stay at Port Natal. In early August, Shaka was accidently stabbed and Fynn was instrumental in nursing him back to health. In gratitude he signed a treaty granting Port Natal and approximately 3,500 square miles of territory adjacent to it to the Farewell Trading Company. Shaka had no intention of permanently alienating this land. The treaty was merely a sign of his respect for the white men.

Until Shaka's death the European community at Port Natal had nothing to fear from the Zulu. They traded beads and other manufactured goods to the Zulu for ivory, cattle, hides, and grain. Henry Fynn was so respected that he became a chief of one of the smaller Zulu clans. Despite the respect given to individuals by the Bantu, the colony did not thrive. The number of settlers at Port Natal until the late 1830s seldom exceeded forty. There was also a drifting African population which numbered approximately 2,000 persons. There were few items of profitable trade which could lure men from more settled areas to a land of such hardship and potential danger. A sandbar blocked the full use of the harbor to all but very shallow draft ships. Despite all these negative factors Port Natal was an established tiny community when Petrus Uys and twenty-one men of a kommissie trek reached it in the winter of 1834. The reports given by these trekkers of the green open country, few natives, and a functioning port played a most important role in the history of the Great Trek. Many of the Boer leaders came to regard Natal as the logical end of their long journey.

The exodus of Boers from Cape Colony began slowly and did not reach maximum proportions until mid-1837. Boer families had to reach individual decisions of the greatest magnitude. They had to decide to give up a settled existence for the unknown. Heads of families who chose to trek placed all their possessions into ox wagons, trailed their herds behind, and committed their families to the rough life of the trek and the danger of death from many sources. Nevertheless, by the midpart of 1836 all of Cape Colony was in ferment as hundreds of families prepared to risk everything rather than continue to be governed by the British. The first party of a dozen families under the leadership of Louis Trigardt left the colony in November 1835 and was soon followed by another small party led by van Rensburg. Trigardt's party settled near the Zoutpansberg range but found this was too isolated for them to get supplies of gunpowder. Eventually Trigardt led them into Portuguese territory where they settled in a fever area near the coast. In 1839 only twenty-nine people of this party were left and they were evacuated to Port Natal. Van Rensburg's party of ten families were simply lost somewhere on the high veld.

The first of the large parties was that of Andries Potgieter and Sarel Cillers with sixty-five families in 1836. At their encampment at Vegkop they met the first Bantu resistance. Matabele impis attacked and, although driven off, the Boer party lost all their cattle. Potgieter and Cillers fell back to Basuto country and in the winter were joined by Gerrit Maritz's party of one hundred families. In January 1837 the combined party fielded one hundred men and forty Griquas against the Matabele. In the ensuing battle which gave portents of the future, the Boers killed over 400 Matabele and recaptured their cattle. In April 1837, Piet Retief left the Cape accompanied by 120 families and he was soon followed by Piet Uys and another large group. By the end of 1837 an estimated 4,000 people had left Cape Colony.

Individualism was the Boer's greatest weakness as well as his great strength. Strong leaders of single treks found it difficult to control the desires of those who followed them. When it became necessary for different parties to cooperate, it was all but impossible to decide on a common policy. This facet of the trek became apparent in June 1837 when representatives of all groups met on the Vet River to establish common planning and unified leadership. Although they formed the United Laagers, there was no common leadership except when extreme danger threatened all the groups. One question more than any other divided the leaders. Where were they going? Retief and Uys were greatly influenced by the reports of the kommissie trek to Natal. They believed they could obtain permission from the Zulu king to settle in the vacant lands. Once settled they would have the advantage of Port Natal for obtaining the necessary

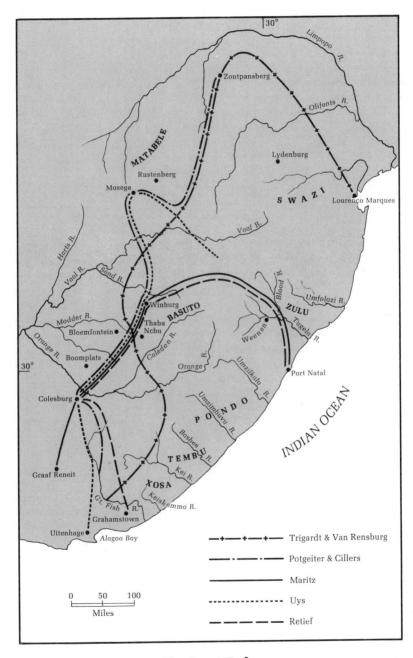

The Great Trek

supplies which they could not produce themselves. Maritz and Potgieter were lured by the high veld north of the Vaal River. It would be nearly impossible for the British to follow them, the land was good and almost completely empty, and Boers had already confronted the major native group, the Matabele, and won.

On the question of direction there was no compromise. Potgieter and those who agreed with him moved north of the Vaal River. In early autumn a Boer commando of approximately 135 men moved against the Matabele beyond the Marico River. In a battle of movement the Boers, without losing a man, drove the Matabele off the inland plateau and chased them toward the Matopo hills. The way was thus cleared for the establishment of the town of Potchefstroom and the peaceful settlement of the Transvaal areas. Meanwhile Retief leading fifty wagons had moved eastward toward Natal. After leading them down the escarpment of the Drakensberg, Retief rode ahead to the newly renamed Durban which had been called Port Natal before 1835. He saw or heard nothing at Durban which would indicate that he had made a bad choice. The settlers at Durban were friendly. The Cape government, although still claiming jurisdiction over the Boers, was engaged in the sixth Kaffir war and in no mood to annex further territory. The harmonious relations between the Durban settlers and Dingane indicated to Retief that he would have few problems in arriving at a settlement with the Zulu king.

Retief and his small escort then proceeded to Dingane's kraal. They were treated well and there were days of feasting and celebration. Finally in a conference Dingane accused Retief of stealing Zulu cattle. Retief denied this and guaranteed to recapture the stolen animals from the real culprit, Sikonyela of the baTlokwa. Dingane promised to give the settlers land if the cattle were returned. Thus emboldened, Retief sent word to his people that Natal was soon to be opened up and went after Sikonyela. The campaign was successful. Sikonyela was captured and ransomed off for cattle. A jubilant Retief led his sixty-nine men back to Dingane's kraal.

Retief's optimism was illusory since Dingane had no intention of allowing a thousand Boers to settle in his territory. Dingane was afraid. He had allowed the settlers at Durban to remain unharmed because they were few in number and therefore weak. These Boers were not weak. The Matabele who had resisted Dingane's best attempts to destroy them had been driven out of their lands by fewer Boers than were already camped in Natal. Dingane had decided, therefore, to kill all the Boers even before Retief returned from the campaign against Sikonyela. On February 4, 1838, Dingane signed a treaty ceding to Retief as governor of the territory all the area from the Umzimvuku River to the Tugela River and from the mountains to the sea. On the morning of February 6, the unarmed Boers were watching a farewell dance given in their honor. At a signal from Dingane the Zulu threw themselves on Retief and his followers and killed them all. The massacre was witnessed by Francis Owen, an American missionary to the Zulu, who brought the news to Durban.

Before word of the tragedy reached the Boer encampments, three Zulu regiments fell upon the unprepared laagers. Some of the larger encampments beat off the attacks, but many were destroyed. The Boers lost forty-one men, fifty-six women, 185 children, and 250 Hottentot servants before the onslaughts were checked. The Zulu drove approximately 10,000 captured cattle back to the king's kraal. In the two months that followed the death of Retief, Boers drifted into Natal from all parts of the interior, and finally a commando of 350 men led by Maritz, Uys, and Potgieter invaded Zulu territory. After an indecisive battle in which Uys was killed, the Boers retreated back to the main laagers. In May the situation had become critical for all Europeans in Natal and the settlers at Durban were evaculated from the town.

At the main Boer laagers over 4,000 people were concentrated. Many were sick and wounded and, after the failure of the previous commando, leadership was more divided than ever before. Then in November Andries Pretorius of Graaf Reinet arrived with sixty men and a cannon. He was elected commandant and almost immediately began another offensive against the Zulu. After a few indecisive skirmishes Pretorius and his small army of 450 men arrived at the Ncome River on December 15. Scouts had reported the presence of the main Zulu army. Pretorius selected a strong defensive position at the junction of the Ncome and another small stream. He had brought along a number of heavy ox-driven wagons which were put into a defensive position every evening. The wagons were placed in such a position that, if the Zulu attacked, they would have to do so on a narrow front. Early the next morning the Boers awoke to see an army of over 10,000 Zulu confronting them. The battle was soon begun by Zulu charging directly at the Boer position. However, the Zulu ox-head formation could not be used and Boer firepower was directed against a restricted area. After a two-hour defensive battle, Pretorius ordered the Boers to mount their horses and charge the Zulu. The Zulu regiments broke and the Boers chased the scattered army for the rest of the day. The Zulu lost over 3,000 men killed while the Boers suffered only four men wounded. From this time forward the Boers would refer to the Ncome as Blood River.

Dingane burned his kraal and moved northward accompanied by a powerful army driving the Zulu and captured Boer cattle before them. Pretorious and his force moved quickly to the king's kraal, but could recover only about one-half of the cattle lost to the Zulu. The commando soon disbanded, some men to return to the high veld, but most to move their families to the now open area of southern Natal. In early 1839 these established their capital approximately thirty miles west of Durban and called it Pietermaritzburg after two of their dead leaders. They proceeded to establish a governing body, the volksraad, elected Pretorius commandant-general, and began the difficult task of apportioning land. The governor of Cape Colony, Sir George Napier, sent eighty men to garrison Durban in December 1838, but since he received no orders to annex the adjacent area, these were withdrawn in December of the following year. It appeared to many Boers that Retief had been correct. They had reached the end of their wandering.

Dingane returned to his area and rebuilt his kraal. Leaving the Boers alone, he directed his armies northward against the Swazi in 1839. Preparatory to this campaign he ordered his brother, Panda, to bring his forces and join the main Zulu force. Panda, instead, learning that Dingane planned to kill him, moved all his people south of the Tugela River into lands occupied by the Boers. Panda, unlike his brothers, was weak by Zulu standards. He was reasonable, passive, and honorable in a European sense. At this time and later he was ignored by his relatives and powerless unless his orders coincided with their desires. The people who followed him south of the Tugela did so not out of loyalty, but because of fear of Dingane. Panda and his entourage traveled to Pietermaritzburg and he appeared before the volksraad on October 15, 1839. The Boers were pleased with the demeanor and promises of this passive Zulu ruler. He promised to stop what Europeans considered to be certain barbaric practices, cease waging war, and submit the choice of his successor to the volksraad. In return the Boers recognized him as Reigning Prince of the Emigrant Zulu and granted him permission to remain south of the Tugela.

The problem of cattle taken by Dingane from the Boers in 1838 proved a continual irritant. Dingane had no intention of returning them, and finally in January 1840 a new Boer commando entered his territory to take them back. The commando was composed of two sections, one Boer and one Zulu hostile to Dingane. On January 30 the Zulu contingent under Nongalaza met Dingane's regiments and after a bloody battle drove them northward. Dingane once again fled north across the Pongola River. This time he had only a few loyal troops and even these began to desert him. Relatively defenseless, he was killed by the Nwayos whose country he was invading. Even before his brother's death, Panda had been recognized by the Boers as king of the Zulu in February 1840.

The Natal trekkers, now safe from the Zulu, turned to the problems of government. The major local problem concerned land allocation. Each Boer male of the 1838–1839 group was entitled to have from one to three farms of 6,000 acres each. Some of the leaders such as Pretorius claimed many more. Many of the veterans of the campaigns of 1838 had not received their second farm when new Boers of the recent campaigns against Dingane demanded land. The disputes over land further divided an already highly individualistic people. Government was also plagued by jealousies between the leading citizens and was chronically short of money. The fees for registering land which provided the bulk of revenue, however low, were still beyond the means of many Boers. The volksraad also confronted the same problem of control over interior people which had hampered the East Indies Company and the British in Cape Colony. It did not have the power to enforce its decrees.

In 1840 the Pietermaritzburg volksraad attempted to weld together all the trekkers in the high veld under its rule. These areas included those closest to Cape Colony which were called Trans-Orangia. Few Boers lived on these hot grassy plains. The southern portion of Trans-Orangia was inhabited by the Griquas organized under their own captains. Thus the Natalians were relatively unconcerned about this area. To the north the area between the Vet and Vaal rivers which came to be called Winburg was fairly well populated and organized. The third area of the high veld was Potchefstroom north of the Vaal. Although Natal appointed a land-drost for this area, the unquestioned leader was Potgieter.

In November 1840 an agreement between all factions created a single republic with the Pietermaritzburg volksraad the chief instrument of government. Pretorius was appointed commandant-general of all Boer forces. Potgieter was named administrator for the north and there was a subsidiary volksraad located at Potchefstroom. In September the Natal volksraad sent a proposal to Sir George Napier at Cape Town asking to be recognized as an independent state. Temporarily united, the Boers sent a more direct and specific request in January 1841. Boer policing actions against scattered Bantu people and the use of the prisoners as apprentices to ease the acute labor shortage in Natal had prejudiced the Cape government against the volksraad. Napier refused their request for recognition in March 1841 and dispatched Captain Thomas Smith and a detachment of regular troops to a position on the borders of Natal. The inability of the Pietermaritzburg government to solve its most acute problems became more obvious in the spring and fall of 1841. This led directly to Napier's proclamation of annexation in December 1841.

The volksraad was divided sharply between those elements which favored acceptance of the inevitable and those who were willing to fight the British. Even when their independence was threatened the Boers continued to pursue their own selfish private goals. It was soon apparent that the Natalians would receive little help from Winburg and Potchefstroom. In May 1842, Smith and 250 regulars arrived and without opposition took possession of Durban. The Boers under Pretorius began to build up their strength at Congella. Smith rashly moved against the Boers and lost forty-nine men. Soon thereafter Pretorius' men captured two British ships and carted away fifty-six wagon loads of booty. Pretorius, however, could not drive the British from their fortified positions and Smith was able to send out a rider for help. The almost unbroken ride of Dick Smith for help to Grahamstown has become a South African legend. In response to Smith's request for help, a fifty-gun frigate and imperial troops under Colonel Cleote raised the siege of Durban in June 1842. By this time many of Pretorius' men had left him, the volksraad was still bickering, and there were rumors that Panda was planning to attack. Therefore, a rump volksraad on July 15 admitted the supremacy of the queen. Although the volksraad lingered on until late 1843, the Republic of Natal was a dead issue. Large number of Boers retreated west across the Drakensberg to the high veld. The volksraad made final the transfer of sovereignty in August 1843, and British troops occupied Pietermaritzburg. The Great Trek was finished and the Natal Boers, despite their hardships and sacrifices, found themselves still controlled by the British. On the high veld British authority was reaching out toward the Boers of Winburg and the Transvaal.

Relationships between Boer, Briton, and Bantu through 1872

The Boer settlements in the high veld in the 1840s and 1850s reflected the individualistic, quarrelsome nature of their leaders. Potgieter who had dominated Potchefstroom moved to Zoutpansberg in 1846 leaving Pretorius as the leader of Potchefstroom and Winburg. In 1846 another republic was briefly created at Ohrigstad in the Transvaal area. The farmers showed few signs of cooperating with one another against the specter of British activity in Trans-Orangia. The weakness of the separate trekker republics, individual jealousies, and the Boer's harsh attitude toward their native neighbors made it easier for the triumph of Britain's expansionist policy in the 1840s.

The same forces in Britain and South Africa which had impelled Governor Napier to annex Natal also pushed Britain to a more expansive policy in Trans-Orangia. In 1845 the Hottentot Griqua leader, Adam Kok, in attempting to arrest a Boer, brought on the threat of a minor war. The new governor of Cape Colony, Sir Peregrine Maitland, led British troops into Griqualand to reestablish order. He made it clear that Britain supported the independence of the Griquas. However, before any further northward expansion took place the seventh Kaffir war diverted the total energies of the Cape military to the eastern frontier.

The seventh war is known as the War of the Axe because its ostensible immediate cause was the arrest of a Xosa charged with stealing an axe. He was liberated from the Grahamstown jail by friends, the British sent troops into Xosa territory, and the war was on. The actual cause was the failure of the Colonial Office to approve D'Urban's settlement after the sixth war. Stockenstrom's treaty system had broken down by 1840. After that date order was maintained on the frontier by Governors Napier and Maitland, forcing the Xosa to accept more direct British rule. The seventh war was a direct result of Xosa dissatisfaction with such a system. The war which lasted almost two years convinced the Colonial Office that a more forward policy beyond the Cape borders was needed. They supported the Cape government with imperial troops and designated the governor as a high commissioner with authority to treat with natives beyond the frontiers.

A new governor, Sir Harry Smith, who had the most distinguished military career of any previous British governor, arrived in Cape Town in December 1847. He brought the Kaffir war to a quick conclusion and sanctioned the selling to Europeans of much of the land between the Fish and Keiskamma rivers. The area between the Keiskamma and Kei rivers he annexed to the crown as a separate entity called British Kaffraria. In order to provide a land bridge to Natal, all chiefs beyond the Kei had to recognize British sovereignty. D'Urban's rejected policy had at last triumphed in a slightly altered form.

Smith immediately turned his attention to the troubled areas north of the Orange River. The constant bickering between Boers, Basuto, and

Griquas posed a continual threat to the stability of the Cape's northern frontier. In February 1848, Smith declared all territories between the Orange and Vaal rivers to be subject to the rule of the queen and sent Major Henry Warden as resident with a few troops into the area to secure the allegiance of the Boers. Although many Boers welcomed an end to the internecine squabbles, many others joined Pretorius who came down from Potchefstroom with a few Transvaalers to oppose the British action. They expelled Warden and began to prepare to defend the area. Retribution was not long coming. Smith marched north and defeated the recalcitrant Boers at the battle of Boomplaats in August 1848. He then constituted the Orange River Sovereignty. British authority by 1849 had thus been extended north to the Vaal. A united British South Africa seemed inevitable.

Smith's dreams, however, were to prove futile. The reduction of the power of the Xosa chiefs in Kaffraria brought on resentment which exploded in 1850 in the eighth Kaffir war. To the dismay of Smith, the Xosa were joined by many Hottentots who felt cheated because of lack of compensation for their support of the British in the previous war. The farmers and burghers on the frontier also found numerous excuses to avoid commando duty. Thus the brunt of the fighting fell on imperial troops. This meant increased expenditure from the British treasury. Major Warden, the British resident in the Orange River Sovereignty, became engaged in an ill-advised war with the Basuto at the same time that Smith was involved with the Xosa. The British government after 1848, dominated by the non-expansion corollary of free trade, began to question the advisability of further responsibilities in southern Africa. Two assistant commissioners who did not have to report through Smith's office were sent to investigate the problem of the northern and eastern Cape boundaries. Smith believed that if they recommended retention of the sovereignty he could still induce the Transvaal Boers to agree to British sovereignty. However, at Sand River in January 1852 the commissioners dashed this hope by recognizing the independence of the Boer territories across the Vaal. The retreat from Smith's policy was continued when in February 1854 another special commissioner, Sir George Clerk, signed the Bloemfontein Convention. This withdrew the British from the Orange River Sovereignty and recognized the independence of that state.

Sir George Grey who became governor of Cape Colony in 1854 recognized immediately the problems of such a reversion. To him a common native policy in southern Africa was of prime importance. In 1856 he inquired of the Colonial Office about the feasibility of revoking the Bloemfontein agreement and received a negative reply. Two years later when his opinion was asked concerning a federation of Cape Colony, Kaffraria, and Natal he exceeded his authority by having the Cape parliament vote to include the Orange Free State in the proposed federation. Grey was rebuked and recalled by the Colonial Office. Although he returned as governor the following year, his reappointment was contingent upon his agreement to forget about any absorption of the Boer states. When Grey left office in 1861 federation seemed far away.

The decade following the Sand River Convention was a stormy period for the Boer states. The Pretorius and Potgieter factions of the Transvaal came together briefly to assure the Sand River Convention in 1852. The truce was short-lived. Andries Pretorius' son, Marthinius, succeeded to the leadership of the Potchefstroom settlers on the death of his father in 1853. His attempt to create a unified republic was rebuffed by other factions who were responsible for creating three small competitive republics— Lydenburg, Utrecht, and Zoutpansberg. Within each of these polities their volksraads had little authority and they were continually without funds. The Boers were little more than a collection of clans constantly involved in small-scale warfare against the Bantu. The Orange Free State was more viable since it was not as wracked by personal quarrels between its leaders and the potential threat of the powerful Basuto forced a more unified government.

In 1857 Marthinius Pretorius attempted to unite the Free State with his South African Republic. President Boshof of the Orange Free State ordered Pretorius from the country, and war between the two areas was only narrowly averted. During the same year Zoutpansberg blended with the South African Republic and in 1860 Lydenburg and Utrecht joined to create a single polity north of the Vaal River. In 1860 Pretorius was elected president of the Orange Free State and thus became the chief executive of both areas. For over two stormy years he tried to bring the two polities together. Finally in 1863 he resigned as president of the Orange Free State in order to retain control of the South African Republic against the challenge of Commandant Paul Kruger.

British activity in the areas beyond the borders of Cape Colony and Natal was at a minimum during this period. Most of their involvement was in Kaffraria where Grey and his successors attempted to convert the Xosa into farmers ruled by white magistrates rather than by their chiefs. This task was made easier by the actions of the Xosa themselves. In 1856 a young girl, Nongquase, the niece of an influential witch doctor, had a series of visions. These promised that a hurricane would be sent to sweep the white man from southern Africa if the Xosa placated the gods by destroying their grain and killing their cattle. If this were done the whites would disappear, all dead Xosa warriors would arise, and fat cattle and grain would be sent to them. Believing the vision, the Xosa launched upon a policy which led to their end as a major power in southern Africa. The vision did not prove true: The dead warriors did not rise and the cattle did not come. Instead an estimated 65,000 Xosa died of starvation.

Two unrelated factors propelled Britain more directly into interior affairs after 1865. Msheshwe of the Basuto had been under pressure from the Boers of the Orange Free State for years. There had been a number of wars between the two polities but none as serious as that of 1865–1867. Fearing the destruction of the Basuto nation, Msheshwe appealed to Sir Philip Wodehouse, the Cape governor, for protection. Not wishing to stand by and do nothing while the Basuto were destroyed, Sir Philip exceeded his instructions and granted Msheshwe's request. The Colonial Office, although displeased, concurred. However, in 1871 the Cape government

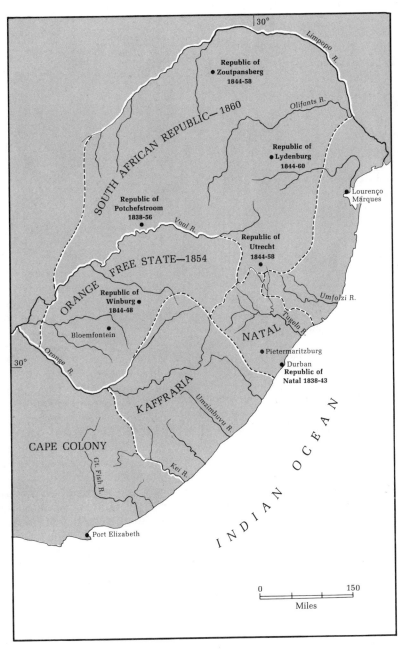

Southern African Polities, 1860

was cajoled into taking over the responsibility of the Basuto. The other event which more profoundly altered British attitudes was the discovery of diamonds in 1867 near the junction of the Vaal and the Orange rivers in Griqualand West. Men from all over the world poured into the diamond areas. By the time the river diggings had been exhausted in 1871, over £300,000 worth of diamonds had been retrieved. The newly founded Kimberley soon became the second largest city in southern Africa.

The area of the diamond fields was claimed by the Griqua chief, Waterboer, and the Orange Free State. The South African Republic also maintained that a portion of the territory was under its jurisdiction. The British government at the Cape supported the Griqua claim. With thousands of miners in the area, some type of government beyond that which the Griquas could provide was necessary. Sir Henry Barkly, governor of the Cape, favored a settlement with Waterboer and direct annexation. Prime Minister Gladstone demurred because of the expense of governing unwanted territory, but agreed that it could be annexed to the Cape. On October 31, 1871, Barkly raised the flag and the area became British territory. However, the Cape parliament refused the honor of bearing the cost of administration and despite Gladstone's objections, Britain had to assume direct control. The British throughout the period prior to annexation had staunchly repudiated the claim of the Orange Free State and had refused to arbitrate the matter. At a time when British interests turned once more toward a peaceful federation of all of southern Africa they had by their stand on the diamond fields alienated one of the necessary units to such a federation.

The fifty-year period after the landing of the Albany settlers witnessed the rapid economic development of Cape Colony. In 1820 there were a few thousand Europeans scattered thinly into the interior. By 1870 the population had grown to over 200,000. The prosperous Boer farmers of the western Cape were being matched by the primarily British farmers in the east. The passing of the Xosa threat in the 1850s expedited the development of the eastern regions. Despite prolonged drought in the 1860s, the Cape farmer was a rich man by comparison to his counterpart in the republics. The wine industry was falling off, but wool exports were worth almost two million pounds. There were banks, schools, and churches in all the major towns and even sixty-three miles of railway between Cape Town and Wellington. Though there was little industry except small firms which catered to specific services, Cape Colony had reached a point where a major infusion of capital could convert it from an agricultural to a proto-industrial society. The discovery of diamonds and less than two decades later, gold, provided the necessary impetus for this change.

The government of the colony had changed radically since the autocratic rule of Lord Charles Somerset. In 1834 there had been created a legislative council nominated by the governors to aid in policy making. Agitation in other colonial areas, particularly in Canada and Nova Scotia, for the colonists to have more voice in their own affairs had an effect on Cape Colony also. In 1842 the Colonial Office turned down the request by

Cape petitioners for representative government. The reason given for this action was the nature of the Cape community and the Colonial Office's fear that an elected government would lead to the oppression of the blacks. This and the jealousy between eastern and western areas of the Cape postponed representative government until 1853, five years after Canada had received responsible government. The tensions between British eastern farmers and their Boer western counterparts, combind with almost a decade of drought, delayed the grant of responsible government to the Cape. In the 1860s the British government had enunciated the principle that with self-government came self-defense. The Cape was in no position to assume the burden of funding the armed forces necessary to guard its frontiers. Finally in the 1870s eastern and western politicians agreed to cooperate with one another, the drought ended, and Britain agreed to maintain imperial troops in Cape Colony. On this basis a formula was worked out whereby the Cape received responsible government beginning in 1873. From this time forward the prime minister of Cape Colony and his ministry had a most important role to play in the development of southern Africa.

The colony of Natal lagged far behind the Cape. Plantation-type agriculture in sugar and tea was not developed until the 1870s. There was a continual labor shortage throughout Natal and the European population in 1870 was only 18,000. Therefore the grant of more self-government to the Natalians was understandably slower than to Cape Colony. Until 1856 Natal was administered as a part of Cape Colony with the chief executive being a lieutenant-governor. In that year Natal was separated from the Cape and given autonomous representative government with a small elected legislative council of sixteen members. Some citizens attempted to gain responsible government for Natal at the same time it was given to the Cape. However, the smallness of the population, lack of revenue, and the threat of the Zulu north of the Tugela River meant that Britain did not seriously consider such proposals. Natal did not receive responsible government until 1893.

Native policy in Natal followed to a large degree the ideas of one man, Theophilus Shepstone. Instead of attempting to westernize the Bantu as Smith and Grey were trying in Kaffraria, the people were segregated into special native reserves. This was done partially to keep them divided, but Shepstone also sincerely believed that their own chiefs could govern them best. The lieutenant-governor of Natal was declared the paramount chief of the Bantu south of the Tugela River. Thus government orders passed to the tribes from the white paramount chief through African leaders. This system kept order and prevented alienation of native lands, but it also created for the native a position as second-class citizen in Natal where there were few attempts made to give him equality with the whites.

North of the Tugela River lived the Zulu who might have remembered Blood River but certainly were not a conquered people. Panda could not control the Zulu in the same way his brother had and there evolved a loose system of government with each chief obeying the king when it seemed to his advantage to do so. Nevertheless, the foundation of the state still rested upon the military. Panda could not have destroyed the warrior system even had he wished to do so. It remained intact although little used during his reign. He sincerely pursued a policy of peace toward the Europeans south of the Tugela. Because of this and partly because of the small numbers of whites in Natal and the native policy of Shepstone, there were few examples of conflict between the Zulu and the settlers.

The somnolent Zulu were, however, revived by one of Panda's sons, Cetewayo. Panda had intended another son, Umbulazi, to succeed him, but Cetewayo gained the allegiance of a large portion of the Zulu and in 1856 declared war on his younger brother. In December of that year Cetewayo's regiments defeated his rival's armies and Umbulazi was killed. At an assembly the following year, Cetewayo was confirmed as the decision maker in the Zulu nation while Panda remained only the titular paramount chief. Cetewayo was more in the mold of his uncles, Shaka and Dingane. He revitalized the army and turned them loose on his native neighbors to the north. When he succeeded to his father's ceremonial title in 1872, he had managed to frighten a large portion of the European settlers in Natal and the South African Republic. Their misreading of Cetewayo's actions led to a disastrous Zulu war in less than a decade.

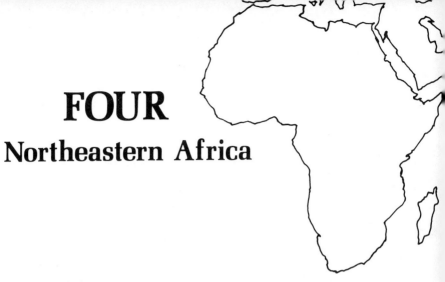

FOUR
Northeastern Africa

The Egyptian problem

Khedive Ismail who came to power in 1863 could not escape from the pressures of an affluent, expansive Europe. The French and British had long had sizable investments in the Middle East. Britain's support of the tottering Ottoman Empire, because of India, had great ramifications for Egypt. British intervention had already prevented Muhammad Ali from extending his influence into Syria at the expense of the sultan, his nominal suzerain. British entrepreneurs, urged on by their government, which was committed to Ottoman hegemony brought their new skills of building railroads, roads, and irrigation systems to Egypt. They were countered by entrenched French political and economic interests. Ismail's predecessor had in 1858 succumbed to Fernand de Lessep's scheme to build a canal linking the Mediterranean and Red seas. This was a diplomatic defeat for Britain which had wanted instead an interlocking system of British-built railroads for the Middle East.

Ismail saw no threat from the Europeans since he wanted for Egypt many of the things which only Europe could provide. He wanted to improve trade, the irrigation system, and with it agriculture. He was concerned with beginning European-style schools to provide a technically competent group as well as a Western-oriented elite. All of these schemes for internal betterment, added to his dreams of a great Egyptian empire, demanded a great amount of money. The Suez Canal by the time it was completed in 1869 cost twenty-six million pounds. The bulk of this had been borrowed by the khedive at high interest rates in the name of the Canal Company. Modernization of his army required large amounts as did his ventures in the Sudan and Ethiopia. In his borrowings he was urged on by French, German, Austrian, Italian, and British bankers who sadly miscalculated Egypt's ability to repay. The 1860s were good years for Egypt. There was a worldwide trade boom and the stoppage of Ameri-

93

can raw cotton for European mills increased tremendously the demand for Egyptian cotton. However, the good years of the 1860s gave way to the troubled 1870s. The reentry of American cotton on the market and a general worldwide trade depression meant that Egyptian expeditures could not continue at a high level without causing economic disturbances. Despite this the tempo of Egyptian spending and borrowing did not abate. Within a year of its opening the Suez Canal was making profits for its shareholders. Otherwise by the mid-1870s the finances of the khedive were in a chaotic state. The public debt which stood at four million pounds at the beginning of Ismail's rule had risen to ninety-one million pounds by 1879.

In November 1875, Ismail was forced to sell his 176,000 shares of the total of 400,000 shares in the Canal Company. The British prime minister, Benjamin Disraeli, by a combination of luck and skill managed to secure these and Britain thus became the largest stockholder in the Canal Company. Ismail's troubles were only beginning since the European bondholders began more stridently to pressure their governments to demand payment from the khedive. In 1876 the management of Egyptian finances passed to a European consortium called the *Caisse de le Dette.* The chief figures of the Caisse were the two secretaries, one French and one British. This dual control brought about only slight improvement in financial affairs and in 1879 when it was discovered that Ismail was plotting against the Europeans he was deposed by the Turkish sultan on the advice of the British.

The new khedive, Tewfik, obviously could not succeed where his predecessor had failed. Europeans kept demanding their money and Egyptians came to believe that they were the cause of all the evils which had befallen the country. The numbers of Europeans resident in Egypt had grown from only 6,000 in 1853 to almost 100,000 by 1882. Egyptian nationalism posed a considerable threat to the security of these Europeans. Arabi Pasha, the minister of war, put himself at the head of the Egyptian nationalists and demanded that Egypt be permitted to rule itself without outside interference. The French premier Gambetta became so perturbed over the danger to French nationals and the specter of Arabi becoming dictator that he proposed to Britain a joint occupation of the country. At first Prime Minister Gladstone refused, but continuing disorders threatening the lives of Europeans compelled him to agree to a joint naval force to overawe the Egyptians. After the killing of Europeans in June 1882 the decision was made to invade Egypt, if necessary, to restore order and rid the country of Arabi. A change in government in France resulted in a reversion of their aggressive policy. Gambetta's successor, Charles Louis Freycinet, refused to authorize the use of French armed forces. Without French assistance the British bombarded Alexandria in July 1882. In August British troops under the command of Sir Garnet Wolseley landed at Ismalia and in the following month defeated Arabi's forces at Tel-el-Kebir. Tewfik was restored to the throne by a British army of occupation and dual control was declared to be ended.

The internal history of Egypt after 1882 is beyond the scope of this work. However, because Egypt was such a key factor in the scramble for Africa it is necessary to outline briefly the international implications of the British occupation. The report of 1883 submitted by Lord Dufferin indicated how archaic and corrupt the Egyptian administration was. The British position then became one of reconstructing the government, employing honest, efficient men in the offices of the state and rebuilding the army around a cadre of British noncommissioned and commissioned officers. Britain contemplated that the reforms would take years to effect and would thus drain away large sums for reconstruction which otherwise would have been applied to pay the bondholders.

The French government, despite involvement in planning for the occupation, assumed that Britain was in Egypt only as agent for the bondholders. Their concept was that the occupying force should not commit itself to any long-term rebuilding. It was merely to act as a means of forcing the money from Egypt to meet the obligations to European investors. As soon as this was done all British troops should be withdrawn. Obviously the French posture was dictated by factors other than merely concern for the bondholders or for Egyptian independence. French financial interests in Egypt were greater than Britain's, and France was beginning to expand its territorial empire throughout Africa. In Egypt, Britain blocked French plans for extension of their own empire. The *Caisse de la Dette* which still functioned was one of the major mechanisms the French used to block Britain's proposed activities in Egypt. British plans for reconstruction of Egypt were saved by the support which they received from Germany. German chancellor Otto von Bismarck was at first relatively uninterested in a territorial empire in Africa. One of his major concerns was to force Britain from its "splendid isolation" into a definite alliance with Germany. In the mid-1880s this long-range German goal dictated support of Britain's Egyptian plans. Therefore by 1887 there came to be a de facto recognition of Britain's premier position in Egypt by all European powers. This concession carried certain disabilities for Britain elsewhere in Africa. As a price for such recognition, France and Germany expected and received little opposition to the expansion of their territorial empires in West and East Africa. In assessing Britain's attitudes toward European encroachment in areas previously considered British spheres, one is led back again and again to its fixed position in Egypt.

Britain's reorganization of Egypt did not at first touch the structure of government. The khedive as a vassal of the Ottoman sultan remained the head of state. An Egyptian ministry was allowed to continue as well as the local government structure. The British merely interposed themselves in the operation of government at all levels. British officials replaced Egyptians on the intermediate levels particularly in offices concerned with finance. The Egyptian army was reorganized according to the British model with the most important positions being filled by British officers. Undoubtedly the most important official in the Egyptian government was

Sir Evelyn Baring (later Lord Cromer) who from 1883 to 1906 was the British consul. Through him the British Foreign Office channeled its high-level decisions which became binding on the khedive's government.

Egypt in the Sudan to 1885

Egypt's dominant position in the Sudan dated from the early days of the rule of Muhammad Ali. This Albanian adventurer, one of the most astute rulers of his day, saw many opportunities in the troubled Sudan. The southern frontier of Egypt was vulnerable to attack from the displaced Mamluks who had fled south after Muhammad's seizure of power. More important than this strategic consideration was the economic factor. Possession of the Sudan would greatly increase the animal and agricultural potential of Egypt. There were also rumors of ancient gold mines in the Sudan which, with the proper care, could be made productive. Then there were slaves which could be taken in the extreme south and either sold or retained as soldiers or forced workers for the state. Obviously an important consideration in the viceroy's planning was the defenseless position of a large portion of the most valuable riverine territory. The Funj rulers no longer exercised any real power over the bulk of territory which had once been their empire. Real power resided in the hands of individual sheikhs who were most concerned with maintaining their privileges against interlopers. It was unlikely that Egyptian forces would meet much opposition if they chose to invade the southern territory.

In 1820 Muhammad Ali dispatched two columns of over 9,000 men into the Sudan. One was under the command of his third son, Ismail, and the other of his son-in-law, Muhammad Bey al Daftardar. Both armies were equipped with the latest in European weapons. As expected, the only effective resistance to this invasion came from the Shukriya. After their surrender the rulers of Shendi capitulated, the Abdullah chiefs surrendered, and Ismail occupied Sennar without difficulty. Al Daftardar's forces immediately invaded Kordofan and in a fierce battle defeated the armies of the representative of the Fur sultan, and this part of the Mussabbaat territory became a part of Muhammad Ali's empire.

Even before the initial conquest had been completed Ismail, assisted briefly by his brother, Ibrahim, began to exploit the territory. Troops were dispatched southward to raid for slaves and a tax levy was imposed many times that which had previously been paid. Despite the fear engendered in the Sudanese by the "Turks" many refused to pay the tax and some fled their homes rather than submit. Ismail's government, although hastily constructed and designed to exploit the territory to the maximum, was not otherwise cruelly oppressive. In most conquered areas the traditional rulers continued to function although under the surveillance of Egyptian officials.

The murder of Ismail changed briefly, but decisively, Egyptian policy to one of direct, violent, oppressive actions against the Sudanese. Ismail in October 1822 paused at Shendi on his way to Egypt after almost two years in the Sudan. At an audience with the local ruler, Ismail demanded the payment of approximately $30,000 and 6,000 slaves. This payment was to be delivered within two days. A brief quarrel ensued over the impossibility of these demands and Ismail struck the ruler with his pipe. Later retainers of the sheikh set fire to the house where Ismail slept and he died in the fire. When news reached al Daftardar of the details of Ismail's death, the reaction was swift and generalized. He sought not to punish those responsible, but to make all Sudanese pay for the action. His armies pillaged and killed from Sennar north to Metemma. Thus the Sudanese learned very early that the "Turks" were violent oppressors, a view which later benevolent actions of Egyptian rulers could not remove.

Following the conquest, Muhammad Ali proceeded to organize a centralized government for the Sudan. The entire area was ruled by a governor-general (hikimdar) who was appointed directly by Muhammad Ali. The governor-general possessed military as well as civil authority and his decisions could be reversed only by Muhammad Ali. In a short time the Sudan was further divided into a number of provinces, each ruled by a governor (murdir) responsible to the governor-general. By the time of Ali's death in 1849 there were seven provinces—Dongola, Kordofan, Berber, Khartoum, Fazughli, Taka, and Sennar. Although there were various experiments by Ali's successors, the provincial type of government remained the basic pattern throughout the period of Egyptian rule. Since it would have been nearly impossible to staff all administrative offices with Egyptians, each province was further subdivided into districts over which traditional rulers presided, subject to control by the governor.

Egyptian rule in the Sudan in the nineteenth century was based upon its exploitation for the benefit of Egypt. The chief administrators were foreigners who generally did not understand or appreciate the cultures of the indigenous people. All Sudanese were taxed heavily and when Egyptian authority spread southward into the Bahr al Ghazal and Equatoria the tribal structure of the people was directly undermined by incessant slave raiding. Government at all higher levels was characterized by corruption, lack of administrative continuity, and open insubordination of officials who could take advantage of the vast distances and poor communications in the Sudan. Other factors must be mentioned in connection with Sudanese misrule. The gold mines proved not to be worth much, agriculture was slow to develop, and therefore the Sudan remained a poor area. Despite high taxes even in years of peace, it was always a drain on the Egyptian treasury. Therefore there was extreme reluctance in Cairo to approve expenditure of funds for improvements in the Sudan.

From the beginning of Egyptian rule the slave trade occupied a prominent position in the affairs of the Sudan. The government until the reign of Abbas Pasha (1849–1854) in Egypt maintained a monopoly of all trade and therefore also of the slave trade. Muhammad Ali's reorganization of the army of occupation in the Sudan was based upon captured slaves trained by European officers. During the entire period of Egyptian rule there was a steady demand for slaves in the northern Sudan, Egypt, and in Muslim territories across the Red Sea. After the late 1850s private companies were organized to tap the human riches of the areas south of Gondokoro. Slaver entrepreneurs such as Zubeir Pasha maintained their own forts and private armies and were laws unto themselves in the frontier areas of the Sudan.

More as a concession to British antislavery pressure than from real conviction, Khedive Muhammad Said (1854–1863) in 1854 issued orders to all his officials in the Sudan to stop the traffic in slaves. A new post was established at Fashoda ostensibly to control the southern trade, but officials in the Sudan merely ignored the khedive's strictures on the trade. By the opening of Khedive Ismail's reign (1863–1879) the only real Egyptian authority in the area south of Gondokoro to the borders of Bunyoro were the slavers.

In the early years of Ismail's term, Egypt's economy improved greatly. This improvement, largely caused by the increased demand for cotton, led Ismail to overcommit himself to European financiers. A substantial portion of the extra funds available to Egypt were spent in furthering the imperialistic ambitions of the khedive. Ismail brought to Egypt many foreigners whom he believed would help him create a modern Western-style army. Many ex-confederate and northern officers from the United States were employed in this task. One, General Charles Stone, became chief of staff of the army. Ismail greatly expanded the size of the army and stationed between seven and ten thousand men permanently in the Sudan during the 1860s. Most of these troops were armed with the latest rifles and, beginning in the 1870s, the army also relied upon various caliber of cannon from Germany.

One of the earliest areas of attempted Egyptian expansion was Ethiopia. In December 1862, Governor-General Musa Hamdi led an expedition of over 7,000 men well into Ethiopia. In 1866 Ismail leased Suakin and Massawa from his Ottoman overlord and in 1870 the coast of Somalia from Bulhar to Berbera was acquired in the same way. In 1874 the Egyptians under Raul Pasha occupied Harar. Two years later the main Egyptian thrust into Ethiopia was permanently damaged when Emperor Johannes IV at Gura defeated an Egyptian army of 12,000 men commanded by the American general Loring and the sirdar Ratib Pasha. Although not abandoning completely the Ethiopian arena, Egypt was forced by internal problems to curtail any further ambitious schemes in this direction after 1877.

The area of Egyptian control over the Sudan was increased in the early 1870s largely by the efforts of the greatest of the Sudanese slavers, Zubeir Pasha. In 1872 his independence and power in the Bahr al Ghazal was challenged by the government. Zubeir's private army defeated the government forces. Instead of being punished for his action Zubeir, after convincing the khedive of his loyalty, was rewarded by being appointed governor of the territory. In 1874 Zubeir's forces, preceding the army of the governor-general, invaded the Fur kingdom, defeated its armies, and occupied El Fasher. Soon afterward, however, the governor-general who feared Zubeir's power convinced the khedive to banish the slaver-captain from the Sudan. Nevertheless, Zubeir's interests were guarded by his son, Suliaman, who reigned supreme in the Bahr al Ghazal.

Another area of great expense which yielded Egypt very few tangible imperialistic gains was the Upper Nile. Sir Samuel Baker, the explorer whom Ismail had first met in 1869, was employed by the khedive and given a twofold task. The first and most important charge was to extend Egyptian influence into the interlacustrine areas of East Africa. Secondly, Baker was to use all means at his disposal to end the slave trade. Baker was well provided with troops and had at his disposal six river steamers and a fleet of sailboats. Almost immediately after his arrival at Gondokoro in April 1871, he set the tone for his relations with the local people by quarreling with Egyptian merchants and confiscating large amounts of cattle from the Bari tribesmen. Baker was henceforth viewed as a danger to the Bari and it took his successor, Charles Gordon, years to gain their confidence. Baker soon moved southward and established a fort at Masiudi from whence he declared Bunyoro an Egyptian protectorate. However, Kabarega, the ruler of Bunyoro, was not favorably impressed by Baker's plans for his kingdom and eventually Bunyoro armies forced Baker to withdraw from Masiudi. Baker also contacted Mutesa, ruler of Buganda, with no more satisfactory results for Egyptian plans. Ultimately Baker had to be satisfied with garrisoning such small places as Fatiko and Folero. Baker left Gondokoro for Egypt in April 1873 with little to show for his two years as governor of Equatoria.

Not warned by his experience with Baker, Ismail employed the hero of the Taiping rebellion in China, Colonel Charles Gordon, to finish the tasks outlined to Baker. Gordon was much more successful than Baker in mollifying the feelings of Africans. Working tirelessly after early 1874, Gordon from his administrative center at Lado extended Egyptian influence deep into Bunyoro. He established a series of military posts between Rejaf and Dufile from whence his boats could travel to Lake Albert. Nevertheless, Gordon's resources were not sufficient for the tasks assigned him. His personality alienated many of his European lieutenants and disease also took a heavy toll of his subordinates. Finally in 1876, near exhaustion himself, he resigned and returned to England. The results of Baker's and Gordon's efforts taken in conjunction with Egyptian failures of the same period in Ethiopia certainly justified the critics of Ismail's government who accused him of spending lavishly without achieving any definite advantage.

Gordon's connection with the Sudan, however, had not ended. There were to be two other acts in the tragedy before his death, at Khartoum, in January 1885. The first of these was when he decided in 1877 to return to his post as governor of Equatoria. By the time he arrived in Cairo he had decided that his major function should be the suppression of the slave trade. To accomplish this aim he demanded that he be appointed governor-general. Surprisingly, Ismail concurred in this request. For almost three years Gordon devoted himself unsparingly to the eradication of the trade. He quelled a revolt against the government in Darfur, and defeated and executed the slaver Suliaman in the Bahr al Ghazal. When he resigned in 1880 in loyalty to his deposed chief, Ismail, Gordon had made severe inroads into the slave trade. However, he had not succeeded in infusing efficiency into the government of the Sudan nor had he taught the Egyptian staff the dangers of a corrupt government.

Egyptian misgovernment brought on a reaction against foreign rule which, coinciding with the British occupation, swept Egyptian authority from the Sudan. The leader of this revolt was Muhammad Ahmed, a religious teacher who in his mid-thirties proclaimed himself the Mahdi. To the Sudanese who are Sunni Muslims this term means the "guided one" who would bring justice to society as the head of the Islamic community. Muhammad Ahmed, the son of a boat builder, had early distinguished himself by his piety and learning. After his studies under a number of famous Sudanese holy men were completed, he became a religious teacher of the Sammaniya sect. From his base at Abba Island in the Nile he began to carry his message of self-denial and purity throughout the central Sudan. One such trip through the Kordofan in 1879 was particularly fruitful in gaining converts and spreading his fame. Sometime before 1881 Muhammad Ahmed began to believe himself the Mahdi. Aided by the Sudanese expectations of the appearance of the chosen one, he soon gathered about him a number of persons who believed him. Among these early converts was Abdullah, the future khalifa.

Muhammad Ahmed spent most of 1881 in Kordofan preaching the need for purity and criticizing the activities of the Egyptian rulers. By mid-1881 he had openly declared himself the Mahdi. In August Governor-General Rauf Pasha sent two companies of troops to Abba Island to arrest the troublemaker. A series of tragicomic events culminated in the Mahdists, with sticks and spears, routing the better-armed soldiers. Muhammad Ahmed then retired to Kordofan. The Egyptian commander at Fashoda, ignoring orders, dispatched 400 regular troops and 1,000 Shilluk to pursue him. On December 9, 1881, the troops were ambushed by Abdullah's irregular forces. Egyptian losses were heavy. These triumphs over established authority earned the Mahdi prestige and gained him many more volunteers.

Governor-General Rauf Pasha was recalled by Tewfik and before his replacement arrived the acting governor-general decided to crush the Mahdi. In the spring of 1882 a military expedition of over 4,000 troops left Fashoda for Kordofan. The Egyptian military commanders took no defensive precautions and they too were ambushed by the Mahdists. Very few Egyptian troops escaped and the Mahdists for the first time secured large stores of modern arms. More important, most of the tribes of the Western Sudan, the Fur, and the Beja joined Muhammad Ahmed. He declared a jihad against the Sudan's Egyptian rulers and his forces immediately laid seige to the towns of El Obeid and Bara.

The Mahdist success was due to more than Muhammad Ahmed's charismatic personality or the ineptitude of the Egyptian authorities. The various crises which led eventually to the British occupation engaged the

attention as well of the Egyptian leaders. Even had there been good leadership in the Sudan, Arabi Pasha was not likely to send any significant
reinforcements to the Sudan in 1882. The defeat of the Egyptian army at
Tel-el-Kebir further reduced the ability of the Egyptians to crush the
Mahdi. Nevertheless, the British advisers to the khedive gave their consent
to sending another large army in pursuit of the Mahdi. A pickup army was
formed and concentrated at Khartoum in the early months of 1883. Winston
Churchill writing a few years later called this army "perhaps the worst
army that has ever marched to war." General Hicks, a retired officer of the
Indian Staff Corps, commanded this force of slightly over 7,000 men.
Ostensibly they were to relieve El Obeid, but this city fell to the Mahdi
before Hicks left Khartoum. However, Hicks' force still left for that area
presumably to relieve pressure upon the governor of Darfur, Slatin Pasha,
who was still resisting the Mahdists. Plagued by dissension, bad leadership,
and poor knowledge of the terrain, Hicks' army met the Mahdist's forces
on November 3, 1883. In a series of confrontations over the next two days
the Egyptian army was almost completely destroyed. Only about 500
Egyptians escaped and Hicks and the European officers were killed.

The fate of the Sudan was sealed after this battle. Slatin surrendered
in Darfur, the riverine tribes joined the Mahdi, and leaders of the eastern
Sudan such as Osman Digna also joined. At this juncture the British
advisers to the khedive, faced with the shambles of the Egyptian economy,
persuaded Tewfik to abandon the Sudan. Prime Minister Gladstone's
government refused to commit any more British troops than absolutely
necessary to hold Suakin and the southern approach to Egypt. Two courses
were open to the khedive. He could follow the stern advice of the British
and evacuate the Sudan or he could attempt to reestablish government in
the Sudan under a strong dynamic leader such as the slave entrepreneur
Zubeir Pasha. The decision was made to withdraw all Egyptians from
various garrisons still holding out. Most of them were concentrated in the
capital city of Khartoum. The final decisions were made in London in
January 1884. Gladstone, against his better judgment, bowed to public
opinion and asked the popular hero, General Gordon, to return to the
Sudan to effect the pullback of Egyptian forces. Only Wadi Halfa and
Suakin were to be kept as military bases to check the further expansion of
Mahdism. The instructions given Gordon in London remain something of
a mystery, but it appears that the ministry was convinced that Gordon's
objectives were clear and that he would carry them out.

On his arrival in Egypt, however, Gordon had developed a counter-
proposal which he felt would continue Egyptian hegemony over some of
the Sudan. This scheme involved the establishment of his old enemy,
Zubeir Pasha, as a counterforce to the Mahdi in the Sudan. The British
Foreign Office, appalled at the idea of using such a notorious slaver,
refused and Gordon left for the Sudan. From Berber in February he sent
gifts to the Mahdi, named him the king of Kordofan, and declared the
government's intention of evacuating the Sudan. Arriving at Khartoum,
Gordon effected a number of changes designed to placate the Sudanese

such as reform of the taxing system and abolishment of the new laws relating to the slave trade. Finally he announced the separation of the Sudan from Egypt. He began to send officials, civilians, and sick soldiers down the river. However, the Mahdists, flushed with success, had no intention of accepting from Gordon favors which were theirs for the taking anyway. The active operations of the British and Egyptians in the eastern Sudan against Osman Digna seemed to cast doubt on Gordon's sincerity.

By the end of March 1884, Khartoum was heavily besieged by the Mahdists. Only steamers operating under hazardous conditions gave Gordon a link with the north. Even this link was severed when Berber fell to the Mahdists in May. The future of Khartoum became a foregone conclusion unless the British intervened. Muhammad Ahmed arrived at Khartoum with over 60,000 men in October. Gordon held on to Khartoum doggedly with approximately 7,000 troops, expecting that a relief column would be sent to relieve him as soon as his plight became known. However, the British government procrastinated during the summer and it was not until late August that the decision was made to rescue Gordon. The commander of the relief expedition, Sir Garnet Wolseley, spent almost two months preparing for the campaign and his main army did not leave Cairo until October. When it became apparent in December that the army would not reach Khartoum in time, a specially organized camel column raced ahead of the main body, cutting across the desert from Korti to Shendi. They fought two major battles with the Sudanese and arrived within sight of Khartoum on January 27, 1885, where they learned that the city had been stormed the day before and Gordon had been killed.

British public reaction to the death of Gordon, predictably, was bellicose. It is doubtful whether Prime Minister Gladstone could have long resisted public demands for revenge. However, the Russian occupation of Penjdeh in Afghanistan in March 1885, which resulted in a brief war scare in Britain, gave him an excuse for withdrawing Wolseley's troops from the Sudan. Nevertheless, the shame of Gordon's death going unrevenged rankled a growing imperialistic Britain. As the scramble for Africa increased in intensity it became only a matter of time before Britain in conjunction with Egypt attempted the reconquest of the Sudan.

The Mahdi, after establishing a new capital city at Omdurman across the Nile from Khartoum, began to consolidate his power. He called upon other Islamic rulers to recognize him as the Mahdi and join him in his jihad. However, he died less than six months after his forces had captured Khartoum. On his recommendation he was succeeded by Khalifa Abdullah. In the twelve years respite given him before direct European intervention, Abdullah wasted much of the potential of the Mahdist movement by internal purges and a series of conflicts with Ethiopia. This latter interest of the khalifa directed the full force of his armies away from Egypt and in the direction of Ethiopia. This gave the British time to rebuild the Egyptian army. The death of Johannes IV of Ethiopia in battle against the khalifa in 1889 was crucial to the developing expansion of Europe in Africa.

Ethiopia through the reign of Theodore

After the death of Yasu II in 1730 Ethiopia quickly drifted into a type of anarchy whose closest European analogy was Merovingian France. The great nobles of the state quarreled with one another and the leaders of the church used their considerable influence on one side and then on another. Emperors came to be figureheads controlled by kingmakers. Warfare between factions continued intermittently and the military literally "ate up the land." The emperors once more abandoned a stationary capital and moved with their courts and followers from one part of the kingdom to another. The glorious palaces at Gondar and Debra Tabor, like the stable dynasty they represented, began to fall apart. In this troubled period the Galla leaders assumed more power than ever before. There is considerable knowledge of a portion of this period because the explorer James Bruce visited Ethiopia in 1769 and much later wrote of the reign of Emperor Takla Haimanot II. The young emperor was controlled by Ras Michael Sehul, the strongest of the Ethiopian nobles. Ras Michael and the imperial armies were continually at war with competitive forces. Eventually in 1779 Takla Haimanot was killed and the central authority broke down completely.

The period between 1779 and 1855 has been called somewhat euphemistically "the era of judges." In actuality this was a time when the emperors had little power, the church declined, and the united kingdom was split into powerful substates. Shoa cut off from the northern provinces by the Wollo Galla obtained almost total independence under the rule of Sahale Selassie (1813–1847). In some of the provinces many of the rulers were either Galla or Muslims. By 1840 there were four main competitive states—Shoa, Gojjam, Tigre, and Begameder. A puppet emperor, Sahela Dengel, presided ineffectually and impotently over all these.

In the late 1830s a young leader with all the attributes of a tillak sew, a strong man, first made his appearance on the political scene. This was Ras Kassa who had originally been destined for the church. However, in one of the many skirmishes his monastery was burned and he was forced to take refuge with his uncle who was one of the emperor's officials. This was the period when Muhammad Ali, the Egyptian khedive, was seeking to expand his control over areas adjacent to the Nile Valley. Ras Kassa became a leader of irregular troops which made raids into the Sudan. His success in boldly raiding as far as Metemma gained him fame and many adherents. The widow of Emperor Johannes III, Manon, became fearful that such a popular powerful figure would upset the control her son, Ras Ali II, exerted over Begameder. However, Ras Kassa defeated her armies and forced a marriage with Tawabatch, the daughter of Ras Ali.

Ras Kassa briefly joined forces with Ras Ali and Ubye of Tigre to meet the further attacks of the Egyptians. After the British brought pressure upon Muhammad Ali to abandon his plans of conquering Ethiopia, Ras Kassa found that he had a parity of power with the other leaders of divided Ethiopia. He then compelled Ras Ali to recognize his authority

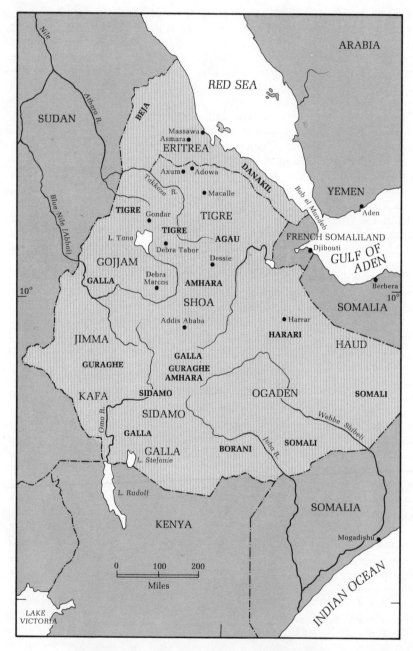

Political Divisions and Peoples of Ethiopia

over his uncle's lands, imprisoned Empress Manon, and established himself at Gondar. In the early 1850s Ras Kassa was in a position finally to attempt to dominate his competitors. He demanded that the ruler of Gojjam, Ras Goshu, submit to his overlordship. When this was refused, Kassa invaded Gojjam and in November 1852 defeated and killed the ras. Moving swiftly he forced Ras Ali from the throne in Begameder. In 1855 Ras Kassa's armies overran Tigre and Ubye was captured. Soon afterward Malakot, king of Shoa, was deposed and sent to a monastery. His son, the young Menelik, was kept as a hostage at Ras Kassa's court. Thus by the mid-1850s through military skill, cunning, and ferocity, Ras Kassa reimposed unity on Ethiopia after over a hundred years of disorder and schism.

The puppet Emperor Sahela Dengel was forced to abdicate even the shadow of authority which he had. Ras Kassa, although not of the Solomonic line, justified his seizure of power by referring to an ancient prophecy that a new ruler, blessed by God, would arise to deliver Ethiopia from its bondage. Kassa took the royal name Theodore which betrayed his sense of divine mission. He was the last ruler to be crowned at the old capital of Gondar even though he did not like the city. The city had been allowed to decay. Only the castle of Ras Michael Sehul and part of the palace of Fasilidas were in livable condition. Theodore preferred Debra Tabor and very early in his reign decided to build a new city which would reflect the glory of his rule.

European interest in northeastern Africa was just beginning to develop when Theodore came to power. The focal point of this interest was Egypt, the Sudan, and the Red Sea. Specific interest in and knowledge of Ethiopia were slow in developing. In 1843 two British travelers, Walter Plowden and John Bell, visited the highlands. Five years later they returned with Plowden as British consul. These two men became close friends of Theodore. They told him of the wonders of European technology and tried to obtain for the emperor some share of these wonders. He trusted them and they, together with his wife, helped to stabilize the brilliant but emotionally erratic ruler. In retrospect what the "mad" ruler of Ethiopia wanted does not seem unreasonable or much different from what the khedive Ismail of Egypt was planning. Theodore wanted a commercial treaty with Britain and more than anything else he wanted modern equipment of war and European instructors. With this equipment Ethiopia could take the offensive against the unbelievers and Theodore could give Britain, his ally, the friendship of a power which controlled all of northeastern Africa from the Nile to the Red Sea. Unfortunately the only section of the British government really concerned with events in Ethiopia was the India Office and they did not approve of any expansion by a powerful Ethiopia. It is doubtful whether anyone above the rank of a junior clerk in the Foreign Office paid any attention to Plowden's extremely detailed account of Ethiopia and the plans of its ruler.

Theodore, master of an Ethiopia he had welded together by force, believed with considerable justification that he was surrounded by enemies. He had taken steps to limit the power of local nobles and to centralize control of the government and the army. In his need for a larger state income, Theodore had undermined the privileged position of the landowning church. Always unstable, Theodore, further, felt isolated with no one he could trust. His first wife had died in 1859 and in the following year both Plowden and Bell were killed by bandits. Theodore became more cruel and erratic and began to harbor deep suspicions of European intentions. The French had established themselves at Oback in 1862 and in 1865 the khedive had negotiated the cession of Massawa to Egypt. From these bases the French and Egyptian consular agents were attempting to extend their authority into Ethiopia. Theodore expelled all Catholic missionaries from Ethiopia, believing them to be French agents, and began to spy upon the activities of all other missionaries.

Whether or not the British consul, Charles Duncan Cameron, who arrived in 1861, was the fool Lord Palmerston called him, he did nothing to calm Theodore's fears and the emperor began to dislike him intensely. In 1862 Theodore attempted to awaken British and French interest in cooperating with him in a projected war against Egypt. The government of Napoleon III avoided Theodore's plea for military assistance and instead reproached him for excluding Catholic missionaries from Ethiopia. From the British government he received no reply. Attributing this to Cameron's actions, he had the consul arrested and placed almost all Europeans under custody. When this information reached Britain the government dispatched two political officers, Hormuz Rassam and Dr. Henry Blanc, to Ethiopia to negotiate the release of the prisoners. The diplomats reached the imperial camp in January 1866. At first Theodore treated them well, although he was disappointed that they had not brought him artisans and gunsmiths. Very soon he arrested them both. In April he directed Rassam to write the British government asking formally for workmen and machinery to help him make guns.

Beginning in the early 1860s Theodore's attention turned more and more toward Magdala. This was a stone outcrop located approximately seventy miles west of modern-day Desse. It was an extremely defensible position and its one-mile-square flat top provided the necessary land for the emperor's followers. As he worked to strengthen his fortress and as his attention was diverted by the Egyptians and the perfidy of Europeans, his kingdom began to fall apart. In 1865 Menelik escaped from Magdala and soon Shoa's loyalty to Theodore was negligible. In 1866 Theodore was forced to take the field against rebels in Gondar. As punishment the churches of the city were plundered of their art treasures, the inhabitants were driven out, and the city was set on fire.

In the autumn of 1867 the British government finally took notice of Theodore. Parliament appropriated two million pounds to support an invasion force to release the prisoners. Sir Robert Napier in command of 62,000 men of the Bombay army landed in Ethiopia in December. Napier marched inland across the Danakil plains and up the escarpment arriving before Magdala with 4,000 effectives in early April 1868. On his march he met no resistance. Kassai, the future Johannes IV, ruler of Tigre, met with

Napier and agreed not to oppose the invasion. Gojjam and Shoa rose against the emperor. At Magdala hundreds of Theodore's troops deserted him. Accepting the inevitable with his typical dual attitude toward reality, Theodore dismissed his European prisoners after massacring hundreds of Ethiopians who were also captives. On April 13 the final British assault began. The gates were easily forced and Magdala was taken, with the British suffering only fifteen wounded. Theodore committed suicide before his fortress fell.

With Theodore's death Ethiopia reverted to the same divided condition as before his imposed unification. General Napier had accomplished his mission and did not mean to become involved in the morass of trying to reestablish order. He installed the queen of the local Gallas as ruler of Magdala, blew up the fortress, and retreated to the coast where the last British troops were evacuated before mid-June 1868. Ethiopia in the 1870s was thus left to two strong competitors for power—Kassai of Tigre and Menelik of Shoa. Kassai had by 1872 negated his major foes in the northern provinces and was crowned as Johannes IV. Shoa became, in theory, a part of a united empire. In fact Menelik, like a medieval European feudal vassal, obeyed the emperor only when it was to his distinct advantage to do so. Ultimately more important to Ethiopia than this rivalry during the reign of Johannes IV was the loss of Ethiopian isolation. Egyptian imperialism, the Mahdist revolt in the Sudan, and the establishment of European bases on the Red Sea coast threatened the independence of the state. Ethiopia thus became enmeshed in the complicated politics of the scramble for Africa.

Ethiopia and the scramble to 1906

Johannes IV was too occupied with consolidating his power in the north and meeting the threat of Egyptian invasions to bring Menelik under control in the decade following his coronation. Finally in 1882 on the eve of the Mahdist uprising in the Sudan, Johannes reached an agreement with Menelik which recognized the local autonomy of Shoa in exchange for Menelik's promise to support the emperor. In return Johannes recognized Menelik as the heir apparent to the Ethiopian throne. To seal the bargain Ras Area Selassie, Johannes' son, was married to Menelik's daughter, Zauditu. The eventual path to the throne seemed clear for Menelik, particularly after the death of Ras Area in 1885.

The reign of Johannes was marked by the growing intrusion of foreign influence in Ethiopia. The kingdom was subjected to increasing pressure from three different but closely interconnected sources—Egypt, Europeans along the Red Sea, and the Mahdists in the Sudan. Khedive Ismail, as a part of his dream of a greater southern empire, attempted for fifteen years to expand into Ethiopia. In 1866 he purchased the port of Massawa from his suzerain, the Ottoman emperor. Four years later, by the same process, he acquired the Somali coastline between the ports of Bulhar and Berbera. An even more aggressive Egyptian policy began in 1874 when Rauf Pasha's troops occupied Harar. In the following year Egyptian forces under Werner

Münzinger Bey attacked and occupied Bogos province and its capital Keren. By then Johannes had gained sufficient control over Ethiopia to thwart further Egyptian advances. In 1875 Münzinger's forces were routed at Awassa. In the following year a much larger Egyptian army was cut to pieces at Gura. These victories halted Egypt's immediate plans of conquest. Internal problems in Egypt and the development of the rebellion in the Sudan finally ended Egypt's threat. However, Egyptian forces continued to hold Bogos, Harar, and Massawa.

Muhammad Ahmed's success against the Egyptians in the Sudan which culminated in the taking of Khartoum and the death of General Gordon had profound effects upon Ethiopia. Western Begameder and Gojjam, abutting upon the Sudan, were areas of increasing conflict with the Mahdi's successor, Khalifa Abdullah. In the crucial five-year period after 1884 Johannes' attention was diverted from Italian activities along the Red Sea coast by the operations of the khalifa's armies. In 1889 Johannes gathered a large army to counter the Mahdist forces which had penetrated Ethiopia as far as Gondar. Menelik did not contribute to the emperor's army. At Metemma the Ethiopians won a decisive victory but a Sudanese sniper mortally wounded Johannes. Before his death he summoned Ras Aloula and other powerful nobles and proclaimed that Ras Mangasha, ostensibly his nephew, was in reality his natural son. Johannes asked that they recognize his son as the next emperor. Although no agreement had been reached or oath sworn to Ras Mangasha before Johannes' death, it was obvious that the emperor had repudiated the 1882 agreement with Menelik.

The struggle for supreme power between the king of Shoa and Ras Mangasha came at a crucial period in the attempted consolidation of European control over the Red Sea coast and its immediate hinterland. The French had been the first European power to acquire territory there when they purchased the small port of Obock in 1862. They planned to use it as a coaling station for their ships en route to their newly opened possessions in Indochina. Later they moved their main base to Djibouti. The opening of the Suez Canal in 1869 increased the importance of Obock and the British station at Aden. In the same year the Italian firm, the *Societa di Navigazione Rubbattino,* leased the port of Assab in an attempt to increase Italy's share of the Red Sea trade. In 1882 the Italian government purchased the port from the company. This was the modest beginning for the later Italian ventures in Ethiopia. For almost fifteen years after this action Ethiopia became the focal point of Italian activities during the scramble.

The failure of Egypt to meet its debts brought about a major crisis there in the late 1870s and finally the forcible British occupation in 1882. The British consul, Sir Evelyn Baring, subsequently became the actual fulcrum of power in Egypt. Confronted with a bankrupt government which had greatly overextended itself, he sought to reduce all unnecessary expenses. The increase in the Mahdi's power in the Sudan was a closely related problem. Britain's solution to the unnecessary expense of the Egyptian empire was to force the new khedive, Tewfik, to abandon any plans for further expansion. In pursuance of this policy Gordon was sent to evacuate the Egyptian garrisons from the Sudan. At the same time Egypt decided to abandon its enclaves in Ethiopia. In May 1884, Britain sent Admiral Sir William Hewett as head of a mission to inform Johannes that Egypt was withdrawing its forces from Keren, Massawa, and Harar. An agreement between the emperor and Hewett formalized Ethiopia's right to use Massawa. In return for this open invitation to reoccupy these former Ethiopian areas Johannes promised to take the field against the Mahdi with a great army.

British foreign policy in regard to northeastern Africa in the decade following Hewett's mission was not simple. The essence of that policy was to assure that no unfriendly power could gain control of the Upper Nile or the Red Sea. Since Britain did not wish to assume the financial burdens of reconstituting the old Egyptian empire, its policy had to be directed toward allowing other states to provide the necessary stability. The obvious inheritor of this role was Ethiopia. However, its history of political instability and factionalism seemed to make it a poor choice to defend British interests. Most qualified observers expected Ethiopia to be continually wracked by civil war and then eventually become easy prey for some expansive European state. France then committed everywhere in Africa to a militant imperialism was the greatest threat to Britain's aims in northeastern Africa. If Ethiopia fell into chaos France would certainly gain strategic territory. To block this, Britain began to support Italy's claims to larger areas of the Red Sea hinterland adjacent to Ethiopia. By encouraging Italian ambitions while maintaining friendly relations with the emperor, Britain hoped to achieve the kind of stability necessary for the maintenance of her interests, whatever developed.

In February 1885, an Italian expedition led by Admiral Caimi occupied the port of Massawa. This action denied Ethiopia the use of the port and therefore was a violation of the agreement made by Admiral Hewett. Nevertheless, Britain openly supported the Italian move. The Italians after consolidating their position at Massawa, took advantage of Johannes' growing preoccupation with the Mahdists on his western frontier. Italian forces occupied Saati, a village on a major caravan route located a few miles inland. Saati was important primarily for its wells. Johannes protested this action as he had earlier the occupation of Massawa. He had never agreed in any manner to the cession of land to any foreign power. The first setback to Italian plans and a portent of future actions occurred in January 1887, when a 460 man column of Italian military on their way to Saati were intercepted by the most powerful Ethiopian chief in northern Tigre, Ras Aloula. Less than a dozen of the reinforcements survived the so-called battle of Dogali. Ras Aloula with over 16,000 men at his command, many armed with the latest rifles, was restrained from further advances toward Massawa only by the direct order of the emperor.

Italian pride, wounded by the massacre, called for revenge and in the months following Dogali they began to build up their forces at Massawa. This threatening situation called forth British efforts to mediate. Sir Gerald

Portal was sent to Ethiopia late in 1887 to visit Johannes with proposals which, if accepted, would end the possibility of war and give Italy a demarcated bloc of territory in the Massawa hinterland. Portal's party was halted by Ras Aloula at Asmara. Johannes refused Aloula's request that he be allowed to kill the British visitors. Portal finally met the emperor on December 6 and proposed that Saati and Keren be ceded to Italy and that Johannes recognize an Italian protectorate over territory one-day's-march inland from Massawa. In return Portal promised continuing British and Italian friendship. Johannes' reply was succinct. He would not give the Italians "an inch of land."

After the failure of Sir Gerald Portal's mission the British restrained the Italians and there were no further confrontations during Johannes' reign. However, after Johannes' death the Italians took advantage of the disorders within Ethiopia to occupy Keren. In 1890 they officially proclaimed the colony of Eritrea. Although the extent of the colony was not definitely stated, it marked a further step toward isolating Ethiopia. In the previous year the Italians had, they believed, gained the support of Menelik of Shoa who had just proclaimed himself emperor. In May 1889, in return for a gift of twenty-eight cannons and 38,000 rifles, Menelik signed the Treaty of Uccialli. Menelik had recognized the Italians' occupation of Massawa and by implication also their ambitions in the interior. The Italian foreign minister Crispi chose to interpret Article Seventeen of the treaty as giving Italy a protectorate over Ethiopia. There were two versions of the treaty, one rendered in Amharic and the other in Italian. The Italian version stated that Ethiopian foreign policy "shall" be conducted through the Italian government. The Amharic text, however, stated that the emperor "might" avail himself of the services of Italy. Despite their knowledge of Menelik and Ethiopia, the Italians in the early 1890s, using the treaty as an excuse, attempted to convert the theory of a protectorate into a reality.

With a greater power base in Shoa and the central areas, Menelik disregarded the deathbed wish of Johannes to be succeeded by Ras Mangasha and was proclaimed emperor in spite of the opposition of the majority of the nobles of Tigre. Although contacts continued between Menelik and Mangasha, the northern areas acted as if they were independent of the emperor. The Italians led Mangasha to believe that they supported him while at the the same time they continued their ostensibly good relations with the emperor. In the early period of Menelik's reign the centrum of the state shifted southward and Shoan affairs overshadowed those of Tigre. This shift was exemplified by Menelik's establishment of his capital at the old town of Entoto newly renamed Addis Ababa.

Italian troops took up the responsibility of campaigning against the Sudanese in the north. In 1893 they defeated the Mahdists and occupied Agordot; and in the following year the new commander, General Baratieri, took Kassala in the Sudan. They also pushed their occupation southward toward Axum as far as the Mareb River. From this point Baratieri began his disastrous forward policy against Tigre. This decision in 1894 was caused primarily by a series of uprisings against Italian authority in Eritrea.

Captured letters written by the leader of one major revolt, Batha Agos, revealed him to be in close contact with Mangasha. The Italians then determined to end the Tigrean threat to their supremacy and authorized the occupation of Tigre. They had received tacit British approval for this action by an agreement in 1891 which designated the bulk of Ethiopia an Italian sphere of influence. Communications with many powerful Ethiopian leaders such as Ras Michael of Wollo and Ras Makonnen of Harar led the Italian command to believe that they would gain the active support for their occupation from many Ethiopian leaders. Thus in the spring of 1895, Baratieri's forces established themselves at Adigrat in Tigre. Later that year they took Macalle and the strategic pass of Alagi. However, the force of 2,000 men detailed to hold this pass was inadequate given the strategic importance of Alagi which barred the main route into Tigre from the south.

Menelik had meanwhile, in 1893, repudiated the Treaty of Uccialli and had settled most of his differences with Ras Mangasha, and the ruler of Tigre had agreed to recognize him as emperor. Thus the disunity which the Italians had hoped for in 1895 was more apparent than real. Menelik and his lieutenants throughout the rest of the year were busy with their preparations to drive the Italians from Tigre. Ras Makonnen's troops from Harar were the first to arrive in the contested area and on December 7 they cleared the Italians from Alagi Pass. Italian Askari casualties were over 1,300 of the 2,000 man force. Makonnen's army then joined with other units from the south and Mangasha's forces to besiege Macalle. After a forty-five day siege the Italian garrison surrendered. They were escorted northward by a large segment of Makonnen's army which also screened the slow parallel movement of Menelik's main force.

Baratieri had gathered all his forces in Tigre and the reinforcements from Massawa at the town of Sawria, sixteen miles northeast of Adowa. Had the general understood the organization of Ethiopian armies he could have won the campaign by avoiding battle. Menelik's army was literally eating up the countryside. With time and this lack of supply, the divisive pressures within the Ethiopian army would have forced a retreat. Baratieri, however, pressured from Rome for a quick victory and having little respect for the Ethiopian army, decided to risk a battle. Baratieri's intelligence service was poor and he had no good maps of the area. He believed the Ethiopian army to number approximately 40,000. Since he had almost 18,000 men of whom 10,500 were European and his army possessed superior weapons, it was not unnatural to believe in the positive outcome of the campaign. On February 29, 1896, Baratieri's army, divided into three brigades, moved southward. On the morning of the next day it was discovered that one brigade was separated from the main body by four miles. Before the error could be adjusted, the Ethiopian army of over 100,000 began the battle of Adowa. By the end of the day Baratieri's army was destroyed. Italian losses were over 6,000 dead and 2,000 wounded while their Askari troops had lost over 4,000 dead. The stragglers retreated northward with their general toward Massawa. The Italians had lost more men in a single day than in all the wars of unification (risorgimento) and Europeans had suffered their greatest defeat at the hands of Africans. The

Ethiopians could sing in triumph. "The Corn of Italy, that was sown in Tigre, has been reaped by Abba Dagno [Menelik's horse] and he has given it to the birds."

Why did Menelik not drive the Italians from their coastal possessions after Adowa? Although no final answer can be given, there were a number of factors which contributed to his decision not to pursue the defeated Baratieri. The state of his own army was such that he could probably not have held it together very long. To the already mentioned problems of supply and dissension had to be added the very heavy losses sustained by the Ethiopians at Adowa. Menelik, always sagacious, probably realized that new Italian troops could be sent to defend Massawa and that in all probability Britain would have intervened on behalf of Italy. Finally, Menelik was at that time more concerned with expanding his influence over the areas immediately adjacent to Shoa. Thus he was magnanimous in the Treaty of Addis Adaba which ended the war. It repealed the Treaty of Uccialli but confirmed the Italians in possession of Eritrea. This included the area up to the Mareb River which the Italians had occupied at the beginning of the campaign. The new Italian foreign minister, Rudini, who had replaced Crispi after Adowa, recognized Ethiopia as an independent, sovereign state.

In the years immediately following Adowa, Menelik's armies brought under control the western areas of Wollega. The king of Kaffa was conquered and Ethiopian authority extended south and southeast toward Lake Rudolf and in the Sidamo Borana area bordering upon Kenya. In the north the death of Takla Haimanot, ruler of Gojjam until 1901, brought that troublesome area firmly under imperial control. Ras Mangasha continued to rule unimpeded in Tigre until he became involved in a small conflict with Menelik's favorite, Ras Makonnen, in 1899. Mangasha was defeated and forced to appear before Menelik with a stone upon his head as a token of submission in order to have the emperor spare his life. By 1901 Menelik had filled out of the borders of Ethiopia by conquering large numbers of non-Amharic, non-Christian people. In a series of agreements from 1897 to 1908 he made treaties with European powers in which they recognized the new, fixed, expanded boundaries of Ethiopia. Only the border of Italian Somaliland remained undelineated, a fact which gave rise to the incident that began the new war with Italy in 1935.

Before the emperor became incapacitated in 1906, he successfully played off the European powers against one another. He tended to favor the French who had received the right to build a railroad from Djibouti to Addis Ababa. The French Compagnie Franco-Africaine brought to Addis Ababa electricity, the telegraph, and telephone. Menelik's capital, sheltered by newly introduced eucalyptus trees, was an outpost of modernity in an otherwise conservative, highly formalized, Ethiopian state. Menelik for all his success had managed to create only a veneer of a modern nation state. When Menelik, the tillak sew, could no longer function adequately the old schisms rose and again threatened the destruction of Ethiopia.

FIVE
The scramble for Africa

Introduction

Direct European involvement in Africa had been minimal during the first three-quarters of the nineteenth century. As detailed elsewhere, Britain, France, and Portugal were the only European states which could have followed a policy of territorial expansion in this period. The rest were either too small, too divided, or concerned primarily with imperial ambitions on the European continent. Portugal was politically moribund and its economy was such that it could have supported large scale military campaigns or the staff necessary to rule a vast territory only with great difficulty. Its coastal possessions from Benguela to Luanda in Angola and near the mouth of the Zambesi River in East Africa suffered from lack of money and enterprise. France in this period was rent by civil dissension. The Bourbon restoration in 1815 had been followed by the revolution of 1830 which brought the Orleanist king Louis Philippe to power. He was unseated by a revolution in 1848 and the short-lived Second Republic gave way to the era of Napoleon III whose ambition except for his brief venture in Mexico was to make France dominant in Europe. The ill-timed war with Prussia destroyed his regime. The pent-up fury of the liberal and working classes then led to the fractricidal Commune of 1871. With such a stormy domestic history it is not surprising that France did not actively seek an overseas empire. Only Britain could have easily carried out territorial expansion during this period. However, both conservative and liberal governments rejected such costly ventures. During the first seventy-five years of the nineteenth century Britain was actively imperialistic, but in an economic not a territorial sense. Possession of African land would not have increased the wealth of Britain. On the contrary, it would have subtracted from the total wealth of the nation.

Why, then, did European states change their attitudes

113

toward acquiring African empires in the period after 1875? The answers to this question are complex and can, in most cases, be examined best by observing the events in individual territories. However, it is necessary to understand some general principles which tended to determine the timing, direction, and degree of European imperialism in the various sections of Africa. First, the reasons for the change of attitude toward Africa were primarily concerned with Europe and not Africa. For European statesmen the focus of power was still Europe. Therefore the reasons for the scramble for Africa must be sought in Europe.

Undoubtedly the most important cause for acquisition of African territory was economic. Prior to the scramble most European governments could see little economic advantage to be gained in Africa, particularly since its greatest export, slaves, had been curtailed. The British, economically dominant throughout the world, had very little money invested in the continent. The argument of the Manchester school was that if any of these areas wished to trade with Europe they would buy primarily British goods and would sell their exports to Britain. The dominant theory of economics in Europe particularly after mid-century was that of free trade. However, by the 1870s the opposing theories of men such as List of Austria were being accepted by many French and German businessmen and traders. Briefly stated, List called for national self-sufficiency. By extension this meant protective tariffs and a return to a mercantilistic empire which would provide for the mother country a steady source of raw material and presumably also guaranteed overseas markets.

French statesmen such as Jules Ferry were among the first to accept the imperatives of the new protectionism. Still fresh from the disastrous defeat in the Franco-Prussian War, they were concerned for the long-term future of France. They came to believe that France would continue as a great power only by acquiring a new empire. At approximately the same time Leopold II, of the small, relatively new state of Belgium, came to similar conclusions concerning his kingdom. He was willing to gamble on the future wealth of the territories of the Congo basin so recently explored by Stanley. In Germany in the early 1880s some businessmen and traders accepted List's conclusions. Many patriotic Germans viewing the economic dominance of Britain came to the erroneous conclusion that its prosperity depended upon the possession of a large territorial empire. For some German imperialists the solution to Germany's problems was simply to acquire an empire.

These more generalized and theoretical approaches to the economic advantages which could be gained from an African empire were reinforced by the experience of a few entrepreneurs actively engaged in trade with Africa. European firms anxious to secure more access to inland markets were active in pressing their governments for more direct support. In the Senegambia, the Gold Coast, and along the Niger coast the merchants had maintained the European presence throughout the early part of the century with little official encouragement from their governments. In the last quarter of the century they added their support to the expansionists. In Egypt, a territory crucial for the scramble, European investors created the conditions which led to the British occupation. In other instances business leaders, impatient for their governments to adopt more forward policies, agreed to their companies assuming government functions. Such was the case in the revival by Britain of the chartered company. Goldie's Royal Niger Company, MacKinnon's East Africa Company, and Rhodes' South African Company were designed as much to hold African territories for Britain as to make a profit.

There are many other factors which acted to create a favorable atmosphere for the "new imperialism." One was the acquisition of more knowledge of the African continent and the inevitable romanticizing of this Dark Continent whenever the explorers wrote of their adventures. West Africa was the first area to be considered by the geographic societies of Europe and particularly by the British African Association. During the thirty-five year period between Mungo Park's first expedition and Richard Lander's discovery of the mouth of the Niger, intrepid adventurers had cleared away much of the ignorance and myth concerning West Africa. This urge to explore was transferred to Central and East Africa in the 1850s with the same results. Livingstone, Burton, Speke, Stanley, and many others suffered terrible hardships to provide for their European audiences data concerning the human and physical geography of the continent. While there was much territory yet to be explored, the main outlines of Central and East Africa had been exposed by 1880.

Most of the explorers were British or were in the employ of a British agency. They therefore reflected the predominant feelings of Evangelicalism and the self-assurance that European culture, particularly British, was best. The European observer was appalled at many aspects of African societies. Human sacrifice, killing of twins, and various religious practices convinced Europeans that what portions of Africa required was the firm, just control of a Western state. The cruel and dehumanizing slave trade was recorded by every traveler whether in West or in East Africa. So deeply ingrained in African society were these practices that individual Europeans felt powerless to end this evil and they, therefore, called for more direct action from their governments. In West Africa this greater involvement took the form of the West African Naval Patrol and a growing interference with the internal affairs of coastal states. In East Africa the British government sought at first to end the trade by convincing the sultan of Zanzibar to act against the trade. It became obvious in the 1870s that such pronouncements by titular rulers of an area could, at best, only divert the trade.

Christian missionaries who were at work in significant numbers in Africa by the 1840s were influential far beyond what their numbers would indicate. Western Europe and particularly Britain was committed to advancing the cause of Christianity in all the "pagan" areas of the world. Explorers, traders, humanitarians, and government servants all considered the implantation of Christianity one of their major tasks. In Nigeria the missionaries at Badagry, Abeokuta, and Ibadan played a crucial role in the more direct intervention of Britain in the Yoruba wars. Missionaries who responded to Livingstone's message and example in Central Africa soon became convinced that peace, order, and an end to "barbarism" would come only with British annexation and they joined the chorus of those who demanded a more expansionist policy. Similar actions by the missionaries can be noted in other African territories. The missionary commitment was crucial in later determining British annexation of the areas near Lake Malawi, Bechuanaland, and Uganda.

Strategic considerations also played a small role in the scramble. Britain more than any other state was affected by this reasoning. Almost immediately after its opening in 1869 the Suez Canal became a major factor in British diplomacy. British occupation of Egypt in 1882 was largely conditioned by concern that France, a potentially hostile power, would become dominant there and be in a position to threaten the canal. Later fears of another state controlling any portion of the middle and upper Nile helped the Salisbury government decide to occupy the Sudan and Uganda. However, throughout most of Africa the military or strategic importance of certain areas had little effect upon the decision of European states to control the territory.

The last general factor to consider is the almost indefinable term "national pride." The French had been humbled by Prussia in 1870. The conservative forces of the state had been temporarily discredited. One key to the foreign policy of the new German empire led by Bismarck was their desire to isolate France diplomatically. Thus in the two decades following the creation of the Third Republic, French statesmen were not able to exercise power in the manner of their counterparts in the second empire. However, they discovered that their ambitions to create an overseas empire met with the general approval of Bismarck. Thus the French could gain in Africa not only a new mercantilistic empire, but could also regain a measure of their lost prestige. To a lesser extent national pride affected Germany. Bismarck did not wish an overseas empire. However, many Germans in the full flower of their dominance of Europe looked jealously toward Britain and erroneously concluded that British power depended upon its empire. Some important Germans, therefore, lent their influence to the formation of colonization societies. Rather than gain the enmity of these factions, Bismarck in the early 1880s supported their desires for African territory. British national pride from the mid-1880s onward forced reluctant governments to adopt a more active role in the race for territory. After 1895 the openly imperialistic sentiment of the "jingoes" had become the attitude of the government. Portuguese reaction to the scramble in areas which Portugal claimed because of historic connections were determined in large measure by a sense of proprietary pride.

With these general principles in mind one can turn to the African scene and attempt to detail the most important events connected with the scramble in each geographic segment. It is necessary to point out that events relating to European imperialism in Africa during this period are so intertwined that it is always necessary to look beyond these arbitrary geographic divisions and to attempt to consider the total picture of expansion.

West Africa

As detailed in an earlier chapter, European interest in West Africa, although small by comparison with the commitments of those states elsewhere, nevertheless grew considerably in the period after mid-century. The British, despite disclaiming officially any desire to acquire a territorial empire, had interfered directly in the domestic affairs of many African states. They had acquired Lagos in 1861 and slightly over a decade later the Dutch forts on the Gold Coast. This latter development involved them in a major war with Ashanti. The French government, ostensibly echoing British nonexpansionist policy, had extended its territory in the Senegambia and allowed its merchants to establish quasi-governmental stations on the Ivory Coast. French merchants in the late 1860s and early 1870s were also responsible for committing their government to protecting their spheres of influence on the Mellacourie River adjacent to Sierra Leone and at Cotonou and Porto Novo in Dahomey.

The French government in the decade after 1875 concentrated its minor expansionist efforts on the coastal areas of West Africa and its immediate hinterland. They extended their influence over Whydah by means of a blockade and in 1878 were firmly established at Cotonou. Four years later the French declared a protectorate over Porto Novo. By 1885 the French coastal sphere in Dahomey extended as far west as Anecho in Togoland. In 1878 French claims to the Mellacourie River territory were expanded and Matacong Island was occupied. The British administration at Freetown reluctantly accepted this larger French sphere. After 1881 the French area near Grand Bassam on the Ivory Coast was slowly but systematically extended.

This coastal occupation was in part military and was done primarily to assure French merchants a dominant position in trade. However much both protagonists might deny the accusation, Britain and France were engaged in a protectionist war in Africa. Customs houses were opened soon after the declaration of a French protectorate and British merchants found themselves at a trading disadvantage. Some British administrators such as Sir Samuel Rowe wanted to react to such tactics with an immediate show of force. However, they were restrained from any hasty action by the Colonial Office. The nonexpansion dictum of the 1860s remained in effect. Britain did not covet territories beyond that which was already controlled. Colonial Office opinion held that most of Africa was economically worthless and, therefore, its occupation would be a liability. Between 1875 and 1882 British officials attempted to arrange a line of demarcation between the spheres of influence of the two nations. To this end they were willing to concede Bathurst and the Gambia river possessions.

Proposals for an exchange of the Gambia were kept alive until the Convention of 1889, but no suitable line was ever agreed upon. In the 1880s the British were content to allow French expansion in areas not considered vital. Those territories defined as important were the hinterlands of Freetown, the Gold Coast, Lagos, and the Oil Rivers.

The situation in West Africa was further complicated by the entrance of Germany into the imperial race. Germans had been active along the Togo coast since 1847 when the *Norddeutsche Missionsgesellschaft* opened its first station. Later merchants had followed and by the early 1880s they controlled the bulk of the Togo palm oil trade. In the Camerouns a number of German firms based at Hamburg and Bremen operated very profitably even though British missionaries and traders there outnumbered them. The British government refused, in 1881, the offer of some powerful Douala chiefs to take their territories under British protection. In early 1884, Chancellor Bismarck ceased to oppose the desires of his more territorially minded countrymen and in May authorized the extension of protectorates over those areas where German traders were threatened by encroachment from foreign competitors. Areas specifically mentioned by Bismarck in his instructions to Consul Nachtigal were Angra Pequeña in Southwest Africa and the territory east of the Niger delta. The consul was instructed to avoid any friction with France. Acting partially on his own discretion on July 5, Nachtigal proclaimed a protectorate over Togo and one week later declared the Cameroun under German protection.

The rapid acceleration of French and German activities along the Niger coast caused a swift reaction from the British. Edward Hewett, British consul to Calabar, although unable to ward off Nachtigal's protectorate over the Cameroun, did conclude a series of agreements with rulers of the coastal areas west of the German protectorate. These formed the basis for the British Oil Rivers protectorate proclaimed later in 1884. The major factor forestalling German and French penetration into British spheres in Nigeria was not the British government but George Goldie Taubman (later Sir George Goldie). Coming to Nigeria first in 1877, he was instrumental in creating the United African Company by merging together the four largest British trading firms. By the time the company's name was changed to the National African Company in 1882, it had more than one hundred trading stations on the Niger and Benue rivers and exercised a near monopoly of riverine trade. Goldie and other officials of the National African Company who were avowed imperialists were alarmed by the forward activities of the French and Germans. To block any counterclaims to territory dominated by the company its agents entered into a number of treaties with African rulers. These were accepted by the conferees at the Congress of Berlin as primary evidence of British paramountcy in southern Nigeria. In June 1885, Joseph Thomson further extended the company's sphere by signing treaties of cession with the sultan of Sokoto and the emir of Gwandu.

In the context of West Africa the scramble was already far advanced before the Congress of Berlin in 1884–1885. However, the congress, because of the rationale for its decisions, speeded up the imperial process. It established rough rules by which European states could be secure from claims by its competitors. The congress thus seemed to be encouraging the rapid partitioning of the continent. The decade following the break-up of the congress was the most aggressive period during the scramble.

The most dramatic example of this increased European imperialism was the French military occupation of the interior. By early 1885 French officials had decided to resume their advance into the Western Sudan which had been temporarily halted after Gallieni had reached Bamako. In early 1885 they were operating a gunboat on the upper Niger and in the following year French forces defeated the followers of Mahmadou Lamine, a leading marabout of the upper Gambia. Gallieni signed a treaty of protection with Aguibou of Dinguiray in 1886 and two years later the Alimamies of Futa Jallon placed their territories under French protection. The explorer Captain Binger carried out a thorough two-year exploration of the Mossi areas which showed that the "Mountains of Kung" were no barriers to trade between the Ivory Coast and the Western Sudan.

In 1886 the French began a long series of campaigns against Samory Touré who after 1866 had built a major empire from his small Mande state in upper Guinea. After being defeated by the French in one campaign he sued for peace and presumably accepted French protection in 1886. However, his followers returned to harassing the French within two years of the treaty. In 1889 he was again beaten and promised once more not to oppose the French, but the war was soon renewed and in 1891 a military column under Colonel Louis Archinard occupied Kankan. Thereafter Samory continued a war of mobility against the invaders which did not end until his capture in the Ivory Coast in 1898.

Long before Samory's kingdom had been completely occupied French armies were attacking the western borders of the Tucolor empire. In 1890 the French occupied Dinguiray and then Segu. Ahmadu, the son of al Hajj Umar, fled eastward to continue the struggle. French armies then moved slowly into the heart of his kingdom taking Djenne and Macina in 1893 and Timbuktu the following year. From their dominating position in the Western Sudan, French forces turned southeastward and occupied the bulk of the Mossi territories in 1896 even though they would not be completely masters of the area until 1902.

While pursuing their aggressive policies in the interior, the French did not ignore the coast. By a convention with Britain in 1889 they received recognition of their claims to territory in the Senegambia, Ivory Coast, and Dahomean territory. In Dahomey the French had turned the coastal vassals against their Fon ruler. King Behanzin who came to the throne in 1889 insisted upon dominating the coast, particularly Cotonou. This made conflict inevitable. In 1892 war began between the well-armed, powerful African kingdom and the French. Despite bitter fighting the French occupied the capital, Abomey, in November 1892, deposed Behanzin, and in the following year declared Dahomey a French protectorate.

British official attitudes toward expansion slowly changed in the decade of the 1880s. This was partially the result of administrators such as Rowe, Carter, and Johnston who, whenever possible, pursued an activist policy. More pertinent, however, was the necessity to react against the French and Germans whenever territory considered vital was threatened. This reactive process was applied even to the Gambia which the Colonial Office was still hoping to trade for more meaningful territory elsewhere. There the French were openly negotiating with some of the war chiefs on the north bank of the river and had sent troops to intervene in the later stages of the internecine wars. It appeared that Britain might lose its favorable position on the river and have little left with which to bargain later. The Foreign Office finally arranged a high-level conference with the French to settle the Gambian question as well as boundary disputes elsewhere in West Africa. When the British delegation to Paris in April 1889 discovered that the French were not amenable to territorial exchange they pressed for unequivocal control of the Gambia River. The French, expecting that eventually they would gain control of the river, did not question British hegemony. However, both sides viewed this as a temporary arrangement. The British administrator, Gilbert Carter, was nevertheless instructed to enter into treaties of protection with the Gambian chiefs and to begin the design of a protectorate system of government. Boundary teams between 1891 and 1904 traced the snakelike borders. With the ending of the scramble and a return to friendly relations between Britain and France, a suitable exchange was never decided upon. The temporary boundaries became permanent, monuments to the arbitrary way European states divided the African continent.

The British position regarding the hinterland of Freetown was clearer than in other areas of West Africa. The Creole population of the colony had been viewed as a special charge since freed slaves had first been landed there. Even the parliamentary report of 1865 which had recommended a nonexpansion policy had recognized the unique position of Freetown. Therefore French activities in Guinea were watched carefully. The agreement with France over the Mellacourie secured the northwest boundary of the Freetown hinterland. The Convention of 1889 extended the agreed upon boundary between French and British spheres along the coast into the interior as far as the 13° longitude. Despite some worry over French aims, the Colonial Office was not called upon to react to direct French threats in the decade of the 1880s. The success of the war against Samory, however, brought the French dangerously close to the Temne and Mende country adjacent to the colony. Thus threatened, the British in 1896 responded by declaring a protectorate over these areas. There had been little if any British consultation with the major interior chiefs prior to the annexation. When the newly appointed district commissioners attempted to collect a Hut Tax in 1898 some chiefs refused to pay. One of these, Bai Bureh (a Temne chief), gave his name to the revolt which followed. Troops were sent into the protectorate and taxes were forcibly collected. The Poro secret society of the Mende was particularly important in resisting British authority. Creole traders and missionaries in the interior were considered agents of the British and hundreds were killed before the revolt was crushed. After the hanging of over thirty chiefs for their part in the actions, the new protectorate area was finally considered by the British to be pacified. Following the rebellion a distinct division between the coast and the interior continued to exist for over fifty years with the coastal Creole minority dominating the country.

The development of the dominant British presence on the Gold Coast has already been discussed through the Ashanti War of 1874. Technically that war had caused little change in the relationship between the British and the Ashanti. After assessing an indemnity and receiving pledges from the Ashanti for future good behavior and the abolition of "barbaric" practices, British troops were withdrawn from Ashantiland. The asantahene, Kofi Karikari, was destooled by his people and a new ruler, Mensa Bonsu, was chosen. His policy was to avoid, whenever possible, conflict with the British. Therefore the Ashanti presence in coastal politics was minimal. Mensa Bonsu's cautious attitude was denounced by many important Ashanti leaders as servile capitulation to British power and in 1883 Mensa Bonsu was destooled. There followed a five-year period of near anarchy in Ashantiland. Finally in 1888 the Ashanti asked the British to help them unravel the complexities of the succession to the throne. On the advice of a British commission, sixteen-year-old Prempeh was chosen asantahene.

Britain's relatively dominant position which carried no correlate political responsibility was threatened in the late 1880s by French and German success elsewhere along the coast and in the interior. The first example of British recognition of this change came in the treaty of protection proposed to the Ashanti in 1890. Prempeh and his advisers rejected the treaty and in the following years the asantahene began to utilize his considerable military power to reimpose Ashanti rule over disaffected areas. French activities in the Mossi areas north of Ashanti led to the two-year treaty-making expedition of George Ferguson in 1892. Ferguson was able to gain treaties from most of the Mossi states, but the French refused to recognize the validity of such treaties, insisting instead on effective occupation. The British then realized that, if the French were to be forestalled in the Upper Volta region, Britain had to assume a more active political role in Ashantiland which now blocked the way to their occupation of any of the Mossi areas. The first example of this more aggressive British policy toward the Ashanti was the demand that Prempeh reject the use of force in his foreign policy. They further demanded that he accept a British resident since residents had been used elsewhere by the British to control policy making by native rulers. Prempeh refused, and by the end of 1895 the more imperialistic Conservative government decided to use force on the Ashanti.

In January 1896, 2,000 British troops invaded Ashantiland. Prempeh decided to offer no resistance to the invaders and Kumasi was occupied without fighting. Prempeh was ordered to pay an indemnity of 50,000 ounces of gold. Upon his statement that the sum was too great for him to pay, he, the queen mother, and a number of influential Ashanti were taken to the coast and finally sent into exile. The British authorities then proceeded to break up the Ashanti Union by entering into separate treaties with individual rulers. There was no new asantahene appointed to replace Prempeh. Pushing beyond Ashantiland, the British conquered Bole and Wa and occupied Dagomba and Mamprussi. Subsequently border agreements were concluded with France and Germany, and the British created the administrative unit called Northern Territories.

The humiliation inherent in the British treatment of the asantahene combined with the activities of the authorities in enforcing rules against slavery and the slave trade had, by 1900, driven the Ashanti to the point of rebellion. Governor Sir Frederic Hodgson had decided to tax the Ashanti and assured them that the measures against slavery would continue and the asantahene would never return. On a visit to Kumasi he completely outraged the Ashanti by demanding: "Where is the Golden Stool? Why am I not sitting on the Golden Stool at this moment?" This unfortunate statement indicating the governor's wish to sit on the collective souls of the Ashanti precipitated a full-scale war. The governor and 700 British troops were besieged at Kumasi for over two months. British units from throughout West Africa were diverted to the Gold Coast and they eventually were successful in defeating the Ashanti and relieving Kumasi. Following the uprising Britain annexed Ashanti as a crown colony.

By the mid-1880s the scramble had effectively separated the British possessions on the Gold Coast and in Nigeria. At the time this did not perturb the decision makers in London. Despite the actions of men such as Johnston and Goldie, the British were content to maintain trading control in specific areas with a minimum of expenditure. In the decade of the 1890s British expansion in Nigeria was accelerated because the French were increasingly in a stronger position to threaten the previously secure hinterland.

In Yorubaland the British administration at Lagos in 1886 acted to bring about a truce in the half-century Yoruba civil wars. Two years later an agreement was reached with the alafin of Oyo whereby a paper protectorate was proclaimed over his kingdom. Nevertheless, hostility between various Yoruba states continued. The Ijebu were responsible for a number of incidents construed by the British as disrespectful to their officials. Sir Gilbert Carter, the administrator of Lagos, reacting to this and also feeling the potential French threat from the west, sent a military column into Ijebu country in 1892. The following year on something of a "grand tour," Carter entered into treaties with Oyo, Abeokuta, and Ibadan whereby British judicial authority was extended into those areas. By 1896, of the Yoruba states, only Ilorin remained independent from British rule. Except for the Ijebu campaign and a small expedition to Oyo in 1895, the northward extension of the Lagos protectorate was peaceful.

The Lagos government, disturbed by the interference of Ilorin in the affairs of Yorubaland and its support of the slave trade, wanted to conquer the town. However, Sir George Goldie claimed that Ilorin was within his and the Royal Niger Company's sphere of influence. Previously in 1894 Goldie had sent Captain Frederick Lugard to Nikki in Borgu to forestall French designs on that area. Despite Lugard's presence, the French continued as a threat to Borgu and Ilorin. Finally the colonial secretary, Joseph Chamberlain, ordered Goldie to conquer Ilorin, and company troops subjugated Ilorin and neighboring Nupe in 1897.

The company, however, was under attack from the press and from government officials. Its trade policy, notwithstanding official prohibition of the practice, was monopolistic. In the eastern areas this led to the choking off of trade for independent coastal cities such as Brass as well as diverting trade from merchants operating in the Niger coast protectorate. By 1895 the more expansionist-minded British were unhappy with the inability of the company to confront the French on equal terms. Thus in 1897 the company police were replaced by an imperial armed force commanded by Lugard. In 1898 a convention between Britain and France fixed the western and northern boundaries of Nigeria. The eastern line of demarcation with Germany had been established in 1893. In this new British imperialistic atmosphere there were few reasons to continue the company. Negotiations were begun in 1898 to purchase the company's political and territorial claims in Nigeria. An agreement was finally reached and on January 1, 1900, Britain assumed control of company territories and Lugard became high commissioner of the new protectorate of Northern Nigeria.

Britain had by 1900 resolved its international differences over Nigeria and the boundaries were theoretically fixed. There were vast areas within these limits where no European had ever been. This was particularly true of the hinterland of the Niger coast protectorate. British functional control extended only a few miles into the interior. In 1899 Sir Ralph Moor planned and finally three years later executed the military occupation of Ibo territory. British authorities expected major opposition from the Aro who controlled the great oracle Aro-Chukwu and who were suspected of holding the Ibo in subjection. However, little resistance was offered to the British military and by 1906 most of the Ibo territory had been absorbed by the British. In 1906 the Yoruba and Ibo hinterlands were amalgamated into one government entity called the Protectorate of Southern Nigeria.

In the northern areas Lugard moved to make effective the protectorate proclaimed in 1900. The first series of campaigns were directed against the slave-trading emir of Kontagora. Lugard then gained effective control over many smaller kingdoms which welcomed the British as a counter force to the Fulani. A military expedition to the Lake Chad area secured a large portion of Bornu for Britain. Lugard played upon the Fulani emirs' fear of the French and promised them minimal changes in their system. He encountered only a small degree of resistance mainly from the sultan of Sokoto. In areas which had submitted to Britain, Lugard confirmed the local rulers in their rights and privileges. This system, later called indirect rule, became the general pattern for the north and played a large role in the peaceful occupation of the area.

By the early twentieth century European rule was firmly established in all West African areas. A bewildering number of meetings, conventions, and verbal agreements had resulted in the division of the vast areas among the competitive powers. Once these divisions had become effective European states ceased to vie with each other in acquisition and turned to the far more difficult task of establishing governmental systems to make effective their rule in the conquered territory.

The Congo

European traders had been in contact with the coastal portions of the Congo basin since the late fifteenth century. At one time the Portuguese appeared to be on the verge of converting the Bakongo to Christianity. However, the slave trade and the growing impotence of the Portuguese crown meant an end to any such philanthropic experiments. Portuguese interests receded southward to the immediate hinterland of Luanda and with the passing of time even their Angolan possessions became moribund. Until the early nineteenth century other European states were concerned with the territory near the Congo River only as a fruitful area for the collection of slaves. As in West Africa, this did not imply territorial acquisition. In the 1830s some chiefs near the mouth of the Gabon River ceded a small amount of territory to the French for use by their anti-slavery naval squadrons. In 1849 the French released a cargo of slaves from a captured vessel on the Gabon coast. These slaves formed the nucleus of the town of Libreville. In the years following, the territory near Libreville was increased slightly, but the French showed no desire until 1875 to explore the interior or to increase substantially their small enclave. In that year a naturalized Frenchman, Pierre Savorgnan de Brazza, began to explore the interior adjacent to the Ogowe River.

In 1877 Henry Morton Stanley reached the mouth of the Congo at the conclusion of his long, arduous, three-year exploration of East and Central Africa. The knowledge of his discoveries and optimism concerning the future of the Congo basin preceded him to Europe. One very interested observer of Stanley's exploits was King Leopold II of Belgium who was the guiding spirit behind the ostensibly philanthropic African International Association. This association was composed of separate national committees in European countries and the United States. In 1877 at the only plenary session of the association ever held, its major funciton was defined as suppressing the slave trade in Central and East Africa. Its announced intention was the establishment of a series of posts linking the Great Lakes with the Indian Ocean coast. The Belgian committee of the association approached Stanley soon after his return to Europe and in time convinced him to return to the Congo as its chief agent for furthering

Christianity and civilization there. With Stanley's return to the Congo in 1880, the focus of the international association was irrevocably shifted from East Africa to the Congo. By 1885 Leopold II had bought out the other stockholders in the Belgian committee and thus had practically separated it from the other national groups. The previous Committee for the Study of the Upper Congo was reconstituted the International Congo Association.

Before Stanley reached the Congo a second time, de Brazza had explored further up the Ogowe River, established the post of Franceville, and later crossed from the Ogowe to the Congo. There he obtained from local rulers the cession of a small amount of territory and established the post of Brazzaville before returning to the coast and Libreville. Stanley, who arrived in the Congo in 1880, began immediately to establish the association's claim to the left bank of the Congo from Stanley Pool to the sea, to gain the grant of territory between these points from African chiefs, and to improve communications in those areas. Stanley's major bases on the Congo were Matadi and upriver a new town called Leopold-ville located across the river from Brazzaville. Stanley was too late to secure the right bank because of de Brazza's earlier activities. De Brazza returned to the region in 1883 as a commissioner for France with troops and financial support from the Third Republic. There ensued in the following year a race between Stanley and de Brazza to secure the cession to their governments of as much African territory as possible.

These activities by the agents of France and Leopold caused the Portuguese government to become active and it laid claims to the lower Congo based upon its long history of contact with the area. In 1884 Portugal was assured of a short-lived triumph when Britain agreed formally to support these historic claims. The Anglo-Portuguese treaty which ignored the claims of both France and the association focused the attention of the chancellor of Germany, Otto von Bismarck, upon the Congo arena. Acting in his assumed capacity of the "honest broker" seeking to avoid international problems, he summoned all interested European parties to convene in Berlin to solve the Congo dilemma. In answer to Bismarck's invitation, representatives of fourteen European nations and the United States met in Berlin in November 1884. For thirteen weeks the delegates confronted not only the Congo problem, but a full range of questions relating to the entire African continent. Britain soon ceased its support of Portugal and gradually veered toward the acceptance of Leopold's claims. Leopold's agents came to the conference with full support from the United States. More important was Leopold's modus vivendi arranged with France. Not having the backing of Britain or Germany and believing that Leopold would not have the funds to carry out his aims in the Congo, France agreed to support his claims to the left bank of the lower Congo. In return Leopold recognized French rights to the area claimed by de Brazza and promised to support French claims to the entire basin if in the future the association proved inadequate to the task.

At the close of their deliberations the conferees had defined the "conventional basin" of the Congo and had recognized the association's primacy to the left bank of the river below Stanley Pool. They also confirmed French claims to the Gabon and to the right bank of the Congo River. The conference declared that navigation on all rivers of the Congo basin as well as the Niger River and all future roads and railroads of the Congo would be open to traders of all nations. Of more importance for the future of European activities in Africa was the stress placed by the congress on the necessity for European states to prove "effective occupation" when claiming African coastal territory. French opposition to the application of this doctrine in the interior regions was sufficient to assure its defeat. In sum, the most important decisions of the congress related to the various agreements concerning the Congo basin. Contrary to the popular view, the Congress of Berlin did not begin the scramble nor did its concepts of effective occupation have much influence on the future development of European imperialism in Africa. However, because the congress had met and reached some decisions on Africa, the scramble was given legitimacy. All important Western states were represented and there were few delegates who defended the rights of the African to be left alone. Although in time most of the doctrines agreed to in Berlin were ignored by European imperialists, all agreed that there was a moral as well as economic imperative to divide the continent.

After the Berlin decisions de Brazza moved rapidly to extend French control over the Gabon and middle Congo regions. His lieutenants explored the hinterland far beyond any established post. Paul Crampel investigated the Sangha River area obtaining treaties from African rulers which bound them to France. Another aide, Albert Dolisie, explored the Sangha and Ubangi territory and established the post of Bangui on the Ubangi River. In the 1890s French explorers moved northward from the Congo area toward Adamoua and Lake Chad, attempting to link up with the southward-moving French columns from the Sudan.

Leopold II wasted no time in assuming the premier position on the lower Congo assigned the association by the conference. He received permission from the Belgian parliament to declare himself sovereign of the association's territories. He then proclaimed, without consulting other members of the association, the existence of the Congo Independent State. In the five years after the congress, Leopold spent a large portion of his fortune in constructing bases on the lower Congo and in creating an administration for the area flexible enough so that it could later be expanded to include other larger areas of the Congo basin. In doing all this he attracted other European entrepreneurs, particularly Belgian investors. Although the Independent State was theoretically free from Belgian control, it actually was tied closely to the fortunes of that state.

The creation of towns, roads, and an administrative structure, as well as the cost of the military campaigns in the deep hinterland, cost more than Leopold had imagined. In 1889 at the Brussels conference, he received the right to charge a ten percent ad valorum duty on all goods brought to the Congo. However, this did not begin to meet the expense of the construction of the railway being built from Matadi to Leopoldville or the telegraph line or regular steamer service from the Congo. Such unexpected expenditures meant that all possible means of extracting revenue had to be pursued. Leopold was instrumental in organizing concession companies which were given monopolies to work certain areas of the Congo basin. Government agents were instructed to expedite the collection and transportation of raw rubber to Matadi. These two factors changed irrevocably the nature of the government of the Congo. Free trade in the Congo ceased to be the practicing ideal of the government. The harsh, cruel treatment of Africans by Leopold's agents while collecting rubber made a mockery of the humanitarian theories on which the state was theoretically based. By 1900 Leopold, Belgian financial interests, and some great companies ruled a greatly expanded Congo in an autocratic fashion never imagined by the signatories of the Berlin conference.

One of the first hinterland territories acquired by the expansive Independent State was Katanga. There Msiri, a crafty king, kept a great variety of different peoples pacified by means of his superior intelligence and firearms. Rumors of great mineral wealth in the Katanga grew as more European missionaries entered the area after 1885. Msiri's kingdom became an eminently desirable area for the Portuguese who were eager to link up their possessions on the east and west coasts. However, their dreams of such a solid bloc of territory was thwarted by the joint labors of the British prime minister Salisbury and the capitalist prime minister of Cape Colony, Cecil Rhodes. Rhodes, the driving force behind the British movement into the interior from Cape Colony, had learned of the potential of the Katanga soon after the pioneer column of his British South Africa Company moved into Rhodesia. He commissioned the explorer Joseph Thomson to visit Msiri and secure the Katanga for the company. Thomson never reached the Katanga because on the way he encountered a smallpox epidemic. However, later in 1890, Alfred Sharpe, the British vice-consul in Nyasaland, arrived there. Msiri made it clear that he had no intention of signing away his country to the British. His attitude, however, changed radically the following year due to a series of rebellions of his subjects which he believed were fomented by the Congo Independent State government and the newly formed Katanga Company. Three separate Independent State expeditions were sent to Msiri's court in 1891. The king decided to invite Sharpe back to discuss a protectorate and had written him a letter to that effect. The letter fell into the hands of one of Leopold's agents, Captain Stairs, who decided to act swiftly to forestall the British. After a meeting with the king, Stairs quarreled with Msiri and in the scuffle which followed, shot the king. Stairs immediately declared the territory annexed to the Independent State.

Meanwhile upriver from Stanley Pool there was open warfare between the armies of the Independent State and the Arab slavers who had turned the eastern Congo region into a huge slaving ground. By the early

1890s the presence of the great slave trader, Tippu Tib, for whatever unity it might earlier have brought, was no longer felt in the territory west of Lake Tanganyika. Initially the wars went in favor of the Arabs. By the close of 1892 they had forced the Independent State to abandon all its posts above Stanley Pool. The tide was turned the following year with the success of Baron Francis Dhanis and his Zanzibari troops operating in the Kasai region. Slowly the Arabs were pushed out of their favored slaving grounds. Warfare continued between the two groups until 1900 but, by 1895, the Independent State was dominant in the eastern Congo.

Explorers and leaders of military columns in the latter 1890s penetrated into the area along the Luapula River, in the high Katanga, and up the Kasai and Kwango rivers. Independent State troops even occupied briefly a part of the Bahr-al-Ghazal until a high level agreement with France forced them to retire in late 1894. By the beginning of the new century Leopold's agents had established a rudimentary form of government throughout most of the territory claimed by the association. The limits of the Independent State was also established by conquest and boundary agreements with other European states. Britain declared a protectorate over the area from the Kafue River to Lake Nyasa in 1894 and Germany claimed Ruanda and Burundi after the Heligoland Treaty in 1890. A series of agreements with Portugal between 1891 and 1914 established the southern boundary with Angola.

The vicissitudes of Leopold's administration of the Congo in the 1890s were the results of two conflicting objectives. As stated at the Congress of Berlin, his motives were to end the slave trade, maintain free trade, and spread Christianity and Western civilization throughout the basin. These theoretical goals foundered upon the harsh realities of the need for money to maintain the state and to extend its influence. Until the opening of the twentieth century the administration of Leopold's empire was a curious blend of efficiency, idealism, and cruelty. Reports from missionaries of the exploitation of Africans in the collection and transportation of rubber was confirmed in 1902 by the report of the British consul, Roger Casement. From that date onward pressure from British and Belgian liberals and the British government forced Leopold to institute reforms and eventually to negotiate the transfer of the Independent State to Belgium in November 1908.

Angola

Although his effect on Angola was only temporary, Sousa Coutinho, governor in the 1760s, was the first modern administrator of the Portuguese empire. He wanted to halt the trade in slaves and secure the systematic occupation of the interior by Portuguese immigrants. He was responsible for beginning the colonizing of the Bié highlands. By 1800 there were over 250 Portuguese and 15,000 Africans in the vicinity of the fortress of Caconda. As with so many of Coutinho's ideas, this colonizing effort was not effectively supported by his successors and by the mid-nineteenth century there were few evidences of Portuguese settlement. Coutinho also wanted to make Luanda a city based upon a viable agricultural hinterland, supported by trade and commerce other than slaves. This, too, failed and Luanda for all its exterior appearance of wealth and beauty continued throughout the nineteenth century to be only the chief city of a listless and growingly decadent colony. The major source of income in Angola was the relatively stable trade in slaves to Brazil.

The disturbances associated with the Napoleonic Wars and their aftermath were deeply felt in Angola. Brazil became independent from Portugal in 1822. The revolutionary ardor reached Luanda where the garrison troops mutinied. A junta ruled for a short time in Luanda and the merchants and leaders of Benguela briefly toyed with the idea of joining Brazil. Portugal was wracked by conflicts between absolutists and liberals for over a decade. Only with the triumph of the liberals in 1834 did stability return to the Portuguese empire. They proceeded to develop an idealistic program which would eventually lead to Portuguese citizenship for the population of their overseas territories. Most of these plans foundered because of the resistance of entrenched interests and lack of funds to carry out the proposals. This can be clearly seen in the attempts of the Marques Sá da Bandiera to end the slave trade. A decree of 1836 made it illegal to trade in slaves. Angolans ignored the provisions of the decree and there was no perceptible decrease in the traffic until the British West African Squadron began to seize Portuguese ships suspected of engaging in it. After 1845 one can see a definite decrease with the actions of the more aggressive governor Cunha. By mid-century the trade from Angola had been perceptibly lessened.

In 1858 a compromise decree was issued which was to end domestic slavery in twenty years. No person could become a slave during this period and after 1869 the slaves became *libertos*. As in Mozambique, there was resistance to this law both openly and covertly. The vagrancy provisions of the decrees allowed government agents to assign Africans who were not employed to work for either the government or private employers. The system of contract labor to São Thomé and Principe which caused such a scandal in the early twentieth century was begun at this time. The abolition of both traffic and slavery itself was closely tied to the difficulty of creating an alternative source of capital. All attempts to get Portuguese to colonize areas such as the Bié highlands failed because of the counter lure of Brazil. Only after the revolt of 1848 at Pernambuco in Brazil was it possible to get significant numbers of Portuguese to migrate to Angola. The ports of Benguela and Luanda prospered in the latter part of the century after they were opened to ships of all nations. Slowly traders such as Silva Porto penetrated into the territory adjacent to the Bié highlands to exchange goods with the Ovimbundu people. Trade with different African groups in the territory inland from Luanda became more important in the same period.

Despite the slowly developing prosperity of Luanda there was little contact with Africans in the more remote interior. One observer of Angola commented that the Portuguese knew more of the inland kingdoms in the seventeenth century than they knew in the nineteenth. Before the spate of explorations in Africa just prior to the scramble there seemed little reason to the Portuguese to expend funds on territories already proven to be uneconomic. There were a few major expeditions undertaken by the Portuguese in the first part of the century. The nine-year adventure of Pedro Baptista and Amaro José in crossing the continent began in Angola. Silva Porto traveled throughout the Bié highlands in the 1840s and attempted a journey across Africa in 1852. In the 1850s the government sponsored Friedrich Welwitsch in making a botanical survey of Angola. Hermenigildo Capelo and Roberto Ivens in the late 1870s made a thorough survey of Kasanje. However, these few efforts were not given much publicity and they were not followed by missionary or trading ventures. When the other European powers became interested in African territory, Portugal could claim historic rights to certain areas but could show little activity in Central Africa after the eighteenth century. Some Portuguese administrators in the last two decades of the nineteenth century attempted to counter these deficiencies by sponsoring expeditions by Pinto, Cordoso, Carvallo, Ivens, and others. The goal of Foreign Minister de Barros Gomes in the 1880s was to assure for Portugal the bulk of the interior between the twelfth and eighteenth parallels. In 1884 the Anglo-Portuguese treaty recognized Portugal's claims to the Congo basin. However, the Berlin conference which assigned the greater part of the area of the Congo to Leopold II destroyed this hope. Between 1885 and 1891 Portugal was forced to abandon its claims to the Katanga, Barotseland, and the Nyasa territory.

Although denied the opportunity to link its Atlantic and Indian Ocean possessions, the area assigned to Portugal in Angola was far greater than they had ever governed before. In the two decades after the settlement of the majority of the boundary questions, Portugal made effective its control over most of Angola. Utilizing metropolitan and African troops and many convicts, the Humbe region of the Cuanhama was pacified by 1910. The last major Ovimbundu revolt on the Bié plateau in 1902 was put down with a huge loss of African lives. Between 1907 and 1910 Dembos territory was entirely brought under Portuguese control. The last serious reaction against Portuguese rule was the Bakongo uprising of 1913. After this the major problem faced by Portuguese officials at Luanda and Lisbon concerned the creation of viable governmental structures which would enable Portugal to rule the vast area of Angola. By the close of World War I these institutions based upon historic philosophical concepts were in effect in Angola. They remained relatively unchanged until the massive African uprising in northern Angola in 1960.

Mozambique

Portugal, as late as the mid-nineteenth century, held only nominal control of the areas immediately behind the coastal towns of Ibo, Mozambique,

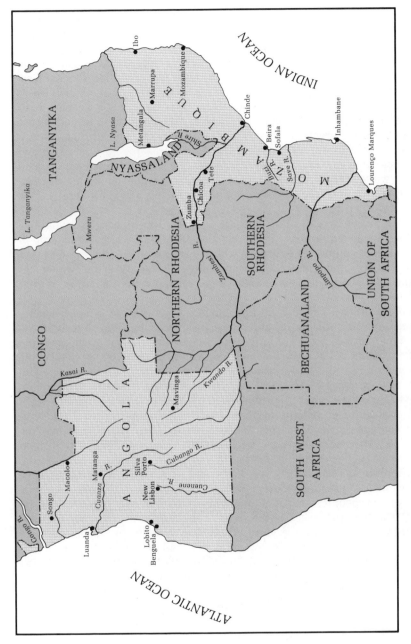

Portuguese Central Africa

Sofala, and Lourenço Marques. Some idea of the importance of those towns can be seen in the population of the largest—Mozambique. There were approximately 5,000 Africans and 800 Portuguese, Goan, and mixed residents on the island. Christianity which had been such a dominant force in the initial Portuguese expansion clung only to the towns. It has been estimated that in 1825 there were only ten priests in the Zambesi hinterland. Seven of these were Goan. The governor-general and lesser Portuguese officials had no power to enforce on interior peoples their decrees or those decided upon in Lisbon. The Portuguese armed forces were composed largely of African levies or convicts. Later in the century when the government attempted to negate the prazeros' (described below) influence, the governors discovered how poor the Mozambique armed forces were. The farthest practical inland extension of Portuguese authority throughout most of the century was the town of Tete on the Zambesi River.

The inland areas of the Zambesi were held by powerful, feudal-like landlords called prazeros. These estates or prazos were begun first in the sixteenth century as a way by which Portugal could control and make profitable the lands adjacent to the Zambesi River. With the waning of Portuguese influence in the Indian Ocean area and the limitation of support to the governors, the prazeros became a law unto themselves. The size of the prazos varied from three-square leagues to over eighty-square leagues. It was possible to cultivate only a small portion of these areas and thus the masters lived by taxes, some legitimate trade, and the traffic in slaves. They were complete masters of their lands and people and maintained their own standing armies. Throughout the nineteenth century they obeyed Portuguese decrees only when it was to their advantage to do so. Originally Portuguese, the prazeros had by intermarriage with Africans and Indians lost much of their European racial and cultural characteristics. Men such as Joaquim da Cruz ruled their empires more as African chiefs than as European administrators. The Lisbon government recognizing the nature of the prazo system, outlawed it in 1832 and re-enunciated this in 1836, 1841, and 1854. These legislative actions had no practical effect upon the continuance of the prazo system.

African peoples in the hinterland were relatively undisturbed by the Portuguese presence on the coast. Even in the seventeenth century, when the Portuguese were more active, they had exerted little influence on African polities. The exception to this had been the empire of the Monomotapas which had been destroyed partially because of Portuguese interference. However, by the nineteenth century, African groups were deeply affected by the upsurge in demand for slaves in the coastal areas. Chief among African slavers were the Makua, Yao, and especially the Nguni people. One of the most dramatic events in interior history concerned the migrations of the Nguni caused by the mfecane in South Africa after 1820. One group of Nguni under Zwangendaba invaded the Delagoa Bay area and joined briefly with other Nguni led by Soshangane. After threatening Lourenço Marques and absorbing many of the peoples of its interior, the Nguni under Zwangendaba moved north into the Shona area of the Changamire. After crushing this empire they crossed the Zambesi in 1835 and disrupted the Nsenga and Cewa near Lake Nyasa. One group of Nguni migrated even further north to the Nyamwezi areas before circling back through Bemba and Bisa lands and settling in northern Rhodesia. Another segment of the Nguni moved eastward into the lower Rufiji River territory. Meanwhile the Nguni under Soshangane had con-solidated their control in the extreme south. By the 1840s his men were threatening the prazos as far north as Sena and many of the prazeros were paying tribute to these Nguni. After mid-century the bulk of the Nguni had ceased their migrations and became less of a threat to the prazos and the Portuguese.

The slave trade was the one major problem in Mozambique which had international significance. In the three decades before mid-century the coastal slave trade had been in a gradual decline. The opening up of new lands in Cuba and the needs of French planters on the Indian Ocean islands of Nossi Be, Mayotte, and Reunion reversed this trend. In order to circumvent the government decree against the slave trade the French utilized the guise of the émigré system where they claimed that African workers were colonists entering the island of their own will. The Portu-guese minister of overseas, the Marques Sá da Bandeira, prohibited the use of the émigré system as a pretext for continuing the trade. This had little effect in Mozambique. Even the decree by the French emperor, Napoleon III, abolishing this system in 1864 did not keep the sugar planters from continuing to import Africans. By 1875 it was estimated that the Mozambique area was absorbing 7,000 Africans a year under the name of émigrés. Livingstone reported in the mid-1860s the continuing slave raiding activities of the prazeros and the open selling of these Africans at Quelimane. He accused the Portuguese officials of complicity although he recognized that they had little power to end it. The slave trade continued throughout the last quarter of the century in a much modified form. Pressure from Britain and renewed Portuguese interest in Africa was partially responsible for its demise. However, the major reason was the drying up of the markets for either slaves or émigrés.

Closely allied to the slave trade was the question of slavery in Mozam-bique. In 1869 the institution was abolished in all Portuguese territories. However, the slaves did not become free automatically. They were de-clared *libertos* but still subject to punitive action. In 1875 and finally in 1878 the position of the *libertos* was further defined. They became free persons but were required to be employed. The vagrancy clause of the edict of 1878 gave the government the power to assign unemployed *libertos* to labor for the government or private employers for a maximum of two years. Throughout the rest of the century there was much under-handed dealing by private labor contractors in utilizing the services of *libertos*.

The onset of the scramble for Africa forced Portugal into a more active role in both the Mozambique and Angolan areas. Livingstone opened up the interior of Africa in a way that no previous Portuguese explorers had done. By the 1870s it was obvious to many Portuguese officials that they would have to expend more effort and funds if they hoped to maintain claims to their historic empire. Prior to this period there had been, in the nineteenth century, few explorations sponsored by the Portuguese. In 1798 Francisco Lacerdo had explored the Luapula Valley and made contact with the Kazembe empire. Pedro Baptista and Amaro José were the first to cross the continent. They left the Kasanje district of Angola in 1802 and were detained for over four years by the Kazembes before reaching Tete in 1811. In 1831–1832 a government expedition led by José Monteiro and António Gamitto reached the headwaters of the Zambesi. None of these expeditions had major commercial or political significance since the discoveries were not followed up by traders or government agents.

The renewed interest of Portugal in the hinterland was symbolized by the creation in 1875 of the Geographical Society of Lisbon. It sponsored Hermenigildo Capelo and Roberto Ivens in 1877 to survey thoroughly the Kasanje and Malange areas. Alexandre de Serpa Pinto explored the Zambesi area while traveling from Angola to Durban. Capello and Ivens, in 1884, established potential basic trade routes between Angola and Mozambique while Augusto Cardosa reached the Katanga and obtained the signature of Mutianvua, chief of the Katanga Lunda, to a treaty of protection. Pinto explored further the Shire areas adjacent to Mozambique. However, much of this renewed activity was for nothing since Britain, France, and Leopold II had become interested in the same interior areas. The Berlin conference of 1884–1885 dealt a major blow to Portuguese aspirations in the Congo basin. By 1894 final agreement on borders had been reached with the Congo Independent State. The activities of Rhodes' British South Africa Company in Central Africa and Harry Johnston's expeditions in the Nyasa area denied finally the Portuguese hope to link their Atlantic possessions with Mozambique. The treaty of June 1891 solved most of the major border problems with the British. Although Lisbon was blocked from achieving its most grandiose schemes, it obtained recognition of its primacy over a huge interior area where few Portuguese had ever been.

The first task of the Lisbon government, if it was to extend its influence over the areas assigned to it by agreements with other European powers, was to negate the power of the prazeros. The Mozambique government during the 1880s concentrated its major efforts against the huge Massangano prazo of the da Cruz family. This prazo located forty miles below Tete was in a position to block downriver communications to Sena. Mozambique had attempted in the 1850s and 1860s to crush the da Cruz power but with no success. Five major expeditions were sent against the prazero Bonga in the two-year period after 1867. Each one was either cut to pieces by Bonga's troops or the expedition was decimated by disease. The conflict between Portugal and the Massangano prazo began again after 1885. Augusto du Castillo, the governor of Mozambique, an excellent soldier with a major force of trained soldiers, took the Massangano fortress in September 1887. A further campaign the following year pitted the

Portuguese against the da Cruz—supported by the African population of the mountain area. The ferocity of the fighting can be seen in the casualties. Approximately 6,000 were killed before Massangano was conquered. The Portuguese had also moved against the other prazeros and had by the 1890s brought them under control. The last of the great prazeros to be tamed was Manuel Antonio da Sousa. His prazo was located near Barué inland from Sofala. He had become chief of the Macombe in the 1880s and later served the Mozambique Company. Da Sousa was killed in 1892 and his interior empire fell apart. With his death the prazero resistance against Portuguese authority came to an end.

Elsewhere in Mozambique, Portuguese military columns were active against African rulers. Lourenço Marques was attacked in the mid-1890s by Africans, but this was a desperation move. Within a year the immediate hinterland was pacified. The paramount chief of Gaza was captured in 1895 and sent into exile. The Barué area south of the Zambesi continued to resist the Portuguese until a major campaign in 1902 pacified the territory. The hinterland behind Mozambique Island was occupied by the military between 1906 and 1910. The Yao of the Niassa district were systematically brought under Portuguese control by 1912. While this pacification went on, men such as António Enes, Freire de Andrade, and Mousinho de Albuquerque were evolving the new mechanisms of control which replaced the older structures of government that were totally inadequate for the large areas then dominated by Portugal.

East Africa

European interest during the last quarter of the nineteenth century in East Africa came from three different directions. Baker and Gordon in the 1870s in their operations in Equatoria had as one of their objectives the annexation of the interlacustrine areas to the empire of the Egyptian khedive Ismail. In the decade of the 1890s these same kingdoms were briefly threatened by the forces of Leopold II moving from the eastern sections of the Congo. However, most European activity, and thus the greatest threat to the continued independence of East African states, came from the sultan of Zanzibar's possessions along the coast of the Indian Ocean. As has been noted previously, the sultan's East African empire was primarily a commercial one. Although his influence was felt deep into the hinterland, he did not attempt to conquer the Bantu or Nilotic people of the interior or to subvert native polities. Due largely to the plantation system established along the coast and on Zanzibar which provided greater commercial opportunities, the slave trade increased enormously in the fifty years after Sultan Said established his hegemony on the coast. This increase in the slave traffic brought the area to the attention of the British government. Long before Burton, Livingstone, and Speke wrote of the horrors of the trade some British officials had attempted to limit it by entering into agreements with the sultan. By the terms of the Hamerton Treaty signed in 1845 Said agreed to prohibit transportation of slaves from his

African to his Asian possessions. In 1873 the near ultimatum of the British government delivered by Consul Sir John Kirk led Sultan Barghash to abolish the trade throughout his territories. In return for the sultan's official aid in controlling the traffic, British officials in London and Bombay assumed the role of protector of the sultan's territories from the ambitions of other European states. In the late 1870s Kirk was not only the British representative on Zanzibar but also the sultan's most trusted advisor.

European interest in and knowledge of eastern Africa was greatly enhanced by the work of the explorers of the 1870s. Most of these adventurers commented that only European occupation would halt the trade in slaves. Official pronouncements notwithstanding, Arab slavers from the coast and from the southern Sudan continued to ravage the interior. Thus the imperative for European direct intervention in hinterland affairs was present before the scramble. The British who were in the best position to take advantage of this situation had no intention of underwriting any costly military or political venture despite their concern with the trade. This attitude was clearly indicated by the official attitude toward the so-called MacKinnon Concession. Sir William MacKinnon, the founder of the British India Steam Navigation Company which operated a number of ships in the Indian Ocean area, was a confirmed expansionist. In 1877 Sultan Barghash offered to turn over the administration of all his mainland territories to MacKinnon and his associates for a share of the customs revenue. MacKinnon was willing to assume this responsibility if the British government would recognize such an arrangement and promise to support it. This, London refused to do and the entire scheme fell through. Consul Kirk was also convinced that Britain should do much more to support the sultan in consolidation of his hinterland possessions. He particularly wanted the sultan, with British aid, to establish a series of posts stretching as far into the interior as Ugogo. Prime Minister Gladstone's liberal government in 1880 refused to cooperate in this scheme.

The activities in 1884 of a twenty-eight year old German adventurer and nationalist, Carl Peters, fundamentally altered power relationships in East Africa. Peters who had spent some time in Britain was convinced that its greatness lay in its empire and therefore Germany, if it wished to challenge Britain for supremacy, would have to acquire overseas territory. In pursuance of this goal, Peters and a number of other young activists had formed the Society for German Colonization. Despite warnings of non-support from Chancellor Bismarck, Peters, Karl Juhlke, and August Otto traveled in the autumn of 1884 to Zanzibar. Crossing to the mainland, they had by December secured over 120 "treaties" with chiefs and headmen in the immediate interior from Bagamoyo. Peters claimed that each of these men was a free agent and not in any way a subject of the sultan. Hurrying back to Germany, Peters used these treaties to gain a *Schützbrief* or charter for his company from a still reluctant Bismarck. This *Schützbrief* granted the company the right to administer a large undefined area between the sultan's territories and Lake Tanganyika. Armed with this recognition, Peters returned to Africa and renewed his treaty making with new fervor.

Sultan Barghash protested Peters' activities directly to the German emperor. Sir John Kirk also recommended that the British government intervene to halt Peters. The British vice-consul to Zanzibar while in Britain urged MacKinnon and others to form a chartered company to secure a protectorate over the rich territory in the vicinity of Mt. Kilimanjaro. Reports from Harry Johnston and the explorer, Joseph Thomson, had been enthusiastic about the area. Nevertheless, the British government refused to support such a scheme and within a few months the Germans had extended their theoretical control over Kilimanjaro and the territory of Witu. The German government, now more openly imperialistic, dispatched gunboats to Zanzibar in August 1885 to show the sultan that it was prepared to back Peters' claim to Witu by force if necessary. The Gladstone and, later, Salisbury governments, far from seeking a confrontation with Germany to protect the territory of their friend, the sultan, welcomed German intervention. They believed Germany would bring order to the territory, stamp out the slave trade, and introduce Western ideals. For a period of approximately two years British statesmen supported German expansion since it would achieve certain desired ends without costing the British taxpayer a shilling.

In 1886 a mixed commission was appointed to study the conflicting German, British, and Zanzibari claims. The members of the commission agreed to a convention which recognized the sultan's control only over a ten-mile deep strip between the Rovuma and Tana rivers. This convention represented the almost complete British abandonment of the sultan since the hinterland, which Barghash claimed, was divided into two spheres of influence. The Germans gained recognition of their premier position in the southern part and in 1888 they forced the sultan to lease to them all his mainland possessions in their sphere.

Peters and his associates continued to expand the territory controlled by the company. For over a year after 1888, German occupation of the coastal towns was resisted by Abushiri ibn Salim and his followers. African troops, askaris, trained and led by Germans, ultimately defeated Abushiri and hanged him. Afterward there was sporadic coastal resistance but the towns were soon overawed by German power and the willingness of men like Peters to use it. In 1890 Emin Pasha, by then in the service of Germany, led an expedition into the interior and hoisted the imperial flag over the major trading center of Tabora.

Peters' attempt to utilize the disturbances in Buganda to extend German influence was eminently successful. The treaty of protection obtained from Kabaka Mwanga was nullified only by his own government which, by the Heligoland Treaty, recognized Britain's supremacy there. The company was not able to meet its financial responsibilities, and in 1891 the German government assumed the direct administration of its East African possessions and Hermann von Wissmann was sent out to become the first commissioner of the territory. Between this date and 1894 the Germans pushed into Hehe country despite the hard-fought resistance of some of their chiefs. The most inflexible of the Hehe leaders was Mkwana who continued to fight the Germans long after most of the Hehe area had been conquered. Hehe resistance came to an end only with Mkwana's capture in 1898. Meanwhile Peters and other German leaders had subdued the Gogo in central Tanganyika; and the Chaga in the region of Mt. Kilimanjaro were brought more firmly under German control. Von Wissmann as early as 1895 led expeditions into the deep interior and also campaigned against the Yao in the extreme south. By 1898 the Germans had asserted their authority over the native peoples in most of the areas in German East Africa. Between 1898 and 1900 the Germans, in the face of opposition from Leopold II's troops, occupied the small heavily populated areas of first Ruanda and then Burundi.

While the Germans were skillfully utilizing diplomacy mixed with open force to consolidate their sphere of influence, the British to the north were much more halting in their interior expansion. In 1887 MacKinnon's British East Africa Association received from the sultan full political control over his northern mainland territories. The situation in Egypt and Buganda had changed substantially since the British government had refused to support MacKinnon and Johnston's ideas of expansion. By 1888 the British began to fear active encroachment by a foreign power on the headwaters of the Nile. Salisbury's government was not yet prepared to sanction the unlimited use of government funds to secure African terrritory. However, Salisbury agreed to grant a royal charter to MacKinnon's company. The Imperial British East Africa Company, unlike the other chartered companies operating in Africa, was undercapitalized from the beginning. The lack of operating capital combined with the relative poorness of the immediate interior restricted what the company could attempt. Most of the company's interests in the late 1880s was concentrated near the coast. They attempted to establish a few customs posts and forts in the interior, but the company had very little influence on the people east of Lake Victoria until the decision was made to construct a railroad in the late 1890s. Far more important to the company and the British government was the kingdom of Buganda.

European influence on Buganda began with the arrival of the first missionaries in 1877. These Church Missionary Society workers had responded to Stanley's plea that Christianity be brought to the kabaka and his people. Two years later White Fathers, a French based Catholic group, reached Buganda. It appears that Buganda was one area particularly receptive to the Christian message because within a very short period there were a significant number of converts. Unfortunately the missionaries and their growing following proved to be a divisive and not a unifying force. The Church Missionary Society group were Protestant and English while the White Fathers were Catholic and French. Each of the missionaries, although they denied it, tended to reflect the nationalistic aims of their respective European states. Very soon there were two Christian factions at the kabaka's court—the Ingleza and the Fransa. The numerically superior non-Christian element in the country and at court resented the influence wielded by the Christians. They, therefore, plotted to rid the country of the Christians.

A further important faction in Buganda were the Arab slave traders. Deeply suspicious of the Christians and the attitudes they held toward slavery, they also opposed the missionaries. At first this opposition was verbal. It later became physical because the slavers, although few in number, commanded large contingents of well-armed troops.

Kabaka Mutesa managed to placate these hostile elements, but Mwanga who succeeded him in 1884 was younger, weaker, and less experienced. Faced with great potential for civil war and watching the encroachment of Carl Peters in East Africa, he decided to act to clear Buganda of the threat of European intervention. Overjoyed at their success in eastern Africa, the Church Missionary Society appointed James Hannington as Bishop of Equatorial Africa and he left for Buganda in 1885. Because of disturbed conditions along the usual route, Hannington and his companions decided to use the way through the highlands which had just been discovered by Joseph Thomson. Mwanga, already apprehensive of the activities of Peters and the Germans, read this as a further threat to his security. He therefore ordered Hannington and his party killed in Busoga, and followed this by killing many Ingleza converts. In 1886 the Church Missionary Society was reduced to only one missionary in Buganda and the Catholics had only three. However, the missionary societies, far from being willing to abandon their projects, immediately sent more missionaries.

By mid-1888 Mwanga felt himself more threatened than ever and decided to kill all foreigners and their supporters. Before this could be done the Christian factions in Buganda joined briefly with the Arabs in support of Mwanga's brother, Kiwewa. Mwanga was forced to flee Buganda in September 1888. The coalition between Christians and Arabs was short-lived and the Arabs seized power, drove out the missionaries and their supporters, and burned the mission stations. When Kiwewa showed signs of independence of the Arabs, he was starved to death and his brother Kalema became the kabaka recognized by the Arabs. The bulk of the Christians took refuge in Ankole and there they eventually made peace with Mwanga. Supported by many of the traditional elements in Buganda society and both Christian factions, Mwanga's forces were strong enough to invade Buganda in late 1889. In four major battles the majority of the Arabs were driven from the country and Mwanga was restored to power. He then granted religious liberty to his subjects.

Before his final victory, Mwanga, soon after invading his kingdom, wrote a series of letters pleading for help from the British East Africa Company. One official of the company, Frederick Jackson, was at that time near Buganda. His party was too small and weak to intervene on behalf of Mwanga and Jackson proceeded northward without becoming involved. Some of Mwanga's letters for help fell into Carl Peters' hands and he decided that Germany could profit by the difficulties in Mwanga's kingdom.

Peters, therefore, traveled immediately to Kampala. Mwanga, whose fortunes by this time had been restored, was nevertheless prone to accept
Peters' offers of German protection. With the reluctant approval of the
Church Missionary Society, Mwanga signed the proffered treaty. Peters
left Buganda immediately for the coast to register his triumph only to
discover that his government had signed the Heligoland Treaty which
renounced all German claims to Buganda.

In August 1890, the British East Africa Company sent Captain
Frederick Lugard to Buganda to secure a definitive agreement of protection from Mwanga. Lugard's small command included fifty Sudanese
soldiers and 270 porters. Arriving in early December, Lugard entrenched
his force in a fort overlooking the kabaka's capital. Despite his weak
military position, he secured the necessary agreement from Mwanga
which gave legality to the company's claims over the area. In the following
months he intervened continually in the domestic affairs of Buganda.
One of his greatest problems was trying to maintain a balance between
the Protestant and Catholic factions, each of which wanted his support.
The agreement signed by the kabaka in December provided that the great
offices of the state would be shared between the two groups. Despite his
efforts at impartiality, Lugard was continually criticized by the Catholic
faction for favoring the Protestants.

Lugard, in conjunction with Mwanga's troops, cleared the western
areas of the country of the Muslim threat. He made contact with Selim
Bey's Sudanese troops near the southwest corner of Lake Albert and
induced them to take service with the company. Ostensibly, in order to
protect Buganda from threats from Kabarega, the ruler of Bunyoro, he
supported the young chief Kasagama in Toro and secured in August 1891
a treaty which placed Toro under company protection. He also entered
into a similar agreement with the Mugabe of Ankole. All of his fragile
successes, however, were threatened by the imminent bankruptcy of
the company. The extra cost of the Buganda venture proved too much
for its finances and in December 1891 he was ordered to retire from
Buganda. Since such a withdrawal would spell probable disaster to their
proselytizing endeavors, the Church Missionary Society in the following
month agreed to meet the company's expenses for an additional year.

The crucial area for decision making in 1892 was London where Lord
Rosebery, the liberal foreign secretary, was attempting to gain enough
popular and parliamentary support to have the government assume the
company's responsibilities. He was able, despite the opposition of most
of his colleagues in Gladstone's ministry, to have the company's expenses
guaranteed until March 1893. Lugard arrived in Britain in October 1892
and, through a series of lectures, committee meetings, informal discussions, and letters he added his support to the Church Missionary Society's
arguments for retention of Buganda. In November the government authorized that a special commissioner be sent to Buganda to determine the
situation there. Sir Gerald Portal was selected as commissioner and left
for the interior on New Year's Day 1893. He reached Kampala on March 17

and spent a total of ten weeks there. On April 1, he declared Buganda, Busoga, and Kavirondo to be under the protection of the British crown. By extension, this temporary state of affairs also applied to Toro and Ankole. In May Portal signed a new agreement with Mwanga which confirmed the premier position of the British government in Buganda rather than the company. Commissioner Portal left for the coast soon after the treaty was signed and reached Britain in early 1894.

Portal's report which supported the imperialists' position was presented to parliament in April 1894. It is doubtful whether the report did much more than change the attitudes of a few. Portal's importance lies in the time it took for him to proceed to Buganda and return with his observations. Rosebery and his supporters used that year to build solid support for the assumption of the company's position in East Africa. Rosebery became prime minister in March 1894 and by that time direct British action in Buganda was a foregone conclusion. Parliament approved the government's plan to declare a protectorate only over Buganda, and following the declaration of the protectorate, the government paid the shareholders of the Imperial British Africa Company £250,000 for their rights. MacKinnon and his associates who had acted to hold East Africa for the crown when the government was reluctant to act lost money since the government refused to pay for debts of approximately £190,000 incurred by the company.

On July 1, 1895, Britain declared the East Africa Protectorate over the hinterland territories lying between the coastal strip of the Zanzibar Protectorate and that of Buganda. On Zanzibar itself British authority had rapidly relegated the sultan to a position of impotence. In 1896 Seyyid Ali, who had held office for six years, died unexpectedly and the office of sultan was occupied by Seyyid Khalid, a son of Barghash. Khalid ordered the British consul to leave and made it clear that he expected to rule, without British help, what little was left of his dominions. However, the appearance of a British naval squadron and its bombardment of the palace forced Khalid to flee to Dar es Salaam. His elderly, placid cousin, Hamed bin Muhammad, was chosen by the British to be sultan.

While the British government was debating what action it should take in regard to Buganda, the situation there continued unsettled. Lugard before leaving for London had been confronted with potential civil war again in January 1892. Fighting between Protestants and Catholics broke out in Kampala and Lugard sided with the Protestant party. He gave arms and ammunition to the Protestants and lent the support of his machine gun to their cause. Mwanga who was the titular head of the Catholic group fled the city and was not reconciled to Lugard until March 30 when he returned to Kampala. Lugard thereupon renegotiated the treaty of 1890. In this Lugard reserved the fertile area of Buddu for Catholic activity but retained five-sevenths of the country for Protestant proselytizing. Lugard's departure later that year left a vacuum in European leadership in Buganda until Sir Gerald Portal arrived. After Portal left Kampala, he appointed Major J. R. L. MacDonald as the British representative with instructions not to interfere in Buganda politics. The instructions were almost immediately shown to be shortsighted. Captain W. F. Owen was dispatched to Toro to withdraw the British Sudanese troops from there. Later MacDonald discovered that his Sudanese garrison at Kampala had been approached by the Buganda Muslims. He disarmed the garrison just in time to prevent it from joining the revolt. The precarious nature of the British occupation convinced MacDonald to end any pretense at neutrality and to end finally the Muslim menace and also check Kabarega's designs on Toro. In December 1893, a joint force of Buganda and Sudanese troops invaded Bunyoro and in less than a year drove Kabarega north of the Nile. There followed a five-year lapse in African rule of Bunyoro until the British recognized Kabarega's twelve-year-old son as the ruler of the state. Even then all major decisions were made by a British subcommissioner while the ruler was a minor.

In 1897 Mwanga, who had never really accepted the realities of British paramountcy, left Kampala and began a final revolt against the Europeans. Although the kabaka raised a considerable force, British authority was so firmly established by then that the bulk of the people did not support their kabaka. Mwanga was deposed and his one-year-old son was declared the kabaka. Mwanga escaped northward and joined his old enemy, Kabarega, in exile north of the Nile. In April 1899, both ex-rulers were captured by the British and subsequently exiled.

Also in 1897 a large portion of the Sudanese military force in Uganda rebelled against the British. Major MacDonald, leading a force of Sudanese northward to counter what was believed to be French designs on the upper Nile, was presented with a series of demands by the Sudanese. They were generally unhappy because their salaries had not been paid and they had been prevented from bringing their women with them. The mutineers retreated to Busoga and joined other Sudanese there. The Baganda who could have taken advantage of the crucial military situation instead supported the government and helped drive the mutineers from Busoga northward beyond the Nile. Their threats to the northern border was not ended until 1901 when the British sent another military expedition against them.

In 1895 the Conservative government of Lord Salisbury, obviously impressed by Portal's description of the difficulties of carrying supplies into the interior, decided to build a railway linking the coast with Buganda. In June 1896, an initial appropriation of £3,000,000 was made. The railway builders were confronted with the full range of technical difficulties in constructing a meter gauge railroad nearly 600 miles over an escarpment over 9,000 feet high. The builders were also hampered by the opposition of the Nandi. In 1896 an expedition to Nandi country failed to defeat these warlike pastoralists. In response to continuing cattle raids and attacks on mail and other convoys, a second expedition was sent against them by the protectorate government in 1900. The troops aided by some Masai spent a number of frustrating weeks chasing the Nandi without any decisive results. The railroad eventually was built through their country only because of an agreement between the Nandi and W. W. Hobley, a subcommissioner for Kavirondo. The Nandi resumed their warlike activities in mid-1905 and it was not until the following year that the British, using Somali troops and Masai warriors, finally subdued them.

The Kikuyu and Kamba, as with the Luo, put up no resistance against the imposition of the British protectorate or the railway builders. This was partly because many of the Kikuyu, plagued by drought and rinderpest, had temporarily moved northward before the arrival of the Europeans. The lack of a heavy Kikuyu population later became an important factor in the alienation of Kikuyu lands in what came to be known as the '"white highlands." The lack of a central organization also prevented the Kikuyu from taking effective joint action against the invaders.

The warlike Masai who could have caused the British considerable trouble instead became supporters of the protectorate regime and British administrators many times used Masai warriors in punitive expeditions. The British, however, encountered great difficulty incorporating the Somali of Jubaland in the protectorate. A series of costly campaigns were necessary after 1898 before they finally capitulated.

Construction of the railway did not interest many Africans and as a result the bulk of the labor force was recruited in India. At one point over 15,000 men were working on the railroad. The Indian workers were given the option of returning to India or staying in East Africa after the expiration of their contracts. Some elected to remain and the additional complicating factor of a substantial Indian population was added to the East Africa scene. The builders of the railroad encountered a series of unusual problems ranging from jiggers to lions since in 1898 work was brought to a complete stop in the Tsavo district by the depredations of two man-eating lions. Despite the difficulties, the road reached Nairobi, a former Masai kraal chosen as one of the major rail camps, in June 1899. The final inspection of the completed railroad was in October 1903, eight years after the initial decision had been made and after the expenditure of almost £8,000,000.

The last act in the assumption of British control over their East African protectorates occurred in the early twentieth century. In 1899 Sir Harry Johnston was sent to Uganda as a special commissioner to report on the future government for the area. By an agreement of 1900 Johnston settled the land question according to Indian models. The complex agreement further recognized the peculiar nature of the institutions of Buganda and the supreme authority of the kabaka, subject to British control, in the definite geographic area called Buganda. Later, in 1900, a simplified version of this type of agreement was extended to Toro and in the following year a similar treaty was made with the Mugabe of Ankole. Thus by the time of the promulgation of the Uganda Order in Council of 1902 there were three specific types of relationships between the peoples of Uganda and the British government. Bunyoro was conquered territory, the ruler of Ankole and Toro had a special position due to the treaties made with Johnston, and Buganda was, in theory, a semiautonomous state.

By the year 1900 Britain and Germany had effectively occupied most of the areas within their respective spheres of influence. There developed in the twentieth century many differences with African subjects which necessitated the use of force. However, with the exception of the Maji-Maji Rebellion in 1905 against the Germans, any disaffection of the conquered people did not develop into major revolts. Therefore, the first few years of the new century were devoted to creating structures of government which would enable the colonial power to dominate their territories as effectively and as cheaply as possible.

The Sudan

The fall of Khartoum and the death of Gordon in January 1885 ended briefly Egyptian hegemony over the Sudan and ushered in thirteen years of rule by the Mahdists. British prime minister Gladstone, using the excuse of renewed trouble in Afghanistan, immediately removed Wolseley's relief force from the Sudan. Within a year after Gordon's death there was only a skeleton force of British troops left in Egypt. The small Egyptian garrisons at Kassala and Sennar had been quickly overrun by the Mahdists, and Muhammad Ahmed's chief lieutenant in the northeast, Osman Digna, began to occupy the Red Sea littoral. Only one port, the small enclave of Suakin, was held by a combination of British and Egyptian troops.

Muhammad Ahmed survived Gordon by only five months, dying in June 1885. He had chosen the khalifa Abdullah as his successor before the fall of Khartoum. Despite this recognition, Abdullah was forced to spend the first months of his reign consolidating his position. He transferred potential rivals such as Wad el Nejumi, the victor of El Obeid, to the frontiers and reduced the Mahdi's relatives to minor positions within the government. Abdullah was a member of the small, fierce, nomadic Baggara tribe and he elevated members of that group to almost all the important positions in the state. He used them openly and skillfully to gradually negate potential opponents. Abdullah put down two minor uprisings headed by men claiming to be the true khalifa. A rebellion in Darfur in 1887 was smashed with such ferocity that many towns were burned and whole areas depopulated.

Abdullah used the memory of the departed Mahdi to further secure his control of the Sudan. He constructed a great tomb with an eighty-foot dome at Omdurman. A large rectangular area approximately one-half mile by three-fourths mile was cleared and roofed over near the tomb. This was the mosque where the khalifa prayed and instructed the people in his hopes for continuing the Mahdi's work. Abdullah, in adding to the myth of Muhammad Ahmed's invincibility, assured that much of the Mahdi's grandeur would reflect upon him. Omdurman became the chief city of the Sudan largely because of Abdullah's desire to concentrate the bulk of his armed forces there and keep its leaders under surveillance. Khartoum, by order of the khalifa, was razed in 1886 and the population forced to move to the new city. Omdurman by 1890 had an estimated population of over 150,000 persons.

The khalifa's rule was harsh, and in many cases brutal, although not as much so as was pictured in European journalistic accounts. During the khalifa's rule there was no mass exodus from the Sudan and the leaders remained loyal to Abdullah even when his theocracy was threatened by an Anglo-Egyptian invasion. The success of Abdullah's policy can be measured by the length and relative stability of his rule. However, the stories of the khalifa's cruelty which circulated throughout Britain supported the new imperialist mood of the nation and caused pressure to mount on the British government to reconquer the Sudan and avenge Gordon.

By 1888, secure in his control of the state, Abdullah began a more aggressive frontier policy. Wad el Nejumi with over 10,000 men invaded Egypt near Wadi Halfa. A large segment of the khalifa's army began to penetrate the exposed western frontiers of Ethiopia. In mid-1888, Abdullah dispatched a large force of 4,000 men and three steamers to the upper Nile to destroy the last Egyptian forces in the Sudan. There at Lado, Emin Pasha (Edward Schnitzer), the governor of Equatoria Province, with over 10,000 Egyptian men, women, and children, still resisted the Mahdists. All the other European governors who had served the khedive had seen their territory overrun and they had been taken prisoner. Henry Lupton, the Egyptian administrator of Bahr-al-Ghazal, died in captivity at Omdurman. Rudolph Slatin, governor of Darfur, survived captivity because he amused the khalifa and he also became a Muslim before his escape in 1895. Emin Pasha's situation in Equatoria was exaggerated in European accounts and Henry M. Stanley was commissioned to lead a large, well-financed expedition to rescue him. Stanley's venture, marred by dissension and hampered by disease, accident, and unexpected hardship, took almost three years of marching from the Congo to the upper Nile and eventually to Bagamoyo. Stanley finally arrived on the east coast with a reluctant Emin in December 1889. The departure of Emin and his followers from the Dufilé area of the upper Nile in February 1889 left the territory to the khalifa's forces.

The succession of almost uninterrupted success of the Mahdists was halted in 1889. Three major defeats placed the khalifa's armies on the defensive and further isolated the Sudan from the outside world. In August Wad el Nejumi's troops were destroyed by British-led Egyptian forces at Toski, sixty miles inside Egypt. This engagement ended the threat of a Sudanese invasion and gave the British time to construct in Egypt a large, well-trained army. Earlier in the year Emperor Johannes of Ethiopia had inflicted a major defeat on the khalifa's forces at Metemma. The third setback occurred when a British offensive launched from Suakin cleared a large area of the adjacent coast of Osman Digna's forces. To this list of defeats in 1889 was added increasingly serious internal problems in the khalifa's state. Diseases such as smallpox were endemic and these in combination with continual warfare had depopulated vast areas of the Sudan. Demands by the khalifa for a large army and the concentration of population at Omdurman meant that much of the arable land of the Sudan had not been under cultivation for years. Food supplies had already become critical when the locusts descended upon the Sudan in 1889. Untold thousands died in the aftermath of this catastrophe. Although the khalifa's theocracy managed to survive these blows, his economic and military situation worsened with each passing year.

In the decade following Gordon's death the shattered Egyptian economy was restored. Under the direction of Sir Evelyn Baring, the British consul, the administrative structure of Egypt was radically altered. British officials held most of the important posts in key agencies such as tax collecting and customs. Even before 1890 there was a budget surplus which could be devoted not only to paying off the foreign debts, but for major development projects in Egypt. Despite the strenuous opposition of the French members of the *Caisse de la Dette,* some of this surplus was devoted to the reconstruction of the Egyptian army. That army, under the direction first of Sir Evelyn Wood and after 1892 Herbert Kitchener, slowly began to develop into a modern, well-equipped, Westernized striking force. Kitchener was the perfect commander for the new army. Although British attitudes were shifting toward a more aggressive imperial policy, the British government insisted that the Egyptian government pay the expenses of modernization. Kitchener pared all unnecessary frills from the army and, to save money, arranged for much of his supplies to be manufactured in Egypt. He was a strict disciplinarian and, although he had great personal ambitions, he never openly challenged the decisions of his superiors. Kitchener had served a long period in the Sudan, commanded troops at Suakin, and appreciated the special problems of undertaking a campaign against the khalifa.

The transitional period in British imperial policy had ended by 1895. The Conservative government of Lord Salisbury after that date was prepared to follow an aggressive policy of territorial imperialism throughout Africa. The major question relating to the Sudan had ceased to be whether a reconquest should be attempted but when it should begin. The memory of Gordon which had never ceased to be a factor in British politics was now invoked to give legitimacy to this changed attitude. The collapse of the intricate British foreign policy in the Horn of Africa following the Italian defeat at Adowa meant to the active British imperialists that the invasion of the Sudan could not be postponed. Rumors of a French expedition whose objective was to claim a portion of the upper Nile were also a spur to the British government. Thus in March 1896, Kitchener was given permission to begin an open campaign against the khalifa.

Kitchener, fully appreciating the difficulty of the coming war, worried about advancing his career, and operating within a restricted budget, decided to secure his supply route by building railroads in the north before attempting to penetrate deeply into the Sudan. One rail line was planned to follow the course of the Nile to Kerma. When this was almost completed, Kitchener in September 1896 captured the major town of Dongola. In January 1897, a new line across the desert from Wadi Halfa to Abu Hamed was begun. Kitchener's strategy in 1897 was the same as the previous year. As soon as the desert line had advanced far enough, Kitchener launched an attack which secured Abu Hamed on August 7 and Berber on August 31, 1897. The railhead reached Berber in July 1898, two years after the con-

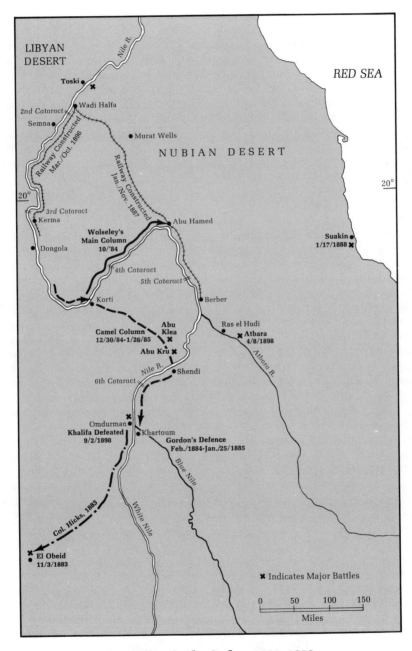

Campaigns in the Sudan, 1883–1898

quest had begun. The khalifa's forces, concentrated at Omdurman, had seriously challenged the Egyptian army only once. In April 1898, Emir Mahmoud advanced down the Atbara River to halt the Egyptian advance. Kitchener's disciplined force with its modern weapons destroyed Mahmoud's attempt, killing over 2,000 and capturing the emir. The khalifa continued to wait at Omdurman, confident that he would destroy his enemies in one great battle. His chance occurred when Kitchener's well-rested Anglo-Egyptian force of over 15,000 men took position near Omdurman in early September 1898. During the morning of September 2 the huge but ill-equipped and relatively inefficient army of the khalifa attempted to overwhelm Kitchener's force. The results were disastrous for the khalifa. The Mahdists suffered appalling casualties—9,000 killed and over 10,000 wounded from a total force of 60,000 men. The khalifa escaped from Omdurman and joined a large force of his followers at El Obeid.

Kitchener had little time to enjoy his victory since intelligence reports indicated that Captain Marchand had reached Fashoda on the Nile and had proclaimed the area adjacent to this town as French territory. Marchand had left Brazzaville two years before with a contingent of a dozen French officers and a hundred African troops. After a journey of over 3,000 miles he arrived at Fashoda in July 1898, completing his portion of a daring political plan. The French government hoped by this venture to gain support from Emperor Menelik and arrive at some compromise with the khalifa in order to block the British and Egyptian control of the upper Nile. On the basis of past negotiations the French had every expectation that the British would succumb to French diplomacy. However, Salisbury's government, after all the difficulties and expense of securing the Nile from a potentially hostile power, had no intention of backing down. Thus the small insignificant town of Fashoda became the focal point of the most serious crisis between France and Britain during the scramble.

Kitchener with five steamers, two battalions of troops, artillery, and machine guns arrived at Fashoda on September 18. Despite his overwhelming superiority, he handled the conferences with Marchand most diplomatically. He informed Marchand that his instructions were to reoccupy the Nile Valley for Egypt and that Marchand's claim for France had no validity. Marchand replied that he and his men were prepared to die at their posts and he could not withdraw without direct orders from his government. Before leaving, Kitchener put the British communications system at Marchand's disposal and left behind Colonel Jackson and a contingent of troops to keep the French under surveillance. The question was then referred to the higher echelons of two governments.

For almost two months the crisis simmered in Europe. Journalists on both sides fed the nationalistic flames. However, the French position both strategically and diplomatically was very weak. Even their army was deeply riven by the results of the Dreyfus affair. Confronted with the united, unmoving position of Britain, the French government capitulated in early November. On December 11 the French flag was lowered at Fashoda, their troops evacuated northward, and the crisis was ended. In March of the following year an agreement was signed between the two powers which reserved the valley of the Nile to Britain and Egypt. In the same month Britain and Egypt agreed to rule the Sudan with a condominium form of government and Kitchener was appointed the first governor-general.

During the entire period of the Fashoda crisis the khalifa was still operating in Kordofan with a considerable force. Finally, in October 1899, Kitchener learned that Abdullah with his major advisers were in Baggara country at Jebel Gedir, 400 miles south of Khartoum. Sir Reginald Wingate and 8,000 troops were immediately sent in pursuit. On November 24 the Egyptian forces, having surrounded the khalifa, rushed the camp. The Mahdist losses again were very heavy. After the battle the bodies of the khalifa and his chief lieutenants were found in one place where, after their retreat was cut off, they waited to be killed. Although punitive expeditions continued, the death of the khalifa spelled the end to the Mahdist dream of dominance in northeastern Africa. Finally, in January 1900, the last of the major Mahdist leaders, Osman Digna, was captured.

SIX
Consolidation of British power in Southern Africa, 1872–1910

General economic and political developments

The domestic political history of Cape Colony after 1872 is a story of important but generally unexciting decisions made by competent, if not flamboyant, personalities. Sir John Molteno was the dominant figure in Cape politics until his resignation as prime minister in 1878. He quarreled with the governor, Sir Bartle Frere, on the use of colonial troops in the war against Kreli, the Xosa leader. He was succeeded by Sir Gordon Sprigg whose government tended to represent the eastern Cape settlers against the more populous and prosperous western area. Sprigg's ministry was cut short by the adverse reaction to his attempts to disarm the Basuto. Sir Thomas Scanlon, backed by the moderate Boers, became prime minister only to be succeeded by Sprigg once again. Specific domestic issues rather than major philosophical differences determined the composition of Cape political parties. Of far more significance to the history of southern Africa than the actions of any of these political leaders was the influence of two men—Cecil Rhodes and J. H. Hofmeyer.

Rhodes had become by 1884 a political figure with considerable power. His mission to Goshen and Stellaland and his subsequent activities in Bechuanaland indicated how far he was willing to go to further his dreams of imperial expansion from the Cape. His success in finance and politics can be attributed, in large measure, to his understanding of events and men. His idea that anyone could be "squared," meant that all men were amenable to reason and all had their price. To achieve one's goal it was necessary to find out the price, offer to meet it, and then be patient. This concept, however cynical, enabled him to create De Beers Company, the British South Africa Company, Consolidated Goldfields, and finally in 1890 to become prime minister of Cape Colony.

J. H. Hofmeyer in many ways operated similarly to Rhodes.

He believed in reason, compromise, and was content to work behind the scenes. In 1883 he gained control of the Afrikander Bond, a heretofore anti-British organization. He converted it from its narrow adherence to the dream of Boer nationalism to an organization devoted to partnership between Boer and Briton. He envisioned, for the future, a united South Africa wherein each national unit had a meaningful, constructive role. Hofmeyer and the Bond cooperated with Rhodes, supporting him for prime minister twice. Hofmeyer utilized his talents and prestige to help create friendly relations between the British and the Boer republics, particularly with the Orange Free State. The cooperation between Rhodes and Hofmeyer and between moderate Boers and Britons was shattered by the disastrous Jameson raid of 1895.

Political activities in all the states of southern Africa were conducted in the last quarter of the century against a background of rapid economic development. White population in all areas increased dramatically during this period. Cape Colony's white population was almost one-half million by 1899, an increase of almost one hundred percent over the figure in 1872. Natal's European population rose from 20,000 to approximately 90,000 in the same period while the Orange Free State recorded a rise from 27,000 to almost 100,000. The South African Republic showed the greatest increase in its white population from 40,000 in 1873 to 250,000 by the beginning of the Boer War.

These increases in population were closely related to economic developments. Total railroad mileage in 1872 in all of southern Africa was only sixty-three miles. By 1899 it had grown to almost 3,600 miles. Correlate developments could be noted in harbor, telegraph, and road facilities. The railway opened up lands, heretofore unprofitable, for agriculture, particularly cereal crops. Diamonds provided an annual export from the Cape in the five years before the Boer War valued at over $20 million while the average annual export of gold was valued at over $55 million. The export of diamonds alone exceeded the total value of annual exports from the Cape in 1870. The development of sugar and tea plantations in Natal raised its exports from approximately $2.5 million in 1872 to almost $10 million by 1895.

The area under direct European administration grew tremendously in this same period. Cape Colony assumed jurisdiction from Britain over Griqualand West in 1880 and British Bechuanaland in 1895. Continuing problems related to the uprising of the Xosa led by Kreli culminated in the absorption of the Transkei by the Cape; and Natal acquired Tongaland and Zululand in 1897. The expansionist dreams of the South African Republic were largely blocked by the northward thrust of Cecil Rhodes' British South Africa Company, but in 1885 Kruger managed to gain temporary control over Swaziland. Matabeleland, Mashonaland, and much of the area across the Zambesi were secured for Britain before 1895 by the actions of the British South Africa Company.

Two opposing native policies developed in southern Africa. In Cape Colony, while recognizing the uniqueness of African institutions, legislation was aimed at integrating the Bantu into the state. This was but a continuation of a historical trend dating to the passage of the Fiftieth Ordinance in 1828. A special native penal code for the Transkei was established, the peculiar position of chiefs recognized, and the machinery for basic legislation by the governor created. In 1894 the first of the district councils for Xosa in both the Ciskei and Transkei regions was formed. In Natal, native policy continued to follow the general outlines formulated by Theophilus Shepstone during his long tenure as chief native commissioner. This had envisioned the creation of separate native reserves with traditional rulers controlled indirectly by Europeans. Natal formulated a code of Bantu law in 1878 to be supplanted by a more comprehensive code in 1891. On the economic level the Cape's concern with ultimate integration led to the introduction to the Bantu areas of European methods of industry and agriculture. In Natal, except for the intervention of European political officers, the Bantu were left to themselves on their reserves.

The Zulu War and the Transvaal question

Events in southern Africa in the late 1870s were contingent upon two main interconnected themes. One, already noted, was the continuing desire of some British administrators, notably the governor and high commissioner, Sir Bartle Frere, to extend the influence of the crown over the Boer republics. The other concerned the revived martial spirit of the Zulu and the distinct possibility that their impis would spill across the frontier in an orgy of killing. The man most responsible for keeping alive this fear was Theophilus Shepstone, the long-time chief native commissioner in Natal. He was, to the inexperienced Bartle Frere, the recognized expert on the Zulu. He was also trusted by the Zulu who believed he would present their case to the governor with truth and understanding. Shepstone, instead, aligned himself with the alarmists after 1876 and used the Zulu "menace" to excuse the British occupation of the South African Republic.

The Zulu ruler was Cetewayo who had officially succeeded his ineffectual father, Panda, in 1872. Cetewayo, however, had been the actual ruler of Zululand after 1856. In that year Cetewayo's warriors defeated and killed his younger brother, Umbulazi, and the majority of his enemies in a bloody battle on the Tugela River. Centralization of authority returned to Zululand under Cetewayo. The military regiments assumed an importance not seen since the time of Dingane. Cetewayo could not be manipulated easily either by the British in Natal or by the Boers in the north. Although his impis raided to the north and west, Cetewayo was scrupulous to avoid any massive intrusion into British territory. The Zulu also respected the farms of the Boers of the tiny republic of Utrecht.

In 1868 Utrecht was absorbed into the larger South African Republic and almost immediately there arose difficulties concerning the boundary between the Republic and the Zulu. Cetewayo maintained that much of the territory of Utrecht belonged to the Zulu who had allowed the Boers simply to use the land. The South African Republic was a study in contrasts. Their officials were bombastic and at the same time afraid. By the time that Frere arrived in South Africa it was generally feared that Cetewayo was ready to send his 10,000 celibate warriors north against the Boers who continued to press their claims for the land adjacent to the Zulu. Eventually a commission was appointed to investigate the counter claims of the Boer and Zulu to the land. Although no Zulu was represented on the commission, Cetewayo agreed to accept its findings.

Sir Bartle Frere had arrived as governor of Cape Colony and high commissioner in March 1877. He had previously distinguished himself as an administrator in India, but had no African experience. He was an ardent champion of Lord Carnarvon's ideas concerning confederation of all southern Africa united under the crown. Furtherance of this was always foremost in his thoughts. He depended for advice upon African experts, particularly Theophilus Shepstone. Frere and Shepstone both saw in the Boer fears and Zulu resurgence a chance to extend British control northward and also end the potential menace of the Zulu.

The South African Republic was bankrupt. Its prodigal land policy, aggressive attitudes toward neighboring Bantu, lax taxation system, and no important exports combined in 1876 to render the territory economically impotent. An ill-timed war with Sekukuni, chief of the Bapedi, was the final act in the developing insolvency of the republic. In the face of the mounting Zulu threat, President T. F. Burgers invited British aid. Shepstone rode northward to Pretoria with only twenty-four soldiers in December 1876. After discussions with members of the volksraad and against a strong minority feeling exemplified by Paul Kruger, Shepstone on April 12, 1877, raised the Union Jack and declared the state annexed to the crown. Such were the fears of the Zulu menace that few Boers protested this action. One link toward the confederation scheme which had so recently failed had been forged. The next step was to negate the Zulu menace.

A lesser chief of the Zulu in July 1878 crossed into Natal after two of his unfaithful wives, seized them, and took them back to be executed. This incident together with the continued "barbarous" practices of the Zulu and the use of their impis against neighboring peoples served as the ostensible reason for direct military action against them. Frere's schemes were almost upset by the announcement of the land commission that most of the Zulu claims to the disputed northern lands were justified. Frere, instead of using this as a basis for rapprochement with Cetewayo, attempted to mask the decision, and delivered instead an ultimatum to Cetewayo. If the Zulu chief had accepted the demands in the ultimatum, particularly those relating to Zulu military organization, and receiving a British president, Zululand would have ceased to be independent. It would have become a de facto dependency of Britain. Cetewayo was given twenty days to comply. He announced his reservations to the ultimatum and the date (December 31, 1878) for compliance passed. Thereupon Frere ordered General Thesiger (later Lord Chelmsford) to occupy Zululand.

Thesiger who had been alerted to his task some months before was

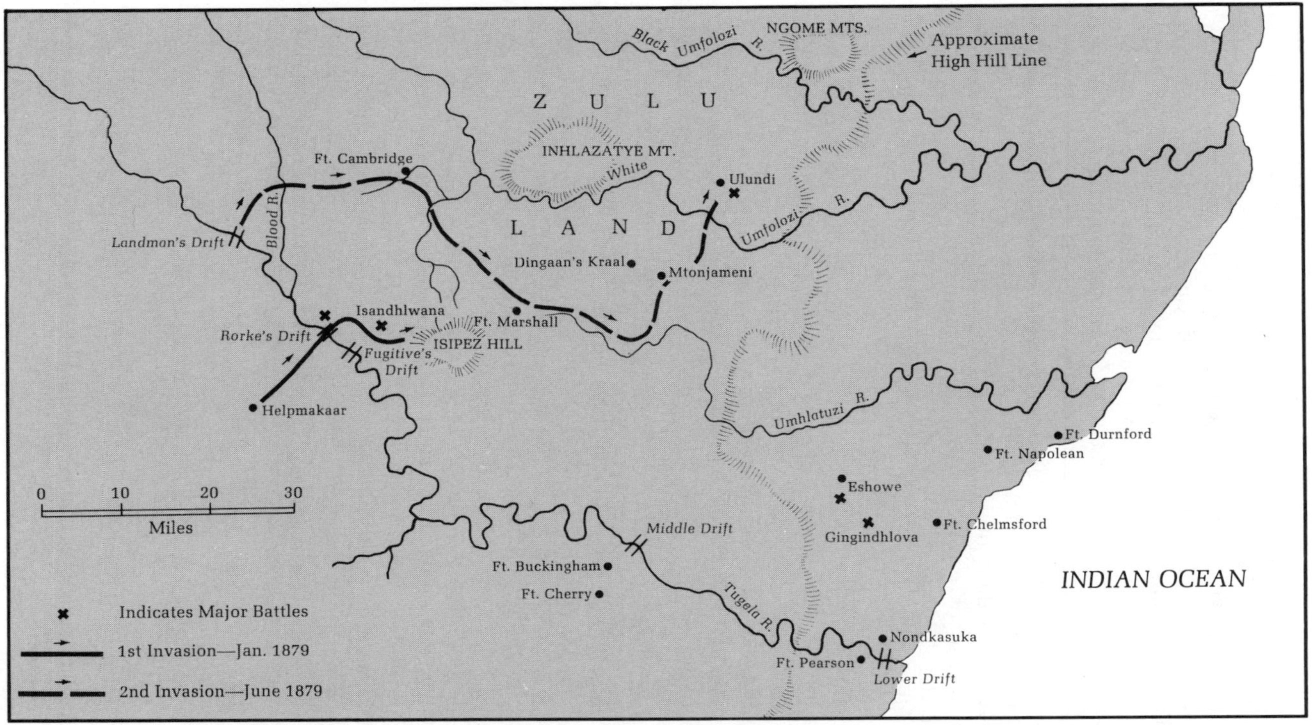

British Operations in Zululand, 1879

INDIAN OCEAN

Ft. Durnford

Ft. Napolean

Ft. Chelmsford

Noodkasuka

Lower Drift

Eshowe

Gingindhlova

Ft. Pearson

Umhlatuzi R.

Tugela R.

Middle Drift

Ft. Buckingham

Ft. Cherry

Helpmakaar

Rorke's Drift

Fugitive's Drift

Isandhlwana

Ft. Marshall

ISIPEZ HILL

Ft. Cambridge

Blood R.

Landman's Drift

Dingaan's Kraal

Mtonjameni

Ulundi

Umfolozi R.

White Umfolozi R.

INHLAZATYE MT.

Z U L U   L A N D

Black Umfolozi R.

NGOME MTS.

Approximate
High Hill Line

Miles

0   10   20   30

Indicates Major Battles

1st Invasion—Jan. 1879

2nd Invasion—June 1879

155

not eager for a campaign in the hilly, stream-crossed country adjacent to Natal. He asked for reinforcements of men and material, most of which were refused him. Nevertheless, on January 11, 1879, he invaded Zululand, dividing his 12,000 man army composed of some regulars, Natal and Cape militia, and native troops, into three columns. The plan was for these three to converge on the Zulu capital of Ulundi. Commanding the middle column of 1,600 Europeans and 2,500 natives, he advanced from Rorke's Drift to Isandhlwana. On the morning of January 22, Thesiger took a small force to reconnoiter ahead. The remaining force, occupying an extremely defensible position, was attacked by approximately 10,000 Zulu. There is evidence that the Zulu did not plan to fight at Isandhlwana, but simply chanced on the British force. Nevertheless, the Zulu commanders reacted intelligently to their opportunity. British leadership was never worse. A tragic parade of errors negated the bravery of the individual soldier. Before the day was finished 806 Europeans and 471 African troops had been killed, Thesiger's army was shattered, and except for the heroic defense of Rorke's Drift, Natal itself would have felt the wrath of the Zulu. The defense by less than 200 men, mainly Welsh Borderers under the command of Lieutenants Chard and Bromhead, saved one of the main crossings over the Tugela River for the British.

After Isandhlwana, Thesiger received the support in men and equipment which he had earlier requested. Regrouping his forces, he reinvaded Zululand in May. Armed with field guns, rocket tubes, and gatling guns, his forces defeated the Zulu at Dingane's old capital of Umgungundhlovo. The Zulu lost 1,200 men in this engagement while the British lost two. The campaign continued for almost three months until the final Zulu defeat at their burning capital of Ulundi on July 4. Thesiger had been officially replaced in command by Sir Garnet Wolseley, but Wolseley had not yet arrived in southern Africa. Thus Thesiger avenged Isandhlwana and was responsible for the capture of Cetewayo.

Cetewayo was sent into exile, lived a part of this time in London, and eventually was allowed to return to his country where he died in 1884. But Zulu power was broken. Britain did not annex the territory; it was divided into eleven chieftaincies. Soon these chiefs were quarreling with each other. The royal house was almost destroyed by these disputes. A Boer, Lukas Meyer, and his followers proclaimed one of Cetewayo's sons, Dinizulu, a puppet king of the Boer New Republic in 1884. After British protests over this action that section of Zululand was incorporated into the South African Republic as the Vryheid area. Finally in 1897 Britain, concerned with the possible eastward expansion of Kruger's South African Republic, formally joined Zululand with Natal.

The defeat of Cetewayo removed the major threat to the security of the Boers of the high veld. The high-handed attitudes of Sir Garnet Wolseley, who had been appointed high commissioner for Southeastern Africa and administrator of the former South African Republic, alienated many of the Boer supporters of British rule. Thus within a year after Ulundi the majority of Boers north of the Vaal supported Paul Kruger in demanding an end to British control. In Britain Lord Carnarvon's successor as colonial secretary, Sir Michael Hicks-Beach, was not a confirmed advocate of confederation. The cost in lives and money of the Zulu War had discredited Bartle Frere. Therefore there was no high British official who was willing to defend the previous policy of expansion. In the parliamentary campaign of 1880 William E. Gladstone denounced the imperialism of Disraeli and the Conservatives and promised if elected he would remove the British presence from beyond the Vaal. Gladstone and his Liberal party won the elections. However, other problems occupied his attention and nothing was done to implement his promise concerning South Africa.

In December 1880, abandoning peaceful means, the Boers reconvened their volksraad and proclaimed the restoration of the republic. Paul Kruger, Marthinius Pretorius, and General Joubert were appointed a triumverate to guard the interests of the new state. The first shots of the renewed conflict with Britain were fired on December 16 at Potchefstroom. The British had only 3,500 men in all of South Africa to oppose the uprising. The small British garrisons in the republic were beleaguered and a larger force at Bokhurst Spruit was defeated by Boer marksmen. The lieutenant-governor of Natal, General George Colley, attempted twice to force entrance into the republic but was forced to turn back. In late February, Colley took up a new position in northern Natal on Amajuba, "Hill of Doves," rising over 2,000 feet above the plain. On February 26 Commandant-General Joubert's troops stormed the hill, killing eighty-five regulars and General Colley. Kruger received the British armistice proposals the day after the Majuba action and he immediately accepted them. By the Pretoria Convention signed later in the year the Transvaal received its independence subject to acknowledgment of British suzerainty. This meant that Britain continued to control the foreign and native policies of the new state. In 1883 the rule of the triumverate over the Transvaal came to an end and Kruger was elected president. By the London Convention of the following year the republic was allowed to make its own treaties and Britain gave up the right to veto native legislation. After seven years for all practical, if not legal, purposes, the South African Republic was once again independent.

British activities north of the Limpopo

Imperialism in southern Africa more than any other area of the continent depended upon decisions made by Europeans resident in Africa rather than on officials at home. The man who was the driving force behind British expansion northward from Cape Colony was Cecil John Rhodes. A sickly boy of sixteen when he arrived in Africa in 1870, he had made a fortune in diamonds before he was thirty. From his early twenties Rhodes had been convinced that British culture represented man's highest development. The later popular phrase "white man's burden" was an imperative to action from him. Thus he was prepared to expend his own personal fortune to secure the future of the British empire in Africa. In the period of transition before 1895, Rhodes' willingness to finance imperial schemes enabled him to receive permission to proceed from the home government whereas imperialists with little wealth such as Sir Harry Johnston or Sir Samuel Rowe would be denied such permission. Rhodes, active in all areas of Cape finance, became in the late 1880s deeply involved in the exploitation of gold on the Rand. As head of Consolidated Goldfields, he became the most powerful voice demanding that Kruger ameliorate conditions for the Uitlanders. He combined financial power with political influence, becoming prime minister of Cape Colony in 1890.

In 1881 Rhodes was first elected to the Cape parliament from a predominantly Boer district. Almost immediately he assumed a major role in the debates and actions concerning Bechuanaland. Boers from the South African Republic had established two ostensibly independent governments, Stellaland and Goshen, in the lands of the Tswana people. This, combined with German annexation of Angra Pequeña, aroused fears in Rhodes and other imperialists that the road for British expansion to the north would be blocked. Rhodes played an important role in convincing the British government to send Sir Charles Warren into Bechuanaland in 1885. Subsequently the southern portion of that territory was annexed as a crown colony while a protectorate was declared as far north as the Zambesi. There was little trouble with the Africans since the major Tswana chiefs such as Khama had already requested that the British protect them from the South African Republic. For Rhodes, although he disagreed with the methods used, Warren's actions assured that the narrow strip of fertile land between the South African Republic and the Kalahari Desert would remain in British hands. Thus he could continue to plan on an all "red" map of east and southern Africa so necessary for his later concept of a Cape to Cairo railway.

SOUTHERN RHODESIA

The pursuance of his imperial ambitions led Cecil Rhodes to look beyond the Limpopo to the lands controlled by the Matabele ruler, Lo Bengula. Discovery of gold on the Rand in 1886 lured many gold prospectors and entrepreneurs north into Matabeleland in the hope of duplicating this rich gold find. In 1887 Piet Grobler, an official of the South African government, entered into a treaty with Lo Bengula which would have given Kruger's government the preeminent position in Matabeleland. However, John Moffat, a former missionary and the assistant commissioner in Bechuanaland, secured a repudiation of this treaty in February 1888. This reopened his territory to many concession hunters who came to Lo Bengula's kraal at Bulawayo during 1888. Among them were representatives of a number of powerful German and British concerns. Lo Bengula resisted the advice of his more practical-minded advisers and refused to kill the Europeans. He did not grant any major concessions until October 1888. With advice from Sir Sydney Shippard, the commissioner for Bechuanaland, the Bishop of Bloemfontein, and the missionary Charles Helm, the king finally decided to give Rhodes' representatives, Charles Rudd, Rochefort Macguire, and

Francis Thompson, the sole right to look for gold in his country. Armed with the so-called "Rudd Concession," Rhodes went to London, formed a company, and eventually in October 1889 secured a royal charter. Rhodes' new venture, the British South Africa Company, was ostensibly designed to search for gold, but to Rhodes it was the necessary vehicle to carry the flag northward to the Zambesi. After securing the charter, he and his close associate, Leander Starr Jameson, went north in early 1890 and secured from an alarmed Lo Bengula the assurance that the pioneers "could have the road." In June the pioneers accompanied by 400 mounted men, the nucleus of the company police, entered Matabeleland. Despite the assurance given Jameson by Lo Bengula, there was great danger that the war party at Bulawayo would gain the upperhand and force Lo Bengula to launch his 18,000 warriors against the pioneers. However, there were no incidents and Jameson proceeded to establish Fort Victoria, Fort Charter, and Salisbury and began to parcel out town and farm sites to the volunteers.

The company had hardly been established north of the Limpopo when the question of Portuguese claims to Manicaland became very important. In September 1890, Jameson traveled to Manicaland and entered into a treaty with one of the great chiefs, Mtasa, which gave the company a preeminent position in his country. However, the Anglo-Portuguese agreement of August 1890 undermined the company's position. Fortunately for Rhodes, the Portuguese Cortes, in a flurry of patriotic indignation, rejected the treaty. The Portuguese dispatched Manuel de Souza, with a small armed force, to occupy Mtasa's village. The Portuguese had hardly settled in when British South African Company troops stormed the village, arrested the Portuguese, and raised the "Union Jack." Thus Manicaland was secured for the company. However, Rhodes' ambitions toward Gazaland were blocked by the Anglo-Portuguese agreement of June 1891 which assigned that area to the Portuguese.

Lo Bengula's initial suspicion of European motives had become a certainty. Although the pioneers had skirted Matabeleland and had settled in Shona territory, this had not eased the king's mind. Why had they settled down and begun to farm and why did more arrive every month? He had only given permission to dig for gold; he had not alienated his control over Shona territory. To the British government there was no doubt that the Foreign Jurisdiction Act applied to Mashonaland. In May 1891, an Order in Council declared all the company territories to be under the protection of the crown. Thus the high commissioner or the administrator could declare, when they so desired, that the Shona were under British protection. The Matebele considered Mashonaland to be theirs—a place to send their regiments to steal the Mashona cattle. This jurisdictional dispute over the Shona led Lo Bengula to discard his caution; and he decided to use his army against the Shona who felt secure in their new-found British protection near Fort Victoria.

A minor incident in June 1893 led to full-scale war. The company administration had confiscated cattle from some Shona, and Lo Bengula claimed the cattle as his. The king at first sent approximately 1,000 men to the area to show the Shona who held the real power. Shona workers were killed on European farmsteads. Thoroughly frightened, many Europeans took refuge at Fort Victoria. Jameson decided not to compromise but to attempt finally to destroy Matabele power in the trans-Limpopo territory. The reasons for Jameson's decision had little to do with the threat of the moment. The presumed rich gold reefs of Mashonaland had proved an illusion. The price of the company stock had fallen to less than one-third of its previous value on the London exchange. If Lo Bengula were defeated, the promise of potential riches in his country would give the company a much-needed financial boost.

By October 1893, Jameson had gathered a force of 600 men near Fort Victoria. He promised them land and cattle in the new territory whenever the Matabele power was broken. Crossing into Matabeleland, Jameson's mounted irregulars fought two major engagements with Lo Bengula's regiments. Repeating rifles and machine guns proved as effective against the Matabele as they had against the Zulu fifteen years before. Lo Bengula burned the royal kraal and fled northward with some of his cattle and the remnants of his army. He died before reaching the Zambesi and within a short while most of the Matabale returned to their homes. Jameson made Bulawayo the administrative center of the area and allocated farms and town sites to his victorious followers. In 1894 the company received permission from the crown to administer Matabeleland. The fortunes of the company had improved so much that in the following year a railroad was begun from Mafeking north to Bulawayo.

Although most of the Matabele had returned to their home areas, their warlike spirit was not completely broken. They were prepared to take orders from the white man as long as they believed them just and as long as the Europeans had superior coercive power. In the eighteen months following Lo Bengula's defeat there were a number of decisions which alienated the Matabele from their governors. The newly formed police force was drawn largely from the Shona, many of whom used their positions to revenge themselves on their former oppressors. European officials who knew little of the Matabele law of property made a number of mistakes in allocation of the nearly one-quarter million head of royal cattle. The policy of forced labor which could be ordered by district commissioners was resented. Finally a serious rinderpest epidemic hit the cattle herds in 1895. Chiefs and religious leaders became convinced that prosperity would return to the Matabele only when the white man was driven out. Their opportunity for this direct action against the Europeans came early in 1896.

Jameson in October 1895 had withdrawn all but forty of the company police from both Mashonaland and Matabeleland in preparation for the hoped rising of the Uitlanders in Johannesburg. The abortive Jameson Raid not only damaged Britain's position vis-à-vis the South African Republic but also offered the Matabele their chance to be rid of the Europeans. By the end of March the Matabele were everywhere in arms. In the early stages of this second Matabele war over one hundred Europeans, mostly traders or farmers in isolated districts, were killed. The settlers flocked to Bulawayo which became the major European defensive bastion in the territory. A small force under Colonel Plummer arrived from Bechuanaland in early May. These troops together with volunteers fought a series of small violent actions against the Matabele. Rhodes was informed by the military that total pacification would depend upon the completion of the railroad and the deployment of several thousand troops. The financial condition of the company did not allow for such a prolonged campaign. Rhodes decided to attempt a quick peaceful solution by direct negotiations with the Matabele chiefs. After five weeks trying to make contact, Rhodes and three companions finally met with the Matabele leaders. He listened to them and agreed to rectify most of the abuses they complained about. On that basis the war in Matabeleland ended. Rhodes later shipped huge amounts of grain at company expense northward to ward off starvation among the Matabele. It is, therefore, understandable that the Matabele in 1902 stood along the route from Bulawayo to Matapos in silent respect for the funeral train of the "great man" who had taken away their freedom.

The uprising in Matabeleland was duplicated by a similar series of events in Mashonaland beginning in June 1896. Handicapped by lack of police and the fact that many of the men were campaigning against the Matabele, the Europeans flocked to Salisbury and other townsites. The fighting against the Shona was in many ways more difficult than against the Matabele. They had no chiefs of large districts so, therefore, all actions fought were small-scale and ultimately peace came not by one general agreement, but by several with individual chiefs. By October 1896, however, the company had restored order in Mashonaland and the Europeans were dominant once again.

Rhodes, in desperate trouble after the failure of the Jameson Raid, nevertheless managed to keep the company intact. He had to accept more direct intervention from the crown in the form of a resident commissioner after 1898. In the last years of his life he devoted most of his time to Rhodesian affairs. In these formative years the pattern of economic development for Southern Rhodesia was set, as well as relationships between the minority white farmers and the once dominant Matabele and Shona people.

NORTHERN RHODESIA

British expansion in the far northern segment of Rhodesia was largely the result of the activities of Cecil Rhodes and his agents. However, the area was so large and the initial contacts so diffuse that it is convenient to consider separately the northeast and northwestern portions of Rhodesia. Although the company agents were active in the northwestern region earlier, this region was not effectively occupied and administered until after the northeast. Until 1894 the northeastern section was considered to be a part of the sphere of imperial influence controlled by Harry Johnston from Nyasaland. In that year an agreement between the British government and the British South Africa Company reserved for the company rights of administration in the northeast. In 1894 a veteran of the pioneer column's march to Salisbury, Major Forbes, became the company's administrator in the territories north of the Zambesi. With his headquarters at Zomba, he was theoretically in charge of the whole north. However, his actual administrative influence never expanded to Lewanika's territory. There after 1897 the resident, Robert Coryndon, although a subordinate of Forbes, was constrained to act on his own.

Company administration from Zomba was, at first, very weak since the powerful Nguni, Bemba, and Lunda chiefs had not asked for British protection and did not recognize British authority. All of the Nguni territory of Chief Mpezeni had been assigned to Britain by the June 1891 agreement with Portugal, although the Nguni ruler never agreed to accept a subordinate position. Major Forbes' situation was made more difficult by the arrival in Nguni country of a number of prospectors who hoped to discover a new gold strike. Their presence as well as Forbes' governmental activities created a genuine fear among the Nguni which in January 1898 resulted in an attempt to drive all Europeans from Nguni country. The company's position was saved by the arrival of 650 men of the Central African Rifles from Nyasaland. Within a short time these troops had defeated the Nguni in a series of small but costly battles. Mpezeni's men were even less able to stand up to modern rifles than had been the Zulu or Matabele. The legal position of the British regarding the Nguni who had never agreed to their overlordship was extremely questionable. Nevertheless, British authorities captured Mpezeni's son, the most important Nguni military leader, and publically executed him for the crimes of murder and instigation to murder. Over one-third of all the tribal herds of the Nguni were then confiscated as indemnity for the "rebellion."

In Bemba country Europeans were in no position to exert much authority until after 1897. "Arab" slavers driven out of their forts near Lake Nyasa had taken refuge among the Bemba and had built a number of stockaded places. European administrators used the divided state of the Bemba to gain ascendancy over them. In 1897 a company force broke the slavers' power over the Senga and in the following year they were driven out of the territory between the Luapula Valley and Lake Mweru. The final campaign against them was conducted by Sharpe in October 1899, directed against those in the Kazembe Lunda area. With its conclusion company authority was dominant in the northeast.

Most of the northwestern area was ruled by Lewanika, the Lozi chief. However, the actual limits of his territory was undefined and this later caused serious international complications. In the 1880s Lewanika, who had been consistently bothered by Matabele raids, first became interested in placing his country under British protection. He inquired of Khama, the Bamangwato chief, regarding his opinion of the British. After Khama had reported favorably, Lewanika formally requested protection. In the same year Lewanika granted rights to look for minerals outside of Barotseland proper to Harry Ware, a prospector. This concession was ultimately purchased in October 1889 by Rhodes for the British South Africa Company. In March of the following year Rhodes sent F. E. Lochner to Lewanika's village. This visit resulted in a treaty whereby the Lozi would receive the company's protection, represented by a British resident at Lewanika's court. For any loss of status Lewanika was to receive a salary of £2,000 annually from the company. In return the company received proprietary rights to minerals in his country and also, by implication, it became the dominant political force in Barotseland.

Despite the central position of the resident in this agreement of 1890, none was sent until 1897. The explanation for the delay must be sought in the list of priorities established by Rhodes. Barotseland was far away and relatively secure. The South African Republic, Matabeleland, Mashonaland, and the Nyasa territories were all more important. Finally, in 1897, Robert Coryndon arrived among the Lozi to become the first resident. In the following June a detailed, well-prepared, final agreement between the Lozi and the company was signed. In 1900 the Northwest Rhodesia Barotseland Order in Council confirmed the area as a British protectorate under the administration of the company. It included the area between the Kafue River and the Katanga which later proved immensely valuable because of the minerals discovered there.

The remaining major problem which was left unresolved after 1900 was the boundary line of Portuguese Angola. The 1891 agreement had stated that the line should follow the western boundary of Barotseland. Unfortunately no one knew where this was and the territory of the Lovale was disputed by Lewanika and the Portuguese. Finally in 1903 an arbitration committee headed by the king of Italy drew the present boundary along conventional geographic lines which separated groups of the Lovale from one another. The question of the possession of the northwest, although never violently contested, was at last settled.

NYASALAND

Long before Cecil Rhodes' company became concerned with expansion north of the Limpopo there were British missionaries living among the Maravi people near Lake Malawi. The peoples of the Lake Malawi area provided a large portion of the slaves for the East African trade in the 1870s and 1880s. The missionaries noted with disgust and a sense of futility the slave trade since they were powerless to halt the raidings of Nguni, Yao, and "Arab" traders. From the date when Livingstone first investigated the lake area, missionary groups had appealed to the British government to intervene. As has been noted previously, the policy of all British governments prior to the early 1880s was hostile to expansion. However, in 1883, as a token of support for the missionaries, they appointed a consul to the "territories of African Kings and Chiefs in the Districts adjacent to Lake Nyasa." The consul had no police and, therefore, little authority. His presence solved none of the pressing problems for the missionaries. Attempting to teach the Africans that profits could be made in legitimate trade, the missionaries aided in the formation of the African

Lakes Company. The company in the 1880s made no headway against the slave trade and was in continual financial difficulties.

Company agents in late 1887 became involved in hostilities with Mlozi, an Arab half-caste who terrorized the Nkonde district. Early the following year the skirmishing between Mlozi and the Europeans was resumed. After June the Europeans were joined by an officer on leave from the British army whose later African exploits became legendary. Captain Frederick D. Lugard's first African experiences were far from successful. Despite considerable bravery, the Europeans and their allies found that they could not take Mlozi's main stronghold of Kota Kota and Lugard was seriously wounded. A situation of armed neutrality prevailed until after Harry Johnston, the new British consul to Mozambique, arrived in the interior in October 1889.

Johnston's name must rank very high in the pantheon of empire builders in Africa. Although only thirty-one years old when he arrived in Mozambique, he was already experienced in African affairs. He had toured the Congo in 1883, and had been greatly influenced by Stanley. Johnston later traveled extensively in East Africa in 1885. His recommendations to the Foreign Office concerning annexation of the area adjacent to Mt. Kilimanjaro came close to being accepted at that time. Johnston was known in London as an exponent of imperial expansion and was important in the ultimate formation of the British Imperial East Africa Company. After his work in East Africa, he had been appointed vice-consul to the Oil Rivers Protectorate where he had been responsible for instituting the forward policy which had overthrown King Jaja of Opobo. It is obvious that the Foreign Office by appointing Johnston was not in a mood to concede hinterland Nyasaland to the Portuguese.

The Portuguese in the late 1880s laid claim to a vast but undefined section of Central Africa which would have linked their Atlantic and Indian Ocean possessions. The bases for their claims were historic connections and some very early interior expeditions. In the Shire River area the most important of these explorations was that of Lacerda in 1798. However, the Congress of Berlin had destroyed the validity of such historic claims. The Portuguese after the conference were forced into a belated effort to secure sovereignty over the Nyasa area. One way of showing their power over the hinterland was to block needed supplies to the missionaries. Another way was to interfere with missionary attempts to control the slave trade. Such activity was facilitated by Portuguese control over the Quelimane mouth of the Zambesi River. This favored position was partially neutralized by the discovery in 1889 of the Chinde mouth. In the same year the Portuguese sent a large expedition under the command of Major Serpa Pinto up the Shire River to establish a modern-day claim to the highlands. However, Johnston intercepted Pinto's column near the confluence of the Shire and Riro rivers and warned him that any further penetration of the territory would be a direct flaunting of British claims. Pinto then found it expedient to withdraw from the highlands. Early in 1890 Lord Salisbury, the British prime minister, removed the

potential Portuguese threat to the Nyasa area by a warning to send gunboats to Mozambique if Portugal did not withdraw from the territory
adjacent to the Shire River.

Even without Portuguese rivalry, Johnston still faced a near impossible task. In October 1889, he arranged a truce with the slavers near
Karonga and then spent the rest of the year traveling northwest of the
lake making treaties wherever possible with African leaders. Johnston
was later very fortunate in convincing Alfred Sharpe, a big game hunter,
to accept the position of temporary vice-consul. In 1890 Sharpe made
two important treaty-making journeys. The first, undertaken in March,
in the Nguni country ruled by Chief Mpezeni was not productive since
the chief refused to consider a treaty of protection. Sharpe was more
successful in Nsenga and Cewa territory. Still another trip in July took
him to Karonga and thence northwest through the Luapula Valley and
finally to the Katanga Kazembes. African chiefs in the Luapula Valley
accepted British protection. However, Msiri of the Katanga would not
consider any diminution of his influence. In the following year Msiri
was killed by an agent of Leopold II and the Katanga was declared to
be under Independent State control. Despite the loss of the Katanga,
the treaties gained by Johnston and Sharpe bolstered Lord Salisbury's
position in negotiations with Germany and Portugal. In July 1890, by
the Heligoland Treaty, Germany recognized Britain's claims to the territory between Lakes Malawi and Tanganyika, and the Anglo-Portuguese
treaties of 1890 and 1891 confirmed Britain's hold on the Shire highlands.

Johnston's tasks after the treaties with Germany and Portugal ceased
to have international implications, but he was still confronted with the
problem of ruling a large territory controlled mainly by "Arab" slavers
and their African allies such as the Nguni and Yao. Johnston had little
money and fewer troops to implement his decisions. His activities were
furthered by Cecil Rhodes who in 1890 came to the rescue of the African
Lakes Company by granting it an annual subsidy of £9,000. In February
1891, this subsidy agreement was renegotiated with the imperial government as the recipient. In return for grants of mineral and commercial
rights to the British South Africa Company, Rhodes promised to provide
£10,000 per year to maintain a police force in Nyasaland. In May 1891,
the imperial government declared a protectorate over the Nyasaland
district and the area which later became northeastern Rhodesia was separated from Nyasaland and given over to the administration of Rhodes'
chartered company. The old African Lakes Company was phased out
by 1893.

After 1891 Johnston had a police force of over 200 men of whom
seventy were Sikhs from India and in 1892 he received two gunboats for
use on the lake. He utilized this force first to overawe the people in
those areas where the chiefs had submitted. Then, if necessary, he used
force to break the slavers' hold on certain districts. By the end of 1895
most of the Nguni and Yao chiefs had submitted to British authority.
The last major campaign in the Nyasa area was fought in late 1895

against the "Arab" slavers in the northern territory. With the taking of Karonga, Johnston effectively ended slaving activities in the protectorate. He soon returned to England ill and exhausted by his seven-year campaign, leaving behind the rudiments of an administrative system and the certain knowledge that British power was recognized by all Africans in Nyasaland.

The Rand gold strike and its consequences

There is evidence that the Boers were aware of the presence of gold in the hilly, eroded region near Johannesburg as early as the 1850s. Thus the discovery by the Struben brothers of the huge Witwatersrand deposits in 1884 was not a complete surprise. The Witwatersrand gold was found in microscopic quantities along with pyrites in the intrusive conglomerate rocks of the reef. This was not the type of alluvial deposit which had earlier lured thousands to the gold fields of California and Australia. Fifty years before it would have been impossible to extract the gold profitably from the quartz rocks. Science and technology had provided the methodology and there was sufficient capital in Cape Colony and Britain to underwrite the expensive, complex machinery necessary to mine the gold. Within a few months of the announcement of the discoveries in 1886, companies were already paying high dividends to their investors. However, the more complex the procedures for mining became, the more it was apparent that larger, more viable companies were needed. Thus such giants as Cecil Rhodes' Consolidated Goldfields dominated the mining scene by the early 1890s.

The continual problem of all the Boer republics had been lack of funds. Always impoverished, they had been at the mercy of the more affluent Cape Colony. The South African Republic had never been able to work out a satisfactory rebate system for imports with Cape Colony. In 1885 Paul Kruger had decided that he could not obtain enough capital to construct his own railway to the sea through Mozambique. He had reluctantly agreed to a continuation of the Kimberley railroad line into the republic. The discovery of gold changed all this. Kruger's government which was hardly solvent in 1884 had later a yearly revenue of over $7,000,000. Land transfers, customs payments, license fees, and stamp duties provided Kruger with funds beyond his most fantastic dreams of a few years before. He now had the economic power to secure the political and economic independence of his country from Britain.

Kruger, after the gold strike, began the construction of a railway that would make him independent of the Cape. The line from the border of the republic to Delagoa Bay was finished in 1889 and was connected to Pretoria in 1894. Meanwhile, a railway line from Natal had reached the border in 1891 and one from Port Elizabeth the following year. The Cape line was extended to the Rand in 1892 while the Natal line was not completed until 1895. All rail shipping through the republic was controlled by the Netherlands South African Railway Company which juggled rates and priorities to its own advantage. When the Cape line in 1894 cut the freight rates in the section across Cape Colony, the Netherlands Company increased them threefold in the republic. In the following year the Rand mining companies attempted to bypass the Transvaal section of the Cape line by off-loading their goods to ox wagons for the trip through the republic. A major crisis arose in 1895 when President Kruger closed the fords across the Vaal River to these shipments. This action showed conclusively that Kruger intended to keep control of the economic mechanisms of his state.

Gold was not an unmixed blessing for the farmers and burghers of the republic. Necessities connected with extracting and refining the gold brought a flood of foreigners to the Transvaal area. With them came the industrial world of the nineteenth century. Men whose entire lives had been bounded by the veld, their farms, families, and their strict religion now confronted a mass intrusion of foreigners. Kruger and his volkraad if they wished the newfound prosperity to continue could not prevent the entry of those necessary to work the mines. However, they could attempt to exercise strict control over them. The two most obvious examples of Kruger's attitude are the rule established for the operation of companies and the government's attitude toward the mass of outsiders or Uitlanders.

The government maintained its control of the mining operators by forcing them to deal with state monopolies for essential goods. Particularly onerous to the operators was the dynamite monopoly. Operators were forced to purchase what they considered poor material at inflated prices for this most necessary product. Railway rates would have been high under any circumstances, but Kruger's policies and the actions of the Netherlands South African Railway Company made them even higher. State control and the distance of the mines from the sea combined to limit the profits of the British and Cape entrepreneurs.

The Uitlander population which by 1895 numbered approximately 175,000 posed a threat to the republic if laws were not passed restricting their participation in political affairs. Until the discovery of gold there were no rigorous tests to determine citizenship. Men could travel freely, do business, and own property in all areas of southern Africa. Three presidents of the South African Republic had been British citizens. After the gold strike the Boers began to emphasize *Het Volk*, the people, and their uniqueness as a nation. Kruger's government systematically raised the citizenship and franchise requirements to the point where after 1895 it was almost impossible for an Uitlander to become a citizen. This disenfranchised class, twice the size of the Boer population, paid nine-tenths of the taxes.

The reaction of Kruger's government toward the mine operators and the Uitlanders created tensions by the mid-1890s which would have to be resolved if the republic were not to be torn apart. The expansion of British influence northward into Central Africa complicated the resolution of the Uitlander problem within the republic. The failure of Kruger to moderate his internal policies combined with increasing British imperialism throughout Africa were the major factors which led to the Boer War.

The Jameson Raid and preliminaries to war

Cecil Rhodes had followed a moderate course of action in wooing the Boers within Cape Colony and in the republics until 1894. Although one of the "Rand lords," he had given scant attention to the complaints of the Uitlanders concerning the franchise and other alleged abuses by the Kruger government. However, by 1895 he had emerged as one of their defenders and had openly assumed a more bellicose attitude toward the Transvaal government. Finally, in late 1895, he abandoned all caution and sanctioned military intervention in the internal affairs of the South African Republic. Why this sudden shift in policy? One answer is obviously the worsening condition of his health. The illness which had brought him to South Africa had never been completely cured and after a serious influenza attack in 1891 he seemed less vigorous. He stated a number of times that he did not expect to live past forty-five. If he were to achieve his aims of a unified South Africa, then he could not afford to wait much longer. Correlated with this was his fear of the growing strength of the South African Republic and the possibility of its alliance with Germany. Perhaps he realized that Kruger could not be "squared"; he wanted nothing which Rhodes could give him.

Rhodes was not the first high British official to think seriously of direct imperial intervention into the Transvaal with an uprising of the Uitlanders. The governor and high commissioner, Sir Henry Loch, after his visit to Pretoria in 1894 became convinced that the Uitlanders were ready to begin a revolt. Loch formulated a plan for intervention by imperial troops in the eventuality of such an uprising. These plans were communicated to the colonial secretary, the Marquis of Ripon, who appears to have restrained the aggressive high commissioner.

In December 1894, Rhodes went to London to lend his support to the selection of Sir Hercules Robinson to replace the retiring Loch as governor. Robinson had previously been governor from 1881 to 1889. He had supported Rhodes over the issue of granting a charter to the British South African Company and was deeply involved in the operations of that company and also that of De Beers. Further, he was over seventy years old and was in poor health. He could obviously be used to further Rhodes' plans. Despite a few minor notes of protest, Robinson was appointed governor and high commissioner.

Rhodes' plans for direct intervention were basically the same as Loch's. The high commissioner was pressured to turn over a strip of British territory connecting the Cape with the Rhodesian frontier to the company. This ostensibly was to further the construction of the railway and was accomplished in October 1895. Rhodes could then strip Matabeleland and Mashonaland of company police and concentrate these at Mafeking under the command of Dr. Leander Starr Jameson. The key to the plan was the actions of the Uitlander leaders in Johannesburg. In 1892 they had formed a National Union to agitate for Uitlander rights. Financed in 1895 by Rhodes and other "Rand lords," they began to organize for an armed uprising. Guns and ammunition were smuggled into the Transvaal. At the signal the Uitlanders were supposed to stage their revolt, seize the armory at Pretoria, and keep Kruger's forces tied down. Jameson, on the pretext of protecting British lives and property, would then invade the western Transvaal. At this juncture Robinson ostensibly acting as a peacemaker would go to Pretoria. Backed by imperial troops, he would then dictate terms to Kruger.

By mid-December 1895, everything was in readiness and the date for the uprising was set for the end of the month. Jameson's force at Pitsani on the border eagerly awaited the signal. Then the leaders in Johannesburg began to quarrel among themselves. In the light of harsh reality they began to see that most Uitlanders, although dissatisfied over some things, were in no mood for armed rebellion. The date for the revolt was postponed until after a general meeting to be held on January 8. Rhodes, fully informed of these events, decided on December 28 to call off the invasion. He sent an ambiguous telegram to Jameson informing him of this. Jameson was also visited by representatives of the Johannesburg committee and told of the developments there. Jameson, nevertheless, on his own initiative decided to precipitate the general revolt and took his armed force across the Transvaal border on the last day of the year.

Kruger, who was aware of the general outlines of the proposed action, kept the Johannesburg area under surveillance. Piet Cronje, hearing of the invasion on Sunday, December 30, called up a commando of some 200 men and later joined a force of approximately 300 under H. P. Malan and F. J. Potgieter. Jameson's force attempted to fight its way through a narrow valley and was later surrounded at Doornkop. Poorly led and attempting to implement an ill-conceived plan, the tired invaders surrendered to Cronje. The column lost fifty-eight men dead and wounded. More important, Jameson's precipitous action all but destroyed any chance of peacefully resolving the differences between Britain and the South African Republic.

The raiders were taken to Johannesburg and tried, most of them escaping with heavy fines. A few were sentenced to death, but these sentences were immediately commuted to prison terms and a fine. Dr. Jameson and his immediate staff were turned over to the British government for trial. By this shrewd move Kruger placed the responsibility for punishment on the British. The leaders were duly convicted and given light terms, and Jameson served only four months. Far more important than these actions was the question of determining who was officially responsible. Rhodes immediately resigned as prime minister of the Cape. Never again would his influence be such that he could expect the British government to accept automatically his solutions to South African problems. A committee of inquiry of the Cape parliament did not assess guilt. A further commission of the House of Commons investigated, condemned the actions of Rhodes and Jameson, but exonerated other high British officials including Robinson and Joseph Chamberlain, the colonial secretary.

Afrikaner leaders such as President Steyn of the Free State and W. P. Schreiner of the Cape who had previously followed a moderate policy moved to support the Transvaal. Kruger's harsh attitudes and suspicions of British motives appeared to be vindicated. The volksraad of the Orange Free State committed their nation to an alliance with the Transvaal. Kruger's government passed new harsh legislation directed at the Uitlanders and their position became even more untenable than before the raid. Kaiser Wilhelm's telegram congratulating the Transvaal on the Jameson action and subsequent German actions disturbed Britain and gave Kruger hope for definite German support in case of future difficulty. Before 1896 there was a large body of Afrikaner opinion which disagreed with Kruger's policies toward the Uitlander. After the raid this opinion was all but silenced. Kruger had little difficulty winning the presidential election of 1898.

In 1897 Sir Alfred Milner replaced the aged Robinson as governor of Cape Colony and high commissioner. A trusted friend and confidant of Chamberlain, he became the key figure in a growingly aggressive British policy in southern Africa. Heretofore the attitude of the London government toward imperialism had been cautious, allowing men such as Rhodes to plan and finance expansion. Chamberlain brought a new aggressiveness to the Colonial Office. This was shown in his willingness to support Rhodes' plan for the raid. Milner transferred this aggressiveness into action as the chief representative of the crown in South Africa. After 1897 he, rather than Cape politicians, made the major policy decisions.

Although convinced from the beginning that conflict was inevitable, Milner proceeded very carefully until after the Transvaal elections of 1898. After that date he began to press the Uitlander case upon the Kruger government. Kruger refused to grant any significant concessions. Milner was aware that the Uitlander issue was only a mask to cover the British decision to control all of southern Africa. A final attempt at compromise was made by moderate elements who brought Milner and Kruger together at Bloemfontein in June 1899. The failure of the conference spurred such advisers to Kruger as the young Jan Christian Smuts to urge the acceptance of major modifications of the franchise laws. By early fall of 1899, the Transvaal had granted Milner the majority of his demands concerning Uitlander rights. However, Milner had shifted his attack to the question of suzerainty. Milner claimed that the Transvaal had been given only conditional independence by the London Convention and that Britain had retained ultimate control over the republic. This contention was too extreme even for Boer opponents of Kruger to accept. In September and October both sides were preparing for the inevitable conflict. The war came when the Transvaal delivered an ultimatum calling for the withdrawal of all British troops from the frontier by October 11. The ultimatum was ignored by Milner and Chamberlain, and the Boer War began.

The Boer War

The onset of the war caught the British totally unprepared. If Milner and his superiors had any intention of carrying out the implications of their planned ultimatum, they were guilty of gross negligence in building up the military. Total British strength in South Africa was 29,000 men of which over 10,000 were volunteers. These forces were scattered from Natal in the east to Mafeking in the west. The bulk of the British forces were in Natal. There Sir George White commanded over 13,000 regulars and 3,000 volunteer troops. Approximately 8,000 of these were concentrated in the town of Ladysmith. Small garrisons were scattered along the northern border. Colonel Robert Baden-Powell commanded 1,250 troops at Mafeking while Colonel R. G. Kekewich deployed not quite a battalion of regulars at Kimberley.

Even before hostilities started, the Transvaal began to call all adult males to serve. Kruger's forces thus at the beginning of the war numbered over 85,000 men. They were supplied with the finest equipment available from European arms manufacturers. Their Mauser rifle was superior to the British Lee-Enfield and the Afrikaner field guns were also better than those of the British. The Afrikaners from both Boer republics were hardy outdoorsmen used to hard work and long hours in the saddle. Boer leaders were very familiar with every section of the country and they were operating on short supply lines. The deficiencies of the Afrikaner armies which became apparent soon after the war began were related to their informal militia organization. There were few regular troops, officers were elected, and none had ever commanded large units before. The major commanders, Joubert and Cronje, were old, conservative, and not prepared to act with the same dispatch as the younger officers, Botha, de Wet, de la Rey, and Smuts.

The Boer offensive in the opening phase of the conflict was designed to keep pressure on the long northern front while Commandant Joubert with 20,000 troops drove through Natal and secured the port of Durban. By mid-October Mafeking and Kimberley were invested and Joubert's forces had met no real resistance in Natal. Sir George White attempted to break out of Ladysmith and fall back to join expected reinforcements from Britain, but the Boers forced him into the city after White's troops had suffered over 1,500 casualties. Joubert failed to follow up his advantage and settled into a siege of Ladysmith.

Sir Redvers Buller arrived in Cape Town on October 31 with the only organized army corps then available to Britain. The situation was so crucial that Buller decided to break up the corps and sent part of it north under the command of Lord Methuen to relieve Kimberley, and another segment under General Gatacre to Molteno. Buller, with the bulk of the reinforcements, proceeded to Natal where twenty years before he had won a Victoria Cross in the Zulu War. Now, over sixty, conservative, and with years of sedentary duty at Whitehall behind him, he was called upon to accomplish a near miracle.

Methuen's forces on November 25 were briefly halted by Cronje on the Modder River. British casualties in this engagement numbered over 450 men. Regrouping, Methuen pushed north only to lose another battle at Magersfontein on December 11 with twice the number of casualties of the previous battle. Gatacre at Stormberg on the previous day had been defeated by another Boer force. There British casualties amounted to over 700 men. The final blow came when Buller in Natal attempted to cross the Tugela River near Colenso. In two coordinate actions the British lost almost 1,700 men and were forced to retreat. This "Black Week" was to be the height of Boer success and the lowest point of British fortunes. The only good news for Britain was the tenacity with which the defenders of Ladysmith, Kimberley, and Mafeking held out.

Joubert and Cronje, by besieging certain cities, halted the war of movement and gave the British government time to build up their forces. Lord Roberts, the most outstanding British general, was given command of all troops in southern Africa. Sir Herbert Kitchener, fresh from his victory over the Mahdists in the Sudan, was appointed second in command. Reservists were called up and offers of assistance from all parts of the British empire were accepted. In the late months of 1899 troops from all parts of the empire flowed into South Africa. Martial law was proclaimed in Cape Colony largely because of the fear of the large numbers of Boer sympathizers resident there. Kruger, who had expected more direct aid from Germany, was sadly disappointed. All the Transvaal received from the rest of the world were expressions of sympathy.

Roberts and Kitchener reached Cape Town on January 10, 1900, just before Buller attempted another movement into northern Natal. At Spion Kop Buller lost over 600 men and once again was forced to retreat. By the end of the month, however, Roberts had completed his plans for counterattack and deployment of the necessary forces. Since the bulk of the Boer armies was in the east, Roberts decided to force the center, invade the Orange Free State, and then drive directly toward Pretoria. The offensive began on February 11, and despite considerable resistance, broke Cronje's front and relieved Kimberley. The Boer army's retreat was cut off and on February 27 Cronje was forced to surrender with 4,000 men. The following day Buller's army which had finally managed to cross the Tugela River relieved Ladysmith. In one major stroke Roberts had smashed the old Afrikaner army organization. Boer forces retreated in considerable disorder, particularly those operating in the Orange Free State.

On March 13, 1900, Bloemfontein fell and British troops pressed inexorably on toward Pretoria. Mafeking was relieved on May 17 after being under siege for 217 days. Baden-Powell's troops there had lost over 300 men and over 460 civilians had died, but they had pinned down a much larger Boer force. Louis Botha succeeded to commandant-general of the

Afrikaner forces on the death of Joubert on March 25, and began to organize the Boer armies into smaller striking forces. However, he could not prevent the fall of Johannesburg on June 1 and Pretoria three days later. Paul Kruger left the Transvaal for Europe in August, broken in health but still hoping to find European support for his battle. Lord Roberts formally annexed the Transvaal in September. Believing the war to be over, he relinquished his command to Kitchener and returned to England. The British government assumed that all that was left to be done was the formality of a peace treaty.

The Boers under the leadership of ex-President Steyn of the Orange Free State and Botha, however, had no intention of surrendering. Smaller mobile units under brilliant commanders such as de Wet, de la Ray, and Smuts harassed the British. They tore up railway lines, attacked smaller British forces, burned supplies, and their cavalry audaciously moved even into Cape Colony. Operating in friendly country, these guerrilla forces were almost impossible to apprehend. Kitchener, with an army greatly depleted by a government which believed the war to be over, evolved new tactics. He converted a large portion of his forces to mounted infantry to increase their mobility, built blockhouses along the rail lines, burned farmsteads, and instituted the century's first concentration camps. Knowing that he had to deprive Botha's groups of the help of civilians, he cleared whole districts and put them in a number of camps. By mid-1902 there were over 125,000 civilians in these detention areas. Poor sanitation facilities and the inadequacy of medical science to treat many diseases rather than British cruelty combined to kill over 26,000 women and children in these camps before the war ended.

In March 1901, Kitchener met Botha at Middelburg and offered lenient terms to the Boers if they would surrender. However, the terms also dictated a yielding of their independence and this the Boer leaders refused, and the war dragged on for another year. Finally exhausted and convinced of the futility of further resistance, thirty representatives of each republic on May 15, 1902, discussed at length the British terms. After almost two weeks of conferences with Milner and Kitchener the five Boer generals, Botha, Smuts, de Wet, Hertzog, and de la Rey signed the Treaty of Vereeniging on May 31. The Boer War was over.

Reconstruction

The war had caused profound changes not only in southern Africa, but also in Britain. Liberal opposition to the war was at first masked by the initial disasters and the quick counterthrust of Roberts in early 1900. Nevertheless, in the so-called "Khaki" election of 1900 the Conservative party received only fifty-three percent of the votes. As the war dragged on and civilian casualties increased, more Englishmen became openly pro-Boer. The war also showed how dangerously alone Britain was. Only the Dominion areas supported the Conservative action. No major state expressed sympathy with Britain's position. The Anglo-Japanese treaty of

1902, the French Entente of 1904, and a similar agreement with Russia in 1907 flowed directly from Britain's sense of isolation during the Boer War.

In South Africa the war which had first seemed so simple had caused tremendous problems. Loyalties were not clear cut. Men with English names had fought with the Boers while most Cape Boers remained loyal to Britain and many had joined the British forces. By the Treaty of Vereeniging, Milner had become the chief executive officer of two new crown colonies. But these new additions were impoverished. Whole areas had been depopulated, farmsteads burned, and the mines had ceased production. The immediate economic task confronting Milner was to resettle the land, begin mining operations, and restore the railways to working order.

By the treaty the British provided £3,000,000 immediately; and later a £35,000,000 loan with extremely low interest was floated to continue development. With the cooperation of most of the Boer leaders, Milner and his "Kindergarten" began immediately to direct the huge task of reconstruction. This so-called "Kindergarten" was composed of brilliant young men such as John Buchan, Lionel Curtis, and Philip Kerr who were later to forge distinguished careers in government and the law. In the years immediately following the war they provided Milner with a competent, idealistic administrative nucleus for the two defeated areas. By the time Milner left South Africa in 1905 the major task of economic reconstruction was completed. The Transvaal area, with the mines once again producing, was able to assume a major financial role in southern Africa.

Political development which involved reconciliation betwen Boer and Briton was more difficult to achieve. By the Treaty of Vereeniging Britain promised to grant responsible government to the two conquered areas as soon as possible. Martial law was ended and normal civilian government reinstituted in Cape Colony in 1902. Responsible government had continued in Natal during the war. Lord Milner was afraid that the institution of responsible government in the Transvaal and Orange Free State would result in a resurgence of Afrikaner nationalism. In the Orange Free State, Fischer and Steyn had already begun the *Oranje Unie* party and in the Transvaal Botha and Smuts had started the *Het Volk* party. Lord Selborne, who succeeded Milner, favored responsible government and after the Liberal victory in the British elections of 1906 this became a reality. The Transvaal received responsible government in 1906 and the Orange Free State the following year.

One of the purposes of the Boer War had been to provide one government for all of southern Africa. That had only been partially achieved by bringing the ex-republics under the crown. There still existed four different governments administering four differing sets of laws. The old divisive factors of customs and railroads which had contributed so much to disunity in the past were still operative. Each colony also had its own separate policy toward black Africans and Asiatic immigrants. To rationalize some of these problems Governor Selborne issued his famous memorandum on closer unity, and the political leaders of the colonies agreed to meet and discuss a full range of problems relating to cooperation.

The convention to consider common problems met at Durban on October 12, 1908, and later in November moved to Cape Town. Each area was represented by its prime minister, leading figures in the government, and also some members of the opposition. Key figures were Botha and Smuts from the Transvaal, Jameson and Sauer from the Cape, Hertzog and Steyn from the Free State, and Morcom and Smythe from Natal. It soon became obvious that closer economic cooperation would be nearly impossible without a concomitant political reorganization. The convention thus constructed a draft cónstitution in early 1909 which was then considered by the parliaments of the four areas. After approval it was passed by the British parliament as the South Africa Act of 1909. By its terms on May 31, 1910, just eight years after Vereeniging, the Union of South Africa became a political reality.

The South Africa Act provided for a unitary government system with one parliament and ministry. The parliament consisted of an elected house of assembly and a partially nominated and partially indirectly elected senate. The executive consisted of a governor-general to represent the crown who initially had substantive powers over the defense, trade, and foreign affairs. The ministry, headed by a prime minister, was responsible to the lower house. To protect certain interests of the smaller colonies there was created provincial councils with powers of control over local matters among which was education. A supreme court with appellate and provincial divisions was also established. The high court very soon established the principle of judicial review.

Three questions almost destroyed the functioning of the convention. One concerned the location of the capital. A compromise was reached by which Cape Town became the legislative center, Pretoria the executive capital, and Bloemfontein the seat of the appellate court. Another factor concerned the national language while an even more difficult problem related to franchise qualifications. The problem of national language was solved by designating both Dutch and English as official languages. No workable compromise could be reached for reconciling differing attitudes toward the black African and his potential use of the franchise. The Cape was the only area which allowed the vote to nonwhites, and the Cape delegation refused to abandon this principle. Botha, Smuts, and Hertzog would not accept the granting of the vote to blacks, even in theory. In the South Africa Act, therefore, voting regulations were left as they had been before the act, although it was stipulated that only Europeans could serve in parliament. Language equality and the franchise regulations were guaranteed by the so-called "entrenched clauses" of the act. These stated that to change either stipulation required not a simple majority vote of the Assembly, but a two-thirds vote of both houses sitting togeher. Thus in one crucial area, native affairs, the Union Act left unchanged the four separate attitudes toward Africans and Cape Colored.

SEVEN
European mechanisms of control in Africa

Political activity in most of the territories of Africa were minimal until after World War II. Egypt, Ethiopia, South Africa, and Liberia were the only independent states. The rest of the vast area was directly controlled by European powers. These European states ruled their dependencies in differing ways. Since African traditional societies had largely been governments of consensus there was little African experience upon which the leaders of African political opinion could draw. Thus the rapid advancement of African areas toward independence was accomplished in a political environment almost totally European. The nationalist leaders had been educated in European schools either in Africa or Europe, worked in European firms, and drew their concepts of the nature of the state from European models and philosophies. Perhaps even more restrictive was the fact that the various concessions leading to independence were granted in sequential modifications to an existing colonial system. The colonial systems of France, Britain, Belgium, and Portugal differed radically in their form and philosophy. Thus African states after independence were various reflections of European educational and political systems present in Africa. Before detailing the development of political movements in African territories, one must look carefully at the different political systems created by the European powers to control their African empires.

British Africa

Before introducing the skeleton of the British form of rule in Africa one must be aware of certain factors implicit within the British system. The most obvious of these is the stress placed on the workability of any administrative unit. The British of the nineteenth century operated on the presumption that their system was best and that they could bring law and order to "lesser breeds without the law." This did not mean that individual

177

administrators understood completely what their system was. They were not ideologists and therefore did not attempt to rationalize their control of a given territory with any preconceived ideology. Their experience in the older portions of their empire had confirmed for them the rightness of their approach. Thus the British could be very flexible in the establishment of their control systems in Africa without feeling it necessary to follow exactly a standardized model.

A second point to stress is the decentralized nature of British institutions. Although theoretically the British parliament retains supremacy of legislative, executive, and judicial functions, in practice this power by the mid-nineteenth century had been shared for over a hundred years with local officials of the shires and the boroughs. Any dependent government system designed by the British would, therefore, leave a large measure of power in the hands of the governor and councils of a given territory. The Colonial Office did have the authority to make crucial decisions without consulting lesser officials. However, in practice it seldom acted this way, preferring to consult directly with the governors of its empire before arriving at any major decision. The Colonial Office came to depend upon this advice and they generally allowed such strong governors as Lord Frederick Lugard or Sir Donald Cameron to exercise almost total practical control over the territories which they administered.

After the scramble, there were three differing systems of control practiced by the British in Africa. The first form of possession was the eighteenth-century colony where large numbers of English persons had actually migrated to the overseas area. Cape Colony, with its large Boer and, later, English population, and Natal, settled largely by the English, conformed to this type of colony. In both areas advanced forms of representative and, later, responsible government was granted freely to the white population before the so-called scramble for Africa began. With the successful conclusion of the Boer War, the two Boer republics of the Transvaal and the Orange Free State were soon associated with the British areas to form the Union of South Africa. The union from its inception had responsible government with an almost total control of its own domestic affairs. By 1926 the union had gained the right to manage its own foreign affairs; and, as a member of the Commonwealth, it was to all extents an independent state freely associated with Britain.

The second type of British possession was Egypt where Britain did not legally exercise sovereign powers until 1914. Before that date the khedive and Egyptian government agencies were ostensibly in control. The reality was considerably different. The British consul was the real power in Egypt although he worked behind the facade of Egyptian and Turkish legalism. During World War I, Britain was the open, legal protector of Egypt. However, they accepted a large portion of Egyptian governmental practice and institutions, modifying these only when it became necessary. The reconquest of the Sudan had been completed in 1898 based upon Egyptian, not British, claims to the territory. The condominium government which was established for the Sudan was a hybrid system and made of the Sudan, as with Egypt, a special case.

The third type of British possession in Africa was what could be called the dependent empire. These territories had largely been gained in the period from 1880 to 1900 even though British possession of some of the coastal areas predated the scramble. These older enclaves were generally designated colony areas while the much larger hinterland territories were normally called protectorates. In the areas under direct administration the form of rule was a modified crown colony system. This consisted of a governor, secretariat, executive council, and legislative council. In the much larger protectorates, the British early adopted the system of utilizing indigenous rulers to carry out most of the processes of local government. This system, called indirect rule, could be conducted with a minimum of British personnel and at very little expense. Customary law was accepted as was African land tenure. The theory was to upset the life of the people as little as possible. Traditional rulers were supervised and directed by representatives of the central government. A typical British dependent area would be governed thus:

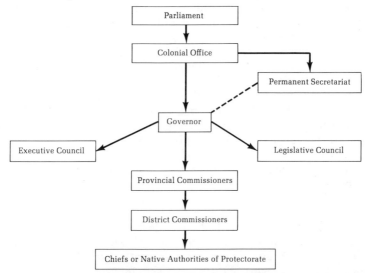

British colonial administration in the dependent empire in Africa until the grant of independence to a territory is a study of unity and diversity. The unity was that of similar structures of government established in all areas of British Africa. These institutions were basically simple and extremely malleable. Thus, while the outline of government of a colony or protectorate was of the same type as imposed elsewhere, its actual function could be quite different. Contrary to the French attempt to create unity, the British were normally pragmatic, attempting to modify the structure to fit a given environment.

This diversity within a common framework can be seen most clearly in the protected areas where there were already established highly structured and efficient African systems such as in Uganda and Northern Nigeria. In such territories the British attempted few administrative changes. Most of the changes instituted were designed to bring the administrative and judicial practices in rough alignment with British policies. District officers in Uganda and Northern Nigeria performed a dual role. Where the central government wished a specific reform enacted, the district officers became in fact the real rulers of their areas. However, in most cases district officers were content to allow the traditional authorities to govern while they assumed advisory roles. In less developed areas the British authorities tried to recreate what they believed to be the traditional system. In some cases the British organized what they thought to be an African system of government indigenous to an area but which was really foreign to the people. In many places the British created their own chiefs who were not totally accepted by the people. With native rulers of such questionable traditional antecedents, provincial and district officers played a more direct role in all areas of local government. They became, in fact, paramount chiefs. Thus, although the facade of indirect rule was maintained, the reality of power rested with the British local officers.

Indirect rule in British Africa was, at first, a pragmatic solution to the problem of governing large territories with a minimum of expenditure. One must remember that of all the imperial powers Britain had possessed a large empire before the scramble. It had already considerable knowledge of governing nonwestern people. Indirect rule of various kinds had already been used throughout the empire, particularly in India. Thus the British system of rule in its African protectorates was not a new creation but rather a modification of an already extant, successful one. Even as British control over African territory progressed, the governors and administrators were applying indirect rule to the conquered or ceded areas. After expansion had ceased, the Colonial Office and governors attempted by a series of modifications in all their protectorates to organize the ad hoc systems into comprehensive, more rational entities. Later Lord Frederick Lugard and other theorists provided the philosophical underpinning for the system and indirect rule came to be regarded by the Colonial Office in the interwar period as an almost sacrosanct institution. It did seem to fit the needs of both the governors and the governed. Its costs were minimal and it apparently did not disturb the Africans' traditional pattern of social, economic, and political life. Indirect rule throughout the British dependencies thus tended to become static and in some cases moribund. Needed improvements in land utilization and conservation, health, communication, and education were often delayed or in many cases never effected because it was feared that these reforms would upset the balance of traditional rule. The practicalities of protectorate rule became contrary to the wishes of such administrators and theorists as Lord Lugard and Sir Donald Cameron. They had envisioned indirect rule as a vehicle for change compatible with African institutions: a system which would preserve the best of African culture while allowing for progress. However, despite the efforts of a few colonial administrators, the protectorate systems remained static and progressively isolated from developments in the colony areas.

Almost all the machinery of the government was concentrated in the colony area. Despite the reluctance of Britain to spend money, these sections were the most developed in British Africa. Streets were paved, modern sewage and drainage systems were built, harbors improved, and the railway and road systems began there. Most of the medical and educational facilities were concentrated in the colony area or in the larger, Westernized cities. All the important firms and banks maintained their main offices near the seat of government.

In time there developed in the colony and urban areas, without direct government encouragement, an African intellectual elite generally composed of the professional middle class. Small in numbers, these lawyers, doctors, and teachers had been educated in Britain and some were steeped in the ideas of European liberty. In the 1920s and 1930s they began to demand that the autocratically appointed government be modified to give the African a voice in his government. By 1939, in the Gold Coast and Nigeria particularly, there had been formed the nucleus of colony-based political parties.

The British administration prior to World War II had in some cases begun to modify the central government apparatus by appointing Africans to positions on the legislative councils and executive councils. Further, the British utilized large numbers of European-trained Africans in the civil service. Most of these held only the lower echelon positions, but their numbers complemented the smaller, more influential group of native traders and professional men. In some areas such as in Northern Rhodesia, African schoolmasters and teachers formed the leadership segment of early political movements. The coalescing of all these groups provided the nucleus of the post-World War II political parties.

It is important to note that all African political parties in British Africa before 1945 were created by a Westernized middle class and had no popular base either in the cities or country areas. The British administration was convinced that the key to the future for their African dependencies lay in modifying the system of indirect rule already established. Thus educated Africans were carefully watched to make certain they did not interfere with the functioning of the protectorate systems. Whenever an organization appeared to be gaining broad popular support, the British authorities would ban it. It was not until the 1950s that the Colonial Office finally abandoned its support of traditional rulers and began to make real concessions to the educated few who controlled the urban political parties.

A factor even more important for the dependent empire than Britain's commitment to indirect rule after World War I was its dedication to frugality. The most sacrosanct rule for governments of British territories was to "live within one's income" and not to expect the British taxpayers to support development schemes, no matter how worthwhile, beyond the financial capability of a territory. Reeling financially from the excessive expense of World War I, Britain could not afford her dependencies. This dictum enunciated by the home government caused all British African administrations to plan their finances in a most conservative manner. Thus a combination of caution and penury damned such poor areas as Sierra Leone and the Gambia to only minimal programs of harbor, road, and city improvements. The backwardness of the educational and health facilities in all British African territories is attributable, to a large degree, to lack of money. As one commentator noted, Britain ran her administration in tropical Africa "on the cheap."

When Britain ruled a multiracial society the forms of dependent government were modified. The actual development of Southern Rhodesia and Kenya will be detailed elsewhere. It is sufficient to note here only a few salient points concerning these territories. Southern Rhodesia, which enjoyed responsible government after 1923, was controlled entirely by the white minority. The government of Northern Rhodesia was also complicated by the presence of a large European population which was either engaged in farming or mining. Kenya, whose politics were complicated by both European and Indian minorities, ostensibly had the typical crown colony protectorate system. Actually the presence of the influential farmers of the white highlands precipitated in 1919–1920 demands for self-government. Although these demands were refused, the white minority was confirmed in its special prerogative in the highlands. They controlled the economic wealth, and white representatives were the first to be nominated to the executive and legislative councils. The presence of a white resident population in all these areas complicated and, in the case of Rhodesia, prevented the devolution of authority to the African majority.

French Africa

French colonial administration until World War II was direct with ultimate control over colonial areas resting with the minister of colonies in Paris. Not surprisingly, it reflected domestic governmental organization and showed the French penchant for detailed organization and centralization. Although there were many changes in the form of government in France in the nineteenth century, there was no change in the concentration of government power in Paris which had been so noticeable after the revolution of 1789. French constitutions, whether monarchical or republican, tended to be complex structures reflecting general theories and goals. It is, therefore, not surprising that where British administration was distinguished by its pragmatism, French government in colonial areas was derived from ideological concepts. With the exception of Senegal, French occupation of West and Central Africa occurred in the brief period from 1880 to 1900 during the early years of the Third Republic. Much of this occupation had been accomplished by the military whose approach to governing these territories was simple and direct. These ad hoc military regimes were soon replaced by relatively complex civilian structures which, however, retained the major decision-making powers for French authorities in Paris.

Important factors which contributed to the decrees which created civil government in much of Africa were the political and cultural goals which France hoped to achieve in her empire. Frankly stated, Frenchmen felt they must not only maintain order and financial stability, but they should also civilize the Africans under their control. This led to a policy of attempting the assimilation of some Africans concurrent with a policy of association with the mass of the population. By establishing the machinery of French culture in Africa, France made it possible for educated Africans to associate themselves directly with France. They could, by renouncing their African heritage, become Frenchmen with all the rights and privileges of citizens of metropolitan France. To be sure, only a small minority of Africans prior to 1944 had made this transition. However, for those who had become assimilated, it was necessary to provide for their inclusion into the political system, even to allowing them to become members of the metropolitan government.

Assimilation was an all inclusive goal and did not apply to only one territory, although Senegal was the prime beneficiary of the policy. The government organization of French Africa was relatively uniform and does not present the diversities which one notices in British Africa. The early decision to create two large federations also facilitated the adoption of a uniform policy for all of the African territories. This uniformity continued until the adoption of the *Loi cadre* in 1956 and the hope for some measure of uniformity existed in France through 1958.

By a decree of 1895 the Ivory Coast, Guinea, and Soudan were placed under the governor-general of Senegal. However, each territory had its own governor and the power of the governor-general was therefore minimal. Dahomey which had recently been conquered was not included, even theoretically, under his control. There were many shifts in attempting to federate these various territories until 1904 when the French West African Federation (AOF) was declared. This was composed of five territories— Senegal, Guinea, Dahomey, the Ivory Coast, and Upper Senegal-Niger. In 1920 Mauritania was declared a colony and added to the AOF, and by shifting boundaries and renaming territories, there emerged three new areas— the Soudan, Niger, and Upper Volta. In 1910 a similar grouping of the four territories of Chad, Ubangi-Shari, Gabon, and the Middle Congo was created. This was the Federation of French Equatorial Africa (AEF). These were entirely administrative entities with no independent rights and powers for the component territories. The chain of command was simple and direct, very similar to a military organization. However, the administrative officers at all levels were advised by councils whose powers were minimal but whose composition was quite complex. Government practices in each of these federations was modified until by 1920 they assumed the form which they retained until World War II.

With the exception of Senegal which will be discussed later, the system of government established in the AOF and AEF was the following:

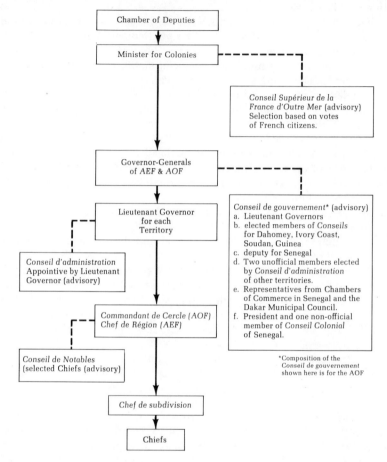

The administrative structure of each federation resembled a pyramid. At the apex was the governor-general, the only official in the federation empowered to deal directly with the colonial ministry in Paris. He was required, in theory, to gain approval for most of his actions from the minister. In actual practice, particularly in the earlier years of the century, the governor-general because of poor communications often acted on his own initiative. This factor combined with his discretionary power in issuing decrees decided upon in Paris into action in the federation enabled the governor-general to offset partially the undue centralization of the system. Each colony within the federation also had a lieutenant-governor and a staff of French civil servants. Under normal circumstances they served to carry out orders passed on to them by the colonial ministry and the governor-general's office.

Within each colony the largest administrative unit in the AOF was called a *cercle* and in the AEF a *région*. These were further divided into smaller units called subdivisions which were in turn composed of cantons, a collection of African villages. Each of the segments of a federation was administered by French officials whose primary responsibilities were to maintain law and order and to see that the decrees from higher authority were carried out by the African rulers.

At the level of local government, direct administrative control by the *Commandants de Cercles* and the *Chefs de subdivision* was more obvious than in most British territories. Although it is true that the British form of indirect rule was more direct than is often believed, the traditional chiefs in British areas were allowed a large measure of autonomy from direct administrative guidance. In French territories the chiefs were maintained and supported but left with little discretionary powers of their own. In time they became paid servants of the administration and as such were expected to carry out orders of their superiors in the hierarchy.

At each successive level of government there existed advisory councils. These councils had no power to act independently of the responsible authority and each executive from the minister for colonies down to the *Commandant de Cercle* could accept or reject the advice of his councils. In 1925 the *conseils d'administrations* of the Ivory Coast, Dahomey, Soudan, and Guinea were increased by having two French citizens elected for the *conseil* by the Chambers of Commerce and Agriculture and by three non-citizens elected by a special African electorate. All other members continued to be appointed. In Mauritania and Niger the members of the *conseils* remained totally nominated until 1945.

Municipal government also was welded into the central administration. There were basically two types of municipalities. The first type had an elected council and an elected mayor with considerable administrative powers. Until 1955 there were only three cities of this type—Dakar, St. Louis, and Rufisque. The reasons for granting these cities more responsibility are to be found in the earlier grant of freedom to the communes of Senegal. The second type of municipal organization was one in which the French administration exercised a large degree of control. There were three different grades of cities in this latter type of system. The first grade had its municipal commission totally nominated by the lieutenant-governors. The second grade had the commission elected by a small portion of the electorate, while the third had its commission elected by universal suffrage. Cities in all three grades of this second type had mayors appointed by the lieutenant-governors and they could also be removed by the same process. Thus except in rare instances the cities in French colonial Africa were controlled by the French central administration.

Senegal differed from all other territories in French Africa because of its long association with metropolitan France. In April 1848, *originaires* of annexed territory were given the right to vote for a representative to the Chamber of Deputies in Paris. In the nineteenth century this area was divided into four communes—St. Louis, Goree, Rufisque, and Dakar. Citizens of these four communes were regarded as French citizens and these divisions were legally confirmed in 1916. In the beginning only Europeans and Creoles were chosen as deputies. The first African deputy, Blaise Diagne, was elected in 1914. To secure this seat and maintain it, Diagne created a powerful political organization which dominated Senegalese political life until the 1930s. Councils headed by an elected mayor were elected within the four communes to deal with municipal affairs. The powers of the elected councils were limited by the central administration. In other communes throughout French Africa there was a form of representation allowed, but the average African could not meet the requirements to vote.

In Senegal there existed from 1879 onward a *Conseil Général* of twenty members elected by the French citizens in the four communes and in the territory under direct French control. All other areas were considered protectorate areas and were not represented on the *Conseil*. Its powers were basically advisory except in budgetary matters. Here they exercised real control. Between 1890 and 1920, during the reconstruction of the government of Senegal and the creation of the federations, the financial and advisory powers of the *Conseil Général* were greatly restricted. In 1920 the protectorate which had been under separate jurisdiction since 1890 was again joined to the direct control areas and the *conseil* became once again the major legislative body. The name was changed in 1920 to the *Conseil Colonial* and was expanded to include twenty chiefs representing the protected areas. Various changes were made in the ratios between the numbers of chiefs and elected members before 1939. In that year a substantial addition of eighteen elected French subjects was made to the *Conseil Colonial*. The *conseil,* although supervised by the administration and checked by the veto power of the governor, played an important role in Senegal. It affected policy making because it could withhold funds necessary for the implementation of new projects. It also served as an important training ground for Africans in the exercise of government on a high level. Taken together with elected deputies to the French legislature, municipal government, and the French type of indirect rule, the *Conseil Colonial* gave the Senegalese a voice in their government prior to 1939 unique in French Africa.

Belgian Africa

In the decade prior to the end of World War I, Belgium had a twofold problem in the Congo. One was the creation of a viable political system to rule the huge area of the Congo basin. The second closely interrelated problem was the repeal of those punitive measures enacted by the regime of King Leopold II. The constitution of the Congo for almost fifty years was the Colonial Charter of 1908. This charter established the basic framework of the reconstructed government with a resident governor-general and governors for each of the four provinces which were later expanded to six. The charter and subsequent legislation curtailed the use of forced labor, labor taxes, and abolished producer monopolies. Land controlled by concessionaire companies was also reduced in size and agents of the companies were prohibited from exercising government functions. The size of the Congo, the lack of staff, and Belgium's deep involvement in World War I delayed the implementation of many of these paper reforms. However, by 1920 the paternalistic Congo government which continued until independence had become a reality. This paternalism was predicated upon a strong centralized form of government with the locus of decision making in Belgium. Although the governor-generals had discretionary powers in administration and legislation, they acted in most cases as agents of policies decided upon by the colonial ministry in Brussels.

Belgian colonial policy was only partially motivated by the desire to exploit efficiently the mineral wealth of the Congo. It was also based on a series of assumptions, most of which were valid through the late 1950s. On the theoretical plane, Belgium assumed a relative equality of the African with the European. Colonial authorities viewed the Congo as a trust, an area where they, as representatives of a more advanced state system, should plan for the present and future well-being of the African. The Congo was by far the most planned for of any dependency of any European power. Belgian paternalism demanded this type of planning to effect ends held to be beneficial for both Africans and Belgians.

Europeans who entered the Congo had to prove that they had future employment and post monetary guarantees for their return to Europe if they should lose their positions. As a result, relatively few whites became permanent Congo residents. Those who did were, normally, government employees, skilled and professional persons, businessmen, or missionaries. In order to develop industry, particularly mining, a proportionately larger number of African workers were utilized in semiskilled positions than in French or British areas. This policy was quite important for thousands of Africans since companies such as *Union Minière du Haut Katanga* were exploiting systematically the mineral wealth of the Congo in the period after 1920. No European could own land in the Congo. Even the large companies held only long-term leases. This again was fully in accord with Belgian ideas of protecting the African.

Aside from maintaining law and order, the government saw its first responsibility to be the economic welfare of the African. Wage scales for urban and government workers were excellent by comparison to other territories. The government supervised building and attempted to maintain wherever possible reasonable living conditions. Medical facilities, government-run and those operated by missionaries, were among the best in Africa both as to size and quality, particularly in urban areas. In the field of education the Belgian government supported primary, secondary, and technical education through grants to missions and directly by operating its own schools. The Congo by the 1950s could boast a literacy rate of over forty percent while most dependencies of other European powers could show only a rate of between ten and thirty percent. However, little provision was made for advanced education in secondary schools and universities. Few Congolese attended European universities and until 1954, when Lovanium University was opened, the government actively discouraged higher liberal education.

This benevolent paternalistic attitude was carried over into the political organization of the state. European residents had no special rights as existed in other multiracial territories such as Rhodesia. Congolese were associated in large numbers with their government only on the lowest levels. Decision making in the Congo was reserved for Belgian appointive officials. The councils which existed on all levels of government were purely advisory and had no powers even comparable with the French advisory councils. The basic organization of the government of the Congo was as follows:

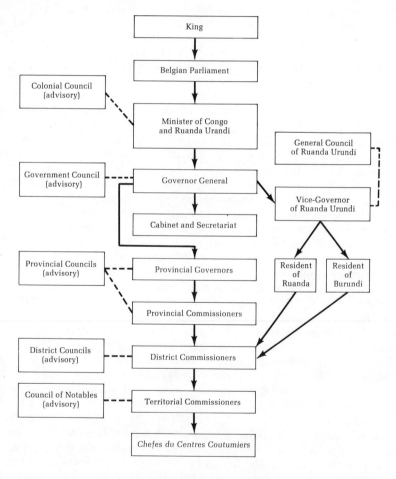

As the chart indicates, the government of the Congo was a European autocratic system with its center of control in Belgium. Only on the lowest levels were the Africans allowed to participate directly in political affairs. Over seventy-five percent of the Congolese population lived under a modified system of traditional rule. Here in these *Centres Coutumiers* traditional authorities were allowed to govern, subject to the control of officers of the central administration. Belgium before World War I followed a policy of supplanting traditional rulers with either European officers or government-appointed chiefs. Although these traditional rulers were later allowed to exercise more jural and executive authority than before, the district and provincial commissioners still retained ultimate power. In the 1950s certain further changes were instituted which created larger administrative units under the direction of appointed paramount chiefs. Also in the 1950s there were changes in the composition of the various councils to include a broader spectrum of representation from other social and economic groups within the African community.

The Belgian system of traditional chiefs met the needs of the majority of the agricultural people of the Congo. However, it was tightly controlled and did not serve as a school for future government leaders. Nor did the system give to the people of the Congo a sense of unity. The territory was so large and the peoples so diverse that the Belgians never considered inculcating in the people a feeling of loyalty to a political entity higher than the tribe. Therefore the ancient hostility between segments of the Bantu people of the Congo continued to thrive. Whatever unity existed in the Congo prior to independence was only that of the Belgian administrations, laws, and police.

A second type of governmental procedure was provided for the Africans who had left their native villages to work for Europeans or in industry or mining. Most of these partially detribalized Africans lived in towns close to urban centers in the large cities. Such areas were called *Centres Extra Coutumiers* by the Belgians. They were administered by native chiefs appointed by the central government and advised by an appointive council under the direction of district officers. The nature of government in these areas differed from the strict traditional rule of the rural districts because of changes occasioned by the detribalization of the majority of the people living in these *centres*. It was in these *centres* that the Belgians planned to begin a slow process of democratizing the administration of the Congo. Although many high officials in Belgium and the Congo had been considering political reforms for years, prior to 1958 no serious proposals were ever made for extensive grants of power on the central level before implementing changes on the lower levels.

After 1919 Belgium received a League of Nations mandate over Ruanda and Burundi which had been carved from German East Africa. Belgian administration of the two territories was subject, in theory, to control by the League of Nations. In actual practice the League interfered very little in the government of any of its mandates. Belgium linked the administration of Ruanda and Burundi to the Congo and made its chief executive officer, the vice-governor, subordinate to the governor-general. However, because of distance and the special conditions of the mandate, the vice-governor was in many ways independent of his superior. Finance was kept separate from the Congo and the judiciary was also independent. The vice-governor had decree-making powers as well.

Ruanda and Burundi are among the most densely populated areas in Africa. The society of the two territories was highly structured and had hardly been affected by the German occupation. There were three distinct people in each territory, each with a specific place in society and a definite function. Most of the people were Bahutu who were Bantu agriculturists. The second largest group was the dominant Nilotic Watutsi who had invaded the highlands centuries before. They were pastoralists and controlled the wealth and politics of both territories. The third and smallest population was the Pygmy Batwa who acted as servants of both others groups.

All the higher offices in each state were held by the Watutsi and each was ruled by an autocratic king or mwami. Belgium retained the traditional structure, modifying it only by the assignment of a resident to the court of each mwami. The only counterbalance to the autocracy of the mwami and the aristocracy was the power of the vice-governor and his staff, particularly that exercised by the residents. European settlement was prohibited and almost all the land except for two huge parks was reserved for African use. There were no urban areas except those towns which grew up around the Belgian administrative centers. Most of Belgian activity in each area was concentrated upon the improvement of agriculture and animal husbandry. Little attention was paid to education. The authorities were willing to leave elementary education to the missionaries. Therefore there was not developed in either area a nucleus of Western-trained Africans. Belgium was content to do nothing to broaden the base of representation until after 1950 when it was decided to experiment with change in each of the regions.

Portuguese Africa

The Portuguese empire in Africa was not constructed in the same manner as colonial governments of the other European states. Except in rare instances, the British, French, and Belgian territories in Africa were the results of late nineteenth-century imperialism. However different their colonial systems, they were the product of a similar time and similar challenges. Because of the competitive nature of late nineteenth-century expansion, the governing instruments of most African areas were hastily arrived at and were pragmatic to the extent that the governments were a compromise between that of the mother country and existing African forms. The Portuguese empire by contrast had existed in the coastal areas of Angola and Mozambique since the fifteenth century. Time, therefore, hallowed many theories of Portuguese rule in Africa and their application, and even though many of these were out of step with the demands of the modern world, they were clung to tenaciously by the Portuguese.

Except for a brief period in the early sixteenth century, the Portuguese were interested in Africa for the single purpose of its economic value. At that time the Portuguese in dealing with the Bakongo were motivated by the desire to Christianize the African and inculcate him with Portuguese culture. However, the growing demand of her colonies (primarily Brazil) for slaves almost totally negated the cultural aspect of Portuguese occupation. Slaves became the most important product of Africa and the Portuguese from their bases in Angola and Mozambique entered directly into not only the overseas distribution but also the gathering of slaves. For over three centuries the slave trade was the major occupation of the Portuguese in Africa. Their attitudes toward Africans were formed in this period. Of all the European powers, only Portugal retained her large permanent establishments from the mercantilist period to modern times. Britain and France were deeply affected by the economic revolution of the eighteenth and nineteenth centuries and they discarded, at least for a time, mercantilist economic organization. Portugal did not. Although the slave trade is gone, the Portuguese territories in Africa still exist economically for the good of Portugal.

Portuguese desires to dominate a major portion of Central Africa during the scramble were frustrated by the ambitions of more powerful European states. Partially because of European competition, but more because of its weak economic position, Portugal was not able to make good its occupation in many territories assigned to her until just before World War I. The Dembos area and the territory of the Cuanhama people in Angola, and Yao country in Mozambique, were not pacified until the first decade of the twentieth century. The stringencies of such conquests reinforced the Portuguese belief that because of their long contact with Africa they alone knew how to govern the African. Despite such confidence in their ability to rule, the Portuguese did not evolve any coherent colonial system until the 1890s. Central to the new system as enunciated by the Colonial Regulation of 1899 was the emphasis placed upon teaching the African the sanctity of work. Much of the responsibility of lower echelon civil servants in all the colonies was directed toward the recruitment of African workers. This recruitment could take the form of demanding that Africans work on public works in their districts or rounding up eligible males to be exported to work outside the territory as contract laborers. Despite widespread criticism of the system of overseas recruitment, particularly in the period just before World War I, Portugal continued the practice.

Over ninety-eight percent of the population of Portuguese Africa are *indigenas* and they have borne the full weight of the authoritarian Portuguese regime. The *shibalo* system of compulsory labor was particularly harsh since it was based upon the premise that the African should be forced to accept the European concept of work. The system was also necessary for the Portuguese to show a profit from their territories. All natives were required to offer proof that they were employed for at least six months of the year. *Indigenas* were exempt from compulsory labor if they could show a certificate from the agriculture department stating that they worked their own farms or were employed in urban work or in mining. Only a small proportion of the population could qualify for this exemption. The rest could be forcibly compelled to work. In theory, workers so recruited were to be utilized only on government projects. In actual fact large numbers were recruited by the government and presented with mass contracts which enabled the government to assign them to work for European farmers. In addition, by the 1950s over one-quarter of a million Africans a year were provided for work in the mines in South Africa and the Rhodesias. These workers were initially supplied by Mozambique as its part in a commercial agreement signed with the Union of South Africa. By this treaty the Union agreed to employ a maximum of 80,000 workers a year and in return ship a certain portion of their products on Portuguese railroads to the port of Lourenço Marques. Later agreements were reached which helped the Portuguese to build up the ports of Lobito and Beira with foreign capital so the one cost to the government in recruiting was that of gathering the natives while the government profited in three ways—from higher taxes and increased use of its rail facilities and its ports.

Far more onerous and more feared than the *shibalo* and contractual work was the transporting of Africans to work the cocoa plantations on the island of São Thomé. A number of observers have pointed out that the so-called *contractos* did not volunteer for this service. They were generally collected in Angola although some came from Mozambique. Natives who were on such service were totally at the mercy of their employers and a long sea voyage separated them from the mainland. As late as the 1940s former Inspector General Galvão of Mozambique reported that the death rate of these workers was over thirty percent.

In addition to these policies, there were numerous other indignities which the African had to suffer from the Portuguese. He had to carry a pass and in urban areas abide by the curfew. Portuguese prisons and jails were far from being models of modern penology. Although, in theory, African traditional rulers continued to function, they were servants of an authoritarian regime whose local agents in some cases used harsh, brutal methods in carrying out their duties. The practice of beating the palms of the hands, the *palmatario,* was outlawed by the 1950s, but some observers even at that late date reported its continued use by Portuguese authorities.

The Portuguese empire in Africa constitutes a closed mercantilistic system. Portugal, one of the most economically backward European states, created a structure which welded the colonies to the mother country politically as well as economically. After 1951 the Portuguese territories were officially known as overseas provinces and considered by the government to be an integral part of Portugal. This action merely solidified the long-held belief that there could be no evolution of the African areas separate from Portugal itself.

A complicating feature of the Portuguese empire is the presence of relatively large numbers of Europeans in the colonies. This factor alone would make difficult the devolution of power to Africans even if Portugal had not been so poor that its future prosperity was considered tied to its empire or if its regime were more liberal. The history of other multiracial areas such as Kenya and the Rhodesias in the 1950s illustrates this. By the mid-1950s there were almost 70,000 Europeans in Mozambique and over 100,000 in Angola. Many of these became increasingly dissatisfied with the nature of their authoritarian government after World War II. However, their dissatisfaction with the regime of Prime Minister Salazar never reached the point where they wished to exchange his rule for that of an African majority.

It is a mistake to believe that the authoritarian, centralized, and inflexible colonial system of Portugal was a product of the Salazar dictatorship. It was a creation of the liberal republic and predated Salazar's regime by a generation at least. The system in general resembles those established by France and Belgium in the early twentieth century. However, the government of Salazar which concentrated power in the hands of a few persons in Portugal simply increased the degree of control and made the system less flexible to respond to the sweeping changes occurring elsewhere in Africa. The Portuguese colonial system as it existed in the early 1950s is shown by the chart below:

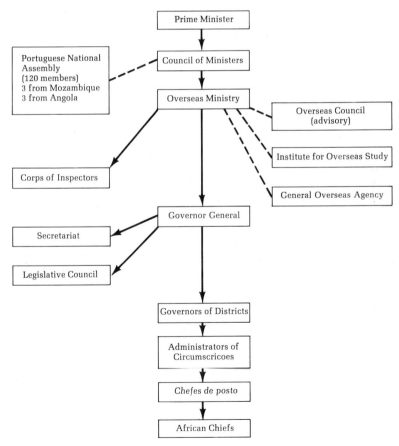

The real authority in the Portuguese government is the council of ministers controlled by the prime minister. This has not been a responsible ministry since the overthrow of the liberal republic in 1926. The council of ministers has the right to legislate as well as to direct the policy of the state. The elected national assembly does not have policy-making powers. Its function since 1932 has been to legislate on matters referred to it by the council of ministers or any individual ministries. The national assembly is composed of 120 elected members. Three members represent Angola and three Mozambique. The influence of elected members from Africa would be negligible even if the government was not as autocratic as it is.

Direction of colonial policy is determined mainly by the overseas ministry. In discharging this responsibility, the ministry is aided by a permanent advisory overseas council and two subsidiary agencies, the Institute for Overseas Study and the General Overseas Agency. The institute exists primarily to train administrators while the agency acts as an information and propaganda center. The chief official resident in a colony is the governor-general appointed for a four-year term of office. He is unchecked in his legislative and executive power by any agency other than the overseas ministry. He is responsible for finances, heads the colonial bureaucracy, directs the native authority system, and sees that the orders of the council of ministers are carried out. The legislative councils in Angola and Mozambique have a majority of elected members, but they have only advisory powers. They do not have the usual right of scrutinizing the budget.

In each district the governors have similar autocratic powers except on a more restricted scale. There have been many regroupings of districts since 1930, but by 1950 there were twelve districts in Angola and nine districts in Mozambique. To ninety-five percent of the Africans in Portuguese territories, the most important European officers are the administrators of the Circumscricoes and the Chefes de Posto, positions roughly comparable to the British provincial and district officers. They act as registry officers, judges, tax collectors, finance officers, and general coordinators. Traditional African rulers are subordinate to the European officers. These chiefs are simply the lowest officials in the government hierarchy with little power to act on their own, and they can be replaced at any time by higher authority. All officials are either appointed by the governor-general or the home officials and they are directly responsible to the governor-general.

Partially obscuring the authoritarian, centralized nature of Portuguese rule has been its stated assimilado policy. Portugal has never had rigid prohibitions against intermarriage between the races. This attitude has resulted in a substantial mixed population. The assimilado system as a natural political extension of this racial attitude has been official Portuguese policy since 1917 and was restated in the Colonial Act of 1930 and the Organic Charter of 1933. Briefly this theory holds that all persons, no matter what their race, will be accorded the same status if they meet certain qualifications. To qualify for this status, an African had to adopt the European mode of life, speak and read Portuguese fluently, be a Christian, complete military service, and have a trade or profession. To many European observers unacquainted with the total picture of Portuguese colonialism, this seems a reasonable, even enlightened policy. The failure of this policy, however, can be measured statistically. In 1956 there were 4,550 *assimilados* in a population of six million in Mozambique and approximately 31,000 in a population of four million in Angola. The major reason for the small numbers of *assimilados* is the difficulty in achieving this station. The Portuguese government does not support education to any extent. Even in Portugal the illiteracy rate is over thirty-three percent. In Africa there are few secondary schools with a total enrollment measured in the hundreds. Elementary education is similarly neglected, most emphasis being given schools specifically designed to impart only rudimentary levels of training. Here the students are taught a few moral principles and basic Portuguese. Such an educational system makes it nearly impossible for a young African, even if he wanted to, to become an *assimilado*.

EIGHT
Colonial Africa: the interwar period

Economic development and social change

The basic impetus which had propelled European powers into Africa had been economic. The economic reasons for any European power's territorial expansion in a given area had been either to dominate assured markets or mineral wealth, or to be in a position to control future discoveries. The latter attitude was the most widespread of the two. French expansion and that of Leopold II had been predicated largely upon the gamble that there were unfound riches in the new territories. They had been spurred on in this belief by the discoveries of gold and diamonds in areas of southern Africa previously considered almost worthless. These factors combined with an uncertain knowledge of the interior and myths of riches were enough to convince many European statesmen and businessmen to support a forward policy in Africa. After the scramble had been completed it became necessary to open up the hinterland of Africa to government and business agents. Prior to World War I there was a considerable investment of private and government capital in all areas of sub-Saharan Africa. This was the period when the bulk of the railway and telegraph lines were constructed. Harbors were improved, docks built, river transport subsidized, and a host of trading companies loosed on Africa.

Railway construction had high priority on the list of economic improvements. There was a twofold reason for this. New government stations in the hinterland demanded a steady supply that, in the very earliest days, could be maintained only by large, expensive, slow-moving caravans. Effective government control in most areas demanded a more efficient system of communications. Northern Nigeria, Buganda, the Rhodesias, and the Congo are good examples of territories where railroads were begun for this purpose long before there were materials or products of known economic value. Later when mineral deposits were discovered in the Katanga, Sierra Leone, and the Rhodesian copper belt, the railways were either extended or spur lines built to facilitate the exploitation of the areas. Correlate with the construction of railway lines was the improvement of the road system which in most African territories, by 1940, linked the major interior towns with the coastline. The imperial powers in the interwar period cut back drastically on major government expenditures in the territories. Nevertheless, where there was sufficient economic justification all would invest money in harbor improvements, better railway rolling stock, or an extension of railway and road lines.

Government and private investment tended to be concentrated on extraction of minerals or trade goods in most areas of Africa, and this, in conjunction with other factors, resulted in a tremendous growth of cities and towns. In order to exploit diamond, manganese, copper, or iron discoveries, it was necessary to concentrate a large number of skilled and unskilled workers in one place. The copper belt of Rhodesia and the Katanga and the full range of mining activities in South Africa are the best examples of this type of industrially induced urbanization. Another reason for the growth of cities and towns was the need to service the new mines or in some cases the developing argicultural sectors. Seaports such as Dakar, Lagos, Abidjan, Luanda, and Lourenço Marques had a phenomenal growth rate in the first fifty years of this century. Similar developments could be seen in the size of cities and towns selected to be the site of national, provincial, or district headquarters. Here were concentrated not only the government services, but major offices for trading or mining companies and banks. One of the most phenomenal examples of developing urbanization is Nairobi which did not even exist when the decision was made in the 1890s to construct the railway through Kenya. By 1940 it was one of the major cities of East Africa with a population in excess of 25,000.

Each step in improving economic or government efficiency in a given territory was accompanied by changes, often subtle, in the traditional African political and economic system. Something as simple as the construction of a railroad or a laterite road near a village facilitated, at the least, the greater mobility of the population. Men who previously had never imagined traveling more than a few miles from their village soon found it easy to visit areas hundreds of miles from their homes. Even traditional markets were affected in the time, locale, and nature of the product sold. In a much more direct way all European-controlled areas soon became converted to a money economy. Young men found it much easier to obtain money by working in the towns, at first for government and then later in a full range of jobs in the civilian sector. Greater mobility combined with greater economic opportunity facilitated the rapid growth of urban centers. In the beginning a man who had worked for government or European firms might be content after a time to return to his village and reassume his place in the traditional order. However, many found that a traditional agricultural existence was stultifying after the excitement of the cities, and many more refused to be constrained within the older political and societal framework. Thus in most African states, although there continued to be migrations between cities and countryside, an ever-increasing number of Africans became urban dwellers.

Urban life wrought many changes upon the African. Familial and tribal ties were loosened and in some cases ceased to be a factor in behavior. Their jobs provided many Africans not only with money and the Western products this would buy, but also introduced them to a new scale of values and gave them the necessary skills to move into more important positions. Some Africans became traders either with European firms or on their own, and with luck and hard work a few could become affluent or even wealthy men. Those Africans in good positions with government, private firms, or who had their own business acted as an incentive to other young village or city Africans. The cities as lodestones did not always fulfill the expectations of Africans. There was only a limited number of jobs and therefore there was an increasingly high unemployment rate which contributed to the feeling of grievance many Africans had against the imperial government. There was little government planning in the organization of these new cities and very soon they were overcrowded with minimal sanitation facilities. Around the centrum of each major city there developed unplanned African communities which in some areas soon deteriorated into slums. In such communities crimes which would have been reprehensible in traditional society became commonplace. Here the normal pattern of life to many became a form which combined the worst elements of both European and African societies.

In many areas where agriculture remained the most important export product, there were significant changes in the economic structures of the country. Cocoa planters in the Ivory Coast, Gold Coast, and Nigeria, coffee growers in Tanganyika and the Ivory Coast, and peanut cultivators throughout West Africa found an ever-increasing demand for their product. Better methods of cultivation, better varieties of plants, and more improved selectivity brought farmers large profits. Where such was the case there evolved a definite agricultural African middle class which in many cases had goals at variance with the traditional structures of authority.

Detribalization became a fact of African life. Urban Africans came to measure success not in traditional terms, but in those of the colonial power. On one level it could be the ownership of European clothes or a bicycle while on a higher level it was to live in the European style, own a car, and educate one's children. Thus while all European governments continued to use the traditional ruler in governing their African possessions, the chiefs' authority even in British territories had been undermined by the new economy and urbanization. Educated Africans, or even those who believed themselves skilled, began to be more vocal in their criticism of a system which excluded them from political power yet rewarded a chief who could not read or write. The policy of European governments and businesses of reserving the upper echelon positions for whites came increasingly under attack by Africans who either were prepared for such responsibility or thought they should have these jobs. Double standards in employment convinced many Africans to join a variety of pressure organizations seeking better opportunities.

Western education and Christianity began to advance in sub-Saharan Africa only after the scramble had been completed and urbanization begun. Christianity had made few converts when the village African could see little advantage in abandoning his traditional ways. In the twentieth century with the added impetus of economic gain, more detribalized Africans began to find advantages in at least a partial adherence to Christianity. Except in the Belgian Congo, the bulk of African education was shifted by a penurious government to missionary societies. In the new atmosphere of the towns and cities education for the African was immediately translatable into economic advantage. Prosperous Africans were willing to invest the necessary money in school fees with the assurance that their sons would be able to compete in the new world. In some cases whole villages, as among the Ibo, would subsidize the entire cost of educating a promising young man. In return the student would bring his village honor, prestige, and later money. This interest evinced by some Africans in education should not be construed to mean that there were ever many schools in Africa. Approaches toward giving a primary education to all African children had to wait until the latter 1950s. But to the more affluent Africans, Christianity came to mean education, and education was provided through the secondary levels for an ever-increasing number of African boys. The more promising could, if financing was available, get university degrees in Britain or France.

The demand of government for more Africans to staff the lower range of the civil service also was translated into a form of education. This type of on-the-job training in public works, agriculture, marine, treasury, and other departments meant that in time diligent Africans could become reasonably skilled in a variety of European-type occupations. Belgium was particularly interested in this form of education. In the Congo many positions in industry and the mines normally associated with whites were filled by Africans. To a lesser extent this was true also in British and French areas. Clerks and junior storekeepers throughout their areas were invariably African.

It was then the juxtaposition of a Westernized economy and government structure on Africa which created the need for more educated and trained Africans. These in turn were much more aware of the political and economic injustices of colonial rule. African doctors, lawyers, and teachers who had encountered the fundamental documents of European freedom and had read widely in liberal or Marxist literature began to question the dichotomy between European theories and colonial practices. African civil servants began to wonder why their upward mobility was arbitrarily blocked and why certain positions were always reserved for Europeans. Even workers in the mines, on the railroads, and on the docks began to question why their wage rates were so much lower than European workers. Once introduced to the competitive wage system, it was a short step for some Africans, whenever their economic aspirations were thwarted, to turn to European-inspired trade union activity or political parties.

Until after World War II the colonial administrations pursued administrative policies which might have been adequate a quarter of a century before but which had become out of step with reality. The new reality had been created, sometimes inadvertently, by the demands of government agencies, economic exploitation, and the advance of education. The cities and towns provided the intellectual leadership, the African economic underpinning, and the unsatisfied partially detribalized masses which in combination became the potent anti-imperialist political movements that eventually forced rapid and revolutionary changes throughout Africa. Political parties, themselves a Western idea, had their origins in the centers of the economically new Africa—the urban areas.

Separatist church movements

The activity of dedicated missionaries in the nineteenth century produced differential results throughout the continent. Although the early optimism of many mission societies proved to be unwarranted, there were many areas which proved to be very receptive to Christianity. Most of these, until the twentieth century, were coastal areas. A combination of factors such as poor communications, disease, and the advance forces of a proselytizing Islam tended to minimize the conversions of interior people. In only a few hinterland areas did the missionaries have great success. Uganda and Nyasaland were the best examples of such fertile fields.

By the beginning of the new century there were many Christian Africans in certain areas. Continually expanded mission activities in the fifty years after 1900 made even further inroads on traditional African religions. It should be emphasized that a convert to Christianity was required to deny himself many things which his clan or tribe considered normal and proper. The greatest general effect of Christianity was the stress placed upon the native community and the extended family system. Christianity required a man to limit himself to one wife. If he already possessed more than one, he was forced to divest himself of the others, sending them and their children back to their families. Christian converts were also taught to look upon the society from which they had been emancipated as heathen and to pride themselves on achieving a higher level. In all conversions there was a factor, unconnected with pure theoretical religion, of accommodation of the African to the white man's world. Such emulation also added to the feelings of superiority a Christian African held for his unconverted relatives. Thus there was present, from the very earliest periods, pressures to accommodate Christianity to the cultures and needs of the African. Such syncretistic movements became particularly effective in the twentieth century and they represented one of the earliest forms of African rejection of complete Europeanization.

At the same time as this type of accommodation was proceeding there developed among the better educated, urban African, a different and less subtle type of reaction to the European. Missionary activity, however, varied from one Christian group to another and in differing places, normally had one common factor. It was firmly controlled by Europeans, although Nigeria was one seeming exception. The conversion of so many of the Niger River peoples to Christianity had been due to the activity of black Christians. However, after 1890 the decisions of the Church of England and its associated missionary society relegated Africans in Nigeria to only secondary positions within the church. Everywhere in Christian Africa this pattern was repeated. Europeans were the administrators, preachers, teachers, and doctors; Africans were only their active, willing supporters. Christian missionaries preached egalitarianism and practiced supremacy.

Throughout Africa breakaway or so-called Ethiopian churches developed in response to the twin pressures of the need to accommodate Christianity to the needs of African societies and the reaction against European domination. African churches represented one of the earliest anti-European manifestations by their stress upon the worth and uniqueness of African culture. However different these churches were from one another, they all emphasized the Old Testament. There they could find sanctions for many practices which European missionaries found distasteful in African society. Most of the churches were only covertly anti-European, but some participated directly in early political movements designed to dislodge the European from power. There were a wide variety of these native churches and it is impossible to do more than to mention a few of these organizations.

One area particularly susceptible to African reforming church movements was central and south-central Africa. One of the most receptive areas for a new synthesis was Nyasaland and the catalyst there was an American fundamentalist missionary, Joseph Booth. Arriving in Nyasaland in 1892, he was immediately struck by the divergence between the theory of Christianity and the practices of European Christians. He noted the wide differences between the economic and social position of whites and blacks. Booth later stressed the Christian imperative for egalitarianism in his writing and preaching at the Zambesi Industrial Mission. In 1899 he petitioned the British government for an end to colonial rule since it perpetuated the differences between the races. Such overt actions stamped him as a radical and the government attempted to arrest and deport him in 1899. He was allowed to return the following year and continued his propaganda campaign against the government in favor of African rights until 1902 when he left the area for South Africa. Five years later he planned to return to Nyasaland, but the government refused to allow him to enter the territory.

Booth's teachings and activity had made a deep impress upon a young Yao convert, John Chilembwe. He became Booth's servant in 1892 and learned to read and write while at the mission. Due to Booth's influence he was admitted to a Baptist seminary in the United States where he trained for the ministry. Chilembwe returned to Nyasaland in 1899 as a missionary for the National (Negro) Baptist Convention. He was largely responsible for constructing and directing the Providence Industrial Mission at Mbombwe. At first conservative in dress and manners and reluctant to lend himself to political causes, Chilembwe gradually adopted more radical concepts. By 1914 his position was that European colonial rule was a mockery of Christianity and further that the only way that Africans could free themselves from European control was by force. Thus Chilembwe lent his considerable local prestige and that of his followers to an attempt to overthrow the government of Nyasaland in 1915. This revolt will be treated in more detail later. It is sufficient to note here that Chilembwe's power base was slight. The revolt failed and Chilembwe was killed. His movement is important, despite the failure of its immediate goals, because it was the first nationalistic movement led by an African which had as its goal the idealistic motives of Christianity.

Meanwhile in Barotseland another charismatic African, Willie J. Mokalapa, was organizing his separatist church. Mokalapa, a Suto evangelical, had previously assisted white missionaries working among the Lozi. He obviously had reacted to the inferior treatment of African Christians since, at a later date in South Africa, he joined a church organization, first founded in the United States in 1816, which opposed the color bar within the church. A group of Africans in 1892 disaffiliated themselves from the South African Wesleyan Church and formed their own extension of this group and took the name South African Ethiopian Church.

Mokalapa returned to Barotseland as the presiding elder in Rhodesia. He persuaded the powerful Lozi chief, Lewanika, to offer protection to the new church. Mokalapa gained a large number of converts but challenged British authority only in an indirect fashion. Instead, he concentrated upon the church and on starting a number of African controlled schools. Nevertheless, the authorities viewed him as a threat and attempted to influence Lewanika to order him from the country. This the chief refused to do. However, in 1904, Mokalapa visited South Africa on business, was swindled of the funds entrusted to him, and never returned to Lozi country. Without Mokalapa to guide it, his church rapidly declined in numbers and potential influence.

Another important religious movement in Central Africa was associated with Jehovah's Witnesses. This Christian fundamentalist group taught that all human governments were doomed. All men would soon be judged after the imminent cataclysm at which God would institute a divine rule among men. African adherents to this doctrine such as Elliot Lamwana, founder of the Free Church and another associate of Booth, believed in the peaceful revolution of the masses. In Nyasaland and Rhodesia the believers were referred to as belonging to the Watchtower movement. In the Belgian Congo the movement was called kitwala. During World War I the movement was proscribed in Northern Rhodesia and Nyasaland. After the war it was allowed to continue and soon became quite strong in certain districts. The Watchtower movement was given much of the blame for the minor disturbances on the copper belt in 1935.

Black ministers from the United States were viewed by the imperial powers as carriers of revolutionary social and political beliefs. Reference has already been made to the activities of Booth, Chilembwe, and Mokalapa, and the reactions which they caused in Central Africa. In 1908 Belgian authorities detained missionaries of the African Methodist Episcopal Church when they attempted to enter the Congo. In 1914 the British also prevented missionaries from this church from working in the Gold Coast. Despite such precautions, Ethiopian churches continued to flourish in most African areas. In Nigeria the decision in 1890 to relegate African ministers and laymen to secondary positions resulted in the rapid growth of break-away churches at first in Yoruba and later in Ibo areas. Schismatic movements among educated Nigerians were greatly influenced by the writings of Edward Wilmot Blyden, a West Indian who migrated to Liberia in the mid-nineteenth century. Not only did he approve of the religious motivations behind the Ethiopian churches, but he stressed the anti-imperialistic doctrine of Africa for Africans.

The Watchtower movement or kitwala in the Congo changed considerably in time. Leaders there tended to stress the degradation of the black man under the existing colonial regime. All this would be rectified by the apocalypse when black men would be changed to white. In the early 1920s the movement had a very powerful anti-Belgian base in the eastern Congo. Later in some places, it blended with the Kimbanguiste sect which owed its beginnings to the prophet Simon Kimbangu. Simon who had been baptized a Protestant, began in 1921 to preach, and according to his followers, he performed miracles. Although he stressed the Bible and the next world in his preaching, the Belgians saw in his popularity a threat to the state. He was arrested, charged with disrupting order, and sentenced to death. The sentence was commuted to life imprisonment, and until his death thirty years later, Kimbangu was confined in exile in the Katanga. Kimbangu was deified by his followers and despite the loss of their leader, the movement flourished and spread throughout the western Congo and into Angola. It took the name of The Church of Jesus Christ on Earth by the Prophet Simon Kimbangu. Kimbanguiste churches modified the liturgy, admitting many African details to the worship ceremonies. It also encouraged African dissatisfaction with Belgian rule and took an active part in Congolese politics in the 1950s. In August 1969, the church began by Kimbangu, having grown to over three million members, was admitted to the World Council of Churches.

In Kenya in the 1920s Henry Thuku led the first organized Kikuyu political agitation against British authority. This blended into the reaction of the Kikuyu to missionary endeavors to end female circumcision. As a result a series of separatist churches were created. Some segments of this reaction became fanatically anti-Western. One example of such a group was the watu wa mungu (People of God) who attacked police stations in 1934 and were later prosecuted by the government. Of more lasting significance was the founding of a number of Kikuyu Independent Schools as an adjunct to the separatist churches. These schools attempted to perpetuate Kikuyu tradition and ideals while at the same time preparing students to function in the increasingly Westernized world of Kenya. Jomo Kenyatta in the days prior to Mau Mau was closely associated with the management of these schools. In this connection it should be noted that in the five years before Mau Mau a whole series of men claiming to be prophets appeared among the Kikuyu. These were both a symptom of the dissatisfaction with British rule and a warning for the future.

One should note a few sailent points from these few examples of separatist churches. First the movements were not localized. Separatist churches were found in all places where Christianity had made substantial gains from African religions. Secondly, almost all these churches attempted to accommodate Christian teachings with the religious and social practices of the African. The existence of these churches was a testimonial to the failure of white Christians, either through their missionaries or government authorities, to live up to the doctrines which were taught the African. Those factors which led large numbers of Africans to associate themselves with these churches were normally worldly rather than spiritual differences. Segregation, poor education, differential standards of opportunity and salary, combined with the urbanized African's feelings of loss of identity, caused these churches to flourish. These same factors encouraged the African to associate himself with embryo political parties and agitate for an end to colonial rule. The separatist churches early served the function of channeling the African's discontent with his lot normally in the direction of the other world. They also prepared the African later to demand of his masters a larger share of responsibility in governing himself and to restate the worth of his own particular culture.

Early political parties

European systems of rule in Africa north of the Limpopo River, however different from each other, had one feature in common. They were all authoritarian. Responsibility for all except the lowest level of decision making was retained by European officers appointed by the home government. Belgian and Portuguese rule did not provide any method by which Africans other than traditional rulers could become a part of the machinery of government. The French pursued a policy of assimilation which created a few well-educated Africans who could compete with their European counterparts for positions in the civil service. In Senegal the presence of the four communes gave Africans a chance to participate directly in municipal government, and after 1871 Senegal chose one representative to the French chamber of deputies. Elsewhere in French Africa it was more difficult for Africans to participate directly in political affairs. Nevertheless it was the practice to appoint Africans to the various advisory councils. The educated elite in French Africa were more involved with the power structure than their counterparts in British Africa. The British Colonial Office by the early 1920s had not only accepted the practical necessities of indirect rule, but its philosophic rationale as well. Thus there existed a deep-seated distrust of Africans who tried to imitate Europeans. Emphasis in all territories was placed upon what the British considered the traditional rulers, and the central administration tried to protect them from the inroads of the educated African. These educated, urban-based Africans, as one means of protesting their inferior status in some British territories, began to form political parties. Except for Senegal this type of protest was confined exclusively to British areas. Belgium and Portugal would not allow such activity and the French African elite were too satisfied with their positions to form political parties.

Africans of the four communes in Senegal had the right to elect one representative to the French chamber of deputies. Until 1914 this position as well as control over municipal politics had been dominated by the Creole population. In that year, however, Blaise Diagne, a black ex-customs official, was elected to the chamber of deputies. The political organization which he constructed gave him and his adherents control of the Senegalese politics until the 1930s. In 1917 Diagne became the undersecretary of state for colonies in the Clemenceau government. His example set the tone for later cooperation between the French African politicians and the metropole. Until the end of World War II politically conscious French Africans associated themselves with French political parties rather than forming their own organizations.

Even though the policy of assimilation worked to keep political parties from developing, it did not assume complete submissiveness of the African elite. In the 1930s many Africans joined the Socialist and Communist parties and thus were introduced to Marxism and its concepts relating to capitalism and imperialism. Perhaps as important for the future development of political parties was the uncomfortable feeling of many Africans who felt caught between two cultures. Léopold Sédar Senghor is perhaps the best example of this. He was given an excellent education in Senegal and Paris, and became the first African *aggrégé* qualified to teach in French secondary schools. He taught in French *lycéés* before the war, and in 1939 joined the army, later being captured by the Germans. Senghor was also a poet of merit and a nationalist. His poetry is filled with nostalgia and longing for Africa and stressed the importance of being African. Senghor and the French West Indian Aimé Césaire were responsible for creating the concept of *Négritude* which stressed the value of African culture distinct from any European taint. Later Senghor and another Senegalese, Alioune Diop, founded the magazine *Présence Africaine* to acquaint the world with these values. The duality between French and African culture so noticeable in Senghor was felt in varying degrees by every French African who later entered politics. This tension was in large part responsible for the course of nationalist development in French Africa in the 1950s.

In contrast to the French territories, nationalist evolvement in parts of British Africa resulted in the early development of African political parties. Political parties in British Africa generally shared certain common features. They were usually urban-based, and their programs were aimed at securing for a small African middle class some share in decision making. The colonial governments in the interwar period were hostile toward the leaders of these movements as well as toward the fundamental concept of African political parties. The urban politicians were accused of being an elite minority who could speak only for a few similar Africans and not the mass of the people who were governed by indirect rule. This official opposition to African political parties managed to restrict early politically organized activity to British West Africa and Kenya. Elsewhere there was not even rudimentary political organizations until after World War II.

Educated Fante in the Gold Coast had been encouraged before the Ashanti War of 1873 to work out differences between the various groups in order to create a Fante confederation. The coming of the war and subsequent imperial moves into the interior relegated the coastal elite to an ineffectual political position. The precedent remained, however, and in the 1920s the coastal elite who aspired to a stronger political voice found a spokesman in Joseph E. Casley-Hayford. He and his followers protested against the British plans to further strengthen the powers of the traditional rulers at the expense of the Western-educated minority. Casley-Hayford was one of the organizers of the National Congress of British West Africa and an important figure in the Pan African movement. He was not able to substantially affect British policy in the Gold Coast since he traditional rulers at the expense of the Western-educated minority. Casley-Hayford's opponents was Nana Ofori Atta, the powerful paramount chief of the Akim Abuakwa. He spoke for many when he argued that future political development had to depend upon cooperation with the British authorities and would be an evolvement of traditional practices. In 1927 Casley-Hayford won one of the three elected seats to the Legislative Council. This marked the end of real opposition in the Gold Coast to British concepts of rule. In the 1930s Joseph Danquah, a younger brother of Ofori Atta, formed the Gold Coast Youth Conference. This was primarily a coastal organization which believed in cooperation rather than opposition to the British authorities.

In the Gambia and Sierra Leone there were no early political parties, but there was a significant number of Africans who participated in political activities. In Sierra Leone the Creole population of the Freetown area, thoroughly Anglicized, formed the nucleus for later political parties. Due largely to the efforts of Sir Samuel Lewis, after 1893 Freetown was a self-governing municipality. Thus the politically active Creoles had some outlet for their desires to participate in government. British authorities ended this experiment in 1926 partially because of the lack of interest shown by the Creoles in participating and also because the authorities were concerned more with strengthening the traditional rulers than the educated Creoles. Political life in the colony area of the Gambia was restricted to a few educated Africans. Despite the efforts of men such as Edward Small, the Bathurst Creole or Aku population was never powerful enough to even create a political party. The protectorate was unrepresented on the Legislative Council until 1932 and even after that the British district officers and the many chiefs were the salient factors in the government of the Gambia.

Of the four British West African territories, only Nigeria had enough nationalist leaders in the interwar period to create significant political parties. Even there African political activity was concentrated in the cities and a large number of the nationalist leaders were West Indians. Early in the century such men as J. P. Jackson, editor of the *Lagos Weekly Record*, campaigned against British authoritarianism. Later Herbert Macaulay, a grandson of Bishop Samuel Crowther, became the most active opponent of Lugard's attempts at creating an efficient administration which, however, excluded the educated Nigerian from participation. He was the driving force behind the creation of the Nigerian National Democratic party (NNDP) in 1923 which won every election in Lagos to the Legislative Council from that date until 1938. Macaulay was involved in the dispute over the recognition and support of the eleko, the traditional ruler of Lagos. Macaulay's protestations over the deposition of the eleko by the British gained him a short prison term in 1928. His position was weakened since he did not represent all the factions of the educated in Nigeria. Men such as Sir Kitoyi Ajasa, owner of the *Nigerian Pioneer*, and Henry Carr, the resident of Lagos, represented and defended British policy and vehemently opposed Macaulay. Macaulay and other early nationalists were viewed by the authorities as dangerous subversives and their movements were carefully monitored and restricted. In 1923 Macaulay was given only seventy-two hours to leave Oyo Province and the ban upon his visiting the province was never lifted.

In 1934 nationalist protests against the quality of education at Yaba Higher College resulted in the formation of the Lagos Youth Movement. The organizers soon founded branches in many of the cities of southern Nigeria and the name was changed to the Nigerian Youth Movement (NYM). This organization gained the adherence of young men such as Samuel Akintola, Obafemi Awolowo, and H. O. Davies. In 1937 a new figure was introduced to the Nigerian political scene. This was Benjamin Nnamdi Azikiwe, educated in the United States, who was very active in politics. Through his newspaper, the *West African Pilot*, he began to preach a more radical nationalism, one that transcended the parochialism of the NNDP. With Azikiwe, an Ibo, the NYM could fairly claim to represent a large portion of the educated southern Nigerians. A quarrel between Azikiwe and other leaders led to the fragmentation of the NYM in 1941 and Azikiwe led most of the Ibo out of the party. In 1944 he formed a new movement called the National Council of Nigeria and the Cameroons (NCNC). Ostensibly a national party, it represented, in fact, the Westernized Ibo and eastern peoples of Nigeria.

All these early nationalists in British West Africa were thinking of limited advance for Africans. They did not demand independence, but instead they fought against the exclusiveness and racial bias in the crown colony system. They did not make radical demands, but they did wish to participate more fully in government. This can be clearly seen in the actions of the National Congress of British West Africa. Inspired by the activities of Du Bois and other Pan Africanists, Casley-Hayford and a few other nationalists created the organization in 1920. Its purpose was to bring together West African nationalists for periodic meetings to discuss common problems and to petition the British government for redress of grievances. The first meeting at Accra resulted in a memorial to the

Colonial Office which stressed four requests. These were for: (1) a legislative council for each area with one-half of the members being elected Africans, (2) control of taxation by the African members of the legislative council, (3) appointment and deposition of chiefs by the people, and (4) abolition of racial discrimination in the civil service.

Moderate as these statements appear now, they were considered revolutionary by the British. Lord Milner, the colonial secretary, dismissed the requests as representing the opinions of a small minority of Africans. The governor of Nigeria openly denounced the conference and the participants. At subsequent meetings at Freetown in 1923, Bathurst in 1925, and Lagos in 1929 the delegates restated the original resolutions and the British government continued to ignore the congress. Far ahead of its time, it expired after 1930 because of official apathy, the coming of the depression, and the death of Casley-Hayford, its most forceful member.

The only British dependent territory outside of West Africa which had any significant African political movements was Kenya. There the major question, particularly among the Kikuyu people, was land alienation. The Kikuyu maintained that Europeans could not claim the land since no Kikuyu was even authorized to sell it. The rapid growth of the African population in the two decades before World War II increased the tension between Europeans and Africans on this subject. There were other factors which disturbed the Kikuyu. One was the presence of large numbers of Indians in Kenya who occupied the lower echelon of the business and mercantile establishments. Thus the Kikuyu, the most Westernized of all Kenya's peoples, found their upward mobility in agriculture and government service blocked by Europeans, and by the Indians in trade. In response to their frustrations the Kikuyu in the 1920s joined a number of protest organizations. The first of these was the moderate Kikuyu Association formed by farmers of the Kiambu district. Its aim was to cooperate with the government to prevent further land alienation.

In 1921, Harry Thuku, a young Kikuyu civil servant, was the main organizer of the more militant Young Kikuyu Association. Thuku's organization soon had a large following and many times he spoke to thousands of Kikuyu at mass meetings near Nairobi. He urged direct action against the government's decision to raise the hut and capitation tax. Other complaints concerned a wage cut for African workers and the government requirement that all Africans carry a pass card. Underlying all of this was the Kikuyu feeling that the small politically dominant European population had stolen the land of the Kikuyu. In 1922 Thuku was arrested as a danger to the peace and security of Kenya, and without the benefit of a trial was exiled to the northern territories. Thuku's arrest triggered riots in Nairobi which resulted in the killing of over twenty Africans by the police. Without Thuku, the Young Kikuyu Association collapsed. A corollary organization, the Young Kavirondo Association in the Nyanza area, composed primarily of Luo was taken over by the missionaries in the following years. Thus it lost its potential as a protest movement.

In 1924 Joseph Kangethe and others formed a new organization, the

Kikuyu Central Association (KCA). Within a short period it had become a powerful force in Kikuyuland. The association appealed particularly to the young, better-educated Kikuyu. One of the young men early attracted to the organization was Jomo Kenyatta who was its secretary in 1928. The aims of the KCA were the same as Thuku's organization, but its leaders were milder in their expressions of dissatisfaction. In 1928 Kenyatta was sent to London to present the association's grievances to the Colonial Office about Kikuyu representation on the legislative council and land alienation. His mission unsuccessful, Kenyatta stayed in London as the KCA representative in Britain. There he attended the London School of Economics, did the research for his book, *Facing Mt. Kenya,* and avoided the struggles for power within the KCA. The association had gained more adherents with its opposition to government plans to end female circumcision. To Harry Thuku, released in 1930 and more conservative, the association seemed too radical, and he attempted to impose his ideas on the leadership. Failing in this, he broke with the KCA and formed the pro-government Kikuyu Provincial Association which was never popular with the bulk of the educated Kikuyu.

The KCA's stand on female circumcision resulted in a break between the educated Kikuyu and the missionaries. This led in the 1930s to the KCA and the various Kikuyu Associations creating and controlling their own schools which attempted to blend Western training with traditional Kikuyu values. In 1939 the Kenya Teacher Training College was opened. Within a decade the Kikuyu schools were an important factor in spurring on Kenyan nationalism. The failure of the prestigious Morris Carter Commission of the early 1930s to alter significantly the land settlement pattern in the highlands increased the alienation of the Kikuyu from the government. By 1940 when the government banned all political activity for the duration of the war, the KCA leaders had become the spokesmen of the younger, more radical Kikuyu rather than the British-supported chiefs. The groundwork for a violent protest against the white-oriented policy of the government had been laid.

In retrospect, early African political parties achieved few of the immediate goals of their founders. However, they provided a mechanism whereby Africans could protest against the authoritarian structure of European rule. They acted as training grounds for a new generation of African leaders. In some cases political parties such as the KCA and the NCNC were merely modified after World War II to confront the changed political environment. During the interwar period, in conjunction with the Pan African movement, they provided many Africans with hope for a better future.

Pan Africanism

A generation before viable African political parties were formed, Pan Africanism was being sponsored by black intellectuals as inevitable because of shared experiences of black men. The origin of the term Pan

Africanism is obscure. One of the first men to use it was Joseph Booth, the Baptist missionary to Nyasaland. His book, *Africa for the African*, and his actions in Central and South Africa underscored the theme of Africa for black men and an ultimate return to Africa of those whose ancestors had been taken away in slavery. In 1897, Booth, along with his Nyasa pupil, John Chilembwe, was responsible for the formation of one of the first African organizations dedicated to African unity—the African Christian Union.

However vague the origins of the term, its definition and use in the first half of the twentieth century is relatively precise. The ideal was supported by Western-educated blacks who resented their inferior status, and those who mourned their exile from Africa and had deep feelings of attachment for their theoretical homeland. Black writers and professional men, particularly in the United States, and the West Indies, reacting to white domination, saw a close parallel between their status and the lot of African peoples living under imperial control. The poets Countee Cullen and Langston Hughes found inspiration and solace in their kinship to Africans. Later the Senegalese poet Léopold Senghor and Aimé Césaire from Martinique coined the phrase *Négritude* to state the importance and uniqueness of blackness and the culture of Africa. The attitude expressed in the works of these and many other black writers was paralleled by the statements and actions of blacks in other professions. Typical were Dr. Edward Blyden, the West Indian-Liberian teacher and diplomat, Dr. Albert Thorne, West Indian founder of an African colonization scheme, and Reverend Charles Morris, Baptist missionary to South Africa. All of these intellectuals created, in their opposition to white control and customs, a hypothetical Africa which never was and a projection of a theoretical unity based upon the non-European nature of the African and his blackness. It is important to note that the driving force behind early Pan Africanism were non-Africans.

The man most responsible for taking the emotions related to Pan Africanism and transferring them into the arena of political action was W. E. B. Du Bois, a researcher and social scientist of great merit. In his many published works he had stressed the unity of the black world and the need for the ultimate freedom of blacks from white control. He assisted in the formation of the National Association for the Advancement of Colored People in the United States and was for many years the editor of its publication, *The Crisis*. In 1900 he attended the first Pan African Congress in London called by the Trinidad lawyer, H. Sylvester Williams. However little that was accomplished by this first meeting, it gave Du Bois the key for further concerted action by concerned black intelligentsia. Du Bois was the prime mover in convening four other Pan African conferences.

Black contributions to World War I and the subsequent problem of disposing of Germany's African empire presented Du Bois with a unique opportunity. In 1919 he proposed the convening of a conference to be held in Paris at the same time as the Versailles discussions. The conference was held despite the negative attitudes of most Allied statesmen because of the intervention of Blaise Diagne. Diagne was the most influential Senegalese politician and a member of the French ministry, and he persuaded Clemenceau to grant permission for the conference. It was attended by fifty-seven black representatives from all over the world, and they ultimately passed a lengthy resolution. This resolution was moderate, asking for such things as international laws to protect Africans, and the rights of Africans to participate in government as quickly as their development permitted. Nowhere did it demand the ultimate right of Africans to independence from European control. The representatives of the major powers ignored the conference and its resolution.

Du Bois was responsible for the convening of three other congresses. One called in 1921 was held in London and Brussels, the fourth Pan African congress met in London and Lisbon in 1923, and the fifth was held in New York in 1927. The resolutions of each of these congresses showed little advance over the Paris meeting of 1919. They asked for local self-government for "backward groups," interracial cooperation, and that "black folk be treated as men." The discussions and resolutions of all the congresses showed that despite the depth of their feelings, the black representatives were prisoners of their class and culture. Their demands were moderate and perhaps because of the lack of a popular base, they did not threaten. Thus the Pan African congresses of the 1920s had little effect upon the policies of the imperial powers. However, the conferences were not failures because they focused the attention of educated blacks, both African and non-African, upon the reality of one shared experience—control by whites. The congresses and the concomitant reporting of them in connection with continuing articles, novels, and poems by black authors conditioned the thinking of a new generation of educated Africans.

Although Marcus Garvey took no part in the Pan African congresses, he exercised a potent influence upon black attitudes and Pan Africanism. Garvey, a black Jamaican with a charismatic personality, built, by 1920, a large following in the northern United States. He stressed black exclusiveness and rejected Du Bois' ideas of cooperation with whites and ultimate black integration into white-dominated societies. His interest in Africa was largely conditioned by his hope of establishing a reverse migration of blacks from the Western Hemisphere to that continent. In 1920 he founded his "Negro Empire," called a black parliament which met in New York, and named himself Provisional President of Africa. Garvey organized a number of services, among them the Black Star Line to help expatriates return to Africa. His ideas foundered upon mismanagement of funds, hostility of European powers and the United States government, and the resistance of the New World blacks and African politicians to cooperate with his back-to-Africa schemes. Garvey was ultimately sentenced to prison, lost his large following, and died in 1940 in London without ever visiting Africa.

Garvey's influence did not depend upon the success or failure of his proposals but upon his writing and speeches of the early 1920s. This was also true of Du Bois and the others associated with the Pan African congresses. Pan Africanism never had a mass following in any African territory. It was always the concern of a very few educated Africans. These followed the developments of the congresses and extracted from the published works of Du Bois and Garvey those items which seemed to reflect their own problems or which dwelt upon conditions prevalent in their areas. Thus Kwame Nkrumah later could state that Marcus Garvey had been one of the most important influences upon his life and career.

World War II marked a dividing line between the older generation of Pan Africanism and the new African leadership. This is clearly seen in the fusion in Britain in 1944 of thirteen student and political organizations to form the Pan African Federation. The federation was responsible for calling the Sixth Pan African Congress which met at Manchester in 1945. Although Du Bois, aged seventy-three, was present, the meeting belonged to the young Africans. Such men as Kwame Nkrumah, Dr. Kuronkyi Taylor, and Joe Appiah of the Gold Coast, S. L. Akintola and H. O. Davies of Nigeria, and Jomo Kenyatta of Kenya, although then unknown, were the major forces within that congress. George Padmore, the West Indian ex-Communist, was also one of the organizers, and the South African novelist Peter Abrahams and the Togolese poet Raphael Aramttoe were present.

The conference marked the end of the patience of African elites with European imperialism. Its demand was for ultimate freedom for the African and independence from European rule. The conference resolution did not mention socialism, but stressed the protection of Africans from exploitation by the creation of what was termed economic democracy. The representatives at Manchester by implication rejected traditional African rule when they opted for the principle of one man–one vote. They agreed that the future of all African territories should be controlled by the Western educated and not left to the chiefs who had become tainted by acting as agents of the imperialists.

Thus a new strident note was added to Pan Africanism. The young Africans generally accepted Gandhi's ideas of nonviolence, but their statements foreshadowed active campaigns against the colonial powers which would result in confrontation. The Pan African movement after 1945 was controlled by African nationalists and they used its rhetoric to advance the cause of independence for their particular states. This led to an ambivalence not recognized by many observers in the 1950s. It became normal for political leaders such as Julius Nyerere and Jomo Kenyatta to speak of the inevitability of African unity but, nevertheless, to take part in the destruction of a potential Federation of East Africa. Almost all the French politicians supported Pan Africanism and yet accepted the dismemberment of the two large organizations—the French West African Federation and the French Equatorial African Federation.

African politicians in the 1950s were forced to assign priorities to their demands. Confronted with an ever-weakening European power structure, they chose the acceptance of colonial boundaries as the borders of independent states. Pan Africanism was used as a weapon against the Europeans in order to achieve national self-determination. The African ruling elites came to subscribe to the long-range hopes for African union, but considered this a secondary goal to independence and development of individual states. Once independence was achieved a host of new problems arose which took precedent over Pan Africanism. Thus while the Casablanca and Brazzaville groups still publicized their devotion to unity, the necessities of political life in the newly independent polities dictated policies which were hostile to Pan Africanism.

NINE
Northeastern Africa
to 1965

Ethiopia, 1906–1965

The Emperor Menelik suffered his first cerebral hemorrhage in early 1906 and the next year his most trusted lieutenant, Ras Makonnen of Harar, died. The seven-year interval between Menelik's stroke and his death was a period when the various factions in Ethiopia maneuvered for power. This factionalism, so typical of Ethiopia, was not halted by Menelik's creation of a council of ministers in 1907 to aid him in governing. In June 1908, he proclaimed before a meeting of the great nobles of Ethiopia that his successor would be his grandson, Lij Iyasu. Later that year another stroke completely immobilized the emperor. However, he formalized the recognition of Lij Iyasu under the regency of Ras Tamara. With the emperor unable to act, the Empress T'aitu tried to maintain the centralized state by attempting to gain power herself at the expense of the powerful feudal nobles. Bribery and corruption increased alarmingly. By 1911 the major factions in the country were those who supported the empress and the traditional church, and those who supported Lij Iyasu and his powerful father, Ras Michael of Wollo. Ras Michael supplanted Ras Tamara as regent in 1911. The young emperor-designate had shown a decided preference for Islam and many of his most ardent supporters were Muslim.

In 1906 British, French, and Italian representatives, concerned over a return to anarchy in Ethiopia which might threaten their separate interests, concluded the Tripartite Treaty. This divided Ethiopia into spheres of influence and each European power agreed to protect the spheres of the other parties. If a given situation in the future necessitated a military expedition this would be undertaken jointly. Britain's sphere included the area around Lake Tana and the headwaters of the Blue Nile. Italy's area was the largest and was described by an arc stretching from Eritrea to Somaliland. The westward limits of the arc were beyond Addis Ababa. The French sphere was over the area traversed by the railway from Addis Ababa to Djibouti. It is perhaps fortunate for Ethiopia that the collapse of central authority in Ethiopia coincided with the coming of World War I. The major energies of the contracting power were thus diverted elsewhere and no serious attempt was made to put into effect the Tripartite Treaty. However, France and Britain had agreed officially to Italy's premier position in Ethiopia. One Italian official in 1932 could, therefore, state that the Tripartite Treaty was Italy's "Magna Charta" in Ethiopia.

Lij Iyasu was not a strong man (tillak sew) who could force his will upon all factions in Ethiopia. His sympathy for Islam and his association with German and Turkish interests during the early stages of World War I also undercut his authority. The Allied powers welcomed the coalition against Lij Iyasu formed mainly by the church and Shoan nobles. The emperor's fortunes dipped low in 1916 and he abandoned the capital for the city of Jijiga in eastern Harar where he attempted to gain more Muslim supporters for his cause. The Shoan nobility took Addis Ababa in September and proclaimed Zauditu, Menelik's daughter, as empress. They declared the twenty-five year old governor of Harar, Ras Tafari, the son of Ras Makonnen, as heir presumptive. Zauditu was crowned in February 1917. However, Tafari, because of his youth and his progressive views, was not included in the triumvirate which ruled Ethiopia. This included the empress, Ras Wolde Giorgis, the negus (highest rank below emperor), and Habta Giorgis, the Minister of War. Lij Iyasu's forces continued an intermittent war against Zauditu which was only ended with his capture in 1921. He was confined in Harar until his death in 1935.

In the decade following World War I, Ras Tafari slowly built up his power base in Harar and also at the court in Addis Ababa. He emerged as a tillak sew who had the loyalty of a large segment of the army. Some of his more conservative opponents died and he was able to replace others with men loyal to him. The empress and her major advisers, Ras Kassa of Tigre and Dejazmach Balcha of Sidamo, were finally negated after the failure of an abortive palace coup in 1928. The last active violent opposition to Tafari was in 1929 when his forces surrounded those of the major rebels and compelled their surrender. Secure finally as the most powerful man in Ethiopia, he had been crowned negus in 1928, and on the death of Zauditu in 1930 he was proclaimed Emperor Haile Selassie I.

Long before he was crowned, Ras Tafari had attempted to associate Ethiopia more closely with other states. He had visited Europe in 1925 and brought back Theodore's crown from Britain which had been taken by General Napier in 1867. He was the leader in the abortive move to join the League of Nations in 1919. However, the practice of slavery in Ethiopia blocked this attempt. Four years later Zanditu under pressure proclaimed the death penalty for trading in slaves and in the same year Ethiopia was admitted to the League. Italy supported Ethiopia's request; only Britain had reservations about the weak central institutions of Ethiopia. In 1925 Britain sought to revive the Tripartite Treaty by securing Italy's support for a plan to build a dam on the Blue Nile below Lake Tana.

Ras Tafari, immediately upon being appraised of this scheme, protested to the League of Nations. Italy and Britain did not attempt to defend their actions, and finally, in 1928, he concluded a twenty-year Treaty of Friendship with Italy.

Haile Selassie's role in Ethiopia after his coronation was that of the strong man who supported reforms considered by many of the nobles as extremely radical. An analysis of the reforms instigated by the emperor since 1930 shows that measured by Western standards he remained an autocrat. However, it was the emperor who promulgated the Constitution of 1931 against the desires of the majority of the ruling classes. This was duplicated again in 1955 by Haile Selassie's sponsorship of a much more liberal instrument of government. It was the emperor who encouraged the reorganization of government agencies according to Western patterns, sent students overseas for education, and brought in European technical, government, and military advisers. Even had the emperor been more radical, the modernization of Ethiopia's government would have been delayed for years by the Italian invasion and the disorders attendant upon the campaigns of World War II.

The European situation in 1934 was such that Mussolini's government believed the time had finally come to bring Ethiopia completely under Italian control. The rise of Hitler, the quiescence and pacifism of France, Britain, and the United States, and the weakness of the League of Nations made Mussolini believe that no major power would intervene on behalf of Ethiopia. Colonel Vittorio Ruggero, the Italian consul at Addis Ababa, was ordered in early 1934 to begin a program of political subversion in Ethiopia. In February the Undersecretary of War was instructed to begin plans for the quick subjection of Ethiopia. Despite this decision to exploit latent border problems with Ethiopia to bring on the war, Italy reaffirmed the 1928 Treaty of Friendship. Mussolini found his reason for war two months later in the Wal Wal incident.

Wal Wal was the site of wells used by Ethiopians and Somali tribesmen in the sparsely populated desert area of eastern Ogaden province. Although the border with Italian Somaliland had never been clearly defined in this area, Wal Wal was well within Ethiopian territory. But in 1930 the Italians established themselves there and built fortifications. They assumed that since no official protests had been lodged their position was recognized by Ethiopia. In 1934 a joint British-Ethiopian commission was formed to survey the Ogaden since the emperor had been considering ceding part of it to Britain in return for territorial concession elsewhere. In November the commission arrived at Wal Wal, but withdrew after the Italians had made clear they considered Wal Wal to be Italian. However, the commission's Ethiopian military escort of approximately 400 men under Fitaurari Shiferra remained behind. Later reinforcements brought the number of Ethiopian troops to approximately 550 men. The Italian garrison at Wal Wal numbered approximately 430 men. The two sides faced each other without particular incident until the afternoon of December 5 when firing commenced. When the battle was over the

Ethiopians had lost 107 dead and forty-five wounded while the losses of native troops under Italian command were approximately thirty dead and one hundred wounded.

The Italian government immediately demanded redress. Ethiopia on December 9, 1934, invoked the clause in the 1928 agreement which called for arbitration of disputes between the powers. Italy ignored this and demanded formal recognition of their right to Wal Wal, the payment of 200,000 Maria Theresa dollars, and the surrender of the Ethiopian commander. Britain and France both suggested to the emperor that he accept Italy's demands, but Haile Selassie refused. On December 14, Italy rejected the arbitration clause of the treaty whereupon the emperor brought the matter before the League of Nations. On December 20, Mussolini drew up a directive which ordered the Italian military to be prepared to move at least 100,000 metropolitan soldiers and sufficient numbers of allied native troops into Ethiopia not later than October 1935.

The discussions on the Ethiopian crisis in the League were conducted against the background of worsening conditions in Europe. France, concerned primarily with the German question, did not wish to alienate the Italians. The United States wanted nothing to do with problems beyond its borders and reflected this by the passage of the Neutrality Act in August 1935. Only Britain of all the great powers seemed to be committed to opposing Italy. In June 1935, Britain offered the League a compromise solution which would have given a large part of the Ogaden and the British port of Zeila to Italy. In August a three-power conference promised Italy what amounted to a full economic protectorate over Ethiopia. Mussolini rejected both offers, and it is doubtful whether Haile Selassie would have accepted either alternative. Later in August a League committee of five recommended much the same solution as had the three power conference. This, too, was rejected by Mussolini. His war plans were by then almost complete. The modern warriors of a revived Italy would avenge the shame and defeat suffered by the Italian army at Adowa in 1896.

Haile Selassie ordered mobilization of Ethiopian forces on September 29, 1935. This was followed on October 2 by Italian mobilization. The next day the Italian army under the command of the high commissioner for Eritrea and Somaliland. Emilo De Bono, crossed the Mareb River and the Ethiopian War began. Nine Italian divisions with the latest in modern equipment, first under De Bono and later under Marshal Pietro Badoglio, operated on the northern front. General Rudolpho Graziani invaded the south with an additional division. Despite the previous Italian planning and the Ethiopians' poor equipment, the campaign did not add to the repute of the Italian army. De Bono was replaced on November 28 because of the slowness of his advance. His successor, Marshal Badoglio, utilizing more energetic tactics and freely using poison gas, advanced more quickly. Between January and March 1936, the Ethiopian armies were shattered. On May 2 the emperor left Djibouti on a British ship. Three days later the Italians entered Addis Ababa and the main campaign ended.

In adding Ethiopia as a new colony to the Italian empire, Italy had broken the Tripartite Treaty of 1906, the Gas Protocol of 1925, the Italo-Ethiopian Treaty of 1928, the Pact of Paris of 1928, and openly flaunted the League of Nations. It would seem that this list of accomplishments would have brought some measure of assistance for Ethiopia from other states. The League immediately after the war began declared Italy an aggressor and, in November 1935, voted sanctions against it. However, only Britain seemed prepared to enforce sanctions and this position was later modified by the Hoare-Laval agreement of early December. This plan, evolved by the British Foreign Secretary and the French Premier, proposed an exchange of territory which would have given to Italy northern Tigre, most of the Danakil, and Ogaden. After Laval disclosed the details of this agreement to the press it was obvious that no major power would aid Ethiopia and the oil sanctions imposed by the League against Italy became a dead issue. It is ironic that despite this appeasement on the part of all the democracies, Italy decided in 1936 to cast its lot with Germany, and Laval's grand scheme for an Italo-French front against Hitler collapsed. A further example of the comic-opera nature of the latter years of the League was the fact that Ethiopia continued to be a member of the organization which had proved so impotent in defending Ethiopian territory against Italian ambitions.

In June 1936, a new constitution was issued by Italy which joined Ethiopia to the other Italian territories in northeastern Africa. Italy's African empire was then divided into six provinces. The new viceroy, General Graziani, instituted policies aimed at continuing the animosities between different tribes in Ethiopia. Many of the Galla and Somali people had supported the Italians during the war and they were favored by the Graziani regime. However, the Ethiopian unity forged by the war continued during the occupation and active resistance was endemic throughout the country. After an attempt to assassinate Graziani in February 1937, there were reprisals against the younger, educated Ethiopians. These harsh policies were, in a sense, repudiated when Graziani was replaced as viceroy by the Duke of Aosta.

By 1938 Italy had decided upon a conciliatory policy toward Ethiopia. This was evidenced by its generous allocation of funds for public works projects. Many Italian farmers were also sent there as colonists to attempt to increase the export potential of the territory. During its short occupation, Italy expended great sums and continuous effort to modernize their new imperial appendage. New roads, telegraph lines, hospitals, clinics, and agricultural stations became the positive heritage of the Italian occupation.

Italy's entry into World War II against the Allies in June 1940 was followed initially by success in northeastern Africa. British Somaliland was early overrun by the Italians. British leaders in the Middle East, however, could not afford to allow a large Italian force to remain in a position to threaten Egypt and the Red Sea route. Haile Selassie joined the British at Khartoum and, in January 1941, two British divisions invaded Ethiopia and were so successful that the major portion of the campaign was over in six months. The Duke of Aosta finally surrendered on May 18, 1941, at

Amba Alage. This short campaign resulted in the destruction or surrender of the greater part of the 220,000 man Italian force in Ethiopia. In Gondar the last Italian force surrendered to the British and Ethiopians in January 1942. The emperor had reentered Addis Ababa on May 5, 1941, five years to the day after the city had fallen to the Italians, and began immediately to restore his authority throughout the kingdom. British military and civil personnel on all levels cooperated with him and his government. These ad hoc wartime arrangements were regularized by a convention between the two countries on January 31, 1942. The terminology of the convention and the attitude of Britain indicated clearly that she supported Ethiopian independence. A further agreement between the powers in December 1944 placed Britain and Ethiopia on a level of complete equality.

Eritrea was administered by Britain after its conquest in 1941 and continued even after the territory was placed under the general supervision of the United Nations. In 1952 Britain and the United Nations agreed to the federal incorporation of Eritrea into the Ethiopian state. This gave Ethiopia direct access to the Red Sea and the excellent port at Massawa, which Italy had in the course of sixty years converted into a Westernized city. Their expenditures upon roads, wharves, and general agricultural and training facilities had made Eritrea far more prosperous, and from a Western point of view, more advanced than Ethiopia. The Eritrean population, early influenced by Islam and then later by contact with the Italians, are an alien people within the state. Eritrean social, political, and cultural values are far different from those of the dominant Amhara and since 1952 this has increasingly become the centrum of discontent against the rule of the emperor.

The Sudan, 1900–1965

The 1899 agreement with Egypt did not establish a true equality between Egypt and Britain in the governing of the Sudan. The supreme authority there was a British governor-general nominated by the British. He was the executive authority, could legislate by proclamation, and was until the death of Sir Lee Stack in 1924 the sirdar or commander in chief of the Egyptian army.

The Sudan was divided into provinces each under a British governor and these were subdivided into districts with at first an Egyptian officer in control. In time British inspectors came to be the actual administrators of the districts with the Egyptians shoved into the background. Not until after World War I were many Sudanese recruited into government service.

In the beginning most of the administrative personnel were of the military. Very soon it became necessary to establish a more regular formal procedure for recruitment. The Sudan civil service was developed which operated in a manner comparable to the Colonial Office and India Office. The Sudan government staff was chosen annually in London by a board from hopefuls who had finished their university education. The Sudan service was small with much scope for individual initiative and, since most officers spent their entire careers in the Sudan, they gained considerable expertise in their areas and took great pride in their work.

Sir Reginald Wingate became governor-general when Kitchener was ordered to South Africa in 1899. Wingate was responsible for laying the groundwork for civil government and the establishment of a law system based on Indian models. His administration completed the rail network begun during the 1896–1898 war and began the experiments in irrigation which later resulted in the very profitable cotton-producing area of the Gezira.

The coming of World War I had profound effects upon the Sudan. In the winter of 1914 the khedive of Egypt, Abbas II, was deposed and Britain proclaimed a protectorate over Egypt. This action exposed the shallowness of condominium rule since Britain now directly controlled both Egypt and the Sudan. The war also gave Wingate the excuse to conquer the autonomous sultanate of Darfur. After the defeat of the khalifa, Sultan Ali Dinar had ruled Darfur without interference from the British. But his alleged pro-Turkish views were considered a threat to the Sudan so Wingate sent 2,000 troops into Darfur. El Fasher was taken in May 1916, and Ali Dinar was killed in November. (Final boundary agreements with the French territory of Chad were made in 1919.)

The southern areas of the Sudan had been almost cut off from control by Khartoum during the Mahdia. Imposition of condominium rule in the south was followed by years of ferreting out of the small-scale slave trade. Slavery was not directly attacked since the British hoped that with improved economic conditions it would fade away. One precaution against it was the virtual exclusion from the south of northern Sudanese. This factor added to differences in race, religion, and historical development further estranged the northern segment of the Sudan from the south.

Following World War I nationalist disturbances wracked Egypt and these culminated in British recognition of its independence. Some of the nationalist feelings found supporters in the educated minority of the Sudanese. The first political movement reflecting such ideas was the United Tribes Society led by Abd al Latif. He later formed the White Flag League which hoped eventually to form a united Nile state of Egypt and the Sudan. This league was secretly supported by Egyptians. There were disturbances at Omdurman and in Khartoum in June 1924, and an Egyptian battalion mutinied at the same time.

Sudanese nationalists were dealt a severe blow by the assassination of Sir Lee Stack, the governor-general and sirdar of the Egyptian army, in November 1924. Field Marshal Edmund Allenby, the British high commissioner, ordered all Egyptian troops out of the Sudan and thus Egyptian participation in the practical affairs of the condominium were almost ended and a radical element in Sudanese nationalism was removed. Subsequent British actions showed a deep mistrust of the Western-educated

Sudanese. Education on all levels was not adequately supported and military training of Sudanese lagged as British administrators began to depend for support much more on traditional rulers.

The fifteen-year period after the conclusion of the Anglo-Egyptian Treaty is a complex melange of forces. Egypt sought to maintain its special theoretical position in the Sudan and resist what it considered any British attempt to sever these historical ties. Britain, concerned for many years with the many problems in Europe prior to World War II, considered the Sudan merely an adjunct to other more pressing Middle Eastern questions. The Sudanese middle classes associated themselves with one of two major parties which evolved in the 1940s. These parties were the result of a split in an older organization, the Graduate General Congress. Ismail al Azhari in 1943 formed the first genuine Sudanese political party, the Ashiqqa, which stood for cooperation with Egypt looking toward the creation of a new larger Nile Valley state. The other party, the Umma, was more moderate and was prepared to cooperate with the British toward the goal of Sudanese independence. Each party, to give the British evidence of mass support, associated itself with a major Islamic brotherhood. The Ashiqqa was supported by the Khatmiyya, the most important sect in the Sudan before the mahdi's triumph. The Umma received the sanctions of the mahdi's posthumous son, Abd al Rahman, and the Mahdists. These connections between political parties and religious brotherhoods meant a widening rift between the nothern Sudanese political groups.

In May 1944, the British administration created an advisory council composed of twenty-eight Sudanese members, eighteen of whom were elected. Most of those on the advisory council were Umma party members, but they did not take over the role of the governor-general's council which continued to be, as it had since 1910, the major legislative body. The Ashiqqa was not satisfied with the advisory council and remained suspicious of Britain's plans for the future of the southern Sudan and the Sudan's relationship with Egypt.

In 1946 British Foreign Secretary Ernest Bevin issued a "draft Sudan protocol" which called for ultimate Sudanese self-government but under the "common crown of Egypt." This attempt to please both Sudanese groups failed since it alienated the Umma without placating the Ashiqqa politicians. Despite the growing British-Egyptian difficulties the liberalization of the Sudanese government continued rapidly before 1950. In 1948 the British unilaterally authorized the establishment of a Legislative Assembly which would represent the entire Sudan. Fifty-two members represented the northern areas and thirteen were either directly or indirectly elected to represent the south. An Executive Council, half of whom were Sudanese, replaced that of the old governor-general's. Negotiations between Britain and Egypt over the future of the Sudan produced nothing. Britain's position by 1950 was the same as the Umma-dominated assembly while Egypt and the Ashiqqa wanted a larger Egyptian dominated Nile polity.

In March 1951 the governor-general appointed an Anglo-Sudanese Constitutional Amendment Commission to develop plans for future self-government. However, in 1951 Egypt announced the abrogation of the condominium agreement and introduced into the Egyptian parliament bills which proclaimed Farouk "King of Egypt and the Sudan." The Sudanese Constitutional Commission completed most of its work by the end of 1951 and it recommended a transitional government with the governor-general acting on the advice of a prime minister who would head an all Sudanese council of ministers. It also planned for a bicameral legislature. This constitution was never fully implemented because of the July 1952 revolution in Egypt which deposed King Farouk. A final agreement was reached between the military regime in Egypt and Britain in February 1953 which gave self-government to the Sudan. This statute provided for a Sudanese House of Representatives and Senate, and a ministry under the general guidance of a British governor-general. The Sudanese were to determine at the end of a three-year period whether they wished independence or amalgamation with Egypt.

The major political parties in the Sudan in the early 1950s were the National Unionist party (NUP) led by Ismail al Azhari, and the Umma led by Sidik al Mahdi and Abdullah Khalil. The NUP was created in 1952 out of a number of pro-Egyptian factions, the strongest of which was the Ashiqqa. Another party which represented the Negro southern Sudan was the Southern Unionist Party (SUP). In the elections of November 1953, the NUP won fifty-one of the ninety-seven seats in the House of Representatives, the Umma twenty-two seats, and the SUP nine seats. Ismail al Azhari became the prime minister and minister of interior. The NUP was at first committed to union with Egypt, but Egyptian activities in the Sudan and the approach of the end of the three-year period created factions within the NUP. By mid-1955 almost all the politicians were against union with Egypt and the plebiscite later that year confirmed this feeling. The Sudan gained its independence on New Year's Day 1956. British and Egyptian forces had already evacuated the Sudan. Temporarily the instruments of government decided upon earlier remained in force with the exception of the transference of the governor-general's powers to a supreme commission of five members. Sayyid 'Ali al Mirghani, the head of the Khatmiyya, reached agreement with Sidik al Mahdi, the grandson of the mahdi and leader of the Ansar faction of the Mahdia, and forced Azhari to form a coalition government immediately after independence. Later al Mirghani withdrew support from Azhari and was instrumental in forming a new party, the Peoples' Democratic party (PDP). In July the PDP and Umma party ousted Azhari as prime minister and Abdullah Khalil became prime minister and al Mirghani deputy prime minister of this new coalition government.

In the elections of February 1958, for the reconstituted House of Representatives, the Umma party won sixty-three seats, the NUP forty-five, the PDP twenty-seven, and the Southern Liberal party which advocated a federal system won twenty. The coalition of Umma and PDP continued with Khalil as Prime Minister. However, Khalil's government was not as powerful as the statistics would indicate. Radio Cairo, by then reflecting the Pan African aspirations of Egypt's new leader, Gamal Nasser, continued to assail the prime minister. Egypt invaded a section of disputed territory in northern Sudan and withdrew only after Sudan complained to the United Nations. Other outstanding difficulties with Egypt concerned utilization of the Nile and evidence of subversion by Egypt. The economic situation of the Sudan also continued to deteriorate throughout 1958. In this atmosphere, complicated by differences between PDP and NUP leadership, Khalil appealed to the army to provide the necessary support in order to ward off internal and external threats to the independence of the Sudan. On November 17, 1958, the army commander, General Ibrahim Abboud, staged a military coup, dissolved the cabinet and parliament, and declared a state of emergency. Abboud then created a thirteen-member Supreme Council of the armed forces which controlled all legislative, executive, and judicial power. In addition, a twelve-member cabinet of advisers was constituted to aid Abboud in administering the state.

In 1959 there were three attempts to overthrow the military regime of General Abboud. In March Abboud bowed to the demands of junior officers and reconstituted the Supreme Council to a ten-member organization which included the complaining officers. In May the government arrested leading members of an alleged communist group and fifteen army officers. Two of the persons behind the March ultimatum to Abboud were also arrested on June 1. Another coup in November was also unsuccessful. Abboud's handling of these events together with his successful economic policy made his tenure of power more secure. Khalil, Azhari, and El Mahdi joined together in late 1960 to call for an end to the military regime but this had no effect. In July 1961, Abboud arrested twelve Sudanese political leaders, among them Khalil and Azhari. Abboud announced the creation of a new committee in November 1961, which was to work on the problem of a new constitution for the Sudan, and in January 1962, Azhari, Kahlil, and their associates were finally released from custody. These disturbances caused Abboud to promise a slow guided program leading eventually to the restoration of constitutional government.

In the various crises Abboud showed that his most potent weapon against other politicians was detention, yet he was not able to destroy the popularity of Khalil or Azhari among their followers. Sidak al Mahdi joined Abboud's opponents in demanding more political freedom for the Sudan. Added to all these problems was the revolt of the southern Sudan. This schismatic movement was racially and religiously oriented and was led by a number of revolutionary organizations such as the Sudan African Union and the Anya Nya. After 1956, they carried on a guerrilla war against government forces in the Equatoria, Bahr el Ghazal, and Upper Nile provinces.

In October 1964, attempting to solve the continuing strife in the three southern provinces, General Abboud formed a special commission to investigate the grievances of the rebels. In addition he encouraged public debate on the questions. These events, coming after years of press control and other restrictions, led to a series of demonstrations by students. The students were joined by government employees and other workers in Khartoum. The ensuing riots against the military resulted in the deaths of at least thirty persons. Nine days after the initial outbreaks, General Abboud assumed full power but promised to end the six-year military rule and return constitutional government to the Sudan.

After more disturbances Elkhatem Khalifa was named Premier to head a fifteen-man cabinet. Military rule was ended although Abboud retained his position as president. He was, however, shorn of much of his executive power. This was to be a transitional government pending full elections to be held in 1965. However, the pressures which had resulted in the overthrow of Abboud continued. Guerrilla raids in the south led by the Anya Nya continued. Khalifa was drawn into the vortex of the Congo rebellion by allowing the southern Sudan to be used as a staging ground for supplying Congolese rebels. A leftist minority attempted to sabotage the elections for the new National Assembly which were held in May 1965.

The election results were, therefore, cause for rejoicing. The Umma party led by Sidik al Mahdi won the largest block of seats. He immediately announced his intention not to hold office but to select a moderate who could carry into effect his plans for reconciling the south. He planned to form a coalition conservative cabinet and reserve three of the fifteen seats for southerners. Mahdi also announced that broad powers of local government would be granted to the south. The National Assembly would also be charged with drawing up a new constitution to provide for a presidential form of government. He promised the south that the position of vice-president would be specifically reserved for a southern politician. To carry out these policies the Umma party selected Muhammad Ahmed Mahgoub to be prime minister. A moderate, he had been selected by an Umma and National Union coalition to be premier just before the military coup by Abboud in 1958.

Mahgoub attempted to placate the three southern provinces. He found three southerners willing to become members of the cabinet. However, the offers of increased powers of local government fell far short of that type of autonomy demanded even by southern moderates. All compromise offers were refused. The guerrillas stepped up their activity. Armed with weapons stolen from the arms convoys which had supplied the Congolese rebels, the Anya Nya attacked the provincial capital at Witu. Lesser battles in July 1965 were reported throughout the three disaffected areas. An attack upon Juba triggered a massacre of the African inhabitants of the town by the Arab garrison. Over 1,400 civilians were killed. This event coincided with the announcement by Mahgoub of a new hard line against the rebels. Amnesty would be granted to all rebels who surrendered. Those who did not would face "severe measures." Few guerrillas took advantage of the government's offer.

The government was forced to concentrate over 15,000 troops in the south. These effectively controlled the Upper Nile and Bahr el Ghazal provinces. However, in Equatoria, by the end of 1965, government control was effectively confined to the towns. The activities of the army and the guerrillas caused the mass evacuation of large areas. Over 50,000 refugees crossed the border into Uganda. Moderation of the Khartoum-based government thus foundered on the centuries old hostility between Arab and Negro. Given the attitudes of the Negro leadership in the south, no compromise was possible. The government of the Sudan may crush the revolt, but by doing so it will only reinforce southern hostility toward any government from Khartoum.

Somaliland, 1880–1965

The opening of the Suez Canal in 1869 brought hundreds of ships every year into the Red Sea. European states and trading companies became concerned with establishing ports near the Straits of Bab-el-Mendeb and on the western flank of the Indian Ocean. The French secured Obock and later Djibouti. British interests were maintained at Aden while the Italians were engaged with the Eritrean coastline. It was an extension of European attitudes toward the Far Eastern trade which brought Europeans to the hitherto inhospitable Somali coastline. There were few towns of importance along the entirety of the coast stretching from Djibouti to Mogadishu. The vast interior, made up largely of bush land and semi-desert, was inhabited by many postoral Somali clans who wandered with their animal herds as far inland as the Haud and Ogaden areas. The hinterland Somalis, converts to Islam, relatively small in number and fierce warriors, had never evolved large viable state structures. Only along the coast was there a pretense of centralized control. Near the Horn of Africa the sultan of Mijertein maintained a tenuous rule over an undefined interior area. In the 1880s the ruler of Obbia declared himself independent of the sultan of Mijertein and in the ensuing years tried to extend his influence northward.

In order to strengthen themselves in the Bab-el-Mendeb area, the British occupied the major coast towns from Zeila to Berbera and declared this territory a British protectorate in 1884. They were not interested in the hinterland territories and maintained only casual contact with the Somali clans there. The Italians were at first interested in the Benadir region of the extreme south. A chartered company first secured rights to the coastline near Mogadishu. In 1884 an agent of the company convinced both the sultan of Obbia and the sultan of Mijertein to place themselves under Italian protection. As with the British, this did not imply anything more than theoretical sovereignty. The sultans were interested in obtaining guns and ammunition from the Italians which they could possibly use against one another. They received a cash subsidy from the Italians. The Italian resident at Mogadishu made an annual tour to the north to visit each ruler to pay the subsidy. This was the limit of Italian power until the opening years of the twentieth century despite the proclamation of a protectorate over southern Somalia in 1889. Hostility between the two

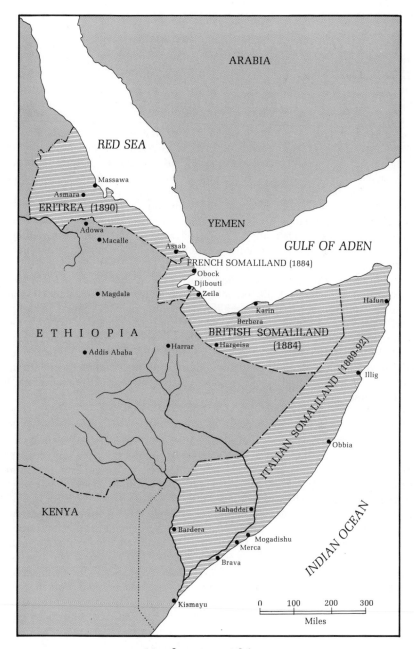

ARABIA

RED SEA

Massawa

Asmara

ERITREA (1890)

Adowa
Macalle

Assab

YEMEN

GULF OF ADEN

FRENCH SOMALILAND (1884)
Obock
Djibouti
Magdala
Zeila

Karin

Hafun

Berbera

E T H I O P I A

BRITISH SOMALILAND
(1884)

Harrar

Hargeisa

Addis Ababa

ITALIAN SOMALILAND (1889-92)

Illig

Obbia

KENYA

Mahaddei

Bardera

Mogadishu
Merca

INDIAN OCEAN

Brava

Kismayu

0   100   200   300

Miles

Northeastern Africa

sultanates became serious in the years after 1897 when adherents of the northern ruler began to raid deep into Obbia. Finally in 1901 the Italians lent military support to the sultan of Obbia and thus the balance between the two areas was restored.

A new factor was introduced in 1895 into this politically confused area. Muhammad Abdullah Hassan, later given the pejorative title the "Mad Mullah" by the British, returned to British Somaliland. He had been born in the Nogal Valley in the 1860s but had migrated first to Aden where he studied Islamic law. Later, after trips to Mecca, he fell under the influence of a famous teacher of the Ahmadiyah sect, Muhammad Salih. Later Muhammad Abdullah became one of the main organizers and instructors in the even more puritanical belief begun by his mentor which was called the Salihiyah. He had already gained considerable fame before he appeared in Somaliland attempting to convince the worldly Qadariyah Somalis to abandon their ways. Muhammad Abdullah's initial success in converting coastal Somali was only minimal and he moved into the interior. As a mullah or judge he soon gained a wide reputation and a considerable following among the Darod Somali. He was strong enough by 1899 to have his forces occupy certain strategic interior watering places and declare a jihad against the unbelievers. He at first directed his war against those who professed Islam but resisted his teaching. However, the British at Berbera believed that he was attempting to establish political hegemony over British Somaliland and the Ogaden areas of Ethiopia and reacted accordingly. Muhammad Abdullah obtained for his followers rifles and ammunition at greatly inflated prices from Sultan Osman Mahmud of Mijertein. By the end of 1900 the mullah's followers had almost halted trade in British Somaliland and had raided deep into the Ogaden for camels and rifles. A combined British and Ethiopian force of 17,000 men penetrated deeply into Somalia to end these attacks. This invasion was the first of a series of failures in the long campaign against Muhammad Abdullah. In 1903 the British with Italian consent used Obbia as the point of departure for another expedition. This too failed to capture the mullah or to end the activities of his followers. The only concrete result of these campaigns was to cause Muhammad Abdullah to occupy briefly the Nogal Valley. However, in 1904 another British expedition drove him into Mijertein.

The Italians had not participated actively in any of these punitive expeditions. In 1905 the mullah made an agreement with the Italians whereby he agreed to accept Italian protection in return for their promise to recognize him as the ruler of Nogal. For three years there was a minimum amount of conflict between Muhammad Abdullah and the Europeans. From his secure base he sent out converts into all Somali areas and these acted as agents of potential revolt. This three-year period witnessed continual quarrels between the two sultans and increasing exercise of authority by Italy. In 1909 an Italian resident was established in Obbia and at Alula. Disputes within the Salihiyah movement weakened the mullah's position. He was even denounced by Muhammad Salih.

Despite this he rejected the proposals brought by Sir Reginald Wingate and Slatin Pasha which would have brought permanent peace to the interior. Perhaps as a belated recognition of the futility of their previous policy, the British abandoned the interior to Muhammad's followers in 1909 and concentrated all their troops in the coastal towns of British Somaliland. Muhammad Abdullah then moved his main base of operations to Taleh, a fortress he constructed in British Somaliland.

During World War I the British and Italians continued to solidify their administrative control over the coast. Increased military force enabled them to intervene successfully in hinterland disputes. At the same time many of the adherents of the mullah began to drift away. His attempt to cement a more definite alliance with Lij Iyasu of Ethiopia was foiled by the overthrow of the young emperor in 1916. At the close of World War I the mullah's direct influence was confined to southeastern British Somaliland. In 1920 the British decided to end the continued threat of raids and warfare posed by Muhammad Abdullah. In January of that year, over 1,500 tribesmen and a cadre of British troops opened the campaign. A new factor was introduced by the British who used aircraft for scouting and bombing. In February Taleh fell to the British, but the mullah and a few of his followers escaped to the Ogaden. The mullah's waning popularity is shown by his inability to gain support for his cause in Ethiopia. British native troops with Ethiopian permission crossed the border and forced the mullah to flee again. The close of the long career of Muhammad Abdullah came in January 1921 when he died of pneumonia. Unlike the mahdi in the Sudan, he had not built a stable state structure nor did he leave behind a competent successor. With his death the political and military overtones of his movement came to an end.

The death of the mullah removed the last major obstacle to British and Italian control of the interior. Each European state established a type of indirect rule over the nomads of interior Somali. Boundaries between both British and Italian areas and Ethiopia remained indefinite. This factor later provided Mussolini with the excuse necessary to begin his war of conquest against Ethiopia. In that war General Graziani with one division operated from Somaliland against the southern flank of Haile Selassie's forces. On June 1, 1936, Italian Somaliland became a partner with Eritrea and Ethiopia in a new government structure called Italian East Africa. After Italy's entrance into World War II, Somaliland was an active theater of operations and British Empire forces completed the conquest of Italian Somaliland in early 1941 prior to their main invasion of Ethiopia.

From 1941 until April 1950, the British administered the conquered area even though after the war the former Italian lands were placed under United Nations control. In 1949 the General Assembly decided to return executive control to Italy and this was effected in April 1950. Italy was to act as the trustee power pending achievement of independence within a period of ten years. Thus it was made clear that the European administration would be temporary and all assistance should be given to Somalian political movements in order to facilitate the granting of independence.

Italian Somaliland was the focus of the earliest political parties and these have had a stormy history. The first political organization was the Somali Youth League (SYL) created in 1943 during the British occupation. The SYL stood for the negation of colonialism and a reunification of all Somalis into one polity. The leading personality in the SYL immediately after World War II was Haji Muhammad Hussein. The SYL was disappointed in their demands for self-determination since the victorious powers could not decide what to do with the Italian colonies. The SYL under Hussein's leadership refused to cooperate with Italian authorities after 1950 and a number of serious disturbances occurred.

In 1953, Hussein left to study in Cairo and his place as president of the SYL was taken jointly by Abdullahi Issa and Aden Abdullah Osman, and they began to cooperate with the Italian administration. In 1956 Somaliland was granted a seventy-member elected Legislative Assembly. In the elections the SYL won forty-two seats and the Hizbia Dighil Mirifle which believed in the retention of tribal organization won thirteen. Abdullahi Issa was chosen as premier of the advisory council. Haji Muhammad Hussein who had returned from Egypt soon after recaptured control of the SYL from those he considered to be conservatives and embarked once again on a program of noncooperation with the Italian authorities. However, in 1958, the SYL executive, tiring of Hussein's activities, suspended him from the movement, and cooperation once more became the policy of the SYL.

A further advance toward self-government in the Italian territory was the expansion in 1959 of the Legislative Assembly to ninety members. Haji Muhammad Hussein, who had been suspended from the SYL, formed a new organization, the Greater Somalia League (GSL), in opposition to the SYL. This organization was militantly pan-Islamic and drew much of its ideological and physical support from Egypt. The GSL announced that it would boycott the elections, and due in part to its activities, there were serious riots in February 1959. Haji Muhammad Hussein was arrested and briefly detained and the GSL was banned. He was soon released and continued his propaganda through the GSL against the conservative leadership of the SYL, particularly against Abdullahi Issa. In the subsequent elections for the Legislative Assembly the SYL won eighty-three of the ninety seats. Issa was again chosen Prime Minister. He was soon replaced by Dr. Abdi-Rashid Shermarke, largely because of the opposition of Hussein. The main accusation against the SYL under Issa was that it was too pro-West and did not concern itself enough with Somali unification.

Meanwhile in British Somaliland a similar political acceleration was taking place. When civil government was restored in 1948 the protectorate was administered by a British governor and an advisory council. In 1957 a new constitution was introduced which provided for a fourteen-member Legislative Council. The council was enlarged again in 1959 to twenty-nine members of whom fourteen were elected. The major political party in British Somaliland was the Somali National League (SNL) which had existed in various forms since the mid-1930s. The SNL was a radical nationalist party with close ties with Egypt. It favored the creation of a greater Somalian state similar to that recommended by the GSL. Its leader by the mid-1950s was Muhammad Haji Ibrahim Egal. The SNL boycotted the 1959 Legislative Council elections because the elected element was not guaranteed a majority. Due largely to this SNL pressure, new elections were held in the protectorate for an expanded elective council in February 1960. The SNL won twenty of the thirty-three seats and Egal served as Prime Minister of the protectorate from February until the unification of both areas in July. Another party in British Somaliland was the United Somali party (USP) which won twelve seats in the 1960 regional election.

Partially in response to political developments throughout Africa and the pressure from Somali nationalist groups, the United Nations moved in 1959 to implement its stated goal of a decade before. Unification of the two Somali areas and independence was effected simultaneously by a joint meeting of the legislative assemblies of British and Italian Somaliland at Mogadishu. There they declared themselves a National Assembly and chose Aden Abdullah Osman as President of the Republic of Somalia. On July 13, 1960, he named Shermarke prime minister to head a coalition government. Abdullah Issa was appointed Foreign Minister and Muhammad Haji Ibrahim Egal became Defense Minister. The government of the Republic of Somalia as constituted in 1960 was confirmed by the electorate in a referendum in June 1961 with Aden Abdullah Osman continuing as president and Shermarke as prime minister. The National Assembly at first refused to certify the constitution and only the resignation of Shermarke in September 1961 forced ratification. Shermarke resumed the position as Prime Minister after ratification. The dominant party in the 123 member National Assembly was the SYL which in 1963 controlled eighty-three seats.

Despite the tensions between the parties which led Premier Shermarke to state in September 1963 that military rule might be necessary, the state remained united. One of the major reasons was that all parties, no matter what their general differences, were in substantial agreement about the long-range goal of creating a greater Somalia. This meant the cession of the Haud and Ogaden regions from Ethiopia, the Northern Territory of Kenya, and French Somaliland. These African states made it clear that they would not concede Somalia's claims. Thus Somalia became a focal point for nationalistic clashes between various African states in the period after 1965.

TEN

Postwar political developments: French Africa

General political changes

The rapid German victory over France in 1940 had serious ramifications for the French territories in Africa. The establishment of the Vichy government dominated by the threat of a victorious Germany split the loyalties of Frenchmen. In the French West African Federation (AOF), Governor-General Pierre Boisson remained loyal to the Petain government until the end of 1942. Felix Eboué, the governor-general of the French Equatorial African Federation (AEF), declared his support for the Free French government of Charles de Gaulle. These divergent policies had a direct influence upon the peoples of the two federations. In West Africa, Boisson, to further his control over the federation, increased the use of the arbitrary penalty system called the indigénat whereby the administration could punish Africans without the formality of a trial. He also intensified practices which were already resented by Africans such as forced labor. The few existing politically oriented organizations were repressed; so were labor groups. Despite these more rigid controls, Governor Boisson was faced with the defection of an increasing proportion of the population as the war progressed. Some chiefs and some of the African soldiers refused to accept the Vichy regime. Many of the latter escaped to the Cameroun or to the AEF to join the Free French. The chief of the Mossi in Upper Volta was the most vocal of African rulers in his opposition to the Vichy settlement. Ultimately he committed suicide after extracting a promise from his heir not to become chief until the "true French" returned. After Boisson led the West Africans into the Gaullist camp in December 1942, many of the active tensions within the federation disappeared. However, his repressive regime was remembered by both the African intellectuals and traditional leaders. Economic dislocation caused by the war was an added stimulus to their demand for a larger voice in their own affairs.

French Equatorial Africa provided an example of loyalty to the Free French. Politically aware Africans realized that they could reasonably demand political rewards for that loyalty. Perhaps as important was General de Gaulle's recognition that the relationship between metropolitan France and its colonies would have to be altered significantly after the war. In January and February 1944, a group of Free French politicians and colonial officials met at Brazzaville and adopted a number of resolutions concerning the future of the French empire. They proposed that Africans be given a larger role in governmental affairs. However, they specifically ruled out self-government for the territories. Instead, they called for a strengthening of the ties binding France to its empire by giving Africans more representation on the colonial level and in the French parliament. After the war Africans should be chosen to the constituent assembly which would be responsible for drawing up the new constitution for France.

The Brazzaville Conference of 1944 set new directions for French colonial policy. However, the hopes of many African leaders for more of a share of power in their territories were blunted in the period 1945–1950 by political considerations in metropolitan France. The reorganization did not result in as much participation as many Africans wished. Nevertheless, there were sweeping changes made in the colonial system by the constitution of 1946 and the Loi Lamine Guèye named for its sponsor, the Senegalese socialist deputy. The major change was the creation of the French Union which consisted of metropolitan France, overseas departments (that is, French Guiana, Réunion, Guadeloupe, and Martinique), and the overseas territories. There was also categories for associated states such as Indochina, Tunisia, and Morocco.

The political structure of the French Union was composed of a president (the president of the Republic), the *Haut Conseil de l'Union Française,* and the *Assemblée de Union Française.* The *Haut Conseil* whose major function was to help the French government in instituting policy for the union was never established. The *Assemblée* was, however, and it was composed of 204 members. One-half of these represented metropolitan France. Two-thirds of the metropolitan members were chosen by the National Assembly while one-third were selected by the *conseil de la république.* Of the 104 overseas members, forty members came from the two African federations with the AOF selecting twenty-seven members. These representatives were chosen by the territorial assemblies. The *Assemblée de l'Union Française* appeared to embody the federal principle, but in fact it had little real power. It was to be utilized generally as an advisory body and decisions which it could make independently relating to overseas territories were not binding on the government.

The overseas territories of France also received substantial representation in the central government by the reforms of 1946. In the National Assembly there were eighty-three overseas deputies. Of these, thirty came from Algeria, ten from the overseas departments, and forty from the AOF and AEF. The territories also were represented in the *conseil de la république*. Deputies to the National Assembly from the AOF and Togoland were elected by the qualified voters in each territory from a common roll. In the AEF and the Cameroun, they were chosen by the two-college system. Representatives to the *conseils de la république* were chosen by the territorial assemblies and the deputies. Although representation in both metropolitan legislative bodies was small, it did associate the leading African intellectuals with the government of France. Thus, far from being disassociated from the central government as in British Africa, these potential leaders were directly involved at the highest level.

Of more direct importance to Africans was the reorganization of the councils which had been designed to aid the governor-general and the lieutenant-governors. In each one of the territories in the AOF, *Assemblées Territoriales* (referred to as *Conseils Généraux* until 1952) were established. In the AEF they were called Representative Assemblies. Their function was a financial one, although they were consulted by the administration on a variety of matters. Like the *conseils* which had existed before the war, they were advisory bodies. The most noticeable improvement of the territorial assemblies over the prewar *conseils* was in the method of selecting the members. They were chosen by a two-college system of direct election. In order to understand this complicated method of election it is necessary to know what changes had been made in citizenship status.

Originally there had been two broad classes of persons in the French African territories. Those who were citizens of France were *citoyens de statut civil*. They could be Africans who met the necessary qualifications as for example the qualified inhabitants of the communes of Senegal. The larger portion of this class, however, were not Africans but Frenchmen. In the previously protected areas the Africans were normally subjects or those persons who were judged by local statutes or customary law. The wording of some of the decrees creating the French Union indicated the intention of abolishing these distinctions and making all persons in the overseas territories citizens of the French Union. In general, these statements tended to confuse the issue because the large mass of Africans kept their customary laws and were not given the same rights of franchise as those holding *statut civil*. Even those persons still under customary law designated *statut personnel* were not all granted the right to vote. Only certain sections of the mass of Africans were allowed the franchise. Through the mid-1950s these categories were expanded until for certain elections in most territories the majority of the Africans did have the vote.

Election to the *Conseils Généraux* was decided on by a two-college system of franchise. The first college was composed of all voters who were entitled to the *statut civil* while the second college was made up of persons of the *statut personnel*. The reasons for this system of voting was the recognition of the differences in education of the people of French Africa. The policy of assimilation was not negated by this system. It merely admitted that the policy had resulted in the conversion of only a relatively few evolved Africans to the class of *statut civil*. Metropolitan French citizens and assimilated Africans were guaranteed the selection of more members to the assemblies than their mere numbers would warrant. The persons who voted in the second college chose more members than did the voters of the first college. The number of representatives chosen by the two electoral colleges varied from territory to territory. However, the voters of the second college chose between three-fifths and four-fifths of the members of the assemblies.

At the federal level the postwar reforms created a new advisory body, the *Grand Conseil*, which represented the entire federation and was chosen by the territorial assemblies of each federation. Each assembly chose five of its own members to the *Grand Conseil*. These bodies in an expanded fashion served the same purpose as had the prewar *Conseil de gouvernements*.

Despite the conservative reaction which occurred in France in late 1946 and lasted for almost a decade, there were three important laws enacted which affected the African federations. The first of these was the Second Loi Lamine Guèye of 1950 which assured Africans of equal conditions of work and pay with their European counterparts in the civil service. The Overseas Labor Code of 1952 guaranteed African workers minimum wages, hours of work, family allowances, and collective bargaining equal to French workers. The third piece of legislation was the Municipal Law of 1955 which provided for the creation of elected mayors and councils selected from a common roll for a number of selected municipalities in French Africa.

The ten-year period of relatively static attitudes by the French government was, nevertheless, marked by events which eventually allowed for a rapid devolution of power to Africans. Outside of the continent the conservative imperial policy of France was rudely shocked by events in Indochina. By 1954 the French had admitted their failure in Southeast Asia by agreeing to the Geneva accords. The revolt in Algeria was well under way by 1956 and the cause of the Algerian guerrilla fighters was receiving considerable support in government circles. Any relaxation of French attitudes toward Algeria also affected the attitude of colonial authorities toward the rest of Africa. It was obvious that France did not wish a reiteration of Indochina and Algeria anywhere else in Africa.

This period also witnessed the creation of the first specific African political parties. Before World War II political parties were present only in Senegal and these tended to be reflections of domestic French parties. The first important postwar party was the intraterritorial *Rassemblement Démocratique Africain* (RDA) organized by Felix Houphouët-Boigny of the Ivory Coast. At first associated with the French Communist party, it had become by 1951 a party of cooperation. The other major party was the loose association of African Socialist deputies put together by Léopold Senghor and called the *Indépendants d' Outre-Mer* (IOM). The 1956 elections to the National Assembly confirmed the RDA as the most important political organization in French Africa and Houphouët-Boigny was made a minister in the French government. This government urged on by the liberal Minister of Overseas France, Gaston Defferre, moved to reform the entire structure of control in Africa. The *Loi Cadre*, or framework law, which accomplished this reflected many of the ideas of Houphouët-Boigny who helped design it. The *Loi Cadre*, contrary to the usual French approach of legislating even the minute details of government procedure, only specified the areas where changes were to be effected. The administration would make the law effective by issuing decrees which would be approved by the territorial legislatures. These decrees framed within the context of the generalizations of the *Loi Cadre* would be the specifics of change in the colonies.

The major intent of the *Loi* and subsequent decrees was to create a decentralization of colonial government. In this aim the framers of the law were breaking with a half-century of colonial legislation that had attempted to create larger units of government directly tied to metropolitan France. The two major reasons for this reversal were the demands for more territorial autonomy from within the two large federations and the pressure created by events elsewhere in Africa. Britain was in the process of moving many of her territories toward independent status. These developments were closely followed by French statesmen and French African politicians. Another force for change was the Algerian revolt which served to divide the allegiance of African leaders and which also predisposed the French government to make sweeping reforms before the spirit of North African nationalism could spread into sub-Saharan Africa. It should be noted that Senghor and the other representatives of the IOM opposed the *Loi* because of its Balkanizing effect upon the federations.

The decrees established the territorial assemblies as the most important institution in the previous federations. The governor-generals became high commissioners, representatives of metropolitan France, and also the chief executive for the *Grand Conseil*. The *Grand Conseil's* area of concern and deliberations was restricted to matters of common concern. Its financial powers were similarly restricted. There was no central ministry provided for the collection of territories. On the territorial level, however, ministries were created called *Conseils de gouvernement* varying in size up to twelve members. These ministries were responsible to the territorial assemblies. The assemblies were given many more powers of legislation in health, education, planning, and economic development for the territory. The chief representative of the administration was the *chef de territoire*, formerly called the lieutenant-governor, who served as the head of the *Conseil de gouvernement*. All acts of the assembly had to be certified by the *chef de territoire*. The chief political figure in the territory was the vice-president of the council who exercised great powers over legislation and through the media of his political party was in a strong position to coerce the French administration.

The *Loi Cadre* was passed over the objections not only of many Frenchmen, but of a large number of important African leaders who wanted to build upon the existing federal structure to achieve a larger working political union than that of territories. Nevertheless, the *Loi* was in the mainstream of African opinion. It established workable territorial units of government at the expense of the federation. Ties of unity to France were shifted from the larger units to the territories. Thus the French Union or later de Gaulle's ideas of the Community were henceforth based on the territory. Where previously the most prestigious and important positions for Africans had been in metropolitan France or in Dakar and Brazzaville, they now became territorial cabinet positions. The expanded duties of the assemblies and the selection of the conseil from the members of the assemblies spurred the formation of political parties and political agitation in the smaller units.

The founding and development of new political parties in the territories which followed the reforms of 1956 will be discussed more thoroughly elsewhere. It is necessary to note here certain developments in metropolitan France that aided the cause of African nationalists. The Algerian conflict had caused France to send over one-half million men there, spend huge sums of money, and it eventually pushed France to the brink of civil war. Charles de Gaulle was called upon to give leadership to a sadly divided France. He agreed, but only on the conditions of a new constitution which would give him the necessary executive power to deal with the crisis. In the summer of 1958 his government prepared the new constitution for a Franco-African Community. As envisioned by de Gaulle, this would be a federal republic with France at the head of a number of all but autonomous states. A plebiscite was to be held in all overseas territories in September to determine the willingness of these areas to become a part of this system. In August de Gaulle traveled throughout Africa conferring with the native political leaders. He informed them that any territory could have its independence from France simply by a majority of its people voting No on the plebiscite. However, any area taking this position could expect to receive no further aid from France. In the ensuing election only Guinea chose this alternative.

By the time of the referendum in 1958, the proposed community had already become that of semi-independent territories tied to France. The defection of Guinea and the differential political movements in the territories convinced even the most adamant defenders of the community such as Houphouët-Boigny that independence was the logical goal of the territories. In retrospect, the Loi Cadre provided the changes necessary to make the final shift to independence in 1960 smooth and easy.

With this general overview of the French method of devolving power to their African territories, one can begin to examine in more detail the development of political parties and nationalistic aspirations in each of the territories.

Devolution of power and consolidation of African rule: the AOF

DAHOMEY

Dahomey, bounded on the west by Nigeria and on the east by Togo, has an area of almost 45,000 square miles and a population of 2,250,000. It is an agricultural state whose main products are cassava, palm kernels, and yams. As with so many of the recently independent West African states, it is too chronically short of funds to undertake any major economic and social projects. France in 1964 continued to support the government financially and took seventy percent of Dahomey's exports and provided fifty-nine percent of her imports.

A key factor in the instability of the politics of Dahomey is the north-south split caused by tribal, religious, historical, and personal factors. Post World War II political activity in Dahomey first centered on a French priest, Father Aupiais, and then on his protégé, a southerner, Serou Apithy, whose political center of power was Porto Novo. Apithy was the dominant political figure in Dahomey until 1959. At first he and his followers associated themselves with the RDA, but they broke with Houphouët-Boigny in 1948 and formed the *Parti Républicaine Dahoméenne* (PRD). Later Apithy affiliated the PRD with the aims of Léopold Senghor of Senegal. The success of Apithy's moderate pro-French policy was confirmed by the implementing elections of the *Loi Cadre* of 1957 when the PRD won thirty-five of the sixty seats in the Dahomean Assembly. In opposition to Apithy was Hubert Maga, a northerner, and Justin Ahomadegbe, another southerner and member of the Fon tribe whose power base centered on Abomey. Maga's party, the *Mouvement Démocratique Dahoméenne* (MDD), won fourteen seats and the *Union Démocratique Dahoméenne* (UDD), led by Ahomadegbe, won eleven.

All three parties in 1958 supported de Gaulle's proposal for the French Community. Apithy attempted to bring Dahomey into the Senghor-Keita designed Mali Federation. However, the political and economic pressure of the Ivory Coast's Houphouët-Boigny upon Niger, Upper Volta, and Dahomey caused Apithy to withdraw his support of Mali and his party from association with Senghor's socialists.

In the election of April 1959, the PRD won thirty-seven seats, the MDD twenty-two, and the UDD only eleven despite the fact that UDD candidates had won almost 30,000 more popular votes than did the PRD. In protest against what they considered unfair districting, UDD supporters displayed a violent reaction which culminated in serious riots throughout the country. These disturbances forced Apithy to concede nine seats to the UDD and join a coalition government with Maga as premier. He and Ahomadegbe agreed to serve as ministers under Maga's leadership. In late 1959 Apithy formed a new front in coordination with Senghor's PFA to secure the independence of Dahomey and this action broke up the coalition. Maga, with MDD and UDD support, removed Apithy from the cabinet.

Dahomey became an independent republic on August 1, 1960, with a seventy-man National Assembly and a president as chief executive. In December 1960, in the first elections after independence, Maga's MDD won a sweeping victory and Maga was elected president. By early 1962 Maga felt strong enough to reshuffle his cabinet "to streamline" the government, ostensibly in order to carry out the recently adopted four-year economic

French West Africa (AOF)

and social development plan. Correlate with the strengthening of Maga's power was a reorganization of parties to form a national front party, the *Parti Dahoméen de l'Unité* (PDU).

Although Maga's power through his control of the government and the PDU seemed at first glance unassailable, there were many disaffected areas. His real power was based in the north, particularly among the Bariba tribe. In the south, Apithy and Ahomadegbe still maintained a large following. The economic sector was basically unhealthy and was maintained primarily with French help. Unemployment, particularly among the white-collar workers, grew, and Maga was accused of squandering money on such projects as a $3,000,000 presidential palace.

This incoherent unrest was increased by a further cabinet reshuffle in September 1963, in which Maga became premier and defense minister in addition to being president. Widespread disorders followed this reorganization and in October 1963, the army, commanded by Colonel Christophe Soglo, intervened and forced Maga's resignation. In November a provisional government was formed. The most important members were Soglo, Maga, Apithy, and Ahomadegbe. This government was an extra constitutional regime whose authority rested primarily on Soglo and his control of the small army of 800 men. In December 1963, Soglo carried the reorganization further by forcing Maga's resignation and placing him under house arrest. On January 20, 1964, Colonel Soglo resigned from politics. On the previous day Apithy had been elected president of the reconstituted government of Dahomey and Ahomadegbe was named president of the council. The government, a forty-two member assembly and ten-man cabinet, was ostensibly a national one. That this was an illusion was shown by the revolt of Bariba tribesmen against the new government in March 1964 in support of the deposed President Maga. The rebellion, after some loss of life, was suppressed by French-trained units of the army. A further source of friction within the state was the problem of the recognition of China. Apithy since 1963 had favored the recognition of mainland China and close contacts with the Ivory Coast and the *Entente* group. Apithy's viewpoint eventually prevailed and Red China was recognized. In the confusing period that followed both Chinese governments maintained embassies in Cotonou. In addition to personal rivalry between Apithy and Ahomadegbe, Dahomey was beset with almost insoluable economic problems which could have been alleviated only by massive aid. Ahomadegbe, attempting to curb spending in July 1965, cut the salaries of the civil service by twenty-five percent. The General Dahomey Workers Union thereupon called a strike. However, Ahomadegbe won his point and the strikes were ended, but these measures provided only partial relief in trying to reduce government expenditures.

The sub-rosa conflict between President Apithy and Ahomadegbe came into the open in November 1965. The two men could not agree over the appointment of the head of the Supreme Court. The coalition government broke apart over this issue and disturbances again rocked the country. General Soglo and the army intervened once more, overthrew the government in December 1965, and appointed an interim president, Tairou Concagou, and a four-man technician government. Soglo also requested that the leading politicians cooperate with one another to create a new stable government. However, in this atmosphere the three leading politicians formed new parties. These were the *Alliance Démocratique Dahoméenne* (ADD) of Ahomadegbe, the *Union National Dahoméenne* (UND) led by Maga, and the *Convention National Dahoméenne* (CND) headed by Apithy. When it became obvious within ten days that the politicians were not going to cooperate with each other to form a stable government, Soglo and the army once more took power and Soglo stated that the military regime was made necessary because of "the incapacity of the politicians to govern." Ahomadegbe and Maga fled to the Ivory Coast and Soglo after the third coup formed a military "technicians" government.

GUINEA

For almost eight years after World War II, Guinea was practically devoid of the political activity so common elsewhere in West Africa. This was largely because the most important native political leader, Yacine Diallo, a school teacher, was a moderate whose political goals were modest and evolutionary. He was supported by one of the most important Muslim leaders in West Africa, Cherif Fanti Mahdi of Kankan, and many of the influential chiefs.

Sekou Touré was one of the founders of the RDA and in 1952 he became the secretary-general of the *Parti Démocratique de Guinée* (PDG), a branch of the RDA. The rise to prominence of Touré and the success of the PDG is closely tied to the trade-union movement in Guinea. Although an extremely poor territory, Guinea did have some iron and bauxite which the French began to mine seriously in the late 1940s. This resulted in a modest-sized African industrial working class. The largest union in Guinea was the *Conféderation Générale des Travailleurs* (CGT) controlled from France and largely Communist-dominated. Touré had become a member of the trade-union movement while still a government employee, and in 1948 had risen to be the secretary-general of the CGT in Guinea and in 1950 secretary-general of the coordinating committee in West Africa. In 1953 Touré and the CGT managed a successful general strike which lasted for over two months. After the capitulation of the movement, Touré became one of the most important politicians in Guinea.

In 1954 Yacine Diallo died, thus removing from the political scene the one important Guinean moderate politician trusted by both the French and Africans. In the elections which followed for the vacant seat in the French Assembly, Barry Diawadou, the leader of the *Bloc Africain de Guinée* (BAG), defeated Touré. The election was marred by charges of election tampering by the officials. In 1955 Touré was elected mayor of Conakry and a deputy to the French Assembly. Despite these victories, the PDG in 1955 did not have a single seat in the Territorial Assembly. In this period there developed serious differences between the PDG and the other RDA branches in West Africa. Houphouët-Boigny had decided after 1950 to rid the party of its radical label and disassociate it from the Communist movement. The logic of the situation in Guinea dictated a totally different approach. Thus while the main RDA was moving to the right, the PDG appeared to become more radical.

In the elections of 1957 occasioned by the *Loi Cadre*, the PDG won fifty-six of the sixty seats in the Territorial Assembly and Touré became vice-president of the executive council. He was now in a position to begin to implement some of his programs for the economic and social development of the country through government planning and control. The major block to such reform was the traditional system of chiefs who resisted the PDG's implementation of agrarian reforms. In 1958 after continuing opposition of the chiefs, Touré's government abolished the system, replacing it with some 4,000 village councils elected by the people. The new system was designed to be more amenable to control by the central authorities than the traditional form of rule.

Touré came into more open conflict with the CGT and in order to stress the African nature of the Guinea unions, he organized the *Conféderation Générale de Travail Africaine* (CGTA) in 1956. In 1957 this merged with dissident union groups to form the one union of Guinea, the *Union Général des Travailleurs d'Afrique Noire* (UGTAN). This union was separate from all metropolitan unions and control of the union was in African hands. Thus by 1958 Touré was the master of the one union in the country, the strongest party, and also controlled the territorial government. His position as an independent agent was not, however, all that secure. This was clearly shown by the referendum of 1958.

As late as his meeting with de Gaulle in August 1958, Touré had not indicated any serious desire for independence for Guinea outside the French Community. His subsequent position against the de Gaulle referendum seems to have been dictated by disappointment in the proposed future union, distrust of de Gaulle, and pressures from the more radical elements within the PDG. These still powerful radical groups could not be ignored, and Touré and the PDG campaigned against the proposed French Community. Guinea was the only area in French Africa to vote No on the referendum of September 28. The vote was a convincing 1,136,000 No to only 57,000 Yes votes. French reaction was swift and emotional. On September 29, Guinea was informed that this rejection meant its separation from French West Africa. French authorities ordered home their teachers, doctors, civil servants, and removed all equipment that could be crated and carted away. Over 4,000 skilled Frenchmen left Guinea.

On October 2, 1958, the Territorial Assembly proclaimed itself a constituent assembly, declared Guinea an independent republic, and named Touré head of state, aided by a sixteen-member cabinet. A new constitution was drawn up embodying these ideas and was adopted on November 12, 1958.

Touré gained desperately needed financial assistance from Ghana in December 1958 and later received loans and technicians from the Communist bloc. This direct aid and guarantees of more support were enough to enable Guinea to weather the first year of independence. By this time Western nations, including France, had reexamined their positions and Touré could begin cautiously to withdraw from what had seemed irrevocable commitments to the Soviet bloc. The quick action of the French after the referendum had strengthened Touré politically. In December 1958, the chief opposition party, the BAG, and the much smaller group, the *Parti Démocratique Socialiste de Guinée*, had merged with the PDG. Barry Diawadou, the leader of the BAG, became a member of the cabinet.

Touré's emancipation from the radical elements within the PDG and the Soviet bloc did not come until late 1961. In November 1961, the Teachers Union precipitated a crisis throughout the country in conjunction with officials of the Soviet Embassy. The disturbances were calmed by Touré and the moderates, and the leaders of the action were arrested and imprisoned. On December 16, 1961, the Soviet Ambassador and key aides were expelled from the country. Soviet Deputy Premier Mikoyan visited Guinea in January 1962 to reassure Touré of the continuing interest of the Soviet Union and to give assurance that its diplomats in the future would not interfere in the political affairs of Guinea. The events of 1961 set the stage for a further loosening of the close ties of Guinea and the Soviet Union. Although the bulk of technicians continued to come from the Eastern bloc, Touré appealed for more Western aid after 1962. This period also witnessed more active participation by Guinea in contacts with other African states and the Western powers.

In November 1964, Touré named resident ministers for the four major regions of Guinea, these ministers to be responsible directly to the central executive. Touré also took steps to restrict membership in the PDG only to the militantly active socialists who had proved themselves. Thus the party was directed away from a mass movement to one that could more accurately reflect the desires of the executive.

The only political opposition to the PDG and Touré was a clandestine one and the party has been vigilant in filling the prisons with those who could be suspect. In November 1965, it announced the discovery of a plot to assassinate Touré and overthrow the government. The chief plotter in the abortive coup was a distant cousin of the president, Mamadou (Petit Touré). Mamadou, who until 1964 was a part of the hierarchy, was one of the leaders of an underground political group, the *Parti de l'Unité Nationale de Guinée* (PUNG).

IVORY COAST

In 1944 Felix Houphouët-Boigny founded a farmers' union, the *Syndicat Agricole Africain* (SAA), which in 1945 grew into the more radical *Parti Démocratique de la Cote d'Ivoire* (PDCI). Partly as a reaction to the second constitution of the Fourth Republic, Houphouët-Boigny and other deputies met at Bamako in October 1946, to found a new, mass, intraterritorial party, the *Rassemblement Démocratique Africain* (RDA). Under the influence of French socialists, the Senegalese did not send representatives and thus began the polarization of nationalistic activity in French West Africa between the Ivory Coast and Senegal. Houphouët-Boigny was chosen the first president of the RDA, and the PDCI became the Ivory Coast branch of the RDA.

From the beginning the RDA associated itself with the Communists. Open clashes with the administration in French West Africa and the Ivory Coast in particular during 1949 and 1950 culminated in widespread loss of life in early 1951. The French administration clamped down on all political activity in the Ivory Coast and the RDA was radically weakened by the mass arrests. Houphouët-Boigny was saved from this because he was a member of the French Assembly. Soon afterward, the PDCI and RDA changed these tactics to cooperation with the French administration and broke their ties with the Communists. Houphouët-Boigny then urged continued cooperation with France and stated that the RDA must become a purely African party. Most of the other territorial political parties associated with the RDA agreed to this change. The weakness of the RDA was shown in the 1951 elections for the French Assembly when only Houphouët-Boigny and two other RDA members were elected. However, the decision to move to a more moderate stance was the correct one since the RDA gained the confidence of the government and the moderate French business community. This confidence was shown in January 1956, when the RDA won nine of the twenty-one contested seats in West Africa for the French Assembly. Houphouët-Boigny was elected mayor of Abidjan and was given cabinet rank by the French government. It was in this capacity that he had so much influence on the Loi Cadre of 1956 which gave universal suffrage based on a one-roll electoral system to French West Africa, created executive councils on the territorial level, and broadened the deliberative powers of the territorial assemblies. In the elections of 1957 for the new territorial assemblies, the RDA swept the elections in most of the areas, winning a total of 236 out of 474 contested seats in the eight assemblies. It gained majorities not only in the Ivory Coast, but also in Guinea, Upper Volta, and the Soudan. In the Ivory Coast the opposition gained only five percent of the popular vote.

The question of the future of the areas of the French Community divided the RDA. Sekou Touré and the PDG-RDA Guinea segment wanted independence quickly, and the Soudan, Upper Volta, and Dahomey were moving closer to Léopold Senghor's position. Houphouët-Boigny, despite his ideas concerning devolution of power to the territories, stood for continuing close association with France and threw his considerable influence in West Africa behind a Yes vote for the 1958 referendum. Houphouët-Boigny utilized the economic power of the Ivory Coast to dislodge the Upper Volta and Dahomey from their newfound agreement with Senegal. This move checked the construction of a potentially powerful federation and resulted instead in the creation of a much weaker Mali Federation. Soon afterward Houphouët-Boigny associated the Ivory Coast with Upper Volta, Dahomey, and Niger in the loosely organized, weak Conseil de l'Entente. This new creation was dominated by the wealthy Ivory Coast.

French agreement for independence for Mali within the Community led Houphouët-Boigny and the other leaders of the member states of the *Conseil* to demand independence also. This was granted, and on August 7, 1960, the Ivory Coast became independent.

The grant of independence to Mali and the *Entente* states effectively ended any chance of a larger territorial unity. This fact and the defection of Guinea minimized the effect of the RDA as an intraterritorial party. The territorial branch parties tended to become more independent of Houphouët-Boigny's control. The PDCI's domination over the Ivory Coast remained. Houphouët-Boigny was elected president in November 1960, and the PDCI-RDA won all seventy seats in the Ivory Coast National Assembly.

All of the smaller parties in the Ivory Coast were either dissolved or absorbed into the PDCI between 1952 and 1958. The *Action Démocratique et Social de la Côte d'Ivoire* was dissolved in 1958 and the small *Parti Regroupement Africaine* disappeared with the deportation of its leader, Camille Adam, in 1959. Earlier the *Parti Progressiste* and the *Bloc Démocratique Eburnéenne* had been absorbed into the PDCI. Houphouët-Boigny continued in this period to strengthen constitutionally his control of the Ivory Coast, particularly since the discovery of plots directed at his assassination in early 1963. In April 1964, another plot to kill Houphouët-Boigny was discovered. The alleged chief conspirator, Ernest Boka, a former minister, later committed suicide in prison. The controls of the PDCI, although less onerous than in most other African one-party states, are just as effective.

However, Houphouët-Boigny's strength lay not in political or police controls, but in the strength of the economy of the Ivory Coast and the success of his domestic and foreign policies. Disdaining a doctrinaire socialistic approach, Houphouët-Boigny made the Ivory Coast into one of the model states of Africa by blending state control with free enterprise. The economy of the Ivory Coast is more balanced than neighboring states. Although coffee is the major export, wood products, cocoa, and palm products also account for over one-half of the exports of the Ivory Coast. Houphouët-Boigny has been one of the most pro-Western of all African leaders, and this attitude has provided a continuing flow of development capital, largely from France.

The PDCI was unopposed in the 1965 elections for president, an enlarged eighty-five member National Assembly, and for 140 local counselors. Of the more than 1,800,000 votes cast, Houphouët-Boigny received all but 332 votes. One might question whether under a contested election the percentage of votes cast for the PDCI would have been so overwhelming, but in Africa, where political success is tied so closely with economic development and prosperity, it is doubtful whether the overall results of the elections would have been different.

MALI (SOUDAN)

The first genuine political party in the French Soudan was the *Parti Soudanais du Progrès* (PSP) formed in the early 1950s by a canton chief, Fily

Dabo Sissoko. This was a very conservative organization and the more radical, educated groups did not find a voice in politics until an ex-teacher, Momadou Konaté, organized a territorial branch of the RDA. Until 1956 Sissoko and Konaté were the dominant native political figures in the Soudan. Konaté's support was in the cities and Sissoko's came from the traditional rural areas. By 1956 the RDA in the Soudan had outgrown its earlier Communist associations and was more acceptable to the authorities and the chiefs. In that year Konaté died and the leadership of the RDA in the Soudan devolved upon a young Bambara politician, Modiba Keita, who had been a close associate of Houphouët-Boigny since 1946. After spending some time in French jails, he had become a member of Soudan's territorial assembly. In 1953 he was elected mayor of Bamako and in 1956 he was the Soudanese representative to the French Assembly.

In the elections of 1957 occasioned by the *Loi Cadre,* the RDA won sixty of the seventy seats for the Soudan Assembly. Sissoko and his deputy, the Socialist Hamadou Dicko, were both defeated. In the referendum of 1958 occasioned by de Gaulle's rise to power, Keita swung the Soudan behind de Gaulle and Houphouët-Boigny's policy of the French Community.

On December 29–30, 1958, at Bamako, Keita met with the leaders of Senegal, Dahomey, and Upper Volta to discuss federation. At a later conference in Dakar in January 1959, the delegates of the four areas agreed upon a federation plan which provided for a federal executive and legislature. This marked a definite break with Houphouët-Boigny's policy of autonomous members with the Community. Houphouët-Boigny brought pressure to bear on the leaders of Upper Volta and Dahomey, and these two states withdrew from the scheme, later forming a loose *entente* with the Ivory Coast. Keita had by this time created out of the Soudan branch of the RDA a new political party, the *Parti de la Fédération Africaine* (PFA). Keita, in conjunction with Léopold Senghor of Senegal, had presided over the Bamako and Dakar conferences. Despite the defection of Dahomey and Upper Volta, Keita and Senghor decided to go on with the plans for establishment of the Mali Federation. Although Keita would have preferred the new polity of Mali to be a unitary state, he bowed to the desire of Senegal for a federal structure. In 1959 the PSP merged with the dominant party led by Keita; and its leaders, including Sissoko, were integrated into the government. In the confirming election of March 1959, the PFA won over seventy-five percent of the popular vote and secured all the eighty seats in the Soudan Assembly. The *Parti Régroupement Soudanaise* (PRS) led by Dicko contested the election but was dissolved soon afterward and Dicko himself abandoned politics.

In April 1959, Keita was named premier of the Federation and Senghor became president of the federal assembly. In September in Paris at a meeting of the French Community's Executive Council, Keita and Mommadu Dia of Senegal presented Mali's wishes for an independent state. In December de Gaulle announced French adherence to the independence of Mali although such a move would mean the effective end of de Gaulle's newly created Community, and in June 1960, the Mali Federation became an independent state. However, stresses which had been overlooked in the emotion of creating the Federation soon divided the two parties. Differences in the economies, social needs, and methods of colonization were the root of the divisions. The immediate reason was a disagreement over apportionment of seats in the Malian federal executive, particularly the position of president. The crisis came to a head on August 19, 1960, when Keita dismissed federal Defense Minister Dia and claimed that the state was in danger. Under the guidance of Senghor the Legislative Assembly of Senegal reacted to Keita's actions on the next day by voting to take Senegal out of the Federation. Keita and other Soudanese leaders were arrested in Dakar and immediately deported. Keita's attempts to save the Federation failed and on September 22 the Soudanese legislature formally pronounced the establishment of a new Republic of Mali. Relations were broken off with Senegal, the frontier sealed, and Malian trade hastily rerouted through the Ivory Coast. The PFA was reconstituted as the *Union Soudanaise* with Keita as its leader. Keita became president of the Republic, and the *Union Soudanaise,* the only party in the state, was Keita's instrument to further his concepts of the socialistic reconstruction of the state. On January 20, 1961, Keita strengthened his control of the government by assuming the portfolios of foreign minister and defense minister. On April 29, an accord was signed with Ghana which aligned Mali with Ghana and Guinea in a union which would, in time, standardize the diplomatic, economic, and monetary policies of the three states. Keita after 1961 followed a policy of radical government control at home and nonalignment abroad. Relations with France were normalized, and with the resumption of friendly relations with Senegal in 1963, Mali once again could utilize the railroad and the port of Dakar. Despite the stringent control of the state by the *Union Soudanaise,* few incidents occurred in Mali which threatened Keita's position. One of these was when Mali merchants in July 1962 demonstrated against the introduction of the new currency regulations. Ninety-one persons were arrested and charged with attempting to overthrow the government. Among those detained were Dicko and Sissoko, and on October 1, 1962, they were sentenced to death on charges of plotting to overthrow the government. One week later their sentences were commuted to life in prison. In July 1964, the government announced that both political leaders had died in prison. Few details were given. In April 1964, the single list of candidates for the Malian National Assembly sponsored by the *Union Soudanaise* received eighty-nine percent of the total possible vote. On May 13, Modiba Keita was reelected president for a new four-year term by the National Assembly.

MAURITANIA

Mauritania is one of the most sparsely settled areas of West Africa, having a population of only slightly more than 700,000 nomadic people. Most of the Mauritanians are Moors and their typical political organization, left relatively undisturbed by the French, was that of rule by emirs. French rule in Mauritania after 1910 was an extremely stormy one. The population was highly mobile and divided by incessant petty wars involving different Berber groups. The stability of French rule was based largely upon control of the great emirs of Trarza, Brakna, and Adrar, and the possession of a first-rate military force which could implement French policy in the more difficult areas of Mauritania. Officially, before World War II the governor was assisted by a territorial council or *Conseil d'Administration*, all members of which were appointed by the governor. After the war, the French introduced a system of elections to choose members of the *Conseils*. This revised system called for a two-college method of voting. The first college was made up of all those electors in Mauritania who were residents of metropolitan France or those Mauritanians who could qualify for the classification of *statut civil*. The second roll was composed primarily of African voters who could qualify for the classification of *statut personnel*. Until 1956 there were twenty-four members in the *Conseil d'Administration*. Of these, eight were selected by the first college and sixteen were selected by the second college, despite the fact that there were only slightly over 700 non-Africans in the territory.

The first political party in the territory was created by Horma Ould Babana who was the first Mauritanian to sit in the French National Assembly. This party was primarily a government sponsored one and was called *L'Entente Mauritanienne*. Some of Babana's programs seemed to be too advanced for the traditional rulers of Mauritania, and they combined with some of the younger men to form an opposition group called the *Union Progressiste Mauritanienne*. The name of this group was later changed to the *Parti du Régroupement Mauritanien* (PRM). The leader of the PRM was Sidi el Mokhtar. In the *Conseil* election of 1952, the PRM won twenty-two of the twenty-four seats on the council. In 1956 el Mokhtar again defeated Babana for the French Assembly and Babana fled Mauritania for the protection of the king of Morocco where he became an adherent of the king's claims to territory in Mauritania. Soon after this, Morocco launched a series of invasions of Mauritanian territory that were contained only with extreme difficulty by the French African troops and paratroopers. In the plebiscite occasioned by de Gaulle's assumption of power, Mauritania followed the pattern of most of the French West African territories and voted to remain within the French Community. Following the referendum, the territory was reorganized and given the name of the Islamic Republic of Mauritania. In this reorganization the legislative body of Mauritania was increased to forty members and the principle of responsible government was instituted. With the flight of Babana in 1956, Mauritania had become for all practical purposes a one-party state. In the confirming elections of May 1959, the PRM gained all forty seats in the Assembly. The premier of Mauritania after 1959 was Mokhtar Ould Daddah, a kinsman of el Mokhtar and the only lawyer in Mauritania. Ould Daddah was educated in France, but he also had close association with the traditional rulers of Mauritania because of his family. After the practical breakup of the French Community in 1960, Mauritania became an independent state with a Legislative Assembly and ministry

Ould Daddah became the first premier, and the PRM the chief political organization of Mauritania. A new constitution was adopted in May 1961 which established a presidential system while retaining the forty-seat National Assembly. Ould Daddah was then elected president unopposed in August 1961.

At the beginning of independence Mauritania seemed to have two basic problems. One concerned the continuing border troubles between Mauritania and Morocco, and the other was the economic nonviability of the state. Since 1960 the border troubles between Morocco and Mauritania have eased in intensity. Many of the African states which had supported Morocco's claim to hegemony over Mauritania have since either adopted a neutral position or have changed sides completely. Although the problem remains, it has become less pressing than in the immediate past. Mauritania's economic position has been strengthened to the point where it is potentially one of the richest of the newly independent states of West Africa because of the discovery and exploitation of iron ore and, to a lesser extent, copper. Ould Daddah's moving of the capital from its long-time location at St. Louis in Senegal to the new city of Nouakchott reflects this growing prosperity.

There were two opposition parties to the PRM, the *Union Nationale Mauitanienne* (UNM) and the *Nahda,* a radical organization. The latter group was banned and Boyagui Ould Abride and other leaders were jailed for a brief time. Later at a series of meetings, outstanding differences between the three parties were adjusted and Ould Daddah formed a new ministry which included Boyagui and Hodrami Ould Khatny of the UNM. An attempt, late in 1964, by three former ministers to form a new political party was thwarted by Ould Daddah who declared that it was a move to destroy national unity. The major threat to continuing political control by the PRM, however, comes not from a Western-organized political party, but from the traditional schismatic elements within the Mauritanian state led by men such as the emir of Trarza and Horma Ould Babana from Morocco.

NIGER

The most outstanding feature of the Niger Republic is its poverty. In 1963 the negative difference between imports and exports was approximately $12,000,000. It is a landlocked state, depending for the export of its crops, primarily peanuts, on the foreign ports of Cotonou and Lagos. The population is ethnically divided between nomadic Tuaregs and Fula in the north and the sedentary Hausa-Songhai people in the south.

Niger gained its independence in August 1960, after voting in 1958 to stay in the French Community. Legislative power after independence was vested in a unicameral National Assembly and executive power in a president who conducts policy, initiates legislation, and has wide powers in times of emergency.

The first major political party in Niger was the *Parti Progressiste*

Nigérien (PPN), which was created in 1946 as the Niger section of the RDA. In 1950 a split occurred in the PPN when the RDA broke with the Communists. The more radical Djibo Bakary split with the party and formed his own *Union Démocratique Nigérienne* (UDN). The major leader of the PPN after the break was Bakary's cousin, Hamani Diori. In the territorial elections of 1957, the UDN in coalition with a smaller party, the *Bloc Nigérien d'Action* (BNA), won forty-one seats while the PPN won only nineteen. Bakary thus became the first premier of Niger. In 1958 he campaigned strenuously against the de Gaulle proposed French Community. The subsequent Yes vote forced his resignation, and Diori and the PPN returned to power. The strength of the new regime was seen in the elections of December 1958 when Diori's party, renamed the *Union pour la Communauté Franco Africaine* (UCFA), won fifty-four of the sixty seats in the legislature.

In October 1959, all opposition parties to the UCFA were banned. The UDN, which had changed its name to the *Sawaba* party and was still led by Bakary, was forced into exile in Mali. Another party which operated clandestinely was the Freedom party whose exiled leader, Andaly Douda, was assassinated in Bamako in May 1962. Douda's party stood for closer association with Mali.

Douda's assassination was blamed on Diori and the Niger government. This was but one of Diori's problems. Economic unbalance and growing tribal conflict made his position in the UCFA far from secure. Serious indications of this could be seen in the conflict between the army and the state in 1963. Certain high officials including the Minister for African Affairs, Zodi Ikhia, were arrested at that time. Bakary from his sanctuary in Mali continued to harass his cousin's government.

Relations with Dahomey became increasingly strained after the deposition of President Maga. Dahomeans living in Niger were expelled and Cotonou was closed to Niger trade. In September 1964, the Niger government announced that a plot, directed against Diori and organized by the *Sawaba* party, had been discovered. In October it was announced that the *Sawaba* party was responsible for a series of violent outbreaks against the government. These abortive attempts to overthrow the government were supposedly led by *Sawaba* "commandos." Diori announced the complete failure of this treasonable plot and that a number of the leaders had been publicly executed. Ghana and Dahomey, particularly, were accused of harboring *Sawaba* members and facilitating their activities against Niger.

In April 1965, while attending the Moslem celebration of Tabasky in Niamey with members of the government, Diori narrowly escaped assassination. A grenade was thrown which killed a child and wounded five other persons. The man arrested for the attempt was linked to the *Sawaba* party and it was alleged that he had been trained in Ghana. The action was denounced by all of the *Entente* members. Thus, while relations with Dahomey had improved, those with Ghana grew progressively worse during 1965.

SENEGAL

In 1945, reacting to the climate of the Brazzaville Conference, Leopold Senghor and Lamine Guèye formed the *Bloc Africain,* affiliated with the French Socialist party, SFIO. Regarding the second constitution of 1946 which established the French Union as insufficient, the African deputies to the French parliament met at Bamako to form the interterritorial RDA. Senghor and Guèye, on orders from the SFIO, did not attend this meeting, thus casting Senegal in a different political mold than the other territories which aided in the founding of the RDA. In 1948 Senghor, demanding more autonomy from the SFIO, began the *Bloc Démocratique Sénégalais* (BDS). In 1951 the BDS won both seats to the French Chamber of Deputies. In the meantime, Senghor had become the dominant force of the *Indépendents d'Outre Mer* (IOM), deputies to the French National Assembly who believed in federalism and rejected association with French political parties. This brought Senghor and the BDS in increasing conflict with the RDA in West Africa. Until 1960 the RDA concept was more popular in France and Africa than Senghor's.

In 1956 the *Bloc Progressiste Sénégalais* (BPS) was formed by blending the BDS with a number of smaller political groups. This became the Senegalese section of the *Convention Africaine* which was the successor to the IOM and was dominated by Senghor and his associates. In 1957 the *Convention Africaine* fused with the *Mouvement Socialist Africaine* (MSA) to oppose the RDA, and in the following year Senghor and Guèye merged their followings to form the *Union Progressiste Sénégalaise* (UPS) as the local agency of the interterritorial *Parti du Régroupement* Africain (PRA). Notwithstanding Senghor's stand against French control, the UPS swung behind de Gaulle's 1958 referendum. In December 1958, discussions were begun in Bamako looking toward a federation of Senegal, Soudan, Dahomey, and Upper Volta which was to be called the Mali Federation. However, pressure from the Ivory Coast caused the defection of Dahomey and Upper Volta. The two remaining partners did form the Mali Federation in March 1959. The UPS was fully in control in Senegal, and Senghor was selected president of the federal assembly of the Federation. With the breakup of the French Union, the Mali Federation became independent in June 1960. However, internal pressures, doctrinal differences, and different pressing social and economic problems brought an end to the Mali Federation in August 1960. Modibo Keita and other Soudanese leaders were deported and Senegal became a separate independent state.

The new constitution for Senegal approved on August 25 called for a president chosen by an electoral college to serve a seven-year term, a premier to act as chief executive, and an eighteen-member cabinet selected by the National Assembly. The legislative power was conferred on the eighty-member National Assembly. All members of the National Assembly were UPS men. Thus power and responsibility in Senegal were balanced between President Senghor, Premier Mamadou Dia, and the president of the assembly, Lamine Guèye. For over two years, with minor exceptions, these three men worked in close harmony to implement economic development under a four-year plan. However, the government system could be utilized by factions within the UPS if harmony among the leaders was lost.

In the period after 1960 there developed two major factions within the UPS. The younger, more radical deputies who were eager for faster economic and social change were led by Dia while the more conservative section of the assembly and the country followed Senghor. The first overt signs of the depth of the rift between Dia and Senghor occurred in the winter of 1961 when the state of emergency first decreed in August 1960 was tightened. Dia was accused of being dictatorial and, in the struggles in the party councils, Senghor proved too popular to unseat. Dia lost some supporters in high places when a cabinet reshuffle of early 1962 replaced them with Senghor adherents.

On December 15, 1962, thirty-nine deputies of the Senegal National Assembly tabled a vote of censure against Dia's government. They accused him of corruption and refusing to lift the unnecessary emergency decrees. On Dia's orders, gendarmes and part of the territorial guards on December 17 surrounded the assembly and members of the assembly were forced to leave. Senghor had meantime ordered loyal paratroops into the city and authorized Guèye to convene a parliamentary session in his home. Forty-eight members of the assembly voted for Dia's overthrow and called upon Senghor to assume dictatorial powers. The bulk of the army proved loyal to Senghor, and Dia and his chief lieutenants were arrested. The assembly immediately authorized Senghor to draw up new constitutional instruments to be submitted to the nation by referendum.

In May 1963, Dia was sentenced to life imprisonment and three of his former ministers were sentenced to twenty years each. The new constitution which was adopted by referendum on March 3 eliminated the position of premier. The functions previously exercised by Dia were taken over by the president who is elected separately from the National Assembly. No vote of censure can bring down the government, nor can the president dismiss the assembly. Thus Senghor gained full control of the executive of Senegal. Within the UPS the elements of Senghor's old party, the BDS, were more powerful than Guèye's following or that of Gabriel d'Arboussier. Senghor thus dominated the UPS. Lesser Senegalese parties such as the *Mouvement de Libération Nationale* (MLN) joined the UPS. The PRA-Senegal which broke with the UPS over the referendum in 1958 still continued its separate existence after the disturbances. Its leaders by restricting themselves to the academic world hoped to avoid conflict with Senghor and thus keep the PRA alive. However, in November 1964, the party leader, Abdoulaye Ly, was arrested and charged with incitement to revolt. The extreme Marxist party, the *Parti Africaine de l'Indepen-dence*, was outlawed. Another small party, the *Front National Sénégalais* (FNS), whose leader was Cheikh Anta Diop, the historian, was dissolved by government order in October 1964. This was probably because a number of former supporters of Dia had drifted into the FNS. Thus Senegal became for all practical purposes a one-party state firmly controlled by Senghor.

UPPER VOLTA

Upper Volta is a large, landlocked area of 105,869 square miles with a population of approximately 4,250,000. It is an agricultural state whose major exports are peanuts, maize, and livestock. It is dependent to a very large extent for extra capital from France which takes eighteen percent of the exports and provides Upper Volta with fifty-two percent of its imports.

The only political force in Upper Volta was the RDA until 1957 when the *Mouvement Démocratique Voltaique* (MDV) was formed. There were two other smaller parties which also contested the *Loi Cadre* election of 1957. These were the *Mouvement Populaire de l'Evolution Africaine* (MDEA) led by Nazi Boni and the *Parti Social d'Education des Masses Africaines* (PSEMA). In the 1957 election for the assembly the RDA won thirty-seven seats, the MDV twenty-seven, and the MDEA seven. The RDA and MDV formed a short-lived coalition under the leadership of Ouezzin Coulibaly. However, later in 1957 this coalition split and the MDV, the MDEA, and the PSEMA coalesced in opposition to the RDA, electing Nazi Boni as president of the assembly. In early 1958, Coulibaly regained control of the government by the defection of several MDV members to the RDA. Chief among these men was Maurice Yameogo. The RDA supported the de Gaulle Community and Upper Volta returned an overwhelming Yes vote in the 1958 referendum. Later in 1958, the death of Coulibaly made Yameogo the head of government of the autonomous republic.

Yameogo led the Volta RDA into a coalition with the opposition parties which allied themselves briefly with Senegal's *Parti Régroupement Africain* (PRA). This movement was the opening wedge in Yameogo's drive to unite Upper Volta with the projected Mali Federation. However, pressures from Houphouët-Boigny of the Ivory Coast rendered these attempts abortive. Later Volta's economic dependence on the Ivory Coast was underscored by its adhesion to the *Conseil de l'Entente* (Ivory Coast, Niger, Dahomey, and Upper Volta). Those who favored the Mali Federation broke with the government. Yameogo's following, now known as the *Union Démocratique Voltaique* (UDV) won sixty-four of the seventy-five seats in the subsequent elections of April 1959.

Yameogo's major political opponent, Nazi Boni, later in 1959 formed the *Parti National Voltaique* (PNV), closely associated with the chief party of Mali, the *Parti Féderaliste Africain* (PFA). This organization underscored Boni's conclusion that Volta's future rested in a close association with Mali. Both were soon banned by Yameogo and the now dominant UDV. Boni created a new party, the *Parti Républicaine de la Liberté* (PRL), which was also banned early in 1960. Boni escaped to Mali where he continued his efforts to undermine Yameogo and his one-party regime.

In July 1960, the necessary arrangements were made in Paris and, on August 5, Upper Volta became a sovereign state. The new constitution adopted by national referendum on November 27, 1960, provided for a presidential system. The first president was chosen by the seventy-five members of the National Assembly. Yameogo was selected in December 1960 to be the first president of the Republic and, in November 1965, was again elected president by gaining 2,132,418 of a possible 2,188,241 votes. Although this vote certainly indicated support, dissatisfaction could be seen in the fact that over one-third of the electorate at Wagadugu did not vote in the elections for the National Assembly. Ostensibly this was in protest to the exclusion of certain persons from the voting list.

Yameogo's major problems in the early 1960s concerned lack of money and the need for an outlet to the sea. Forced out of the proposed Mali Federation and into the *Conseil de l'Entente*, Yameogo, nevertheless, negotiated better economic and political arrangements with Volta's other rich southern neighbor, Ghana. Poverty and its attendant pressures, coupled with government overspending, proved too complex for the UDV government of Yameogo. The president built a sumptuous country palace, and other politicians lived in lavish style while the economic ills of the country went unsolved.

To curb overspending on government services, Yameogo proposed in December 1965 a twenty percent cut in government salaries. This caused four days of demonstrations against the government in Wagadugu. The president reshuffled the cabinet, reduced its size from sixteen members to thirteen, and he assumed the position of defense minister. This precipitated the revolt of the military under the command of Lieutenant Colonel Sangoule Lamizana. The coup was bloodless, and even Yameogo publicly praised the take-over. Lamizana became president, holding in addition five ministries. None of Yameogo's ministers were retained in the new regime. However, no representative of the labor groups which had led the disturbance were included either. Lamizana established a state of emergency, proclaimed a curfew in the cities, and announced his intention of instigating an austerity program. He created a consultative committee composed of civilians to act as an intermediary group under the central government. Despite the obvious military nature of the regime, Lamizana declared that the military take-over was only temporary.

Devolution of power and consolidation of African rule: the AEF

CENTRAL AFRICAN REPUBLIC

The Central African Republic, formerly the territory of Ubangi-Shari, is a landlocked, poor area of 238,224 square miles, composed ethnically of a number of Bantu groups, with a population of approximately 1,300,000. It is primarily an agricultural country, hampered by poor soil and lack of minerals, the exception being diamonds of which 265,000 carats were mined in 1965. The bulk of the nation's trade is with France which in 1965 supplied sixty-one percent of the imports and took fifty-seven percent of the republic's exports. In addition, France supplied the funds to meet the recurrent deficit in the government budget. The major problem facing any government of the newly independent Central African Republic was how to make the necessary social and economic improvements without the proper base.

The Central African Republic attained autonomy in the French Community in 1958 after voting ninety-eight percent Yes to the de Gaulle

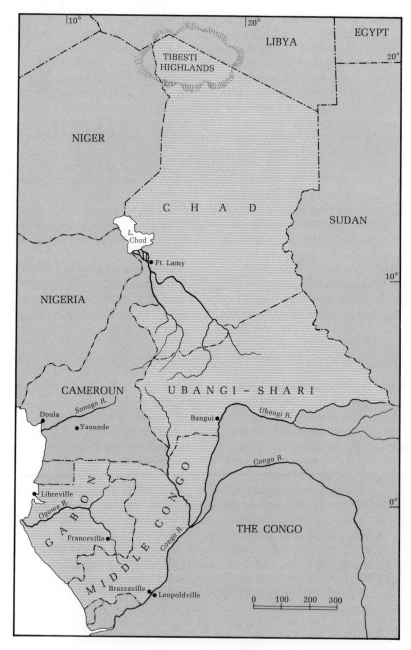

French Equatorial Africa (AEF)

referendum. The first political party in the territory was the *Mouvement pour l'Evolution Sociale de l'Afrique Noire* (MESAN). It was the creation in 1952 of Barthélemy Boganda who was a member of the French Assembly and had the support of the French party, *Mouvement Républicain Populaire*. Boganda wanted a closer federation of the four equatorial republics (Central African Republic, Congo, Gabon, and Chad) but was defeated by affluent Gabon's reluctance to join such a union. However, in 1959 the republic joined with her sister states in the Equatorial Customs Union. In 1965 the range and functions of this union were broadened by the establishment of the Central African Customs and Economic Union. A new constitution of February 1959 established a Legislative Assembly of fifty members and a president elected by the assembly as chief executive. Boganda's death in 1959 threw the politics of the country temporarily into disorder on the eve of elections for the Legislative Assembly in 1959. However, his chief lieutenant and twenty-six year old nephew, David Dacko, succeeded to power as head of the party and was elected president of the republic in April 1959. In July 1960, Dacko signed the necessary constitutional instruments with France, and on August 13 the Central African Republic was proclaimed a sovereign state.

Differences within MESAN led to the creation in 1960 of a rival party, *Mouvement pour l'Evolution Démocratique de l'Afrique Centrale* (MEDAC), led by Abel Goumba. However, in December 1960, MEDAC was ordered dissolved and Goumba and his most important followers were arrested. From that date onward the Central African Republic has been a one-party state. In early 1962, Goumba and another leading politician, Pierre Maleombko, were sentenced to jail for six months for "endangering the state," and later in the year all opposition parties were dissolved. In late 1963, an election for the assembly was held on the basis of a single list of candidates and, in January 1964, Dacko was elected to a seven-year term as president. In March 1964, he was unanimously reelected chairman of MESAN. Thus it appeared that Dacko was finally in full control of the state. However, the economic problems of the republic could not be solved without massive economic reconstruction. The funds provided by France, no matter how important, were not sufficient to undertake such designs. The mode of life of the politicians was not indicative of the poverty of the land. The form of political protest against the government in such a one-party state could only be a violent one.

On January 1, 1966, Colonel Jean Bedel Bokassa, a fourth cousin of Dacko and commander of the 800 man army, led his forces against the government. He charged Dacko and the other politicians with corruption, moral laxity, and becoming pawns of the Chinese Communists. Little resistance to the army was encountered, and as had been true in other military coups in Africa, Dacko and the other leading politicians immediately proclaimed their loyalty to the government. Bokassa dissolved the National Assembly and created a Revolutionary Council which guided by him would establish the laws for the new regime. Bokassa's first acts were an attack upon what were considered the major problems of the republic.

Polygamy was abolished and Bokassa in a number of public statements stressed the ideal of work as a major ingredient in solving the nation's economic problems. Expense allowances for government workers were canceled, taxes were cut, and a government austerity program was announced. Since the key to the republic's shaky future was continued economic cooperation with the West, Bokassa immediately took steps to assure these supporters of his hostile feelings toward the Red Chinese. Alleging the discovery of evidence linking them with paramilitary training and actvity, the new regime broke diplomatic relations with Red China.

CHAD

With an area of almost one-half million square miles, Chad is one of the larger African states. Like some of its neighbors in the former AOF, it is very poor, having a base of subsistence agriculture. Its major export item is raw cotton which provides two thirds of the export income. Chad runs a huge import-export deficit yearly and depends upon continuing French aid and investment for its economic stability.

Chad, together with Gabon, the Congo, and the Central African Republic, formed the pre-World War II administrative federation of French Equatorial Africa. It is a poor, landlocked territory with a sparse population of less than three million persons. It is divided as is Niger and Mali into two broad cultural groups—Muslims in the north and Bantu ethnic groups in the south. Despite its poverty and isolated position, Chad played an important role in the development of African nationalism in French Africa. After the French defeat in 1940, when many of the colonies remained loyal to Vichy, Chad, under the influence of its West Indian governor, Felix Eboué, declared for the Free French. It was later joined by the other component areas of Equatorial Africa. Eboué in this favorable climate was the moving force behind the Brazzaville Conference of 1944 which proposed sweeping reforms in French Africa. The failure to carry through on these promises set the stage for the development of political parties, particularly the RDA, in the ten years after the war.

The first major party, the *Parti Progressiste Tchadien* (PPT), in Chad was created by another West Indian, Gabriel Lisette, in 1947. The PPT became the local version of the intraterritorial RDA. Lisette led the PPT and the government through the reorganization caused by the *Loi Cadre* of 1956. However, mounting pressure from the Muslim north eventually forced his resignation as premier. He was succeeded by François Tombalbaye who was more acceptable to the north. Chad, in the referendum of 1958, voted overwhelmingly to remain in the French Union. Tombalbaye soon ousted Lisette as head of the party and exiled him in 1960. Some of the Muslim support defected from Tombalbaye and formed a separate party, the *Parti National Africaine* (PNA), to contest the elections of 1960. On August 11, 1960, Chad became an independent nation. The National Assembly of eighty-five members was composed of sixty-seven PPT members, ten PNA, and six independents. Tombalbaye became the president of the new republic.

In early 1961, Tombalbaye effected a compromise with his chief opposition, the PNA, and in March a fusion of the two groups, the *Union pour le Progrès du Tchad* (UPT), was announced. In January 1962, Tombalbaye declared all opposition parties a danger to the state and they were dissolved. Not surprisingly in the Chad National Assembly elections of March 1962, the PPT won all the seats and Tombalbaye was again selected head of state by the assembly. From this time Tombalbaye worked to get rid of all his potential political rivals and to further consolidate the power of the PPT. In March 1963, five leading politicians were arrested and the National Assembly was dissolved. In July two of the five were sentenced to death for subversion. Again in September 1963, Tombalbaye declared a state of emergency following clashes between demonstrators and the army. Three major politicians, including Ahmed Koulmallah, former head of the PNA, were arrested. A Chad government in exile with headquarters in Khartoum was later formed; it continued to operate until late 1965.

In April 1964, a quarrel developed between the government and some French nationals. The Chad National Assembly asked that all French troops be removed from the country. However, Tombalbaye rejected the notion that this should be carried out since Chad needed the 1,000 man French force for security as well as for the economic value of the military to the nation.

The periodic violent disturbances in outlying districts directed against Tombalbaye's government continued through 1965. The most serious was located in the Mangalme district northeast of Fort Lamy where seven government officials were killed in October. The movement at Mangalme ostensibly was backed by the Muslim rulers who wanted some of their feudal privileges returned. At the same time less serious antigovernment moves were organized in the south. In November three ministers of state and three members of parliament were arrested and accused of plotting to kill the president. Following upon these events, the National Assembly voted a change in the constitution. The section of the constitution which gave persons the right to form political parties was deleted. Thus Chad officially became a one-party state. Despite this, Tombalbaye's control of the state continued to be fraught with danger. The coups in ostensibly more stable neighboring states acted as a spur to the activities of the dissident elements within Chad.

THE REPUBLIC OF THE CONGO (BRAZZAVILLE)

Immediately after World War II, the only territorial political party in the Middle Congo was the *Mouvement Socialiste Africaine* (MSA) which was a section of the French Socialist party (SFIO). The most important African member of the MSA was Jacques Opangault. The RDA was early represented in the Congo by an efficient organization headed by Felix Tchicaya. In 1956 the *Union Démocratique de la Défense des Intérets Africains* (UDDIA) was founded by Abbé Fulbert Youlou, a Catholic priest and former mayor of Brazzaville. Although the church later defrocked the abbé, he continued to wear the habit, largely because of the effect it had on many of his supporters. Much of this support came from the Bakongo who had elevated one of their deceased leaders, Sergeant Matswa, to the position of semidiety. Some of this earlier allegiance was transferred to Youlou.

In the 1957 territorial elections, the MSA and UDDIA each won twenty-one of the forty-five seats. However, Opangault was called to form the government. Later in 1957, the UDDIA became affiliated with the RDA. Both the MSA and the UDDIA stood for autonomy within the French Community in 1958 and the electorate returned a ninety-nine percent Yes vote on the de Gaulle referendum. By the defection of one MSA supporter, Youlou was named the first premier in late 1958. Rioting between factions supporting each party occurred in January 1959. The riots took on the character of tribal warfare with the M'Bochis supporting the MSA and the Bakongo and Balalis supporting the UDDIA. French troops finally restored order, but only after one hundred persons had been killed. Opangault and other leading MSA figures were subsequently jailed. A new constitution was adopted in February which provided for a legislative assembly of sixty-one members and responsible government. The elections of June gave the UDDIA fifty-one seats and the MSA only ten. Two members of the MSA were included in the cabinet and the MSA was merged into the UDDIA before independence in 1960.

In February 1960, Youlou reshuffled his cabinet to eliminate all Europeans, and on July 12 he signed an agreement with France providing for the independence of the Republic of Congo. Under a new constitution of March, 1961, chief executive authority was conferred on a president elected by universal suffrage. The president appointed the cabinet and the vice-president, and these were not responsible to the National Assembly. Youlou was elected to a five-year term as president on March 26, 1961, and the UDDIA won over ninety-seven percent of the popular vote in the elections for the assembly. Youlou seemed to be at the height of power. He held, in addition, the positions of premier, minister of defense, and minister of the interior.

Youlou espoused a militant foreign policy, demanding freedom for Africans while at the same time developing at home a policy to restrict all opposition to the "nationalist government." The authoritarian bent of Youlou's government became more pronounced after the disturbances of September 1962, when a state of emergency was proclaimed after a disputed soccer game with the Gabon. Youlou's most vocal opponents were the various labor union leaders who were dissatisfied with the economic progress of the country and its close ties with France. Charges of corruption and mismanagement were also made against the UDDIA-dominated government. In the summer of 1963, the most important union leaders were arrested and, despite the growing signs of unrest throughout the country, Youlou persisted in his aim of establishing constitutionally an authoritarian regime. In late August, mobs in Brazzaville stormed the jails and released the unionists and forced Youlou from power. The army intervened to restore order and prevent the establishment of a left-wing unionist government. A provisional government was formed under the leadership of Alphonse Massemba Debat, an ex-minister in Youlou's government. On December 8, a new constitution was approved by a plebiscite. It provided for a one-house legislature of fifty-five members elected for five years. The head of state was to be a president chosen by an electoral college composed of the legislature and urban and provincial councils. His length of office was also five years.

Relations between Brazzaville and Leopoldville worsened in 1964 with the development of civil strife in the larger republic. Part of the rebel forces utilized the Brazzaville area as a staging ground for their invasions. Debat's government was openly hostile to the West and maintained good relations with the Chinese Communists whose regime it had recognized in February 1964. In October Leopoldville expelled all Brazzaville Congolese. In July 1964, the Congo became officially a one-party state with the establishment of the National Revolutionary Movement as the only legal party. Massemba Debat became the secretary-general of the party. On December 22, 1964, the electoral college confirmed Debat as president and made concessions to the radical left by appointing Pascal Lissouba as his prime minister.

GABON

The Gabon Republic is located on the equator with a very small population of less than 500,000. It is extremely rich in hardwood timber, uranium, iron, gold, and oil. The dominant political party in the Gabon has been the *Bloc Démocratique Gabonais* (BDG) which was formed in 1953 as an outgrowth of an earlier group, the *Mouvement Mixte Gabonais*. Both of these parties were the local sections of Houphouët-Boigny's intraterritorial RDA. The leader of the BDG and first head of state was Leon M'Ba. Another important party was the *Union Sociale Gabonaise* (USG) whose leader was Jean Aubame. In the elections of 1957, occasioned by the *Loi Cadre,* Aubame's party won eighteen of the forty seats in the territorial assembly. This was the high-water mark for Aubame; afterward the BDG under M'Ba increased its influence at the expense of the opposition.

Gabon became independent on August 17, 1960. In the first elections neither party gained a majority in the forty-seat assembly. Four independent members, however, supported the BDG and M'Ba was selected premier. Because of the inability of the first government to act decisively in establishing new programs, a new constitution was drawn. The constitution of February 1961 provided for a president to serve a seven-year term and also a sixty-seven member National Assembly whose members serve a term of five years. For the elections of that same month, the two parties agreed to cooperate, and a single list of candidates was submitted to the voters. M'Ba became president and Aubame vice-president, and the ministry was almost equally divided between adherents of the two parties. M'Ba's policy was to discourage close ties with other independent African states and depended heavily economically, culturally, and defensively on France. In February 1963, Aubame's USG was given the choice of merging with the BDG or having their ministers resign from the government. The USG ministers chose to resign and oppose M'Ba's government. They criticized M'Ba for his dependence on France, his budget-cutting programs, and legislation concerning the High Court.

The president dissolved the National Assembly in January 1964, called for new elections under new regulations favorable to the BDG, and arbitrarily reduced the size of the assembly to forty-seven members. Angered by these events, on February 17, 1964, Gabon's 400 man army staged a coup which deposed M'Ba from power. Under duress he resigned and a provisional government headed by Aubame was created. However, the next day in answer to M'ba's request, French and African troops from Brazzaville and Dakar arrived, honoring the 1961 defense treaty, and M'Ba was restored to office. Elections were then held in April under the new rules and the BDG won thirty-one of the forty-seven seats in the assembly. The leaders of the coup were tried in August and received relatively mild sentences, but Aubame was sentenced to ten years for his activity. Thirteen of the opposition members later joined the BDG leaving only three members in the assembly who were not members of M'Ba's party.

Devolution of power and consolidation of African rule: the French trust territories

CAMEROUN

Politics in the Cameroun was complicated by the divisions of the territory between France and Britain as mandatory powers. In the larger French area, the first important party was the *Union des Populations du Cameroun* (UPC) created in 1947 which agitated for an end to mandate status and reunification of all parts of the Cameroun. Because of its activities, French authorities in 1955 resorted to repressive measures against the UPC and it was proscribed. The UPC leader, Reuben Um Nyobe, in the following year launched a guerrilla war to force the French departure. However, the party lost much of its drive with the death of Nyobe in 1958. Felix Moumie succeeded Nyobe as head of the party and continued to follow a terroristic policy.

Another important early party was the *Bloc Démocratique Camerounais* (BDC) led by Andre Mbida and Ahmadou Ahidjo. Benefiting from divisions in the party, Ahidjo broke away in 1956 to form his own party based primarily on northern support called the *Union Camerounaise* (UC). Ahidjo, a Fulani, had been elected to the Territorial Assembly in 1952 and became vice-premier in 1956, serving under Mbida's leadership. Mbida's political strength lay in the largely Catholic areas near Yaounde, but it proved insufficient to stem the mounting criticism over his handling of the UPC and certain of his long range goals. He resigned in January 1958, and Ahidjo and the UC formed a new government. After negotiations in Paris were completed early in 1958, full internal self-government was promised French Cameroun on January 1, 1959, and full independence a year later. Both Mbida and Ahidjo had, with French troops, continued the war against the UPC and Moumie. In 1959 Ahidjo dismissed parliament and ruled by decree. On January 1, 1960, the country became independent and Ahidjo became president with Charles Assale as premier. The power of the UPC was further weakened by the death of Moumie in November 1960.

The British-governed portion of the Camerouns was divided into two parts, both areas administered as a part of Nigeria. The Northern Camerouns until the 1961 plebiscite formed a segment of the Northern Region while the Southern Camerouns had a separate administration under the control of the governor of Nigeria acting as high commissioner for the territory. In both areas two contrary ultimate solutions for the future of the Camerouns were presented to the Africans and the United Nations. One was the unification of the British and French trust areas to form a new state. The other was permanent division with the British trusts becoming a part of the Federation of Nigeria. This latter solution was done irreparable damage by the prolonged government crisis in the Eastern Region of Nigeria in 1953. Prior to this time thirteen elected members from the Camerouns sat in the Eastern House of Assembly and cooperated with the dominant party, the National Council of Nigeria and the Camerouns. The deadlock in the Eastern regional government convinced many of the Cameroun politicians that association with Nigeria would not serve their best interests.

Two different parties were operative in the British areas in the early 1950s—the Kamerun United National Congress (KUNC) and the Cameroons National Federation (CNF). These were eventually merged to form the Kamerun National Congress (KNC) under the leadership of Dr. Emmanuel Endeley. The KNC advocated the absorption of the British Cameroun into a region of Nigeria. In 1955 as a result of the political differences in Eastern Nigeria, Dr. John Foncha resigned from the KNC and created the Kameroun National Democratic party (KNDP) which advocated the union of French and British areas.

On March 13, 1959, the United Nations General Assembly called for a plebiscite in the northern British segment to determine whether it would enter the Federation of Nigeria. The plebiscite, held under United Nations supervision in November 1959, resulted in a vote to continue the trustee status rather than join Nigeria. The United Nations in October 1959, by resolution, called for another plebiscite to be held in the Camerouns to decide its future. On October 1, 1960, the Northern Cameroun was separated from Nigeria and administration was placed under a special British administration. Meanwhile in January 1959, elections to a thirty-two member House of Assembly based on universal suffrage were held. The KNDP won fourteen of the twenty-six contested seats and Foncha became the prime minister. On July 18, 1960, Prime Minister Foncha met with Premier Ahidjo of the French Cameroun and they declared their substantial agreement on a federation of their two areas.

The plebiscites called for earlier by the United Nations were held in February 1961, with the result that the Northern Cameroun chose to join Nigeria and the southern region selected association with the French

Cameroun through a federal system of government. On June 1, 1961, the northern area became Sarduana Province of Northern Nigeria. On October 1, 1961, the southern region became the West Cameroun with its own regional assembly controlled by the KNDP. On the federal level West Cameroun sent ten representatives to the fifty-member Cameroun Federal Assembly. Ahidjo remained the president of the Federal Republic and Foncha became vice-president. Federal elections were held for the first time in April 1964. President Ahidjo's party, the UC, won all forty of the seats allotted to the east. In the west, vice-president Foncha's KNDP won all ten seats.

After unification, both Ahidjo and Foncha worked closely together attempting to weld their respective parties into one national party. In the spring of 1962, the UC and KNDP formed a "National Unity Group" to ensure unanimity in the Federal Assembly. The principle of a united party was accepted by both major groups but the mechanics were difficult to work out and a coordination committee was formed to work out the details of fusion. In East Cameroun most of the lesser political parties such as the *Mouvement d'Action Nationale* (MAN), *Rassemblement du Peuple Camerounais* (RPC), and *Démocrates Camerounais* (DC) declared for a union of all parties. In West Cameroun the Cameroon Peoples National Convention (CPNC), which was organized to fight unification, did not oppose, in principle, a one-party establishment, but again the structure of such a party presented the major obstacle to fusion. In May and September 1964, new meetings were held and a seventeen-man committee was appointed to strengthen cooperation between the parties. The ease with which federation of the two widely differing areas was carried out and the harmony displayed between the UC and the KNDP promised well for Cameroun politics. The only dark spot in this otherwise excellent example of cooperation was the civil war which Nyobe had begun in 1956. Although the French-trained troops of the Cameroun government have had the upper hand since the beginning of the revolt and contained the rebels, it is estimated that some 70,000 people were killed in this little-known conflict in the five years after independence.

TOGO

During the scramble for Africa, Germany claimed direct possession of the coastal area between the Gold Coast and Dahomey. It had taken a long time to penetrate the interior, and German control there was barely effective before the start of World War I. Togoland was one of the most unfortunate victims of the boundary delimitations of the ninteenth century. There are many tribes in Togo such as the Gourmas, Lambas, and Akebas with the largest single group being the Ewe. Tribal boundaries tend to run east and west, while the state boundaries were drawn north and south by the European powers. Thus many of the tribes are also located in Ghana and Dahomey.

After World War I the small sliver of territory was divided between the two major liberating powers. Britain became responsible for the portion adjacent to the Gold Coast which was administered as a part of that territory. The French portion, with a population of slightly over one million, was administered separately from the neighboring French areas of Dahomey or Upper Volta. In 1945 these mandates were transferred to the United Nations to be administered as Trust Territories. The United Nations ordered a plebiscite to be held in the British trust to determine its future. The plebiscite held in 1956 confirmed the territory's long association with the Gold Coast. The voters in British Togoland chose by a substantial margin to have their section integrated with Ghana. Thus the originally small, poor area of Togoland was reduced even further. The future independent state of Togo, therefore, was constructed out of only the French Trust Territory.

The political reforms immediately after World War II gave Togo representatives in the French Union and also in the two representative bodies in metropolitan France. Togoland also was given a representative Assembly of thirty members, chosen by the two-college system of election. Initial nationalist leadership after the war proved to be too radical for the French administrators and some of the conservative chiefs. With some slight alterations, a more conservative group of politicians came to power under the leadership of Nicolas Grunitzky. Grunitzky's party was called the *Parti Togolais du Progrès* (PTP) composed primarily of non-Ewes and opposed to the reconstitution of a Ewe state. The party of Ewe nationalism became the *Comité de l'Unité Togolaise* (CUT). Due to divisions of West Africa from the 1880s, the Ewe peoples were assigned to the Gold Coast, the two Togos, and Dahomey. In 1951, Sylvanus Olympio became the leader of CUT. Realizing that by standing for Ewe unification his party could hope for little support from the other tribes, he changed the party's demands to a unification of the two Togos. Another early party was the *Union des Chefs et des Populations du Nord*. This party was renamed the *Union Démocratique des Populations Togolaises* (UDPT) in 1958. Its power was based on the northern section which is dominated by conservative Muslim chiefs.

By the general reforms instigated by the *Loi Cadre,* France made Togoland an autonomous republic within the French Union. This called for a ministry and a chief minister, and a legislature selected from a common roll. In the ensuing elections the PTP gained the majority and Grunitzky became the first premier. Following the reconstruction of the government, the people were called upon in October 1956 to vote in a referendum whether they wished the new republican statute or a continuation of trusteeship status. Olympio, feeling that his party could not win, called a boycott of the referendum. The United Nations refused to send observers since they maintained that the referendum did not give the voters wide enough choice. Despite these factors, seventy percent of the electorate approved the new status.

On this basis France attempted to have trusteeship status revoked in 1957. However, the United Nations called for UN supervised elections to decide the future of the area and what party really represented the people. Under threats of violence by all parties and fears of a possible *putsch* from Ghana, the elections were held on April 27, 1958. The results surprised most observers. The CUT won nineteen of the twenty-three seats in the south and even ten of twenty-three in the supposed hostile north. The popular vote was over sixty percent of the votes cast for the CUT.

Olympio as premier also surprised the French by his moderate, pragmatic approach to the many problems of Togo. He negotiated full internal autonomy for Togo beginning in January 1959. In late 1959, he received guarantees from France for the independence of Togo in April 1960. Before independence, Olympio's government successfully withstood an attempt by Ghana to integrate Togo into Ghana. Charging a breakdown of law and order in Togo, Kwame Nkrumah came forth as the protector of all Ewes. Nkrumah also charged that Togo was planning an invasion of Ghana and moved troops to the border. Olympio stated that an invasion under whatever pretext would be resisted and he would appeal to France and the United Nations for help. This open power play was thwarted and was one of Nkrumah's earliest major defeats.

The great victory of the CUT in 1958 left the opposition parties shattered. But Olympio's moderate, basically pro-French and anti-Ghana attitude created other forces of opposition within the CUT. His approach to the many problems of economically poor Togo was pragmatic. This called for economy in government, reduction of the armed forces by half, and continued close economic contacts with France in order to keep the budget balanced and continue minimum development of the country. The youth wing of the CUT, Le Mouvement de la Jeunesse Togolaise (JUVENTO), demanded more radical, socialist programs. The leader of JUVENTO, Anani Santos, a brilliant lawyer, had been quite influenced by Ghanaian socialism. In reality, JUVENTO was a separate party even before its open break with the CUT. There were rumors in January 1959 of a JUVENTO coup against the government backed by Ghana. However, despite military precautions supported by the French, nothing occurred.

A new constitution was drawn up and approved by the electorate in April 1961. This new instrument of government provided for a presidential system with a unicameral legislature. The Chamber of Deputies was composed of fifty-one members elected by universal suffrage. In the elections of 1961, Olympio was elected president. Grunitzky formed an alliance with JUVENTO to contest the election. The election lists of the alliance were disallowed and the CUT won all the seats in the legislature. Grunitzky left Togo soon after the elections, and JUVENTO was later outlawed. Previously, in the elections of 1958, the UDPT and the PTP had ceased to be effective political parties. Therefore, after 1961, Togo had only one political party, the CUT, and Olympio seemed firmly in control of the government.

Olympio's conservative approach to the needs of Togo led directly to the overthrow of his government and his assassination in January 1963. Togo is a poor country, and Olympio resisted all demands to increase the budget by adding new government posts. Unemployment, always a problem, increased. By far the most important question concerned the size of the Togolese army. The ex-soldiers demanded an increase in its size and this demand was continually refused. These ex-soldiers served as the nucleus of the revolt. Despite Olympio's record as an administrator, capable of balancing the budget and maintaining excellent relations with Europe, the military forces numbering in the hundreds took over the government on January 13, 1963, and killed President Olympio.

A revolutionary committee of eight officers was formed. Grunitzky, who was in exile in Dahomey, was informed of the coup and arrived in Lome three days after the overthrow of Olympio's government. Until his arrival there was considerable confusion in Togo. However, the committee appointed Grunitzky provisional president and some order was reestablished. New elections were promised within six weeks. Grunitzky calmed the dangerous situation by promising reforms and increasing the size of the army to employ the ex-servicemen who had been so instrumental in the coup.

One of the complicating features of these crucial days was Ghana's possible involvement. Relations between Ghana and Olympio's government had been poor since before the independence of Togo. From December 1959 through May 1960, there was a possibility of armed conflict. In December 1961, eighteen men were arrested by Togolese police and charged with plotting to overthrow the government. They were allegedly supported by Ghana. JUVENTO was actively pro-Ghana, and many of the leaders of the opposition to Olympio had gone to Ghana. Ghana was the first state to offer de jure recognition to the new regime. However, Grunitzky and Antoine Meatchi, the foremost politician from the north, made it clear that they intended to maintain the integrity of Togo.

In conjunction with other members of the provisional government, Grunitzky called for national unity. The constitution was revised to provide for a National Assembly of fifty-six members. Each of the four parties in Togo was to have equal representation in the legislature. These parties were the CUT, the UDPT, JUVENTO, and the *Mouvement des Populations Togolaises* (MPT). This represented a revival of political activity, although the competition was restricted. Each party would nominate proposed members. From this list the voters would choose the legislators. The presidential system was also to be retained. Before the elections of May 5, 1963, there was considerable conflict and confusion among the leaders. Grunitzky was challenged briefly for the leadership of his now revived party, the UDPT, by Meatchi who wanted to be the presidential nominee. Also, from Guinea, M. Mally, the interior minister under Olympio, broadcast charges against the provisional government. Despite threats of a coup against the provisional government, the elections were held. Grunitzky was elected president, the constitution was adopted, and the single list submitted was approved by the electorate. Mally was later arrested and sentenced to twenty years imprisonment for his actions in the days prior to the election.

Subsequently, the Togo government was recognized by most of the African states, and their representatives were present as observers at the Addis Ababa conference. In August 1963, Togo was formally admitted to the Union Africain et Malagache (UAM). Even Ghana opened an embassy in Lome and entered into economic discussions with Grunitzky's government. Although Grunitzky's government could not solve many of the problems which led to the overthrow of Olympio, it did restore law and order, and gave Togo a stability which many observers believed impossible in the spring of 1963. Indicative of this stability was the joint meeting of representatives of the four parties making up the coalition government in December 1965. The congress of the four—JUVENTO, UDPT, MPT, and CUT—called for studies which would perhaps lead to their merging into a single political party.

ELEVEN

Postwar political developments: British Africa

General political changes

The British government indicated an alteration of attitudes toward its dependent empire during World War II by a number of separate actions. The Colonial Development and Welfare Acts showed that the prewar penurious attitudes were at an end. The Colonial Office early in the war sent a directive to the governors of all its territories to design coordinate postwar development plans for all colony and protectorate areas. This was the first time that the Colonial Office was presented with complex, integrated analyses of the situation in each territory and with projections for the future. Despite the economic stringencies of postwar Britain, funds were provided for many of these projected improvements. At the same time the Labor government committed itself to opening more mid-range positions and equalizing pay scales and conditions of work in the civil service for Africans. This Africanization, although it did not proceed as rapidly as many believed necessary, did provide within a decade a much larger cadre of trained personnel at all levels in all British African territories.

Before the end of the war most governors had indicated that the governmental instruments for their areas were inadequate. With the concurrence of the Colonial Office new constitutions were granted to all of Britain's dependent empire in the five years following the war. Before granting these constitutions Britain consulted African nationalists only in a minimal fashion. Thus such reforms as the Richards Constitution in Nigeria were from the outset unpopular because they granted the elite too little power. Nevertheless, these new government instruments brought many more Africans on the upper levels into the legislative and executive councils. On the local level reforms in municipal government gave Africans a larger share in determining local policy. The Colonial Office also tried to improve the all but moribund concept of vital, developing sys-

269

tems of indirect rule for the protectorates. The new emphasis was upon native authorities rather than a chief and his traditional council. An effort was made, wherever possible, to admit the elective principle in the selection of the native authorities. Thus the major question after 1950 was no longer whether Africans should be given more responsibility but concerned the timing for increased authority to the Africans.

Reforms of the central government structure presented the British government with an unforeseen problem. Heretofore the dichotomy between the government of the colony areas and the protectorates had produced few problems. It was apparent that the grant of increased influence to Africans in the central government was incompatible with the older concepts of indirect rule. The now politically influential, educated Africans made it clear that the old and, in many ways, inefficient local government system would have to be modified. Semi-independent states could not function with two such incompatible philosophies of government. Every advance of the British territories toward independence witnessed the commensurate shrinkage in power of the protectorate chiefs. British concerns for the future of the protectorate Africans and their traditional rulers dictated a slower policy of political advance than was desired by the African political parties.

Thus the rate of advance became the key problem in the 1950s. Political agitation such as that first undertaken in the Gold Coast was designed to show the British a united native front and force the Colonial Office to grant concessions earlier than the British authorities wished. But in West Africa, Kwame Nkrumah, Benjamin N'namdi Azikiwe, Obafemi Awolowo, Milton Margai, and other African politicians did not have to convince the British that eventually the African should control the destinies of their territories. Initially British authorities as well as most African nationalists had envisioned a long period of continued, responsible British control which would devolve power to the Africans when they were able to meet the responsibilities of that power. British experience in India and observation of the Dutch in Indonesia and the French in Indochina and Algeria, however, had shown the futility of attempting to maintain control against the wishes of the people. Thus the major contribution of activist parties such as Nkrumah's CPP was to convince British authorities to speed up the granting of authority to Africans. The transition from British to African control was a relatively smooth one even though it was accomplished far faster than many responsible officials believed was safe. The presence in West Africa of only a small number of European residents also facilitated the transfer of power to the Africans. It was more difficult elsewhere.

Once the change was decided upon, the method by which Britain accomplished the shift of power was relatively simple. There was never any attempt to bring all the British territories to the same level of development at the same time or to associate them directly with the mother country. The crown colony system of government was merely expanded and elaborated upon. The change from total dependency to independence was accomplished by a series of modifications. The first was to associate

Africans with the government by nominating more of them to the legislative and executive councils. The next step was to provide for the elections of some Africans to the Legislative Council. The third was to increase the number of Africans, usually elected, to the Legislative Council until they controlled an unofficial majority. Normally at this time ministries were formed having basically advisory functions to the civil service departments. The African quasi-ministers were part of the Executive Council. The next to last step was to increase the size of the legislature and hold elections throughout the territory for its members. A ministry could then be formed responsible to the legislative body. This ministry took the place of the Executive Council and the ministers exercised real executive power over the departments under their control. Normally at this point a chief minister with the responsibility of coordinating policy and legislation was also chosen. It was at this time that the African territory gained full internal self-government. The governor, still appointed by the Colonial Office, exercised some powers of review and veto over domestic matters, but these were seldom exercised. Only in the areas of foreign trade, defense, and foreign affairs did the British government still retain its preeminent position. The final step was complete independence of the territory and voluntary association in the Commonwealth.

This is a generalized pattern of evolution of the British African states toward independence. In non-multiracial areas this evolution proceeded in an orderly fashion with a minimum of friction. This was not the case where the British government attempted a compromise between the demands of Africans and Europeans. There were only two areas of Britain's African empire where there was a significant resident, white population—Kenya and the Rhodesias.

In 1944 Kenya's population was slightly over four million. Of these only 32,000 were Europeans. Yet they possessed an inordinate amount of political and economic power and influence. Although it is a mistake to believe that the Nairobi government was a rubber stamp for these colonists, one cannot deny that basically it reflected the desires of the Europeans. Thus the postwar government reforms came late to Kenya and they were much less sweeping than in West African areas. By 1948 there were only four nominated Africans on the Legislative Council. The proposed reforms of 1952 contemplated the introduction of a system of indirect election for six Africans on this council while the Europeans had fourteen seats. Long-standing grievances over land, growing urban unemployment, high prices, and the conviction that Britain was not going to grant them the same measure of freedom which it was giving West Africans drove some of the Kikuyu into revolt. Mau Mau was bloody and costly. Although few other tribes in Kenya joined the revolt, it took the British four years to pacify the country, and the era left scars which will take long to heal. However, after 1957, the British government realized that it had to choose between the African majority and the white minority. After deciding for the former, political evolution in Kenya followed the general pattern of development of other British colonies.

The problems in Central Africa were similar to those of Kenya, but due to the creation in 1952 of the Central African Federation they were more difficult to resolve. The Central African Federation of Nyasaland, Northern and Southern Rhodesia was created over the objections of almost all the African political leaders of these territories. The major force which created and held this union together was the white population of Southern Rhodesia and their leader, Sir Roy Welensky. Although the outlook of the whites in Southern Rhodesia and the 38,000 Europeans in Northern Rhodesia was generally not as extreme as the Afrikaners in South Africa, they had no intention of allowing Africans the measure of political authority which their numbers would have indicated. The problem facing political leaders such as Kenneth Kaunda and Hastings Banda was, therefore, more complicated than elsewhere in Africa. The federation had to be broken before independence for its northern territories became a reality. It was not until 1963, after considerable violence in all these areas combined with pressures from the now independent African states, that the Colonial Office decided finally to jettison Welensky and the federation and allow the independence of Malawi and Zambia. The problem of a largely disenfranchised African majority and a controlling white minority, nevertheless, remained in Southern Rhodesia.

Aside from the multiracial areas, Britain's record of colonial guidance in the years following World War II was excellent. Its central government system, pragmatic from the earliest days, was simply expanded to meet the new demands. In the protectorates the traditional systems were changed to function primarily as agencies of local government while the responsibility for the protectorate as a unit was merely shifted from a loose system of direct rule to a more complex method controlled by the newly expanded organs of the central government. A brief examination of each British territory will show how the grant of authority to Africans was accomplished in each area.

Devolution of power and consolidation of African rule: British West Africa

GAMBIA

For such a small area (approximately 4,000 square miles, population 250,000) which was touched late by nationalistic feelings, the Gambia has had a large number of political parties. Until the decade of the 1950s the typical British dual rule of crown colony government for the colony and guided, traditional rule for the protectorate seemed sufficient. Britain granted more liberal constitutions to the Gambia in 1946, 1950, and 1954 with little organized pressure from the Gambians themselves. Not until after 1959 did the leading politicians of the Gambia begin to demand eventual independence for the small, economically poor area. They had previously proposed direct federation with Britain or a federal union with Sierra Leone as their goals. With the creation of the West Indies Federation and independence for other tiny areas such as Malta, the idea of a direct federation with Britain was no longer feasible. Sierra Leone on the eve of independence was not in the mood for adding more responsibilities. The only alternatives left for Gambians became continued dependent status, amalgamation with Senegal, or independence. Growing dissatisfaction with the British administration ruled out the first. Thus the only goals left were independence or absorption by Senegal.

The first political parties in the Gambia were of necessity colony-based and were formed to contest the 1951 election. The first of these was the Democratic party (DP) which served as a vehicle for the election of its leader, the Reverend J. C. Faye, to the Legislative Assembly. The second party also created in 1951 was the Muslim Congress which was formed out of a number of smaller Muslim cultural and political groups. Its leader, I. M. Garba-Jahumpa, wanted to mobilize the Muslim majority of the Gambia not only for the Legislative Council elections but possibly to control the future political development of the Gambia. Formed soon after P. S. N'Jie was defeated for the Legislative Council in 1951, the United party (UP) was also personality oriented. It gained great support from the colony by N'Jie's opposition to the British administration and the fact that he held no government office.

The first constitution to genuinely reflect Gambian articulate opinion was that of 1960. It provided for a greatly increased Legislative Council and appointed ministers. It was the first to apply the elective principle to to the numerically superior protectorate. As such, it was the first definite breach in the authority of the chiefs in the protectorate. A number of changes occurred in political alignments before the election. David Jawara formed the first protectorate-oriented party, the Peoples Progressive party (PPP). Failing support for their programs caused the Muslim Congress and Democratic Party to merge into the Democratic Congress Alliance (DCA) just weeks before the elections. The elections resulted in a standoff between the PPP and the UP. The UP won six seats, five of which were in the colony. The PPP won eight protectorate seats. Neither of the leaders of the DCA was elected, although the party captured three seats. The balance of power was held by eight indirectly elected chiefs. In early 1961, the governor appointed the first chief minister. The role of the chiefs was decisive in this selection and P. S. N'Jie, leader of the UP, was appointed.

None of the political parties were satisfied with the constitution, and constitutional discussions with the Colonial Office were held in mid-1961. A new constitution was put into effect in 1962 and elections were held for a greatly expanded House of Representatives. The colony was to have only eight elected members while the protectorate directly elected twenty-five. The chiefs had only four indirectly elected representatives. In the elections of 1962 th PPP gained eighteen seats, the UP thirteen, and the DCA only one. A responsible ministry was formed by the PPP and David (later Sir Duada) Jawara became premier. Despite considerable confusion and debate over the election registers, this government was confirmed and the PPP has never since been out of power. In the fall of 1963 the Gambia was granted full internal self-government.

One of the major questions that Jawara's government had to deal with was independence or amalgamation. The PPP government instituted a number of discussions with Senegal and asked for a United Nations team to investigate possible courses of action. The United Nations report published in mid-1964 recommended federation with Senegal as the ultimate political solution. However, opposition in the Gambia and a cooling off of Senegal's receptiveness postponed any action in this direction. Therefore, in July 1964, discussions with British officials established the date for independence as February 19, 1965. The form of government for the new independent state was a constitutional monarchy with a governor-general representing the crown and responsible government with a prime minister and ministry based on the Westminster model. No new elections were held for the newly independent state. Thus Jawara carried over into independence the majority he controlled in the House of Representatives.

In 1965 Garba-Jahumpa and his followers withdrew from the DCA which had by then been all but swallowed up by the PPP. They formed their own small but vocal group called the Gambian Congress. The UP continued to be the major opposition but until late in the year, except for the all but defunct election issue, there were few points which they could contest with the PPP. Jawara then proposed a major alteration in the system of government. He wanted a presidential system with the president chosen not by direct election, but by a majority vote of the thirty-six member House of Representatives. Jawara proposed a referendum on this question to be held in November. The UP and the other small groups opposed the measure while the PPP fought for it. Thus it was strictly a political contest. The referendum to amend the constitution required a two-thirds majority and Jawara was certain that he, with better facilities at his disposal and a stronger campaign, would secure the requisite vote. However, the plebiscite showed the PPP failing to secure their goal by 758 votes. Thus Gambia remained a reflection of Westminster. However, this issue along with unification with Senegal was far from settled and Jawara indicated that he would go to the polls again on the issue to bring the Gambia more in conformity with the presidential systems of other African states.

GHANA

Ghana was the first African territory to exchange colonial status for independence. As such it served as a model of political agitation for nationalists elsewhere in Africa. In transforming the Gold Coast colony and protectorate into a nation state, Britain, in cooperation with the political leaders of the Gold Coast, worked out the forms which would later be applied to other British African territories. After independence Ghana, because of its premier position, helped determine, by its policies, the domestic and foreign policies of other newly independent states.

In 1946 the Gold Coast was granted a new instrument of government, the Burns Constitution, which gave the territory the first Legislative Council in Africa with a majority of African members. However, the constitution did not go far enough to satisfy many African leaders. Dissatisfaction with their status led to the formation of the first powerful political voice for Gold Coast Africans, the United Gold Coast Convention (UGCC). The party was created in the fall of 1947 by Dr. Joseph Danquah and other middle-class urban Africans.

In November 1947, a new factor was introduced into Gold Coast politics when Kwame Nkrumah returned from Britain to assume the post of general secretary of the party. Nkrumah, then thirty-eight years old and a member of the Nzima tribe, had been educated at the Achimota secondary school, and in 1935, upon the advice of the Nigerian nationalist, Dr. Azikiwe, left the Gold Coast for the United States. He attended and later taught at Lincoln University in Pennsylvania and did graduate work at the University of Pennsylvania. He was introduced to the writings of Du Bois, Garvey, Ghandi, Marx, and many other Socialist and Communist authors. In addition he had carefully observed the organization and tactics of American political parties. In 1945 he left the United States for Britain where he met George Padmore and other British African nationalists. Nkrumah played a prominent role in organizing the fifth Pan African Congress at Manchester. Thus when he arrived in Accra he was far more politically knowledgeable and radical than the founders of the UGCC.

Nkrumah immediately began to create a mass political party with a European style of organization. This called for Nkrumah and other younger members of the party to address African audiences in all parts of the Gold Coast to prepare them for direct action against the British authorities. In the spring of 1948 economic problems led to demonstrations by ex-servicemen and a general African boycott of European and Syrian traders. Nkrumah welcomed this type of confrontation because it could be utilized to the advantage of the UGCC. British authorities attributed much of the disorder to the inflammatory activities of the UGCC, and the six leaders of the party were arrested. This was the beginning of the split between Nkrumah and his more conservative colleagues. On their release he was removed from the position of general secretary and, although continuing to work for the UGCC, he founded the Committee on Youth Organization (CYO). In June 1949, the CYO converted itself into a new party, the Convention Peoples party (CPP) with Nkrumah as its head.

A commission of inquiry into the disorders of 1948 recommended an increase in membership of the Legislative Council and greater African responsibility in the executive. In 1949 an all African committee was appointed under the chairmanship of Judge Coussey to examine the entire constitutional position of the Gold Coast. The commission report formed the basis for the new constitution issued in 1951. In the months that followed the issuance of the Coussey report, the CPP made clear its opposition to the moderate changes proposed by the commission and conducted positive action against its implementation. In January 1950, after numerous mass disturbances occasioned by CPP demonstrations, the CPP leaders, including Nkrumah, were arrested.

The 1951 constitution provided for a Legislative Assembly partially elected by direct suffrage. Of the eighty-four members, thirty-eight were popularly elected. In the Executive Council six of the eleven members were to be in charge of government departments. The work of the African members of the Executive Council was to be coordinated by a leader of government business. Despite its previous opposition to the constitution, the CPP contested the election held in February 1951 and won thirty-four of the elected seats. Dr. Danquah's UGCC won only three seats. Nkrumah was released from prison to become leader of government, and this office was upgraded to prime minister in 1952. Under pressure from the CPP and its mass organization, Britain announced in 1953 further government concessions. A new constitution promulgated in April 1954 provided for a responsible cabinet and a 104 member, all elective Legislative Assembly. In 1954 the Northern Peoples party (NPP) which, as the name implies, drew much of its strength from the poorer northern regions was created. In the general elections of June 1954, the CPP won seventy-one of the seats while the NPP could gain but twelve, becoming the official opposition. The Gold Coast in 1954 thus had reached the stage before complete independence. The major question which concerned Nkrumah's government and the Colonial Office was what should be the new form of the independent state.

The NPP was afraid that the coastal politicians would dominate the new government and force upon the north measures unpalatable to the traditional society there. Of more actual concern to the CPP government was the National Liberation Movement (NLM) formed by Dr. K. A. Busia in September 1954. This party spoke for the separatist feelings of the Ashanti. Instead of a unitary state, they wanted a federal system. The asantahene and the fifty chiefs of the Asanteman Council signed a petition to Britain demanding this type of government. Nkrumah opposed the federal scheme and the Colonial Office also registered its disapproval.

Disturbances in Ashantiland postponed the smooth movement of the Gold Coast toward independence. In 1955 a commission headed by Sir Frederick Bourne was invited by the Gold Coast government to review the extant government and make suggestions for the future of the Gold Coast. The NLM refused to meet with Bourne and continued to demand a federal system even after Bourne had made his report. The report of 1955 recommended a unitary state with substantial devolution of power from the central government to provincial assemblies in order better to protect the minorities in the state. Nkrumah's government was in substantial agreement with these proposals. However, the CPP leadership never forgot the disturbances and the refusal of the NLM to advise the government. The attitudes of the northerners had postponed the grant of independence. Finally on May 11, 1956, Britain announced its intention of granting independence after the conclusion of the new elections. In May a plebiscite in British Togoland resulted in a favorable vote for integration of that territory with the Gold Coast.

In the elections of 1956, the CPP won seventy-two of the 104 seats including eight of twenty-one in Ashanti and eleven of twenty-six in the northern territories. The NPP gained twelve seats and the NLM twelve. Nkrumah announced in the fall of 1956 his government's intention to call the new state Ghana and set the date for independence as March 6, 1957. After independence, six opposition groups in October 1957 came together to form the United party (UP) under the leadership of Dr. Busia.

Immediately after independent Nkrumah moved to secure control over decision making for the central government in all areas of Ghana. This resulted in a series of confrontations with traditional authorities. The CPP made it clear that it considered opposition a luxury which the new state could not afford. In February 1958, following disturbances in Ashantiland, the government deposed two paramount chiefs. In March six persons including two members of parliament from Togoland were sentenced to prison for creating disturbances. Nine members of the UP in Ashantiland were deported in April. The CPP-dominated assembly passed the Preventive Detention Bill in July which gave the government the right to imprison suspects without trial for up to five years. In September the government took over direct control of the Kumasi region due to alleged misappropriation of funds for the use of the NLM. In November forty-three members of the UP were arrested on charges of plotting against the government, and the government withdrew passports from all opposition members. This reaction of the CPP majority against opponents continued throughout 1959, forty-five persons being imprisoned under the Preventive Detention Act by the end of November. Dr. Busia, the leader of the opposition, was disqualified from the assembly and fled the country. By the end of 1959 Ghana had practically become a one-party state.

In April 1960, by a combined plebiscite and presidential election, Ghana became a republic and Nkrumah, its first president, was given more executive power. The CPP controlled eighty-six seats in the 104 seat unicameral National Assembly. In addition there were ten differentially elected women members. Nkrumah further extended his control by taking over full executive direction of the CPP on May 1, 1961, and instituting a series of austerity measures on the party and throughout the country. In September 1961, a dock and railroad workers' strike, which was briefly dangerous, was settled. The next month Nkrumah reorganized his cabinet and the government arrested forty-nine persons allegedly connected with the strike. On October 30, the National Assembly passed a bill establishing special courts empowered to try political cases with the right to impose the death penalty. By 1962 the CPP controlled one hundred seats in the assembly and the UP only nine.

In 1962 there was an easing of restrictions in Ghana. Several hundred persons held under the detention act were released. This policy was sharply reversed by the first major attempt on Nkrumah's life on August 1, 1962. The grenade blast wounded Nkrumah, killed four persons, and injured fifty-six. Other terroristic attacks in October claimed more lives. Hundreds were arrested including Ako Adjei, the foreign minister, Tawia Adamafio, minister of information, and H. Cofie-Crabbe, executive secretary of the CPP. In October Nkrumah rejected the offer of the assembly for a lifetime tenure as president but reiterated his previous statements that Ghana, in order to survive, would continue to be a one-party state. In April 1963, five of the chief conspirators of the fall of 1962 were sentenced to death, and in August 1963, the trial of the ex-ministers and other alleged conspirators began. In December 1963, the three judges, including Chief Justice Sir Arku Kosah, acquitted Adjei, Adamafio, and Cofie-Crabbe. In the ensuing constitutional crisis, the chief justice was dismissed from office by Nkrumah and the accused were not released.

The New Year's broadcast of 1964 by Nkrumah suggested certain further changes in the constitution which were adopted by a plebiscite and the legislature between January 31 and February 21. These made Ghana officially a one-party state. The president received the power to remove any judge from office, not just the chief justice as had been the case. Subsequently Nkrumah removed three supreme court justices and one lesser judge. Even the national flag was changed to reflect the red, white, and green colors of the CPP. Seven of the eight UP members in the assembly changed to the CPP. The eighth was arrested under the terms of the Preventive Detention Act.

On January 2, 1964, the fifth attempt since 1956 was made on Nkrumah's life. A police constable fired, missed the president, but killed the chief security officer. Partially because of the danger and partially due to Nkrumah's growing feeling of omnipotence, he withdrew himself more and more from the public. The state-controlled press extolled his virtues as the savior of the African people and castigated all who opposed him as agents of neo-imperialism. His active saber-rattling had frightened Ghana's neighbors and the majority of African leaders rejected both Nkrumah and his policies. There was a worsening of Ghana's relations with the United States in 1964 and an improvement of those with Red China. The visit of Chou En-lai in January was followed by a Chinese loan of eight million Ghanian pounds. Despite the attempt on his life, Nkrumah's hold on Ghana seemed secure in 1964. The CPP appeared to be a docile, willing agent for the leader. The young pioneers and students at the Ideological Institute at Winneba were systematically indoctrinated in a manner reminiscent of Fascist Europe. The Volta Dam, one of the great projects sponsored by Nkrumah, was over eighty percent complete, and the cocoa crop brought an excellent price. The government in 1964 announced its seven year plan which envisioned a capital expenditure of 1,017 million Ghanian pounds. More than half of this was to come from the private rather than the government sector. In February 1965, Adamafio, Adjei, and Cofie-Crabbe were found guilty by a jury of twelve drawn from the Ideological Institute. The government also announced the death in a detention camp of Dr. Danquah, founder of the UGCC.

In late 1964 the first indications of a financial crisis in Ghana became apparent. There was a significant fall in the world market price of cocoa, and this, combined with the near exhaustion of the surplus fund, dictated a policy of retrenchment. However, the government continued its policies of establishing ventures of questionable merit heavily subsidized by the state. Many of these were poorly managed and lost great sums. Others such as Ghana Airways attempted too much and were a constant drain on government money. Foreign governments were reluctant to advance funds to Nkrumah to check the growing economic crisis. An investigation agency of the International Monetary Fund in 1965 was extremely critical of the state corporations and short-range inflationary loans and refused to advance funds until Ghana altered its financial priorities. Reluctantly the government agreed to put into effect some of the recommendations of the commission.

Nkrumah's grandiose plans for leadership of larger African political groupings had received repeated setbacks after 1960. The final blow to his prestige as a spokesman for Africa occurred in October 1965. Accra was the host city for the third conference of the Organization of African Unity. The Ghana government spent over fifty million dollars preparing new facilities for the meeting. However, only nineteen heads of state attended the conference and the delegates were divided on almost every issue. The ex-French states of Africa were not represented. This Accra meeting was a stunning expensive defeat for Nkrumah and his dreams of leadership of a united Africa.

Nkrumah left Accra in late February 1966, on a state visit to Peking, seemingly unaware of the growing dissatisfaction with his regime. In his absence the Second Brigade of the Ghana army stationed at Kumasi marched on Accra on February 24. Soon the leaders of the revolt, Colonels Katoka and Ocran, and Major Afrifra, had gained the support of the rest of the army. Overpowering the presidential guard, they assumed control of the state. The junior officers called upon Joseph Ankrah, who had retired in 1965, to become commander in chief of the army and head of a seven man National Liberation Council. A state of emergency was proclaimed, political prisoners were released, the CPP was banned, and the Ideological Institute was closed. The revolution was greeted by large, joyous crowds throughout Ghana.

The new regime announced that the military phase would be temporary until a new constitution could be developed which would provide for a separate executive, legislative, and judicial branch. Political freedom was guaranteed and assurances were given that Ghana would no longer be used as a base for subversion against its neighbors. The new regime labeled Nkrumah a tyrant and began at once to deport Soviet and Chinese technicians. Nkrumah flew from Peking to Guinea and immediately announced his intention to return to Ghana, and Sekou Touré named him honorary president of Guinea. His hopes of ever regaining power were dealt a severe blow with the recognition by the Soviet Union of the new military government.

NIGERIA

Despite encouragement from outside sources and some participation in Pan African conferences, there was very little nationalistic activity in

Nigeria before the early 1940s, and then until the close of World War II it tended to be Lagos based. The first real Nigerian party was the Nigerian National Democratic party (NNDP) created by Herbert Macaulay, the doyen of Nigerian politics, and it was a good example of the Lagos bias. In 1934 the Lagos Youth Movement was formed to agitate for better Nigerian education. In 1936 the name was changed to the Nigerian Youth Movement (NYM) and it became the focal point for the political education of young Nigeria. Based partially upon the popularity of Benjamin Nnamdi Azikiwe's newspapers, the NYM was the major protest party in Lagos by 1938 and had organized branches in many of the major cities. In 1941, however, the NYM was all but destroyed by the defection of Azikiwe and his followers. Only in Ibadan did the NYM remain potentially powerful.

In 1942 Azikiwe formed the Nigerian Reconstruction group, and in August 1944, at a conference in Lagos, the Nigerian National Council was created. The name was changed later to the National Council of Nigeria and the Cameroons (NCNC). It absorbed many separate tribal and cultural organizations and Macaulay's NNDP. The party stood for more African participation at all levels and a definite timetable for an independent federal Nigeria.

In 1945 the Richards Constitution was put into effect by Britain. Although it was an advance over the previous government instruments, it was not designed in consultation with the Nigerians. The NCNC opposed it. Labor disputes rocked the government and the prestige of Azikiwe and the NCNC soared with their protest delegation to London in 1947. The dissatisfaction in Nigeria abated somewhat with the discussions which led to the MacPherson Constitution. In the meantime Obafemi Awolowo and others had formed in London the *Egba Omo Oduduwa* which became the Yoruba cultural base for a new political party. This party, the Action Group, was created to contest the elections of 1951 called for by the MacPherson Constitution. The Action Group based its power on the wealth of the Western Region. In the north the Northern Peoples Congress (NPC) was formed in 1949, first as a cultural union. However, when more radical elements led by Mallam Aminu Kano formed the Northern Elements Progressive Union (NEPU), the NPC converted itself into a political party. Its leader was Ahmadu Bello, Sardauna of Sokoto, who was aided by a young progressive Muslim, Abubakar Tafewa Balewa. Thus by the time of the elections of 1951, Nigeria had its three major parties, each strongly based on an ethnic group with their strength concentrated in different regions.

The 1951 constitution provided for a semifederal system with divisions of power between the central government and the governments of the three regions. The Northern and Western Regions had a two-house system with a House of Chiefs and a predominantly elected House of Representatives. The Eastern Region had only a House of Assembly. Each region had its own Executive Council which was responsible to the lower house for its continuance in power. On the federal level there was a House of

Representatives of 148 members, 136 of whom were elected. There was a Federal Council of Ministers of eighteen members, twelve of whom were nonofficials. Although the governor and his lieutenants in the regions retained wide executive powers, the MacPherson Constitution was a major step forward toward self-government in that Nigerians were given freedom, within certain limits, to enact and carry out government policy for themselves.

Dr. Azikiwe attempted to make the NCNC a national party, but the Action Group which had won the elections in the West prevented his election to the federal House of Representatives in 1951 and Azikiwe was relegated only to leader of the opposition in the West. In 1952 Azikiwe began a purge of those who disagreed with him in the NCNC. This resulted in the formation of the National Independence party (NIP), and when the Eastern Region House of Assembly was dissolved in 1953, Azikiwe returned to the East as undisputed leader of the NCNC. The NIP won only nine out of the ninety-seven seats in the subsequent elections.

Questions not adequately explained by the MacPherson Constitution concerning the regional and central government soon brought demands for a new government instrument to clarify these disputed points. The Action Group in the West and the NCNC in the East both demanded that 1956 should be the date fixed for Nigerian independence. This demand led to conflicts with the North whose representatives wanted a slower development and more guarantees for their institutions. Four members of the Council of Ministers resigned in March 1953 on this issue. Serious riots broke out in Kano in May between Action Group and NPC followers. Also, in May the Eastern assembly defied the government and was dismissed by the lieutenant-governor. With this type of disorder as a background, the Colonial Office convened constitutional discussions in London and Lagos beginning in July 1953, and the new constitution went into effect on October 1, 1954. It called for a strengthening of the federal system, an expanded House of Representatives with 184 elected members, and better definitions of the role of the central and regional governments. The Council of Ministers at the center was reduced in size to thirteen members. The major political leaders chose to remain on the regional level, Awolowo becoming premier in the West, Azikiwe in the East, and Ahmadu Bello in the North. The power ratio in the federal House of Representatives was NPC seventy-nine, NCNC fifty-six, Action Group and their allies twenty-seven, Kamerun National Congress six, and sixteen independents.

In May 1957, a conference held in London resulted in the grant of self-government within the federal structure for the Eastern and Western Regions. Agreement was also reached on further constitutional changes. The most important of these was the appointment of an all-Nigerian Council of Ministers and a federal prime minister. The constitution provided for a greatly expanded House of Representatives and a Senate. Regional governments would also be maintained, each with a premier and elected lower house. The federal government, by consensus, after 1957 was a national government of all three parties. Abubakar Tafewa Balewa of the NPC was chosen to head this coalition as chief minister.

In October 1954, when Awolowo became premier of the West, he tried to extend the Action Group's influence beyond that region by using modern electioneering methods. However, he failed to muster support in the North, and in 1957 when Balewa was selected chief minister, the only way that the southern area could have kept the North from power was by a coalition of the NCNC and Action Group. Dr. Azikiwe had survived another threat to his power in the East, especially from Dr. Mbadiwe, the second vice-president of the NCNC (the name was changed in 1961 to the National Council of Nigerian Citizens), and was in no mood to come to terms with his old adversary, Awolowo. Instead, after the federal elections of 1959, he negotiated an alliance with the NPC which broke up the national government that had existed since 1957. The Action Group was then left in opposition at the federal level. In the House of Representatives after the 1959 elections, the NPC held 142 seats, the NCNC eighty-nine, and the Action Group seventy-three. Each region was still controlled by a specific party with the greatest power in the hands of the sarduana in the North. Because the central government was by then the most important political arena, Azikiwe delegated his authority as premier in the East to his lieutenant, Dr. Okpara. Chief Awolowo trusted the regional government of the West to the leadership of Chief S. L. Akintola. This was the political arrangement in Nigeria when independence finally was granted in October 1960.

Between May and June 1962, a major crisis developed in the Western Region. Differences between Chief Awolowo and Chief Akintola led to the majority of the Action Group requesting Akintola's resignation as Western premier. Akintola refused to comply and the governor of the region dismissed him from office. Disturbances in Ibadan and in the regional legislature were of such seriousness that the federal prime minister, Balewa, declared a state of emergency and suspended parliamentary government in the Western Region. On July 7, 1962, the Supreme Court ruled that Akintola's dismissal was invalid, and on September 17, the federal government arrested Chief Awolowo and fifteen associates, charging them with planning to overthrow the government. The trials of the accused were prolonged through September 1963 when the court found Awolowo and his lieutenants in the alleged plot guilty. Chief Awolowo was sentenced to fifteen years in prison. The Action Group as a power in the West and at the federal level was shattered by these events. Direct federal administration in the Western Region was continued through April 1963.

The Western House of Representatives met in April 1963, for the first time since the emergency. The session was boycotted by thirty-eight members of the Action Group led by their new leader, Alhaji Adegbenro. Chief Akintola remained as the premier. His support came from a new party, the United Peoples party (UPP), composed of former Action Group members who had chosen to support Akintola in the internecine conflict. The UPP after mid-1963 was in coalition with the NCNC on the regional level and, therefore, Akintola's position as premier was far from secure. No elections were held immediately after the emergency and many Yorubas remained loyal to the Action Group and their "lost leader." Their latent strength was shown in the 1963 Lagos municipal elections when the Action Group won all the seats.

A major policy decision was made in 1962 to create a new region, the Mid-West, out of parts of the Eastern and Western regions. Litigation introduced by the Western Region postponed effecting this division until 1963. However, a plebiscite held in 1963 in the areas concerned resulted in a favorable vote for the new region. An interim administrator, Chief Dennis Osadebay, was appointed under federal control until elections could be held for the Mid-Western House of Representatives. All the major parties in Nigeria contested these elections which were held in February 1964. A Mid-West Democratic Front (MDF) was formed which allied itself for this election with the NPC and also the Mid-West branch of the UPP despite the fact that the NPC and the NCNC were allied on the federal level. The NCNC led by Chief Osadebay thus was challenged by a coalition of all parties except the Action Group. The Action Group had an informal understanding with the NCNC for the elections. The result of the elections showed the NCNC winning forty-nine seats and the MDF only ten.

Prior to these elections Nigeria had taken another step away from older British forms of government by becoming a republic. With the exception of the change of name and creating the post of president, little was altered in the structure of government. Dr. Azikiwe became the first president in October 1963 with the same internal powers formerly exercised by the governor-general. The regional governors and other legislative and executive institutions were retained unchanged.

Early in 1964 there were signs that the coalition between the NPC and the NCNC at the federal level was wearing thin. Examples of friction between the parties were the NCNC-UPP coalition in the West and the recent elections in the Mid-West which saw the NCNC and the NPC contesting against one another. In March 1964, it was announced that a merger between the UPP and a large segment of the NCNC in the West had been effected. The new party led by Chief Akintola was called the Nigerian National Democratic party (NNDP). The census taken in preparation for new general elections placed the southern regions at an even further population disadvantage to the North and was sharply criticized by the NCNC. The census showed the North to have a population of 29,750,000 as compared to the 12,333,000 of the East, 10,250,000 of the West, and 2,500,000 of the Mid-West. As of January 1964, however, Balewa was secure with a majority in the House of Representatives even without the NCNC. Although it is difficult to determine exact alignments in the house, a conservative estimate of parliamentary strength at that time was NPC **179**, NCNC 82, UPP 19, and Action Group 18.

In 1964 there was considerable unrest in all of the regions of Nigeria, even in the supposedly secure North. The Tiv country in the extreme southeast of the Northern Region was the scene of widespread violence beginning in February 1964. Over one hundred persons were killed and more than one thousand were arrested for various crimes including murder. Local politicians were restricted and the Northern government appointed a commission to inquire into the disturbances.

Part of the reason for the unrest was the historic differences between the Tiv and the Fulani-Hausa ruling group in the North. The Tiv, a Bantu people, comprise the largest homogeneous minority in the North. They had formed the chief opposition to the NPC in the southern area of the Northern Region. In the 1959 elections the United Middle Belt Congress (UMBC) was formed to agitate for a separate region. UBMC candidates won the Tiv seats handily, but this did not diminish the control of the NPC over the native authority. The defeat of a proposed Middle Belt region further intensified the hostility between the Tiv and the NPC.

The violence in 1964 began over the location of a market and spread rapidly until it involved thousands of people. The NPC finally dissolved the native authority in question and appointed a commission of inquiry. The basic question was far from settled by the end of 1965 and illustrated very well an area of great instability within what was normally considered the most stable political region of Nigeria.

By the fall of 1964 it was apparent that new elections, the first since independence, would soon be held. This accelerated the breakdown of the NPC-NCC coalition and resulted in the formation of new political alliances. Potentially the strongest of these groupings was the Nigerian National Alliance (NNA) which was composed of the NPC, the NNDP of Chief Akintola, the MDF, a small schismatic party, the Niger Delta Congress, an anarchistic new organization, the Dynamic party, and the Lagos State United Front. The chief figure in the NNA was the sardauna of Sokoto, Ahmadu Bello, whose NPC was the dominant party at the center. His confidence in victory was based largely upon the new population figures.

The NNA called forth an opposition alliance of parties, the United Progressive Grand Alliance (UPGA). The main strength of this union was the NCNC which provided the government of both the Eastern and Mid-Western regions. Also prominent in the alliance was the Action Group under the leadership of Adegbenro in the absence of Awolowo. The other two parties joined to the UPGA were the NEPU and the UMBC. The NEPU was the main opposition to the NPC in the North while the UMBC was solidly based in the Tiv areas.

In addition to these two great alliances there were a number of small, localized independent groups. The most important of these was the Socialist Workers and Farmers party (SWAFP) whose leader, Dr. Tunji Otegbeye, was a former leader of the Nigerian Youth Movement. However, the SWAFP contested only about one-fifth of the seats and its chances of success even in those constituencies were minimal.

The alliance systems assured that the coming election would be the first to be nationally contested. This did not mean that the NPC or NCNC was in danger in its region, but there was theoretically a better chance for the opposing parties to make inroads in areas previously closed to them. Thus, even before the date was set, the alliances were already contesting the election. Some of the speechs, including those of President Azikiwe, publicly reminded the people that they were Nigerians and not members of a party, province, or tribe.

The preelection controversies continued through the period of balloting in January 1965. Dr. Okpara, leader of the UPGA, already disturbed over the census figures, declared that the election was being manipulated in many districts. This was believed to be particularly true in the Northern Region where forty UPGA candidates had been jailed and over twenty other candidates had not been allowed to register despite the fact that the Northern Region, already controlled by the NPC, was allotted 167 of the 312 seats in the National House of Representatives. In the minds of Eastern politicians such activities only confirmed their suspicions of the sardauna and the NPC. When the NNA announced that sixty-four of their candidates from the North would be returned unopposed, Dr. Okpara replied that the UPGA would boycott the elections until the question of irregularities had been thoroughly investigated. The boycott was fairly effective in the Eastern and Western regions. However, this decision brought Nigeria to the brink of civil war and dissolution of the federation. Okpara stated that if the political situation continued to deteriorate, the UPGA coalition would consider proposals to break up the federation. Rioting was endemic throughout the southern part of Nigeria, particularly in the Western Region. There was a protest strike by civil service workers in Lagos supporting the UPGA position.

Only last-minute appeals by President Azikiwe and Prime Minister Balewa saved the situation. Balewa agreed to accept UPGA members into his ministry which in effect would create, at the federal level, not a partisan, but a coalition government. While still protesting the validity of the election returns, the UPGA leadership eventually accepted the offer. Thus by a very hasty compromise more bloodshed was avoided and the federation was saved.

The next important test for the stability and unity of Nigeria was the Western regional elections held in October 1965. Due to the suspension of the civil government in the West in 1962 and early 1963, the region had not had an election since independence. Many of the troubles which had plagued the federal elections in January 1965 had their source in the conflict between the Action Group and Chief Akintola's NNDP. There was more than political rivalry involved in the West. Genuine hatreds had been generated by the arrest and subsequent imprisonment of Chief Awolowo. Chief Adegbenro of the Action Group had accused Premier Akintola of a whole range of unfair practices even before the dates for the regional elections had been set. In the early stages of the balloting Chief Adegbenro accused the NNDP of a number of flagrant violations of election rules. The Federal Electoral Commission, however, certified the results of the election which gave the NNDP of Akintola seventy-one of the ninety-four seats in the Western House of Assembly. Such an overwhelming victory was a surprise to many observers who believed that the contest would be close.

Adegbenro, obviously disappointed and distressed, protested vainly to the governor of the Western Region, Chief Fadahunsi. The governor, however, refused to see him and called upon Akintola to form a new government. At this juncture Adegbenro and the Action Group announced their computations of the election results. These estimates, if approximately true, would have reversed the official figures and given the UPGA a majority of over fifty seats. During the exchange of views by the political leaders, the violence which had been endemic during the elections spread. These disturbances were particularly bad in Ondo Province where many public buildings were burned. Ijebu Province and Lagos were also scenes of antigovernment UPGA violent protests. Most observers agree that the majority of the participants of these activities were UPGA supporters. In Ibadan a dusk to dawn curfew was imposed and four of the major newspapers in the region were banned.

The UPGA did not file election petitions challenging any of the contested seats. The leadership obviously believed that federal authorities would intervene in the deeply divided riot-torn region. However, Prime Minister Balewa was not eager to repeat the state of emergency proclamations of 1962 and refrained from utilizing the central government as an agent for either of the contending parties. Therefore, whatever the validity of the UPGA charges, the failure to challenge any of the contested seats officially left Akintola and the NNDP in control of a deeply divided Western Region.

At the same time events in the Mid-Western Region also created tension and a sense of disunity. There, a federal board of inquiry was investigating the activities of the Owegbe cult, a semireligious society composed of Benis. This had been organized to give voice to the desires of the Benis and to protect them from imagined Ibo oppression. The cult had as members some of the most influential men in the region such as the oba of Benin and Chief Omo-Osagie. The Federal board was concerned with the activities of the cult in intimidating candidates for office and the electorate.

Over a year of tension in Nigeria was climaxed by the overthrow of the government by the army. On Friday evening, January 14, 1966, the main elements of the 10,000 man army led by junior officers moved simultaneously against the federal and regional governments. In the North, units commanded by Major Nzeogwu attacked the palace of Premier Bello, head of the NPC. After its capture the sarduana was summarily executed. Other forces in Ibadan concentrated on the major leaders of the NNDP. Chief Akintola was taken from his home and shot. Meanwhile, the commander of the presidential guard in Lagos arrested Prime Minister Balewa and Finance Minister Okotie-Eboh. Three days later their bodies were found outside Lagos. It was later revealed that the army's plan was nonpartisan and Dr. Okpara and Osadebay, premiers of the East and Mid-West, had been scheduled for execution, but the plans went awry. President Azikiwe escaped possible assassination because he was in England. Over seventy-five other influential persons were killed during the coup.

By January 18, the revolt was stabilized by the assumption of leadership of the country by the army commander, Major General John Aguiyi-Ironsi. The constitution was suspended, the offices of president and prime minister eliminated, and military governors appointed for each of the four regions. Ironsi promised a concerted attack upon corruption, inefficiency, and partisanship. To. show that he was serious, many superfluous civil service positions were abolished and travel abroad was severely restricted. The leading politicians in all the regions accepted the military coup and promised their support of the new regime. Even the North where the sarduana's power had been paramount showed no real signs of resistance to the new regime.

SIERRA LEONE

Politics in Sierra Leone through 1957 were dominated by the tension between the colony and protectorate. The colony had been administered by the British from the early eighteenth century with the active support of the Creole population. The Creoles of Sierra Leone, descendants of freed slaves, were the first Africans to develop a large Western-oriented middle class. Throughout recent history many of the doctors, lawyers, ministers, and teachers in West Africa came from, or were trained in, Sierra Leone. The protectorate with a much larger population was by comparison backward, relatively poor, and ruled by the British through traditional chiefs. The Creole attitude toward protectorate natives, developed at an earlier period, seriously prejudiced the development of national political parties.

In accordance with their policy elsewhere in West Africa, Britain put forward proposals in 1947 for an expansion of African representation in the Legislative Council. These proposals called for the protectorate to have a larger representation than the colony. Creole opposition led by Dr. H. Bankole-Bright, head of the colony-based National Council of Sierra Leone, blocked the implementation of the proposals until 1951. Then the British government instituted a Legislative Council of twenty-one elected members as contrasted to seven officials and two nominated members. Members from the protectorate were chosen by an indirect method.

The year 1951 thus signaled a radical change in the government and in the political parties of Sierra Leone. Until then all parties had been small, Creole, and colony-oriented. The formation of the Sierra Leone Peoples party (SLPP) coincided with the shift of political power to the protectorate. The SLPP was an outgrowth of the Sierra Leone Organization Society which had been created earlier to further agricultural development in the protectorate. Under the leadership of Dr. Milton Margai and his brother Albert, this became, with the backing of the chiefs, the major political instrument of the protectorate. Milton Margai blended this organization with the small colony-based Freetown Peoples party to create the SLPP. The new party became the majority group within the new Legislative Council under the leadership of Milton Margai. With the active support of the governor in the period after 1951, the six African members of the Executive Council assumed the status and responsibility of ministers.

The improvements in the government of Sierra Leone, impressive as they were, did not directly affect the majority of the population. No more than 6,000 persons had had an opportunity to vote for candidates. Responsible British and Sierra Leone officials soon began work to advance the territory toward the goal of independence. The Keith-Lucas Commission in 1954 suggested a wide franchise based, however, upon property qualifications and exercised in single member constituencies. The commission recommended that independence be granted in 1961.

In July 1956, the Colonial Office submitted to the Legislative Council a plan to reorganize the legislature. This new legislature, called the House of Representatives, was to contain fourteen elected members from the colony, twenty-five from the protectorate, and twelve chiefs who were to be selected by the district councils. The reorganization of the executive was to be left to the decision of the new house. The plan was adopted by the Legislative Council, although all the colony parties opposed the disparity between the number of colony and protectorate representatives. This plan was assented to by Britain in November and elections were set for May 1957.

The election of 1957 was heavily contested in the colony. The National Council, the Labor party, the Sierra Leone Independence Movement (SLIM), and the United Peoples party (UPP) opposed the SLPP. The results were almost a foregone conclusion since all of the other parties were primarily colony-based and the SLPP was so strongly entrenched in the protectorate that it ran its business with only twelve branch offices. The SLPP won twenty-six of the thirty-nine directly elected seats in the new house. The SLPP even won all six Freetown seats and three of the six in the immediate colony area. The National Council, the official opposition in the old Legislative Council, won no seats and soon disappeared as an active party. The UPP won five seats and became the opposition. With most of the twelve paramount chiefs supporting SLPP policy, Milton Margai's position seemed unassailable.

Immediately after the elections of May 1957, however, in the reconfirmation of the party leadership, Milton Margai was challenged by his brother Albert. Milton was conservative and his political power was strongly dependent on support from the protectorate chiefs. Albert appealed to the younger, more progressive members of the party. In closed balloting for the leadership, Albert was chosen by one vote over his brother. Later arrangements were made, Albert stepped aside, and Dr. Milton Margai continued as head of the SLPP and prime minister of Sierra Leone.

In September 1958, the split within the SLPP leadership so noticeable the previous year was confirmed by Albert Margai's resignation as national chairman of the SLPP. Together with other more radical leaders such as Siaka Stevens, former minister of lands and labor, he formed a new party, the Peoples National party (PNP). This group criticized the SLPP for its slowness to react to the many pressing needs of Sierra Leone. Because of its size, it became the government opposition party. In December 1959, the party alignment in the house was SLPP thirty, PNP-SLIM coalition seven, UPP four, and independents three.

Discussions concerning further constitutional advances were begun as early as December 1957. Serious final talks began at Lancaster House on April 20, 1960 and continued until May 4. Sir Milton Margai led a coalition group, the United Front, to the conference. The United Front was composed of all parties of Sierra Leone. Such an arrangement, it was believed, would show that all factions were united on the question of independence. The conference set the date for independence as April 1961 and decided there was no need for a general election before independence. It was on this latter issue that Siaka Stevens, a PNP delegate, demurred and refused to sign the agreement. In June 1960, Stevens was expelled from the PNP and subsequently formed his own party, the All Peoples Congress (APC).

Independence came to Sierra Leone on April 27, 1961, in the midst of what has been described as the most peaceful state of emergency in Africa. On April 18, Siaka Stevens and fifteen members of the APC were arrested and charged with planning violent acts to disrupt the independence ceremonies. Thirteen of those charged were released in May. Stevens was tried for his activities and sentenced to six months in prison. Later this conviction was reversed and Stevens' party became the chief opposition to the SLPP.

The other parties, never large and with little countrywide following, underwent a series of crises after 1957. The UPP split into two factions. The dissident group called themselves the Independent Peoples party. They were drawn into Margai's United Front of early 1960 and their members subsequently either joined the SLPP or coalesced once again with the UPP in late 1960. Having lost decisively in the elections of 1962, the UPP merged with Stevens' APC in July 1962. The SLIM, which had strength only in the Kono district, also merged with the APC. After independence the PNP was reabsorbed into the SLPP. In the first election after independence held in May 1962, there were only two really effective parties, the SLPP and the APC.

The SLPP itself was but an amalgam of local groups held together by a loose organization and the political sagacity of Sir Milton Margai. This coalition was effective because of the trust placed in Margai by the protectorate authorities and his pragmatic conservatism. The APC, although disagreeing only on a few general policies of the government, appealed to the younger, more progressive elements in Sierra Leone. In the elections of May 1962, the SLPP won twenty-eight seats in the house, the APC twenty, and independents fourteen. However, twelve of the independents associated themselves with the SLPP and it could count on the support of most of the twelve indirectly elected chiefs. Thus on major issues the real voting strength in the house after May 1962 was approximately fifty-two to twenty-two in favor of the SLPP. The closeness of the vote between the SLPP and the APC and the loose party structure of the SLPP indicated that without Milton Margai, the SLPP could well lose any future general elections.

In May 1964, Sir Milton Margai died and was succeeded by his brother Albert as head of the party and premier. The change of leadership was accomplished smoothly. Sir Milton, in a quiet, efficient manner, left a multiparty legacy to his nation. In 1965 only Sierra Leone, Gambia, and Nigeria of all independent West African states maintained a system whereby opposition groups had a legal and effective outlet. However, the new prime minister made a concerted attack upon the multiparty concept. By the end of 1965 shifts of alliances gave the SLPP forty-eight seats to only fourteen for the APC in the seventy-four member house. In December 1965, a private member introduced a motion in the house which called upon the government to consider seriously the introduction of a one-party system. This private motion was approved by the house. It appeared that Sierra Leone was going to follow the example of most other African states in rejecting a multiparty approach to government.

Devolution of power and consolidation of African rule: British Central Africa

CENTRAL AFRICAN FEDERATION

Politics in the Central African Federation in the 1950s was the most complex in Africa. This was not because the problems themselves were more complex, but because in addition to the need to solve the questions posed by a multiracial society there was added the largely unwanted mechanism of a federal government structure. The federation, composed of Southern and Northern Rhodesia and Nyasaland, was not based upon historical precedents, tribal affinity, or political similarity. It was created by the British Colonial Office in response to the pressure of the whites, primarily of Southern Rhodesia, to draw together these territories in a closer economic union and thus covertly postpone the date when Africans would receive full political equality with the whites. When the federation was created in 1953, only the electorate of Southern Rhodesia, a self-governing colony, primarily white, expressed the desire for federation. The decision for the northern territories was made by the British government.

The federal structure reserved specific powers to the central authority whose executive was a ministry and a prime minister, first Lord Malvern and after 1956, Sir Roy Welensky, responsible to a central legislature. However, governmental responsibility in certain areas was shared with the separate states. The white minority of Southern Rhodesia represented by the United Federal party (UFP) and Sir Roy Welensky tended to dominate the association. In 1957, despite the growing nation-

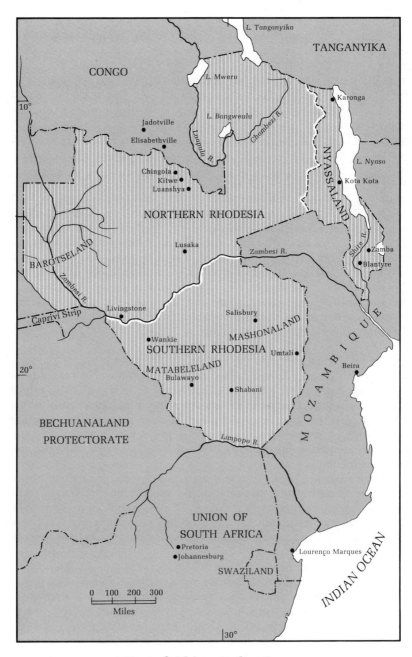

Central African Federation

alist sentiments in all the territories, Welensky began his campaign to have the federation become an independent entity within the Commonwealth. The Monckton Commission, which was charged with investigating the politics of the federation, reported in 1960 negatively on Welensky's proposal and this left the way open for its breakup. Any strength the federation had was based upon its acceptance by the regions. Its final dissolution, in January 1964, was due to its failure to meet the demands of African politicians in Southern and Northern Rhodesia and Nyasaland. Therefore, it is to the regions rather than the center that one must turn to understand the political development in the Central African Federation.

RHODESIA

Southern Rhodesia was the result of the territorial expansion of the Rhodes' controlled British South Africa Company which colonized the area in the 1890s. The company ruled there until 1923, when it surrendered its rights to the crown. After this date the politics of this self-governing colony was dominated by the small white-settler population (3,500 in 1924; 60,000 in 1955). The franchise was ninety-nine percent controlled by them. The earliest political parties were the Rhodesian Union Association and the Responsible Government Association which fought the 1922 referendum on the question of union with South Africa which was favored by the former. The Responsible Government Association governed the colony for ten years until Dr. Godfrey Huggins welded together a number of opposition parties and won the election of 1933. By personal appeal and political patronage, he later formed almost all political groups into one, the United Party (UP). Not until after World War II was there any real opposition to the UP when in 1946 a small group formed the Liberal party which, despite its name, favored a policy of strict paternalistic segregation. The Liberal party posed a serious threat to the UP and Huggins maintained only a slim majority in parliament. After 1948 the Liberal party ceased to have much influence.

Before World War II, Africans were represented by a variety of small, politically powerless organizations such as the Rhodesian Native Association, Commercial Workers Union, and the Rhodesian Bantu Voters Association. In 1938 the Bantu Congress of Southern Rhodesia was created which contented itself with trying to influence the government in matters of education and labor. The party did not challenge the segregation policies of the government. After World War II the name of this organization was changed to the Rhodesian African National Congress (ANC). The ANC absorbed many small African cooperative societies. Among these was the Rhodesia Railways African Employees' Association which brought Joshua Nkomo into the incipient African movement.

A long series of discussions with the Colonial Office concerning possible unification began in 1949 and culminated in 1953 with the creation of the federation. This was done against the fears and protests of African leaders in all areas. Nevertheless, the Colonial Office believed that the compromise by which Britain retained definite powers of intervention in

Northern Rhodesia and Nyasaland would protect African interests. The ensuing federation resulted in a reorganization of the UP. One segment was called the United Federal party (UFP) to contest federal elections, and the other was the United Rhodesians, primarily for Southern Rhodesia. Sir Godfrey Huggins of the UFP was elected federal prime minister and Garfield Todd became prime minister of Southern Rhodesia. The most important African parties carried the names of their respective African national congresses. The key leaders were Nkomo of Southern Rhodesia, Chuime of Nyasaland, and Nkumbula of Northern Rhodesia.

There was no effective opposition to the United parties until 1956 when the Dominion party led by Winston Field was formed. He advocated permanent white supremacy and the expulsion from the federation of all nonviable, non-European territories. In 1957 there was a major crisis in the United Rhodesian party. Garfield Todd had recommended gradual integration and voter privileges for the Africans. Partially for this and partially because of personal conflicts with his ministers, he was expelled from office and the party. In the ensuing election, Sir Edgar Whitehead, Todd's chosen successor as leader of the United Rhodesian party, was barely able to win over Field's Dominion party. On the federal level, however, the UFP held firm control. In 1955, Huggins had retired, becoming Lord Malvern, and his place as federal prime minister was taken by Sir Roy Welensky.

Economic agitation by Africans which had begun as early as 1945 continued to mount and the ANC in Southern Rhodesia benefited from this and the growing African dissatisfaction in the northern territories. Its leader, Joshua Nkomo, had been one of the major opposition leaders to federation in the London discussions in 1952, but four years after federation the ANC was almost moribund. Nkomo's proposals for a united ANC of all the territories had been rejected. However, in 1957, the movement began to revive and Nkomo was elected president-general. In February 1959, due to continued disturbances, a state of emergency was declared in Southern Rhodesia; the congress leaders were arrested and the organization was banned. Nkomo escaped arrest because he was in London and therefore became influential in organizing a new party, the National Democratic party (NDP) in early 1960. Elected president-general in October 1960, he returned to Southern Rhodesia. In late 1959, the British appointed a twenty-five member commission headed by Viscount Monckton to investigate the potential for future development of the federation. It recommended that the federation be retained but that each area be given the right to secede after five years. It also suggested a liberalization of the franchise laws and more African representation in the legislature. After the Monckton Report, the Colonial Office began a series of discussions on the substance of the report and revision of the Southern Rhodesian constitution. Nkomo, a moderate within his party, at first was inclined to accept the compromises agreed upon in the discussions. However, pressure within his party forced him to repudiate the agreement in February 1961. In July the NDP called a general strike during the time of the referendum on the proposed new constitution and organized a referendum of its own. This strike was a failure and the NDP referendum had little effect on the attitudes of the Colonial Office. A group dissatisfied with Nkomo's leadership broke away from the NDP to organize their own more radical party, the Zimbabwe National party (ZNP). In December 1961, when Nkomo was in Tanganyika, the Southern Rhodesian government permanently banned the NDP. Nkomo replied by organizing yet a new party, the Zimbabwe African Peoples' Union (ZAPU). With the increasing intransigence on the part of the Southern Rhodesian government, nationalist leadership became more radical.

The new constitution which went into effect in December 1961 called for a legislative assembly of sixty-five elected on a two-roll system. Fifty members were to be selected from the predominantly white upper roll while fifteen were to come from the predominantly black lower roll. Although the Dominion party and the NDP denounced the constitution for widely differing reasons, it had been accepted by over seventy-five percent of the qualified voters.

Much of 1962 was taken up by discussions on new constitution instruments since the constitution of December 1961 was so unpopular. No real agreement could be reached between Africans and whites. Further adding to the confusion was the coalition of the right-wing parties into the Rhodesian Front party (RF) led by Field. There was an increase in violent activities throughout Rhodesia which led to a tightening of restrictive native laws and these, in turn, produced more violence. It was announced in November that elections under the new constitution would be held in December 1963. Nkomo was arrested and ZAPU was banned which meant that no African party would be officially represented in the new elections. The UFP and Whitehead attempted to get as many Africans as possible enrolled in the lower rolls. However, African leaders effectively prevented this.

In the elections the UFP was placed between the two extremes of white ultraconservatives and African nationalists. The election results clearly showed the fate of a middle-ground party in Southern Rhodesia. The RF won thirty-five seats to twenty-nine for the UFP, with one independent being returned. The decision of the ZAPU leaders that Africans should boycott the elections thus resulted in the election of a more conservative government—a government dedicated to independence for Southern Rhodesia on white-settler terms. The harsh laws of the Whitehead and Field governments and the banning of ZAPU had temporarily disorganized African opposition. Nkomo and his lieutenants upon their release from detention formed yet another African political group called the Peoples Caretaker Councils.

Winston Field carried the demands of the RF for independence to London in February 1964. He and other white leaders believed that their case had been strengthened by the recent breakup of the federation and the promised independence of the other two territories. However, the British government was adamant in demanding a readjustment in the electoral system to give more voice to the African majority. Thus Field came back empty-handed to face a revolt within his party. Field was ousted and Ian Douglas Smith who had served as Field's finance minister became prime minister. Smith represented the most adamant section of the RF. His first official act was to arrest Nkomo and three officers of the Peoples Caretaker Councils. This action resulted in riots in Salisbury and the arrest of 250 Africans.

The breakup of the federation and the promises of speedy independence made by the Colonial Office to Nyasaland and Northern Rhodesia had created demands by the Europeans in Southern Rhodesia for independence within the Commonwealth. Winston Field's failure to secure some type of commitment from Britain had led to his downfall. Smith and the RF refused to consider any major reforms of the electoral laws of Rhodesia which alone would have appeased the sentiments of Great Britain. Instead, he explored the possibility of a unilateral declaration of independence. Although repeatedly stating that his government would pursue negotiations with the Colonial Office, he also said he believed these would be fruitless. His political position in Rhodesia was not strong enough to allow him to do more than make tentative moves toward pressuring Britain. The RF had only a slim five-vote majority in parliament in the summer of 1964. One of the first pronouncements of Harold Wilson's newly elected Labor government in Britain was to reiterate his hostility toward Smith's views of the native question and underline the ill effects that any precipitate independent action would have on Rhodesia's future.

In June 1964, the Rhodesian National party (RNP), formerly the UFP, held a congress and declared against unilateral declaration of independence unless Britain interfered with the internal affairs of Rhodesia. Also in June, Dr. Maurice Hirsch launched a new organization, the Reform party, whose program was much the same as that of the RNP. The major differences were in the personalities of Hirsch and Sir Edgar Whitehead. The Reform party wanted to do away with racial discrimination on the upper roll and entrench the fifteen "B" roll seats in the constitution while making adjustments for wider African representation. Such changes were necessary before Britain would contemplate granting Rhodesia independence. Fragmentation of parties among the Africans continued to hamper any coordinated African protests. The government also made difficult any meaningful opposition. The leader of the Zimbabwe African National Union (ZANU), Ndabaningi Sithole, was in and out of jail during this period. Joshua Nkomo was placed in restricted custody at Gonakudzingwa in southeast Rhodesia.

Although Smith had voiced his skepticism many times concerning an amicable agreement with Britain, the discussions between the governments continued. In March 1965, the Commonwealth secretary, Arthur Bottomley, visited Rhodesia, met various leaders, and reported back to Prime Minister Wilson. The granting of independence to Zambia the previous fall and the seeming intransigence of both the Hume and Wilson governments had created more support for Smith in Southern Rhodesia by midsummer than he had enjoyed before. In October Smith visited

London for a series of discussions with Prime Minister Wilson. Smith announced his willingness to add a senate of African chiefs to the legislature and give the right to vote to perhaps one million Africans. However, he refused to increase African representation in the house immediately over the existing fifteen out of a total of sixty-five. These promises were not sufficient for Britain, and Smith returned to Rhodesia better armed for a unilateral declaration.

The United Nations' General Assembly condemned the concept of a unilateral declaration and the white supremacy concepts of Smith's government by a vote of 107 to two. Three former prime ministers of Rhodesia spoke out to urge caution. In retaliation, former prime minister Garfield Todd, without trial, was ordered by the government confined to his farm for a year. The Rhodesian Chamber of Commerce and Tobacco Trade Association warned that the economic repercussions of any move not sanctioned by Britain could bring on a catastrophe for Rhodesia.

Smith's ministry had already met and ostensibly decided for a unilateral declaration of independence. However, Smith did not announce this immediately, but opened contacts once again with Prime Minister Wilson. He demanded independence on the same terms as before with the exception of offering a "solemn treaty" to guarantee what his government had promised. Prime Minister Wilson decided to fly to Salisbury to continue the discussions. On October 30, 1965, an agreement was reached which called for the establishment of a royal commission to investigate further. However, on November 11, Premier Smith, reacting to pressures within his party, declared the independence of Southern Rhodesia. The governor, Sir Humphrey Gibbs, dismissed Smith, but the premier ignored this and stripped the governor of any real administrative powers.

Britain refused to be stampeded into rash military action by other African states and decided instead to try to bring the Smith regime down by imposing a boycott on all goods to and from Rhodesia. By mid-December this was some ninety-five percent effective. The embargo on oil supplies had the most immediate dramatic effect on Rhodesia. No other state recognized the Smith regime. South Africa and Portugal, although sympathetic to the government, did not find it to their advanage to support directly the de facto government. The Organization of African Unity passed resolutions against the breakaway regime and condemned Britain for not taking more direct forceful action. However, even the African states bordering on Rhodesia showed little inclination for positive direct action.

MALAWI (NYASALAND)

Politics in Nyasaland was simpler than in either Southern or Northern Rhodesia because of comparative lack of resources and small European population. African politics in Nyasaland until 1958 was conducted by the Nyasaland African National Congress (ANC) whose major role had been in opposing federation. Beginning in 1957, however, a new factor galvanized the Africans in Nyasaland into a more active force. This was Dr. Hastings

Banda, a highly respected, reputable physician who had been practicing medicine in England.

The announcement of the plan for the federation aroused Banda's interest in Nyasaland politics. From his office in London and later Ghana, he gave guidance to the leaders of the Nyasaland African Congress. Finally persuaded to return to Nyasaland after an absence of many years, he was elected president-general of the party in August 1958. Banda was welcomed as a deliverer everywhere in Nyasaland, and he urged noncooperation on all levels with the federation until a new constitution could be granted. However, after a number of incidents, the government (in March 1959) declared a state of emergency in Nyasaland. Banda and his chief lieutenants were arrested. While Banda was in prison in Southern Rhodesia, The Malawi Congress party was founded to take the place of the old ANC and Banda resumed leadership of the Nyasaland nationalist movement upon his release in April 1960. In June 1960, the emergency in Nyasaland was ended and in the following month constitutional discussions were begun in London. The Congress party accepted the constitution instruments which provided twenty-eight elected seats out of a total of thirty-three in the Legislative Council. Voting was to be from two election rolls with eight seats chosen from the upper roll. Almost one year later on August 16, 1961, the elections were held and the Congress party won twenty-three of the twenty-eight elected seats. Banda and four of his congress associates joined the Executive Council in September 1961 and formed the first black government within the federation. Banda as leader of the Congress party and minister of local government continued throughout 1962 to oppose the federation even to the refusal in July of a federally planned hydroelectric project. Nyasaland was granted self-rule on November 23, 1962, representing the first great break in the federation. After lengthy high-level discussions, Banda's demands for secession from the federation were granted. A new constitution was promulgated on February 1, 1963, and Dr. Banda became prime minister. A committee to work out the manifold details of secession was formed. The many functions previously performed by the federal government were phased out by January 1, 1964.

The final step in Banda's nation-making was accomplished on July 6, 1964, when Nyasaland became the thirty-fifth independent African nation under the new name of Malawi. The major political force in Malawi was the Malawi Congress party which appeared to be totally dominated by Banda. However, in the summer of 1964, a rift occurred between Banda and some of his most important ministers. The six disaffected members contended that the prime minister was assuming too much personal power. The ministers were dismissed and the leader, ex-Education Minister Henry Chipembere, was restricted to a four-mile radius around his home in Malindi. Soon there was rioting between the pro- and anti-Banda factions in the capital. Banda survived this threat to his leadership and the leaders of the opposition were either arrested or forced into exile. The united front which had sustained Malawi in its drive for independence, however, was broken and Banda would never again have such whole-hearted support of all the people of Malawi. His party, nevertheless, in 1965 controlled fifty seats in the fifty-three member National Assembly, the other three being reserved for Europeans elected on a separate election roll.

ZAMBIA (NORTHERN RHODESIA)

When federation was imposed despite Northern Rhodesian-ANC opposition, the organization turned to boycotts and demonstrations. This led to more conflicts with the European-dominated government and prison for many of the leaders. In February 1958, the ANC proposed that twenty-one of the forty-two seats in the Northern Rhodesian Legislative Council be reserved for Africans elected by direct franchise. Instead, the Colonial Office sanctioned an extremely complex system of franchise. Harry Nkumbula's leadership of the ANC, which had been under fire for some time, was openly challenged because of his seeming noncommittal behavior. The result of this quarrel was the creation of Zambia African National Congress (ZANC) led by Kenneth Kaunda and containing a majority of the influential members of the ANC in the north. While ANC supported the elections of 1959, the ZANC actively opposed them. In March 1959, ZANC was banned and its leaders arrested. Kaunda was not released until January 1960, when he became the leader of a new party, the United National Independence party (UNIP) which announced its aim to force independence by the close of the year. After violence flared in the copper belt, the UNIP was banned from that area. Kaunda held talks with the Colonial Office in May 1960, but it was not until October 1960 that it was announced that new constitutional discussions would take place at the same time as the Federal Review Conference. These discussions began in December, and in February 1961, the tentative complex territorial constitution was announced. Under this constitution there was created a three-part electoral system. Fifteen members of the Legislative Council would be elected from an upper roll, fifteen from a lower roll, and fifteen from the composite of both. It was obvious to the federal prime minister, Sir Roy Welensky, that Africans would gain a majority in the Legislative Council unless the constitution was changed. He demanded further discussions with the Colonial Office which resulted in the revision of the proposed instrument to give a separate electoral roll for Indians, and a percentage factor was introduced which limited the effect of the African votes. Following this announcement violence again erupted in Northern Rhodesia and the UNIP was banned in the northern areas. Faced with such African protest, the Colonial Office agreed in September 1961 to reconsider the entire question. In February 1962, the Welensky revision was again revised partially to compromise with the UNIP demands. This Colonial Office compromise satisfied none of the parties concerned, and Kaunda announced that in any elections, the unwieldy constitution would produce a deadlock. The UNIP rejected the new constitution promulgated in March 1962 but later indicated that it would contest the election as a preliminary to dissolving the federation and independence for Northern Rhodesia. The United Federal party led by Mr. J. Roberts, a supporter of federation and the white party policies, strongly contested the election. Another white-dominated party, the Liberal party, had as its major premise close cooperation with the Africans.

In the elections held in October 1962, the United Federal party won a total of fifteen seats (thirteen upper roll, two national), the UNIP won fourteen (one upper roll, twelve lower roll, one special Asian), and the ANC won five (three lower roll, two national). Ten seats were left vacant on the national combined roll because none of the candidates received the ten percent minimum votes necessary. Of the 104,000 votes, the UNIP gained 64,000. The Liberal party was utterly defeated.

The complicated system of voting, as Kaunda had predicted, produced a complete stalemate, and a caretaker government of officials was appointed by the governor pending by-elections in December. The ANC and UNIP formed a coalition government in December, controlling twenty-one seats, and Kaunda became minister of local government and Nkumbula was named minister of African education. In February 1963, the first major decision of the new Legislative Council was to call for a new constitution and an end to federation. Committees were appointed by the governor to make recommendations on both points and, by June 1963, substantial agreement had been reached by the UNIP and ANC. After a number of higher level conferences, the British decided that with Nyasaland opting out of the federation and violence continuing in Northern Rhodesia, the only solution was to grant what the nationalists wanted—an end to federation.

The federation officially ended in January 1964 and the new constitution for Northern Rhodesia went into effect that same month. It provided for self-government with a ministry responsible to a seventy-five member Legislative Assembly. Elections were held on January 20, with the UNIP winning fifty-five of seventy-five seats, and Kenneth Kaunda became prime minister. Harry Nkumbula's African National Congress won only ten seats. According to the constitution, ten of the seats were to be reserved for the 77,000 Europeans until 1969.

In May Kaunda led a delegation to a further series of conferences in London. During this sixteen-day discussion period, Britain granted Kaunda's request to dispense with the usual period of symbolic rule under a governor-general and agreed upon the immediate establishment of a presidential system. The new state renamed Zambia thus became a republic on October 24, 1964. Kaunda was chosen by the assembly as the first president elected for a five-year term. For all subsequent terms the president would be elected by direct suffrage.

Rich in copper, Zambia's major economic problem is related to its landlocked position and the fact that the railway lines connecting it with the outside world passed through the disturbed Congo and its potentially hostile neighbor, Southern Rhodesia. Kaunda's own moderate position was thus reinforced by the economic situation. He, like Hastings Banda in Malawi, could not immediately afford to take a militantly hostile line toward South Africa, Southern Rhodesia, or Portugal. This type of neutralism was brought to an end by the unilateral declaration of independence by Premier Ian Smith of Southern Rhodesia.

The reactions against Smith's regime by Britain and other African states placed Kaunda in an extremely vulnerable position. The Kariba Dam which supplies power to Zambia as well as Southern Rhodesia was, in the first days after Southern Rhodesia's action, the focal point of most concern. The turbines and generators in this joint venture were on the Rhodesian side of the border. Kaunda's position was, therefore, ambivalent. He wanted Britain to deal with Smith's government, but did not feel that he could sanction the kind of actions which might have detrimental results for Zambia. Prime Minister Wilson's embargo on Southern Rhodesia was followed by a Southern Rhodesia embargo on oil transports to Zambia. Thus in November and December 1965, the British action had as much negative effect upon Zambia as on Rhodesia. To a very large extent the stability of Kaunda's government depended not only upon forces within Zambia but upon the development of events in Southern Rhodesia.

Devolution of power and consolidation of African rule: the high commission territories of Southern Africa

BASUTOLAND (LESOTHO)

The major determinant in the history of this 12,000 square mile territory is its geographic location. It is a predominantly highland area completely surrounded by the Republic of South Africa. In the nineteenth century the Basuto people were in constant conflict first with the Boer trekkers and later with their republics, particularly the Orange Free State. The Basuto, largely because of the easily defensible terrain, were never conquered by the Boers. However, the great Basuto chief, Msheshwe, realized that ultimately they would be conquered if they continued to stand alone. Repeatedly he appealed for protection to British authorities at Capetown. Finally in 1868 the British annexed Basutoland and attached it administratively to Cape Colony. In 1884 the Cape was relieved of the cost of administration and the government of Basutoland was assumed directly by the British crown.

The type of administration in Basutoland in the twentieth century prior to its independence was the dual rule of the British and Basuto. The traditional Basuto rulers have exercised more power in local affairs than was true in other areas under indirect rule. Basuto local government was also more unified since the paramount chief had substantive powers over his chiefs and subchiefs. Although no paramount chief has been as able and had as much influence as Msheshwe, they always were important enough to be consulted by the British before any major policy changes were instituted.

Basutoland was a High Commission Territory, and as such, it was administered since the 1920s under the Commonwealth Relations Office and not the Colonial Office. The chief administrator was a resident commissioner who was assisted by a secretariat and district commissioners. Since 1903 he was advised by the Basutoland Council. After 1910 this council was composed of thirty-six members elected by the district councils, fifty-two members appointed by the paramount chief, five members nominated by the government, and six representing special interests. The council not only acted to give the resident commissioner a wide sampling of Basuto opinion, but also from this body the three chief advisers to the paramount chief were selected.

The most crucial continuing problem of Basutoland concerned its future relations with South Africa. By the Act of Union, South Africa was assured that in due time all the High Commission Territories, after consultation between Britain and the Union, would be returned to South Africa. Britain's reluctance to do more than discuss this matter was based on the known opposition of the Basuto to any such union. Nevertheless, any liberalization in the government of Basutoland in recent years meant further estrangement from South Africa. South Africa completely surrounds Basutoland and a large sector of the Basuto economy depends upon the continued employment of Basutos in South African industry.

Due to the nature of dual rule, political parties in Basutoland were slow to develop. The oldest such organization, the Progressive Association, was founded in 1907 and could not be considered a political party in the usual sense. It stood for more Basuto participation in the central government, but represented a conservative, go-slow, cooperative policy. Any influence which it might have had was more than matched by the Sons of Msheshwe. Composed of the descendants of the great chief, this organization exercised considerable influence over local government and British opinion, particularly concerning association with South Africa.

In 1954 Britain, responding to pressures within Basutoland and carrying out the liberal colonial policy so noticeable elsewhere in British Africa, appointed a commission to study political reforms. The report of the Moore Commission did not recommend major changes in the system. Many of the younger educated Basutos had formed a political party, the Basutoland Congress party (BCP) before the commission had been appointed. The mild report said nothing about the BCP's foremost demand for an elected legislative council. The BCP, while not completely against traditional rule, wanted an end to British control and the grant of more power to elected representatives who in turn would limit the power of the chiefs. In 1958 the British again attempted to find a consensus on constitutional reform. BCP representatives in London made it clear that they expected the normal progression toward independence. Soon afterward Britain announced basic agreement with the BCP ideas of an elected legislature.

This announcement and the subsequent constitution changed the status of Basutoland and South Africa. After the constitution of 1959, any move to incorporate the enclave into the Union would need not just the consultation of the British government with South African officials, but also the consent of the Basutos.

The constitution of 1959 provided for a legislative council, the Basuto National Council, of eighty members. One half of the members were elected by the nine district councils. All 162 members of the district councils were directly elected from a common roll. Therefore, the indirect method of selecting a member of the Basuto National Council, although a compromise, was representative. The council had the right to legislate in all matters except external affairs, defense, police, loans, and public service. In these it acted only as a consultative body. In the elections under the new instrument held in January 1960, the BCP won seventy-three of the 162 seats on the district councils and twenty-nine of the forty elected seats to the National Council.

As was true in many other areas at the same stage of development, Basutoland has had a number of political parties. The only other party besides the BCP with a large following was the Basuto National party (BNP) led by Chief Lebua Jonathan. Another group founded in 1962 was the Marematlou Basuto Freedom party (MFP) whose leader was S. S. Matete. He was replaced in mid-1964 by Dr. Seth Makotoko. There have been other small parties with little popular support that disappeared after a few months. The Communist party was small but extremely active in Basutoland. Although all three major parties denounced Communism as alien to Africa, the BCP was in the past receptive to receiving aid from the Eastern bloc, particularly in the form of education grants. All parties demanded more power for the Basuto, exercised through a fully elected legislature and a ministry. All were opposed to union with South Africa. The differences came in their concepts of the rate and degree of Basuto advance and the position of the traditional native authorities in the future government.

The BCP was a more radical group than its opponents. It was affiliated with the Pan African Freedom Movement (PAFMECA) whose chief goal was independence of all territories from colonial rule as soon as possible. The BCP also was more hostile to granting the paramount chief, Moshaeshoe II, any real substantive powers in an independent Basutoland.

In October 1961, the BCP leader, Mokhehle, called for constitutional revision which would provide for responsible government. When this was not forthcoming, there was, in early 1962, considerable violence in Basutoland. Later twenty-three persons were sentenced in Maseru to terms up to ten years for their part in the disturbances. In May 1962, Mokhehle demanded of the United Nations Committee on Colonialism that they investigate Basutoland, and he again asked for quick independence.

A constitutional commission was appointed by Britain in early 1962. One of its greatest problems was what position the paramount chief should have if more responsible government was granted. Throughout the course of its investigations there grew among the Basutos the feeling that Britain was no longer giving them adequate protection. This was in reference to South Africa which had tightened its border controls considerably. In August 1963, in an unprecedented action, the Basuto National Council rejected the speech from the throne because of this feeling.

In October 1963, the constitutional commission published its recommendations for the future structure of the government after independence. The tentative date was suggested for 1965. The government, as conceived, was to be a constitutional monarchy with the paramount chief acting as head of state. The report called for a two-house system, the upper house mainly composed of chiefs with the lower house fully elected. The ministry, headed by a premier, was to be responsible to the lower house.

In May 1964, the British Commonwealth secretary, Duncan Sandys, announced his government's adherence to the draft constitutional instruments. Further, if the people of Basutoland desired independence, it would follow one year after the legal acceptance of the constitution. Chief Moshaeshoe immediately announced his support of the British proposal. The leaders of the major political parties also agreed to abide by the recommendations. All major political figures in Basutoland made public statements of assurance of future friendly relations with the Republic of South Africa and renounced any scheme of using their territory as a base for subversion within the republic.

On April 29, 1965, general elections were held and the new constitution came into being. Chief Moshaeshoe became the Queen's representative, and the British resident became the British government representative holding important reserve powers. The executive power was to be in the hands of a prime minister and his ministry, dependent upon the confidence of the lower house. The legislature was bicameral. The upper house, or Senate, was composed of twenty-two principal chiefs and ward chiefs, and eleven nominees of the paramount chief. The lower house, or National Assembly, was composed of sixty members elected by the Basuto people.

In the interim period, before the elections, great changes had occurred in the political parties. The BCP which had dominated the political scene for almost ten years encountered internal problems. The creation of the MFP was one result of these stresses. Further quarrels led to the diversion of much of the Soviet funds away from the BCP to the MFP. The MFP then became a force which detracted from potential BCP support. Mr. Mokhehle, the leader of the BCP, was such a dominant personality in the party that a number of younger Basuto were discouraged from supporting it. After Dr. Makotoko became leader, the MFP began to shift its policies from radicalism to a more moderate stance. This process continued so rapidly that by the end of 1964 the party was recognized as the political organ of the great chiefs. It was rumored that the paramount chief actually supported the MFP.

The BNP, led by Chief Jonathan and Mr. C. D. Malopo, represented the middle and lesser chieftains. It was avowedly pro-West and harshly critical of the Moscow and Peking connections of the other two parties. It was also much more realistic in its attitudes toward future relations with South Africa and was supported, although not openly, by the various Christian organizations in Basutoland.

Campaigning for the elections began early with each party well organized and having a considerable amount of modern equipment. Armed clashes between the BCP and MFP, in October 1964, resulted in the deaths of at least four people, and this undoubtedly caused many Basutos to support the BNP. Preelection indications were that either the BCP or BNP could win, but by a narrow margin. The results of the election, where ninety percent of the electorate participated, confirmed this prediction. The BNP emerged victorious with thirty-one seats and a popular vote of over 105,000. The BCP with a vote of more than 103,000 won twenty-five seats. The MFP gained four seats but had a popular vote of over 42,000. Post-election difficulties were avoided by the appointment of Mr. Malopo of the BNP and Dr. Makotoko, leader of the MFP, as senators. Each of these men had been defeated in the general election. Chief Jonathan, who was also defeated, later stood a by-election.

Chief Jonathan decided not to attempt a coalition but to form an exclusive BNP ministry which had but a narrow two-vote majority in the National Assembly. The middle-ground government thus formed was able to avoid an open clash between traditionalists and radicals until independence in the spring of 1966. At that time the name of the state was changed to Lesotho.

BECHUANALAND (BOTSWANA)

Bechuanaland was the largest (275,000 square miles) and most sparsely settled of the High Commission Territories. Unlike the other territories, it is not populated by only a single tribe but has eight different tribes living in separate reserves. The largest and most influential group is the Bamangwato. The Bantu population numbers slightly over 300,000 persons. In addition, there are approximately 3,000 Europeans and half as many Asians in the territory. Much of Bechuanaland is desert where only the Bushmen and Makalahari peoples can exist. Although there is some good agricultural land available, Bechuanaland is the poorest of the territories. This is reflected particularly in its systems of health, public works, and education. In Basutoland a large portion of the population is literate and, therefore, more in contact with political movements outside the territory. In Bechuanaland, however, the numbers of the educated elite are smaller and the unmodified tribal system more in evidence. Bechuanaland presented more problems than the other areas in its movement toward independence. It had a resident European population with its own confirmed rights and prerogatives, eight different tribal systems, and was poorer in resources than the smaller territories.

The British became interested in Bechuanaland in the late nineteenth century in competition with the Transvaal and to ward off German encroachment. The southern portion, since transferred to South Africa, was declared a protectorate in 1885. The territory was important for Cecil Rhodes' plans for expansion northward. After much discussion, the British government assumed, in 1896, direct control over the protectorate of Bechuanaland. This action was largely due to the protests of the chiefs over threatened incorporation into the territories ruled by Rhodes' British South Africa Company. The most powerful of the traditional rulers was

Khama III of the Bamangwato who until his death in 1923 maintained that he owed direct allegiance only to the British crown.

The system of rule in Bechuanaland after 1896 was a dual system. Because of the many tribes, no single chief was as important as in Swaziland and Basutoland. The presence of Europeans also caused a modification in the type of rule. The resident commissioner was the chief executive, operating on instructions given from the high commissioner's office in Pretoria. The resident commissioner was aided by a secretariat and district commissioners who were responsible for implementing indirect rule. In 1920 a European advisory council was created to represent European interests in the government. In that same year an African advisory council was established. It was composed of thirty-five chiefs, subchiefs, or persons appointed by chiefs. Its functions were similar to its European counterpart. In 1951 a joint advisory council was instituted, composed of eight members, each from the European and African councils.

The logical progression from this type of rule to a more liberal form was postponed by the long conflict between the Bamangwato and the British over the chieftainship of the tribe. The Bamangwato chief, Sekgoma, ruled for only two years and in 1925 left his heir the infant, Seretse Khama. His uncle, Tshekedi Khama, acted as regent and became known as one of the most enlightened rulers in southern Africa. In 1948 Seretse married an English woman and this created a crisis among the Bamangwato. However, their loyalty to Seretse eventually prevailed and the elders agreed to accept him as chief. However, the British in 1950, fearing further disturbances, deposed Seretse for a five-year period, and also exiled Tshekedi. This left the Bamangwato without a chief executive, and thus no important business could be transacted. After 1953 the British government attempted in vain to get the Bamangwato to accept a new chief. Eventually, with pressures from Africans and the British Labor party, the government was forced to allow both Seretse and Tshekedi to return to Bechuanaland. However, it was decided not to attempt to reconstruct the office of paramount chief of the Bamangwato but rather to introduce a conciliar system.

Only after the Khama crisis had been settled could Britain begin a reconstruction of the government. This was accomplished by the constitution of December 30, 1960, which established a multiracial Legislative Council. The council was composed of ten government officials, ten elected European members, one elected Asian member, and ten Africans selected by a newly formed African council. The representation to this Legislative Council was unbalanced in favor of the Europeans. Representational ratios were: for the Europeans one to 300 persons, Asians one to 1,500, and Africans one to 30,000. No direct elections were provided for the Africans either at this level or for the thirty-two seats on the African council. They were all selected by traditional authorities.

It is in this context that political parties came into being. These new parties either represented traditionalism and tribalism or reacted against these old methods. The largest party, the Bechuanaland Democratic party

(BDP), was based on the Bamangwato whose leader was Seretse Khama. The Bechuanaland Liberal party (BLP) was mainly representative of the Bangwaketze tribe. Each of these favored a slower program of political development which took account of the traditional order of society. The two most radical parties were the Federal party and the Bechuanaland Peoples party (BPP). The former was affiliated with PAFMECA while the latter was even more radical. The BPP completely rejected the Legislative Council because it was nonrepresentative. Their delegates testified in June 1962 before the United Nations Committee on Colonialism and demanded immediate independence for Bechuanaland.

It became obvious to the British that the old Legislative Council had to be drastically revised to admit the elective principle. In consultation with the politicians, a new constitution which provided for internal self-government was created and accepted by the British government in June 1964. Under the new instruments a two-house legislature was established. The lower house, the Legislative Assembly, of thirty-two members was to be elected by broad suffrage. The upper house, the Senate, was a house of chiefs which was given delaying powers similar to that planned for Basutoland. The functional executive was to be a prime minister and ministry responsible to the Legislative Assembly. A national census was completed in 1964, and a commission demarcated the thirty-two electoral constituencies.

The general election was held on March 1, 1965, and the BDP of Seretse won twenty-eight of the seats in the Legislative Assembly and thus he became the first prime minister of Bechuanaland. Almost immediately he publicly reiterated his position toward the Republic of South Africa. Although disagreeing with the Republic's native policy, he stated that he saw no reason why good economic relations could not be continued between the areas. This was most important when Bechuanaland became an independent state in September 1966 taking the name Botswana. It continued to be tied to the Republic by a customs union, used South African currency, and over 30,000 Tswana earned their living in South Africa. Prime Minister Verwoerd replied to Prime Minister Khama's statements in equally moderate terms.

SWAZILAND

Swaziland was the third of the British territories in southern Africa administered by the high commissioner under the Commonwealth Relations Office. Slightly less than 6,700 square miles in area, it has a population of approximately 280,000. There is only one Bantu group, the Swazi, resident in the territory. Although still a relatively poor area, it has greater economic potential than either Basutoland or Bechuanaland. Asbestos, sugar, cotton, timber, and rice have been the major export products, but iron deposits have been uncovered and an expensive hydroelectric project has been started. Despite these advantages, the problems of converting the political system to a more liberal form were more complex than in the other

High Commission Territories. Although there are only 8,000 Europeans resident in Swaziland, they own almost half the land. They have established economic and political rights. There are also 2,000 Colored residents, most of whom are middle class. Thus any constitutional change had to be such that it would satisfy all these groups.

Throughout the 1950s, the dual government of Swaziland was administered by the Native Administration Proclamation of 1950. The chief administrative officer was the resident commissioner, aided by a secretariat and district commissioners. He was also assisted by a European advisory council of ten members. The native reserve of 3,516 square miles was administered by the paramount chief, Subhousa II, who was assisted by two councils. The first, the Liqoqo, was originally a family body and remained largely aristocratic. The second, the Libandhla, was a more popular council, although the elective principle in the Western sense was not practiced in selecting its members.

Political parties in Swaziland were late in developing, but as constitutional concessions were made to Basutoland and then to Bechuanaland, there was a sudden spurt of political activity. The first powerful Swaziland party was the Swaziland Progressive party (SPP) led at first by Mr. J. J. Nqutu and, after June 1962, by Dr. A. P. Zwane. It was affiliated with PAFMECA, and from the beginnings of constitutional discussions assumed the most radical position in Swaziland. The other early major Swazi party was the Swazi Democratic party (SDP) whose leader was Dr. Allen Nxumalo. Although in basic agreement with the ends announced by the SPP, it was more amenable to compromise with the traditional authorities and the British. Chief Subhousa II commanded the allegiance of more Swazis than any other figure. His position as traditional head of the Swazis was reinforced by his own knowledge of Western forms and, particularly, by his personality. At first the traditional views of the paramount chief were not represented by a political party. However, to contest the 1964 elections, the Imbokodvo party reflecting Subhousa's ideas was formed.

Another quite small Swazi party which emerged in the early 1960s was the Mbandzeni National Convention. The European community at first formed no political party, but was represented in the early political deliberations through the European advisory council. By the time of the first elections for the Legislative Council, they, too, had a party, the right-wing United Swaziland Association. The Colored of Swaziland formed a Eurafrican Welfare Association to present their views. These were basically conservative and constituted an appeal to unity and the idea of Swazi nationhood.

A constitutional committee was appointed by the British in late 1961 to study and make recommendations for a new constitution. From the first the SPP demanded elections to the Legislative Council on the basis of one man, one vote. They also asked for a bill of rights and the guarantee of Chief Subhousa's position as head of state. This position was to be largely ceremonial with the real power in the hands of a chief minister. These recommendations, if adopted, would have removed power not only from the paramount chief, but also from the European residents. Subhousa wanted his present power and prerogatives guaranteed. The Europeans wanted a certain number of seats guaranteed them to prevent being swamped by the numerically superior Swazi. All factions agreed that they wanted a better constitution than that presented to Bechuanaland.

In March 1962, the constitutional committee made its recommendations. They called for a continuation of the dual system. The governor was to be appointed by the British government and responsible to the secretary of state. The position of the paramount chief was to be recognized and protected. His authority in the native areas was to continue relatively unchanged. Executive and legislative councils were to be created and they were to be advisory to both the governor and the paramount chief. Elections of whites to the Legislative Council were to be direct for one-half of the seats. One-half of the seats were to be reserved for Swazis chosen in the traditional way.

Both the SPP and the SDP rejected the proposals as being racialistic and discriminatory. Later in 1962, a great *indaba* or formal meeting of the Swazi was called by Chief Subhousa, the first in seventy-five years. However, the delegates were so divided in their thinking that they were dismissed before reaching any specific conclusions. In 1963 the British government issued a White Paper in which it stated its compromise solution to the selection and composition of the Legislative Council. In January 1964, the British granted a constitution based on its White Paper which created a twenty-four member council. This was to be composed of eight Swazis elected in the traditional manner, eight of any race elected from a common, nonracial roll, and eight whites of which four would be elected by Europeans and four from the common roll. Except for the eight Swazis selected in the traditional manner, the basis of franchise was one man–one vote. For the contested seats on the common roll, voters in a given district had to vote for one European and two Swazi candidates.

This compromise constitution was opposed by all the political parties and even the Europeans protested that Britain was imposing a constitution on Swaziland. The constitution did not solve the political impasse but simply postponed its solution. Despite the protests, the constitution went into effect and elections were held for the Legislative Council in June 1964. The election results were a considerable surprise to most observers because the traditionalists swept all the elected seats. The king was practically guaranteed eight supporters in the Legislative Council by the traditional method of selection. Few persons believed that the Imbokodvo would win all eight of the Swazi seats on the multiracial roll. However, they did, and furthermore the right-wing United Swaziland Association won all the seats reserved for whites. The radical African parties were completely shut out. Thus in the indefinite future, the more modern-oriented African parties on the basis of these elections seemed to have no effective place in Swaziland.

Devolution of power and consolidation of African rule: British East Africa

KENYA

Political activity in Kenya prior to World War II was concentrated almost entirely in the small but dominant white community. From 1907 when the first Legislative Council with two unofficial white members was created until Mau Mau, European colonists managed to obtain from the government most of what they wanted. In the five years after World War I there was considerable disturbance in Kenya related to the future political role of the colony. Many European settlers wanted the home government to grant responsible government to the area which would give the settlers complete control of local decisions. Despite generally pro-European attitudes, no British government was prepared to turn the destinies of millions of Africans over to the rule of a few thousand settlers. Nevertheless, the constitution was changed to give the settlers more voice in the decisions of the legislative and executive councils. Two settlers were appointed as unofficial members of the Executive Council in 1918. The following year the elective principle was admitted in selecting eleven European members for the expanded Legislative Council. The revision contemplated having nominated Indian and Arab members and also one European nominated to represent African interests. The Indians, deeply resentful of their treatment by Europeans, refused to cooperate and for seven years there were no Indian members in the council.

The Indians comprised a significant third population in Kenya even in the 1920s. Brought at first to East Africa to work on the railroad, those who remained occupied a socioeconomic position between the dominant Europeans and the Bantu people. They were restricted from owning land and were forced to live segregated from the whites. In the early 1920s, supported by the government of India, they precipitated a crisis in Kenya. Indians wanted to own land in the highlands and secure abolition of all official discrimination. They wished to be able to compete, on the basis of merit, for positions in the police and civil service. In 1923 after the British government had gone on record as supporting Kenya for the Africans, the Devonshire White Paper supplied a formula for ending the Indian impasse. It provided for the election from a communal roll of five Indian representatives to the Legislative Council. It did nothing to remove the other restrictions which the Indians had complained about. After the Indian community eventually accepted these conditions there were no further important alterations in the Legislative Council until after World War II.

African attitudes in the interwar period were generally constrained within the context of indirect rule. Outwardly docile, the Africans were deeply dissatisfied, although they had no effective organization to present their demands. Their major concern was over the alienation of their land. Though never enunciated as official policy, the practice of government at all levels confirmed Europeans in control of the "white highlands." Despite the British White Paper in 1923 which stated "native paramountcy," there was little done during the next two decades to implement that policy. The most pressing problem for the Africans, particularly the Kikuyu, was land. The early European settlers such as Lord Delamere had purchased large amounts of land from the Kikuyu. Later the Kikuyu denied that they had sold the land. They had only given use rights since no Kikuyu, acting on his own, could dispose of communal land. In 1904 the government drew the boundaries of native reserves. All land not specifically designated as reserves was decreed to be crown land which could be disposed of by the government in any way it wished.

There was no flood of European emigrants to Kenya, but rather a steady stream with the majority coming after the Boer War and World War I. By 1950 the European population of Kenya was less than 35,000 persons yet they controlled over 12,000 square miles of land. At the same time the native reserved areas comprised 52,000 square miles for a rapidly growing population which had reached the four million level. In 1932 a royal commission, the Carter Land Commission, was appointed to investigate the whole range of problems connected with land. The commission, although adding a portion of land to the Native Reserves, did little from the African viewpoint to solve their problems because it accepted the basic European contentions.

African politics before 1945 was concerned primarily with the two factors of land and the clash of multinational interests. Little had been done in the interwar years to adjust the attitudes of the different African tribal units. Most of the African pressure upon the colonial administration had been brought by groups interested in a specific problem rather than in long-range solutions through the media of political parties. Of all African groups in Kenya, the most responsive to European attitudes and methods were the Kikuyu. It is not surprising, then, that the bulk of African political activity should have been initiated by them.

The first Kikuyu political organization was the Kikuyu Association formed by chiefs and trusted by the government. Thus its major function was to mediate between government decrees and the people. In 1921 Harry Thuku, a young telephone operator, formed the Young Kikuyu Association composed mainly of some of the younger, more educated Kikuyu. Although hampered by organizational problems, the association was the first attempt to present Kikuyu grievances through a modern, nontraditional organization. As a result of its activities, moderate though they were, Thuku was arrested in March 1922 and exiled by the government. Members of the Young Kikuyu Association formed the nucleus of a new organization, the Kikuyu Central Association (KCA). Although there were a number of smaller political groups such as the Progressive Kikuyu party, the KCA remained the most articulate spokesman for the Kikuyu. They lost no opportunity to present their complaints to either the Nairobi or London governments. However, they were never able to expand their influence beyond the Kikuyu, and the government, despite evidences of popular support, continued to treat the KCA as unrepresentative. It was in this period that the very influential Kikuyu Independent Schools Association was formed to combine, in their schools, Western concepts of education with the traditional values of the Kikuyu. Weaker, small political groups such as the offshoots of the Kavirondo Association were also operating in the 1930s among non-Kikuyu Bantu and the Luo.

During World War II the British administration in Nairobi considered the KCA a danger and it was proscribed. After the war a new organization, the Kenya African Union (KAU), was formed and Jomo Kenyatta became its president in June 1947. The KAU's influence was greatest among the Kikuyu, but it was not designed to be just a Kikuyu group. Oginga Odinga was particularly successful in his attempts to organize the Luo in Nyanza in the late 1940s. By 1950 the KAU's membership was over 100,000.

Concessions to the African majority in Kenya were slower and more grudgingly granted than to most other British African territories. Finally in 1952 Britain introduced a constitution which would have given Africans six representatives on the Legislative Council. Educated Africans protested that this reform was hardly sufficient since the Europeans had fourteen representatives on the council. Failure of the British to act definitively on such complaints led to Mau Mau.

Mau Mau was a terrorist organization designed to drive the Europeans from Kenya. It was almost entirely a Kikuyu-based movement and it utilized Western organizational practices and warped traditional Kikuyu oathing ceremonies in order to bind its adherents to the group. The first disturbances began in 1951 with attacks upon European cattle and then moved to sporadic raids against white farms. The government in October 1952 declared a state of emergency, flew in British troops, and organized European and Kikuyu militia units. Detention camps were established for all those Kikuyu suspected of belonging to Mau Mau and elaborate de-oathing ceremonies were performed to enable members to feel themselves free from their obligations to the movement. Under continuous pressure, the terrorists were forced further into the Aberdare Mountains. In September 1955, the government announced that the major threat had come to an end. By then the rebellion had cost the government over £30 million and had resulted in the loss of thousands of lives, most of them Kikuyu. The Mau Mau uprising led to the arrest of Jomo Kenyatta in November 1952, and for a brief time the KAU continued legal operation under the presidency of Walter Odede, a Luo, until the government banned all political activity. Kenyatta was tried, convicted of complicity in Mau Mau, and sentenced to seven years imprisonment. There was no legal political activity during most of the period of the state of emergency which was not lifted until early 1960.

During the disturbances in 1954 the colonial secretary, Oliver Lyttelton, announced his intention to issue a new constitution which would leave the composition of the Legislative Council unchanged but would make the African positions elective. This promise was confirmed in 1956 and elections took place in March 1957. In 1956 the Nairobi District African National Congress was formed to contest the election. By then the British government had decided to abandon its previous support of the white minority and speed up the devolution of power to Africans. A new constitution became effective in 1958 which provided for enlarged African representation on the Legislative Council and which also created a Council of State with the function of ensuring nondiscrimination in legislation.

The most important political organization at this time was the Peoples Convention party founded by Tom Mboya, general secretary of the Kenya Federation of Labor. In April 1959, Jomo Kenyatta was freed by the government but kept restricted to the northern territories. As the pace of governmental advance quickened, his release became a major issue. In August 1959, the Kenya National party was created and this soon gave way to the two parties that have since dominated Kenya politics, the Kenya African National Union (KANU) and the Kenya African Democratic Union (KADU). KANU elected Kenyatta president, but the government would not register the party under his leadership. The party was finally recognized when James Gichuru stood in for Kenyatta. Although claiming to speak for Kenya, KANU's power was based upon the urban Bantu, the Kikuyu, and Luo. KADU, led by Roland Ngala, represented the smaller tribes.

The white settlers were almost unanimous in opposing the extension of more authority and responsibility to the Africans. Their failure to achieve this goal was registered in the constitutional conference of 1960. The constitution which emerged from these discussions provided for a greatly expanded Legislative Council with thirty-three members being elected from a common roll. There were also twenty-two seats reserved for differing ethnic groups. The Executive Council was reconstructed as a Council of Ministers with twice as many unofficial as official members. One group of moderate white settlers did follow Michael Blundell's New Kenya Group of 1958–1959 with its concept of cooperation with Africans. But the mechanics of political development, the smallness of the white community, and the deep divisions within it dictated that such a compromise movement would have little success.

The general election of 1961 gave Africans a majority in the Legislative Council. KANU won eighteen seats to eleven for KADU and polled three times as many votes. KANU, however, made the recognition of Kenyatta's leadership a condition of forming the government. KADU eventually agreed to cooperate with the government and became the official government. Kenyatta was moved from the north in March and finally released unconditionally in August in time to prevent an open split in KANU between Mboya and Odinga. Kenyatta again became president of KANU in November 1961, and the rules regarding persons convicted of major crimes were changed to allow him to be elected to the Legislative Council.

A further London conference convened in February 1962, to discuss the future of Kenya. KADU, afraid of the domination of the smaller tribes by the Kikuyu, demanded a federal constitution while KANU stood for a unitary system. The stresses between the parties were important and potentially dangerous. But the conference ended with the Colonial Office deciding to compromise between the groups by providing for a strong central government and six regional governments with considerable local power. There was much disagreement to come over the degree of regionalism, but each party agreed to accept seven ministries in a new coalition government. The whole of 1962 was taken up in KANU by factions and quarrels which threatened to tear the party apart.

This factionalism within KANU led to an abortive attempt by the Kenya Federation of Labor to set up a new Labor party. Although the party was never formed, the Kikuyu-Luo split and the Mboya-Odinga quarrel were highly important. KADU's policies of tribalism undoubtedly led to the creation of the Kenya Land Freedom Army and outbreaks of violence. Charges by KANU that the Colonial Office was procrastinating caused the removal of Governor Renison in November 1962. One of the reasons for delay in granting self-government was the demarcation of the regional boundaries which was finally completed in the fall of 1962, and the boundary commission's report was published in December. Earlier in the year dissidents from the two major parties under the leadership of Paul Ngei formed the African Peoples party (APP) which seemed, at the beginning of 1963, to hold the balance between the large parties. After much delay, the new elections for a really responsible Kenya government were set for May. In the elections, KANU elected sixty-nine members of the House of Representatives compared to KADU's eight. In the Senate, the KANU-Northern Province United Association (NPUA) coalition elected twenty out of thirty-eight, and in the regions KANU won 158 seats to KADU's fifty-one. The new ministry was formed by Kenyatta with Odinga becoming justice minister, Gichuru, finance minister, and Mboya, minister of constitutional affairs.

The period of internal self-government from June 1 through December 11, 1963 was a time of heated debates in the House of Representatives between the APP-KADU coalition and the government over the power to be assigned to the regional assemblies. Ngala and his followers feared a strong centralized regime controlled by Kenyatta. The power of the government opposition in time waned as various opposition members of parliament joined the government party. The first major defection was Ngei and the APP and then finally a number of very important leaders of KADU.

Nevertheless, at the Lancaster House Conference held September 25 to October 19 to decide the final form of the Kenya government after independence, the question of regionalism versus a strong central authority was the main point of debate. At one time Roland Ngala threatened to end the discussions and establish in those regions loyal to KADU a new Republic of Kenya. KANU countered this bombastic threat by promising to break up the conference, return to Nairobi, and declare independence on October 20 without further reference to the British. This threat quickly led to substantial agreement between Britain and the KANU representatives. After the furor, the KADU leaders accepted defeat and urged support for Kenyatta's government. Kenyatta and KANU controlled the newly expanded 130 member House of Representatives. KADU elected only thirty-one persons to the house. Independence finally came to long-divided Kenya on December 11, 1963.

Defections from KADU to KANU continued after independence; KADU was officially disbanded in 1964, and Roland Ngala, its leader, was made a minister in the Kenyatta government. A new constitution was adopted in 1964 which removed the governor-general and established a republican form of government with a president as chief executive. It also created a two-house system—a forty-one member Senate and a House of Representatives of 129 members. On December 12, 1964, the new government with Jomo Kenyatta as president went into effect.

Although after 1965 there was only one party in Kenya, it was far from being homogeneous. The vice-president, Oginga Odinga, a leader of the Luo, was far more radical than the other political leaders. He wished closer contacts with the Communist bloc and was openly critical of the pro-Western attitudes of Kenyatta and Mboya. On a number of occasions in 1965 Kenyatta made clear his opposition to Odinga's ideas, and by extension to Odinga as a possible successor. Perhaps the clearest indication of Kenyatta's intention to stay clear of the Communist bloc and avoid taking sides in the cold war was the seizure, in May 1965, of a convoy of Chinese arms sent from Tanzania to Uganda over Kenya's roads. Although Kenya continued after independence to belong, with its neighbors, to the joint rail, air, road, and postal systems, Kenyatta considered this action a flagrant violation of Kenya's neutralist position. The trucks and drivers were released only after Tanzanian and Uganda officials were fully appraised of Kenyatta's determination to stay clear of Communist influence.

The same practical firmness could be noted earlier in his quick reaction to the mutiny on January 24 of a battalion of the Kenya Rifles. The uprising was a result of dissatisfaction with pay and the continued presence of European officers. The disturbance was of the same order as those which struck Tanzania and Uganda at the same time. Acting quickly, Kenyatta asked for British aid, and thus the mutiny never got beyond the embryo stage. Later sixteen of the mutineers were sentenced to prison and twenty-nine others were discharged from the service. The decisive action by Kenyatta possibly warded off a crisis of the same order as that which shook the foundations of Nyerere's power in Tanzania. Despite Kenya's poor economic position and the many long-range problems facing the state, it soon became one of the most stable of the new African states due to the moderate leadership of Kenyatta, Mboya, and Gichuru.

TANZANIA (TANGANYIKA)

After World War I Britain was confirmed by the League of Nations in its occupation of the bulk of what had been German East Africa. The two territories of Ruanda and Urundi had been detached and given to Belgium as mandates of the League. Theoretically Britain ruled Tanganyika under the direction and guidance of the League as a class "C" mandate. In actuality the League interfered very little in the administration of Tanganyika. The major advantage to the Africans of the League's presence was its reminder to the Colonial Office and British administrators that Tanganyika was held for Africans until they were sufficiently advanced to govern themselves.

In 1920 the government of Tanganyika consisted of the governor, Sir Horace Byatt, a nominated Executive Council, and a skeleton staff of European district officers. Traditional rule throughout the area was in shambles largely because the German system had minimized the importance of chiefs and headmen. Byatt's primary concerns were to bring order to all areas of Tanganyika and to restore trade. His success can be measured by the exports which in 1925 were twice the 1914 levels. It was left to his successor, Sir Donald Cameron, to attempt a reconstruction of local government under traditional leaders. Cameron, with long experience in Nigeria, believed the best format for advancing African people was through the medium of their own institutions. In Tanganyika this necessitated long, complex surveys to discover the varying systems of rule and the actual leaders of the people. Whenever these were known, Cameron constructed his form of indirect rule complete with native courts and in some cases native treasuries. By the time he left Tanganyika in 1930 this system was working in all areas except where the slave trade or the Maji-Maji rebellion had destroyed the older system. Cameron's structure of local government remained relatively unchanged for almost thirty years.

Cameron was responsible for the introduction of the first legislative council in 1926. He opposed the desires of the European community for some type of amalgamation with Kenya and the imposition of the same type of settler-dominated government as in Kenya. Demands from Europeans in Tanganyika and Kenya and the economic stringencies of the postwar years led to a number of commissions appointed by the British government to investigate the federation of some of the British East Africa and Central African territories. The first of these reports, that of the Ormsby-Gore Commission in 1924, had already pointed out that the difficulties of uniting Uganda, Kenya, and Tanganyika outweighed the economic advantages. However, after 1925 the colonial secretary, Leopold Amery, still pursued the idea of federation even against the obvious opposition of the mandates commission. Joined by Lord Delamere, who had called an unofficial conference in 1926 to discuss the union of Nyasaland, Rhodesia, and Tanganyika, Sir Edward Grigg, governor of Kenya, produced in 1927 a plan to federate Uganda, Kenya, and Tanganyika. Cameron believed that African interests, particularly in Tanganyika, would be subordinated to the wishes of the Europeans in Kenya and threatened to resign on this question. Grigg's plan for federation was not adopted, but Amery appointed yet another commission, the Hilton-Young Commission, to make recommendations on union and a number of other related problems. Finally in 1930 the new Labor government laid to rest the possibility of an immediate political amalgamation of the three areas. Despite this, government officials, Indians, and Europeans continued to be perturbed in the 1930s over the future of the territory. In the early part of the decade there was genuine fear that the League was going to end its mandate and hand Tanganyika over to a resurgent Germany. Not until 1938 did it become apparent, even to the German settlers, that Lord Milner had been correct eighteen years before when he had stated that Tanganyika had become "permanently incorporated in the British Empire."

Few alterations were made in the mode of British control in Tanganyika even after World War II. The British Labor government placed the area under United Nations control which continued the earlier pattern of administration that had as its goal the preparation of Africans for independence. Despite this objective, little had been done to help the education system provide more educated leaders; and the country stilll operated on the basis of indirect rule. One reason why Britain did not offer revised constitutional instruments to Tanganyika after the war was because African political leaders were more concerned with local than national politics. The Legislative Council remained totally nominated until 1955, with seven European, four African, and three Asian members. This imbalance reflected harshly upon the theory of British administration since there were fewer than 20,000 Europeans and only 60,000 Asians in a total population of approximately 8,000,000. In 1949 a committee on constitutional development was created which reported in 1951 that the Legislative Council should be enlarged and its influence extended. No changes were made, however, until after the investigations of W. J. M. MacKenzie, a Professor of Government from Manchester University, in 1955. Then the council was enlarged to thirty unofficial members with a rough parity between the races. All members of the council were still nominated by the governor. To offset the lack of elections, the British instituted a system whereby some of the African members became assistant ministers with restricted executive authority.

In June 1956, a bill was passed by the Legislative Council which called for a revised constitution which would allow the elective principle. The instrument which was designed to meet this demand permitted elections to an expanded council. The franchise was granted on a qualitative basis and all voters were placed on a common roll. However, the election system was very complex. Each voter in the districts had three votes and were required to vote for three candidates—one African, one Asian, and one European. The elections held in 1958 were saved from a possible impasse by the rise in importance of a new political party, the Tanganyika African National Union (TANU).

The modern political history of Tanganyika is closely tied to the career of one man, Julius Nyerere, who after returning to Tanganyika from Britain in 1952 became a power in the old Tanganyika African Association which had been created in 1929. In 1954, believing that this association was too restricted, he formed TANU. Within months the organization had branches throughout the country. In 1955 Nyerere took the nationalists' complaints concerning Britain's slowness to reform Tanganyika's political institutions to the United Nations. In the beginning

TANU was primarily a vehicle for African nationalism. However, after its initial successes it became more moderate and Nyerere was able to convince Asians and Europeans that if they cooperated with TANU their interests would be safeguarded. Nyerere's approach did much to undermine the potential of the United Tanganyika party which had been created in 1955 on the platform of multiracism. In December 1957, Nyerere again highlighted TANU's demands for faster developments by resigning from the Legislative Council. TANU cooperated in the implementation of the constitution of 1958 although the party disagreed with the division of African, European, and Asian candidates, and TANU won an overwhelming majority of the elected seats. The members of the new Legislative Council of 1958 formed themselves into the Tanganyika Elected Members Organization (TEMO) to expedite the political liberation of Tanganyika. Backed with solid African support, TANU immediately demanded that Britain grant more responsibility to Africans. Nyerere's pressure and cooperation produced the new constitution of 1960. This constitution provided, for the first time, a majority of elected members to the Legislative Council and also responsible ministerial government. Fifty electoral districts were created which chose seventy-one members. Reservations were made so that eleven of the members elected had to be Asians and ten Europeans. In the elections of August, TANU-supported candidates won seventy seats and Nyerere was asked to form a government. In the spring of 1961 a constitutional conference held at Dar-es-Salaam gave Tanganyika full self-government on May 1 and full independence at the end of December 1961. The Legislative Council was renamed the National Assembly and Nyerere became prime minister of an independent Tanganyika.

In early 1962, tensions within TANU convinced Nyerere that he should not try to hold both the position of prime minister and head of TANU until the country was more stable. There were indications that the tightly knit party which he had created was in danger of breaking apart. Therefore he resigned as prime minister to concentrate on the task of reconstructing the party throughout Tanganyika. His mild-mannered, trustworthy deputy, Rashidi Kawawa, became prime minister. In the interim, constitutional changes were proposed on June 28 to the National Assembly which would enable Tanganyika to become a republic. In early November the first presidential election was held and Nyerere returned as the head of government, and on December 9, 1962, Tanganyika became a republic within the Commonwealth. The constitution provided for a vice-president, an appointive fourteen-member cabinet, and gave the president a veto over legislation.

The first serious threat to the moderate evolutionary government of Nyerere occurred in January 1964 with the mutiny of a large segment of the 1,600 man Tanganyika Rifles. They were discontented with low pay and being still under command of British officers. Nyerere had refused to bow to growing demands to dismiss a number of British senior officers and replace them with Africans. This uprising was probably triggered by the successful military coup in 1963 which ousted the sultan of Zanzibar.

Nyerere, fearing a takeover similar to that which had occurred in Togo and Zanzibar, went into hiding, leaving the minister of external affairs, Oscar Kambona, to deal with the mutiny. Nyerere finally issued a call for British troops, and with their aid the mutiny was quelled. After the revolt Nyerere dismissed large numbers of soldiers and police, but his image had been altered by the revolt. The army was eventually disbanded to be replaced by a militia force, the Tanzanian Peoples Defense Force, which was armed primarily with weapons provided by the Chinese. The revolt of 1964 illustrated how explosive the forces were beneath the surface of even the best-managed, moderate African government.

Nyerere recovered some of his lost prestige by engineering the federation of Zanzibar and Tanganyika. In March 1964, Oscar Kambona flew to Zanzibar to discuss mutual problems with Abeid Karume, head of the new revolutionary regime. Implicit in the discussions was the possibility that Tanganyika would remove its policemen which had enabled Karume to restore order. This would have left Karume with only a mixed irregular force to maintain peace in Zanzibar. Later Karume visited Tanganyika at a time when Abdul Muhammad (Babu) was on a tour of the Far East. This series of discussions led to the announcement of the union of Tanganyika and Zanzibar. The agreements of the two leaders were later ratified by the legislatures of both areas in April 1964. By the agreement, Nyerere became president and Karume first vice-president of the Federation of Tanzania.

The articles of union called for a modification of the constitution of Tanganyika to provide for a separate executive and legislature for Zanzibar. The union was only temporary until a combined commission on the constitution made its report and a constituent assembly was called to redraft the constitution. These actions were to be completed within a year from the initial act of union. Until that time the laws in both areas remained in effect, although the president had the power to repeal any laws of Zanzibar which infringed on the power of the federal government. Areas specifically reserved to the federal government were the constitution, defense, external affairs, trade and customs, police, and emergency powers. Each area of the union maintained its own legislature to deal with specifically local issues.

Actual integration of services were predictably slow. Foreign aid throughout 1964 still came directly to Zanzibar without going through the mechanism of the central authority. As late as September 1964, there were still customs examinations between Tanganyika and Zanzibar. Nevertheless, the federation appeared on the higher levels to be a triumph for Nyerere and moderation, even though Muhammad and Hanga still remained in the government.

In late January 1965, the government of Tanzania charged two United States officials with plotting against Vice-President Karume and requested their removal. The United States retaliated by asking that Nyerere recall one of his attaches from Washington and he, in return, reacted by recalling the Tanzanian ambassador from the United States. This worsening of relations with Nyerere, who was once considered to be one of the most moderate African politicians, was paralleled by friendlier relations between Tanzania and Communist China. Tanzania received $45,000,000 in pledges from China, and in June, Chou En-lai visited Dar-es-Salaam and made a major address from there. The new-found friendliness between China and East African states embroiled Nyerere with his northern neighbor Kenya. Chinese arms designated for use in Uganda were sent from Tanzania by truck across Kenya. This was done without prior consultation with Jomo Kenyatta. The guns were seized and were not released until both Uganda and Tanzania apologized for attempting to compromise Kenya's position by such activities.

In October 1965, elections were held for the expanded 107 seat legislature. President Nyerere also was seeking reelection but ran unopposed. A new feature of elections in a one-party state was introduced. With the exception of six seats reserved for top party officials, all seats were contested. TANU nominated two men for every seat, gave each candidate equal support, and then let the incumbents and their challengers vie for voter's approval. The results were surprising. Only sixteen members of the old assembly were able to retain their seats. Nine ranking party officials, including the finance minister, Paul Bomani, were defeated.

The government of Tanzania in 1965 remained an enigma to Western observers. Nyerere, despite his overtures toward China and the worsening of relations with the United States, seemed essentially a moderate. If the president's statements were taken at face value, all he wished to do was to keep Tanzania as far from cold-war commitments as possible and retain freedom of action for his government. The great unanswered question concerning the future of the federation was how successful he would be in dealing with supporters, particularly on Zanzibar, who were unlikely to be happy under a moderate government.

UGANDA

There have been major alterations in the boundaries of Uganda since Sir Harry Johnston left. These adjustments which ceded great portions of the protectorate to neighboring Kenya and the Sudan had reduced the territory to approximately half its former size by 1926. The area which remained was a compact, well-populated, rich agricultural territory. The divisions of the protectorate based upon the agreements designed by Johnston and his predecessors did not substantially affect the unity of Uganda until the 1950s. In brief, the agreements signed with the rulers of the important kingdoms of Buganda and Bunyoro gave these areas a special relationship to the central British administration. For a half century they made British rule easier in Uganda. The existence of strong kings and their councils, while making consultation imperative, did ensure the adherence of an entire nation to policies agreed upon by the rulers and the British authorities. European colonization in the interwar period was not encouraged, thus avoiding many of the problems of adjacent Kenya.

The two factors of strong African rulers and few Europeans meant that the British governor could exercise more direct authority without the usual restrictions of a meaningful executive or legislative council. It was not until 1921 that these agencies were established with a legislative council composed of only six members, four of whom were officials. No Africans were represented. Not until 1945 were three Africans chosen as a part of the seven-member unofficial group in a fourteen-member Legislative Council. Further adjustments to the Legislative Council were made in 1947, 1948, and 1950 which resulted in increasing African unofficial representation to the level of the combined number of European and Asian members. By the early 1950s it had become apparent that any major constitutional advance by the entire protectorate in the same direction as that taken in other British territories could only come by restricting the significant power of the traditional authorities. There had been some democratization of the Buganda Lukiko (Assembly of Notables) following the disturbances of 1949, but it was still a major force for conservative Buganda nationalism. In 1953 further attempts at reform by the central government precipitated a major crisis with the kabaka.

In June 1953, in an after dinner speech, the colonial secretary, Oliver Lyttelton, suggested the possibility of the development of a meaningful East African Federation. The Baganda, their special status already threatened by Uganda constitutional reforms, reacted to this further intimidation by demanding that their country be placed under Foreign Office control and a plan be devised to grant Buganda its independence separate from Uganda. The governor, Sir Andrew Cohen, one of the architects of the new British African policy, hastily assured the Baganda that Britain had no intention of forcing a federation upon them. The Lukiko would not be mollified by such assurances and pressed its demands. The kabaka, caught between the contending parties, negotiated with the governor a plan for the future development of Buganda within the large polity. However, under pressure from his most powerful subjects, he repudiated this agreement and supported the Lukiko's demands. By not representing the British government's opinion to the Lukiko, he was in violation of the 1900 agreement. Sir Andrew reluctantly ordered the kabaka, Mutesa II, deported to Britain. Not until 1955, when he was allowed to return to Uganda, did he play a significant role in Uganda politics.

In 1954 Sir Keith Hancock of the Institute of Commonwealth Studies and a committee of the Lukiko negotiated a compromise settlement. In November 1954, on the basis of this agreement and after consultation with other segments of Uganda opinion, the government issued a new constitution. The Legislative Council was increased in size to sixty members with the thirty unofficial members being Africans. There would be ministerial government introduced with five ministers, three of whom would be African. At the same time the 1900 agreement with Buganda was modified to establish the kabaka as a constitutional monarch acting on the advice of his ministers. The Lukiko also accepted the concept that Buganda representatives should sit on the Legislative Council. These representatives were to be chosen by indirect election. Britain reiterated its pledge not to force a federation and the Baganda gave up their demand for independence. Britain also promised that there would be no change made in the form of government agreed upon until 1961. On acceptance of the agreement, Kabaka Mutesa II returned to Uganda in October 1955.

A decision in 1957 to have the speaker of the Legislative Assembly preside over its meetings was taken by the Baganda to be a breach of the 1954 agreement and they refused to send their representatives to the central government. By 1958 most African members to the council were being selected by direct elections. Buganda, however, continued its opposition, refusing to allow its five representatives to take part in the Legislative Council. Early in the year Buganda again requested that the Buganda Agreement be terminated and British protection ended. This was refused, but a new constitutional committee was established to plan for the future of Uganda. In May 1959, the government was faced with a boycott of all non-Africans by a new organization, the Uganda National Movement. The organizaton was banned, its leaders sent into exile, and a new constitution was drawn up for a greatly expanded Legislative Council of eighty-two members; and elections were held on a basis of direct suffrage in March 1961.

The general elections of March 1961, which were designed to give Uganda a large measure of self-government, were boycotted by the kabaka and his followers. The Democratic party (DP) which had been created in 1956 won the twenty seats for Buganda with a total of less than 12,000 votes. This gave them forty-four out of the eighty-two seats in the Legislative Council while the rival Uganda-wide party, the Uganda Peoples Congress (UPC) led by Milton Obote, could gain but thirty-five. Therefore, the DP, although the minority party throughout Uganda, formed the first real African government for Uganda under their leader, Benedicto Kiwanuka. In the months that followed, Britain negotiated an agreement with Buganda whereby the kabaka was recognized as the hereditary ruler. Buganda was to be federally associated with the rest of Uganda. Buganda was given twenty-one representatives in the eighty-two seat National Assembly. The Buganda Lukiko, however, was to be directly elected. The agreement was accepted on October 31, 1961, and the elections for the Lukiko were held on February 22, 1962. The Kabaka Yekka party, which had been created in November 1961 as the political extension of the kabaka's traditional power base, won sixty-five of the sixty-eight seats to the Lukiko. The UPC by agreement did not challenge this regional election. In the national election of April 25, 1962, the DP in an atmosphere of growing bitterness was soundly defeated. The UPC won forty-three seats while the DP could claim only twenty-four members in the assembly. The twenty-four selected members from Buganda gave the Kabaka Yekka the balance of power. Kiwanuka, the former head of government, was not even elected to parliament.

The months immediately following the elections of 1962 were devoted largely to discussions concerning total independence for Uganda. Major problems also arose from the demands of Ankole, Bunyoro, Toro, and

Busoga for equal status with Buganda in any federal structure. Formal discussions which opened on June 27, 1962, were troubled further by border disputes between Bunyoro and Buganda. The conference evaded many of the implications of federalism, but it did establish a system encompassing four kingdoms, Busoga, and eleven administrative districts, and October 9, 1962 was established as Independence Day. The president of the republic was to be the kabaka of Buganda, while the vice-president was to be the king of Bunyoro, Sir William Nadiope.

Conflict at the central level quickly arose because of the kabaka's idea of his position in Uganda and his power position in parliament. However, the UPC in the elections in Ankole and Toro gained control of the regional governments. Obote made good use of his position as the head of the only strong party that stood for a Uganda-wide policy against the Buganda-oriented policy of the kabaka. By June 1963, defections from the DP and the Kabaka Yekka made him master of parliament with fifty-five members out of a total of ninety-one. If the UPC could manage a two-thirds majority, then the constitution could be changed to prevent a recurrence of the weak coalition that existed before June 1963.

In January 1964, the army mutiny in Tanzania triggered a smaller outbreak in Uganda. The first battalion of the Uganda Rifles captured the minister of the interior on January 23 and held him hostage, demanding pay raises. Reluctantly Obote called for British aid and the mutiny was suppressed. The Uganda government bowed to the demands of the army and by midsummer most of the European officers had been replaced by Ugandans.

Tribal affairs throughout 1964 continued to disturb the political equilibrium of the state. In Toro, the Bwamba and Bakonjo who insisted on a separate district were attacked by Toro tribesmen. This forced a state of emergency to be proclaimed for the whole area. In August the government announced a referendum to determine the future of the two "lost counties" of western Uganda. Kabaka Yekka members walked out of the National Assembly and their coalition with Obote's UPC was dissolved on the issue. In November the voting took place and the people in the counties elected to return to the kingdom of Bunyoro.

Relations between the kabaka's party and the UPC were repaired in 1965 and Obote continued as prime minister. The major shocks to Obote in 1965 were the seizure of an arms shipment by Kenya and, toward the end of the year, charges of misappropriation of funds captured from Congolese rebels in 1964. Obote settled the former problem by a personal visit to Kenyatta where he apologized to the president of Kenya for the shipment through Kenya and promised that there would not be a recurrence of such activity. The second problem by the end of 1965 threatened to overthrow Obote since many of his own party were joining in criticism of their leader. The Kabaka Yekka and the small DP both demanded investigations of the supposed misappropriation of approximately one-third of a million dollars.

Thus the government of Uganda in practice was as unstable in December 1965 as it had been in theory since the adoption of the complex federal system. Tribalism had been enshrined into the constitution. With the kings of Buganda, Bunyoro, and Toro claiming exclusive privileges in certain areas, it is doubtful whether any politician would have been able to achieve more unity than Obote. Any increase in stability depended upon the outcome of the power struggle between Obote and the kabaka.

ZANZIBAR (SEE ALSO TANZANIA)

The islands of Zanzibar and Pemba, ruled by the sultan under British control until January 1964, had a population of one-third of a million persons, mostly African, although the traditional rulers were the minority Arabs who dominated politics. Much of the wealth of the state was controlled by Indians. Zanzibar was ruled in a dual manner in the first half of the twentieth century. Ostensibly the sultan ruled the country. However, the British protectorate officials effectively curtailed any significant independent action by the sultan. In 1914 control of the protectorate passed from the Foreign Office to the Colonial Office and in the next ten years the sultan's political agents were gradually replaced by British district officers.

In 1924 the theoretical limits of British authority in the protectorate were defined and two years later the sultan established the first executive and legislative councils. All members of the councils were appointed by the sultan. There were seventeen members of the Legislative Council of which eight were unofficials. The ethnic composition of this council—three Arabs, two Africans, two Asians, and one European—indicated the complex ethnic mix of the island. The next major political change occurring in Zanzibar was the 1944 reorganization of the Zanzibar Township Council. All members of the enlarged township council were nominated by the British resident. Membership on this council also reflected the complex mixture in Zanzibar. However, the Africans who have a majority of the population on the island did not receive a commensurate number of seats on any of the councils.

In the reorganization of government following World War II a significant difference of opinion developed between the Arab ruling class and the African majority over the ends to be achieved. The Arabs wanted a quick movement toward self-government while the Africans were more cautious, suspicious of their role in an Arab-dominated government. The British, therefore, proceeded very cautiously in their reforms. In 1956 they enlarged the executive and legislative councils. The Executive Council remained totally nominated, but in the twenty-six member Legislative Council, six of the twelve unofficial members were elected from a common roll.

Political parties in Zanzibar date from 1955 and were responses to mainland nationalistic moves and British reaction to them. The first party was the Zanzibar National party (ZNP) led by Sheikh Ali Muhsen and Abdul Muhammad (Babu). Although Arab-led, it attempted to appeal to all classes and was not originally a narrow Arab party. It stood for rapid constitutional advance toward self-government. In 1955 ZNP called for adult suffrage, a common roll, and all members of the Legislative Council to be elected. In 1957 as a result of the court's investigating commission, the new constitution was implemented and elections were held for six of the Legislative Council seats. The Afro-Shirazi party (ASP) was created to contest this election. The ASP, like the ZNP, was also a conglomerate party which attempted to win both Arab and African support although its leader, Abeid Aman Karume, appealed more to the uneducated, economically depressed Africans. At that time the major difference in the approach of the parties was the speed of approach to self-government since the ASP wanted a slower rate. The ASP won three seats to the Legislative Council in the elections. Two independents later allied themselves with the ASP. The popular voting showed approximately one-third of the voters opting for each party.

Attempts in 1958 to heal the growing breach between the parties were made by the Pan African Freedom Movement of East and Central Africa (PAFMECA). The moving force in this attempt was Julius Nyerere of Tanganyika. This conciliation failed because of the economic and social differences of the populations to which each party made its appeal. From this period onward Zanzibar became a focal point for outside influence from East Africa, the United Arab Republic, and the Chinese Republic. In December 1959, a split occurred in the ASP when Muhammad Shamte formed the Zanzibar Peoples' Party of Pemba (ZPPP). This party also was mostly African in membership and appealed to the African electorate.

Devolution of power by Britain to mainland African territories denied Britain the option of withholding further constitutional advance for Zanzibar, although after 1956 it was apparent that the African majority would no longer be satisfied with a subservient role under Arab leaders. British officials, in conjunction with African nationalists, formulated a new constitution which provided for a larger Legislative Council, a form of ministerial government, and granted the franchise to most Zanzibari. This constitution, issued in 1960, made it possible for the relatively new African-oriented parties to successfully challenge the Arabs for leadership. The Arab position was further weakened in 1960 by the death of Sultan Seyyid Sir Khalifa bin Harub who had ruled Zanzibar since 1911. The new sultan, Seyyid Abdullah, in turn died two years later. His successor, the young Seyyid Jamshid, was made sultan just before Zanzibar became a self-governing state and inherited all the problems of the Arab-African rivalry.

The new constitution, which went into effect in January 1961, provided for elections of twenty-two of the thirty Legislative Council seats. The election of January was very close. The ASP won ten seats, the ZNP nine, and the ZPPP three. Two of the ZPPP men supported ZNP and one the ASP, creating an eleven to eleven deadlock in the Legislative Council which necessitated new elections. In the second election, held in June, twenty-three seats were voted on. The ZNP and ZPPP agreed on constituencies to contest and the results were ASP ten, ZNP ten, and ZPPP three. The coalition ZNP-ZPPP formed a government and the ZPPP leader, Sheikh Shamite Homadi, became chief minister. The June elections were marked by extreme violence on election day with over sixty killed and nearly 1,000 wounded. This was the first major outbreak of racial violence between

African and Arab although the conditions which produced the riots had existed for a long time. A state of emergency was declared which lasted over a year and many important persons were arrested and jailed for their role in the disturbances. Abdul Muhammad, former secretary-general of the ZNP, was sentenced to fifteen months for sedition and eleven other persons of the ZNP were detained. The ZNP, despite being the government party, was very anti-British and was accused by many of being pro-Communist (Chinese). Certainly two of the major trade unions allied with the ZNP had been strongly influenced by the Chinese. In June 1963, Abdul Muhammad broke with the ZNP and became the dominant figure in the Red Chinese-oriented Umma party which was later banned.

Further constitutional advance toward self-government was delayed by the disturbances and the state of emergency. A constitutional conference in London, in March 1962, broke up because of nonagreement between the parties. Finally new constitutional instruments were devised and elections based upon universal adult suffrage were held in July 1963. The ZNP-ZPPP coalition won eighteen of the seats for the Legislative Council while the ASP gained only thirteen. The new government immediately asked Britain for independence. After a conference in September, the date for the independence of Zanzibar was set as December 10. Also on that date the sultan's authority over the coastal areas of Kenya would cease and these territories would come under the authority of the Kenya government.

On January 12, 1964, the Zanzibar army led by self-styled "Field Marshall" John Okello overthrew the one-month independent government of Zanzibar. After one week of rioting, more than 500 Zanzibaris, mostly Arabs, were dead and the Afro-Shirazi and Umma party leaders, Karume and Abdul Muhammad, gained control of the government. Okello was gradually eased out of power and in March, after a visit to the mainland, he was refused readmittance to Zanzibar. The ZNP leaders and the sultan were forced into exile.

Order in Zanzibar was restored largely because of the presence of 300 Tanganyika police loaned by President Nyerere to the new revolutionary government. Although Karume enunciated a moderate course for the government, he was not strong enough to keep his chief lieutenants, Abdul Muhammad and Kassim Hanga, from stating the hope of establishing a Communist regime for Zanzibar. Abdul Muhammad, the foreign minister, was pro-Communist, and Hanga, the vice-president, although less obvious, seemed to be committed to the same policies. Aside from the historic and economic connections with the coast, this drift to the left convinced President Nyerere of Tanganyika that something had to be done to negate potential extremism. In April 1964, Nyerere found President Karume amenable to a closer union. The discussions between Karume and Tanganyika officials resulted in a federation of the two states called the Union of Tanganyika and Zanzibar (Tanzania). In the new union, Julius Nyerere became president and Karume first vice-president. Details of these discussions and the subsequent federation are discussed more fully in the section dealing with Tanzania.

TWELVE

Postwar political developments: Belgian Africa

Belgian authorities, notwithstanding the political ferment elsewhere in Africa in the early 1950s, assumed that they would have time to carry out the Congo's development on an evolutionary basis. Thus, while Britain and France in colonial territories less economically viable than the Congo were granting the Africans political power, the Belgian authorities continued their white-dominated autocratic system. The first concessions to the Africans' demands for democracy came in the reforms of municipal government in 1957. Previously local government in the cities had been of a two-part type. One form was that of the native city (*extra coutumiers*) of the areas surrounding the large cities. The other was the government of the cities themselves. In the native cities chiefs had been appointed by the central authorities to govern under Belgian direction. They were aided by appointive councils which the Belgians had planned to utilize at some future time as a base for extension of democracy. The cities proper had been administered directly by the Belgian authorities. In 1957 the *statut des Villes* abolished these distinctions in Léopoldville, Elizabethville, and Jadotville. The native cities were abolished in these areas. The cities were divided into communes each with its own elected council and mayor. These mayors were appointed from the candidates chosen by the electorate. In Léopoldville less than 50,000 persons out of a population of approximately 350,000 could qualify for the franchise. Election was from a common roll.

The Belgians granted these minor reforms with considerable reluctance after studying the long-range implications of such a move for almost ten years. The functional powers of the mayors and councils were quite limited. Further, a chief mayor was appointed by the central authorities to coordinate municipal government. Minor as these reforms were by comparison with those occurring in French and British Africa, they signaled a change in the direction of Belgian policy. The elections

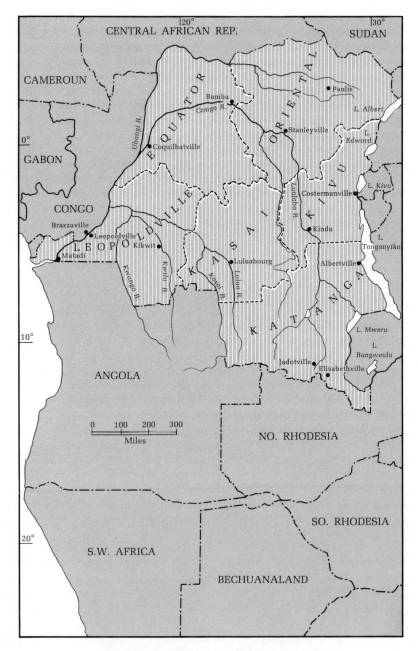

The Congo: Towns and Provinces, 1960

resulted in developing the first political parties which were not only based upon tribal affiliation but on their popularity in the urban centers.

In 1958 the government of Belgium underwent a series of changes which brought more liberal men to office. M. Leo Petillion, former governor-general of the Congo, became minister of colonies. He had long favored political changes in the Congo. Before any specific reforms were announced, Petillion was replaced by the even more liberal van Hemelrijck. In November 1958, the prime minister of Belgium, Mr. Eyskens, stated that a detailed declaration of Belgian reforms would be announced in January 1959. Before the reforms were announced, African political leaders such as Joseph Kasavubu of ABAKO made it clear that they wished no slow evolutionary change but quick independence. In early January, there were riots in Léopoldville which lasted several days and resulted in the deaths of over thirty Africans. Almost fifty Europeans were injured. These riots were triggered in part by the economic recession which had struck the Congo in early 1957. Many urban, partially detribalized Africans were without jobs and were receptive to the new propaganda calls by political leaders who blamed the Europeans and the government for these conditions. Although only a small portion of the population of Léopoldville took part in the riots, the effect upon the Belgian government was electric.

Both the king and the colonial ministers made immediate statements in which Congolese independence was promised. Although the Belgian government had decided before the riots to grant a large measure of self-government to the Congo, it appeared to the Africans that the riots had effected the change. The Belgian announcements of early 1959 resulted in the creation of new political parties and a growing political ferment throughout the Congo. Even though many Belgian officials believed that moderate reforms would suffice, African political leaders wanted a speedy advance to independence. The Belgian government adopted this point of view by late 1959 and the Congo state became independent in June 1960.

In the short period of three years after 1957, the Belgian Congo moved from a government almost totally controlled by the Belgians to complete independence. A nation as large as Europe, populated by diverse tribes actively hostile toward one another, the Congo had not been allowed to develop the proper institutional base for independence. There were few Congolese trained in the political skills of ruling such a heterogeneous state. Belgian policy before 1957 was not necessarily wrong if the Congo had been isolated from the rest of Africa, but it was not. The political advances of territories less economically developed than the Congo could not be hidden from the Congolese political leaders. The change from paternalism to fraternalism could not be achieved in a short period of time. Political education and maturity could not be legislated. When the Belgian semiautocratic regime removed itself from the Congo, the only force that had unified the Congo basin for seventy years was removed. The new Congo Republic had neither the prestige nor the experience to take the place of the old Belgian administration. Unlike British and French territories, the Belgians had not left behind an educated or trained political elite who could peacefully assume the roles of leadership. Thus the Congo, with one of the most advanced social, health, and economic systems, drifted into anarchy.

Devolution of power and consolidation of African rule

THE REPUBLIC OF THE CONGO

Events in the politically quiescent Congo moved with such rapidity and such confusion after 1959 that it is nearly impossible to synthesize them. Belgian policy after 1909 had been based primarily upon the economic interdependence of the Congo and Belgium. The central government, represented in the Congo by the governor-general and the administrative staff, sought to improve living and working conditions for the urban African and protect the rural African from undue exploitation either by Europeans or other hostile tribes. The political system was autocratic and paternalistic and at its best was geared to bringing the African into the government by a slow evolutionary process. As late as the mid-1950s, Belgian authorities had only begun to formulate plans for sharing political power with the urbanized African on the lowest levels of government.

Notwithstanding the economic development of the Congo, the pursuance of a policy of slow evolution kept the Congo politically infantile. The government discouraged higher education for Africans, did not employ them in positions of responsibility in government, and had not by the mid-1950s established a workable framework whereby peaceful transition of power from Europeans to Africans could be effected. The paternalistic Belgian regime had done little to break down tribal differences and hostilities. The reality of the Congo on the eve of independence was not an embryo nation-state but a collection of hostile tribal entities held together by an efficient Belgian administration.

Within a distressingly short period of time Belgian policy was completely reversed. The right of self-determination and the representative principle were admitted and the Congo embarked upon independence without any of the necessary preludes to self-government. All of the political parties of the Congo were formed during this period to take advantage of the weakening position of the Belgian government. These parties tended to represent tribal and regional loyalties and usually were dominated by one man.

The first major political party in the Congo, the *Association des Bakongo pour le maintien l'Unité et l'Expansion et la Défense de Langue Kikongo* (ABAKO), was originally a cultural association of the Bakongo people. Founded in 1950, it had become by 1956 a party in all but name. Joseph Kasavubu became president of the ABAKO, dedicated not to Congo independence but the unification of all the Bakongo people in the Congo, Angola, and Rhodesia.

The other major parties came into being after the Belgian government had granted a measure of political reform. In December 1957, democratic elections were held for the first time for the major urban councils. The ABAKO based its power not only on the Bakongo but also on its strength in Léopoldville. Emboldened by the changed attitudes, a number of the evolués addressed demands for more political power leading to independence. These demands were backed by political agitation in the cities and the countryside. The threat of violence spread throughout the Congo in 1958. Patrice Lumumba, president of the African Staff Association in Stanleyville, requested eventual independence from the Belgian government in August. Similar demands and agitation came from every one of the provinces of the Congo. The visit of Charles de Gaulle to Brazzaville in August and the announcement of the large measure of self-government which was to be granted to the French Congo speeded up political agitation in the Belgian Congo and the formation of new political groups.

In October 1958, the Mouvement National Congolais (MNC) was created by Patrice Lumumba and had its centrum of power in Stanleyville. The MNC soon became the only party to stand for a unitary Congolese state. Its objectives were to promote unity throughout the Congo, combat tribalism, and prepare the masses for eventual control. Branches of the MNC were soon established throughout the Congo.

By 1959 the major African personalities in the Congo began to emerge. Kasavubu and the ABAKO openly advocated separatism or as an alternative a loose federation. Lumumba and the MNC opposed any breakup of the Congo and called instead for the speedy end of Belgian control and the establishment of a strong central government. In January 1959, Lumumba, recently returned from the Accra Conference, addressed a number of large meetings in Léopoldville. Disturbances in the cities grew more commonplace. A march of the unemployed in Léopoldville brought about only one of many clashes with the Belgian government. Kasavubu was briefly arrested and the ABAKO banned. These and other punitive measures were not successful. The Belgian government then decided to compromise and promised immediate and long-term reforms with the possibility of territorial communal elections for December 1959. Instead of carrying through on these elections, the government announced that a round table discussion between the various political factions and the government would be convened in Brussels in January 1960. To present a united front, the major Congolese parties in December 1959 formed the short-lived ABAKO-Cartel. The most important parties in this grouping were the ABAKO, the MNC, a MNC breakaway group in the Kasai headed by Albert Kalonji, and the Parti Solidaire Africaine (PSA) of Antoine Gizenga.

Although the round table conference was stormy, it was the basis on which the Belgian government built the loi fondamentale which established the structure for the future independent Congo state. The loi fondamentale established a bicameral central legislature. The 137 member Chamber of Deputies was to be elected by universal male suffrage. An eighty-four member upper house, or Senate, was to be selected by the provincial assemblies. There was to be a president as titular head of state, but the real conduct of central policy was left to a premier and a cabinet responsible to the legislature. Although the *loi* endorsed the principle of the supremacy of the central government, it nevertheless provided for six provincial legislatures and provincial ministries. The six provinces were Léopoldville, Kasai, Katanga, Kivu, Oriental, and Equator. The system was quite complex and the balance between central and provincial government would have been hard to maintain even with a more sophisticated polity. The conference set June 30, 1960 as the date for Congolese independence.

In the Katanga the *Conféderation des Associations du Katanga* (CONAKAT) had been formed in July 1959, headed by Moise Tshombe. This was a political party which based its popularity and later its power upon the Lunda people. A rival organization, the BALUBAKAT, headed by Jason Sandwe, had been formed which reflected the desires of the Baluba tribe. The major party in Equator Province was the *Parti de l'Unité Nationale* (PUNA) led by Jean Bolikango. Thus by the time of the elections of May 1960, there had been created in the space of three years a great number of political parties which, with the exception of the MNC, reflected only tribal and regional loyalties.

The elections held in May 1960 were for both the central and provincial legislatures. The MNC won forty-one of the 137 seats in the Chamber of Deputies and was the only party to show strength throughout the Congo. Gizenga's PSA won thirteen seats, the ABAKO twelve, and CONAKAT eight. The MNC was also the strongest party in the Senate, holding twenty-two of the eighty-four seats. However, ABAKO dominated the provincial elections in Léopoldville Province winning thirty-three of the ninety seats in the legislature. Together with ABAKO's allies, they controlled the province. In the Katanga, CONAKAT, despite Tshombe's later claims, did not have universal support. His party held twenty-five of the sixty seats in the provincial legislature and only with the aid of smaller groupings was he able to overcome the BALUBAKAT.

The Belgian government did nothing for its image by first ignoring Lumumba's support and asking Kasavubu to form a government. He could not get the requisite parliamentary support and Lumumba was reluctantly called upon to form the government on June 24. On the same day Kasavubu was elected president of the Republic. King Baudouin I of Belgium, at ceremonies conducted in Léopoldville, proclaimed Congolese independence six days later. The newly formed entente between ABAKO and the MNC was short-lived because of the mutiny of the Congolese *Force Publique* against their Belgian officers in June 1960. A series of clashes between these rebellious forces and Belgian civilians brought Belgian troops to the Congo to protect their nationals, and the wholesale evacuation of Belgians from the Congo was begun. This exodus left the government, educational, medical, and social departments without the necessary trained personnel to carry out the ordinary services. The state of confusion bordering on chaos which followed forced Lumumba to call upon United Nations assistance to maintain control over the Republic.

On July 15, the first United Nations caretaker troops landed. By December 1 there were over 19,000 United Nations soldiers in the country. In the months that followed the rebellion of the *Force Publique*, government in the Congo became fragmented with many provincial political leaders acting independently of the central authority. In July 1960, Tshombe declared the Katanga independent, and in August he was elected head of state by the Katanga legislature. Kasavubu gradually moved back to his federalist position and in September attempted to dismiss Lumumba from office and replace him with Joseph Ileo of the MNC-Kalonji. Lumumba in turn tried to oust Kasavubu from the presidency. The Senate overthrew both dismissals. On September 15, Colonel Joseph Mobutu of the Congolese army seized power in Léopoldville, suspended both Lumumba and Kasavubu, and dismissed parliament. This confused situation in Léopoldville caused Antoine Gizenga of the PSA, who had previously reached an understanding with Lumumba, to flee to Stanleyville. There he formed a provisional government which gradually extended its control over the provinces of Oriental, Kivu, and Northern Kasai. Albert Kalonji, a Baluba chief and opponent of Lumumba, had previously formed a new state in southern Kasai.

In late September, Mobutu had reached an agreement with Kasavubu and appointed a nonpolitical caretaker government ostensibly led by Ileo. Lumumba was a virtual prisoner within his quarters, protected only by United Nations guards. Lumumba, the legal functional head of the state whose armed forces had not been successful against the breakaway regime and who felt impotent in Léopoldville, accused the United Nations of refusing to support him and acting as agents of his enemies. Ordered to act only defensively and to be neutral toward the factions, the United Nations forces, because of their inaction, did enable Kasavubu and Mobutu to effectively destroy the constitution. Lumumba, afraid for his safety, attempted to join Gizenga in Stanleyville and was arrested by Mobutu's troops on December 2. On January 18, 1961, Lumumba was transferred as a prisoner to Elizabethville in the Katanga. There under circumstances not yet totally known, he was murdered on February 13. It is known, however, that although a Belgian mercenary was the executioner, Tshombe and Kasavubu were deeply implicated in his death. Despite the United Nations' presumed neutrality, they had, in contravention of the *loi fondamentale*, recognized Kasavubu as head of the Congolese state in November 1960.

The United Nations, following a theoretically defensive course of action, called off a threatened invasion of the Katanga in August 1960. The central government under Kasavubu arrived at a surface rapprochement with Kalonji in the Kasai in February 1961. In March a meeting of all Congolese parties was convened in Tananarive, Madagascar. There a basic agreement was reached for a federal type state. At a further conference in April at Coquilhatville, Tshombe, however, disagreed on the integration plans and left the meeting. He was arrested by the central authorities who immediately announced he would be tried for his crimes. He was, however, released after signing an eleven-point agreement which would have provided for a national Congolese parliament and a federal system. This agreement was repudiated in July 1961 by the Katanga legislature.

Discussions between the central government, the United Nations, and Gizenga's breakaway regime in Stanleyville went on through the summer of 1961. In August Gizenga dissolved his regime and the Congo National Convention was reconvened. A government of national unity was created and Cyrille Adoula was named as the compromise premier in the same month. Adoula had at first been associated with the MNC and later with the Kalonji group, as well as being one of the chief organizers of the *Union Féderation Générale des Travailleurs du Kongo* (FGTK). In the election of May 1960, he had affiliated himself with the PUNA of Equator Province. Antoine Gizenga was associated with Adoula in the government reorganization of late 1961 as first deputy premier. However, Gizenga refused to leave Stanleyville. He had formed a new party there called the *Parti National du Patrice Lumumba*. Two other deputy premiers in the central government were Jean Balikongo of PUNA and Jason Sandwe of the BALUBAKAT. Adoula reduced the size of the unwieldy forty-three member cabinet by nearly half. The new central government survived a shaky beginning which included a near parliamentary defeat in November 1961.

Nevertheless, the Adoula government backed by the United Nations began to take more effective measures to reunify the Congo. The major focus of their efforts was the Katanga. On September 13, 1961, United Nations' military forces attempted to seize Katanga. Tshombe's mercenary forces held them back and a cease fire was arranged on September 20. Again in early November the Congolese forces under Mobutu failed in their military attempt on Katanga. On November 24, the United Nations General Assembly passed a new resolution authorizing the use of force to unify the Congo, and the United Nations launched a general attack on the Katanga on December 5. With Elizabethville surrounded, Tshombe agreed to a conference with Adoula. At Kitona on December 19, Tshombe accepted an eight-point program which would end the Katanga secession and bring the province once again under central authority. Despite these assurances, it was not until February 16, 1962 that the Katanga Assembly accepted the Kitona agreement.

At the same time political and military pressure was exerted on the schismatic regime of the South Kasai. On January 3, 1962, Albert Kalonji was arrested and imprisoned. Antoine Gizenga was also ordered to leave Stanleyville and come to Léopoldville to face charges. Brief fighting occurred between central forces and Gizenga's followers, and Gizenga surrendered. A vote of censure in the Chamber of Deputies was passed, and on January 16, 1962, he was dismissed as deputy premier and arrested. The Katanga, however, was not yet pacified. Details of reunification of the Katanga had not been covered at Kitona, and Adoula and Tshombe met from March 18 to April 17, and May 22 to June 26, to discuss these problems. They represented two extreme positions, particularly with regard to the financial obligations of Katanga to the central government.

When no agreement was reached by August, Adoula attempted to cut off Katanga from the outside world. A compromise financial scheme submitted by the United Nations in August 1962 for sharing revenues was accepted by the central government but not by Tshombe. The total achievement of this one year of discussion was almost nil and military action against Katanga was resumed in December 1962. By December 31, Congo and United Nations forces held all the important centers of Katanga. Tshombe at first fled to Rhodesia but returned to proclaim, on January 15, 1963, the end of Katanga's secession. Soon afterward Tshombe fled the Congo.

By August 16, 1962, President Kasavubu had promulgated laws which created sixteen new provinces out of the six old provinces. Although these measures reduced immediate friction between rival tribes, they were a further concession to federalism and tribalism. On October 16, Adoula introduced a new constitution which gave the provincial governments great autonomy in local affairs while still reserving the most important functions for the central authority.

After January 1963, peace, imposed by the United Nations forces and the Congolese army, had returned to the Congo. All the major factional leaders had either been imprisoned, were dead, in exile, or working for the government. Lumumba was dead, Tshombe and Kalonji in exile, Gizenga in prison, while Kasavubu, Adoula, and Sandwe were in power. The political parties with their schismatic differences were still the major channels of political power. The unity of the Congo was a forced one created by the central government through its control of the *Army Congolaise National* (ANC) and its ability to call upon the United Nations forces in case of trouble.

During 1963 Adoula's government concerned itself with the economic as well as the political situation. The government was impoverished. The rich mines of the Katanga and Kasai had produced little revenue for the central government. The two years of civil war had disrupted trade, destroyed railroads and bridges. The Congo was solvent only because of United Nations' funds. Although not able to completely restore financial stability, the Congo under Adoula was by 1964 moving toward a restoration of order. The United Nations and the United States spent large sums to improve the quality of arms and training for the ANC. The political nature of the Congo, however, remained chaotic, and this threatened any gains made by the new government. In addition to the major parties such as CONAKAT, BALUBAKAT, ABAKO, MNC, and PSA, there were dozens of small splinter groups representing totally local and parochial viewpoints. Later in 1963, a number of exiles in Brazzaville formed the *Comité du Libération National* (CLN) pledged to the overthrow of the Adoula government. Later elements of the CLN were also based in Usumbura. Chief among the leaders of the CLN were Andre Lubaya, Christopher Gbenye, and Emile Soumialot.

Leaders of the major parties within the government attempted to counteract the splinter tendency by trying to organize larger nationwide political parties. A meeting of some fifty political groups in August 1963 resulted in the formation of a new party, the *Rassemblement Démocratique Congolaise* (RADECO). In early 1964, Premier Adoula became the president of RADECO. Another attempt at a national grouping was the formation of the *Comité Démocratique Africaine* in June 1964. This was another alliance of local groups including Kasavubu's ABAKO and the PSA-Kamitatu, a splinter of Gizenga's PSA. A most important grouping was the ABC alliance in the Katanga. This was composed of the former enemy parties of the BALUBAKAT and CONAKAT with the Tshakwe Association of Congo and the Rhodesias (AKTAT).

To work out a more satisfactory and stable government system, President Kasavubu in late 1963 appointed a 120 member constitutional commission. This group headed by Joseph Ileo had made little progress by the spring of 1964. The government, as well as all factions, were aware that June 30, 1964 would be one of the most crucial dates in Congolese history because the United Nations had previously announced the withdrawal of all their troops by that date. The new constitution had to be finished by then and the ANC prepared to take over the full responsibility for policing the state.

The first of a new series of disturbances began in Kwilu Province in December 1963. The leader of the uprising was Pierre Mulele, former minister of the interior in the Lumumba government. He had spent years in Communist areas absorbing details of guerrilla warfare. Returning to the Congo, he organized his guerrilla bands, called the *Jeunesse,* on the model of those in Southeast Asia. In Kwilu he found the native population hostile to the central government and willing to support his irregulars. Although the government announced, in late January 1964, that the area was pacified, this was far from the case. The *Jeunesse* controlled most of Kwilu. The guerrillas believed they were immune from the bullets of the ANC. The ANC seemed to believe it also. By March 1964, central Kivu was also affected. It is doubtful that Mulele was directly responsible for this outbreak, but certainly his success in Kwilu served as a good example. The fighting in Kivu was led partially by the CLN based in Burundi. Another faction in the disturbances in Kivu were the Bafulero pygmies led by Moussa Maranduru. Although better equipped, the ANC proved no match for the insurgents. Many regular soldiers feared the magic of their opponents. Time after time patrols of the ANC, numerically superior, threw away their weapons and fled. Even the appearance and personal bravery of General Mobutu served only as a palliative. To add to the confusion, a three-day riot ripped Albertville in northern Katanga. The ANC was spread so thin that, even if its troops had been more disciplined, the situation would have been critical. By June the United Nations had only 2,000 troops remaining in the Congo and these left on the appointed date.

Adoula's government was being torn to pieces. He no longer could command the allegiance of any but a few high government officials. There was no parliament since President Kasavubu had suspended it in March, probably because it was impossible to gain a quorum of the necessary forty out of a total of 137 elected members. Rumors were that approximately forty members of parliament were in the interior and fifteen had joined the CLN. Late in June 1964, Tshombe and Kalonji were allowed to return to the Congo. Premier Adoula submitted his resignation on June 30 but was persuaded by Kasavubu to remain the head of a caretaker regime. Kasavubu then asked Tshombe to sound out political leaders to see if he could gain their support to form a new government. In early July, Tshombe, who only eighteen months previously had been the chief secessionist, became the premier of the Congo. He freed Antoine Gizenga from his two and one-half year imprisonment on the island of Balambemba and included in his ministry many of his old enemies. In this government of "public salvation," President Kasavubu retained the ministry of defense; Tshombe was premier, minister of trade, and minister of foreign affairs; Albert Kalonji was minister of agriculture; Andre Lubaya was minister of health; and Tshombe's old confederate, Godefroid Munongo, became minister of the interior.

Tshombe claimed that within three months he would put down the uprisings and secure a stable Congo. However, he was hardly in office when a new threat to the state appeared. A "Popular Army of Liberation" guided by one of the CLN leaders, Emile Soumialot, aimed at capturing Stanleyville. Although the second largest city in the Congo was protected by almost 1,000 ANC, the ill-equipped rebel force inspired such fear that most of the ANC fled and Stanleyville fell to Soumialot's forces. Soumialot was soon replaced as head of the Stanleyville regime by Christopher Gbenye who established a rival government which he called the Peoples Republic of the Congo.

Tshombe's position was extremely critical. Rebels controlled Albertville and Bukavu in the east and most of the territory from Kongolo northward along the Congo River to Stanleyville. The ANC, although well-equipped, would fight only in rare instances. Tshombe turned to two sources for aid. His appeal for more material from the United States was soon met by a quantity of aircraft and technical advisers. His attempt to secure aid from the OAU, however, showed that other African states were more consumed with hate for Tshombe and his past actions than with the future of the Congo. In September 1964, he addressed the foreign ministers' meeting of the OAU at Addis Ababa detailing the Congo's position and asking for aid. He wanted African states to provide troops to police-pacified areas so that the bulk of the ANC could be thrown against the rebels. This help would thus enable him to dispense with mercenary soldiers. The foreign ministers rejected his request for troops. In October Tshombe flew to Cairo to lay his case before the heads of state of the OAU. He was not given a hearing but was held prisoner in a Cairo hotel before being deported. Thus Tshombe was thrown back on his own resources, knowing that he would receive no help from other African states. The only concrete action taken by the OAU was to establish a committee headed by Jomo Kenyatta to work for a mediation of differences in the Congo.

Tshombe's decision to use white mercenaries as a spearhead for his armies had been one of the reasons for his reception in Cairo. However, the 400 mercenaries from Europe, Rhodesia, and South Africa were the main reason why the Congo did not collapse. Used as shock troops, they drove the rebels out of town after town. The ANC following behind began to regain some confidence. By November, Bakavu and Albertville had been recaptured. Meanwhile, Gbenye at Stanleyville had seized all Europeans in the area and held them as a pledge for the safety of his regime and the withdrawal of the mercenaries. Daily the position of the Europeans became more desperate. From a moderately harsh position toward them, Gbenye drifted to one which threatened their lives as his military situation worsened. This situation brought forth further European intervention in the form of Belgian paratroopers flown in by planes supplied by the United States. This drop was coordinated with a flying column of mercenaries and ANC from Kindu. Stanleyville was taken, but only after approximately one hundred European hostages were killed by Gbenye's militant followers who had been given the name "simbas." The majority of the 1,000 Europeans in the district were safely evacuated. Gbenye, Olenga, Soumialot, and the other rebel leaders fled to the Sudan. However, when the Belgian troops were withdrawn, rebel soldiers returned and the northern area was far from secure for Tshombe. Confusion was compounded in Stanleyville by the outbreak of a typhoid epidemic in December. The Belgian intervention was condemned by most African states and a full-scale discussion of the Congo was conducted in the United Nations. It is obvious that the Stanleyville affair did not enhance Tshombe's position in Africa.

Tshombe protested to the Security Council of the United Nations the actions of certain African states giving aid to the rebels. Specifically, Burundi and the Sudan were named as areas being used as both a staging ground and training area for the rebel forces. Tshombe gave evidence that Algerian officers were training guerrillas and that Egypt, Ghana, and Algeria had all sent arms to the rebels through the Sudan. The Security Council was content to call for a general cease fire.

By mid-December mercenary and ANC units had rescued over 600 Europeans caught in the midst of the fighting. During early January 1965, over 200 hostages were killed by the hard-pressed "simbas" in the northeastern regions. Over one hundred hostages were still held in June in the Buta region north of Stanleyville after the majority were rescued by Congolese and mercenary forces. The revived ANC and the mercenaries continued their operations in disaffected areas throughout 1965. A major operation was that against Fizi in the mountains near Lake Tanganyika in September and October. The rebels were never able to seriously challenge Tshombe's government after January 1965. Support from the Sudan, Burundi, and other states sympathetic to the rebels slackened. The leaders of the revolt were killed or forced into exile. Gbenye and others were eventually expelled from their sanctuary in Egypt. At the end of 1965, the Congo had been pacified. By June 1965, most of the states of the OAU had reconsidered their previous positions and had accepted Tshombe's regime as the legal government of the Congo.

While world attention was rightly focused upon the efforts of the central government to restore stability, there had been a considerable constitutional change. In July 1964, a new, more simplified, constitution was adopted by referendum. All males over eighteen years of age were made eligible to vote for the members of the National Assembly and members of one of the twenty-one provincial legislatures. The lower house was to have 166 seats with one deputy elected to represent approximately 100,000 persons. Each provincial legislature chose six persons for the upper house or federal Senate. The executive continued to be responsible, depending upon the support of the house. In October 1964, the minister of the interior, M. Munungo, announced that general elections under the new instruments would be held in early 1965. Therefore it became doubly imperative that order be restored to the Congo before these elections.

The elections were held from the middle of March through April 30, 1965. The size of the Congo, the multiplicity of parties, and the number of candidates involved made the elections seem chaotic. There was voting for the National Assembly and for provincial representatives as well. There were sixty separate lists of candidates for office and over 230 parties represented. So complicated did the process become that in places the election had to be postponed to a date later than scheduled. As an example, the elections in Léopoldville originally scheduled to begin on March 25 were postponed until April 25.

The major political groupings involved in the elections were the ABAKO of Kasavubu and the *Convention Nationale Congolaise* (CONACO) led by Tshombe. CONACO was a coalition between the Katanga-based CONAKAT and some fifty smaller political parties. The MNC-Lumumba, once so powerful, was not an important factor in the election. It was allied with other Lumumbist-oriented parties such as the *Parti Lumumbiste Unité* (PALU) created by Gizenga in August 1964. Other important smaller parties were the PSA-Kamitatu which had some strength in Kwilu, the *Union Démocratique du Congo* also in Kwilu, and the BALUBAKAT and FRONKAT, anti-Tshombe parties in northern Katanga.

Tshombe's CONACO emerged from the election as the most important political force in the National Assembly. However, due to the many parties involved, it did not have a majority. President Kasavubu, obviously concerned with Tshombe's success and popularity, decided to act to minimize Tshombe's influence in the months before the presidential elections. Between May and October there developed a definite power struggle between the two men. In October Kasavubu dismissed Tshombe and his ministry, declaring that the tasks assigned in 1964 had been completed and, therefore, Tshombe was no longer needed. Kasavubu called upon Evareste Kimba, one-time foreign minister of the secessionist Katanga, to form a government. Tshombe, looking toward the presidential elections in February 1966, chose to become leader of the parliamentary opposition.

In October and November 1965, there were obvious signs of an active anti-Tshombe campaign. Kasavubu restored relations with Congo-Brazzaville, made definite contacts with Ghana, and promised to get rid of the mercenary forces. The chief of police forces, Nendaka, had begun to supervise pro-Tshombe newspapers. The growing rancor between Kasavubu and Tshombe decided General Mobutu in late November to act to end the power struggle which threatened a further civil war.

General Mobutu and the army forced Kasavubu's resignation as president and guaranteed him instead a permanent seat in the Senate. The Kimba ministry resigned to be replaced by a "government of National Union" with one minister for each of the twenty-one provinces. To head this ministry, Mobutu called upon the most able of the army combat officers, Colonel Leonard Mulamba, who had been serving as the military governor of northeastern Congo. Kasavubu, Tshombe, Kimba, and their adherents, at least outwardly, welcomed the military regime.

RUANDA–URUNDI

These two small mountainous territories were originally a part of German East Africa. After World War I, they were detached from Tanganyika and became separate League of Nations mandates administered by Belgium as a portion of the Congo. The size of each territory was slightly over 10,000 square miles and they had a combined population of almost 6,000,000. The population concentration in these territories was one of the highest in Africa. Although the land available for cultivation was better than in surrounding territories, the pressure of population combined with the ultraconservative political system made the territories poor. The Bahutu, a Bantu agricultural people, comprised over eighty percent of the population of each area. The politically dominant people, however, were the tall, aristocratic, Nilotic Watutsi. The Watutsi owned the cattle, the most obvious source of wealth. In addition, they were the traditional rulers of Ruanda and Urundi. The Watutsi had kept as their servants and workers the Batwa pygmies who comprised about one percent of the population.

The Belgians, as had the Germans before them, did little to upset the aristocratic, feudal system dominated by the Watutsi. The supreme rulers in each territory were the bami (singular mwami) who were advised by appointive aristocratic councils. Below the bami were the chiefs and subchiefs, each with their own appointive advisory councils. Belgian administration was superimposed over this system and until 1956 did not attempt to modify the almost total control of the Watutsi aristocracy over the territories. The chief Belgian administrative authority was the vicegovernor general of Ruanda-Urundi who was assisted by a totally appointed general council and secretariat. In the countryside, Belgian authority was represented by district officers who made certain that Belgian regulations were carried out. However, they normally left local administration in the hands of the Watutsi overlords. There was only one part of Ruanda-Urundi that was a centre extra-coutumier. This was the capital, Usumbura, which had a population of approximately 40,000.

Beginning in 1949, the Belgians utilized Ruanda-Urundi for elections which could serve as tests for possible application to the rest of the Congo. The elections held in 1949, 1951, and 1953 were actually only tests of the preferences of the population for the advisers to the Belgian local officials. The power of appointment was still retained by the Belgians. In 1956 Belgium devised an extremely complex system of direct and indirect elections for all the councils of the territories from the clan councils up through the African councils which advised the bami. The members of the African councils chose the native representatives who sat with the Belgian officials on the general council of the territories. All of these councils remained advisory with no legislative power of their own. However, the general council was empowered to examine the budget and make recommendations.

All of the changes in administrative procedure made by Belgium through 1959 were in keeping with their concept of gradualism. They had been careful not to disturb the traditional pattern of rule and their support of the Watutsi rulers. However, events in the Congo impelled them to apply new approaches in Ruanda-Urundi. They had been too inflexible in recognizing public opinion in the Congo. Thus in Ruanda-Urundi they attempted a new approach by recognizing the aspirations of the Bahutu masses. This was as much a reversal of previous policy as was their actions in the Congo. In Ruanda, particularly, this quick change of attitude did not foster continued Belgian power but rather contributed to a violent upheaval which destroyed not only Watutsi influence but also Belgian control.

RWANDA (RUANDA)

Before 1959 the Watutsi had favored a quick advance toward independence because they were positive that their domination would continue as before. In this period the Bahutu looked upon the Belgian rule as a protection which mitigated the harshness of their Watutsi overlords. In June 1959, mwami Charles Rudahigwa died suddenly. The chief council of Rwanda, fearing that the nationalism rampant in the Congo would spread into Rwanda and take advantage of the vacuum of power, quickly appointed the dead mwami's half-brother, Kigeri, as the new mwami. This action increased the now politically awakened Bahutu's fears, and some Bahutu began to plunder the villages of the Watutsi. Over one hundred persons were killed in late October and the Belgians sent in Congolese army units and paratroops to restore order. Instead of supporting the new mwami and the Watutsi, the Belgian government, reflecting their general Congolese policy, shifted to support the Bahutu and their new political party, the *Association pour la promotion des Masses* (APROSOMA). On November 10 the Brussels government announced plans to create constitutional monarchies in the two trust territories and end their dependence upon the government of the Congo. Popular elections were promised for an enlarged legislature within six months. A United Nations mission recommended in early 1960 a round table conference of all factions which would lead to elections and a speedy independence. The round table conference was never called and the Belgian authorities continued with their own plans. The election for a provisional legislature was held in July 1960.

APROSOMA and the newly formed *Parti d'Emancipation des Hutus* (PARMEHUTU) gained eighty-four percent of the votes, and the old order in Rwanda was broken. Violence between the two peoples was endemic throughout 1960.

In January 1961, Belgium, without prior consultation with the United Nations, concurred with the Rwanda parties in declaring the state independent. The provisional legislature, elected in July 1960, declared itself a parliament. Mwami Kigeri V was formally deposed and the state declared a republic. The first appointed president was Dominque Mbonyemuta, the leader of PARMEHUTU. Gregoire Kayibanda was declared premier. With Belgian aid, the machinery of government was reorganized. All of these actions were taken without consulting the Watutsi. The United Nations was presented with a dilemma. It was on record favoring independence, but the methods of achieving it was not in accord with their concepts. A United Nations investigating commission reported in March 1961 that Belgium was attempting to establish a pro-Belgian government in open defiance of the United Nations. In April the United Nations General Assembly called for new elections under United Nations control for broadly based caretaker governments in both Rwanda and Burundi. They also demanded a referendum to decide whether the mwami of Rwanda should retain his office.

The United Nations-supervised elections were held in September 1961, after a summer of constant violence. Over 300 deaths were reported in July and August. Many Watutsi fled to Burundi or took refuge at the Christian mission stations. Under such conditions it was not surprising that the referendum showed the people definitely opposed to the return of the mwami. The proposed constitution called for a forty-four member legislative committee elected by direct suffrage and for a presidential-type executive. The PARMEHUTU won thirty-five of the seats and Kayibanda became president. During all these political changes Belgium still held executive responsibility under the United Nations. Not until July 1962 did Rwanda become totally independent of outside control.

The quick reversal of power from the Watutsi to the Bahutu had caused considerable violence. Many Watutsi expected after independence to be slaughtered by the now dominant Bahutu. The excesses of July and August and the expectation of more violence caused almost 100,000 Watutsi to flee the country. It is alleged that from their places of refuge in Tanzania, Burundi, and Uganda, these displaced Watutsi continually raided Bahutu farms and villages in Rwanda. In the week before Christmas 1963, thousands of Watutsi crossed the frontier, and some of these armed bands advanced to within a few miles of the Rwanda capital of Kigale. They were repulsed by the regular Rwanda army, and then the Bahutu began a process of slaughtering the Watutsi. The Rwanda government was not directly implicated in the massacres that followed, but the statements by government officials indicated sympathy with the Bahutu terror. No accurate figures exist for the numbers of Watutsi killed during this period, but estimates vary between 10,000 and 15,000 with some 6,000 in the

Kigene district alone. The disorders culminating in these massacres spelled an end to any hope of reconciling the Bahutu and Watutsi to a coalition government similar to that of Burundi.

In June 1964, the army was forced to meet another threat to the sovereignty of the small state. The disorders then current in the eastern Congo almost spilled over into Rwanda. Elements of the rebel forces, intent on capturing Bukavu in the eastern Congo, attempted an invasion through Rwanda. They were met by the army at the Ruzzi River, defeated, and forced to turn back. Although there were sporadic raids in 1965, the year was relatively peaceful since the Congolese government threatened to expel the Watutsi refugees if they did not cease agitating against Rwanda. Disorders in neighboring Burundi occupied the attention of the dominant Watutsi group there. However, the situation was complicated by large numbers of Bahutu refugees who fled Burundi for the safety of the Bantu government of President Kayibanda.

The endemic violence between the Bahutu and Watutsi in Rwanda was made worse by the potentiality of armed conflict with neighboring unstable Burundi. After October 1965, when a revolt of Bahutus within the Burundi army was crushed, the pro-Watutsi group within the government was even more active in supporting plans for an overthrow of the Bahutu government of Rwanda.

BURUNDI (URUNDI)

Although conditions in Burundi since 1959 were similar to those in Rwanda, there were slight differences and these differences were responsible for the separate political development of Burundi. The Bahutu made up approximately eighty-seven percent of the population and were ruled by a Watutsi mwami. However, the traditional rule of the mwami of Burundi was never as centralized as in Rwanda. There was better rapport between the Bahutu and Watutsi. Most important, there was no event similar to the death of the mwami of Rwanda that could be immediately seized upon by the Belgians to change radically the traditional system. Lacking such an opportunity, early political development in Burundi followed a more standard, orderly course. Under the tutelage of the United Nations and Belgium, the once autocratic regime was transformed into a constitutional monarchy. The constitution created in the summer of 1961 established a National Assembly of sixty-four members, a crown council to advise the mwami, and a premier exercising executive authority dependent upon the support of the legislature. One of the key factors in the early relative stability of Burundi was the mwami, Mwambutsa IV, who, even under the revised constitution, still retained a strong residue of power.

The major political party in Burundi was the *Parti de l'Unité et du Progrès National du Burundi* (UPRONA). It was conservative and had the support of both Bahutu and Watutsi chiefs. In the elections of September 18, 1961, arranged by the United Nations and Belgium, UPRONA won fifty-eight of the sixty-four seats. There was also a smaller political party, the *Parti Démocratique Chrétienne* (PDC), but it never became a major factor in the government. The first premier chosen was Louis Rwangasore, son of the mwami. Despite the orderly development of self-rule, violence did not pass Burundi completely by since Rwangasore was assassinated on October 13, 1961. He was succeeded by his brother-in-law, André Muhirwa. The United Nations General Assembly voted ninety-three to zero on June 27 to approve independence for the two trust territories and Burundi became an independent state on July 1, 1962. Muhirwa remained premier until June 1963, when he was forced to resign by a vote of censure by the Assembly which charged him with attempting to assume dictatorial powers by ordering the arrest of the president of the Assembly. His successor, Pierre N'Gendandumwe, was a Bahutu.

The major question which agitated the government in early 1964 was that of the revolt in the Congo and the attitude which the government should assume toward the Red Chinese who had opened an embassy at the capital Bujumbura (Usumbura) in January. This question more than any other issue caused the resignation of pro-Western N'Gendandumwe in March. He was replaced as prime minister by Albin Nyamoya who adopted a most compliant attitude toward the activities of the Chinese. During 1964 Bujumbura was the main focal point for aid to the rebel forces operating in the eastern Congo. Chinese money had made a deep impact on members of the Burundi government and the National Assembly. The mwami finally became so concerned that Nyamoya was dismissed and N'Gendandumwe was returned as prime minister on January 8, 1965. On January 15, 1965, Prime Minister N'Gendandumwe was assassinated on the steps of the hospital in Bujumbura. The assassin was a Watutsi, and it appeared that his action was motivated more by tribal hatred than concern with cold-war issues. Former Prime Minister Nyamoya, a Watutsi, and twenty-three other Watutsi tribesmen were arrested as accomplices. Joseph Bamina, a moderate in domestic affairs and neutralist in regard to foreign policy, became premier. In early February, the mwami, now thoroughly alarmed by possible Chinese subversion, ordered their embassy closed. The Burundi army supervised the departure of the Chinese ambassador and his staff.

Mwami Mwambutsa dissolved the National Assembly in March and elections were held on May 10. These further discredited the pro-Communist faction since all the leading Watutsi figures associated with Nyamoya were defeated. The king retained the powers of the premier through the summer due largely to tensions between the Watutsi and Bahutu which had increased after N'Gendandumwe's assassination. Finally in September, Leopold Biha, a Watutsi who was considered a moderate by outside observers, became premier. Nothing substantial had been done since independence to weld the two racial groups in Burundi closer together. On the contrary, events in Rwanda, as well as Burundi, had only alienated them more from each other. Over 80,000 Watutsi refugees from Rwanda added to the government's difficulties. Many Bahutu in Burundi demanded the ouster of Mwambutsa and the establishment of a republic which would be controlled by the Bahutus. This desire and resentment against the government led, in October 1965, to a revolt of some of the police units backed by Bahutu radicals. Biha was surprised in his home and shot. The mwami hid in the palace and thus escaped the rebels until loyal troops quickly put down the rebellion. Martial law was proclaimed and thirty-four of the rebellious gendarmes were publicly executed. Large numbers of Bahutu politicians and intellectuals were arrested.

The UPRONA government formed by Biha was dissolved by the mwami, and he granted powers of government to Michel Micombero, the defense minister. Then the mwami left the country for a rest in Switzerland. On November 18, Mwambutsa reconstituted the Biha government. However, Biha, in a Belgian hospital recuperating from the attempt on his life, was in no position to effect the changes decreed by the mwami. In March 1966, Prince Charles Ndizeye arrived in Burundi to act for his father, the mwami, and bring some order to the strife wracked state. However, in July he deposed his father and became Mwami Ntare V. In turn, while on a state visit to the Congo, he was deposed by Micombero who declared the monarchy at an end. Instead, there was created a republic controlled by a thirteen-member National Revolutionary Committee. Thus after four years of independence, Burundi's politics were as stormy as ever, the cleavage between Bahutu and Watutsi remained, and the new factor of pro-Western and pro-Communist factions further divided the people.

THIRTEEN
The Portuguese territories: reaction to African nationalism

The political system briefly outlined in Chapter Seven continued in force after World War II. The assumptions upon which Prime Minister Salazar had constructed his system remained unchallenged until the uprising in Angola in 1961. Centralized control over the lives of Africans was actually increased when in 1952 the African territories were designated overseas provinces of Portugal instead of colonial possessions. Thus, while other colonial powers were modifying their rule in response to African pressures, the Portuguese made no concessions. Dual citizenship was maintained. The first class, the *populacao civilizada* (civilized), comprised all Portuguese residents, the mixed population, and the few *assimilados*. Persons in this category participated fully in the limited political life of the territories. The bulk of the population was designated *populacao nâo-civilizada* (uncivilized), and were controlled directly by the full machinery of the appointive European system. Portuguese neo-mercantilism and the *assimilado* system effectively prevented the development of any legal political activity for the indigenous people, the *indegenas*.

The key to Portugal's attitude toward its overseas provinces lies in its poverty. In 1959 Portugal's trade deficit with the rest of the world was over $140,000,000. In order to keep this unhealthy situation from becoming worse Portugal needs desperately the cotton, tea, tobacco, petroleum, and other supplies provided by its provinces. Angola, Mozambique, and Guinea are also constrained to import the bulk of their goods from Portugal. It should not be assumed, however, that Portugal neglected its territories economically. In order to increase their economic potential Portugal has invested millions in port facilities, railroads, roads, and irrigation systems. An integral part of its schemes for economic development has been the re-settlement of Portuguese families in new agricultural communities in Angola and Mozambique. One of the largest of these *colonatos* is located north of the Limpopo River and cost

Portugal over $35,000,000 in the decade after 1954. In 1959 Portugal instituted a six-year development plan which projected the expenditure of $300,000,000 for new agricultural and industrial enterprises. Despite all its efforts to support white colonization, there were less than one-third million Europeans resident in Angola and Mozambique.

In March 1961, Portugal's empire was shaken to its base by a revolt in northern Angola. Salazar was forced to concentrate over 50,000 troops in Angola before African resistance was broken. In mid-1962 a further nationalist uprising began in Guinea and guerrillas trained in Tanzania started to operate in northern Mozambique. The United Nations, Britain, and the United States brought additional pressure to bear upon Portugal to alter its African political system. While implicitly denying the right of any outside agency to interfere in Portugal's domestic affairs, Salazar's government acted as early as June 1961 to moderate some of the worst features of its system. Municipal councils which had previously been appointive were in the future to be elected. Three new seats were assigned to Mozambique, three to Angola, and one to Guinea in the Portuguese National Assembly. The government announced in August 1961 a plan to abolish dual citizenship replacing it with a single set of property and educational standards for the franchise. Events after 1961 connected with the African revolt against Portugal became so complex that only by viewing each province separately can one obtain an understanding of this period.

Angola

The government regime of Dr. Salazar both in Portugal and in the colonies precluded the normal organization and lawful practice of political parties in Angola. The territory was governed by an appointive governor-general and elected legislative council. However, the council was dominated by the white settlers and, moreover, had little real power. African political activity in Angola has, therefore, been of the clandestine, terrorist type which seeks the overthrow of the centralized white regime. The political organizations operative in Angola were never recognized by Portugal and their headquarters were located in friendly African states. The political party which has demonstrated, in the past, that it had a larger amount of African support than the others was the *Uniao das Populacaes de Angola* (UPA). The UPA was founded in 1954 and was led by the Congolese-educated Holden Roberto. Roberto was widely known in African Nationalist circles, having attended all the major conferences after that in Accra in 1958. He had a close relationship with Kwame Nkrumah, and the office of the UPA was located in Léopoldville. The UPA takes credit for the March 15, 1961 uprisings which focused world attention on Angola. Certainly the strength of the UPA was in the agricultural north, particularly among the Bakongo.

Another nationalist party was the *Movimento Popular de Libertacao de Angola* (MPLA) founded in 1957 by Ilidio Alves Machado. Arrested for subversion in 1959, Machado was imprisoned in Luanda during the uprising. One of the other early leaders, Dr. Agostino Neto, also was arrested in June 1960. The movement's next leader in the absence of Neto was Mario Pinto de Andrade whose headquarters was in Guinea. At the All African Peoples Conference at Tunis in January 1960, the MPLA joined three other small nationalist organizations to form the *Frente Revolucionaria Africana para Independencia Nacional* (FRAIN) to gain independence for all Portuguese colonies. This led to a permanent coordinating organization, the *Conferencia de Organizacoes Nacionalistas das Colonias Portuguesas* (CONCP). Most of the MPLA were mulatto and the strength of its movement in Angola was in the vicinity of Luanda.

In March 1959, the government arrested several hundred people including leaders of the clandestine political parties. There were three trials subsequently where fifty-seven persons were charged with "attempts against the external security of the State." Portugal began to reinforce its garrison in Angola. The exiled MPLA in conjunction with the UPA formed a united movement, the *Frente Libertacao Nacional de Angola* (FLNA), in May 1960 and appealed to the government for a peaceful solution to the Angolan problem. The Portuguese answered by more arrests of suspects in Luanda, Lobito, Dalatando, and Malange. In July 1960, troops began intermittent raids on African quarters in Luanda. In November twenty-eight nationalists from Cabinda were executed in Luanda. Leaders of the Liberation Front in London implied in December that only direct action was left to the Africans if they wished to end Portuguese colonialism.

The first direct action was timed to coincide with the return of Henrique Galvão to Luanda. On January 23, 1961, he and seventy followers had seized Portugal's second largest ship, the *Santa Maria,* to dramatize opposition to Salazar's regime. Captured by the Brazilian navy, the *Santa Maria* was scheduled to dock in Luanda on February 4. African nationalists attacked the prisons and a military barracks. The main battle raged for three days before the revolt was quelled with a loss of African life estimated at over 2,000. Throughout February fighting between Portuguese army units and Africans was endemic in northern Angola and there was a major African uprising on March 14.

Despite its militant attitude which predated the February uprising, Portugal had not believed the Africans capable of concerted action. Therefore the entire military garrison of Angola in early March numbered less than 3,000 men. On the evening of March 14, an estimated 60,000 Africans attacked the Portuguese settlers in the provinces of Congo, Malange, and Luanda. Over 300 European men, women, and children were killed in the initial onslaught. There were numerous cases of rape, torture, and mutilation. In the next three weeks approximately 1,000 more Europeans and 6,000 Africans were killed. Dr. Salazar took over the ministry of defense in Portugal and reinforcements were rushed to Angola. Armed civilians in Angola joined the military in counterattacking. Jet planes using bombs, machine guns, and napalm struck at villages and targets of opportunity throughout the disaffected area. The ferocity of the initial African attack was thus matched by the Portuguese counterattack.

Before the end of the initial crisis in October 1961, Portugal had over 15,000 troops operating in the three provinces. Eventually more than 50,000 soldiers were garrisoned in Angola. There is no way of knowing how many Africans died in northern Angola. Estimates have been made of upward of 60,000 dead. It is known that over 100,000 fled northward to join their Bakongo kinsmen in the trouble-wracked Republic of the Congo. Portugal had by the end of the year controlled the uprising at a cost of millions of dollars of its scant reserve fund. Fighting was endemic on a smaller scale in northern Angola through 1965.

Portugal, after the rebellion, responded by liberalizing its rule to a limited extent. The *assimilado* system was abolished and civil rights extended to all residents of Angola. A single set of requirements for the franchise was established. Forced labor for the production of cash export crops was stopped and the government disassociated itself from active participation in recruitment of African labor. The Legislative Council was made elective and three new seats in the Portuguese National Assembly were reserved for Angola. It should be remembered that the grant of franchise and civil rights, while an advance, is not comparable to these practices in British or French areas. The Portuguese government remained firmly in the hands of Premier Salazar and his associates and even Europeans in Portugal had few political rights.

Another result of the uprising was the speeding up of European colonization of Angola. The government announced its long-range goal of attempting to convince many of the 50,000 soldiers in Angola to settle there permanently. The Portuguese relaxed their immigration requirements and began to fund at an even higher level their land settlement schemes. The success of Portugal's colonization efforts can be seen in the following approximate figures for European population: 1940—40,000; 1950—79,000; 1955—140,000; 1960—200,000; 1964—240,000.

In reaction to the disturbances, the United Nations voted on April 20, 1961 to send a five-man fact-finding commission to Angola. The Security Council in June, by a vote of nine to zero, called upon Portugal to cease its repressive measures against the Africans. Portugal bitterly criticized the actions of the United Nations and its fellow NATO ally, the United States, for their positions on this matter. Salazar maintained that these were internal disturbances beyond the scope of United Nations activity and refused to allow the General Assembly's committee to land. Further resolutions of the Security Council in 1962 and 1963 were likewise ignored by Portugal. The pressure of African states, even those which broke relations with Portugal, had even less effect upon Salazar's policies.

The failure of African nationalists to achieve any substantial part of their goals by 1965 was due as much to divided leadership as to Portuguese troops. After the uprising of 1961, there was a fragmentation of the

MPLA and a corresponding loss of prestige of the *Frente Revolucionaria* and the CONCP. The largely mulatto leadership of the MPLA had never been popular with the African masses. There was briefly a shift in Portuguese settler thinking toward a Brazilian solution where the settlers in Angola, not the politicans in Lisbon, would determine policy. This more moderate attitude of the settlers was partially designed to undermine the MPLA. The lack of a single revolutionary organization which could coordinate guerrilla activity in Angola restricted the effectiveness of the revolution. In 1963 the OAU created a coordinating committee to investigate the relative merits of FLNA and MPLA. The investigations indicated that the MPLA had no political structure in Angola. Further, the committee discovered that MPLA militants in Angola numbered only about 200. The goodwill commission previously had imagined that its risk would be to reconcile two revolutionary groups of almost equal power. However, it found that the FLNA was the only really effective political and military force in Angola. Holden Roberto's group at that time still controlled, by the admission of the Portuguese, over six percent of Angola. The OAU commission recommended that all future aid be channeled to the FLNA through its Léopoldville headquarters and suggested that all of the smaller revolutionary groups join the more effective and militant UPA and FLNA. Subsequently, the OAU recognized Roberto's government in exile, located in Léopoldville, as the official government of Angola.

The concentration by the Portuguese of a large, well-trained, modern army in Angola had by 1965 all but negated the guerrilla forces throughout the territory. Only a few bands were still active in the Bakongo country. Further to the south those in the Kimbundu areas either had been liquidated or had vanished. Portugal was thus able to transfer a large portion of her military forces from Angola to the troubled areas of Mozambique and Guinea.

These reversals were paralleled by a loss in prestige for Roberto and the government in exile. Jonas Savimbi, his ex-foreign minister, broke with Roberto over policy. Savimbi maintained that the guerrilla losses stemmed largely from Roberto's failure to give the proper leadership. He also claimed that Roberto's Bakongo separatist sentiments had kept the FLNA from becoming an all-Angolan movement. Other defectors from Roberto's party in 1965 formed the *Congress Popular de Angola* (CPA).

While Roberto's group, perhaps as a reflection of its losses, became more Bakongo-oriented, the MPLA based in Léopoldville recovered some of the prestige which was lost in 1963. Under the leadership of Neto and Andrade, guerrilla bands loyal to the MPLA carried out terrorist activities in Cabinda. At the close of 1965, Roberto still had the support of the OAU, but there was considerable feeling that his group had failed and that the MPLA had a better chance of eventually succeeding in Angola.

Portugal has made it clear in public statements and overt action that it considers Angola the most important of its African territories. The task of driving the Portuguese from the area would be formidable without the frantic competition between rival revolutionary groups. Thus in spite of the heavy loss of life by the guerrillas and heroic pronouncements by FLNA and MPLA leaders, Portugal's hold on Angola was greater in 1965 than it had been before the uprising.

Mozambique

Mozambique is the most populous Portuguese territory in Africa with a population in 1964 of approximately six million of which over 65,000 were Europeans. It has a coastline over 1,500 miles long. In the north it borders Tanzania, in the west Rhodesia and Malawi, and in the south the Republic of South Africa. Most of the European population is located in the south and along the coast.

Portugal's hold over interior areas was extremely tenuous even after the agreements which settled the scramble. Before that the *prazeros,* mulatto descendants of early Portuguese settlers, controlled the Zambesi Valley. Laws unto themselves, they ignored, except when convenient, rules made in Lisbon or Mozambique. With their private armies they fought among each other, against the Africans, and against innumerable Portuguese expeditions. By use of chartered companies, such as the Mozambique Company, and more troops, the Portuguese succeeded in defeating most of the African rulers of the interior and the *prazeros.* By 1914 the Portuguese held nominal control of the interior.

Early in the twentieth century the Portuguese established the practice of sending contract laborers to São Thomé and Réunion. In 1911 the Portuguese government signed an agreement with the Union of South Africa to provide up to 80,000 workers every year for the mines. The use of the hippopotamus hide whip, beating the palms of the hands, and other methods were utilized to enforce Portuguese decrees for forced and contract labor. These methods were outlawed by 1915 but were still being practiced at a much later date.

In 1915 the Lisbon government announced the *assimilado* system which theoretically gave the African the right to rise to the status of Portuguese citizens. The home government under the control of Premier Salazar after 1931 was even less amenable to change than had been the monarchy. Thus Portuguese neo-mercantilism and the *assimilado* system have prevented the development in Mozambique of any legal political activity for the *indegenas* who make up most of the population. Thus all African political groups have been clandestine organizations such as those in Angola and Portuguese Guinea. The Salazar government made clear by its statements and actions even before the uprisings in Angola that there would be no major change in the relationship of the African territories to Portugal.

In 1952 Mozambique was declared an overseas province and an integral part of Portugal. It continued to be directed largely from Lisbon through the offices of the governor-general and his appointive staff. An advisory council and a twenty-four man Legislative Council composed of European appointees gave advice to the executive, but they had little substantive powers. The political reality of life for the *indegenas* was direct control of their affairs by European officers down to the district level. The failure of the *assimilado* system in Mozambique is seen in their numbers. Only 4,500 Africans out of a population of almost six million had become *assimilados*.

Portugal's strict paternalist relations with the African population became critical in the late 1950s when African territories of other European states were being advanced quickly toward independence. One of the main thrusts of the Pan African movement was to oust all colonial powers from the continent and replace them with African rule. It was impossible for Portugal to seal its frontiers against these new ideas. The March 1961 rebellion in Angola was the best evidence of the extent of this Portuguese problem. Following the outbreak of violence in Angola, a number of African political organizations were founded which had as their objective self-determination and independence for Mozambique. In October 1960, Adelino Gwambe and a few followers formed the *Uniao Democratica Nacional de Mocambique* (UDENAMO) with its headquarters in Tanzania. Another political faction, the *Frente da Libertacao de Mocambique* (FRELIMO), was created by Dr. Eduardo Mondlane. Its headquarters was also in Tanzania. In addition there were a large number of local groups operating generally in northern Mozambique which were not directly affiliated with either liberation party. FRELIMO claimed by 1965 to have 9,000 members inside Mozambique and they have had approximately 500 men in training in Tanzania. FRELIMO was affiliated with other freedom groups operating in Portuguese territories which were opposed to Holden Roberto's party in Angola. This loose association was called the Conference of Nationalist Organizations of Portuguese Colonies (CONCP). The OAU has made clear its sympathies with the African revolutionaries.

Portugal replied to this increasing guerrilla activity by enlarging substantially the garrisons in Mozambique and building new forts throughout the border areas. President Tomas on a state visit in 1965 reviewed over 5,000 troops in Lourenço Marques and reiterated Portugal's intention to maintain itself in East Africa. Portugal has continued to send white settlers into reclaimed agricultural areas throughout Mozambique. The largest of these was the Limpopo *colonato* composed of thirteen villages northwest of Lourenço Marques. Since 1954 over 2,000 families have been settled there. A 2,100 foot dam was built on the Limpopo River and thirteen irrigation canals now carry water to the 30,000 acres of the *colonato*. The project by 1965 had cost Portugal almost $40,000,000. Lourenço Marques and Beira reflected the prosperity not only of Mozambique, but also of Rhodesia and the Republic of South Africa. The bulk of Rhodesian goods passes through Mozambique as well as much of the equipment for the mines of the Transvaal.

Portugal's resolve to hold Mozambique has been aided by dissension among the various African nationalist groups. UDENAMO and FRELIMO leaders have often been jealous of one another and, therefore, there has never been a unified command of the guerrilla activities in Mozambique.

Nor does it appear that the organization of the peoples of northern Mozambique has been very effective. These factors were most important for the Portuguese before they could shift large numbers of troops from Angola. The task of holding Mozambique against an effective coordinated African revolt is tremendous. The size of the territory alone makes policing difficult: Mozambique is larger than the state of Texas. Other strategic difficulties relate to the long coastline of Mozambique and the Malawi salient thrust into the heart of the northern area. There are over 700 miles of mountainous bush area along the border with Malawi.

Recognizing the vulnerability of Mozambique, Portugal strengthened its garrisons, particularly in the northern sector. According to reports, there were between 20,000 and 25,000 troops in this area in 1965. In addition, Portugal has constructed five new airfields in the north and there was a considerable number of all types of planes at these stations. A new military road between Palma and Mueda was also constructed. Guerrilla activity was especially strong in the areas immediately adjacent to the Tanzanian and part of the Malawi borders. However, by the end of 1964, Portuguese troop activity and massive arrests had considerably lessened the dangers to Portuguese control. In the summer and fall of 1964, nearly 7,000 refugees crossed the Ruvuma River from Mozambique into Tanzania. The long-expected contest of strength between the rebels and the Portuguese began in early 1965 in Mozambique. Dr. Mondlane at the OAU meeting at Accra in 1965 admitted that the activities of FRELIMO within Mozambique were accelerated during the year. Despite his optimistic statements, the year ended with FRELIMO forces restricted to smaller areas and, because of the divisions within, the freedom movements were forced to assume the defensive.

Portuguese Guinea

Portuguese Guinea, with a population of slightly over one-half million, is the smallest of the Portuguese possessions in Africa. In its 14,000 square miles are numerous tribes, many with warlike histories, and some such as the Puels were only recently subdued by the Portuguese army. It is a poor area producing chiefly agricultural products such as rice, peanuts, palm oil, and timber. Until recently it was considered one of the small, sleepy backwaters of Africa. Since mid-1962, however, the nationalist revolt against Portuguese authoritarianism has wracked the Guinea interior.

Before 1962 Portuguese Guinea was ruled by an appointed governor-general who implemented the decisions made in Lisbon by the council of ministers and the overseas ministers. The assimilado policy was followed as were all the other facets of Portuguese rule in Africa. The distinction can be made, however, that the harsh rule so typical in southern Mozambique and Angola was not in as much evidence in Guinea. Another noticeable difference was the smaller number of Europeans resident in the territory. The educational system can be evaluated by the fact that in 1962 there was only one secondary school in the territory with an enrollment of less than 300 students. There was no framework through which Africans could hope to gain any voice in the government. Thus the African political organizations of Portuguese Guinea were organized outside of the territory as clandestine revolutionary organizations.

A number of different nationalist groups claimed to represent the aspirations of the Africans of Portuguese Guinea. The first and most powerful of these organizations was the *Parti Africana Independencia para Guinea e Cabo Verd* (PAIGC). The nucleus of this group was composed of colonial students who in the mid-1950s began to plan for independence for Portuguese Guinea. The organization of PAIGC was correlate with those organizations formed for the liberation of Angola. The leader of PAIGC was Amilcar Cabral, a native of the Cape Verde Islands. He is quite well-educated since there was no native statute in Cape Verde to restrict African education.

Two smaller nationalist movements were the *Frente Libertacao para Independencia Nacional de Guinea* (FLING) and *Uniao Nacional de Guinea Portuguesas* (UNGP). The former had its headquarters in Dakar and was led by Francisco Mendy and Enrique Labery. The UNGP is an even smaller group whose leader was a mulatto, Benjamin Pinto Bull. Bull's brother was appointed administrative secretary-general of the colony in 1963. The UNGP is a party which tries to compromise between the extreme positions of the inflexible Portuguese and the more radical nationalists. It has practically no popular support.

The first signs of revolt in Guinea occurred in 1959 when a strike for higher wages began in the small capital city of Bissau. The police reacted violently and a number of African workers were killed. An intangible but certainly a key factor in the organization of the nationalist movement in Portuguese Guinea was the granting of independence to neighboring Senegal and Guinea. In the early 1960s, it was apparent that even tiny Gambia was being groomed for independence. To nationalist leaders the only way which seemed open to them to achieve the same ends for Portuguese Guinea was a resort to arms. The uprising in Portuguese Guinea was almost entirely the work of the PAIGC. This organization's headquarters was located in the Republic of Guinea. From there the guerrilla leaders infiltrated southern Portuguese Guinea in an area where there is an extensive network of waterways and which is densely forested. The revolt, which began in June 1962, was based upon the grievances and aspirations of native farmers. Aid was initially supplied primarily by Guinea. The nationalist revolutionaries in the south also received some aid from Algeria, Ghana, and Morocco. At a later date the revolt spread to the northern area which borders on Senegal. Raiders moving across the Senegalese border and utilizing native support did considerable damage. In both the north and the south the terrain was such that the Portuguese forces were at a disadvantage. The guerrilla nationalists knew the areas perfectly and could operate with freedom, totally supported by the African population.

Portugal followed the same procedures in dealing with the crisis in Guinea as was used in Angola and Mozambique. The small garrison of sleepy Guinea soon belonged to the past. With some 10,000 troops operating in the territory by 1965, the Salazar government showed its intention of holding the territory by force. The PAIGC claimed to have over 4,000 guerrillas operating throughout Guinea. They had shifted their activities to the northwestern part of the country, and by the end of 1965 the rebels had pinned down most of the Portuguese troops in Bissau and the other urban centers. The measure of the success of Cabral's guerrillas can be seen in the admission of the Portuguese defense minister in 1963 that the rebels controlled fifteen percent of the territory. The area, dominated by the guerrillas two years later, had been enlarged to over forty percent of the country. The major unanswered question relating to the revolt concerned the ability of the PAIGC to maintain control over its guerrilla forces and thus force Portugal to extend itself beyond reasonable limits to control an unprofitable colony. Another question on the political level which was not resolved was the quarrel between PAIGC and FLING for recognition by the OAU as the recognized revolutionary government of Portuguese Guinea.

FOURTEEN

Supranational organizations

Nowhere is theory and reality of action more at variance than in the different supranational organizations which have recently been constructed in Africa. An observer must carefully weigh statements concerning unity and cooperation made by heads of state or those which are released from conferences of African leaders. These pronouncements normally represented aspirations and took little account of the difficulties of achieving these ends. The most obvious example of this dichotomy is Pan Africanism. Almost every leader in Africa committed himself to the furtherance of the principle of greater unity. However, the realization of even the first steps toward the goal proved to be more difficult than at first envisioned. A further complication arises in attempting to assign reasons for failures. For example, how far are the failures of the *Conseil de l'Entente* or the Union of African States to achieve closer unity among the states directly attributable to the actual difficulties of union and how much simply to the reluctance of political leaders to surrender their own power to a larger association?

On the level of the practical, all of the political associations before the creation of the Organization of African Unity were failures. This sweeping statement is not meant to negate the intangible contributions made by statesmen of Africa meeting together and discussing common problems. However, on the wider plane of establishing viable administrative mechanisms to put into practice the theories of the various organizations, no other verdict can be given. The economic committees established by the various organizations did not really establish policies which limit or direct economic planning and development in the member states. Some of the organizations had a defense council designed to coordinate planning for the group. Strategic and logistical problems prevented any real implementation of a joint military policy. Even the much heralded announcement by the OAU of a boycott of South African goods was largely window dressing since some African states such as Malawi depend too much on South African manufactured products.

It would be presumptuous to dismiss the various movements for larger groupings as a waste of time. Slowly many of the petty differences which have separated the various blocs in Africa have been bridged and, for all its immediate impotence, the nucleus of an organization of African states was created. It would have been unreasonable to expect that African states in little more than five years would have been able to achieve a fully functioning political and economic unity. That they progressed so far, even in theory, augurs well for future development. The real power of any supranational organization in Africa rests not with that organization but with the separate national entities that comprise it. Thus even the OAU, for all of the fanfare surrounding its creation, will succeed or fail on the willingness of the separate states to surrender to it a portion of their sovereignty.

There is no way to present the extremely complex events concerned with supranational organizations in any concise integrated fashion. One must look, therefore, at each individual organization and chart its creation, development, and in some cases demise in relative isolation from the maze of sweeping changes occurring throughout Africa which affected that organization.

Conseil de l'Entente

The *Conseil de l'Entente* was a reaction to the original plans to establish the Mali Federation which was to include Senegal, Soudan, Upper Volta, and Dahomey. The governments of France and the Ivory Coast brought economic pressure to bear upon Upper Volta and Dahomey. France intimated that it might reconsider building new facilities at the harbor of Cotonou. The rich Ivory Coast hinted at economic sanctions, particularly against Upper Volta, if the Mali constitution was adopted. Not surprisingly, the two weaker states revised their previous commitment and chose to continue their economic association with the Ivory Coast. Upper Volta was the first to defect from the proposed federation. Then Dahomey, which depended greatly on its position as the outlet for trade for landlocked Upper Volta and Niger, soon removed itself from its commitment to Mali.

In April 1959, an agreement was reached between the Ivory Coast and Upper Volta which served as the basis of the *Conseil de l'Entente* or, as it is sometimes called, the Benin Union. This agreement guaranteed that the harbor of Abidjan would be utilized in common and the main railway from Abidjan north would be jointly used. Further, a customs union was created to regulate customs and taxes, a common system of road transport was established, and in time it was planned that there was to be common postal service. In addition, the Entente was to regulate affairs common to the states. A *Fonds de Solidarité* was established to aid in development of the two territories.

By the end of May 1959, Dahomey and Niger had joined the *Conseil* and further discussions had evolved basic agreements on civil service, labor, justice, and finance. These agreements were further elaborated upon after long negotiations by resolutions signed, in April 1961, by the premiers of the four states. Continuing disturbances in Dahomey created in 1964 strains on its friendship with other Entente states. By the end of the year Dahomey had been phased out of the activities of the union. Therefore the decisions by the heads of state in December 1964 to establish "dual nationality" applied only to the Ivory Coast, Niger, and Upper Volta. Houphouët-Boigny, Diori, and Yameogo stated that this was the first step in a long-range program to effect a "fusion" of the three areas. In 1965 Houphouët-Boigny utilized the Entente to oppose Ghana and the OAU summit meeting called in October. Each of the members with four other ex-French areas refused to attend the conference and thus focused attention upon the dual role which Ghana was attempting to play.

The development of the Entente to the point where it could act as a working model for other African states was hampered by two interrelated factors. One was the disparity in wealth between the rich Ivory Coast and its poorer northern neighbors. To make the association meaningful, the Ivory Coast would have to bear the major cost of financing the further development of these areas. Not only Premier Houphouët-Boigny, but also powerful factions within the Ivory Coast, did not wish to see their wealth expended for the benefit of other areas. Certainly one of the factors which made the Ivory Coast leaders adverse to keeping, in effect, modified federal mechanisms of the AOF was the feeling that the Ivory Coast had been drained in the past to support the poorer members of the French African empire.

The second reason for the nullification of the Conseil as an effective federation was the attitude of Premier Houphouët-Boigny. For a variety of reasons he opposed political federalism as a solution to African problems. He viewed the Pan African movement as being effective in removing economic barriers and building understanding between African national leaders. He had always opposed political amalgamation as an effective solution to African ills. The Ivory Coast would gain little advantage by merging politically with even its immediate neighbors. Economic liabilities to the Ivory Coast would join the political by creating a larger, less homogeneous, less stable state. The Conseil, by achieving the modest ends Houphouët-Boigny set for it, created more harmonious conditions between the states and their ten million people. Within this existing framework the Ivory Coast could lead by influence without further political commitments. Correlate with the Ivory Coast's reluctance to strengthen federal ties was the development of larger, equally loose associations such as the Afro-Malagasy Union and the Organization of African States. These attempts to meet common problems is a way which agrees with Houphouët-Boigny's philosophy and renders relatively unimportant regional agreements such as that of the Conseil which sought to do the same.

Ghana-Guinea-Mali Union (Union of African States)

The Ghana-Guinea Union, which was born in 1959 and expanded to include Mali in July 1961, was in practice no union. It came into existence in the aftermath of Guinea's No vote to the de Gaulle referendum of 1958. The immediate, almost total withdrawal of French technicians and aid left Guinea in a desperate situation. Under Nkrumah, Ghana was attempting to extend its influence and philosophies throughout West Africa. The situation was tailored for some type of rapprochement. Ghana offered a loan of £10,000,000 which along with credits and aid from elsewhere enabled Guinea to survive the first troubled months of its independence. In May 1959, discussions between Kwame Nkrumah and Sekou Touré resulted in the union. In November 1960, soon after the breakup of the Mali Federation, Nkrumah announced, following discussions with Modibo Keita of Mali, that Ghana would grant Mali a long-term loan. He also stated that Ghana and Mali would establish a political association. The expanded union was formally created in July 1961, after a declaration of joint purpose had been issued in December 1960. Again the catalyst had been Ghanaian money and Nkrumah's desire to create an effective political entity which would forward his ideals of African unity.

The declarations of 1959 and 1960 had been framed in general terms. The major purpose was to "establish a union of our three states." Details of this amalgamation were not mentioned; instead the 1960 statement established two special committees to study "practical methods for achieving objectives." Various proposals which would have created a standard currency were never implemented. Neither was the plan to have a resident minister from each country serve in the ministry of the other states put into effect. Practically speaking, the union had little effect upon the internal policies of any of the states. This inaction represented a setback for Nkrumah who attempted through 1961 to follow a Pan African policy that would lead to an actual federation of states. Thus the Union of African States (UAS) was little more effective than the *Conseil de l'Entente* created by Houphouët-Boigny who had never favored political integration.

Yet the UAS was not a complete failure. The presidents of the three states consulted together a number of times on matters of common interest. The UAS created a spirit of cooperation between the countries which was most notable in the united front presented on nonalignment. In general, Nkrumah, Keita, and Touré were in agreement on foreign affairs. There were noticeable exceptions to this such as the Congo where Nkrumah's policies clashed with those of the more militant Touré. Given the differences in language, culture, and general economic and social problems, it was unrealistic to believe that a real political union could be quickly achieved.

Whatever intangible value the association might have had was lessened considerably by the rapprochement between Mali and Senegal and the creation of the OAU. The final blow to the union as a potentially effective organization was the revolt in Ghana which deposed Nkrumah. The new military government of Ghana began immediately to follow policies which mitigated against the continuance of the union. Perhaps the last feeble act of the organization was the token appointment of Nkrumah as an honorary president of Guinea in early 1966.

Union Africaine et Malagache (UAM) and successors

Most durable of all the supranational organizations were the associations of independent states which had been former French colonies. This is not surprising since there had existed before independence a large degree of geographic contiguity and economic interdependence. With rare exceptions the leaders of these states tended toward moderate policies, both in foreign and domestic affairs, and they remained on good terms with France. French investment and loans for many of the poorer areas allowed them to continue to maintain services that otherwise would have been impossible. The name of the organization representing the ex-French states has changed four times since 1960 and the functions have changed accordingly. However, the degree of cooperation represented has remained fairly constant.

In October 1960, twelve African states acting on the request of the Ivory Coast met in Abidjan. The primary reason for the meeting was to explore ways by which these states, all of which had previously been a part of the French colonial empire, could act as mediators in the Algerian crisis. This initial meeting was followed by another at Brazzaville in December 1960, where it was decided to establish a more permanent organization. The Brazzaville declaration called for a quick solution to the Algerian problem while it reiterated the continuing friendship of the states with France. The declaration made clear the states' sympathy with the FLN and its objective of an independent Algeria. It also stated the support of the signatories for Mauritanian independence and their backing of the United Nations in its attempts to solve the Congo problem.

The declaration provided for a meeting of a representative commission to study the problem of establishing closer economic ties between the states involved. In January 1961, the commission met in Dakar and formed the *Organization Africaine et Malagache Coopération Économique* (OAMCE). It was primarily an economic organization which was designed to coordinate economic policies relating to industry, agriculture, and interstate trade. This establishment led to the creation of Air Afrique, an airline composed of the total aviation resources of the member states and a joint defense command. In March 1961, the charter of the *Union Africaine et Malagache* (UAM) was signed by the heads of state. The association provided for close cooperation between the governments involved and twice-yearly meetings between the heads of state. A permanent secretariat was established at Cotonou to be run by a secretary-general.

Partially as a reaction to the Casablanca Conference, invitations were sent out to all African states in May 1961 to convene for a general conference at Monrovia, Liberia. Of the twenty states attending, twelve were from the UAM. The Monrovia Conference declared for a unity of aspiration attempting to work toward African solidarity based on the realities of the African situation. Thus other African polities represented at Monrovia accepted the principle behind the UAM of not trying to create immediate political unification.

With the addition of Rwanda and later Togo in July 1963, the UAM consisted of fourteen states. Due to the unity of language and culture as well as the nonpolitical approach toward greater unity, the UAM became the best organized of all African supranational groups. It was far more successful and pragmatic than the Casablanca group and, due to its loose political nature, it could associate freely with regional organizations such as the Conseil de l'Entente and take part in wider discussions such as the Monrovia meeting.

By early 1963, many of the differences which separated the so-called Casablanca group from the Monrovia bloc were healed. The relations between Nigeria and Guinea had improved, Senegal and Mali had settled their differences, and the hostility between Ghana and Togo was no longer a bar. In May 1963, all independent African states met at Addis Ababa. This conference resulted in a rapprochement between the two previously hostile blocs and led to a series of important declarations. The Addis Ababa meeting established the framework of the Organization of African Unity (OAU). Many of the duties envisioned by this new organization duplicated those already functioning in the UAM.

It thus became apparent, although the UAM was not to be phased out immediately, that there would have to be major changes if the fourteen member states were serious about the development of OAU. Many of the most important political and permanent officials of the UAM in the summer of 1963 seemed to favor a shift away from the UAM. Two such officials were President Yameogo of Upper Volta and President Senghor of Senegal. In March 1964, at the end of the meeting of the heads of state of the UAM in Dakar, it was announced that the UAM was to be transformed. The new organization was to be called the Union Africaine et Malagache Coopération Économique (UAMCE). This was but a return to the limited aims of the original states when in 1960 they had created the OAMCE. President Tsiranana of the Malagasy Republic stated that this move would "facilitate stronger links with Mali and Guinea" and would be a "far reaching step toward African unity." There were no further meetings of the heads of state of the UAMCE in 1964. The session planned for December was postponed until the spring of 1965. However, 1964 was the year of increasing cooperation between French African leaders, even those who had previously belonged to the more radical group. The Mali-Senegal rapport was made effective and relations between Senegal and the Ivory Coast improved.

In early 1965, the name of the organization was again changed, although ostensibly its functions remained basically the same. The new title was the Organization Common Africaine et Malagache (OCAM). The OCAM, although conceived to be primarily an economic organization, retained considerable residual political power. This was shown by the position taken by a majority of the OCAM states toward the OAU summit meeting at Accra in October 1965. Houphouët-Boigny of the Ivory Coast began his campaign in the spring to boycott the meeting unless Ghana was willing to change its aggressive attitude toward its neighbors. At an extraordinary meeting of the heads of state of the OCAM in May, Houphouët-Boigny's views prevailed and eight members of the organization did refuse to attend the OAU conference. However, this issue and that of the relationship of Congo-Léopoldville to the OCAM sharply divided the members. At the May 1965 meeting, only eight presidents were in attendance. Two other states sent observers. The president of the OCAM, Moktar Ould Daddah of Mauritania, was one of the statesmen who did not appear. He, particularly, opposed any rapproachement with the Kasavubu-Tshombe regime in the Congo and was also hostile to Houphouët-Boigny's attitudes toward the OAU. The triumph of Houphouët-Boigny in the OCAM did aid in keeping the Accra meeting from becoming a triumph for Nkrumah. However, it resulted in the resignation later of Mauritania from the OCAM.

The developments in 1965 showed how potentially powerful the OCAM was as the largest, best-organized economic and political bloc in Africa. At that time Houphouët-Boigny and the Entente group effectively controlled the OCAM, largely because the other leaders of French Africa tended to think and act in the same moderate way as the leader of the Ivory Coast.

The Casablanca group

The Brazzaville Conference in December 1960 acted as a catalyst for those African powers which followed a more activist line toward the West and its supposed neocolonialism. The Congo situation served to isolate these states from the majority of the African states in the United Nations. Supporting the Lumumbist position in the Congo was only one of the reasons why these nations drew together after Brazzaville. Morocco, which had an outstanding quarrel with Mauritania, fearing the results of the Brazzaville group's sponsorship of Mauritania, issued invitations to a select number of states whose foreign policies paralleled its own. This call resulted in the convening of the Casablanca Conference in January 1961. Seven African states attended the conference. These were Morocco, Guinea, Ghana, Mali, the United Arab Republic, Libya, and the Algerian provisional government. In addition, Ceylon was represented at the conference.

The Casablanca meeting necessitated a number of compromises on the part of the attending powers. Morocco was primarily concerned with non-recognition of Mauritania. Three of the other states, Ghana, Algeria, and Libya, for the sake of greater unity, abandoned their previous positions and supported Morocco's claims on Mauritania. The Congo crisis was another heated issue. Most of the states were in favor of withdrawing all their troops from the United Nations' command. Further, they were in favor of open aid to the Stanleyville government of Antoine Gizenga. Only Nkrumah opposed these proposals. In the end a communique was issued which stated in general terms the position of the powers. However, the last paragraph of the communique which reserved the right for each state to take appropriate action if the United Nations did not heed their advice showed that Nkrumah had won his point. Having won on that issue, Ghana relented and supported the United Arab Republic-sponsored resolution again Israel. This was the first time that a group of African states had taken a firm position of record on the Israeli-Arab conflict.

Following the January 1961 meeting, a further conference of the foreign ministers of the Casablanca states met in Cairo in May. There the basic agreements reached at Casablanca were incorporated into a charter. This created the executive machinery of the new union. It established four committees—political, economic, defense, and cultural. The political committee was made up of the heads of state, the economic was composed of the finance ministers of each state, and the defense committee was made up of the chiefs of staff of the armies of the member states. A permanent secretariat was established, located at Bamako, Mali.

Despite the specific statements and commitments to action made by the Casablanca and Cairo conferences, the association proved less durable and homogeneous in its organization than the Brazzaville group. The first major defection from the ostensibly solid front of January 1961 was the refusal of Libya to sign the protocol in May. Four of the original seven African states in the group were northern states with their focus of interest in the Islamic world of the Middle East and only secondarily in sub-Saharan Africa. Although there was a broad area of agreement on nonalignment and the dangers of the new imperialism between the states, there was from the beginning a tacit conflict between the United Arab Republic and Ghana. The three powers most involved in the Casablanca experiment were the nations of the Union of African States—Ghana, Guinea, and Mali. The Casablanca group did not take part in the Monrovia Conference or the follow-up Lagos meeting and seemed to be going contrary to the expressed wishes of the majority of African nations. In retrospect, these differences were more apparent than real. The primary aim of President Nkrumah for some type of immediate real political union had proved illusory; even the Casablanca protocol did not provide for this. Thus after 1961, the major differences between the Casablanca group and the Brazzaville group concerned means, not ends. National and individual rivalries tended to obscure this fact.

Improved relations between Nigeria and Guinea, Mali and Senegal, Ghana and Togo, and even Morocco and Mauritania made possible the rapprochement between the two groups which took place in May 1963 at the Addis Ababa Conference. The Addis Ababa summit meeting which established the OAU ended the Casablanca and Monrovia blocs although the UAM was not disbanded as a political organization until March 1964.

Organization of African Unity (OAU)

The new African states in the period 1960–1963 attempted a compromise between nationalism and Pan Africanism. If their independence was to be permanent and meaningful it was necessary for political leaders in all states to create a sense of nationalism in their people. The synthetic boundaries drawn by European powers in the scramble for Africa had to be accepted as the limits of the new nation states. Tribal and traditional loyalties had to be minimized and the state substituted as the entity which claimed the first loyalty of the citizens. In order to achieve this end, strong central governments were established, usually of the one-party type. Economic and social progress was demanded by the people. To satisfy the real needs of the people as well as their aspirations, the politicians had to foster a sense of particularism. Opposing such nationalism were the claims made by all African leaders that they desired a united Africa. They saw Africa as a whole with all states having common internal problems, all with a heritage of colonialism, and all wishing to avoid the pitfalls of the cold war. Despite the many statements by African leaders favoring Pan Africanism, the solutions to their national problems took precedence over general African or even regional solutions. This led many observers to conclude that Africans, despite their pronouncements, were not overly concerned with African unity.

Reinforcing the apparent disunity of Africa was the rivalry between differing cultural blocs and political personalities. Differential occupation by the French, British, and Belgians for over sixty years had imposed two languages and three sets of institutions on Africa which acted as a major block to any plans for immediate political union. In the period after 1957 there emerged a number of African leaders who were jealous of their new-found prerogatives, each seeking regional or African unity on his terms. Such varied personalities as Nkrumah of Ghana, Senghor of Senegal, Touré of Guinea, Houphouët-Boigny of the Ivory Coast, Balewa of Nigeria, and Nasser of Egypt had their own solutions to African unity. Inevitably the plans formulated by such African leaders clashed. These differences were institutionalized in the formation of a number of hostile organizations such as the Ghana-Guinea-Mali Union, the *Conseil de l'Entente*, and most important, the Casablanca and the Brazzaville blocs. Although generalizations must be made with caution, one can say that the differences between these blocs concerned means and not ends. The Brazzaville (later Monrovia) bloc wanted to build toward possible political unity by rationalizing those divisive elements which could effectively be dealt with immediately. The Brazzaville group attempted economic solutions and, building on a base of common institutions, sought to create a spirit of unity. The Casablanca powers did not have these common institutions and tended to be more radical in their pronouncements of non-alignment and anti-imperialism. The Casablanca group in the statements of their leaders favored steps toward immediate political unity. From 1961 onward, however, both groups began to realize that the ends of African unity were ultimately the same. This awareness led to a conference of delegates from all the independent African nations, with the exception of Togo, at Addis Ababa in May 1963. This meeting resulted in the abolition of the Casablanca and Monrovia blocs and the creation of the Organization of African Unity (OAU).

The speeches of the heads of state at Addis Ababa reflected a newfound maturity. Different though they were, most of the speeches pressed for a charter to define the areas of agreement, an organization to work for the realization of African unity, and a body which would organize efforts to drive the last vestiges of imperialism from Africa. Although there was a recognition of areas of conflict between African states, such as Somalia's claims to Ethiopian and Kenya territory, the stress was upon unity. This spirit of cooperation resulted in the charter which established the OAU.

The charter, later ratified by all independent African states, provided for an assembly of the heads of state, a council of ministers, a general secretariat, and a commission of mediation, conciliation, and arbitration. The assembly of the heads of state or their representatives was to meet at least once a year. The council of ministers was composed of the foreign ministers of the individual states or their representatives. This council was charged with preparing the agenda for the assembly conferences, investigating matters referred to it, implementing decisions of the assembly, and coordinating policies leading to inter-African cooperation. The council of ministers was to meet at least twice a year. The secretariat was under the direction of a secretary-general and was charged with carrying out the administration of the organization. Members of the secretariat were not controlled by one state and received orders only from the organization. All member states were pledged to avoid violence in settling any dispute with another member state. It was the duty of the commission on mediation, conciliation, and arbitration to solve questions involving conflicts between states.

The budget for the organization was prepared by the secretariat and approved by the council of ministers. Contributions from member states were based upon the rate of assessment made by the United Nations. No state was to be charged with over twenty percent of the total yearly budget. In addition to the major subdivisions of the organization, specialized commissions were to be established under the direction of the assembly. These regular commissions covered the areas of defense, health, economics, nutrition, and science and research.

Aside from the establishment of the framework of a general African organization, the most important pronouncement of the Addis Ababa Conference of 1963 concerned South Africa, Rhodesia, and Portugal. The conference urged decolonization of the remaining parts of Africa still controlled by European powers. It urged the United Kingdom to prevent the "white settler" minority from consolidating its power in Southern Rhodesia and promised aid to the nationalist leaders there in securing African political rights. Apartheid in South Africa was condemned and the states pledged themselves to oppose this system through direct aid to nationalists, through mobilization of world opinion in the United Nations, and through a boycott of trade with South Africa. These same forms of opposition were to be applied to Portuguese imperialism in Guinea, Angola, and Mozambique. The heads of state recommended the breaking of diplomatic relations between African states and Portugal and South

Africa. However, a number of states such as Malawi and Zambia later showed a decided coolness toward any such action because of the adverse economic effect it would have on them.

The organization established a coordinating committee with headquarters at Dar-es-Salaam to help national liberation movements. A liberation fund was established to aid the freedom fighters and all states promised to help train volunteers for the national liberation movements. The year following showed how difficult it was to translate these ideals into concerted action.

The second summit meeting of the OAU took place in Cairo in mid-July 1964. After a week of deliberation which had been preceded by conferences of the foreign ministers, the heads of state made a few important announcements. The permanent site of OAU headquarters was established at Addis Ababa. M. Diallo Telli of Guinea was appointed to a four-year term as secretary-general. His position was not defined in terms other than the administrative ones already outlined in the charter. Reluctance to give him more political responsibility to act in urgent cases stemmed from fear of concentrating theoretical power in the hands of the representative of a supranational organization.

There were few concrete successes to report to the heads of state. The dispute between Algeria and Morocco was settled. Little was said of the Kenya-Ethiopia-Somalia dispute except to promise that it would be the subject of special study. Later Somalia announced that it would not be bound by any decisions made by the OAU in respect to her borders. Two functional committees were established, one of which was to coordinate activities of the African states in applying sanctions against South Africa.

Illustrating the wide divergence of opinion among OAU members were the four days of speeches by the heads of state. President Nkrumah of Ghana was particularly critical of the work of the liberation committee in putting into effect any real help for those Africans struggling for freedom. President Nyerere of Tanzania was equally critical of Ghana's attitude of preaching unity but refusing to help the liberation committee.

Perhaps the major failure of the Cairo meeting was their reluctance to deal with the Congo crisis. Moise Tshombe had been appointed premier of the Congo three days before the heads of state were due to arrive in Cairo. The foreign ministers cabled President Kasavubu requesting that Tshombe not come to Cairo. Thus the premier of the most troubled area in Africa was not present. This was more than symbolic; it was an actual rejection of the Congo and undercut the OAU's later position against foreign intervention. If Tshombe was not even to be invited to present the problems of his state, then the OAU was not really the organization it claimed to be.

In September the OAU appointed a ten-member commission headed by President Kenyatta of Kenya to attempt a reconciliation of the warring factions in the Congo. After interviewing rebel leaders, some of the commission members called upon Tshombe to stop receiving outside aid. A delegation flew to the United States to protest to President Johnson any further aid to the Congo. President Kasavubu protested this action by commission members, claiming he was not consulted and the delegation was, therefore, not received by President Johnson. The Kenyatta commission was kept in force after the foreign ministers' meeting in March 1965, although it had accomplished little and its report had been rejected by Tshombe. The commission did more harm to the image of the OAU than would have been the case if they had not acted at all. Not only did they focus world attention on the weakness of the OAU to act decisively, but the commission acted as a focal point for the expression of wide differences of opinion within the OAU itself.

However, in certain areas the OAU was successful. One of its commissions had played a most important role in the resettlement of over 100,000 Watutsi who had fled Rwanda. The Algeria-Morocco border dispute was temporarily settled. The organization acted as a base for a number of bilateral and multilateral groupings concerned with such matters as riverine agreements. The liberation committee still functioned although beset with a host of problems brought on by the fragmentation of resistance movements. Perhaps the one action of the OAU in early 1965 which could have the most far-reaching effects was the establishment of the African Development Bank. By the spring of 1965, $32,000,000 of the initial capitalization of $250,000,000 had been subscribed from African sources.

Despite all of these positive actions, the OAU was deeply divided. At the conference of foreign ministers in Nairobi in March and in the months immediately following, most member states were polarized into a pro- or anti-Ghana faction. One of the reasons for this split was differential attitudes toward the problems in the Congo. Even more serious were the charges made by some political leaders that Ghana was actively supporting subversion against the political regimes of other African states. The leader of the anti-Nkrumah group within the OAU was Houphouët-Boigny of the Ivory Coast, solidly backed by the other Entente members. This conflict was magnified by the fact that the 1965 summit meeting was scheduled for Accra.

In May Houphouët-Boigny launched a "Peace Offensive" to gain support in boycotting the Accra meeting until Ghana would promise to stop encouraging exiles from neighboring states in their subversive activities. This maneuver was successful only in those ex-French states which had tended to follow Houphouët-Boigny's leadership in the past. In the months preceding the Accra Conference in October, various proposals were made to have Nkrumah and Houphouët-Boigny meet at a "little summit" and compromise their differences. All of these attempts were unsuccessful. Thus when the third general conference was held, seven states followed Houphouët-Boigny's guide and were not represented. These were the four Entente states and Togo, Chad, and the Malagasy Republic.

Nkrumah had done everything possible to impress the visiting heads of state. Thousands of banners and signs were erected in Accra. The city itself was cleaned thoroughly and the Ghana government had built a special facility to house the delegates. The main building in this complex was a twelve-story building with sixty presidential suites which cost a total of £10,000,000 to construct.

Despite these preparations, the Accra meeting was a general defeat for Nkrumah's policies. He had wanted the conference to create the machinery for an all-African government. The first step in this direction, he believed, should be the formation of an "Executive Council" to give continuing direction to unified political objectives. This proposal was referred to the heads of state for further study. Thus nothing could be done toward creating a stronger executive for at least one year. The Congo was another issue on which Ghana's position was not upheld. President Kasavubu attended the conference and made it clear that he would leave if the Congo question was made an issue. Perhaps because he had just removed Tshombe as premier and perhaps because of his own popularity, the Congo question was not discussed.

Although not represented, Houphouët-Boigny won a substantial victory when the conference, after lengthy debate, passed a strong resolution on subversion. This resolution was directed not only at non-African powers but also at African states which actively condoned movements in their territory designed to overthrow other African governments. This by implication struck directly at Ghana.

The issue which dominated the discussions was Rhodesia and Ian Smith's unilateral declaration of independence. The conference called upon Britain to use whatever steps necessary, including force, to bring down the white Rhodesian government. It also called upon all African states to utilize all their strength to put an end to the present Rhodesian state. In the resolution there was a veiled threat to Britain if the situation in Rhodesia was not immediately rectified. The resolution asked for African states to reappraise their economic, political, and diplomatic relations with Britain if Prime Minister Wilson's government did not act more speedily in ending the Smith regime.

In December 1965, at the foreign ministers' conference in Addis Ababa, the delegates returned to the question of Rhodesia and decided to implement the implied threat to Britain. In essence they delivered an ultimatum to Prime Minister Wilson to end the Rhodesian problem by December 15. If this was not accomplished, then the member states of the OAU would break off relations with Britain. The British government immediately replied that it would not be coerced into any hasty ill-conceived action. The Tunisian and Upper Volta governments repudiated within a few hours the OAU decision. The old Brazzaville bloc of states made no move toward a break in relations. Not even Rhodesia's closest neighbors, Zambia and Malawi, followed the OAU decision.

At the end of 1965, in reappraisal, the three-year existence of the OAU was a stormy one. It achieved certain of its objectives not the least of which was the phasing out of the Brazzaville and Casablanca groups. No matter how weak the OAU appeared or how divided its counsel, it was the only supranational political organ recognized by all African states. However, the OAU failed to achieve the status hoped for at its inception. There were two major reasons for this. One was a reflection of the immaturity of African statesmen. In two major African crisis situations the OAU failed to give constructive leadership. In both the Congo and Rhodesian questions the OAU was given the opportunity to react constructively in solving extremely complex problems. Instead, in each case, the delegates allowed emotion to govern their actions and assumed extreme positions which could not be maintained and which they later were forced to repudiate. The second reason for the continued weakness of the organization is more fundamental. However unpopular Nkrumah might have been, he had analyzed the OAU correctly when he said that it could never become the hoped for, positive force in Africa until its executive power was strengthened. Its ultimate success in securing the goal of Pan Africanism depends upon how much power the individual members are willing to give to the organization.

FIFTEEN

The special case: the Republic of South Africa, 1910–1965

Political developments to 1948

In 1910 the Union of South Africa was still predominantly rural. This was especially true for the Afrikaner people in each of the provinces. Electoral boundaries were drawn to favor the country vote and this was one factor in the initial success of the Afrikaners at the polls. Once in power a Boer-dominated government was not likely to alter the voting districts which helped give it power. This technical fact must be kept in mind in assessing the continued success of Afrikaner-led parties in all the parliamentary elections in the Union. The major area of political conflict for almost fifty years did not concern Africans or Colored. Rather it was a continuation of the old Boer-British contest of the nineteenth century. Two of the chief political leaders, Louis Botha and Jan Christian Smuts, accepted the necessity for Afrikaners to function, in cooperation with the British population, within the context of the empire. Others such as J. B. M. Hertzog, N. C. Havenga, and Daniel Malan rejected the concept of continued cooperation. Their goal was Afrikaner domination of the political life of the Union and as soon as possible an independent republic free from British interference.

Botha and Smuts had created the South African party by blending their old *Het Volk* group with middle-of-the-road British supporters. Until the elections of 1924 this party dominated the political life of the Union. At imperial conferences, Botha and Smuts made clear their dedication to the empire and the necessity to forget the Boer War. During World War I, Union forces conquered German South West Africa and cooperated in the campaigns in East Africa. Botha led the South African army against many of his old comrades such as de Wet and de la Rey in the abortive Afrikaner uprising of 1914.

J. B. M. Hertzog, formerly minister of justice in Botha's first government, had resigned in 1911 to form the Nationalist party which represented the separatist aspirations of Afrikanerdom. He was joined by younger men like Dr. Daniel Malan who began to publish the influential Afrikaans newspaper, *Die Burgher*. So long as Louis Botha was prime minister, the Nationalists could hope for few gains even in the Transvaal. Botha, the stolid Boer figure, was still a great hero to most Afrikaners. With his death in 1919, Smuts became prime minister. Distrusted for his coldness and intellectual bent, "Slim Jannie" could not demand the same loyalty from the Afrikaners. Worsening economic conditions in the Union and Smuts' penchant for violent unilateral action alienated many. The killing in May 1921 of 163 Israelites, African followers of Enoch Mgijima, convinced many British supporters that they could not continue to support Smuts' government. This massacre at Bulhoek was soon followed by the repression of the Bondelswarts Hottentots in South West Africa. These Hottentots were pastoral people who supplemented their cattle tending by hunting. The government, in an obvious attempt to make them settle in one area, assessed a £1 tax per dog owned. The Bondelswarts refused to pay, whereupon in May 1922, Smuts, known to the outside world as one of the architects of the mandate system, sent a column of 400 men and two airplanes against the Hottentots. The resultant loss of life exceeded one hundred and the incident indicated Smuts' readiness to use maximum force against his opposition.

The Rand strike, already referred to, was the final example of Smuts' use of force. However, on the Rand he was dealing with Europeans and his violent methods there alienated the minority Labor party whose support was crucial if Smuts was to continue in power. The elections of 1924 gave the South African party fifty-three seats, the Nationalists sixty-three, and the Labor party eighteen. The Labor party refused to cooperate with Smuts in a coalition government and Hertzog and the Nationalists came to power for the first time. Hertzog was forced to compromise on his promise to create an Afrikaner republic for two reasons. One was the narrowness of his majority in parliament and Labor's opposition to the republican ideal. The other concerned changes then occurring in the institutional structure of the British empire. World War I and the Irish troubles combined with the growing sense of particularistic nationalism had led to granting de facto independent status to Commonwealth countries. Between 1926 and 1931, the leaders of British colonies worked out the details of the British Commonwealth. The Statute of Westminster of 1931 gave the Union of South Africa the best of both worlds—virtual independence with a continuation of the close economic links with Britain. Hertzog felt justified, therefore, in abandoning Afrikaners' dream of a Boer-dominated republic.

Hertzog's Nationalists retained control of parliament after the 1929 elections partially because they openly advocated the stripping of political rights from the Cape Colored. Thus his government was in power during the early, most stringent years of the depression. Undoubtedly the South African party could have utilized the depression to force an election and probably would have won. However, Smuts refused to use economic distress as a political issue and joined with Hertzog in 1933 to form a national government. The two political parties were fused to create the United party. Only a few Afrikaners refused to belong to the coalition and joined with Dr. Malan to form a new purified Nationalist party. Hertzog remained prime minister with Smuts as his deputy until September 1939.

The onset of World War II highlighted the differences between Smuts and his followers and those of Hertzog. Many of the latter group believed that the Union had no concern with Britain's war and wanted to remain neutral. After a lengthy acrimonious debate, Smuts and the interventionists won, South Africa declared war on Germany, the coalition was destroyed, and Smuts once more became prime minister.

Despite the South African army's distinguished record and Smuts' role in international politics, the war was not popular with the majority of the Afrikaner population. A number of Afrikaner organizations had developed in the 1930s such as the Broederbond, the *Afrikaanse Nasionale Studentebond* (ANS), and the *Ossewa Brandweg*. All of these were devoted to Afrikaner nationalism and the securing of more economic and political power for Afrikaners. Many Afrikaner leaders had become enamored of the Nazi message. J. F. J. van Rensburg, Oswold Pirow, and Johannes Vorster actively supported the Germans. Undoubtedly many other Nationalist leaders who were not as active had great sympathy with the ideas enunciated by the Germans.

At the close of the war the poor white Afrikaner of the late 1920s and early 1930s had been better assimilated into the industrial life of the nation. Their leaders had created a series of organizations to give form to Afrikaner ideals and there were more Afrikaans newspapers and periodicals. Many of the younger Boer politicians such as Dr. Hendrik Verwoerd, Johannes Strijdom, C. R. Swart, and Johannes Vorster were weary of attempts to conciliate the British-speaking population. Economic disturbances following the war, a series of strikes by African workers, and a belated recognition of the numbers of Africans in all the cities gave Dr. Malan's party an issue which in the election of 1948 dwarfed all others.

The position of Africans in the Union is discussed elsewhere, but it should be stressed that they had never been a real political issue between any of the white political parties. Dr. Malan, backed by all the Afrikaner organizations, provided with a philosophical and religious rationale by the South African Bureau of Racial Affairs (SABRA), decided to make the threat of African domination the chief issue in the election of 1948. His party for the first time openly enunciated the need for complete separation of the races. The United party was placed on the defensive on this issue and the aging Smuts never regained the initiative in the election. The results of the 1948 elections surprised everyone, including Dr. Malan. Although winning only forty percent of the popular vote, the Nationalist party of Malan won seventy seats and the smaller Afrikaner party of Havenga won nine. The United party could muster only sixty-five seats. In combination with smaller groups, the opposition to the Nationalists had only seventy-four seats. Thus Dr. Malan formed a government with a slim majority of only five seats. His government was pledged to carry out rigorously the campaign promises to establish apartheid as a way of life.

Economic developments, 1910–1948

The Union of South Africa's unique position in Africa is as much characterized by its economy as by its political development based upon European dominance. It was, even before the Boer War, a proto-industrial state. It possessed excellent harbor facilities, railroads, telegraph lines, and a firm financial base closely linked to the great banking houses of Europe. Gold and diamonds were the central features of South African wealth in the late nineteenth century, but diversified farming in row crops, vineyards, and orchards as well as cattle and sheep ranching undergirded the economies of all the provinces of the Union. Milner's reconstruction plans had restored the mining and transport industries of the Transvaal and Orange Free State. Spurred partially by the demands of World War I, South Africa continued its industrialization. In the half century after 1914 the mining industry assumed a greater role in South Africa. Platinum, iron, coal, copper, uranium, and chromate discoveries added to the wealth of an ever-developing gold and diamond industry. South African entrepreneurs were not satisfied with only an extractive economy. Smelters and fabrication plants were developed, the chemical industry begun, and food and packaging plants started. All these called for a myriad of service industries.

After 1910 the Union of South Africa was all but independent of British political control. Even the areas of political dependence were eliminated by the Statute of Westminster passed by the British parliament in December 1931. Thus the political system of South Africa, contrary to other British African territories, was vitally concerned with the rapid economic development of the country. There was a close relationship between government at all levels and business and banking interests.

The complex evolvement of each major industry in South Africa is beyond the scope of this work. It is sufficient to note that, by the time of the crucial election of 1948, it was an industrial and urban state. The seeming insatiable demands of the mines for more labor were early duplicated by other industries in centers such as Cape Town, Johannesburg, and Durban. Hundreds of thousands of Africans permanently left their home areas and became residents of the sprawling, unplanned towns which sprang up near every city. In the fifteen-year period following World War I, there was a mass exodus of Afrikaners from the farms to the cities. By 1936 almost forty-five percent of South Africa's population was resident in nine major cities. The poor unskilled white in the city, predominantly Afrikaners, came more into direct competition with the black laborer and this reinforced the earlier exclusivist attitudes of the white labor unions.

Although South African industry is highly diverse, the gold mining industry was the bellwether of the economy. Its position as the first support of the economy has waned in the period after World War II, but South Africa in 1969 still produced eighty percent of the world's gold. The historian C. W. de Kewiet reported that in the year 1935–1936, 26.95 percent of the entire government revenue of the Union was derived from the mining industry. Therefore, a brief survey of that industry is necessary to understand modern South Africa. The low quality of the ore of the Witwatersrand early dictated large-scale operations which, to be successful, had to utilize the most modern techniques available. Each producing mine needed in addition large amounts of cheap labor. Even before 1914 competition between mines was kept at a minimum by rationalizing common services. The Chamber of Mines through a series of offices provided a common approach not only to purchases and labor but also to medical research, health conditions, mining regulations, and taxation. A subsidiary of the chamber, the Native Recruiting Corporation, provides the bulk of native workers for all the mines, thus eliminating possible wage inflation. By utilizing this common approach and the latest in techniques and machinery, the productivity of an average African miner was raised from 500 tons per worker a year in 1914 to 1,600 tons a year in 1930. At the same time the cost per ton of the ore milled was reduced from approximately twenty-nine shillings to less than twenty shillings.

Labor had always been a critical problem. Most of the European miners who had held all the skilled and most of the semiskilled positions had left during the Boer War. There was not an adequate number of Africans trained in mining techniques available. The high commissioner, Lord Milner, in order to rapidly restore the mining industry, had imported Chinese workers. By 1907 there were 54,000 Chinese laborers in the Transvaal. Within a short time this policy was dispensed with and the mine operators began to use Africans for most of the unskilled work. Contract laborers were recruited from every nation and tribe in the Union. As industry expanded, Africans from Rhodesia and Basutoland also migrated to the Union to work in the mines. In 1901 and 1910, agreements were signed with the Portuguese for the importation of a maximum of 80,000 African workers per year from their territories. White miners were also used in unskilled as well as skilled positions, although they were from the beginning paid more for their work than Africans. The bulk of white miners before 1918 were of British origin. However, in the 1920s, Afrikaners began to be important in the European sector.

Tension developed very early between the mine owners and white workers. Needing cheap labor to reduce overhead, the mine owners were in favor of employing Africans through at least the level of semiskilled positions. White workers insisted not only upon higher pay for the same job but also that certain vocations be reserved exclusively for them. The government, despite its dependence upon the mines for working capital, has continually supported the concept of the color bar for certain occupations. The Mine and Works Act of 1911 was the first Union law to enshrine the concept that certain occupations were reserved for Europeans. This law was upset by the Supreme Court in 1923, but the industry continued to apply its principles until a new, more comprehensive act was passed. The Mines and Works Act of 1926 was Prime Minister Hertzog's way of paying off labor for its support after the election of 1924. Taken together with the Apprenticeship Act of 1922 which closed many occupations to potential African trainees, the new mines act gave white workers the special treatment which they demanded.

The Mines and Workers Act of 1926, with other mechanisms of control over white labor such as the Industrial Conciliation Acts, made the white unions in the 1930s a respectable part of the industrial scene. This had not always been the case. The first trade unions in southern Africa were modeled upon their British counterparts and in general were led by radicals. Syndicalism, the radical tradition, and after 1917, Communism propelled the early white unions toward direct action against their masters. The strikes on the Rand in 1913–1914 which spread to influence other workers were violent and the Botha government used police and troops to break the walkout. Better wages, better health facilities, and safety improvements were all delayed by World War I. By 1919 shrinkage in the price of gold on the world market necessitated cutting back operational costs. The Low Grade Mine Commission of 1920 recommended not only a reduction of wages but also the employment of Africans in certain positions and thus the removal of the color bar. The mine unions and associated organizations, infiltrated by radical leaders, reacted violently. In January 1922, strikes began in the coal mines and by March a general strike had paralyzed all mining on the Rand. Prime Minister Smuts reacted militantly as he had in 1914 by sending in troops and this time using airplanes against the strikers. The strike was broken, workers accused of being snipers were shot without trial, and others arbitrarily exiled.

The white unions had lost their short-term demands and were forced to accept the government and mine owners' dictates. The Labor party, although not in complete sympathy with the strikers, threw its support behind Smuts' opponents in the election of 1924. The new prime minister, Hertzog, early cemented this temporary liaison by granting the white unions their special position against native competition. The improved economy of the 1920s removed many of the economic demands of the unions from the imperative category. Although there continued to be labor problems, never again would the bulk of the white workers on the Rand confront the government with a potential revolution.

African workers have always suffered under almost insurmountable handicaps in their attempt to organize into effective unions. All the institutions of the state opposed strikes by Africans. Government joined management and white unions in attempting to break any significant black union movement. The most important attempt to accomplish a general black union was the Industrial and Commercial Union of Africa (ICU) first organized immediately after World War I by Clements Kadile. By 1928, Kadile's union claimed over 250,000 members. However, the ICU was always relatively impotent. The Hertzog government used every means at its disposal to destroy its power. White workers were always available to break any black strike. In the latter 1920s the union became fragmented because of quarrels between Kadile and other leaders. The depression delivered the final blow to the ICU. No other African union has since had such appeal or success. Strikes and industrial disturbances by African workers, nevertheless, continued. Work stoppage became so serious during World War II that the Smuts' government, in 1942, passed War Measure 145. This made all strikes by Africans illegal. Despite this, there were continued disturbances on the Rand during the war. In 1946 a major strike involving over 74,000 workers closed almost half the mines. Utilizing War Measure 145 and the Riotous Assembly Act, the government sent in the police and drove the strikers back to work. Over fifty leaders were subsequently arrested and charged with a variety of disorders.

Prior to the election of 1948, the Union was already the industrial power of sub-Saharan Africa. Its preeminence was based not only upon capital and expertise but also upon the ready availability of cheap African labor. A series of laws and entrenched practices in government and industry had established firmly the principle of the subordination of the African worker. In a state where integration of the labor force was a key to continued success, the African had been segregated, his unions rendered ineffective, and his leaders proscribed. Long before apartheid became the official policy of the government, segregation had become the practice at all levels of industry and mining throughout the Union.

Developments in the non-European sector through 1948

Prior to 1948 there were few responsible officials who opposed the basic principle of separation between whites and blacks. Every government of the Union had made clear by significant acts of legislation its support of the white South African against the threat, real or imagined, of black predominance. These actions can be considered under four separate although interconnected headings of labor, land, urban problems, and political rights. In each of these categories the Bantu and to a lesser extent Cape Colored and Indians were relegated to the role of second-class citizens. Reference has already been made to the Mines and Works Acts of 1911 and 1926, the Apprenticeship Act of 1922, the Industrial Conciliation Act of 1924, and War Measure 145. All had been directed at curbing the Bantu's aspirations for better jobs and wages throughout industry. These acts had given the white laborer a superior, guaranteed position, in many cases to the direct detriment of economic establishment.

Despite the growing need for African workers in the urban areas, the majority of the Bantu during the first half of the twentieth century lived in rural areas. Beginning with the policies of Sir Harry Smith in the Transkei and Theophilus Shepstone in Natal, there had developed, in a haphazard manner, the concept of native reserves—areas of land guaranteed to the Bantu by the government in which, in theory, they could develop politically, socially, and economically in their own fashion and at their own speed. In these reserves indirect rule through chiefs or elected councils was the goal of administration. However, white officials could and did intervene directly in African affairs in the reserves. Major changes could also be instituted without consulting Bantu leaders which totally altered African traditions. The Glen Gray Act in the Cape in 1894 offers a good example of this since the act converted tribal ownership of lands to individual holdings and also instituted the rule of primogeniture.

The first comprehensive measure which established a standard reserve policy for the Union was the Native Land Act of 1913. This act demarcated areas on which various groups of Bantu had historic claims and made provision for later additions to the reserves by government purchase. This act did not of itself segregate the rural Bantu. It only recognized the de facto segregation which already existed. White public opinion in the next twenty years opposed any substantial appropriations to add to the size of the reserves although they were obviously inadequate for the growing Bantu population. In 1936 the Native Trust and Land Act finally provided for the purchase of an additional fifteen million acres of land to be added to the reserves. However, by 1961 only slightly more than ten million acres had been purchased. When the 1936 act is finally complete, the total area reserved for African occupation will be approximately 65,000 square miles or less than fourteen percent of the available land of the Union.

The African population increased from approximately seven and one-half million persons in 1936 to almost eleven million in 1961, indicating very clearly that population increase had outstripped the addition of new lands. Adding to the African dilemma is the condition of much of the land. Poor conservation techniques in many areas have converted previously fertile land to marginal land. Over ninety-four percent of African land is communally owned. Subsistence agriculture is the prevailing practice which prevents the utilization, even if funds were available, of most modern farming techniques. Thus the African population, notwithstanding government claims to the contrary, cannot live on the lands assigned to them. This is clearly seen by the fact that in 1961 only 3.6 million Africans were resident on the reserve land. The bulk of the adult male Bantu population were working outside the reserves either as farm laborers or in the cities.

The use of Bantu as workers in the cities caused the African urban population to increase dramatically. By 1961 almost three million Africans were resident in the urban centers with almost one million living in the Witwatersrand area. Such a concentration of population early brought severe problems related to housing. The Native Urban Areas Act of 1923 empowered local authorities to establish locations for African settlements with the understanding that these be segregated from white areas. Housing, sanitation, and control of the local population also became local responsibilities. Even before World War II, only about half the urban African population lived in controlled locations. The rest either lived with their employers or had simply "squatted" illegally on municipal and other unoccupied areas. There they built houses of scrap lumber, tin cans, and galvanized iron. Needless to say, water, electricity, and modern sewage facilities were absent. These shanty towns were a feature of every large city and were a reflection on the government's inadequacy in solving the African's housing problem. World War II speeded up the movement of Africans to the cities and made an already bad situation much worse.

Most of the African population was rendered politically impotent by the South Africa Act. Instead of enunciating a common policy within the Union relating to African rights, the act enshrined the differences inherent in the four separate areas prior to unification. Only in Cape Colony was the African given theoretical rights equal to the white citizen. Even this was hedged by proscribing Africans from standing for election to the Union House of Assembly. However, if the Bantu and Colored met the educational and property qualifications of the Cape, they were guaranteed the franchise. The most important entrenched clause in the South Africa Act specified that in order to remove them from the common roll a two-thirds majority of both the House of Assembly and Senate was required. However, the South Africa Act did not provide for guaranteeing non-Europeans equal treatment if at some later date the franchise rules were broadened. Thus in 1931 when white women were given the right to vote in Union elections, it was decided that it was not necessary to include Bantu or Colored women in this reform.

In 1936 the Representation of Natives Act disenfranchised approximately 15,000 qualified Bantu in Cape Colony. Instead of being on the common roll with all other voters, they were given special representation. A twenty-two member Native Representative Council was created for the entire Union. It had only advisory powers in matters relating to African affairs. To replace the Cape Bantu's loss of political equality three special seats were created in the House of Assembly. Only whites could stand for these offices, but they were to represent the interests of the Bantu. Four senators were also chosen to watch over the rights of non-Europeans. Given the nature of these reforms and the relatively powerless position of the Senate, the arguments that the Bantu were given better representation had a hollow ring.

Thus in brief, the Bantu majority, long before 1948, were living in a society of apartness. There were two separate sets of rules governing whites and blacks in all important areas of life. However, the position of the Cape Colored and Indian, although affected by segregationist legislation, had not been seriously attacked before World War II. Since much of the thrust of Prime Minister Malan's program after 1948 concerned the Cape Colored, their peculiar situation within the Union should be briefly noted.

Numbering approximately one and one-quarter million by 1948, the Cape Colored are racially a very mixed group. Their historical antecedents date to the liaisons between slaves and Europeans in the seventeenth century. Later admixtures of Hottentot, Bushmen, Malay, and Bantu helped create the present population. Over eighty-five percent of the

Colored live in Cape Colony where they had been guaranteed theoretical equality before the law as early as 1828. The Colored population is more urban than the Bantu and because of the more favorable government attitude toward them, they hold positions normally closed to the Bantu. They are represented as artisans in the building and printing trades and hold semiskilled and skilled positions in industry. The majority of the non-European doctors, lawyers, and teachers in Cape Province are Colored. With the increasing race consciousness which began in the 1920s, many Afrikaner leaders looked hopefully to the time when the Colored would be put in their place. Standing between the Afrikaners and these desires was the entrenched clause of the South Africa Act. After Malan's election victory in 1948, a major goal of his Nationalist party was to remove the special privileges of the Colored.

There is another minority group in southern Africa, the Asian population, which is largely concentrated in Natal. Of the almost one-half million Asians, only approximately 20,000 live in the Cape and another 60,000 in the Transvaal. Indians were first brought to Natal in the 1860s as indentured servants to work the sugar plantations. Many chose the option of remaining in a territory which offered them more economic opportunity than India. They were later joined by their families and friends who also recognized the greater advantages of Natal, despite the color bar. Even before the Boer War there were many restrictions placed upon Indians. They could not even live in the Orange Free State. Although they could reside in the Transvaal, they could not individually own property. As soon as responsible government was granted to Natal, their right to vote was taken from them. Only in Cape Colony did the Indians continue to enjoy political freedom.

Mohandas Gandhi began in Natal to use passive resistance against discriminating legislation which would later become so much a part of the Indian scene. Before World War I, he was successful in removing some of the petty annoyances imposed on the Indians and also in preventing the enactment of more punitive measures against them. However, Smuts' government, responding to demands of white merchants and municipalities in the 1920s, introduced a Class Areas Bill which would have segregated Indians throughout the country. Smuts' government fell before this could become law, but in 1926 Hertzog introduced an even more severe measure. Extreme pressure from Britain and from the government of India prevented this from being enacted. By the Cape Town agreement, Indians were promised better treatment in South Africa and the Union government provided funds for repatriation of those who wished to return to India. Europeans remained unhappy with the Indians' way of life, their poverty, their aptitude in business, and their desire to own real estate. Finally in 1946, the Smuts government passed the so-called "Pegging Act" which attempted to restrict the sale of real estate to Indians in Natal. As a concession to the liberals within the United party, the Indians were granted the right to elect three European members to the House of Assembly.

What was the political reaction of the three nonwhite sectors of the population to all the legislation which relegated them to inferior status within the Union? Their major problems in attempting to organize effectively to oppose any action of the government was lack of unity and weakness to implement any decisions. In 1902 the Colored formed the African Peoples Organization which reflected the hopes and aspirations of the professional, moderate middle classes. They believed in cooperation with the white governments and attempted to alleviate their problems by arguments, petitions, and persuasions. The consciousness of their special position prevented them from active cooperation with Bantu or Indian political groups. The Indian community also had similar problems of diffusion of aims. The South African Indian Congress created in 1918 was a development from Gandhi's earlier movement. It, too, was dominated by professional and upper-class businessmen whose methods were strictly within the law. Smuts' and Hertzog's class bills in the 1920s were defeated not because of the Indian Congress, but because of pressures from Britain and India. The Indian Congress by 1948, due to the desires of its leaders to please the white government, was almost powerless.

The traditional leaders of various Bantu tribes increasingly became government spokesmen since their continuation in office depended upon Johannesburg. Even had they wished, they were not prepared to exercise leadership roles which transcended their own groups. There were few Western-educated Bantu and they found it difficult to communicate their ideas to the mass of tribal Bantu. Until 1912 there was no overall political organization through which they could express their hopes and fears. The early potential leaders of the Bantu were men of their times. They were middle class and believed in the efficacy of reason and peaceful petition. Perhaps as important were the jealousies between some educated Bantu. The career of John Tengo Jabavu is a good example of the pressures imposed on an educated Bantu. He was educated by missionaries, became a teacher, and edited a number of newspapers. The last was the very influential Xosa-English newspaper *Imvo*. In it he campaigned against the double standard of justice, pass laws, and general antinative legislation. In politics he supported a succession of white liberals who promised to alleviate the condition of the Bantu. When Jabavu's position as spokesman for the educated Bantu of the western Cape seemed to be threatened, he reacted against the imagined threat. Thus he opposed a Bantu, Reverend Walter Rubasana, for the seat to the provincial council from Tembuland in 1913, and this assured Rubasana's defeat and the election of a European. Jabavu was against the founding of the South African Native National Congress in 1912 and campaigned for the Land Act of 1913. These actions removed any influence he might have had over the form of the emerging Bantu political organization.

The South African Native National Congress was formed to oppose the Land Act of 1913. Its delegations to the governor-general, Lord Gladstone, and to the Colonial Office were ignored. This set the pattern for relations between the organization, renamed the African National Congress (ANC), and the government. Its leaders, such as John Dube of

Natal and Reverend Rubasana, could only petition the government. By the terms of the Act of Union the ANC could form no power base in the legislature, and the ANC rejected the radicalism and potential violence inherent in the program suggested by the Communists in the 1920s. The struggle to keep Communists and radicals from gaining control weakened the ANC further in the 1930s. Given that weakness and the attitude of the government, it is not surprising that the ANC opposition to the Cape Native Franchise Act of 1935, which removed the Bantu from the common roll, was ineffectual.

Perhaps the best example of the weakness of the ANC was the anti-pass agitation which began at the annual Congress in May 1944. Under Dr. Alfred Xuma, the ANC leadership confidently predicted that they would collect over a million signatures to a petition protesting the pass laws. Over a year later the petition was presented with only about 100,000 signatures, and it was ignored by the government. In June 1946, the ANC promised to continue the collection of signatures to indicate their disapproval of the passes. Partially because of government opposition, but also because of poor organization, the campaign was a failure.

In 1943 a number of younger educated Bantu under the leadership of Anton Lembede formed the Youth League. Its membership included Walter Sisulu, Robert Sobukwe, and Nelson Mandela. Because the Youth League had a definite coherent program of action, it was able to exercise a profound influence on the ANC in the immediate postwar years. This culminated in 1949 with the adoption by the ANC of a program of action designed to end "the idea of white domination or the domination of white over black." This more militant stand of the ANC, however, was too late because in 1948 the Nationalist party with its watchword of apartheid came to power.

South Africa since 1948

The election of 1948 represented a watershed in South African life. Heretofore the non-European had played a small role in the determination of elections. Dr. Malan's Nationalists, however, in all the campaign oratory, stressed that this was the major issue. They had been provided with a systematic theory of exclusion by the professors of Stellenbosch University and SABRA. Economic disorders following the war and the greater militancy of black workers and some Bantu intellectuals was also a convincing factor in the election. Afrikaner nationalism was focused by Malan on this one issue. Smuts' United party had no definite answers to the call for apartheid. He could not accept the full program of exclusiveness without alienating a large portion of the liberal electorate nor could he afford to adopt a meaningful liberal retort to Malan's program. Although the United party won fifty-three percent of the popular vote, it gained only sixty-five seats in the Assembly. The Labor party, allied to Smuts, won six seats. Together with the three seats guaranteed for Africans, the Smuts coalition could muster only seventy-four seats.

Countering this, Malan's Nationalists won seventy seats and Havenga's Afrikaner party won nine. Malan thus formed a government with a slim majority of five and a mandate to carry out his program of apartheid. The factionalism within the United party and their lack of a suitable alternative program became more evident with every subsequent election. In 1950 Smuts died and was succeeded as party leader by J. G. N. Strauss whose leadership was so ineffective that he was replaced by Sir de Villers Graaf in 1956. In 1951 the Afrikaner party was absorbed by the Nationalists and the six representatives from South West Africa added to Malan's majority. The degree by which Nationalist control has been extended after 1948 can be seen by comparing the election statistics of that year with those of 1961. In 1961 the Nationalist party, although gaining less than fifty-five percent of the popular vote, won 105 seats in the Assembly. The United party could win only forty-nine.

Specific acts of the Nationalist government and a growing sense of frustration caused the creation of a number of small political parties in the 1950s. In 1953 Mrs. Margaret Ballinger, one member of parliament who represented Africans, became the leader of the Liberal party. Some of its members such as Patrick Duncan and Alan Paton gave the movement worldwide publicity. However, the party, because of its position reflecting the idea of one man—one vote, was never a threat to the Nationalists. Another group formed in 1953 which had little impact was the Federal party mainly based in Natal which wanted to break up the unitary system. In 1954 a conservative revolt within the United party resulted in the short-lived National Conservative party. All the members of parliament who joined this group either lost their seats or joined the Nationalist party.

A more significant creation occurred after the United Party Congress in 1959. Twelve United party members of parliament resigned to form the Progressive party. Its platform was Rhodes' old concept of "equal rights to all civilized men." In the 1961 elections only one of these members of parliament, Mrs. Helen Suzman, was returned to office. Aside from the obvious fact that all the small new parties of the 1950s represented new approaches to the problem of race relations, their main effect was to further weaken the United party. There were, during this period, no serious defections from the Nationalists. Thus during the crucial phase of implementing apartheid, the only major opposition party was further divided and rendered almost impotent.

With this background of political development, one can better examine the policies of the Nationalists. Malan's major contributions to apartheid were the Suppression of Communism Act (1950), The Immorality Amendment Act (1950), The Population Registration Act (1950), The Group Areas Act (1950), and the Bantu Authorities Act (1951). The Suppression of Communism Act defined Communism in such a broad manner that the state could ban any organization which was remotely suspected of Communism. It was under the terms of this act that the long drawn out Treasons Trials of over 150 people were begun in 1956. The

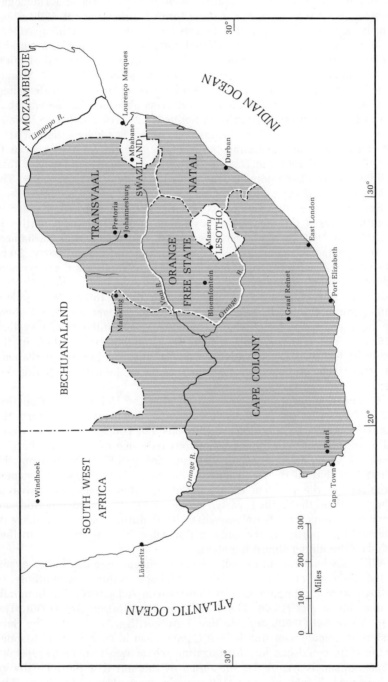

The Republic of South Africa

Immorality Act made any type of miscegenation a criminal offense. The Population Registration Act provided for the registration of all persons according to race—based upon the 1951 census. An identity certificate was then issued. The definition of a white person was anyone who was obviously white by appearance or by general repute and acceptance. Anyone can object to the race classification of another person. A board operating under the jurisdiction of the interior ministry then hears evidence and can reclassify any person according to the evidence. A white classification carries with it all the economic and political preferences, so since 1951 the government has heard thousands of cases. Aside from the mental anguish caused by such classification, the terms of the act are so ambiguous that persons of the same family have been given differing classifications. However, the act did what the government hoped. It gave them a fairly accurate detailed breakdown of the population according to race. They could then proceed to other acts necessary to implement apartheid.

The Group Areas Act which Dr. Dönges, the minister of the interior, referred to as the "cornerstone of apartheid" restricted races to "full" areas already occupied. No member of one race could acquire property in areas reserved for another. It was the aim of the act eventually to restrict the residence of all persons to distinct areas and thus minimize contact between Bantu, Colored, Indians, and whites. A 1954 amendment gave the minister of native affairs power to expel Africans from zones declared white. Dr. Hendrik Verwoerd, armed with this authority, moved over 100,000 Africans from the immediate environs of Johannesburg to new group areas farther from the outskirts of the city.

The Bantu Authorities Act became the basis for the later Bantustan developments. It regularized the older system of indirect rule in the native reserves. Instead of assuming the economic interdependence of white and black in a growing industrialized South Africa, the Malan government made it clear that as soon as practicable all Bantu would have only one place of permanent residence—one of the native reserves. By 1955 the chiefs of the Transkei area had accepted the implications of the act. Chiefs from other areas reluctantly followed this lead. In 1960 the government removed the three special representatives of the Bantu from the House of Assembly.

In 1954 Dr. Malan retired from politics and was succeeded as prime minister by the even more conservative Johannes Strijdom. It was his government which devised the means by which the Cape Colored were removed from the common voting roll. In 1951 Malan had attempted to accomplish this by the Separate Registration Bill passed by a simple majority of the Assembly. In March 1952, the Supreme Court declared this act invalid since the procedure was not in accordance with the South Africa Act. In May parliament declared itself the highest court in the land when dealing with constitutional matters. This action was also negated by the Supreme Court in September 1953. In 1954 the Nationalists attempted three times to secure the necessary two-thirds majority and failed each time. Strijdom's government then reorganized the Appellate Court in 1955 by increasing its numbers from six to eleven members. In June the Senate Act reapportioned the seats in the Senate and increased the number of by increasing its numbers from six to eleven members. In June the Senate assured the necessary two-thirds vote for the South Africa Amendment Act of February 1956 which finally removed the Colored from the common roll in Cape Colony. The courts held that this action was legal as defined by the original South Africa Act, and thus the Colored lost the political rights which they had possessed for over a century.

Eight years after their victory in 1948 by means of these acts and a host of lesser supporting legislation and executive decisions, the Union had been converted into a state where segregation was the basis of political action. Hendrik Verwoerd who succeeded as prime minister after Strijdom's death in 1958 carried on the tradition of his two predecessors largely by administering the legislation already passed and thus made apartheid a working system. Mounting pressure from newly independent African states and other Commonwealth nations convinced Verwoerd in 1960 that South Africa could not continue to function within the Commonwealth. A referendum to decide whether it should become a republic was then conducted. Fifty-two percent of the voters agreed to the change and the Republic of South Africa was proclaimed May 31, 1961.

The African National Congress, although not completely converted to an action program, entered into an agreement of cooperation in 1945 with the Indian National Congress and the Colored Peoples Organization. This alliance called for brief work stoppages in 1948. In 1953 they collaborated with the Indian National Congress in an open campaign to challenge segregated public facilities. South African police reacted by arresting almost 9,000 of those involved in civil disobedience. In 1956 there was a long campaign by Africans against using buses in Johannesburg. In the following two years the ANC was involved in supporting a series of activities directed against government policies. In all these actions the leaders were dominated by Gandhian concepts of peaceful resistance. However, many of these protests were marred by bloodshed. In 1950 eighteen Africans were killed in Johannesburg and the 1953 campaign was finally cancelled because of the violence.

Traditional leaders of the ANC such as Chief Luthuli and Dr. Alfred Xuma were considered too moderate by some younger Africans. Led by Robert Sobukwe, a lecturer at Witwatersrand University, these radicals formed the Pan African Congress (PAC) in 1959. They favored direct action to create a situation which would force the Nationalists from power. Their first objective was the pass laws. They encouraged thousands of persons to refuse to show their passes to the authorities. Such a demonstration would thereby fill the jails and prisons. This type of passive resistance culminated in the Sharpeville Massacre in March 1960 where the police fired upon thousands of peaceful demonstrators, killing sixty-nine people. The outrage in the world press over Sharpeville played an important role in causing South Africa to withdraw from the Commonwealth. A state of emergency was declared in South Africa and both the ANC and PAC were declared illegal. Most of the leaders of the organizations were arrested or went into exile.

Verwoerd's government utilized every facet of its power to contain the protest movements. Chief Luthuli was placed under house arrest, Sobukwe was arrested, and later two other PAC leaders, Nelson Mandela and Walter Sisulu, were tried for sabotage. All nonwhite political organizations were proscribed and therefore their effectiveness was greatly limited. Verwoerd also announced his intention of proceeding with the Bantustan policy which would ultimately create a federal South Africa composed of black and white states. This ultimate in apartheid, however economically unrealistic, was advanced by the creation of the Transkei Bantustan under the leadership of Chief Kaiser Mantazima.

World opinion grew increasingly hostile to the racial policies of South Africa in the 1960s. African states individually and collectively through the OAU have condemned South Africa and called for a boycott of the Republic. The open and covert criticisms of other members of the Commonwealth drove Verwoerd to break with the crown. The United Nations, particularly after Sharpeville, has attempted to moderate Republic policy, and its intervention in the affairs of South West Africa has made it an open foe of the Nationalist government. United States policy has been ambivalent in practice as has that of Britain. However, the major leaders of both states have openly supported the aspirations of the nonwhite population of the Republic. The result of this type of pressure appears not to have changed any policy of the Nationalist government. Rather, it has intensified their feelings of isolation and convinced them that their program of action is correct.

South West Africa is a good example of the impotence of the United Nations and individual states when confronting the Nationalist government. South West Africa was turned over to the Union to be administered as a class "C" mandate under the general guidance of the League of Nations. The Bondelswarts Massacre in 1922 was the first occasion of conflict between the League and South Africa over management of the mandate. However, the League did nothing practical to enforce their rule and the Union government came to look upon the vast territory as theirs. In 1946 Smuts' government requested the United Nations to allow South West Africa to be incorporated within the Union. This was refused because of the past administrative history of the mandate. In 1950 the International Court of Justice gave a nonbinding decision that the United Nations had inherited the mandate responsibilities of the old League of Nations. South Africa disputed this, claiming that the mandate had lapsed. All attempts by the United Nations to implement their theoretical control have failed. The South West Africa Amendment Act of 1949 provided for six representatives elected by the white inhabitants to sit in the Union's House of Assembly. For practical purposes, therefore, the mandate has been absorbed into South Africa. The last blow to the United Nations' claims was the refusal of the International Court of Justice in 1966 to rule on the question of South West Africa brought before it by Liberia and Ethiopia. Failing the use of force by the United Nations, the Republic will not relinquish South West Africa.

South Africa's racial policies have resulted in defeating its aims in one direction—the absorption of the High Commission Territories. In 1910 it appeared to British and South African statesmen that the logical development of these territories was toward incorporation within the Union. The evolvement of exclusive racial policies in the Union in the thirty-five years following the enactment of the South Africa Act postponed, but did not destroy, the possibility of reversion. However, the actions of the Nationalist government after 1948 combined with the devolution of political power to Africans elsewhere in Africa meant that no British government in the 1950s would seriously consider handing Basutoland, Bechuanaland, and Swaziland over to South Africa. The development of Britain's new attitudes toward the High Commission Territories has been detailed elsewhere. It is sufficient to note here that these territories, when they became politically independent, were still dependent economically on the Republic. Their future is still closely linked to South Africa. Lesotho (Basutoland), totally surrounded by the Republic, is particularly vulnerable. If the Republic feels threatened by events in the ex-territories, it may well yet absorb them despite adverse world opinion.

SIXTEEN
Troubled independence, 1965–1970

In the latter years of the 1950s there were two diverse, extreme attitudes held by observers of the African scene. One view held that Africans were not prepared technically, philosophically, or psychologically to manage their affairs as independent entities. These critics pointed to the small number of persons with a university education even among the politically elite. Most of them had never exercised political power and were completely unfamiliar with the mechanisms of government. Even more critical was the extreme shortage of competent, well-trained personnel who could staff the mid-range white collar positions and perform competently as technicians for the railways, telegraph services, port facilities, and other vital services. These critics pointed to the dichotomy between the small, politically active, and now dominant urban political elite and the traditional rulers of the African masses. With the manifold health, educational, and economic problems of almost every area, the new, untried, naïve political leadership seemed an invitation to disaster.

At the opposite extreme were the European liberals who saw independence for Africa as the logical continuation of the anticolonial struggles for liberty and self-determination. They believed that African statesmen would continue the development of Western-style political democracies. Such free governments based upon an expanding African middle class would be able, with disinterested outside assistance, to guarantee civil liberties for all and guide their states peacefully through the transition from traditionally based rule to a new, viable African synthesis. This optimistic attitude was shared by the largest numbers of African politicians.

In the decade after independence was gained by most African states, the liberal attitude was shown to be unrealistic. Kwame Nkrumah and the CPP in Ghana showed the way for others to move toward the negation of parliamentary democracy. After less than three years, Ghana had ceased to have an actively functioning legal opposition party. The good of the party became synonymous with the good of the state. Disagreement with the CPP was tantamount to disloyalty. Other polities, not all for the same reasons, soon after gaining independence became one-party states where deviation from a preestablished party position could mean prison or exile for the individual. In states such as Guinea, Mali, and Ghana mechanisms of domination associated with European totalitarian states were used very efficiently to make certain that the party program was carried out with a minimum of opposition.

The omnipresence of the ruling elite was noticeable even in polities such as those of Senegal, Ivory Coast, Kenya, and Nigeria. Less ideologically committed than the members of the Casablanca group, politicians in these states nevertheless sought to protect their position and tended to consider criticism of their policies as threats to them and their programs. The variety and complexity of the reactions of political leaders to real or imagined threats has already been described in detail in Chapters Eleven and Twelve. However different the responses were, one factor emerged very clearly by 1965. Politicians in power had come to view their high positions as a type of reward for previous services. They and their political parties had, in a short period, become entrenched and much of their energy was devoted to protecting themselves. By making disagreement and dissent either illegal or dangerous, they were assured that their most implacable political opponents could only resort to violence to change the structure of the state. Violence in some form became the only way to secure a change in a corrupt, moribund government.

The manifold problems of each independent nation would have been difficult enough had all the politicians involved been as honest and idealistic as they appeared during the anticolonial struggle. By 1965 it was obvious that a larger number of high-placed politicians were using their offices for personal profit and many showed little interest or aptitude for doing their jobs well. Where there were elections, corruption of all forms existed to assure that the dominant party would stay in power. In many independent states the life of the ordinary African was little, if any, better than it had been when the Europeans ruled. The rising expectations of millions of Africans were succeeded by growing frustration. The great majority of the people were helpless to change the political situation. Only those who could command a coercive force superior to the government had the potential to overthrow the entrenched political machines. Once this was realized, the military throughout Africa were quick to take advantage of their special position within the state structures to oust moribund, unpopular, or ineffective civilian governments. The depth of estrangement between the people and their elected governments can be measured by the immediate popular support given to most new military regimes.

As previously noted, the military reacted in many different ways once they had ousted the politicians. In some cases the army announced that it was playing only a caretaker role and would withdraw once certain deficiencies had been corrected. Some of the military regimes such as in Ghana and Sierra Leone actually followed through with these promises. In other areas such as the Congo and Mali, the military leader gave a sense of civilian legitimacy to his rule by issuing a new constitution and continuing on as the civilian head of state while elsewhere the military ruled openly with no apparent plans ever to return to a form of civilian rule.

It seems clear that in most cases the assumption of control by the military, far from being a setback, actually marked an advance in the fortunes of the state. The military replaced political regimes which had either been discredited or could not solve the pressing problems of their polities. Thus the extreme pessimists who expected Africa to disintegrate once European leadership was removed have also been proved wrong. Economics seems to be the key to the future. Those states such as the Ivory Coast, Gabon, and Tanzania, where there was either great economic potential or where the government was deeply involved in providing the people with a more promising future, have avoided military take-overs. If military regimes can minimize corruption and utilize better the resources of their states, then they will be able to survive, no matter what constitutional form they assume. A brief survey of political developments in each geographic area of Africa since 1965 may help to underscore these very tentative generalizations.

West Africa

The most significant phenomenon noted in West Africa in the five-year period after 1965 was the new role assumed by the military. In Ghana early in 1966 the long-time one-party regime of Kwame Nkrumah was overthrown by a portion of the military led by junior officers. The subsequent regime of General Ankrah provided the necessary conservative leadership to stabilize Ghana's economic drift. True to its promise, the military in November 1968 appointed a constituent assembly to create new constitutional instruments for a return to civilian rule. General Ankrah resigned in April 1969, and his place as head of government was taken by a triumvirate led by Brigadier-General Afrifa. In 1969 political parties again began to function in Ghana. The two most important were Dr. K. A. Busia's Progress party with its main strength in Ashantiland and the National Alliance of Liberals based upon the Volta regions and headed by Komla Gbedemah. In the August 1969 elections for the legislature, the Progress party won 105 of the 140 seats and Dr. Busia became prime minister of the new Ghana government on October 1.

In Sierra Leone the government of Albert Margai did not measure up to the standards established by his brother, Sir Milton Margai. In the elections of early 1967 the ruling Sierra Leone Peoples party was challenged by Siaka Stevens' All Peoples Congress. The elections, marred by corruption and violence, was extremely close. Governor Lightfoot-Boston declared the All Peoples Congress the victor and called upon Stevens to form a government. However, the head of the armed forces, Brigadier-

General Lansana, and a small number of adherents overthrew the government on March 21 and arrested Stevens and Governor Lightfoot-Boston. Two days later a counter-coup organized by junior officers deposed Lansana. The new junta or National Reformation Council eventually invited Lieutenant-Colonel Juxon-Smith to act as head of state. The military immediately launched a series of investigations into alleged mismanagement of the previous regime. One report of the disputed election confirmed that Stevens had indeed won. Juxon-Smith repeatedly promised a return to civilian government as soon as possible and he appointed a committee to study the full range of problems connected with the transfer of power. Many Sierra Leoneans did not believe these promises. Among the disbelievers were junior officers who in April 1968 staged another military coup and thus forced a return to civilian control. They jailed Juxon-Smith, Lansana, and other members of the former military regime and invited Siaka Stevens to return. After conferences between the two major parties, Stevens was chosen the leader of a national government. Widespread disorders followed and a state of emergency was declared in November 1968. However, despite many problems, Stevens has continued to strengthen his party's control of the state.

In Nigeria, after the second military coup, Colonel Yakuba Gowon replaced the assassinated Major-General Ironsi on August 1, 1966. He retained the old structure of military rule and kept the governors of the four regions, including Colonel Odemegwu Ojukwu in the East. Gowon promised a speedy return to civil rule and appointed a constitutional conference to facilitate this. His plans were upset in September by the killing of thousands of Ibo in the Northern Region. Within a month a flood of Ibo refugees inundated the East. Ojukwu ordered northerners out of the East for their safety and openly questioned whether one Nigeria could exist when over seven million citizens could not travel freely in any part of the country. After that time, Ojukwu began to govern the East with little reference to the government at Lagos and started to build up that portion of the army under his command. He stated that for reasons of safety he would not meet with the other military leaders outside of the Eastern Region.

After many attempts, a conference between the military commanders including Ojukwu was finally convened at Aburi, Ghana, in January 1967. Agreement was reached at Aburi on a number of salient points. Chief among these was that the future structure of the federation should have a weaker central government and more power should be devolved to the regional authorities. However, Gowon made no attempt to put the agreement into effect and, in early March 1967, Ojukwu announced that he would do so on a unilateral basis.

From this point on, Nigeria edged toward civil war. Both sides increased their military forces and attempted to create a feeling of patriotism in their people. On May 27, Gowon announced the government plans for a new federation of twelve regions with the central government retaining supreme authority. The Ibo would be restricted to one landlocked region. Ojukwu had not been consulted before this declaration and he considered the plan a negation of the Aburi agreements. Therefore, the Eastern Consultative Assembly declared its secession from Nigeria on May 30, 1967 and took the name Biafra for their new state.

Actual hostilities began on July 6 when federal troops invaded Biafra on two fronts. The initial numerical superiority of approximately three to one remained constant throughout the war although the Nigerian army grew, by 1969, in excess of 80,000 men. Early in the conflict the Biafran ports of Bonny, Port Harcourt, and Calabar were captured, thus preventing Ojukwu from receiving large quantities of war material and food supplies. Except for the August 1967 Biafran offensive which resulted in the occupation of a part of the Mid-West, Ojukwu's forces were always on the defensive. Enugu was lost to the federal army in October 1967, and despite heroic efforts, the Biafran forces were driven from Aba, Okigwi, Owerri, and Onitsha in 1968. Biafra was thus reduced to only a small fraction of what had been Eastern Nigeria. Despite its inferiority in numbers, supplies, and equipment, the Biafrans refused to surrender. To Gowon and his chief advisers this was an embarrassment since almost everyone had believed that the war could be quickly won. Instead it had become a nightmare, killing thousands of federal troops and draining the credits of a once prosperous state.

Biafra's only hope by mid-1968 lay in gaining recognition from a significant number of other states. However, only Tanzania, Zambia, the Ivory Coast, Gabon, and Haiti recognized Ojukwu's regime. The United States maintained a neutral position while Britain and Russia supplied Nigeria with war materials. France, although refusing to alienate Nigeria by supporting Biafra diplomatically, did allow its nationals to provide arms to Biafra. All such aid had to be funneled into one bad, temporary airstrip at Uli. Attempts by various nations and the OAU to mediate the dispute proved fruitless. Meetings at London, Kampala, Niamey, and Addis Ababa had no influence toward ending the conflict. In addition to combat casualties, untold thousands of Biafran civilians died in the conflict. Many of these were children, most of whom died of starvation despite the efforts of national and international relief agencies to abate the suffering. When Biafra finally capitulated on January 12, 1970, Nigeria was once again a united state, but the once rich Eastern area had been thoroughly devastated.

The independent states of what had been French West Africa were no more stable after 1965 than their English-speaking counterparts. In Senegal, Guinea, Niger, the Ivory Coast, and Mauritania the politicians who had been responsible for gaining independence were able to maintain control. But even in these polities evidence of unrest and dissatisfaction was expressed in a number of ways, many of them violent. Assassination plots against Houphouët-Boigny of the Ivory Coast and Sekou Touré of Guinea were foiled by authorities. The poor economic position of Senegal led to a series of confrontations between Senghor's government and students and workers. President Hamani Diori of Niger, by restructuring his government, managed to avoid any serious threat to his domination of the state. Elsewhere military overthrow of the civilian, one-party governments became the pattern.

In Upper Volta, Sangoule Lamizana, leading the army, overthrew the government of President Maurice Yameogo in January 1966. Etienne Eyadema, the chief of staff of the Togolese army, deposed President Grunitzky in January 1967 and outlawed all political parties. Troubled Dahomey, which had witnessed a series of previous mlitary coups by Colonel Soglo, witnessed a further takeover in December 1968 when Major Maurice Kouandete and other junior officers overthrew President Soglo. President Modibo Keita of Mali, long viewed as one of the stronger rulers of a one-party state was deposed in September 1969 by the army under the control of Lieutenant Moussa Traore. In all these territories the excuse given by the army officers was the need to restore national unity and end the corrupt rule of the politicians. Each military leader promised a return to civilian rule as soon as conditions permitted. Despite the formalities of appointing constitutional commissions, only one of these military leaders has surrendered his power to the civil authorities. This was Kouandete of Dahomey who invited Emile Zinsou to become president of the Republic. A later referendum confirmed this choice and Kouandete was made chief of staff of the army. Eyadema, Lamizana, and Traore continued to function as heads of state and showed little inclination to relinquish power to any other leader.

Central Africa

In the five years after 1965, most of the independent states of what had been French Equatorial Africa were politically unstable. The Gabon, one of the richest areas in Central Africa, which has since independence maintained extremely close relations with France, had only one serious crisis. This was in the period immediately after the death of long-time President Leon M'Ba in December 1967. M'Ba's chosen successor, Vice-President Albert Bongo, became president with only minimal opposition. To most casual observers the Central African Republic in 1965 appeared to be firmly controlled by the conservative president Jean Bokassa. However, he was forced to call for French troops in 1967 to help thwart a planned coup, and his government survived another abortive takeover in May 1968. Colonel Alexandre Banza, a close friend of Bokassa, attempted, in April 1969, to get other army officers to support his attempt to overthrow the government. Although this power play failed and Banza was executed, Bokassa's regime remains extremely vulnerable.

In the Republic of the Congo (Brazzaville) the factors which had created instability before 1965 continued to cause problems. In mid-1966 Marien Ngouabi and other junior officers failed to unseat President Massamba-Debat. Their power base was such that most of the would-be rebels were able to continue in their positions without retribution. In early August 1968, Ngouabi and his associates were finally able to overthrow

Massamba-Debat. Until January 1969, Ngouabi was content to be the power behind the new military-based regime. Then he replaced Major Alfred Raoul as president, crushed a counter coup in February, purged the army and police, and established a hand picked Council of the Revolution to aid him in ruling the Congo.

Chad with a mixed population of Semitic nomads in the north and black agriculturists in the south has been the scene of a series of crises. President Tombalbaye in 1966 and early 1967 was confronted with a number of raids across Chad's eastern frontier from the Sudan. No sooner had this problem been diplomatically resolved than Chad army units in the Tibesti area mutinied (in March 1968). Some joined the nomads who were already hostile toward the government. Unable to check the growing rebellion with his own forces, Tombalbaye, in August, requested France to honor its defense treaty with Chad and send troops to the Tibesti area. The revolt spread to other areas of northern and eastern Chad despite the actions of French troops. The main political force behind the uprising is ostensibly the Chad Liberation Front led by Dr. Abba Sick with its headquarters in Libya. By the close of 1969, the French had over 2,500 troops including elements of the Foreign Legion operating against the rebels. Nevertheless, the rebels continued to control much of the northern area. Without French assistance it is doubtful whether Tombalbaye could continue to dominate even the southern area of Chad.

The former Belgian areas, which had been the scene of so much warfare and bloodshed in the early years of the decade, had become relatively quiescent by 1970. In the Republic of the Congo (Kinshasa), General Mobutu, who had earlier seized power from Tshombe and Kasavubu, was able to restore peace throughout most of the Congo. Potentially the most serious threat to Mobutu was the action in 1967 of approximately 150 white mercenaries and 900 Katanga gendarmes. For over six months they held a large portion of the eastern Congo based upon their control of the town of Bukavu. Eventually the mercenaries crossed into Rwanda where they were repatriated. Mobutu's old rival for power, Kasavubu, died in March 1969. Moise Tshombe, who had been detained in Algeria for two years, died the following June. Mobutu had executed Pierre Mulele the year before. Thus the most important Congolese leaders who could have rallied support against Mobutu were removed from the political scene. Even before the mercenary threat ended, Mobutu had renegotiated, for the new Congolese government company, favorable terms with Belgian mining concerns in the Katanga. With the return of peace throughout the Congo, the economic position of the state rapidly improved and this as much as any other factor solidified Mobutu's regime.

The same pattern of relative peace was noticeable in the neighboring state of Rwanda. Although the Hutu-Tutsi problem within the state remained, there was no repeat of the bloodletting of the early years of the decade. Peace in the Congo meant a relaxation of tensions between Rwanda and Mobutu's government after the crisis over the white mercenaries was surmounted in 1968. President Gregoire Kayibanda in the elections of September 1969 was supported by over ninety-nine percent of the electorate. Neighboring Burundi has been more politically restive. Michael Micombero seized power from the royalists in a bloodless coup in November 1966 and has survived many plots to overthrow his government. In May 1967, Major Albert Shibura and other officers were implicated in planning a coup against Micombero. A second attempt was made in September 1969 and again failed. The Belgian ambassador was dismissed when Micombero tried to link Belgium to this plot; but normal relations between the two states were restored after Micombero's government absolved Belgium of complicity.

The three areas which comprised the old Central African Federation were stable in their internal politics in the period after 1965. Zambia, the largest and potentially wealthiest of the three, was firmly ruled by Kenneth Kaunda's United National Independence party. In the December 1968 elections UNIP candidates won control of eighty-one of the 105 seats in the Assembly and Kaunda was reelected president, soundly defeating the leader of the opposing African National Congress, Harry Nkumbula. In 1967 in the wake of the Rhodesian crisis, Zambia disassociated itself from the joint railway and airline company. The following year Kaunda began a cautious policy of nationalization when the state took control over twenty-five smaller companies and renegotiated a new royalty formula with others. This policy was extended by the general nationalization of the copper industry in 1969 with the state taking over control of fifty-one percent of the stock of the companies.

Hastings Banda in 1966 presided over the conversion of Malawi to a republic. As president, his major problem remained the lack of resources and relative poverty of its four million citizens. Banda has negotiated trade agreements with South Africa and communications agreements with the Portuguese in Mozambique. He has also maintained friendly relations with Israel. Because of Banda's foreign policy, Malawi has been viewed by many other African leaders as a betrayer of the cause of black Africa. This attitude has not been translated into any effective overt or covert political activity within Malawi, and Banda appears to be as secure as ever as head of state.

The territory which offered the most potential for violence and instability was Rhodesia. The actions of members of the United Nations and the OAU, after Ian Smith's government declared its independence in November 1965, was an open invitation to activists. The economic boycott of Rhodesia did not support British Prime Minister Wilson's contention that this would bring the Rhodesians into line. It has damaged the economy of the breakaway state and made Smith's followers in the Rhodesian Front party more convinced that their actions were correct. All attempts by Britain to negotiate the problem foundered on its demands that the four million Africans be given a larger share in the government. The militant attitude of Kenneth Kaunda of Zambia who pressed the British to crush Rhodesia militarily did nothing to ease tensions in Central Africa. From May to August 1967, there were a series of guerrilla raids into the northern areas of Rhodesia. In the largest action in August, Rhodesian police killed over eighty guerrillas. This hit-and-run action continued well into 1968 but was eventually contained by the Rhodesian armed forces. The feeling of being assailed by the world has led to a hardening of white Rhodesian attitudes. The new constitution of 1969 approved by a referendum confirmed this. Rhodesia became a republic with a two-house legislature. The new instruments provided for complex voting procedures to choose black and white representatives, but the white minority arranged to retain ultimate political authority in the foreseeable future.

East and Northeastern Africa

President Julius Nyerere's government in Tanzania has been involved in a far-reaching political and economic reorientation of the state since 1967. This plan was announced after a high-level conference between government and TANU party leaders at Arusha in February 1967. The government subsequently took over all banks, the food processing industry, and many businesses to assure the continued socialization of the economy for the good of all the people. Foreigners were to be eased out of jobs which Tanzanians could hold. Swahili was also to be utilized wherever possible in government, business, and the elementary schools. However revolutionary these government actions were, there was little obvious opposition. There were only two examples of a potential deep-seated dissatisfaction with Nyerere's regime. In 1968 Oscar Kambona, the minister of local government, resigned and fled to London where he accused Nyerere of dictatorship and dogmatism. Far more serious as an indication of future trouble was the arrest in September 1969 of Abdullah Hanga and the former Tanzanian ambassador to the United States, Othman Shariff, along with sixteen others. They were executed in October with two others who also had been charged with conspiracy against the state. Although Nyerere and Vice-President Karume announced in April 1969, on the fifth anniversary of the Tanzanian union, that the merger was working well, Zanzibar continued as a possible source of division to Tanzania.

Kenya was, until mid-1969, a model of political decorum and stability in East Africa. In 1966 at President Kenyatta's urging, the two-house parliament was converted into a 168 seat unicameral legislature. The government's handling of the Indian question, although gaining some adverse commentary in the world press, was obviously popular in Kenya. Britain's imposition of a limit on Indian immigrants from Kenya forced Indians to make a decision within two years whether they would become citizens of Kenya. President Kenyatta was able by his firmness to minimize the incursion of Somali guerrillas in the northern territories and, in October 1967, the Somalia government promised to stop its support of any organization that sought to unite these areas with Somalia. A further triumph for Kenyatta was the change in the method of selecting the president which was adopted in early 1968. This provided that the vice-president upon the death of the president was automatically to succeed to that office until a general election could be held.

The Luo-Kikuyu jealousies within KANU which, except for the dismissal of Oginga Odinga, had been well-masked, erupted in 1969. Tom Mboya, the young Luo minister of economic planning, was assassinated in Nairobi in July. Many Luo believed this had been planned by Kikuyu within the party to further cut into Luo influence in the government. Despite government assurances and pleas for calm, there was a series of confrontations between police and Luo. The discovery that the assassin was a Kikuyu seemed to lend veracity to the worst rumors. Not even his execution in September quelled the Luo feeling of estrangement. On October 25, following a speech by President Kenyatta, a major riot occurred which resulted in the death of eleven persons. Kenyatta immediately declared the Luo-based Kenya Peoples Union proscribed and Oginga Odinga and many other party leaders were arrested. By the close of the year the worst of the crisis was over. However, the unrest was reflected in the KANU primary elections in December when many members of the government were defeated. Kenyatta's position remained secure, but the Mboya affair indicated how delicately balanced the forces were in what had previously seemed a politically stable African state.

In neighboring Uganda, the question of the relationship between the rights of sovereignty of the kabaka of Buganda and the power of the central government prevented any real political stability. In May 1966, Prime Minister Obote sent the army into Buganda and forced the kabaka, Sir Edward Mutesa II, to flee the country. A state of emergency was proclaimed throughout Buganda which enabled the central government to dispense with the usual formalities of democratic rule. In September 1967, a new constitution was issued which gave Uganda a republican government with an executive president. The traditional kingdoms of Bunyoro, Buganda, Toro, and Ankole were abolished. The existence of large numbers of supporters of the kabaka in Buganda kept the state of emergency in force until the beginning of 1970. In September 1969, former Prime Minister Benedicto Kiwanuku was arrested and charged with sedition and libel. The death of the kabaka in London in November increased the tension within Uganda. On December 18, President Obote was seriously wounded in an attempted assassination.

The pattern of unrest and violence so noticeable throughout the continent was continued in northeastern Africa. Somalia which had earlier in the decade followed an active expansionist policy was forced to abandon the dream of uniting all Somalis under one state. The closing of the Suez Canal, which had an adverse effect upon Somali's economy, along with the firm stand of Haile Selassie and Jomo Kenyatta, meant that President Abdirashid Ali Shermarke and Prime Minister Muhammad Ibrahim Egal's government had to become more moderate. The more militant Somalis opposed this and created a minor crisis within the ruling Somali Youth League in 1968. Egal, nevertheless, retained control. In the election of March 1969, the SYL was challenged by sixty-three different political parties, but nevertheless won seventy-three seats in the 123 man National Assembly and Egal formed a coalition government. On October 15, President Shermarke was assassinated and six days later Egal's government was overthrown by the army and police. A Supreme Revolutionary Council was formed headed by army chief Major-General Muhammad Said Barre. The council promised to restore trust in a purified Islamic government and the state was renamed the Somali Democratic Republic.

Since the abortive coup of December 1960, Haile Selassie, by utilizing his great power, has been able to keep internal opposition to his regime in Ethiopia to a minimum. Difficulties with the Sudan occurred in 1967 over the border area near Falasha. In the same year Ethiopia was forced to rush troops to the Somalia border to counter subversive activities there. In the following year tensions with both parties were eased due largely to a change of policy by the new governments in Somalia and the Sudan. Haile Selassie has not been able to assuage the hostility of many Eritrean Muslims and their demands for a separate state. In 1967 the Eritrean Liberation Front, coordinating the efforts of guerrillas, temporarily closed road traffic in Eritrea. The Ethiopian army swept through a number of villages and forced several thousand inhabitants to flee into neighboring Sudan. The guerrilla raids nevertheless continued throughout 1968 and 1969. The separatists attacked Ethiopian air facilities in Germany and Pakistan and attempted to steal an Ethiopian airliner in December 1969. By the end of the year, guerrillas had managed to shut down, by attacking road convoys, a large portion of normal road traffic in Eritrea. Another source of trouble for the emperor was student unrest. Ostensibly demanding educational reform, the student groups were also demonstrating against a broad range of government policies. At one time in mid-1969 the university and all secondary schools in Ethiopia were closed and the government arrested or detained thousands of students. So, despite the outward semblance of the continued order of traditionalist rule, Ethiopia is far from a serene polity.

The two salient facts in the recent history of the Sudan have been religious and political factionalism and the ongoing civil war in the south. The government of Sadik al Mahdi, which had seemed so powerful in 1966, had broken apart by May 1967 primarily because of opposition to his policies by the ultraconservative wing of the Ansar sect. Muhammad Ahmed Mahgoub replaced al Mahdi as premier to head a coalition government which attempted to associate members of the Southern Front party with its rule and thus bring an end to the hostilities in Equatoria. Although elections had been held in the south in March 1967, in the southern Sudan for the first time in ten years, the recognized political parties did not represent the rebels and the war continued. In February 1968, Mahgoub asked for the dissolution of the National Assembly rather than face a vote of confidence. A major conflict between the government and the followers of al Mahdi who streamed into Khartoum to protest Mahgoub's action was barely averted. In the general elections of April, Mahgoub continued as prime minister because his party won 101 of the 218 contested seats. The war in the south continued to be a constant drain on resources. A revolutionary southern Sudanese government in exile led by Aggrey Jarden was formed in Uganda and all attempts at pacification seemed to fail since the rebels controlled most of the countryside in the three disaffected provinces. Finally on May 25, 1968, young army officers led by Colonel Jaafar Muhammad al Niameiry, despairing of improvement in the political future of the Sudan, overthrew the civilian government. A revolutionary council and a twenty-one man cabinet was created to aid al Niameiry in ruling the country. Peoples military courts were established to try persons accused of crimes against the state. Press censorship was imposed and in October al Niameiry was named prime minister as well as head of the council. The new government, attempting to reconcile the southerners, extended the 1968 amnesty provisions and promised a number of political and educational reforms for Equatoria. The southern rebel leadership did not appear impressed by the new regime and the fifteen-year civil war continued.

Epilogue

By concentrating on the political aspect of recent Africa one can draw a pessimistic view of the future for sub-Saharan states. This conclusion would be as premature as those projected by observers a decade ago who envisioned a swift, onward and upward movement toward economic well-being and political democracy for the newly independent African states. The past few years have been a period of transition from colonial rule toward viable political structures designed by Africans to meet the specific problems of their states. In the long reach of African history, this time of adjustment has been woefully short for anyone to make any but extremely tentative judgments on the ultimate success or failure of African states. To counterbalance the specter of political instability, there are those polities, such as Zambia, the Ivory Coast, Tanzania, Senegal, and Malawi, which have been almost untouched by violent political turmoil. Further, states whose names were once symbolic of violence—the Congo, Ghana, and Nigeria—appear to have evolved, at least temporarily, governmental forms which are able to match their performance to the aspirations of the people.

There are many other signs of growing maturity and responsibility. Julius Nyerere's program aimed at placing Tanzanians in responsible posts throughout the nation is a reflection of the success of that government's education policies. This is duplicated by most African states whose pool of educated and trained personnel is far larger than when independence was granted. Another portent of maturity is the greater degree of cooperation apparent among them. This cooperation is much more practical than the idealistic proposals for united action espoused by political leaders a few years ago. It recognizes the primacy of nationalism and seeks to find areas, particularly in the economic realm, where states can mutually benefit from concerted action. The OAU is an imperfect structure, but its very existence as with the United Nations represents a tremendous advance over what had gone before.

Economic development must assume a key role in the future of every African state. Here, too, one can point to great advances. The iron ore deposits of Liberia and Mauritania and the petroleum of Nigeria are recent discoveries and have already gone far toward transforming the economy of those states. Hydroelectric projects such as those in Ghana, Nigeria, and Zambia are necessary prerequisites for any real advance in industrialization. Close cooperation between African states and foreign investors as in the case of the Ivory Coast, Zambia, and the Congo has allowed millions in investment capital to flow into an otherwise capital deficient area. The economic base of most African polities is agriculture. An analysis of the type, variety, quality, and quantity of agricultural goods exported from almost any African state in 1970 will show considerable advance over 1960. The interplay between government policy and the economic realities of African states will determine to a large degree whether this huge continent will achieve its full potential or be continually hampered by the internecine strife so typical of the period since 1965.

Glossary

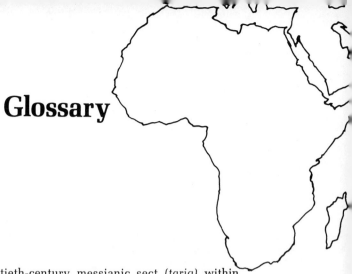

Ahmadiyah A twentieth-century messianic sect (*tariq*) within Islam. Founded by Mirza Ghulam Ahmad in the Punjab area of India. Ahmadiyah missionaries have been very active in the coastal parts of West Africa.

Aku Gambian term for Sierra Leone creoles who migrated to Bathurst.

Alafin Title of the ruler of Oyo empire.

Askaris African troops trained and armed in the European fashion by the Germans and Italians.

Assimilado A system by which Africans could gain rights equal to Portuguese citizens in Portugal's African territories.

Basorun The king's chief minister in the kingdom of Oyo.

Boer Dutch term for farmer, it came to be applied to all persons of Dutch descent in South Africa.

Cercle Name of the largest administrative unit within a colony of the AOF.

Chitimukulu Title of the paramount chief of the Bemba.

Commando A Boer military unit of varying size and composed of volunteers. Commandos were used with great effect in the unsettled areas of the eastern frontier of Cape Colony.

Contractos Laborers recruited and signed to contracts by the Portuguese to work on São Thomé.

Dash A gift or unofficial payment to a chief or official which enabled European traders to conduct business.

Destooling The act of removing Akan chiefs from office.

Drotsdy A large unit of local government in Cape Colony in the early nineteenth century.

Emir A title of nobility common to Islamic states. In northern Nigeria the emirs were rulers of city states subject only to the control of the sultan of Sokoto.

Eleko The hereditary ruler of Lagos.

Feld cornet In a Boer district in South Africa the feld cornet was the elected leader of commando operations.

Heemraaden In the early nineteenth century the elected legislative body of a drotsdy.

403

Hukimdar Egyptian title for the governor-general of the Sudan.

Imam A title which originally meant the leader of an entire Muslim community. In some places the term came to signify only a tribal leader.

Impi A regiment of Zulu or Matabele warriors.

Indaba Formal meeting of all responsible citizens in Swaziland.

Indigenas Portuguese term for the bulk of the African population of its territories.

Indigenat French system by which Africans could be punished without the formality of a trial.

Jihad A holy war or a war sanctioned by the religious authorities in Islamic states.

Kabaka Title of the ruler of Buganda.

Kaffir Originally the term meant a stranger. Afrikaners applied the term, sometimes in a perjorative sense, to all Bantu, but particularly to the Xosa.

Khalifa Arabic word for caliph or prophet. In Africa the term is generally associated with the career of Abdullah, one of the four khalifas appointed by the Mahdi.

Khedive Title meaning viceroy given to Muhammad Ali of Egypt by the Ottoman emperor in early nineteenth century. Later khedives were almost independent of Turkish control.

Khatmiyyah Most important Islamic sect *(tariq)* in the Sudan prior to the rise of Mahdism. It was founded by Ahmad ibn Idris in the early eighteenth century. Greatest teacher and missionary of this *tariq* was Muhammad al-Mirghani.

Kitwala Congolese name for the twentieth century Watchtower movement.

Landdrost Chief executive officer of a drotsdy, appointed by the central authorities at Cape Town.

Liqoqo Swazi aristocratic council whose composition was based on family ties.

Libandhla Swazi council where general populace was represented.

Litunga Title of the paramount ruler of the Luyi.

Loi Cadre An enabling act passed by French National Assembly in 1956 which was the first step toward a breakup of the two major federations—the AEF and AOF.

Lukiko Council of great nobles in Buganda.

Mahdi In certain sects of Islamic mysticism the Mahdi was the awaited prophet. In Africa the term is generally associated with Muhammad Ahmed, the Sudanese religious and political leader.

Mai The title of the ruler of Bornu.

Marabout An Islamic teacher of the Western Sudan. The name was also given to the puritanical reform movement which caused a series of wars in the Senegambia in the latter nineteenth century.

Mfecane Means the "time of crushing" and refers to the fifteen year period of internecine conflict between Bantu groups in southern Africa.

Mugabe Title of the ruler of the kingdom of Ankole.

Murdir Egyptian title for a governor of a province in the Sudan.

Mwami Title of the Watutsi ruler of Ruanda and of Burundi.

Mwato Kazembe Title of the paramount ruler of the Kazembe kingdom.

Mwato yamvo Title of the ruler of the Katanga Lunda.

Nilo-Hamitic Pastoral invaders of East Africa after the sixteenth century. Original home was probably the southern Sudan. Modern examples are the Nandi and Masai.

Nilotes Pastoral inhabitants of the upper Nile region and after the tenth century, invaders of East Africa. Modern examples are the Shilluk and Nuer.

Oyo mesi Major councilors of state and advisers to the alafin of Oyo.

Palmatario In Portuguese territories the punishment of beating the palms of the hands of Africans convicted of crimes.

Prazeros The owners of large interior land grants (prazos) made by Portugal in the eighteenth century. Intermarriage with the Bantu and isolation changed the prazeros. In nineteenth century Mozambique they were powerful enough to defy the central government.

Quadariyah An Islamic religious fraternity founded in Baghdad in the twelfth century. It is the most widespread Islamic sect in West Africa.

Ras Ethiopian title of nobility given to the great nobles who ranked just below the emperor in power and prestige.

Région Name of the largest administrative unit within a colony in the AEF.

Salihiyah A puritanical sect of Islam organized in the latter nineteenth century by Muhammad Salih. Very important in Somalia because of the efforts of the Mullah Muhammad Abdullah.

Sarkin Hausa title for a ruler of one of the city states before the jihad of Usuman dan Fodio.

Shibalo The system of compulsory labor practiced in Portuguese African territories.

Soninke The warrior class of a chief's retainers in the Gambia in the latter nineteenth century. They were the most committed opponents of the marabouts.

Tijaniyya A Muslim elitist order founded in North Africa which through the activities of Al Hajj Umar became one of the major Islamic sects in West Africa.

Vizier Normally the ruler's closest advisor and head of the bureaucracy in Islamic societies.

Watu wa mungu "The people of God," an anti-Western religious movement among the Kikuyu in the 1930s.

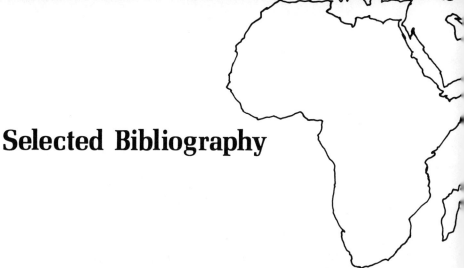

Selected Bibliography

The following list of books is not meant to be exhaustive. Rather, it is a selection of books and articles which the author found most useful for reference for specific subdivisions of the book. Many of these can also be utilized by students who wish to do reading corollary with the text. Those which might prove most useful have been marked with an asterisk (*). Books available in paperback editions have been noted with a plus sign (+). A number of books, particularly general histories, have application to several topic areas covered in this textbook, although each work is cited only once under the most appropriate chapter heading.

Chapter One
WEST AFRICA BEFORE THE SCRAMBLE

ISLAMIC RESURGENCE

*Boahen, A. Adu. *Britain, the Sahara, and the Western Sudan, 1788–1861.* London: Oxford University Press, 1964.
Hodgkin, Thomas. "Uthman dan Fodio," *Nigeria Magazine,* October 1960.
Hunwick, J. O. "The Nineteenth Century Jihads" in J. F. Ade Ajayi and Ian Espie (eds.), *A Thousand Years of West African History.* New York: Humanities Press, 1965.
Ifemesia, C. C. "Bornu Under the Shehus" in Ajayi and Espie (eds.), *A Thousand Years of West African History.* New York: Humanities Press, 1965.
Johnston, H. A. S. *The Fulani Empire of Sokoto.* London: Oxford University Press, 1967.
*Kirk-Greene, A. H. M. *The Emirates of Northern Nigeria.* London: Oxford University Press, 1966.
Last, M. *The Sokoto Caliphate.* New York: Humanities Press, 1967.
*Trimingham, J. S. *A History of Islam in West Africa.* London: Oxford University Press, 1962.

EUROPEAN ATTITUDES

Coupland, Reginald. *Wilberforce.* Oxford: Clarendon Press, 1923.
*Curtin, Philip D. *The Image of Africa: British Ideas in Action, 1780–1850.* Madison, Wis.: University of Wisconsin Press, 1964.
Flint, J. E. "The Growth of European Influences in West Africa in the Nineteenth Century" in Ajayi and Espie (eds.), *A Thousand Years of West African History.* New York: Humanities Press, 1965.
*Hallet, Robin. "The European Approach to the Interior of Africa in the Eighteenth Century," *Journal of African History,* IV, 1963.
Hodgkin, Thomas. *Nigerian Perspectives.* London: Oxford University Press, 1960.
Martin, E. C. *The British West African Settlements 1750–1821.* London: Longmans, Green & Co., 1927.

EUROPEAN EXPLORATIONS

Baikie, William B. *Narrative of an Exploring Voyage up the Rivers Kwara and Binue . . . in 1854.* London: John Murray, 1856.
Barth, Heinrich. *Travels and Discoveries in Northern and Central Africa,* 5 vols. London: Longmans, 1857–1858.
Burton, Richard F. *A Mission to Gelele, King of Dahome.* London: Tinsley Bros., 1864.
Clapperton, Hugh. *Journal of a Second Expedition into the Interior of Africa from the Bight of Benin to Soccatoo.* London: John Murray, 1829.
Denham, Dixon, H. Clapperton, and W. Oudney. *Narrative of Travels and Discoveries in Northern and Central Africa in the Years 1822, 1823, 1824.* London: John Murray, 1862.
*Lander, Richard, and John Lander. *Journal of an Expedition to Explore the Course and Termination of the Niger,* 3 vols. London: John Murray, 1832.
Lupton, L. "The Death of Mungo Park at Bussa," *Nigeria Magazine,* March 1962, p. 58.
*Park, Mungo. *Journal of a Mission to the Interior of Africa in the Year 1805. . . .* Philadelphia: Edward Earle, 1815.

WEST AFRICAN NAVAL PATROLS AND THE SLAVE TRADE

*Coupland, Reginald. *The British Anti-Slavery Movement.* London: Thornton Butterworth, 1933.
Curtin, Philip D., and J. Vansina. "Sources of the Nineteenth-Century Atlantic Slave Trade," *Journal of African History,* V, 1964, p. 185.
Donnan, Elizabeth (ed.). *Documents Illustrative of the History of the Slave Trade to America,* 4 vols. Washington: Carnegie Institution, 1930–1939.

Duignan, Peter, and C. Clendenen. *The United States and the African Slave Trade 1619–1862.* Stanford: Stanford University Press, 1963.

Forde, Daryll (ed.). *Efik Traders of Old Calabar.* London: Oxford University Press, 1956.

*Lloyd, Christopher. *The Navy and the Slave Trade.* London: Longmans, Green & Co., 1949.

FREETOWN

*Fyfe, Christopher H. *A History of Sierra Leone.* London: Oxford University Press, 1962.

Gallagher, John. "Fowell Buxton and the New African Policy, 1838–1842," *Cambridge Historical Journal,* X, 1950, p. 36.

Haliburton, G. "The Nova Scotia Settlers of 1792," *Sierra Leone Studies,* No. 9, 1957, p. 16.

Kup, Peter. *A History of Sierra Leone, 1400–1789.* Cambridge: Cambridge University Press, 1961.

*Porter, Arthur T. *Creoledom: A Study of the Development of Freetown Society.* London: Oxford University Press, 1963.

LIBERIA

Boyd, Willis D. "The American Colonization Society and the Slave Recaptives of 1860–61: An Example of United States-African Relations," *The Journal of Negro History,* XLVII, 1962, p. 108.

*Hargreaves, John D. "African Colonization in the Nineteenth Century: Liberia and Sierra Leone," *Boston University Papers on African History,* I, 1964, p. 55.

Johnston, Harry H. *Liberia,* 2 vols. London: Hutchinson & Co., 1906.

Laughon, Samuel W. "Administrative Problems in Maryland and Liberia, 1836–1851," *The Journal of Negro History,* XXXVI, 1941, p. 325.

Lynch, Hollis R. "Sierra Leone and Liberia in the Nineteenth Century" in Ajayi and Espie (eds.), *A Thousand Years of West African History.* New York: Humanities Press, 1965.

*Staudenraus, P. J. *The African Colonization Movement, 1816–1865.* New York: Columbia University Press, 1961.

THE GOLD COAST

Amenumey, D. E. K. "The Extension of British Rule in Anlo (South-east Ghana), 1850–1890," *Journal of African History,* IX, No. 1, 1968.

Coombs, Douglas. *The Gold Coast, Britain and the Netherlands, 1850–1874.* London: Oxford University Press, 1963.

*Metcalfe, G. E. *Maclean of the Gold Coast: The Life and Times of George Maclean, 1801–1847.* London: Oxford University Press, 1962.

*Ward, William E. *Short History of Ghana.* New York: Humanities Press, 1966.

OYO AND THE YORUBA

*Ajayi, J. F. Ade. *Yoruba Warfare in the Nineteenth Century*. New York: Cambridge University Press, 1969.
*Akinjogbin, I. A. "Dahomey and Yoruba in the 19th Century" in Anene, Joseph, and B. Godfrey (eds.), *Africa in the Nineteenth and Twentieth Centuries*. New York: Humanities Press, 1967.
Biobaku, Saburi O. *The Egba and Their Neighbours*. New York: Oxford University Press, 1957.
+Bradbury, R. E. *The Benin Kingdom and the Edo-Speaking People of South-Western Nigeria*. London: International Affairs Institute, 1957.
+Forde, Daryll. *The Yoruba-Speaking Peoples of South-Western Nigeria*. London: International Affairs Institute, 1951.
Johnson, Samuel. *History of the Yorubas*. Lagos, Nigeria: C. M. S. Bookshops, 1960.
McIntyre, W. D. "Commander Glover and the Colony of Lagos, 1861–73," *Journal of African History*, IV, No. 1, 1963.
Phillips, Earl. "The Egba at Abeokuta: Acculturation and Political Change, 1830–1870," *Journal of African History*, X, No. 1, 1969, p. 67.

FRENCH ACTIVITIES TO 1870

Deschamps, Hubert J. *Le Senegal et la Gambie*. Paris: Presses Universitaires de France, 1964.
Faidherbe, Louis L. C. *Le Senegal: la France dans l'Afrique occidentale*. Paris: Hatchette, 1889.
O'Brien, Rita Cruise. "France in Senegal in the Nineteenth Century," *Tarikh*, II, No. 4, 1969, p. 21.
Quinn, Charlotte A. "Maba Diakhou Ba: Scholar-Warrior of the Senegambia," *Tarikh*, II, No. 3, 1968, p. 1.
Sabatie, Alexandre C. *Le Senegal: sa Conquête et son organisation, 1364–1925*. St. Louis, Senegal, 1926.
Schnapper, Bernard. *La Politique et le commerce Français dans le Golf de Guinée de 1838 à 1871*. Paris: Mouton, 1961.

Chapter Two
EAST AND CENTRAL AFRICA BEFORE THE SCRAMBLE

THE PEOPLES OF EAST AFRICA AND THE ARAB TRADERS

Beachey, R. W. "The East African Ivory Trade in the Nineteenth Century," *Journal of African History*, VIII, No. 2, 1967.
+Beidilmann, T. O. *The Matrilineal People of Eastern Tanzania*. London: International African Institute, 1967.
*Coupland, Reginald. *East Africa and Its Invaders*. London: Oxford University Press, 1961.
+Fallers, Margaret. *The Eastern Lacustrine Bantu*. London: International African Institute, 1960.

*Freeman-Grenville, G. S. P. "The Coast, 1498–1840" in Oliver, Roland, and G. Mathews (eds.), *History of East Africa*, I. London: Oxford University Press, 1963.

Gavin, R. J. "Sayyid Said," *Tarikh*, I, No. 1, 1965, p. 16.

Gray, Sir John M. *History of Zanzibar*. London: Oxford University Press, 1962.

*Gray, Sir John M. "Zanzibar and the Coastal Belt, 1840–84" in Oliver, Roland, and G. Mathews (eds.), *History of East Africa*, I. London: Oxford University Press, 1963.

*Low, D. A. "The Northern Interior, 1840–84" in Oliver, Roland, and G. Mathews (eds.), *History of East Africa*, I. London: Oxford University Press, 1963.

+Middleton, John, and Greet Kershaw. *The Kikuyu and Kamba of Kenya*. London: International African Institute, 1953.

+Middleton, John, and Jane Campbell. *Zanzibar*. London: Oxford University Press, 1967.

Oliver, Roland. "Discernible Developments in the Interior ca. 1500–1840" in Oliver, Roland, and G. Mathews (eds.), *History of East Africa*, I. London: Oxford University Press, 1963.

Posnansky, Merrick. *Prelude to East African History*. London: Oxford University Press, 1966.

Prins, A. H. J. *The Swahili-Speaking Peoples of Zanzibar and the East African Coast*. London: International African Institute, 1967.

Redmayne, Alison. "Mkwawa and the Hehe Wars," *Journal of African History*, IX, No. 3, 1968.

*Smith, Alison. "The Southern Section of the Interior, 1840–84" in Oliver, Roland, and G. Mathews (eds.), *History of East Africa*, I. London: Oxford University Press, 1963.

Trimingham, J. S. *Islam in East Africa*. London: Oxford University Press, 1964.

EUROPEAN EXPLORATIONS

Baker, Samuel W. *Albert Nyanza, Great Basin of the Nile and Explorations of the Nile Sources*, 2 vols. New York: Macmillan, 1866.

Burton, Richard F. *The Lake Regions of Central Africa*, 2 vols. London: Longmans, Green & Co., 1860.

*Coupland, Reginald. *Livingstone's Last Journey*. London: Collins, 1945.

*Farwell, Byron. *Burton*. New York: Avon, 1965.

Krapf, Ludwig. *Travels, Researches and Missionary Labors during an Eighteen Year Residence in Eastern Africa*. London: Trubner, 1860.

Livingstone, David. *The Last Journals of David Livingstone in Central Africa*, 2 vols. (ed. by Horace Waller). London: John Murray, 1880.

+*Moorehead, Alan. *The White Nile*. New York: Harper & Row, 1960.

Perham, Margery, and J. Simmons. *African Discovery*. London: Faber & Faber, 1949.

Speke, John Hanning. *Journal of the Discovery of the Source of the Nile*. London: Blackwood, 1863.

Stanley, Henry M. *Through the Dark Continent or the Sources of the Nile around the Great Lakes of Equatorial Africa*, 2 vols. New York: Harper & Brothers, 1878.

CONGO BASIN

+*Davidson, Basil. *A History of East and Central Africa*. New York: Anchor Books, 1969.
Vansina, Jan. "The Foundations of the Kingdom of Kasanje," *Journal of African History*, IV, 1963.
Vansina, Jan. *Kingdoms of the Savannah*. Madison, Wis.: University of Wisconsin Press, 1966.
Vansina, Jan. "More on the Invasions of Kongo and Angola by the Jaga and Lunda," *Journal of African History*, VII, 1966.
+*Willis, A. J. *The History of Central Africa*. London: Oxford University Press, 1964.

Chapter Three
SOUTHERN AFRICA TO 1872

Bond, John. *They Were South Africans*. London: Oxford University Press, 1956.
Gailey, Harry A. "John Philips' Role in Hottentot Emancipation," *Journal of African History*, III, No. 3, 1962.
Lye, William F. "The Difeqane: The Mfecane in the Southern Sotho Area, 1822–24," *Journal of African History*, VIII, No. 1, 1967.
Lye, William F. "The Ndebele Kingdom South of the Limpopo," *Journal of African History*, X, No. 1, 1969.
*Macmillan, William M. *Boer, Bantu and Briton*. Oxford: Clarendon Press, 1963.
Marais, J. S. *The Cape Coloured People, 1652–1937*. Johannesburg: Witwatersrand University Press, 1962.
Millar, Anthony K. *Plantagenet in South Africa: Lord Charles Somerset*. London: Oxford University Press, 1965.
*Morris, William. *The Washing of the Spears*. New York: Simon and Schuster, 1965.
Okoye, Felix N. C. "Dingane: A Reappraisal," *Journal of African History*, X, No. 2, 1969.
Rose, J. H., A. P. Newton and E. A. Benians (eds.). *The Cambridge History of the British Empire*, VIII, South Africa. Cambridge: Cambridge University Press, 1929.
Sanders, P. B. "Sekonyela and Moshweshwe: Failure and Success in the Aftermath of the Difeqane," *Journal of African History*, X, No. 3, 1969.
Theal, George McCall. *History of South Africa, 1795–1872*, 5 vols. London: George Allen & Unwin, 1908–1910.
Walker, Eric A. *A History of Southern Africa*. London: Longmans, Green & Co., 1957.
Walker, Eric A. *The Great Trek*. London: Adam and Charles Black, 1965.

Chapter Four
NORTHEASTERN AFRICA

THE EGYPTIAN PROBLEM

Baring, Evelyn (Lord Cromer). *Modern Egypt.* London: Macmillan, 1908.
Blunt, Wilfrid S. *Secret History of the British Occupations of Egypt.* London: Unwin, 1907.
Holt, P. M. *Egypt and the Fertile Crescent, 1516–1922.* Ithaca, N.Y.: Cornell University Press, 1966.
+Stevens, Georgiana G. *Egypt: Yesterday and Today.* New York: Holt, Rinehart and Winston, 1963.
*Tignor, R. L. *Modernization and British Control in Egypt, 1882–1914.* Princeton, N.J.: Princeton University Press, 1967.

EGYPT IN THE SUDAN TO 1885

Allen, Bernard M. *Gordon and the Sudan.* London: Macmillan, 1951.
Baker, Samuel. *Ismailia: A Narrative of the Expedition to Central Africa for the Suppression of the Slave Trade.* London: Macmillan, 1874.
Chaille-Long, Charles. *Three Prophets.* New York: Sampson Low, 1884.
*Collins, Robert O., and R. L. Tignor. *Egypt in the Sudan.* Englewood Cliffs, N.J.: Prentice-Hall, 1967.
Hill, Richard L. *Egypt in the Sudan, 1820–1881.* London: Oxford University Press, 1958.
Holt, P. M. *A Modern History of the Sudan.* New York: Praeger, 1963.
+*Moorehead, Alan. *The Blue Nile.* New York: Harper & Row, 1962.

ETHIOPIA THROUGH THE REIGN OF THEODORE

Abir, Modechai. *Ethiopia, The Era of Princes.* London: Longmans, Green & Co., 1968.
Abir, Modechai. "The Origins of the Ethiopian-Egyptian Border Problem in the Nineteenth Century," *Journal of African History,* VIII, No. 3, 1967.
Ceruli, Ernesta. *Peoples of South-West Ethiopia and Its Borderland.* London: International African Institute, 1956.
*Crummey, Donald. "Tewodros as Reformer and Modernizer," *Journal of African History,* X, No. 3, 1969.
Darkwah, Kofi. "Emperor Theodore II and the Kingdom of Shoa, 1855–65," *Journal of African History,* X, No. 1, 1969.
Darkwah, Kofi. "Shoa before the Reign of Menelik," *Tarikh,* II, No. 3, 1968.
Doresse, Jean. *Ethiopia.* New York: G. P. Putnam, 1959.
Hooker, J. R. "The Foreign Office and the Abyssinian Captives," *Journal of African History,* II, No. 2, 1961.
Huntingford, G. W. B. *The Galla of Ethiopia.* London: International African Institute, 1955.

+Jesman, Czeslaw. *The Ethiopian Paradox*. London: Oxford University Press, 1963.
*Mathew, David. *Ethiopia, the Study of a Polity, 1540–1935*. London: Eyre & Spottiswoodie, 1947.

ETHIOPIA AND THE SCRAMBLE TO 1906

Jones, A. H. M., and E. Monroe. *A History of Ethiopia*. London: Oxford University Press, 1960.
Marcus, Harold G. "Ethio-British Negotiations concerning the Western Border with Sudan 1896–1902," *Journal of African History*, IV, No. 1, 1963.
*Marcus, Harold G. "The Foreign Policy of the Emperor Menelik 1896–1898, a Rejoinder," *Journal of African History*, VII, No. 1, 1966.
Pankhurst, Richard. "Italian Settlement Policy in Eritrea and Its Repercussions 1889–1896," *Boston University Papers in African History*, I, 1964.
Rubenson, Sven. "The Protectorate Paragraph of the Wichale Treaty," *Journal of African History*, V, No. 2, 1964.
*Sanderson, G. N. "The Foreign Policy of the Negus Menelik 1896–1898," *Journal of African History*, V, No. 1, 1964.

Chapter Five
THE SCRAMBLE FOR AFRICA

INTRODUCTION

Bodelsen, Carl A. G. *Studies in Mid-Victorian Imperialism*. Copenhagen: Gyldendalske Boghandel, 1924.
Brunschweg, Henri. *Mythes et réalités de l'impérialisme colonial français 1871–1914*. Paris: Librairie Armand Colin, 1960.
*Crowe, Sybil Eyre. *The Berlin West African Conference, 1884–1885*. London: Longmans, Green & Co., 1942.
Gallagher, John, and R. Robinson. "The Imperialism of Free Trade," *The Economic History Review*, VI, 1953, p. 1.
Gifford, Prosser, and W. R. Louis. *Britain and Germany in Africa*. New Haven, Conn.: Yale University Press, 1967.
*Hargreaves, John D. *Prelude to the Partition of West Africa*. London: Macmillan, 1963.
Keith, Arthur Berriedale. *The Belgian Congo and the Berlin Act*. London: Oxford University Press, 1919.
+*Langer, William. *The Diplomacy of Imperialism 1890–1902*. New York: Alfred Knopf, 1951.
Langer, William. *European Alliances and Alignments*. New York: Alfred Knopf, 1950.
Newbury, Colin W. "The Development of French Policy on the Lower and Upper Niger 1880–1898," *Journal of Modern History*, XXXI, 1959, p. 16.

Nowell, Charles E. "Portugal and the Partition of Africa," *Journal of Modern History,* XIX, 1947, p. 1.

Power, Thomas F. *Jules Ferry and the Renaissance of French Imperialism.* New York: King's Crown Press, 1944.

Roberts, Stephen H. *History of French Colonial Policy, 1870–1925.* London: Frank Cass, 1963.

+*Robinson, Ronald, J. Gallagher, and A. Denny. *Africa and the Victorians.* New York: St. Martin's Press, 1961.

Townsend, Mary Evelyn. *Origins of Modern German Colonialism, 1871–1885.* New York: Columbia University Press, 1921.

WEST AFRICA

Ajayi, J. F. Ade. "The British Occupation of Lagos 1851–61," *Nigeria Magazine,* August 1961.

Alagoa, Ebiegberi Joe. *The Small Brave City-State: A History of Nembe-Brass in the Niger Delta.* Madison, Wis.: University of Wisconsin Press, 1964.

Anene, J. C. *Southern Nigeria in Transition 1885–1906.* Cambridge: Cambridge University Press, 1966.

+*Crowder, Michael. *A Short History of Nigeria.* New York: Praeger, 1966.

Flint, John E. *Sir George Goldie and the Making of Nigeria.* London: Oxford University Press, 1960.

Gailey, Harry A. "European Rivalry and Diplomacy in the Mellacourie 1879–1882," *Sierra Leone Studies,* No. 15, 1961, p. 135.

*Hargreaves, John D. "The Establishment of the Sierra Leone Protectorate and the Insurrection of 1898," *The Cambridge Historical Journal,* XII, 1956, p. 56.

Hargreaves, John D. "The French Occupation of the Mellacourie, 1865–67," *Sierra Leone Studies,* No. 9, 1957.

Idowu, H. O. "The Establishment of Elective Institutions in Senegal 1869–1880," *Journal of African History,* IX, No. 2, 1968.

O'Brien, Donal Cruise. "Toward an Islamic Policy in French West Africa 1854–1914," *Journal of African History,* VIII, No. 2, 1967.

Perham, Margery. *Lugard: The Years of Adventure 1858–1898.* London: Collins, 1956.

THE CONGO BASIN

+Abraham, R. G. *The Peoples of Greater Unyamwezi, Tanzania.* London: International African Institute, 1967.

Burton, Richard F. (ed. & trans.). *The Lands of Cazembe.* London: Royal Geographic Society, 1873.

Cookcy, S. J. S. "Tippu Tib and the Decline of the Congo Arabs," *Tarikh,* I, No. 2, 1966, pp. 58–69.

+*Davidson, Basil. *A History of East and Central Africa.* New York: Doubleday, 1969.

Flint, Eric. "Trade and Politics in Barotseland during the Kalolo Period," *Journal of African History*, XI, No. 1, 1970, p. 71.

McCulloch, Merran. *The Southern Lunda and Related Peoples.* London: International African Institute, 1951.

Rotberg, Robert I. "Plymouth Brethren and the Occupation of Katanga 1886–1907," *Journal of African History*, V, No. 2, 1964.

Vansina, Jan. *Kingdoms of the Savannah.* Madison, Wis.: University of Wisconsin Press, 1966.

*Vansina, Jan. "Long-Distance Trade Routes in Central Africa," *Journal of African History*, III, No. 3, 1962.

Webster, J. B. "Mirambo and Nyamwezi Unification," *Tarikh*, I, No. 1, 1965, p. 64.

Whitely, Wilfred. *Bemba and Related Peoples of Northern Rhodesia.* London: International African Institute, 1950.

THE PORTUGUESE EMPIRE

Akinola, G. Akin. "The Mazrui of Mombasa," *Tarikh*, II, No. 3, 1968, pp. 26–40.

Boxer, Charles R. *Race Relations in the Portuguese Empire, 1415–1825.* London: Oxford University Press, 1963.

*Cunnison, Ian. "Kazembe and the Portuguese, 1798–1832," *Journal of African History*, II, No. 1, 1961, p. 61.

*Duffy, James. *A Question of Slavery.* London: Oxford University Press, 1967.

Liesegang, Gerhard. "Dingane's Attack on Lourenço Marques in 1833," *Journal of African History*, X, No. 4, 1969, p. 565.

+McCulloch, Merran. *The Ovimbundu of Angola.* London: International African Institute, 1952.

Newitt, M. D. D. "The Portuguese on the Zambesi: An Historical Interpretation of the Prazo System," *Journal of African History*, X, No. 1, 1969, p. 67.

*Newitt, M. D. D. and P. S. Gailake. "The Aringa at Massangano," *Journal of African History*, VIII, No. 1, 1967, p. 133.

EAST AFRICA

Coupland, Reginald. *Exploration of East Africa.* London: Faber & Faber, 1939.

*Flint, John. "The Wider Background to Partition and Colonial Occupation" in Oliver, Roland, and G. Mathews (eds.), *History of East Africa*, I. London: Oxford University Press, 1963.

*Freeman-Grenville, G. S. P. "The German Sphere, 1884–94" in Oliver, Roland, and G. Mathews (eds.), *History of East Africa*, I. London: Oxford University Press, 1963.

Hemphill, Marie de Kiewiet. "The British Sphere, 1884–94" in Oliver, Roland, and G. Mathews (eds.), *History of East Africa,* I. London: Oxford University Press, 1963.

Johnston, Henry Hamilton. *The Uganda Protectorate,* 2 vols. London: Hutchinson, 1902.

Lugard, Frederick D. *The Rise of Our East African Empire,* 2 vols. London: Blackwood, 1893.

Lugard, Frederick D. *The Story of the Uganda Protectorate.* London: Blackwood, 1901.

Chapter Six

CONSOLIDATION OF BRITISH POWER IN SOUTHERN AFRICA, 1872–1910

Bryce, James. *Impressions of South Africa.* New York: The Century Co., 1900.

Caplan, Gerald L. "Barotseland Scramble for Protection," *Journal of African History,* X, No. 2, 1969.

Cloete, Stuart. *Against These Three.* Boston: Houghton Mifflin Company, 1945.

Denoon, D. J. N. "The Transvaal Labour Crisis 1901–06," *Journal of African History,* VIII, No. 3, 1967.

French, Gerald. *Lord Chelmsford and the Zulu War.* London: Bodley Head, 1939.

Gandhi, M. K. *Satyagraha in South Africa* (trans. V. G. Desai). Stanford: Academic Reprints, 1954.

Gibb, Henry. *Background to Bitterness.* New York: Philosophical Library, 1955.

*Hanna, A. J. *The Story of the Rhodesias and Nyasaland.* London: Faber & Faber, 1965.

Marks, Shula. "Harriette Colenso and the Zulus, 1874–1913," *Journal of African History,* IV, No. 3, 1963.

Marquard, Leo. *The Story of South Africa.* New York: Ray Publishers, 1955.

Maurois, Andre. *Cecil Rhodes.* London: Collins, 1954.

Millin, Sarah Gertrude. *Rhodes.* Capetown: Central News Agency, 1952.

Ranger, T. O. *Revolt in Southern Rhodesia 1896–1897.* Evanston, Ill.: Northwestern University Press, 1968.

*Thompson, Leonard M. *The Unification of South Africa, 1902–1910.* Oxford: Clarendon Press, 1960.

Van der Poel, Jean. *The Jameson Raid.* London: Oxford University Press, 1951.

+*Williams, Basil. *Botha, Smuts and South Africa.* New York: Macmillan, 1948.

Williams, Basil. *Cecil Rhodes.* London: Constable, 1938.

Wills, A. J. *An Introduction to the History of Central Africa.* London: Oxford University Press, 1964.

Chapter Seven
EUROPEAN MECHANISMS OF CONTROL IN AFRICA

BRITISH AFRICA

Bourret, F. M. *Ghana, the Road to Independence*. Stanford: Stanford University Press, 1960.

*Ehrlich, Cyril. "Some Social and Economic Implications of Paternalism in Uganda," *Journal of African History*, IV, No. 2, 1963.

Gailey, Harry A. *A History of the Gambia*. London: Routledge & Kegan Paul, 1964.

*Gailey, Harry A. *The Road to Aba*. New York: New York University Press, 1970.

Huxley, Elspeth. *White Man's Country*, 2 vols. New York: Macmillan, 1935.

*Mungeam, G. H. "Masai and Kikuyu Responses to the Establishment of British Administration in the East Africa Protectorate," *Journal of African History*, XI, No. 1, 1970.

Ogot, Bethwell A. "British Administration in the Central Nyanza District of Kenya 1900–1960," *Journal of African History*, IV, No. 2, 1963.

Twaddle, Michael. "The Bakungu Chiefs of Buganda under British Colonial Rule 1900–1930," *Journal of African History*, X, No. 2, 1969.

Wight, Martin. *British Colonial Constitutions*. London: Oxford University Press, 1952.

Wylie, Kenneth C. "Innovation and Change in Mende Chieftaincy 1880–1896," *Journal of African History*, X, No. 2, 1969.

FRENCH AFRICA

*Cowan, L. Gray. *Local Government in West Africa*. New York: Columbia University Press, 1958.

Crowder, Michael. *Senegal, a Study in French Assimilation Policy*. New York: Barnes & Noble, 1967.

*Delavignette, R. *Freedom and Authority in French West Africa*. London: Frank Cass, 1968.

Johnson, G. Wesley. "Blaise Diagne: Master Politician of Senegal," *Tarikh*, I, No. 2, 1966.

Newbury, Colin W. "The Formation of the Government General of French West Africa," *Journal of African History*, I, No. 1, 1960.

Robinson, Kenneth E. "French West Africa," *African Affairs*, I, 1951.

Weinstein, Brian. "Felix Eboué and the Chiefs," *Journal of African History*, XI, No. 1, 1970.

BELGIAN AFRICA

*Anstey, Roger. *King Leopold's Legacy*. London: Oxford University Press, 1966.

*Brausch, George. *Belgian Administration in the Congo.* London: Oxford University Press, 1961.
Buell, R. L. *The Native Problem in Africa,* 2 vols. London: Frank Case, 1965.
Gravel, Pierre Bettez. "Life on the Manbi in Gisaka (Rwanda)," *Journal of African History,* VI, No. 3, 1965.
Ryckmans, Pierre. "Belgian Colonialism," *Foreign Affairs,* XXXIV, 1955.

PORTUGUESE AFRICA

+*Duffy, James. *Portugal in Africa.* Baltimore, Md.: Penguin, 1963.
Duffy, James. *Portuguese Africa.* Cambridge, Mass.: Harvard University Press, 1959.
Easton, Stewart C. *The Twilight of European Colonialism.* New York: Holt, Rinehart and Winston, 1960.
Egerton, F. Clement. *Angola in Perspective.* London: Routledge and Kegan Paul, 1957.

Chapter Eight
COLONIAL AFRICA—THE INTERWAR PERIOD

ECONOMIC DEVELOPMENT AND SOCIAL CHANGE

Blair, T. C. V. *Africa: A Market Profile.* New York: Praeger, 1965.
Cowan, L. Gray, James O'Connell and David G. Scanlon. *Education and Nation Building in Africa.* New York: Praeger, 1965.
Davis, Kingsley. *Economic Development and Cultural Change.* Chicago: University of Chicago Press, 1954.
Little, Kenneth. *West African Urbanization.* London: Cambridge University Press, 1965.
Marris, Peter. *Family and Social Change in an African City.* Evanston, Ill.: Northwestern University Press, 1962.
McCall, Daniel F. "Dynamics of Urbanization in Africa," *Annals of the American Academy of Political and Social Science,* No. 29, March 1955.
Munger, Edwin S. "Adam Smith in East Africa," *African Field Reports, 1952–1961.* New York: American Universities Field Staff, 1955.

SEPARATIST CHURCH MOVEMENTS

Hodgkin, Thomas. *Nationalism in Colonial Africa.* New York: New York University Press, 1957.
*Hooker, J. R. "Witnesses and Watchtower in the Rhodesias and Nyasaland," *Journal of African History,* VI, No. 1, 1965.
Lynch, Hollis R. "The Native Pastorate Controversy and Cultural Ethno-Centrism in Sierra Leone," *Journal of African History,* V, No. 3, 1964.

Rotberg, Robert I. *The Rise of Nationalism in Central Africa.* Cambridge, Mass.: Harvard University Press, 1965.
*Shepperson, George. *Independent Africans, John Chilembwe and the Origins, Settling and Significance of the Nyasaland Native Revolt of 1915.* Edinburgh: Edinburgh University Press, 1958.
Shepperson, George. "The Politics of African Church Separatist Movements in British Central Africa, 1892–1916," *Africa,* XXIV, 1954.

EARLY POLITICAL PARTIES

+*Awolowo, Obafemi. *Awo.* London: Cambridge University Press, 1961.
+*Azikwe, Benjamin Nnamdi. *Zik.* London: Cambridge University Press, 1961.
Hargreaves, J. D. *Life of Sir Samuel Lewis.* London: Oxford University Press, 1958.
Leys, Norman. *Kenya.* London: Hogarth Press, 1925.
*Nkrumah, Kwame. *Ghana: the Autobiography of Kwame Nkrumah.* New York: Nelson, 1957.
Perham, Margery, and Elspeth Huxley. *Race and Politics in Kenya.* London: Faber & Faber, 1956.
Thomas, Issac B. *A Life History of Herbert Macaulay.* Lagos: N.P., 1946.

PAN AFRICANISM

Cronon, Edmund David. *Black Moses.* Madison, Wis.: University of Wisconsin Press, 1969.
Du Bois, W. E. B. *Color and Democracy.* New York: Harcourt, Brace & World, 1945.
Du Bois, W. E. B. *The World and Africa.* New York: Viking Press, 1946.
Hooker, James R. *Black Revolutionary.* New York: Praeger, 1970.
Hughes, Langston. *The Langston Hughes Reorder.* New York: Braziller, 1958.
+*Legum, Colin. *Pan Africanism.* New York: Praeger, 1965.
Lynch, Hollis R. *Edward Wilmot Blyden: Pan-Negro Patriot.* New York: Oxford University Press, 1970.
*Padmore, George (ed.). *History of the Pan-African Congress.* London: Hammersmith Bookshop, 1963.
Rudwick, Elliot M. *W. E. B. Du Bois.* Philadelphia: University of Pennsylvania Press, 1960.
Shepperson, George. "Notes on Negro American Influences on the Emergence of African Nationalism," *Journal of African History,* I, No. 2, 1960.

Chapter Nine
NORTHEASTERN AFRICA TO 1965

Del Boca, Angelo. *The Ethiopian War, 1935–1941.* Chicago: University of Chicago Press, 1969.

Doresse, Jean. *Ethiopia.* London: Elek Books, 1959.

Greenfield, Richard T. *Ethiopia—A New Political History.* New York: Praeger, 1965.

Matthew, David. *Ethiopia: The Study of a Polity, 1540–1935.* London: Eyre and Spottiswoodie, 1947.

Mosley, Leonard. *Haile Selassie, the Conquering Lion.* London: Weidenfeld and Nicolson, 1964.

Pankhurst, E. S. *Ethiopia: A Cultural History.* Essex, England: Lalibela House, Woodford Green, 1955.

Toynbee, Arnold J. *Survey of International Affairs, 1935: Abyssinia and Italy.* London: Oxford University Press, 1936.

Ullendorf, E. *The Ethiopians.* London: Oxford University Press, 1965.

Chapter Ten
POSTWAR POLITICAL DEVELOPMENTS—FRENCH AFRICA

Adamolekum, Ladipo. "The Road to Independence in French Tropical Africa," *Tarikh,* II, No. 4, 1969.

Alexander, A. S. "The Ivory Coast Constitution," *Journal of Modern African Studies,* I, No. 3, 1963.

Berg, Elliott J. "The Economic Basis of Political Choice in French West Africa," *The American Political Science Review,* LIV, 1960.

Carter, Gwendolen. *African One Party States.* Ithaca, N.Y.: Cornell University Press, 1962.

LeVine, Victor T. *The Cameroons from Mandate to Independence.* Berkeley: University of California Press, 1964.

Morgenthau, Ruth Schacter. *Political Parties in French Speaking West Africa.* London: Oxford University Press, 1964.

Morgenthau, Ruth Schacter. "Single-Party Systems in West Africa," *The American Political Science Review,* LV, 1961.

Munger, Edwin S. "The Ivory Coast," *African Field Reports, 1952–1961.* Cape Town: C. Struik, 1961.

Senghor, Léopold Sédar. "West Africa in Evolution," *Foreign Affairs,* XXXIX, 1960–1961.

Skurnik, Walter A. E. "France and Fragmentation in West Africa: 1945–1960," *Journal of African History,* VIII, No. 2, 1967.

Skurnik, Walter A. E. "Senghor and African Socialism," *Journal of Modern African Studies,* III, No. 3, 1965.

*Thompson, Virginia and Richard Adloff. *The Emerging States of French Equatorial Africa.* Stanford: Stanford University Press, 1960.

Thompson, Virginia and Richard Adloff. *French West Africa.* Stanford: Stanford University Press, 1958.

Wallerstein, Immanuel. "Elites in French-Speaking West Africa," *Journal of Modern African Studies,* III, No. 1, May 1965.

Zolberg, Aristide. *One Party Government in the Ivory Coast.* Princeton, N.J.: Princeton University Press, 1964.

Chapter Eleven
POSTWAR POLITICAL DEVELOPMENTS—BRITISH AFRICA

WEST AFRICA

Austin, Dennis. "The Working Committee of the United Gold Coast Convention," *Journal of African History*, II, No. 2, 1961.
Munger, Edwin S. "Ghana's Finance Minister: Komla Agbeli Gbedemah," *African Field Reports, 1952–1961*. Cape Town: C. Struik, 1961.
Robson, Peter. "The Problem of Senegambia," *Journal of Modern African Studies*, III, No. 3, 1965.
Rothschild, Donald S. "Safeguarding Nigeria's Minorities," Duquesne University Institute of African Affairs, *African Reprint No. 17*, 1964.
Smythe, H. H., and M. M. Smythe. "Subgroups of the New Nigerian Elite," Duquesne University Institute of African Affairs, *African Reprint No. 5*, 1960.

CENTRAL AFRICA

*Clegg, Edward. *Race and Politics, Partnership in the Federation of Rhodesia and Nyasaland*. London: Oxford University Press, 1960.
Clutton-Brock, Guy. *Dawn in Nyasaland*. London: Hodder & Stoughton, 1960.
Cohen, Andrew. *British Policy in Changing Africa*. London: Routledge & Kegan Paul, 1959.
Franck, Thomas M. *Race and Nationalism: The Struggle for Power in Rhodesia and Nyasaland*. New York: Fordham University Press, 1960.
*Franklin, Harry. *Unholy Wedlock: The Failure of the Central African Federation*. London: G. Allen & Unwin, 1963.
Hanna, A. J. *The Story of the Rhodesias and Nyasaland*. London: Faber & Faber, 1960.
Kaunda, Kenneth. *A Humanist in Africa*. London: Longmans, Green & Co., 1966.
Leys, Colin, and R. Cranford Pratt (eds.). *A New Deal in Central Africa*. London: Heinemann, 1960.
*Mason, Philip. *Year of Decision*. London: Oxford University Press, 1960.
+Powdermaker, Hortense. *Copper Town: Changing Africa*. New York: Harper & Row, 1965.

THE HIGH COMMISSION TERRITORIES

Ashton, Edmund H. *The Basuto*. London: Oxford University Press, 1962.
Benson, Mary. *Tshekedi Khama*. London: Faber & Faber, 1961.
*Hailey, William M. (Baronet). *The Republic of South Africa and the High Commission Territories*. London: Oxford University Press, 1963.
Halpern, Jack. *South Africa's Hostages*. Baltimore, Md.: Penguin, 1965.

⁺Kuper, Hilda. *The Swazi: A South African Kingdom.* New York: Holt, Rinehart and Winston, 1963.

Munger, Edwin S. *Swaziland, the Tribe and Country.* New York: American Field Services, 1962.

Rosenthal, Eric. *African Switzerland: Basutoland of Today.* London: Hutchinson, 1948.

Sillery, A. *The Bechuanaland Protectorate.* London: Oxford University Press, 1952.

*Stevens, R. P. *Lesotho, Botswana and Swaziland.* New York: Praeger, 1967.

Stevens, R. P. "Swaziland Political Development," *Journal of Modern African Studies,* I, No. 3, 1963.

BRITISH EAST AFRICA

Chamberlain, John. "Kenyatta's Kenya," *American-African Affairs Association Paper,* April 1968.

Glickman, Harvey. "Some Observations on the Army and Political Unrest in Tanganyika," Duquesne University Institute of African Affairs, *African Reprint No. 16,* 1964.

*Ingham, Kenneth. *The Making of Modern Uganda.* London: Allen & Unwin, 1958.

Lansdale, J. M. "Some Origins of Natonalism in East Africa," *Journal of African History,* IX, No. 1, 1968.

Low, D. A., and R. C. Pratt. *Buganda and British Overrule, 1900–1955.* London: Oxford University Press, 1960.

Mboya, Tom. *Freedom and After.* London: Andre Deutsch, 1963.

*Rosberg, Carl G., and J. Nottingham. *The Myth of Mau Mau: Nationalism in Kenya.* New York: Praeger, 1966.

Tordoff, William. "Regional Administration in Tanzania," *Journal of Modern African Studies,* III, No. 1, May 1965.

Chapter Twelve
POSTWAR POLITICAL DEVELOPMENTS—BELGIAN AFRICA

Hennessy, Maurice N. *The Congo.* New York: Praeger, 1961.

*Hoskyns, Catherine. *The Congo since Independence.* London: Oxford University Press, 1965.

Lefever, E. W. *Crisis in the Congo.* Washington: Brookings, 1965.

⁺*Legum, Colin. *Congo Disaster.* Baltimore, Md.: Penguin, 1961.

Munger, E. S. "Conflict in the Congo," *African Field Reports, 1952–61.* Cape Town: C. Struik, 1961.

⁺*O'Brien, Conor Cruise. *To Katanga and Back.* New York: Simon and Schuster, 1962.

Young, Crawford. *Politics in the Congo.* Princeton, N.J.: Princeton University Press, 1965.

Chapter Thirteen
THE PORTUGUESE TERRITORIES
*Ehnmark, Anders and Per Wastberg. *Angola and Mozambique.* New York: Roy Publishers, 1963.
+Kitchen, Helen. *A Handbook of African Affairs.* New York: Praeger, 1964.
*Mason, Philip, et al. *Angola: Views of a Revolt.* London: Oxford University Press, 1962.
Munger, Edwin S. "Mozambique: Uneasy Today, Uncertain Tomorrow," *African Field Reports, 1952–61.* Cape Town: C. Struik, 1961.
Segal, Ronald. *Political Africa.* London: Stevens, 1961.

Chapter Fourteen
SUPRANATIONAL ORGANIZATIONS
+*Adam, Thomas R. *Government and Politics in Africa.* New York: Random House, 1965.
+Burke, Fred G. *Africa's Quest for Order.* Englewood Cliffs, N.J.: Prentice Hall, 1964.
+Dia, Mamadou. *The African Nations and World Solidarity.* New York: Praeger, 1962.
Haile Selassie I. "Toward African Unity," *Journal of Modern African Studies,* I, No. 3, 1963.
Hovet, Thomas. *Africa in the United Nations.* Evanston, Ill.: Northwestern University Press, 1963.
*Nkrumah, Kwame. *Africa Must Unite.* London: Heineman, 1961.
Nye, Joseph S., Jr. "East African Economic Integration," *Journal of Modern African Studies,* I, No. 4, 1963.
+Rivkin, Arnold. *Africa and the West.* New York: Praeger, 1962.
Segal, Aaron. "Africa Newly Divided," *Journal of Modern African Studies,* II, No. 1, 1964.

Chapter Fifteen
THE SPECIAL CASE: THE REPUBLIC OF SOUTH AFRICA, 1910–1965
Bjerre, Jens. *Kalahari.* New York: Hill & Wang, 1960.
Carter, Gwendolen. *The Politics of Inequality.* New York: Praeger, 1959.
Crafford, F. S. *Jan Smuts.* Garden City, N.Y.: Doubleday, Doran, 1943.
+*Davis, John A., and James Baker (eds.). *Southern Africa in Transition.* New York: Praeger, 1966.
De Beer, Z. J. *Multi-Racial South Africa.* London: Oxford University Press, 1961.
+De Kiewiet, C. W. *A History of South Africa: Social and Economic.* London: Oxford University Press, 1966.
+Drury, Allen. *A Very Strange Society.* New York: Pocket Books, 1968.
*Feit, Edward, *African Opposition in South Africa.* Stanford: Hoover Institution, 1967.
+*Feit, Edward. *South Africa: The Dynamics of the African National Congress.* London: Oxford University Press, 1962.

+*First, Ruth. *South West Africa*. Baltimore, Md.: Penguin, 1963.

Hammond-Toke, W. D. "The Transkeian Council System 1895–1955," *Journal of African History*, IX, No. 3, 1968.

+*Hepple, Alexander. *Verwoerd*. Baltimore, Md.: Pelican Books, 1967.

Hill, C. R. *Bantustans*. London: Oxford University Press, 1964.

+Louw, Eric H. *The Case for South Africa*. New York: MacFadden Books, 1963.

Luthuli, Albert. *Let My People Go*. New York: McGraw-Hill, 1962.

+Marquard, Leo. *The Peoples and Policies of South Africa*. London: Oxford University Press, 1962.

+Mbeki, Govan. *South Africa: The Peasants' Revolt*. Baltimore, Md.: Penguin Books, 1964.

+Roux, Edward. *Time Longer than Rope*. Madison, Wis.: University of Wisconsin Press, 1966.

+Segal, Ronald. *Sanctions against South Africa*. Baltimore, Md.: Penguin Books, 1964.

South African Bureau of Racial Affairs. "Apartheid—a Slogan or a Solution," *Fact Paper No. 30*, March 1957.

South African Bureau of Racial Affairs. "Bantu Education Policy," *Fact Paper No. 39*, August 1957.

South African Bureau of Racial Affairs. "Bantu Labour in Industry," *Fact Paper No. 12*, June 1956.

South African Bureau of Racial Affairs. "Implications of the Separate Development Policy," *Fact Paper No. 17*, August 1956.

South African Bureau of Racial Affairs. "Is Separation the Answer to South Africa's Race Problem?" *Fact Paper No. 16*, August 1956.

South African Bureau of Racial Affairs. "The Origins and Essence of the Race Pattern in South Africa," *Fact Paper No. 61*, July 1958.

Thomas, Elizabeth M. *The Harmless People*. New York: Alfred Knopf, 1959.

+*Thompson, Leonard. *Politics in the Republic of South Africa*. Boston: Little, Brown, 1966.

+Vatcher, William H. *White Laager: The Rise of Afrikaner Nationalism*. New York: Praeger, 1965.

Chapter Sixteen

TROUBLED INDEPENDENCE

Barber, James. *Rhodesia: The Road to Rebellion*. London: Oxford University Press, 1967.

Grundy, K. W. *Conflicting Images of the Military in Africa*. Nairobi: East African Publishing House, 1968.

Kaunda, Kenneth. *Independence and Beyond*. London: Thomas Nelson, 1966.

Kenyatta, Jomo. *Suffering without Bitterness*. Nairobi: East African Publishing House, 1968.

+*Legum, Colin. *Africa: A Handbook to the Continent*. New York: Praeger, 1967.

Mazrui, Ali. *Toward a Pax Africana.* Chicago: University of Chicago Press, 1967.

Mungai, Njorge. *The Independent Nations of Africa.* Nairobi: Acme Press, 1967.

Nkrumah, Kwame. *Neo-Colonialism: The Last Stage of Imperialism.* London: Thomas Nelson, 1965.

Nyerere, Julius. *Freedom and Unity.* Dar-es-Salaam: Oxford University Press, 1966.

Odinga, Oginga. *Not Yet Uhuru.* London: Heinemann, 1967.

+Ojukwu, C. Odemegwu. *Random Thoughts of C. Odemegwu Ojukwu,* 2 vols. New York: Harper & Row, 1969.

+Sithole, N. *African Nationalism.* London: Oxford University Press, 1969.

+Wallerstein, Immanuel. *Africa, the Politics of Unity.* New York: Random House, 1967.

Index